ELLIOTT'S
GOLF
FORM
1999

Keith Elliott

This Edition First Published in 1998 by
Portway Press Limited
Halifax West Yorkshire HX1 1XE
Tel: 01422 330330 Fax: 01422 358645

Paperback ISBN 1 901570 08 8

Cover photographs
Front: Vijay Singh by David Cannon, Allsport.
Back: Michael Bradley by Jamie Squire, Allsport; Russell Claydon by Richard Sellers, Sportsphoto; David Duval by David Davies, Sportsphoto; Vijay Singh by Harry How, Allsport

Printed and bound by The Charlesworth Group
Huddersfield UK 01484 517077

About The Author

Keith was first attracted to golf betting because, being a game played between the ears, he could apply to it much of his knowledge from the positive thinking, personal motivation and mental skills courses, workshops, and broadcasts that he had given for many years.

Throughout the nineties he has applied his statistical ability, analytical skills and knowledge of mental processes to sports betting. Indeed while working at the Liverpool Business School, he was the only University lecturer in the country who had permission to run a sports service from his professor.

He chose early retirement in late 1995 to focus on his sports betting, horse racing and positive thinking interests.

He is the author of 'How To Win At Golf Betting' and this is his fifth successive golf betting annual.

He currently runs Timeform's Sportsview Service.

While BBC Radio Merseyside's Racing Correspondent he raised over £19,000 in successful charity bets with the money going to his favourite charity, the Samaritans.

In September 1997 he was appointed by the Home Secretary to be an independent member of the British Horserace Betting Levy Board. He has a deep and passionate interest in all matters relating to punter protection.

Keith has been happily married to Tik for 32 years, and has two sons, Steven (20) and Martin (18).

FOREWORD by Jimmy Tarbuck

My dad was a bookmaker so I grew up understanding betting, and now as a golfing 'nut' I play the world's greatest game as often as I can. So I am very pleased to have the opportunity to write the foreword for this, the only book on golf betting, because it combines my family background in bookmaking with my passion for golf.

The opening chapter's definition of golf is dead right—golf is a 'deliciously old-fashioned game' as it is surely the one sport above all others which does not allow its rules to be bent, in which fair play is expected and through which character is built. I firmly believe it is the last great game of honour.

Interest in golf has really increased in recent years with the massive expansion in television coverage, so more and more people are watching the professional game and many of them are increasing their enjoyment by having a bet.

Indeed many punters believe that golf is a game that starts with a tee and ends with a profit. However, whether you bet for fun or profit I feel sure that the punter guides to the tournaments, the player profiles and the countless tips in **Elliott's Golf Form 1999** will help you succeed.

It's a fascinating book full of insights into the world's top players and I'm sure you'll enjoy it.

Wishing you a good read, good golf and good punting. Golf is like sex, when it's bad—it's still good. I see the rough is clear, so I can tee off.

Cheers.

INTRODUCTION

Although last year's volume was very well received with first-class reviews there are a number of improvements and changes this year.

- There is a brand new Part Two, entitled 1999 the Golf Betting Year in Prospect. It includes all tournaments scheduled for the European and American tours as well as those scheduled for the 1998-99 Australasian tour. There are also previews of the 1999 Majors, the Ryder Cup and players to follow.
- Part One now focuses solely on issues of importance to the golf punter.
- With nearly all firms now paying, either one quarter or one fifth the odds a place the first five all tournament results now include the first five players rather than the first four.
- In Part Six there are now a total of 152 American, and 132 European player profiles – far, far more than ever before.
- The stats in Part Seven have also been expanded to include the top 40 (from top 30) in all categories.

Overall I hope you will agree that this, the fifth annual, is better than ever before.

This year I would like to thank the European PGA for agreeing for us to use their GUARDIAN PERFORMANCE DATA stats from the 1998 European tour.

I am also particularly grateful to Jimmy Tarbuck for agreeing so readily to write the Foreword. A bookies' son who's a golf nut seemed an inspired choice and Jim's foreword tells you so much about him, his passion for the game and, of course, his great humour......and how refreshing that the question of payment was never raised, although I have offered to caddie for him!

Ladbrokes have again provided a free competition with superb prizes, including a £500 first prize, so do enter now while it's on your mind. The competition is on page xix.

To produce this book by the end of November within four weeks of the end of the European and American seasons is, I can assure you, a minor miracle so I must thank Timeform, and particularly Nigel Townsend for his help. It was even his idea to contact Jimmy Tarbuck re the Foreword.

And, of course, this book would not have been possible without the incredible efforts of my wife, Tik, and my sons Martin and Steven (who inspired my creation of 'the nappy factor').

My thanks also go as always to my great friends Stevie B, Meggles, Mike Rad, Beryl and the Pifs, and this year to Alison and Dave for that unforgettable Saturday in August.

Finally, many thanks if you wrote in to say kind things about the book, particularly to Michael S from West Leederville, Western Australia (yes, really a fan from down under!) who said "I enjoyed reading the book and was most impressed with Keith's ability to tip winners for the season."

Thanks to M.S. and no matter where you are reading this I do hope this volume will once more continue to help you make winning bets in 1999.

If you would like to comment I would, as always, be delighted to hear from you. You can write to me c/o Timeform, Halifax, West Yorkshire, HX1 1XE, or fax me on 0151 – 608 – 4860, or send your E-mail to KEVApositive@BTInternet.com

DEFINITIONS and ABBREVIATIONS

PMA	Positive Mental Association
MLD	Mental Let Down
IBC	Inspiration By Comparison
DYM	A DYM player is one who is quoted by a bookmaker at odds that are at least double the odds quoted by another e.g. a player is 50/1 with bookie A, only 25/1 with bookie B. By backing with bookie A you can Double Your Money.
TYM	A TYM player is one who is quoted by a bookmaker at odds that are at least triple as high as the odds quoted by another e.g. a player is 100/1 with bookie A, only 33/1 with bookie B. By backing with bookie A you can Triple Your Money.
*	Next to any players' odds mean that he is a DYM or TYM.
33/1	The odds quoted, unless otherwise stated, were the biggest in the market at the time.
PWW	Previous Week's Winner.
PWW2	Winner for the previous two weeks.
DC	Defending Champion.
HTWAGB	How To Win At Golf Betting – the title of my book.
DNP	Did Not Play.
MC	Missed the Cut.
O/M	The European Order of Merit.
M/L	The US Money List.
GIR	Greens in Regulation.
R1	Round one i.e. first round of a tournament. The fourth round would be R4.
T2	Tied 2nd. The T shows that one, or more, players were tied at that position.
!	The exclamation next to a point is to illustrate that it is a surprise.
Rookie	A player in his first year on the US or European tour.
Jolly	Refers to the favourite.....as in the 'jolly old favourite'.
The Cut	The reduction of a tournament field, usually at the halfway stage. All those then finishing the tournament receive a cheque so they are 'in the money'.
Par	The regulation or expected number of shots to be taken at a hole.
Birdie	1 under par – e.g. a three on a par 4.
Eagle	2 under par – e.g. a three on a par 5.
Albatross	3 under par – sometimes called a miracle!

Bogey	1 over par.
Double Bogey	2 over par.
Q.School	Qualifying School for either the European or American tour.
Draw	Moving the ball from right to left.
Fade	Moving the ball from left to right.

PLEASE NOTE In Parts Three, Four and Five in the tournament results there are lines drawn after the top 10, the top 20, and the last player to beat par.

CONTENTS

THE DYM SYSTEM – AN UPDATE

- DYMs and the way the Racing Post gets its golf odds

LIES, DAMNED LIES
AND (CHIP'S) GOLF STATISTICS

- Be wary of final round golf stats

AND FINALLY.......

ELLIOTT'S GOLF FORM SPECIAL COMPETITION
WITH
Ladbrokes

FIRST PRIZE
£500 of Free Bets from Ladbrokes on the
1999 US MASTERS

RUNNER-UP PRIZES
FIVE RUNNERS-UP will each receive a £20 Free Bet from
Ladbrokes on the **1999 US MASTERS**

TO ENTER
Simply name the player who won the 1997 US Masters
by a record breaking 12 shots

Please send your answers (postcards only) to:

**ELLIOTT'S GOLF FORM LADBROKES COMPETITION
PORTWAY PRESS, TIMEFORM HOUSE, HALIFAX,
WEST YORKSHIRE, HX1 1XE**

CLOSING DATE
All entries must be received by Wednesday 31st March 1999

THE RESULT
Winners will be notified within seven days of the closing date.
Full competition rules available from the above address.

AWARDS FOR 1998

'SMILE' AWARD

This year there are FIVE awards.

The 'SMILE' Award was given last year to CARL WATTS for his cheerful demeanour in defeat in the BMW International on the day Princess Diana died.

This year I was planning to scrap the award. However one reader, an avid fan of the book, wrote in to nominate DAVID CARTER when winning the Irish Open.

"For his attitude on the 18th green I would like to nominate DAVID CARTER. I had backed Monty so I knew that once the play-off came that was my money down, but Carter's attitude with the gallery on the 18th when he needed to make that putt was nice to see, he was smiling and saying to the crowd 'hey look it's not that bad', and all this after the worst 4 holes of his life. Brilliant to see and a splendid example of true sportsmanship."

SO A BIG THANK YOU TO READER STEVE BRADLEY for that.......so the 'SMILE' AWARD THIS YEAR GOES TO DAVID CARTER.

'QUOTE OF THE YEAR' AWARD

The 'QUOTE OF THE YEAR' award must go to JOHN DALY who shot an 18, yes an eighteen, at the sixth hole during his final round in the Bay Hill Invitational in Orlando in March. When asked why he took an 18? He replied, "I missed a putt for a 17."

Some quote. Some man!

JOHN DALY WINS THE 'QUOTE OF THE YEAR AWARD'

BEST GOLF SENTENCE OF THE YEAR AWARD

He may not be a golf journalist or indeed a golfer, yet I always enjoy SIMON BARNES' writing in the Times.

He wins the award for the BEST GOLF SENTENCE OF THE YEAR when he wrote a brilliant piece entitled 'Fortune favours brave youth' about youth in sport, focusing on Michael Owen, Tim Henman, Andrew Flintoff and Sachin Tendulkar. However, the winning sentence referred to Justin Rose and the player's performance in the British Open.

"If Justin Rose were an England cricketer he would have been dropped after his third round." Nice one, Simon!

GOLF SENTENCE OF THE YEAR: AWARD WINNER IS SIMON BARNES (THE TIMES).

BEST GOLF PARAGRAPHS OF THE YEAR AWARD

I always enjoy the excellent GOLF WEEKLY and the BEST GOLF PARAGRAPHS OF THE YEAR AWARD goes to its Managing Editor, Bob Warters, for his superb piece on Russell Claydon after the popular 32-year-old had gained his first tour win in the BMW International.

But it was his swing that really fascinated me. It was all his own with a unique, almost ham-fisted hold on the club which he subtly re-grips at the top of the backswing and a follow through that resembles Santa Claus heaving a sack of presents over his left shoulder on his way to the next lucky recipient. He hasn't changed a bit – though Christmas came early for Russell Claydon on Sunday.

Nice one Bob!

GOLF PARAGRAPHS OF THE YEAR: THE WINNER BOB WARTERS (GOLF WEEKLY).

TV QUOTE OF THE YEAR AWARD

Two contenders here were Peter Alliss (BBC) and Steve Livingstone (Sky).

> Steve Livingstone during the Doral Ryder Open in March described Vijay Singh who was making his fiftieth successive cut as "one of the tour's regular grinders."

Some grinder! Vijay went on to win his first major, the USPGA in August!

> Peter Alliss commentating at Augusta as Mark O'Meara holed that superb putt to win his first major. A moment of true sporting drama, pure theatre and yet Alliss' remark....."Well, I'll go to the foot of our stairs" was neither funny nor relevant. Surely it merited a different comment.

THE TV QUOTE OF THE YEAR GOES TO PETER ALLISS (WHO PROVIDED THE FOREWORD TO LAST YEAR'S BOOK).

THE FREE TRANSFER OF JEREMY CHAPMAN

If one of the saddest features of 1998 for all punters was the demise of The Sporting Life one of the best features was the 'free transfer' of Jeremy Chapman from The Sporting Life to the Racing Post.

Those involved in the closed world of professional sports betting and tipping inevitably have strong opinions, a belief in their own judgement and a confidence (at least superficially) that they can succeed in the hazardous world of sports forecasting. The insecurities inherent in such a speculative business inevitably bring out the insecurities inherent in its individual practitioners.

I discovered this after I became a publicly known sports-betting and golf tipster when the Racing Post, having given my first golf book a very highly favourable review, never reviewed, or even referred to, the following three years' annuals. That 'cold shoulder' told me so much about the pressures and jealousies of the world of professional sports-betting advice.

However it has always seemed to me right to be as objective as you can about others who pursue the same line of business as yourself. So I have no hesitation at all in saying that Jeremy Chapman is the best golf-betting writer and analyst I've ever read. I always enjoy his style, his wit and have the highest professional respect for his judgement.

There can be no doubt if he'd been a footballer he'd have fetched a Dwight Yorke size fee. As it was the Racing Post pulled off the season's best 'free transfer' when signing up 'the 'ole fella'. Whether he got a football-style signing-on fee I don't know. He certainly deserved one.

CONGRATULATIONS TO THE RACING POST FOR ENSURING THE SECOND COMING OF J.C.

A BETTER DEAL FOR GOLF PUNTERS

A CHALLENGE TO THE RACING POST

The RACING POST certainly did golf punters a big favour in securing Jeremy Chapman. However, their golf coverage, although first class, can still be improved in two main ways:

1. GIVE THE TEE TIMES FOR ALL PLAYERS IN EACH TOURNAMENT.

It is always valuable to have the tee times for the first two days of any tournament because 'early' starters nearly always have an advantage.

> They play the course when it's in perfect condition before the 'heavy traffic' from the vast majority of the other 150 plus players has started to create spike marks and scuff up the greens.
> Players don't have to 'hang around' burning up nervous and physical energy so a player can be fresh after a minimal amount of practice.
> Early starters often, although not always, gain a weather advantage as they often play when conditions are still before any wind develops later.

Given the acknowledged importance of tee times the request is simple:

GIVE THE FULL LIST OF TEE TIMES FOR ALL PLAYERS

2. PROVIDE THE FOUR-DAY WEATHER FORECAST FOR THE AREA IN WHICH THE TOURNAMENT IS HELD.

The importance of the weather in assessing a golf tournament cannot be over emphasised.

> It is necessary to interpret the tee times to assess which players are likely to get the best of 'the draw'
> It can point to the windy wet conditions in which some players thrive, or to the dry warm weather which give a comparative advantage to other players.

Such forecasts are on the Internet and readily available so my second request is:

PROVIDE A FULL FOUR-DAY WEATHER FORECAST FOR EVERY TOURNAMENT

A CHALLENGE TO THE BROADCASTERS

The television companies can also play an important part in improving things for the golf punter.

3. SCRAP THE NEWS!

The BBC's infuriating on-the-hour news bulletins that interrupt their sporting and golfing coverage especially on a Friday, must go! Let me take you back to Friday, 10th July, the third round of the Standard Life Loch Lomond Invitational tournament. It was the last European tour event before the British Open.

Any golf enthusiast or golf punter sitting down to enjoy the golf from the Bonnie Banks found the coverage interrupted on the hour by national news followed by local news, and the national weather forecast.

I believe the reason this is done is simply because the BBC sees itself now as it always has seen itself, as a training ground for the production of top-quality news journalists. We must suffer the news interruptions during our Friday because the BBC is in essence a producer-driven organisation concerned with supply not demand. The BBC's concern for its sporting customers is on a par with Bill Clinton's concern for the truth.

Now let's be clear, I thoroughly enjoy current affairs and politics, however I get an early-afternoon 'fix' at 1 pm on Radio 4 through its superb PM programme, which has incidentally suffered a 25% cut in its timeslot! However when watching afternoon golf that's what I want to see—golf, not news, and so I believe do millions of others. I've yet to meet anyone, or hear of anyone who is a sports enthusiast, particularly a golf enthusiast who wants his sports coverage interrupted by news bulletins. It's not, as if any concession is made to the sport being interrupted. For example, the weather forecast in mid-afternoon on the third day of the Loch Lomond tournament avoided any reference whatsoever to the weather for the tournament!

Indeed if the BBC's policy is right and we sports fans must have news forced on us against our will perhaps someone can explain why on the Saturday, the final round of the Loch Lomond tournament, there was no mid-afternoon news despite the fact that the Drumcree stand-off was rapidly developing as a very big news story.

After all the BBC does not have (as Sky News has) a sports slot within its news as a regular definite feature. So sport doesn't always interrupt the news, yet news always interrupts the sport!

The BBC had **B**etter **B**e **C**hanging.......and soon.

SCRAP NEWS BULLETINS THAT INTERRUPT GOLF COVERAGE

4. LET'S HAVE CLEAR AND ACCURATE TV INFORMATION

One improvement to TV golf coverage that could be made by all stations is to improve the display of the leaderboard. So often we see a seven-man leaderboard with, for example, the last three players shown in T5th position at 3 under par. However this can give a totally-false impression because there may be, say, another five or six players who are also at 3 under who are not shown.

This really can be very misleading because either you think your player on the leaderboard is T5th with only one other, or you don't see his name and presume he's out of contention when he may well also be T5th yet not shown!

CREATE LEADERBOARDS THAT GIVE A CLEAR AND ACCURATE PICTURE

Golf fans want to know three things at any particular time about the players they are watching.

> the number of the hole he has just completed
> his score (to par) for the current round
> his score (to par) for the whole tournament to date.

These three pieces of information are available and could be provided TOGETHER whenever a player is shown on tee, fairway or green yet they are not <u>all</u> shown.

If they were we would have a complete picture which would enable us at a glance to know the progress of any 2-ball or 3-ball bet, as well as any outright wager.

LET'S HAVE ACCURATE PUNTER-FRIENDLY STATS WHENEVER A PLAYER IS SHOWN

THE EROSION OF ODDS –
THE NEED FOR PUNTER VIGILANCE

MATCH BETTING

Let's take a hypothetical match – FALDO v MONTGOMERIE. On such a bet the traditional odds are shown in Column A with the bookmakers' overround 11.43%. However by shaving the odds to 9/10 from 10/11 that overround goes to 11.93%; and through further shaving 9/10 becomes 5/6 with the overround then up to 15.77%. (I am assuming a three-outcome situation without the tie a 'runner' and so no possibility of a dead heat).

A		B		C	
FALDO	10/11	FALDO	9/10	FALDO	5/6
MONTY	10/11	MONTY	9/10	MONTY	5/6
TIE	14/1	TIE	14/1	TIE	14/1
Overround	11.43%		11.93%		15.77%

B compared to A   overround + 0.5% – an increase of 4.37%
C compared to B   overround + 3.84% – an increase of 32.18%
C compared to A   overround + 4.34% – an increase of 37.97%

Already this process of shaving the odds for match betting has started as bookmakers seek to gain every possible advantage they can at the expense of the punter.

The move from 10/11 to 9/10 in and of itself is bad for punters. However it is surely only a staging post on the road to 5/6 each of two which is the bookmakers' big prize. Let's remember from 10/11 to 5/6 (via 9/10) increases the bookmakers' overround by a colossal 37.97% (15.77 minus 11.43 divided by 100).

The effect of this shaving of odds is shown particularly in doubles and trebles

	10/11 each of two	9/10 each of two	5/6 each of two
DOUBLE pays	2.65-1	2.61-1	2.34-1
TREBLE pays	5.97-1	5.86-1	5.13-1

And let's be clear, pushing the tie out from 14/1 to 16/1 is no consolation. Stand up the punter with half a brain who bets on 72-hole match bets being tied?

THE SIMPLE TRUTH IS PUNTERS WANT TO BACK ONE PLAYER TO FINISH AHEAD OF ANOTHER OVER 72 HOLES AND TO DO SO ON THE 'TRADITIONAL TERMS' OF 10/11 EACH OF TWO AND 14/1 THE TIE.

GROUP BETTING

Group betting enables punters to back their fancy in a 'small field' rather than in the 154-runner races they usually face in the outright betting markets.

Traditionally there are five players grouped together, all priced at 7/2, which gives the bookmakers an overround of 11.1% which, as you can see, is comparable to the traditional match-bet overround of 11.43%.

A		B		C	
FALDO	7/2	FALDO	10/3	FALDO	10/3
MONTY	7/2	MONTY	10/3	MONTY	10/3
WOOSY	7/2	WOOSY	7/2	WOOSY	10/3
TIGER	7/2	TIGER	7/2	TIGER	10/3
ERNIE	7/2	ERNIE	7/2	ERNIE	10/3
Overround	11.1%		12.82%		15.4%

B compared to A	overround + 1.72% – an increase of 15.5%
C compared to B	overround + 2.58% – an increase of 20.12%
C compared to A	overround + 4.3% – an increase of 38.74%!

Once more here you can see the same process of erosion of the odds as bookmakers move from A to B as a staging post to C which will surely be their medium-term goal. Here let's note that the move from 7/2 to 10/3 for each of the players in the group increases the bookmakers' overround by a huge 38.74% (15.4 minus 11.1 divided by 100).

We can now see a pattern.

* The move from 10/11 to 5/6 via 9/10 in match betting would increase the bookmakers' overround by 37.97%, and the move from 7/2 to 10/3 (each of five) in group betting would increase the overround by 38.7%. In both cases bookmakers are seeking to move their overrounds in these submarkets from the range of 11 – 11½% to the range $15^2/_5 - 15^4/_5\%$.

However bookmakers are often very cute and will put one group together as follows.

D	
FALDO	3/1
MONTY	3/1
WOOSY	7/2
TIGER	7/2
ERNIE	4/1
Overround	14.44%

By pushing Ernie out to 4/1 while reducing Faldo and Monty to 3/1 they are creating confusion cleverly to enable them to push up their overrounds. I expect they will use this device rather than that shown in C because it appears a swings and roundabouts change making little difference when in effect it boosts the overround very significantly.

D compared to A	overround + 3.33% – an increase of 29.73%

The answer for the punter is simple.

* KEEP YOUR EYE OPEN FOR BOOKIES SHAVING ODDS
* COMPLAIN WHEN THEY DO, AND
* ALWAYS 'SHOP AROUND' FOR THE BEST ODDS

WILL AN ENTERPRISING BOOKMAKER OFFER 'THE FIELD' AS A BET?

In this volume a couple of years ago under the above heading I suggested that an enterprising bookmaking firm seeking to gain an edge in the expanding golf betting market could offer 'the field' as a bet.

I was reminded of this, earlier this year, when one foreign firm quoted the following odds for the US Open won by Lee Janzen.

Tiger Woods	8-1	Jesper Parnevik	33-1	Tom Kite	50-1
Ernie Els	10-1	Vijay Singh	33-1	Andrew Magee	50-1
David Duval	12-1	Tom Watson	33-1	Jumbo Ozaki	50-1
Davis Love III	15-1	Thomas Bjorn	40-1	Loren Roberts	50-1
Colin Montgomerie	18-1	Mark Calcavecchia	40-1	Bob Tway	50-1
Justin Leonard	20-1	Stewart Cink	40-1	Ian Woosnam	50-1
Fred Couples	22-1	Steve Elkington	40-1	Paul Azinger	75-1
Tom Lehman	22-1	Nick Faldo	40-1	Mark Brooks	75-1
Phil Mickelson	25-1	Brad Faxon	40-1	Jay Haas	75-1
Mark O'Meara	25-1	Steve Jones	40-1	Hale Irwin	75-1
Nick Price	25-1	Bernhard Langer	40-1	Robert Karlsson	75-1
Lee Westwood	28-1	Frank Nobilo	40-1	Scott McCarron	75-1
John Cook	33-1	Payne Stewart	40-1	Jack Nicklaus	75-1
Jim Furyk	33-1	Stuart Appleby	50-1	Corey Pavin	75-1
Scott Hoch	33-1	John Huston	50-1	Costantino Rocca	75-1
Lee Janzen	33-1	John Daly	50-1	Scott Simpson	75-1
Jeff Maggert	33-1	Glen Day	50-1	Paul Stankowski	75-1
Jose Maria Olazabal	33-1	Bill Glasson	50-1	THE FIELD	11-1

As you can see all the 'rank outsiders' are lumped together as 'the field' and quoted at 11/1, so creating a 55-runner race. This effectively reduces the bookmakers' overround yet still leaves it, in the example, at a very healthy 64.45%!

There have been examples of 'the field' being introduced (usually at 7/1 – which in the example would have pushed the overround up to 68.5%) in this country so it can be done.

SO THE CHALLENGE IS THERE FOR ANY ENTERPRISING, PROBABLY SMALLER, BOOKMAKING FIRM THAT WANTS TO BOOST ITS MARKET SHARE – TO INTRODUCE 'THE FIELD' AS A BET IN THE OUTRIGHT MARKET

EACH-WAY GOLF BETTING

The bookmaking industry shows all the classic signs of what economists call an 'oligopoly' – an industry with the mass of the market dominated by three or four large firms who tend to compete on service, advertising and promotional offers rather than on price itself.

Each of the large firms in such an industry knows that if it cuts its price its rival firms will follow suit with the result that there will be a benefit to the industry's customers but little for the price-cutting firms. For that reason the firms don't tend to cut their prices relative to their rivals.

Each of the big bookmaking firms act exactly like this in their approach to taking a unilateral decision to give improved terms to punters. So when I decided to press the main bookmakers to improve their each-way terms on golf betting, and to follow the example of Victor Chandlers and Sunderlands and pay one quarter the odds on the first five, rather than the traditional first four, I was only slightly hopeful rather than wildly confident.

In the event Ladbrokes decided to extend their each way terms on pre-tournament golf outright betting to pay on the FIFTH player but to offer only one-FIFTH the odds. In essence, for the first time they gave each-way punters a choice.

> 1/4 odds 1,2,3,4

OR

> 1/5 odds 1,2,3,4,5

Very soon Hills, Stanleys and the Tote followed Ladbrokes' lead, although Corals and Stan James did not.

Although this was a mini-success the emphasis was on the mini rather than the success. Nevertheless punter choice had been extended. As Jeremy Chapman commented at the time 'we should be grateful for small mercies'.

WHEN TO TAKE ONE FIFTH THE FIRST FIVE

The first priority for the each-way punter must be to bet at ONE QUARTER the odds the first five. However if you are unable to do so you now have the choice of one quarter 1-4, or one fifth 1-5.

There can be no obvious 'right' answer to this alternative without looking at the specific details of the player and the tournament

If you fancy an 80/1 outsider at 1/5 1-5 you get 16/1 a place, at 1/4 1-4 you get 20/1 a place. On balance it may be wiser, if you can't get 1/4 1-5, to take 1/5 1-5 and that 16/1. Sure, if your player finishes in the front four you've lost 4 points on the place bet, however 'the insurance' provided by the 5th place payout is fair compensation.

Incidentally in this example you can compare the 'value' of your outsider being in the first five at 16/1 with another name player who may be only 16/1 to win the whole tournament.

* WHEN BETTING EACH WAY (IF YOU CAN'T BACK AT 1/4 FIRST FIVE) ALWAYS CONSIDER THE ONE FIFTH THE FIRST FIVE OPTION.

THE FUTURE OF CORALS

Golf punters are well aware that over the years Corals have probably priced up more tournaments worldwide and created more speciality submarkets than any other firm. Jon Wright, their senior compiler together with James Farley and Karl Schaum 'know' their golf, know their computer and know punters enjoy variety.

So one aspect of the proposed Ladbrokes merger and the future of Corals for golf punters was the continuation of these markets. I sought and received an unequivocal assurance from Ladbrokes in this regard which was included in their press release dated Tuesday, 20th January 1998 and covered in the Racing Post.

Elliott chips in for punters

We soon found out what Keith Elliott, who sits on the Levy Board and is a noted golf fanatic and author, though of Ladbrokes' decision to squeeze golf margins.

After the uproar quite rightly created by Derek McGovern in the Racing Post, Elliott rang to say he had already discreetly made the point, on behalf of the punters in general, to Ladbrokes. Elliott said he had also raised the issue of paying the first five, a concession A R Dennis' punters lost when the company was acquired by Ladbrokes a year ago.

"They told me they were reviewing the situation and would consider paying the first five, albeit to a fifth the odds.

"They also have undertaken to maintain the creativity Coral brought to golf betting around special and long-term markets—something which added much to my own pleasure and that, I am sure, of many punters."

He will have been delighted at Ladbrokes' subsequent announcements, first reverting to 10-11 take your pick in match betting and then, this week, that punters could have the standard quarter the odds, first four, or opt for fifth the odds, first five.

The end result to a PR nightmare for Ladbrokes is punters' choice has been expanded. Elliott, unusually, was directly praised in Ladbrokes' press release. It all suggests that the Levy Board's publicised concern for punters is not just window dressing.

Following the announcement of the acquisition of Coral, Elliott was again in contact asking Ladbrokes to commit to increasing the number of golf events on which prices are available. Coral have priced up more senior's, women's and Australasian golf events and have offered a number of novelty markets. Ladbrokes committed not only to price up these events but to surpass the Coral range of golf markets.

You will see in this volume, and will know from previous volumes, of Corals' wide range of markets which this year included the 'pricing-up' of the Qualifying Rounds for the British Open the full details of which are in Part 3, as well as the odds for individual players to play in the 1999 Ryder Cup.

Ladbrokes merger with Corals was blocked by the Government after the report of the Monopolies and Mergers Commission. So, at the time of writing, we do not know the future of the Corals company.

However you can be certain that once it is known I shall press very hard indeed for the assurance I got from Ladbrokes to be honoured by Corals' new owners.

* CORALS' RANGE OF SPECIALITY MARKETS MUST BE ALLOWED TO CONTINUE.

HOW TO WIN AT GOLF BETTING

THE NAPPY FACTOR REVISITED

In 'Elliott's Golf Form 1996' I introduced the idea that becoming a father, especially for the first time and especially of a son, acts as a real inspiration to a young player. So the 'nappy factor' was born.

'The nappy factor' in essence is to note such players in the first full year or the next full season after the birth and I quoted countless examples of winning players to back up the point.

Indeed in a memorable article in the March 1996 GOLF WORLD the late Peter Dobereiner stated, after his own detailed research found many examples to support the theory, "the accumulating body of evidence – and there is plenty more where that came from – does seem to establish a connection between fatherhood and achievement".

33-year-old Davis Love III is a classic example. Before his son, Davis Love the fourth, was born in December 1993 Davis had won eight tournaments yet he'd never recorded a single top 10 in twenty-three starts in majors. However from 1995 to 1997 he played in all twelve majors and his record was superb.

1995   2nd US Masters; T4th US Open
1996   T7th US Masters; T2nd US Open
1997   T7th US Masters; T10th British Open; Won USPGA

So from no top 10s to seven top 10s in twelve starts including his first major win in the 1997 USPGA. Davis Love the fourth had some impact on Davis Love the third!

Russell Claydon's first win in August came in his first 'nappy factor' season after son Alex was born, and that victory came only a couple of weeks after Darren Clarke had clearly stated that first-time fatherhood of a first-time son has a mega-effect. He missed the USPGA to be with his new son Tyrone (named after the Irish County) and then went on to play the European Open at the K Club in Dublin where he finished 4th at 18/1.

"As you are aware, I tend to get upset occasionally with my golf when I don't play so well. I think when Tyrone was born that all changed. My perspective on life now is completely changed. I've got a beautiful wife and son now at home who are much more important than my golf. That takes the pressure off my golf and let's me go and play and accept whatever happens as opposed to getting annoyed about my bad shots".

Darren proved just how significant 'the nappy factor' was when he won the Volvo Masters at 22/1, and at once took his new son Tyrone in his arms as he walked off the green. It was his first win as a dad, and it sure won't be his last.

The nappy factor will be referred to where relevant in the Player Profiles.

* THE 'NAPPY FACTOR' STILL RULES O.K.!

THINK TWICE AFTER THE WINDS BLOW

In 'How To Win At Golf Betting' (p.39) the point is made that playing in high winds can destroy a player's rhythm. As a result, his performance the following week can be poor, or at best average.

> A classic example was the 1996 Scottish Open when the winds were so severe not even the winner, Ian Woosnam, could beat par. Of the first ten in that tournament nine played the next week in the warm, dry conditions at Royal Lytham in the British Open and eight of them missed the cut by an average of almost 4 shots.

> This year the AT&T in late January was ruined by gales. The following week, seven of the players in the AT&T top 10 played in the Buick Invitational. Although the Buick itself was rain-reduced the players did not

have to face the same windy conditions of the previous week. Their subsequent poor performances are shown.

	AT&T Position	Buick Invitational position
Tim Herron	T1st	Missed cut (by 6 shots)
Jay Haas	T3rd	T76th
Phil Mickelson	T3rd	T49th
Davis Love III	T6th	T3rd
Chris Smith	T6th	Missed cut
Tom Pernice Jr	T6th	T27th
Paul Azinger	T6th	T57th

> The wind-affected British Open this year certainly took its toll on some of the leading players who admitted that their swings had been adversely affected, with Lee Westwood a notable example.

* BE PREPARED TO OPPOSE PLAYERS THE WEEK AFTER THEY HAVE HAD THEIR SWINGS RAVAGED BY THE WIND.

FOLLOW PLAYERS ON THE COMEBACK TRAIL

In 'How To Win At Golf Betting' Chapter 4 contained 37 tips for successful golf betting and No. 25 was to 'follow players on the comeback trail'.

THE MAGNIFICENT SEVEN ON THE COMEBACK TRAIL

Number of wins before the winless streak began		No wins in	On the 'Comeback Trail' in America
JOHN COOK	6	1993,1994,1995	Won 1996 (twice) Won 1997 Won 1998
HAL SUTTON	8	1996, 1997	Won 1998 (twice)
MARK O'MEARA	7	1993, 1994	Won 9 times since!
LEE JANZEN	7	1996, 1997	Won 1998 US Open
NICK PRICE	14	1995, 1996	Won 1997 Won 1998
JOHN HUSTON	3	1995, 1996, 1997	Won 1998 (twice)
STEVE JONES	4	1990s injured	Won 1996 US Open Won 1997 (twice) Won 1998

We need to find players who possess an 'extra' inner drive for success. Players on the 'comeback trail' have this. Golfers can lose form because of injury, changing clubs or a descent into a 'comfort zone' of mediocrity. However once such a player with a proven winning record overcomes illness or recovers from injury, or readjusts his mental approach, he can provide value betting opportunities. Refocussed, rededicated and refreshed they have real incentive, deep anticipation and a heightened appetite for success.

The chart below shows recent examples of some of golf's 'comeback kids'. I believe the point to be of sufficient significance to have added a symbol (CT) to indicate in a Player's Profile that he's now on the 'Comeback Trail'.

Number of wins in career to date		Last win	
Corey Pavin	14	1996	Loss of form and confidence. Changed clubs
Paul Azinger	11	1993	Overcame cancer
Payne Stewart	9	1995	Just three winless years
Tom Lehman	4	1996	Two years without a US victory

Four American players on the 1999 comeback trail are shown. It will be interesting to see how they do.

* FOLLOW GOLF'S 'COMEBACK KIDS'.

THE DYM SYSTEM – AN UPDATE

I introduced the DYM system in my very first golf book. I had found it appealing because essentially it enabled the punter to use the knowledge and insights of golf odds compilers for 'free'.

Bookmakers produce sets of prices for each of the golfers in a tournament. These odds represent the compilers' views of the players' chances. On the day before the tournament, charts appear in the Racing Post showing the odds that the different firms offer. The heart of the system is to use the different odds given by the different firms as the basis for making a 'value' bet.

The rules therefore are:

1. From the bookmakers' odds chart in the Racing Post note any player whose highest price is at least double his lowest price e.g. if one firm quotes 66/1 when another offers 33/1.

2. The system is called the DYM system because effectively one firm is offering to Double Your Money compared to another firm by offering at least double the odds.

3. The system will give you a short list, sometimes a long short list, of players which you will then have to prune.

The logic behind the system is essentially simple. When professional odds compilers disagree they are in fact giving punters vital pieces of information.

For example in the 1998 USPGA championship in the Top European player market the Swede Per-Ulrik Johansson was only 14/1 with Victor Chandlers while he was 25/1 with Hills and Ladbrokes and a massive 33/1 at Stanleys.

Johansson therefore was clearly a DYM player. However was the 14/1 or the 33/1 the more logical price? Delving deeper the shrewd punter would have noted that

* The Swede, after a poor season dogged by ill health, returned to form in his last tournament when a fine 7th in the Scandinavian Masters.

* In the last six American majors he had been one of the top 3 European three times – a 50% strike rate.

* He obviously enjoys the USPGA having finished 8th in 1996, when he was 2nd in the Top European market.

* The conclusion had to be that Johansson was very generously priced at 33/1 in a 14-runner field.

However there will be many examples where you find that even at his best price the player is not worth a bet.

For example in the 1998 European Open at the K Club, Dublin in late August American raider Payne Stewart was 20/1 with Stan James (their joint fifth favourite) while 40/1 was on offer from Ladbrokes.

Although he had played well in Europe before when winning the Dutch Open that was seven years ago and Stewart was playing the K Club for the first time and was probably on a 'jolly' even if he would try his best.

So the reasonable view was that 20/1 was too cautious and the 40/1 quote probably realistic. Stewart was a DYM player yet not one to give the bookies some Payne!

In the event the nattily-dressed American missed the cut!

THE WINNING RECORD OF THE DYM SYSTEM

The US Money List

1995 Greg Norman	8/1	
1996 Tom Lehman	33/1	

1994		1995	
Brett Ogle	40/1	D A Weibring	50/1
Kenny Perry	50/1	Paul Broadhurst	66/1
Scott Hoch	80/1	Vijay Singh	33/1
John Huston	50/1	Ted Tryba	80/1
Hale Irwin	66/1	Andrew Oldcorn	66/1
Mark McCumber	50/1	Alexander Cejka	66/1
David Gilford	50/1	Jim Furyk	66/1
Stephen Ames	66/1		

1996		1997	
Guy Boros	100/1	Phil Blackmar	100/1
Steve Stricker	80/1	Clinton Whitelaw	100/1
Mark Brooks	66/1	Frank Nobilo	80/1
Jonathan Lomas	100/1	Scott McCarron	50/1
Raymond Russell	100/1	Paul Stankowski	50/1
Padraig Harrington	80/1	Jeff Sluman	100/1
Diego Borrego	80/1	Billy Ray Brown	100/1
Costantino Rocca	50/1	P U Johansson	40/1
Paul Stankowski (Nov)	100/1	Davis Duval	40/1
Bill Glasson	66/1		

1998 DYM WINNERS

USA		EUROPE	
Michael Bradley	80/1	Tony Johnstone	100/1
Olin Browne	200/1	Stephen Leaney	66/1
Steve Pate	125/1	Mats Lanner	80/1
Billy Mayfair	125/1	Sam Torrance	80/1
John Huston	50/1	Stephen Leaney	125/1
		Stephen Allan	100/1
		Retief Goosen	40/1
		(A Dunhill Cup)	

Majors

British Open   Mark O'Meara 40/1
USPGA   Top European Player: P U Johansson 33/1

So 1998 has been the best DYM year to date both for the number of winners and for their prices with thirteen tournament winners including six at odds of 100/1 plus.

THE FREQUENCY OF DYMS

As golf betting becomes ever more popular so golf odds compilers are making fewer mistakes than in the past.

However, often the golf odds compilers also create odds for other sports so find real pressure on time.

So DYMs can occur

* In the first tournaments after a Bank Holiday Monday
* When compilers have paid more attention to other big events.

> 16th – 19th July 1998 there were ten DYMs among the twenty-one players priced at or below 66/1 in the Deposit Guaranty Classic in America because compilers were too busy in British Open week.

> 9th – 12th July 1998 thirty-eight (over 51%) of the seventy-four players in Racing Post's golf pricewise column for the Quad City Classic were DYMs as attention focussed on the World Cup.

Over a period of time you will 'get a feel' of the different firms' compilers, noticing which are the more clued up and which make the most 'ricks'.

PRUNING THE SHORT LIST

The DYM winning record really is excellent on both sides of the Atlantic. However, we must not get too excited although some degree of excitement is appropriate with such a simple system regularly unearthing huge–priced winners.

The real skill lies in pruning the shortlist of DYM players. You can apply the THIRTY-SEVEN tips given in my book, 'How To Win At Golf Betting' to each tournament's DYM players.

With the DYM system providing the raw material for the short list your pruning skill will then provide the final selections.

OPERATING THE DYM SYSTEM

You will need

> The pricewise golf chart from the Wednesday or Thursday morning editions of the Racing Post.

> To be able to place your bet with one of the range of bookmakers who quote odds on golf tournaments. To do this you will have to open credit accounts, switch/delta card accounts or have a friendly independent bookmaker who will accept other firms' prices.

> Keep up to date on the players on both the European and American tours to enable you to prune your DYM shortlist.

This year, for the first time, every DYM player in any market or submarket is shown with an asterisk * against his name.

DYMs AND THE WAY THE RACING POST
GETS ITS GOLF ODDS

So often in life we find that our innocent, and often well-intentioned, actions have unintended consequences. The way the Racing Post get the outright golf odds from the bookmakers for its golf pricewise chart is a case in point.

One method for getting the odds in from the various bookmakers would be to send every firm an A–Z list of the full field of players. If this was done the returns would then have to be studied at the Racing Post to create a rank order from favourite and second favourite downwards to the real long shots. Such an operation when time and staff are scarce would be expensive, so this method is not used.

What actually happens is that the first firm to price up, possibly by Monday early afternoon, has its rank order used as the basis for the list of 'runners' faxed to the bookmakers. So the compilers receive a list which is, in fact, giving them free information. For example, if a player is tenth in the rank order on the list sent out then the compiler who was going to quote 100/1 will immediately wonder why the guy is tenth on the list. He may then quote him at 50/1 rather than 100/1 as a 'defensive' measure. As a result this method of collecting odds tends to have an inbuilt mechanism that reduces differences in odds between firms, and creates a more uniform market. However when the odds are received at the Racing Post they can be tabulated relatively quickly.

For some time my suspicion had been that inadvertently this odds-gathering mechanism actually worked in a punter-hostile way. So I rang Bruce Millington, the Sports Editor, first to explain the point, and second to see if any action could be taken to alleviate its unintended effects.

Bruce understood the point straightaway, and for the following week's tournament (the Greater Milwaukee Open) changed the system to 'A–Z' from 'odds rank order'. As a result of that mini-experiment it became clear that it was too expensive in terms of staff time to continue, and that it is probable that the unintended effect that I had pointed to did exist as the Greater Milwaukee Open had 12 DYMs among the 37 players best priced at or under 100/1, which was a much higher proportion than usual.

Now I do appreciate that compilers may be able to get rival's prices from teletext. However that is an uncertain and time costly method compared to having a rank order presented to you directly. Golf compilers are always under time pressure because they have so many other events to price up, so a system which saves time and gives them assistance is clearly preferable to them than one that doesn't.

Nevertheless we've already lost The Sporting Life, and I certainly don't want to see extra costs placed on the Racing Post. However fewer DYMs, and a greater market uniformity, is the price we are probably paying in the golf outright markets.

LIES, DAMNED LIES AND (CHIP'S) GOLF STATISTICS

Golf being a game of numbers is a game that is saturated with statistics, and very valuable they are too. Indeed they are an absolutely essential part of the golf punter's armoury.

Potentially one of the most valuable avenues open is the (usual) 2-ball betting on the final round, particularly on American golf. One of the main statistical tools available is the R4 scoring averages. Now if we really can spot the 'bottlers', the guys who can't stand the heat of the Sunday kitchen, then we are quids in.

However turning to the final rounds stats, before the Las Vegas Invitational, who did I see in pole position, the USPGA tour's Number 1, the player we can be sure can be backed on the final day? Tiger? Duval? O'Meara? Elk? Furyk? .....guess on.....indeed ask your mates to guess, and given them 20, 30 or 40 guesses.....will they produce the right answer? I doubt it..... it was CHIP BECK, who can hardly make a cut if you give him a machete and who had had just one final round all year when, nowhere near the leaders, he had shot a 68.....so his average was 68....and he was top!

Well in 1999 I shall be creating my own R4 index for every player because, apart from the Beck absurdity, the key weakness of the statistics is that they average all R4 scores irrespective of (a) whether, or not the player was in contention, and (b) whether the scoring conditions were hard or easy.

So a par 72 in very tough conditions when starting the final day in third place is clearly better than a 70 when conditions are easy and you're under no pressure starting in 50th place!

Next year I'll explain its creation and use. During the year I shall be using it for my Timeview Sportsview clients and callers.

* BE WARY OF **FINAL ROUND** GOLF STATS.

AND FINALLY

Every year I make the same point in concluding the opening chapter and I make no apology for doing so again. Golf is now unquestionably the last game of honour left, played for a living by professionals. It's an oasis in an amoral desert of commercial professional sporting sleaze.

So let's always remember as we watch the players drive for show and putt for dough that they are going through all sorts of mental torment. To you and I it's a bet, a very important bet, yet to the players, and their families it's their future and their place in the history books.

So enjoy having a golf bet, admire the incredible skill and feel the tension. To be a part of it through a credit account, switch card or betting slip is to be involved in the greatest sport on the planet. Enjoy it, have fun.....and I hope you pile up profits by perusing these pages!

1999 – The Golf Betting Year In Prospect   Part 2

THE 1999 RYDER CUP

Will Faldo play?

When Nick first made the decision to play full time in America I expected the change in his lifestyle to have an impact. Indeed I predicted in this book, four years ago, that he'd win one of his first six tournaments in the States and he did just that.

So if Nick's slump in form was to be reversed it would surely have been in October in the Belgacom Open. After all he made another 'fresh start' with the announcement of his parting from his girlfriend, and his split from his long-standing golf coach David Leadbetter. In this climate of change there would surely be an 'impact' effect on Nick's golf.

His chance came in the Belgacom Open, on one of his favourite courses where he has a superb record. He opened with a most encouraging 65. However 'normal service' was resumed as Nick ended T30th as the 'old magic' in the most favourable of circumstances simply did not return.

With Ryder Cup points available from the monies to be won in the new 1999 World Golf Championships Nick will be very keen to play in the Andersen World Consulting Match-play in February, open to the World's top ranked 64 players, and Nick is currently (29th October) 66th.

However should he miss out on that tournament his chances of breaking into one of the top 10 automatic places will, I believe, be slim, and slim's left town.

So would Nick then be granted a wild card by 'Jesse' James in the last-chance saloon? If that was the choice open to Mark James–and I think it probably will be–then the media would have a real feeding frenzy.

Much would obviously depend on the players in the top 10, and the other in-form players available for wild-card selection by James. However it really is possible to envisage a 1999 European Ryder Cup team without Faldo.

The Captains

When Mark James was announced as the European captain on the eve of the BMW International in late August I was delighted as I'd tipped him at Corals' very generous 3/1. His vice captain was to be Sam Torrance with Sky commentator Ken Brown his assistant.

His opposite number will be 'Gentle' Ben Crenshaw who, like James, has proved himself to be a fierce competitor. Crenshaw has 19 US tour victories including the US Masters twice, whilst James has 18 European tour successes.

They will both have the respect of their players, although I fear 'Jesse' James will be outfought at Brookline in September 1999.

THE BROOKLINE, MASSACHUSETTS 1999 MATCH

One initial point to note is that a combined-odds bet on each side to win by one or two points, and on the tie (five bets in all) would have won in seven of the last eight Ryder Cups. That combined-odds bet (on a 'betting-to-figures' basis) in 1997 was between 6-5 and 11-10.

Nevertheless the 1999 Ryder Cup may just change that pattern as

> The potential American team (with Duval, Woods, Love, Furyk, O'Meara and Mickelson all looking certain to play) seems to have far more strength in depth than the Europeans.
> Ryder Cup stalwarts such as Langer (42), Woosnam (41), Rocca (42) and Faldo (42) have been suffering from losses of form and confidence, or a variety of injuries. (Their ages here will be those at the time of the 1999 Ryder Cup.)
> America with home advantage, will be really focussed to ensure they 'stop the rot' and prevent a third successive defeat.

Admittedly European team spirit, and the possibility of 'media pressure' on the home players may help our guys, however the expectation with just under a year to go must be for the US to win, and by more than 2 points.

WELL DONE CORALS

As usual Corals opened books on which players would make the European and American teams. The prices are shown in the profiles of the relevant players in Part 6.

Three initial thoughts on inspecting their prices were:

Surely 5/1 Justin Rose was a joke. It was the first time ever a prospective Ryder Cup player was given a quote before he had made a professional cut.

> Seve at 16/1 is another laugh. Come on Jon Wright 66/1 or 80/1, but sixteens?
> 13/8 Johansson seemed the best initial 'value' and on the first day of trading his price went to odds on. The news that the new World Golf Championships will count for Ryder Cup purposes should also help the young Swede.

THE ODDS

The best odds available on the two sides after James's appointment were:

USA: 4/6 Hills, 2/5 Corals, Surrey
GB & Europe: 11/8 Hills, 5/2 Corals
Tie: 10/1 Chandler, Hills, Surrey, Tote

THE PLAYERS TO FOLLOW IN 1999

Last year my "7 to follow" kept up the good record of this feature.

David Duval (four times), Jim Furyk (once), Vijay Singh (twice), and Lee Westwood (five times) all won. Retief Goosen with his 25/1 win as top points scorer in the Dunhill Cup, and Per-Ulrik Johansson with his 33/1 win as top Euro in the USPGA also rewarded their selection.

This year I'm changing tack. It would be easy to tell you that Duval, Woods and Furyk will win in the States or that Westwood, Clarke and Monty will also succeed on the European tour......and they will.

However let's go for players who will be at 'value' prices, guys who can be expected to land 'shock' wins at tasty odds.

So my magnificent seven for 1999 are:-

SCOTT VERPLANK – American amateur champ in 1984, this guy is a very good player who has had all sorts of injury and health problems. He re-established himself by easily being the top player at the 1997 US Q School and then notched four top 5 finishes in 1998. Top 30 for greens in regulation, top 25 for putting, and as an 'unexposed' player he'll be on offer at big prices. I expect him to win in 1999.

BILL GLASSON – He's been in operating theatres more times than Dr Kildare. However this guy now seems in full health and can be expected to make a series of high finishes in 1999. Like Verplank he'll often be available at tasty prices.

STEVE STRICKER – Back to form after a poor spell last year. Won twice in 1996 when he was 4th in the Money list at 100/1. In 1998 he was T5th in the US Open, and 2nd in the USPGA. In 1999 with 'nappy factor' inspiration I expect he'll do really well, especially in July as you'll see in his player profile.

BRANDEL CHAMBLEE – In each of the last three years he's either won or finished second. Now he's got his first win another in 1999 at a juicy price wouldn't be a surprise.

ALEX CEJKA – Number 1 on the 1998 European tour for greens in regulation yet he couldn't buy a putt. A proven winner, with 'nappy factor' inspiration expect him to get back to winning ways in 1999.

ANDREW COLTART – In 1998 he won his first European tour event, was top of the Australian Order of Merit, and played well to end the season 2nd in the Volvo Masters. He's got a fine swing, and can go on to win again in 1999.

PETER BAKER – Ryder Cup year 1999 could well see the re-emergence of the 1993 Ryder Cup 'hero'. He's working very hard on his short game and surely he'll get into contention in 1999, and post a victory.

'NEW KIDS ON THE BLOCK' – This annual feature has given five players so far with 1996 Thomas Bjorn (W 80/1) and 1997 Stewart Cink (W 50/1) being the big winners.

In 1999 expect SERGIO GARCIA to make a big impact on the European tour. In the States STEVE FLESCH can build on his fine rookie year. He very nearly gave me my biggest-ever winner when 2nd at 200/1 as an 'unknown' in the Freeport McDermott Classic when the stats were already pointing to his accuracy. SERGIO and STEVE should make their mark in the coming season.

THE MAJORS

The four majors are always the highpoints of the golfing year, so let's look well in advance at the prospects for 1999.

THE US MASTERS

Augusta — 8th – 11th April

The only major to be played on the same course each year and with a relatively small field (87 in 1998 including amateurs and old codgers) this is probably the most punter-friendly major of all.

TIGER WOODS is the advance selection as Augusta clearly is tailor made for his long-hitting game as he proved with his record-breaking 1997 victory when he was 18 under par and the 12-shot winner. Even this year when only T8th he had four par or sub-par rounds, although his iron play was way below his best. In 1997 he was T1st for greens in regulation whereas in 1998 he was T16th! So long as his back is in good shape and his dad is in good health I expect the Tiger to play really well at Augusta in 1999.

Another player to note would be PAUL AZINGER. The Zinger was T5th in 1998 just 3 shots behind Mark O'Meara yet he took 14 putts more than the winner. Fully recovered now after his cancer problems the 38-year-old was only 2½ yards behind the Tiger for driving distance this year, and also 3rd for greens in regulation. If he can improve his putting he will surely go close and let's remember he's already won a major, the 1993 USPGA.

The best value bets of 1998 were surely on PER ULRIK JOHANSSON to be top European in the US Masters (T3rd 33/1) and in the USPGA (won 33/1). Both were well tipped in last year's volume. The 31-year-old Swede when fully fit is a very good player with lots of bottle. T12th in the last two US Masters – he was 5th for greens in regulation in 1997 and 6th for putting in 1998. If he can combine those two performances in 1999 he'll improve on those 12th place finishes. Certainly in the top European betting he's a cracking each-way bet.

One top player to oppose would be NICK PRICE who has missed the Augusta cut three times in the last six years. He admits himself he'd rather win the US Open than the US Masters and says that he can't reach all the par 5s like Woods or Els, and can't really handle the greens. In his last two completed finishes at Augusta – he was T32nd (of 46) for putting in 1997 when finishing T24th, and T26th (of 44) for putting the previous year when finishing T18th.

When teelng off at Augusta Nick has low expectations, and although he holds the course record, he can be opposed. A world-class player yes, an Augusta winner no!

THE US OPEN

Narrow fairways, severe rough and fast, undulating greens are the usual mixture that we can expect at Pinehurst No. 2, in North Carolina from 17th – 20th June 1999.

The best bet is probably that TOM LEHMAN will play well and post a high finish. The 39-year-old gears his first half of the year to this tournament in which his recent record is stunningly consistent – T5th 1998: 3rd 1997: T2nd 1996: 3rd 1995. He may never win it because of his putting and his apparent inability to vary from his stock shot (a draw). Nevertheless on the record of the last four years he is a rock-solid spread-betting proposition.

One young player to note is STEWART CINK. In his three US Opens he's finished T10th 1998: T12th 1997: T16th 1996 to suggest that his straight hitting, sound temperament and solid all-round game will continue to enable him to notch top 20 finishes and so encourage spread betters to have him on their side.

The player to oppose must be ace putter BRAD FAXON whose inaccuracy off the tee always finds him out in the US Open. The five-time tour winner has now played in 13 US Opens with his highest ever finish T33rd!

THE BRITISH OPEN

From 15th – 18th July Carnoustie will host the final British Open of the nineties. The course was last used on the European tour for the windswept 1996 Scottish Open.

If BRAD FAXON is to be opposed in the US Open he sure can be supported on the spreads in the British Open. In the last five years he's made every cut to finish T11th 1998: T20th 1997: T32nd 1996: T15th 1995: 7th 1994. That's a superbly-consistent record in a tournament he really enjoys and looks forward to.

At Carnoustie in 1999 make a note of the 32-year-old Texan BOB ESTES. In that 1996 Scottish Open he finished T11th and was the 11/1 Top American, and in 1995 at 66/1 he was T3rd in the Top American player when the British Open was last played in Scotland. If he plays in 1999 he'll be at a big price to be Top US player.

SHIGEKI MARUYAMA has a fine British Open record – T29th 1998: T10th 1997: T14th 1996. He's a superb putter, a stocky player with a low centre of gravity well suited to links golf. He can be followed in 3-ball betting (nice 3/1 R1 win this year) and in the top Japanese market in which he was the 1998 9/4 winner.

Do note GREG TURNER in the Top Australasian market which he has won twice – 14/1 1998: 18/1 (d.heat) 1996 – in the last three years, and interestingly he was also top Aussie at Carnoustie in the 1996 Scottish Open.

The player to oppose must be COLIN MONTGOMERIE. In ten starts he has missed six cuts and posted only one top 20 finish when 8th in 1994. It is particularly noteworthy that in the last six years he's only been placed once (when T3rd at 6/1 in 1994) in the top British and Irish player market.

THE USPGA

The Medinah Country Club, Chicago, Illinois hosts the 1999 USPGA, a tournament that shows a distinct-predictable pattern.

In last year's volume not only were the key criteria given for finding the winner VIJAY SINGH, he was also clearly named and provided readers with a juicy 50/1 success. Indeed one reader rang to tell me of his spread-betting profit on Singh based on the book's analysis.

One quality player who is in his thirties, seeking his first major win and with a fine 1998 major record is STEVE STRICKER. T5th in the US Open, and 2nd in the USPGA in 1998, he'll be under the influence of 'the nappy factor' in 1999 when the USPGA will be played in the state of Illinois, where he went to

University. If he's in form come mid-August and is still waiting for his first major he can be expected to make a bold show.

"I always feel comfortable playing this tournament," and STEVE ELKINGTON's USPGA record gives the reason – 3rd 1998: T3rd 1996: WON 1995: T7th 1994: T14th 1993 and T18th 1992. In the last seven years he's only once finished outside the top 20 (when T45th in 1997) and his average position has been 13th. Such astonishing consistency can be backed either on the spreads or in the top Australasian market where he was an 11/2 winner in 1998. If he's fit in mid-August the 35-year-old, with arguably the best swing on tour, must be backed.

The best 'value' in the 1999 USPGA will surely be JEFF SLUMAN – a straight-hitting consistent player, inspired by the nappy factor, a winner in each of the last two years, a winner already of this major, and crucially in 1999 it will be held in his home town of Chicago, Illinois. He'll surely be worth an interest as an outsider 'playing at home'.

Back to JOHANSSON, T8th in 1996 and T23rd in 1998 he has provided a PER of tasty bets in the top European player market when 2nd at 40/1 in 1996, and when, in a 14-runner field, he was the 1998 winner at an incredible 33/1! Again if he's fit in mid-August in the top Euro market he must be followed.

THE NEW WORLD GOLF CHAMPIONSHIPS

In 1999 there will be three new world golf championships (WGC). The five major golf tours, the PGA of Australasia, the European Tour, the PGA Tour of Japan, the USPGA Tour and the South Africa PGA tour constitute the PGA Tours International Federation who are behind this new initiative.

ANDERSEN CONSULTING MATCH-PLAY

Date: 24th – 28th February 1999, La Costa Resort & Spar (Carlsbad,CA)

Eligibility: Top 64 players on the Official World Golf Rankings

Format: 64-player Match-Play event
Wednesday 32 matches
Thursday 16 matches
Friday 8 matches
Saturday (am) 4 quarter-finals
Saturday (pm) 2 semi-finals
Sunday Consolation match
Final 36-hole match

Purse: Prize money awarded will be considered 'official' on the respective money lists of each of the five Tours. In addition, contestants will earn world ranking points

NEC INVITATIONAL

Date: 26th – 29th August 1999, Firestone Country Club (Akron, OH)

Eligibility: All members of last-named Presidents Cup and Ryder Cup Teams

Format: 4-day, 72-hole competition, no cut
Minimum field is 36 players and maximum field is 48 players:

12 US players from the Ryder Cup
12 US players from the Presidents Cup
12 European players from the Ryder Cup
12 International players from The Presidents Cup

Purse: Prize money awarded will be considered 'official' on the respective money lists of each of the five Tours. In addition, contestants will earn world ranking points

AMERICAN EXPRESS STROKE-PLAY CHAMPIONSHIP

Date: 4th – 7th November 1999, Club de Golf (Valderrama, Spain)

Eligibility:
1. Top 50 players on the Official World Golf Ranking
2. Top 30 from the PGA Tour Money List, not otherwise exempt, to a floor of 100 on the Official World Golf Ranking
3. Top 20 from the European Tour Volvo Ranking, not otherwise exempt, to a floor of 100 on the Official World Golf Ranking
4. Top 3 from the Australasian Tour Order of Merit, not otherwise exempt, to a floor of 100 on the Official World Golf Ranking
5. Top 3 on the Japanese PGA Tour Money List, not otherwise exempt, to a floor of 100 on the Official World Golf Ranking
6. Top 2 from the Southern Africa PGA Tour Order of Merit, not otherwise exempt, to a floor of 100 on the Official World Golf Ranking
7. If not otherwise exempt, the top player on the money list of each five Tours

Estimated field size is between 60-65 players

Format: 4-day, 72-hole competition, no cut

Purse: Prize money awarded will be considered 'official' on the respective Money Lists of each of the five Tours. In addition, contestants will earn world ranking points

PUNTERS' POINTS

- The prize money awarded for each event will be considered 'official' on the respective money lists of each of the five world tours.
  As a result if you are considering placing a bet on either the US Money list, or the European Order of Merit you must consider whether your selection is likely to play or not.
- Also the WGCs will definitely count towards Ryder Cup points.
- The World Rankings are therefore very important. The Top 64 will qualify for the Andersen Consulting Match-play, and the top 50 for the American Express Stroke Play.

As a guide, THE WORLD TOP 70, as of 18th October, were:

1	Tiger Woods	36	Brandt Jobe
2	Mark O'Meara	37	Billy Mayfair
3	David Duval	38	Ian Woosnam
4	Davis Love III	39	Shigeki Maruyama
5	Ernie Els	40	Bob Estes
6	Colin Montgomerie	41	Jeff Sluman
7	Nick Price	42	Thomas Bjorn
8	Lee Westwood	43	John Huston
9	Phil Mickelson	44	Mark McNulty
10	Fred Couples	45	Stewart Cink
11	Vijay Singh	46	Loren Roberts
12	Jim Furyk	47	Glen Day
13	Jumbo Ozaki	48	Joe Ozaki
14	Greg Norman	49	Andrew Magee
15	Steve Elkington	50	Frank Nobilo
16	Justin Leonard	51	Craig Parry
17	Jesper Parnevik	52	Hal Sutton
18	Mark Calcavecchia	53	Carlos Franco
19	Scott Hoch	54	Patrik Sjoland
20	Tom Lehman	55	Scott Verplank
21	Tom Watson	56	Frankie Minoza
22	Lee Janzen	57	Miguel Angel Jimenez
23	Jose Maria Olazabal	58	Craig Stadler
24	Brian Watts	59	Paul Stankowski
25	Payne Stewart	60	Eduardo Romero
26	Darren Clarke	61	Michael Bradley
27	Steve Stricker	62	Fred Funk
28	Bernhard Langer	63	Greg Turner
29	John Cook	64	Per-Ulrik Johansson
30	Jeff Maggert	65	Paul Azinger
31	Stuart Appleby	66	Nick Faldo
32	Bill Glasson	67	David Toms
33	Steve Jones	68	Robert Karlsson
34	Bob Tway	69	Stephen Leaney
35	Brad Faxon	70	Scott McCarron

THE 1999 USPGA TOUR

January
7-10   **Mercedes Championship**
         The Plantation Course at Kapalua, Lahaina, Hawaii
14-17*   **Sony Open in Hawaii**   Waialae Country Club, Honolulu, Hawaii
20-24   **Bob Hope Chrysler Classic**
         Indian Wells/Bermuda Dunes/LaQuinta, Indians Wells, CA
28-31   **Phoenix Open**   TPC of Scottsdale, Scottsdale, AZ
February
4-7   **AT&T Pebble Beach Natl Pro-Am**
         Pebble Beach Golf Links/Spyglass Hill/Poppy Hills, Pebble Beach, CA
11-14   **Buick Invitational**
         Torrey Pines Country Club, South Course/North Course, LaJolla, CA
18-21   **Nissan Open**   Riviera Country Club, Pacific Palisades, CA
24-28   **WGC – Andersen Consulting Match Play**
         La Costa Resort & Spa, Carlsbad, CA
24-28   **Tucson Open**   Omni Tucson National Golf Resort, Tucson, AZ
March
4-7   **Doral-Ryder Open**   Doral Resort & Country Club, Miami, FL
11-14   **Honda Classic**   TPC at Heron Bay, Coral Springs, FL
18-21   **Bay Hill Invitational**   Bay Hill Club & Lodge, Orlando, FL
25-28   **The Players Championship**   TPC at Sawgrass, Ponte Vedra Beach, FL
April
1-4   **BellSouth Classic**   TPC at Sugarloaf, Duluth, GA
8-11   **Masters Tournament**   Augusta National Golf Club, Augusta, GA
15-18   **MCI Classic – The Heritage of Golf**
         Harbour Town Golf Links, Hilton Head, SC
22-25   **Greater Greensboro Chrysler Classic**
         Forest Oaks Country Club, Greensboro, NC
29-May 2 **Shell Houston Open**   TPC at The Woodlands, The Woodlands, TX
May
5-9   *****Entergy Classic**   English Turn Golf & Country Club, New Orleans, LA
13-16   **GTE Byron Nelson Classic**
         TPC at Las Colinas/Cottonwood Valley CC, Irving, TX
20-23   **MasterCard Colonial**   Colonial Country Club, Fort Worth, TX
27-30   **Kemper Open**   TPC at Avenel, Potomac, MD
June
3-6   **Memorial Tournament**   Muirfield Village Golf Club, Dublin, OH
10-13   **FedEx St Jude Classic**   TPC at Southwind, Memphis, TN
17-29   **US Open Championship**
         Pinehurst Country Club No. 2 Course, Pinehurst, NC
24-27   **Buick Classic**   Westchester Country Club, Rye, NY
July
1-4   **Motorola Western Open**   Cog Hill Golf & Country Club, Lemont, IL
8-11   **Greater Milwaukee Open**
         Brown Deer Park Golf Course, Milwaukee, WI
15-18   **The Open Championship**   Carnoustie Golf Links, Carnoustie, Scotland
15-18   **Deposit Guaranty Golf Classic**   Annandale Golf Club, Madison, MS
22-25*   **John Deere Classic**   Oakwood Country Club, Coal Valley, IL
29-Aug 1 **Canon Greater Hartford Open**   TPC at River Highlands, Cromwell, CT
August
5-8   **Buick Open**   Warwick Hills Golf & Country Club, Grand Blanc, MI
5-8   **PGA Championship**   Medinah Country Club, Medinah, IL

19-22   **Sprint International**   Castle Pines Golf Club, Castle Rock, CO
26-29   **The Reno Open**   Montreux GC, Nevada
26-29   **WGC – NEC Invitational**   Firestone C.C., Akron, Ohio, USA
September
2-5   **Greater Vancouver Open**
     Northview Golf & Country Club, Surrey, BC, Canada
9-12   **Bell Canadian Open**   Glen Abbey GC, Oakville, Ontario, Canada
16-19   **B.C. Open**   En-Joie Golf Club, Endicott, NY
23-26   **Westin Texas Open at LaCantera**
     LaCantera Golf Club, San Antonio, TX
24-26   **Ryder Cup**   The Country Club, Brookline, MA
31-3 Oct   **Buick Challenge**   Callaway Gardens Resort, Pine Mountain, GA
October
7-10   **Michelob Championship at Kingsmill**
     Kingsmill Golf Club, Williamsburg, VA
13-17   **Las Vegas Invitational**
     TPC at Summerlin/Desert Inn Golf Club, Las Vegas, NV
21-24   **National Car Rental Golf Classic at Walt Disney World Resort**
     Magnolia, Palm & Lake Buena Vista Golf Courses, Buena Vista, FL
28-31   **The Tour Championship** Champions Golf Club, Houston, TX
November
4-7   **WGC – American Express Stroke-Play Championship**
     Club de Golf Valderrama, Cadiz, Spain

PUNTERS' POINTS

- The tournaments with an asterisk (*) have been retitled yet remain at the usual courses.
- The brand new tournament will be the Reno Open in August. It will be played opposite the World Golf Championship – NEC Invitational.

     The 7,552-yard, par 72 mountain course is Jack Nicklaus designed.

     It has been likened to the Castle Pines course in Colorado. So form from that course's Sprint International should be studied when assessing the 1999 Reno Open

     PLEASE NOTE

     * Prize Money on the 1999 USPGA Tour will be over 22% up on 1998.

     * The exemptions for winning the Players Championship has been cut to 5 years, and for winning the Tour Championship to 3 years.

1999 EUROPEAN TOUR SCHEDULE & APPROVED SPECIAL EVENTS

January
14-17   **Alfred Dunhill S.A. PGA**   Houghton GC Johannesburg, South Africa
21-24   **South African Open**   Stellenbosch GC Cape Province, South Africa
28-31   **Heineken Classic**   The Vines Resort, Perth, Australia
February
4-7   **Kuala Lumpur**
11-14   **Dubai Desert Classic**   Dubai Creek Golf and Yacht Club
17-20(Sat)   **Qatar Masters** Doha GC
24-28   **WGC – Andersen Consulting Match Play Championship**
     La Costa Resort & Spa Carlsbad, CA, USA

March
4-7   **Portuguese Algarve Open**
11-14   **Turespana Masters**
18-21   **Moroccan Open**   Golf Royal D'Agadir, Agadir, Morocco
25-28   **Madeira Island Open**   Santo da Serra, Madeira
April
1-4   **TBA**
8-11   **Masters Tournament**   Augusta National, Georgia, USA
15-18   **TBA**
22-25   **Peugeot Open de Espana**
29-May 2   **Fiat and Fila Italian Open**   Circolo Golf, Torino, Italy
May
6-9   **Open de France**
13-16   **Benson & Hedges International**
           The Oxfordshire GC, Thame, Oxon
21-24(Mon) **Deutsche Bank – SAP Open**
           TPC of Europe St Leon Rot, Heideburg
28-31(Mon) **Volvo PGA Championship**   Wentworth Club, Surrey, England
June
3-6   **English Open**
10-13   **German Open**   Sporting Club Berlin, Berlin, Germany
17-20   **US Open**   Pinehurst No. 2, North Carolina, USA
24-27   **Compaq European Grand Prix**
           De Vere Slaley Hall, Northumberland, England
July
1-4   **Murphy's Irish Open**   Druids Glen, Dublin, Ireland
7-10(Sat) **The Standard Life**   Loch Lomond, Glasgow, Scotland
15-18   **128th Open Golf Championship**   Carnoustie, Angus, Scotland
22-25   **TNT Dutch Open**   Hilversumsche GC, Hilversum, Amsterdam
30-Aug 2   **Smurfit European Open**   The K Club, Dublin, Ireland
(Mon)
August
5-8   **Volvo Scandinavian Masters**   Barseback G & C.C., Malmo, Sweden
12-15   **US PGA Championship**   Medinah C.C., Chicago, Illinois, USA
19-22   **BMW International Open**
           Golfclub Munchen Nord-Eichenried, Munich, Germany
26-29   **WGC – NEC Invitational**
           Firestone Country Club (South Course), Akron, Ohio, USA
September
2-5   **Canon European Masters**   Crans-sur-Sierre, Switzerland
9-12   **One 2 One British Masters**
16-19   **Trophee Lancome**   Saint-Nom-La Breteche, Paris, France
24-26   **The 33rd Ryder Cup Matches**
           The Country Club, Brookline, Massachusetts, USA
30-3 Oct   **Linde German Masters**   Gut Larchenhof, Cologne, Germany
October
7-10   **Alfred Dunhill Cup***   St Andrews, Fife, Scotland
14-17   **Cisco World Match Play Championship***
           Wentworth Club, Surrey, England
14-17   **Open Novotel Perrier***   Golf du Medoc, Bordeaux, France
21-24   **Belgacom Open**   Royal Zoute, Belgium
28-31   **Volvo Masters**   Montecastillo, Jerez, Spain
November
4-7   **World Golf Championship – Stroke-Play Championship**

Club de Golf Valderrama, Cadiz, Spain
11-14   **Johnnie Walker Classic#**
18-21   **World Cup of Golf***
Mines Resort & Golf Club, Kuala Lumpur, Malaysia
18-23   **European Tour Qualifying School Finals**
San Roque Club & Sotogrande Golf Club, Spain
* *Denotes Approved Special Events*
# *Denotes 2000 Volvo Ranking*
TBA Cannes Open

THE 1998-99 AUSTRALASIAN TOUR SCHEDULE

There will be 12 tournaments on the 1998-99 Australasian Tour Schedule. The defending Australasian tour O/M champion is Andrew Coltart.

Oct 22-25   **Ford Open**   Kooyonga GC, Adelaide
Nov 19-22   **PGA Championship**   New South Wales Golf Club, Sydney
Nov 26-29   **Players Championship**   Royal Queensland Golf Club, Brisbane
Dec 3-6   **Australian Open**   Royal Adelaide Golf Club, Adelaide
Dec 10-13   **New Zealand Open**   Formosa Auckland Golf Club, New Zealand
Dec 17-20   **Coolum Classic**   Hyatt Coolum Resort, Queensland
Jan 7-10   **Victorian Open Championship**   The Victoria Golf Club, Melbourne
Jan 28-31   **Heineken Classic**   The Vines Resort, Perth
Feb 4-7   **Greg Norman International**   The Lakes Golf Club, Sydney
Feb 11-14   **Australian Masters**   Huntingdale, Melbourne
Feb 18-21   **Canon Challenge**   Terrey Hills, Sydney
March 4-7   **The Tour Championship**   Royal Canberra, Canberra

THE 1998 PRESIDENTS CUP

- The third Presidents Cup match between the United States and an International side will be held from 11th – 13th December 1998 at the ROYAL MELBOURNE GOLF CLUB.
- The event follows the same format as the Ryder Cup
- Previous results:
  1994 US Won 20-12
  1996 US Won 16.5 – 15.5

TOUR FORM 1998   Part 3
EUROPEAN

THE EUROPEAN ORDER OF MERIT

Date	From 22nd January in Thailand to 1st November at Montecastillo
Courses	Assorted
Par	70 – 72
Yardage	Various
First Prize	Europe's Number 1 position

The Order of Merit is simply the monetary league table of all the European Tour players based on their prize money winnings over the full European season.

1998 ODDS

fav	4/1	Colin Montgomerie	25/1	Padraig Harrington
	6/1	Lee Westwood	33/1	Thomas Bjorn*
	8/1	Bernhard Langer	40/1	Andrew Coltart
	14/1	Darren Clarke*	40/1	Ernie Els*
	14/1	J M Olazabal	40/1	Ignacio Garrido
	14/1	Ian Woosnam*	50/1	Nick Faldo
	20/1	Per-Ulrik Johansson	66/1	Paul McGinley
	25/1	Robert Allenby*	66/1	Mark McNulty*
	25/1	Retief Goosen	66/1	Eduardo Romero
	25/1	Costantino Rocca	66/1	Raymond Russell

20 players were best priced at or under 66/1.

BOOKIES AT ODDS

Colin Montgomerie 11/4 Hills, Ladbrokes, Sunderlands, Stanleys: 4/1 Tote

Lee Westwood 4/1 Tote: 6/1 Hills

DYM Darren Clarke 7/1 Tote: 14/1 Ladbrokes, Surrey

1998 RESULT

1	4/1	Colin Montgomerie
2	14/1	Darren Clarke
3	6/1	Lee Westwood
4	80/1	M A Jimenez

PUNTERS' POINTS

- Three players have dominated the front four in the last two years, Monty, Clarke and Westwood.

  > Monty's SIXTH successive win is surely one of sport's truly great achievements. Can he make it a magnificent seven?

  > Lee Westwood (3rd 6/1 1998: 3rd 25/1 1997) will surely finish in the first four virtually every year from now on.

  > Darren Clarke (2nd 14/1 DYM 1998: 4th 33/1 1997) can also be expected to finish in the front four again in 1999.

1997 RESULT

1	5/2	Colin Montgomerie
2	20/1	Bernhard Langer
3	25/1	Lee Westwood
4	33/1	Darren Clarke

1996 RESULT

1	7/2	Colin Montgomerie
2	33/1	Ian Woosnam
3	66/1	Robert Allenby
4	12/1	Costantino Rocca

WINNERS IN THE '90s

1990	Ian Woosnam
1991	Seve Ballesteros
1992	Nick Faldo
1993	Colin Montgomerie
1994	Colin Montgomerie
1995	Colin Montgomerie
1996	Colin Montgomerie
1997	Colin Montgomerie
1998	Colin Montgomerie

PUNTERS' GUIDE

- The large prize money on offer for the new 1999 World Championship events will count towards the European Order of Merit so this must be borne in mind when making your selection.

- Monty, Darren Clarke and Lee Westwood will surely all be 'in the frame' again. However Jesper Parnevik who will be playing on the European tour as well as in all the new world tournaments will provide a better-priced alternative. If his putting improves (as it has in 1998 for Vijay Singh) Jesper could have a very big year in 1999.

Top 5 finishes on the PGA Tour

1	2	3	4	5
Johnnie Walker Classic				
5/1 T Woods	10/1 E Els	40/1 R Goosen	50/1 A Coltart 12/1 L Westwood 80/1 A Cejka 66/1 P O'Malley	-
Heineken Classic				
33/1 T Bjorn	22/1 I Woosnam	16/1 J M Olazabal 25/1 P Harrington 7/1 E Els 66/1 P Baker	-	-
South African Open				
9/2 E Els	33/1 D Frost	50/1 P Sjoland	200/1 N Henning 100/1 M Gortana 12/1 B Langer	-
South African PGA				
100/1 T Johnstone	5/1 E Els	33/1 R Goosen 8/1 N Price	-	100/1 S Dunlap
Dubai Desert Classic				
16/1 J M Olazabal	200/1 S Allan	8/1 E Els 100/1 R Karlsson	-	20/1 I Woosnam
Qatar Masters				
33/1 A Coltart	66/1 P Sjoland 200/1 A Sherborne	-	200/1 V Phillips	40/1 R Goosen 125/1 R Muntz 80/1 D Carter
Moroccan Open				
66/1 S Leaney	12/1 R Karlsson	100/1 M Gronberg	33/1 M A Martin 150/1 M Davis	-
Portuguese Open				
66/1 P Mitchell	80/1 J Sandelin 33/1 D Gilford	-	33/1 E Romero 66/1 S Torrance 125/1 J Lomas	-
Cannes Open				
150/1 T Levet	66/1 P Price 50/1 S Struver 33/1 G Turner	-	-	40/1 C Whitelaw 150/1 S Webster
Peugeot Spanish Open				
40/1 T Bjorn	80/1 G Chalmers 8/1 J M Olazabal	-	33/1 E Romero 66/1 M James	-
Italian Open				
66/1 P Sjoland	8/1 J M Olazabal 80/1 J Haeggman	-	20/1 T Bjorn	66/1 P Baker

Turespana Masters

22/1 M A Jimenez	16/1 M A Martin	80/1 K Tomori	125/1 V Phillips	66/1 M Long
		P McGinley*		66/1 S Luna

* Non-runner for bookmaking purposes

Benson & Hedges Open

33/1 D Clarke	100/1 S Luna	150/1 M Florioli	-	10/1 C Montgomerie
		20/1 T Bjorn		33/1 R Goosen

Volvo PGA

10/1 C Montgomerie	9/1 E Els	-	-	50/1 A Coltart
	40/1 P Sjoland			150/1 P Lonard
	150/1 G Orr			20/1 T Bjorn
				250/1 M Hallberg
				200/1 D Robertson

Deutsche Bank Open

22/1 L Westwood	20/1 D Clarke	25/1 M O'Meara	200/1 P Walton	-
			16/1 B Langer	
			100/1 P Senior	

English Open

10/1 L Westwood	200/1 O Karlsson	-	7/1 C Montgomerie	40/1 P Sjoland
	80/1 G Chalmers			

Compaq European Grand Prix   Tournament Void

Madeira Island Open

80/1 M Lanner	80/1 S Scahill	80/1 A Beal	25/1 T Gogele	-
			66/1 F Cea	

Peugeot French Open

80/1 S Torrance	125/1 M Florioli	-	-	-
	150/1 O Edmond			
	14/1 B Langer			
	66/1 M Goggin			

Murphy's Irish Open

125/1 D Carter	8/1 C Montgomerie	80/1 P Baker	-	250/1 C Hainline
		250/1 J McHenry		

Loch Lomond Invitational

10/1 L Westwood	66/1 R Allenby	-	-	-
	25/1 I Woosnam			
	66/1 D Howell			
	50/1 E Romero			
	200/1 D Edlund			

The British Open

40/1 M O'Meara	250/1 B Watts	12/1 T Woods	200/1 R Russell	-
			500/1 J Rose	
			28/1 J Furyk	
			50/1 J Parnevik	

TNT Dutch Open

125/1 S Leaney	22/1 D Clarke	14/1 N Price	-	40/1 C Rocca
		10/1 L Westwood		

Scandinavian Masters

14/1 J Parnevik	16/1 D Clarke	200/1 S Field	100/1 J Van de Velde	-
			125/1 M Jonzon	

German Open

100/1 S Allan	125/1 M Roe	-	-	-
	40/1 I Garrido			
	125/1 S Webster			
	40/1 P Harrington			

The USPGA

50/1 V Singh	66/1 S Stricker	100/1 S Elkington	20/1 N Price	-
			100/1 F Lickliter	
			33/1 M O'Meara	

European Open

125/1 M Gronberg	66/1 M A Jimenez	-	18/1 D Clarke	125/1 A Cabrera
	125/1 P Price			100/1 C Hainline

BMW International Open

125/1 R Claydon	125/1 J Spence	125/1 T Gogele	80/1 A Cabrera	-
			12/1 B Langer	

Canon European Masters

80/1 S Struver	40/1 P Sjoland	14/1 D Clarke	22/1 C Rocca	80/1 A Cjeka
				100/1 G Brand Jr

One 2 One British Masters

10/1 C Montgomerie	125/1 P Fulke	-	200/1 A Oldcorn	-
	40/1 E Romero		66/1 I Garrido	
			125/1 P Quirici	

Lancome Trophy

50/1 M A Jimenez	14/1 D Duval	-	-	-
	16/1 M O'Meara			
	150/1 J Sandelin			
	66/1 G Turner			

German Masters

10/1 C Montgomerie	16/1 V Singh	-	150/1 S Webster	33/1 P U Johansson
	80/1 R Karlsson			

Belgacom Open

8/1 L Westwood	150/1 F Jacobson	33/1 R Karlsson	-	66/1 P Mitchell
		33/1 G Turner		33/1 J Sandelin

Alfred Dunhill Cup

8/1 South Africa	16/1 Spain	-	-	-

World Match Play

6/1 M O'Meara	7/2 T Woods	-	-	-

Novotel Perrier Paris

10/1 J Sandelin &	33/1 R Boxall &	12/1 S Ballesteros &	50/1 J Remesy &	-
O Karlsson	D Cooper	M A Jimenez	R Jacquelin	

Volvo Masters

22/1 D Clarke	66/1 A Coltart	9/1 C Montgomerie	80/1 P Baker
			50/1 P O'Malley

THE JOHNNIE WALKER CLASSIC

Date	22nd-25th January
Course	Canyon Course, Blue Canyon C.C., Phuket, Thailand
Par	72
Yardage	7,099
First Prize	£133,330
Total Purse	£800,000

The Canyon course was last used for this tournament in 1994 when Greg Norman was the winner. It is built on the site of an old tin mine and rubber tree plantation so water hazards from the flooding of open mine excavations and rubber trees provide the main hazards.

1998 ODDS

fav	5/1	Tiger Woods	50/1	Patrik Sjoland
	10/1	Ernie Els (DC)	50/1	Paul McGinley
	12/1	Lee Westwood	50/1	Andrew Coltart
	18/1	J M Olazabal	66/1	Peter O'Malley
	20/1	Nick Faldo	66/1	Robert Karlsson
	25/1	Ian Woosnam	66/1	Raymond Russell
	33/1	Robert Allenby	66/1	Greg Chalmers
	33/1	Thomas Bjorn	66/1	Michael Long
	33/1	Padraig Harrington	66/1	Wayne Westner
	40/1	Retief Goosen	66/1	Peter Lonard*
	40/1	Greg Turner		

Just 21 players were best priced at or under 66/1.

BOOKIES AT ODDS

Third placed Retief Goosen 25/1 Ladbrokes, Stan James: 40/1 Corals

Tied fourth Andrew Coltart 33/1 Chandlers, Hills, Stan James: 50/1 Corals and Surrey

Winner Tiger Woods 7/2 at Ladbrokes was best priced at Corals' 5/1.

1998 RESULT

1 fav	5/1	**Tiger Woods**	72 71 71 65	279
		(Woods won at the second play-off hole)		
2	10/1	**Ernie Els**	67 65 74 73	279
3	40/1	**Retief Goosen**	71 71 69 69	280
T4	50/1	**Andrew Coltart**	71 68 72 70	281
T4	12/1	**Lee Westwood**	71 66 73 71	281
T4	80/1	**Alexander Cejka**	67 68 74 72	281
T4	66/1	**Peter O'Malley**	69 68 72 72	281

T8	S Leaney	70 68 72 72 282		T-P Chang	73 72 78 69 292
	P Harrington	69 67 73 73 282		T Sriroj	70 75 74 73 292
	P Marksaeng	67 72 69 74 282		Z Moe	72 75 72 74 293
	N Faldo	71 67 69 75 282		No-Seok Park	72 72 76 73 293
T12	P Lonard	70 71 71 71 283		J Cooper	71 70 71 81 293
	R Allenby	75 70 66 72 283		M Wheelhouse	72 74 72 76 294
T14	M Long	76 71 67 71 285		J Lomas	72 74 75 73 294
	P Baker	73 69 68 75 285		M Harwood	73 72 73 76 294
T16	S Alker	68 71 72 75 286		S Laycock	76 69 77 72 294
	B King	71 72 68 75 286		V Phillips	78 69 73 74 294
	J M Olazabal	72 72 70 72 286		R Chapman	77 70 74 73 294
	P Price	69 72 71 74 286		C Jones	72 75 73 74 294
	R Pampling	73 72 73 68 286		D Chopra	68 73 76 78 295
T21	S Tait	69 75 70 73 287		S Allan	76 69 76 74 295
	P McGinley	69 71 76 71 287		C V D Velde	75 72 78 71 296
T23	F Minoza	73 70 74 71 288		P Haugsrud	74 73 74 75 296
	H Meshiai	73 71 71 73 288		N-S Park	73 72 74 78 297
T25	S Struver	73 70 75 71 289		D Howell	74 72 72 79 297
	F Casas	72 72 76 69 289		M Allen	68 75 82 72 297
	A Atwal	70 71 73 75 289		G Orr	73 74 77 73 297
	G Turner	73 71 73 72 289		J L Guepy	74 71 76 76 297
	I Garbutt	74 73 68 74 289		M Ecob	75 68 76 79 298
	W Smith	69 75 75 71 290		D Fardon	73 73 76 76 298
	L-W Zhang	70 72 74 74 290		D Ecob	73 74 77 75 299
	J Payne	75 72 74 69 290		P Lawrie	71 75 76 77 299
	L Parsons	68 75 76 71 290		J O'Keefe	76 70 73 80 299
	G Chalmers	72 68 76 74 290		L Wastle	71 75 77 77 300
	F Tarnaud	73 69 77 71 290		E Boult	71 76 76 77 300
	R Gibson	72 74 69 75 290		G Evans	73 73 75 79 300
	P Sjoland	71 75 74 71 291		J Senden	75 72 77 78 302
	D Cole	70 75 71 75 291		M Gates	75 72 74 84 305
	A Gilligan	73 73 73 72 291			

The 36-hole cut was made at 147 – 3 over par – 70 players qualified.

ROUND BY ROUND LEADERBOARD

FIRST ROUND

E Els	5 under
T Bjorn	5 under
P Marksaeng	5 under
A Cejka	5 under
M Allen	4 under
S Alker	4 under
D Chopra	4 under
L Parsons	4 under
T WOODS	level

SECOND ROUND

E Els	12 under
A Cejka	9 under
P Harrington	8 under
L Westwood	7 under
P O'Malley	7 under
N Faldo	6 under
S Leaney	6 under
T WOODS	1 under

THIRD ROUND

E Els	10 under
N Faldo	9 under
P Marksaeng	8 under
P O'Malley	7 under
P Harrington	7 under
A Cejka	7 under
T WOODS	2 under

FINAL ROUND

T WOODS	9 under
E Els	9 under
R Goosen	8 under
A Coltart	7 under
L Westwood	7 under
A Cejka	7 under
P O'Malley	7 under

PUNTERS' POINTS

- Starting the final round 8 shots back Tiger Woods shot a 65 to set a clubhouse target which only Ernie Els with a final-hole birdie could match.
- Tiger Woods made a birdie at the second play-off hole to Els's par to land an astonishing victory. Once more we saw the red shirt, the red peaked cap and the clenched right fist on the final green.
- Woods had shown two characteristics in this tournament – first his love of a challenge and his 'never-say-die' spirit, and second his occasionally poor course management when he takes unnecessary risks.
- Last year in his Player Profile I noted that Ernie Els had often 'thrown away' tournaments on the final day that he had previously dominated. Here he did it again with an over par 73 in R4 to give Woods his chance.
- 66/1 Peter O'Malley, 10 under with two holes to play made double bogey, bogey to slip back to finish T4th.
- 50/1 Andrew Coltart ended his opening round with two double bogeys which were ultimately to prove very costly. However, the sweet-swinging Scot is in fine form 'down under' and looks set for a successful season.
- It was good to see 1993 Ryder Cup hero Peter Baker play well for the first three rounds. However he must have been very disappointed with that final round 75.
- A final-round 75 plunged Nick Faldo down the leaderboard from second place to T8th. However, Nicholas Alexander's overall tee-to-green play looks in good shape.
- Talented Alexander Cejka's T4th showed that the 27-year-old who had three wins in 1995 is back in really sound form following his fine second place in the individual rankings in the World Cup of Golf.

- Ryder Cup star Thomas Bjorn's rounds of 67-81 led to the 26-year-old Dane slipping out of contention and out of the tournament! However he was suffering from food poisoning during that second round.
- Only two players, Retief Goosen and Peter Lonard showed the consistency necessary to beat par in every round.
- With the European tour venues changing constantly, particularly for this event, it is very important to be aware of any relevant past course form. Sadly the Racing Post did not select Tiger Woods because ".....he is no good thing on a course he has yet to experience". Indeed in their Spread Betting column the advice was to buy Woods' finishing position mainly because "....this is a 156-runner race and he has no previous experience of the course".

  Woods as an 18-year-old in early 1994 had played the course, in that year's Johnnie Walker Classic scoring 74-71-74-73 for 292, to finish T34th as the top amateur.
- Among those to miss the cut were 25/1 Ian Woosnam, 33/1 Thomas Bjorn and 66/1 Wayne Westner.

1997 RESULT

1	12/1	Ernie Els
T2	80/1	Michael Long
T2	66/1	Peter Lonard
T4	16/1	Nick Faldo
T4	14/1	Fred Couples
T4	66/1	Anthony Painter

WINNERS IN THE '90s

1990	Nick Faldo
1991	No tournament (Gulf War)
1992	Ian Palmer
1993	Nick Faldo
1994	Greg Norman
1995	Fred Couples
1996	Ian Woosnam
1997	Ernie Els
1998	Tiger Woods

PUNTERS' GUIDE

- Tiger Woods' victory maintained the record that throughout the nineties (1992 excepted) this tournament has been won by a world-class player who has won a major.
- When looking for an outsider it is wise to go for players who are in form from the Australasian tour.

THE HEINEKEN CLASSIC

Date	29th January – 1st February
Course	The Vines, Perth, Australia
Par	72
Yardage	7,101
First Prize	£105,300
Total Purse	£555,500

Hosting the tournament for the ninth time, this Graham Marsh designed Vines course can provide a severe test, especially when the wind blows.

This tournament was being played on the European tour for the third successive year.

1998 ODDS

fav	7/1	Ernie Els
	12/1	Bernhard Langer
	16/1	J M Olazabal
	20/1	Robert Allenby
	22/1	Ian Woosnam
	22/1	Retief Goosen
	25/1	Craig Parry
	25/1	Padraig Harrington
	33/1	Andrew Coltart
	33/1	Peter O'Malley
	33/1	Thomas Bjorn
	40/1	Greg Turner
	40/1	Peter Lonard
	40/1	Paul McGinley
	40/1	Stephen Leaney
	50/1	Alexander Cejka
	50/1	Patrik Sjoland
	50/1	Steve Alker
	66/1	Bradley Hughes
	66/1	Peter Baker*
	66/1	Greg Chalmers
	66/1	Michael Long*
	66/1	Phillip Price
	66/1	Rodney Pampling

24 players were best priced at or under 66/1.

BOOKIES AT ODDS

DYM Michael Long 28/1 Chandlers: 66/1 Corals

DYM Tied third Peter Baker 33/1 Tote: 66/1 Corals

Winner Thomas Bjorn 25/1 Stan James, Chandlers: 33/1 Corals, Hills, Stanleys

1998 RESULT

1	33/1	Thomas Bjorn	70 68 68 74	280
2	22/1	Ian Woosnam	66 69 70 76	281
T3	16/1	J M Olazabal	67 72 68 75	282
T3	25/1	Padraig Harrington	74 71 71 66	282
T3 fav	7/1	Ernie Els	70 71 70 71	282
T3	66/1	Peter Baker	73 71 67 71	282

7	T Gogele	68 73 70 72 283	S Scahill	70 69 75 76 290
T8	D Howell	72 68 69 75 284	J Payne	73 68 73 76 290
	G Chalmers	73 72 70 69 284	D Chopra	71 73 73 73 290
	J Sandelin	77 68 67 72 284	G Evans	73 72 70 76 291
T11	P Broadhurst	71 70 71 73 285	M Long	70 71 77 73 291
	S Laycock	69 72 70 74 285	N O'Hern	71 71 72 77 291
	G Dodd	70 71 72 72 285	R Willis	72 73 74 72 291
	B Langer	69 66 76 74 285	J Robson	70 71 77 73 291
T15	T Price	69 71 72 74 286	R Jacquelin	74 71 72 74 291
	J Townsend	73 69 77 67 286	P Eales	72 72 71 77 292
	A Beal	70 70 73 73 286	P Senior	69 73 74 76 292
	A Coltart	68 70 71 77 286	R Muntz	70 72 80 70 292
	J M Singh	69 70 75 72 286	D Carter	73 72 72 75 292
T20	P McGinley	69 70 74 74 287	R Pampling	71 71 72 78 292
	R Karlsson	70 74 72 71 287	R Byrd	73 69 72 78 292
	C Parry	71 67 70 79 287	S Conran	74 69 76 73 292
	P McWhinney	74 70 75 68 287	R Davis	71 70 77 75 293
	G Joyner	71 71 72 73 287	J J West	69 75 77 72 293
T25	G Coles	70 74 71 73 288	C Jones	69 76 71 78 294
	R Allenby	68 71 75 74 288	L Wastle	71 74 73 76 294
	A Cejka	71 73 70 74 288	G Orr	71 73 70 80 294
	E Boult	74 71 71 72 288	L Parsons	73 72 73 76 294
	D Smail	74 71 71 72 288	S Struver	76 68 75 75 294
	K Druce	70 74 71 73 288	P Walton	72 73 74 75 294
	P Lonard	73 68 75 72 288	P Price	72 73 74 76 295
	R Green	72 72 68 77 289	B Davis	71 71 73 81 296
	I Garbutt	72 70 71 76 289	J O'Keefe	71 73 74 78 296
	P O'Malley	72 68 73 76 289	D Dunakey	74 71 77 74 296
	M Gates	68 75 72 75 290	J Wagner	72 72 71 82 297
	G Turner	71 74 69 76 290	M Wheelhouse	72 73 80 76 301

The 36-hole cut was made at 147 – 3 over par – 66 players qualified.

ROUND BY ROUND LEADERBOARD

FIRST ROUND

I Woosnam	6 under
J M Olazabal	5 under
A Coltart	4 under
R Allenby	4 under
M Gates	4 under
T Gogele	4 under
T BJORN	2 under

SECOND ROUND

I Woosnam	9 under
B Langer	9 under
C Parry	6 under
A Coltart	6 under
T BJORN	6 under
S Scahill	5 under
J Singh	5 under
P McGinley	5 under
J M Olazabal	5 under
R Allenby	5 under

THIRD ROUND

I Woosnam	11 under
T BJORN	10 under
J M Olazabal	9 under
C Parry	8 under
D Howell	7 under
A Coltart	7 under

FINAL ROUND

T BJORN	8 under
I Woosnam	7 under
J M Olazabal	6 under
P Harrington	6 under
E Els	6 under
P Baker	6 under

PUNTERS' POINTS

- "You get the feeling the entire field would give the trophy back to Heineken, nobody wants it," commented Steve Beddow as the field bunched up on the final day as one player after another dropped shots in the difficult blustery conditions.

- Ian Woosnam had an eagle putt at the last to force a play-off however, he couldn't make it, so his Ryder Cup partner Thomas Bjorn's final hole birdie gave the young Dane his second win at 33/1.

- Woosie can be followed in match bets here as he obviously enjoys this course where he's now 31 under par over the last 3 years in which he's finished 2nd-T6th-Won.

- Yet the spread firms were at odds over the Welshman – City Index's finishing position for Woosie was 29th-32nd whereas Sporting Index went 19th-22nd! What an arb!!

- With its tight dog legs this course tends to nullify the length advantage usually enjoyed by the big hitters. Nevertheless long-hitting Thomas Bjorn's aggressive approach, especially on the greens, paid off.

- One conundrum for punters: of the front seven in this tournament four had high finishes in the Johnnie Walker Classic – Els (2nd), Harrington (T8th), Baker (T14th), and Olazabal (T16th) whereas the first two, Bjorn and Woosnam, and 7th-placed Gogele all missed the cut last week.

- Robert Karlsson's 71 in R4 confirmed what a fine wind player he is.

- When evaluating the form do remember that R4 was played in very tough conditions so the rounds of Harrington (66), Chalmers (69), Townsend (67) and McWhinney (68) were worth noting.

- Among those to miss the cut were 22/1 Retief Goosen, 50/1 Patrik Sjoland and 80/1 course specialist (in the first three in the last two years) Jean Van de Velde.

1997 RESULT

1	80/1	Miguel Martin
2	12/1	Fred Couples
T3	28/1	Frank Nobilo
T3	66/1	Jean Van de Velde
T3	80/1	Marc Farry

WINNERS IN THE '90s

1991	Blaine McCallister
1992	Ian Baker Finch
1993	Peter Senior
1994	Mike Clayton
1995	Robert Allenby
1996	Ian Woosnam
1997	Miguel Martin
1998	Thomas Bjorn

PUNTERS' GUIDE

- Large undulating greens, tight dog legs that reward accuracy rather than length, and gusting windy conditions make The Vines a severe test.
- Proven ability on the course is, therefore, very important, so in 1999 one player with a real chance must be Padraig Harrington – T11th in 1997 after being the halfway leader thanks to a course record 63 in R2; he was a T3rd in 1998 after a superb final-round 66.

THE SOUTH AFRICAN OPEN

Date	5th – 8th February
Course	Durban C.C., Johannesburg
Par	72
Yardage	6,642
First Prize	£72,000
Total Purse	£460,000

For the second successive year the South African Open appeared on the European tour fixture list. The venue, the Durban Country Club, is relatively short with undulating tight fairways bordered by out-of-bounds fences and dense bush. So accuracy off tee and fairways, rather than length and power are the requirements

1998 ODDS

fav	9/2	Ernie Els	40/1	Clinton Whitelaw
	12/1	Bernhard Langer	40/1	Patrik Sjoland
	14/1	Vijay Singh (DC)	40/1	Greg Chalmers
	14/1	Mark McNulty	50/1	Sven Struver
	16/1	Frank Nobilo	66/1	Adilson da Silva
	18/1	Retief Goosen	66/1	Daniel Chopra
	25/1	Costantino Rocca	66/1	Jarmo Sandelin*
	28/1	Wayne Westner	66/1	Anders Forsbrand
	33/1	David Frost*	66/1	Jamie Spence
	33/1	Ignacio Garrido	66/1	Thomas Gogele
	33/1	Alexander Cejka	66/1	Tony Johnstone
	40/1	David Howell	66/1	Warren Schutte

24 players were best priced at or under 66/1.

BOOKIES AT ODDS

DYM David Frost 16/1 Stan James: 33/1 Ladbrokes

Ignacio Garrido 18/1 Stan James: 33/1 Corals

DYM Jarmo Sandelin 25/1 Stan James: 66/1 Tote

Winner Ernie Els was best priced 9/2 with Stan James's, 10/3 the shortest price.

So Stan James were clearly taking no chances!

1998 RESULT

1 fav	9/2	Ernie Els	64 72 68 69	273
2	33/1	David Frost	68 66 71 71	276
3	50/1	Patrik Sjoland	69 74 68 69	280
T4	200/1	Nic Henning	69 71 70 71	281
T4	100/1	Marco Gortana	70 71 70 70	281
T4	12/1	Bernhard Langer	71 68 71 71	281

T7	I Garrido	66 72 72 72 282
	M McNulty	66 79 67 70 282
T9	R Kaplan	69 73 72 69 283
	B Liddle	71 71 71 70 283
	J Kingston	74 70 70 69 283
	A Cejka	73 72 70 68 283
	V Singh	71 72 67 73 283
	D Howell	72 72 70 69 283
	M Florioli	72 72 68 71 283
	T Gogele	69 69 73 72 283
T17	C Williams	70 69 71 74 284
	G Chalmers	66 71 74 73 284
	A Wall	73 72 71 68 284
T20	G Orr	71 71 76 67 285
	S Webster	69 76 68 72 285
T22	M Mouland	72 75 67 72 286
	H P Thul	70 74 72 70 286
	R Wessels	73 71 74 68 286
	J Remesy	68 73 73 72 286
	A Cruse	69 71 74 72 286
	K Storgaard	72 71 73 70 286
	J Van de Velde	70 68 73 76 287
	S Dunlap	73 74 67 73 287
	A Hunter	69 73 74 71 287
	A Da Silva	70 73 69 75 287
	C Kamps	72 69 70 76 287
	D Van Staden	74 72 67 74 287
	D Pappas	70 75 74 69 288
	C Davison	69 72 75 72 288
	J Lomas	74 68 71 75 288
	A McLardy	69 75 74 70 288
	T Johnstone	70 73 71 75 289
	J Spence	72 75 73 69 289
	B Vaughan	73 74 71 71 289
	T Immelman	73 70 70 76 289
	J Hawkes	70 72 73 75 290

F Nobilo	70 73 72 75 290
R Muntz	73 74 71 72 290
P Affleck	69 75 75 71 290
M Archer	72 71 75 72 290
S Struver	72 75 70 74 291
P Price	70 69 75 77 291
D Botes	72 73 70 77 292
D Lynn	71 76 74 71 292
W Bradley	72 73 77 70 292
A Pitts	74 72 72 74 292
P Blaikie	72 74 75 72 293
A Sandywell	73 72 72 76 293
K Stone	73 74 76 70 293
T V D Walt	67 75 73 78 293
M Hallberg	66 72 75 80 293
V Phillips	73 74 70 76 293
U V D Berg	70 72 77 74 293
W Abery	73 71 78 72 294
M Scholz	72 74 68 80 294
I Palmer	69 72 75 78 294
S Kjeldsen	72 74 73 75 294
S V Vuuren	74 72 72 77 295
P Panagopoulos	74 70 77 74 295
F Jacobson	76 70 72 77 295
G Evans	70 73 73 80 296
C Rocca	76 71 71 78 296
S Shearer	74 73 77 72 296
M Mackenzie	77 70 70 80 297
W Riley	76 68 74 79 297
A Forsbrand	74 72 75 77 298
C Watts	75 70 78 76 299
W Schutte	73 71 79 77 300
A Kankkonen	71 76 79 75 301
H Inggs	74 73 78 76 301
H Buhrmann	74 73 81 77 305

The 36-hole cut was made at 147 – 3 over par – 74 players qualified.

ROUND BY ROUND LEADERBOARD

FIRST ROUND		SECOND ROUND	
E ELS	8 under	D Frost	10 under
G Chalmers	6 under	E ELS	8 under
I Garrido	6 under	G Chalmers	7 under
M McNulty	6 under	G Hallberg	6 under
T V D Walt	5 under	T Gogele	6 under
D Frost	4 under	J Van de Velde	6 under
J Remesey	4 under	I Garrido	6 under

THIRD ROUND		FINAL ROUND	
E ELS	12 under	E ELS	15 under
D Frost	11 under	D Frost	12 under
N Henning	6 under	P Sjoland	8 under
B Langer	6 under	N Henning	7 under
I Garrido	6 under	M Gortana	7 under
T Gogele	6 under	B Langer	7 under
C Williams	6 under		

PUNTERS' POINTS

- The Durban Country Club course was set up in "a US Open" style with narrowed fairways and tough rough and as the winds did not blow both the course and climate enabled the in-form Ernie Els to win comfortably.

- On the final day, despite a bogey at the first hole, big Ernie was clearly determined not to throw away the lead as he had done in the Johnnie Walker Classic. With his putting much improved he never looked in real danger.

- 33/1 David Frost could never really mount a final-day challenge. Nevertheless for the second successive year (2nd 25/1 in the 1997 Data Dimension Pro-Am) he had secured a top 4 finish at rewarding odds early on in the European tour.

- The value to be had in golf betting was illustrated by Marco Gortana. T2nd in the previous week's Wild Coast Challenge, and T5th in the 1997 S.A. Players' Championship when this course was last used for a big tournament, he was an in-form, course-proven, DYM player available early at Stan James's 100/1. After I tipped him he was backed down to 50/1 and he justified the confidence with an ultra-consistent display to finish T4th.

- Thomas Gogele, T3rd at half way when 6 under, was 1 over for his final two rounds. He is clearly an improving player with real ability. The challenge he faces is to maintain his early-round form when the pressure is turned up over the final 36 holes.

- Course specialist Wayne Westner "loves this course" having won two South African Opens here. However, even the strong PMAs he has for the Durban course could not overcome his sluggish current form as the peroxide-blonde South African missed the cut.

- Aussie left hander Greg Chalmers had a 10 (yes, a ten!) in R3! If that ten had been a six he'd have finished T3rd!!

- Among those to miss the cut were 18/1 Retief Goosen, 28/1 Wayne Westner and 66/1 Jarmo Sandelin.

1997 RESULT

1	25/1	Vijay Singh
2	11/1	Nick Price
T3 fav	7/1	Ernie Els
T3	12/1	Mark McNulty
T3	50/1	Fulton Allem

WINNERS IN THE '90s

1990	Trevor Dodds
1991	Wayne Westner
1992	Ernie Els
1993	Clinton Whitelaw
1994	Tony Johnstone
1995	Retief Goosen
1996	Ernie Els
1997	Vijay Singh
1998	Ernie Els

PUNTERS' GUIDE

- Anyone with an honours degree from the University of the blindingly obvious will tell you that Ernie Els (won 1998, T3rd 1997, won 1996) will make a stout defence of his national title in 1999.
- The advantage enjoyed by the 'home' players is shown by the fact that in 1997 five of the first six, and in 1998 four of the first six were regular South African tour players.

THE SOUTH AFRICAN PGA

Date	12th – 15th February
Course	Houghton Golf Club, Johannesburg
Par	72
Yardage	7,035
First Prize	£63,280
Total Purse	£400,000

The South African PGA was held at the Houghton Golf Club for the third successive year. It is a long, testing course with five of the first six holes having water hazards. This time the rough was thicker than it was last year when Nick Price was the winner.

1998 ODDS

fav	5/1	Ernie Els (PWW)		40/1	Thomas Gogele
	8/1	Greg Norman		40/1	Costantino Rocca
	8/1	Nick Price (DC)		40/1	Patrik Sjoland
	16/1	David Frost		50/1	Marco Gortana
	18/1	Mark McNulty		50/1	Wayne Westner*
	33/1	Retief Goosen		50/1	Sven Struver
	33/1	Alexander Cejka		66/1	Jarmo Sandelin
	33/1	Ignacio Garrido		66/1	Adilson da Silva
	40/1	David Howell		66/1	Clinton Whitelaw
	40/1	Greg Chalmers			

Just 19 players were best priced at or under 66/1.

BOOKIES AT ODDS

DYM Wayne Westner 25/1 Hills: 50/1 Ladbrokes

Fifth-placed DYM Scott Dunlap 50/1 Stan James, Sunderlands, Tote: 100/1 Hills, Ladbrokes, Stanleys

The winner DYM Tony Johnstone 40/1 Corals, Tote: 100/1 Hills, Ladbrokes, Stanleys

1998 RESULT

1	100/1	**Tony Johnstone**	68 64 67 72	**271**
2 fav	5/1	**Ernie Els**	69 69 66 69	**273**
T3	33/1	**Retief Goosen**	71 70 69 65	**275**
T3	8/1	**Nick Price**	71 67 69 68	**275**
5	100/1	**Scott Dunlap**	69 66 71 70	**276**

6	P Price	69 71 66 71 277	I Hutchings	71 69 69 78 287
7	A Wall	71 72 67 69 279	M Mouland	70 73 69 76 288
8	A Forsbrand	68 70 72 71 281	H P Thul	71 73 73 71 288
9	M Gronberg	73 68 71 70 282	C Watts	72 73 74 69 288
T10	B Vaughan	75 68 71 69 283	C Whitelaw	71 72 72 73 288
	A McLardy	72 71 70 70 283	N V Rensburg	74 68 73 73 288
	M McNulty	71 74 70 68 283	P Affleck	67 76 70 76 289
	S V Vuuren	70 72 67 74 283	M Reale	70 73 76 70 289
	R Muntz	72 67 72 72 283	J Remesy	72 73 72 72 289
	T Gillis	69 69 73 72 283	G Levenson	72 73 70 74 289
T16	G Chalmers	74 70 69 71 284	A Cejka	74 69 73 73 289
	N Henning	72 72 68 72 284	B Lincoln	74 68 74 73 289
	D Gammon	71 72 72 69 284	J Sandelin	71 68 80 70 289
	A Cruse	70 72 69 73 284	D Pappas	73 70 73 74 290
	P Quirici	70 72 70 72 284	M Florioli	73 71 72 74 290
	M MacKenzie	74 68 70 72 284	L-W Zhang	72 73 75 70 290
	B Dredge	69 72 72 71 284	O Edmond	69 73 78 70 290
T23	C Kamps	74 69 70 72 285	C Davison	72 69 75 74 290
	A Clapp	74 69 72 70 285	W Druian	72 73 72 74 291
	G Owen	70 73 70 72 285	M Murless	74 71 72 74 291
	G Petersen	71 71 71 72 285	J Mashego	74 69 74 74 291
	R Wessels	68 74 70 73 285	B Collins	73 69 71 78 291
	B Liddle	71 71 70 73 285	A D Silva	70 74 76 72 292
	R Jacquelin	72 68 73 72 285	H Buhrmann	75 69 74 74 292
	M Wilshire	69 70 72 74 285	F Quinn	72 72 72 76 292
	S Struver	69 70 76 70 285	I Giner	72 73 74 73 292
	J Kingston	69 74 69 74 286	M Hallberg	78 67 78 69 292
	M Gortana	73 72 70 71 286	T V D Walt	70 75 75 72 292
	J Hawksworth	71 71 76 68 286	R Burns	74 68 73 77 292
	S Webster	71 69 73 73 286	D Edlund	76 68 74 75 293
	G Hutcheon	70 73 72 72 287	J Van de Velde	73 70 73 77 293
	J M Singh	69 75 71 72 287	A McLean	69 74 75 76 294
	C Rocca	68 76 73 70 287	S Kjeldsen	71 72 75 76 294
	A Roestoff	71 74 74 68 287	P Golding	73 70 75 77 295
	W Bradley	71 74 75 67 287	E Darcy	77 68 74 80 299
	M Archer	71 74 75 67 287	M Lafeber	72 73 77 78 300

The 36-hole cut was made at 147 – 3 over par – 74 players qualified.

ROUND BY ROUND LEADERBOARD

FIRST ROUND

P Affleck	5 under
C Rocca	4 under
A Forsbrand	4 under
R Wessels	4 under
T JOHNSTONE	4 under
E Els	3 under
P Price	3 under
S Dunlap	3 under
9 other players	3 under

SECOND ROUND

T JOHNSTONE	12 under
S Dunlap	9 under
A Forsbrand	6 under
E Els	6 under
T Gillis	6 under
N Price	6 under

THIRD ROUND

T JOHNSTONE	17 under
E Els	12 under
P Price	10 under
S Dunlap	10 under
N Price	9 under
S Van Vuuren	7 under
I Hutchings	7 under

BEFORE THE FINAL NINE OR TEN HOLES WERE PLAYED ON MONDAY

	Holes Left	
T JOHNSTONE	10	17 under
E Els	10	14 under
S Dunlap	9	13 under
R Goosen	9	11 under
N Price	9	10 under
P Price	10	10 under

FINAL ROUND

T JOHNSTONE	17 under
E Els	15 under
R Goosen	13 under
N Price	13 under
S Dunlap	12 under

PUNTERS' POINTS

- Tony Johnstone brought a smile to bookies' faces. The out-of-form 41-year-old entered the tournament unhappy with his game and on a course he had felt was too long for him in 1997.

  However with his confidence boosted by solid early putting and undisturbed by the regular weather interruptions he went on to win despite big Ernie 'breathing down his neck'.

- Johnstone was just a single shot ahead of the reigning US Open champion when they stood on the tee of the demanding 465-yard par 4 final hole. Both players put their approaches into a greenside bunker. However, Johnstone produced a magical bunker shot to 18 inches from the pin.

- Although 5/1 Ernie Els could never quite catch Johnstone, his season's winnings (£236,020) put him into a commanding lead in the European Order of Merit for which Hills went 5/1 when Ladbrokes went 16/1 about Els finishing 1998 as Europe's Number 1.

- Playing on the back of successive missed cuts Retief Goosen, 4th last year on this course, shot a superb 65 in R4 to finish T3rd at 33/1, and to move to third place in the European Order of Merit.
- 80/1 Philip Price here confirmed the fine form he showed at the end of 1997 when he was T7th in the individual placings in the World Cup of Golf at Kiawah island in November. His improved play on and around the greens was the basis for his creditable position as top European player when he finished 6th.
- Anders Forsbrand finished an eye-catching 8th to suggest that the tall Swede in his 'nappy factor' year could be a player to follow.
- Among those to miss the cut were 16/1 David Frost, 40/1 chances Patrik Sjoland and Thomas Gogele, and 50/1 Wayne Westner. Ignacio Garrido withdrew during R1 when 3 over par.
- Greg Norman 8 under par, with 9 holes to play on Monday, flew to America in his own plane instead. He was disqualified.

1997 RESULT

1 fav	4/1	Nick Price
		(Price won at the first play-off hole)
2	14/1	David Frost
3	125/1	Nico Van Rensburg
4	28/1	Retief Goosen

WINNERS IN THE '90s

1990	Fulton Allem
1991	Roger Wessels
1992	Ernie Els
1993	Mark McNulty
1994	David Frost
1995	Ernie Els
1996	Sven Struver
1997	Nick Price
1998	Tony Johnstone

PUNTERS' GUIDE

- For the second successive year all the leading positions were filled by acclimatised 'home' players with experience of the local weather, the course and the nap of the greens.
- This course, long at over 7,000 yards, is tailor made for Retief Goosen (T3rd 1998: T4th 1997) who is 29 under par for his eight rounds in the last two years in which he has twice 'burned' up the course with a 65 (R4 1998: R1 1997).

THE DUBAI DESERT CLASSIC

Date	26th February – 1st March
Course	Emirates Golf Club, Dubai
Par	72
Yardage	7,079
First Prize	£130,000
Total Purse	£770,000

The Emirates course is relatively easy with wide fairways and large flat greens making low scores the norm. This year, with virtually no rough, the course was criticised as the tournament was said to be 'a putting contest'.

1998 ODDS

fav	8/1	Ernie Els	40/1	Retief Goosen
	9/1	Colin Montgomerie	50/1	Paul McGinley
	12/1	Greg Norman	50/1	Costantino Rocca
	16/1	J M Olazabal	50/1	Andrew Coltart
	16/1	Lee Westwood	50/1	Ignacio Garrido*
	20/1	Ian Woosnam	50/1	Eduardo Romero*
	28/1	Thomas Bjorn	66/1	Joakim Haeggman
	33/1	Padraig Harrington	66/1	Peter Baker
	33/1	Robert Allenby	66/1	Alexander Cejka
	40/1	P U Johansson	66/1	M A Jimenez
	40/1	Darren Clarke		

21 players were best priced at or under 66/1.

BOOKIES AT ODDS

DYM Defending champion Richard Green 40/1 Tote 100/1 Ladbrokes:

DYM 1993 winner Wayne Westner 40/1 Stan James 100/1 Ladbrokes:

Tied third DYM Robert Karlsson 50/1 Tote 100/1 Corals:

Second placed DYM Stephen Allan 66/1 Stan James 200/1 Sunderlands:

Winner J M Olazabal 16/1 or 14/1 across the market with Corals' 12/1 the shortest quote.

1998 RESULT

1	16/1	J M Olazabal	69 67 65 68	269
2	200/1	Stephen Allan	67 70 67 68	272
T3	8/1	Ernie Els	71 63 67 72	273
T3	100/1	Robert Karlsson	66 65 67 75	273
5	20/1	Ian Woosnam	68 69 65 73	275

T6	I Garrido	67 67 66 76 276	S Tinning	74 67 73 70 284
	L Westwood	69 69 68 70 276	V Phillips	69 73 66 77 285
	G Norman	67 68 68 73 276	R Boxall	71 71 70 73 285
9	A Cejka	75 67 66 69 277	S Richardson	73 69 66 77 285
T10	A Oldcorn	71 66 68 73 278	R Goosen	75 68 66 76 285
	S Ballesteros	68 68 69 73 278	S Struver	70 72 76 67 285
	C Montgomerie	70 69 70 69 278	P Fulke	70 73 68 74 285
T13	D Carter	72 70 67 70 279	M Mouland	69 67 74 75 285
	D Clarke	68 68 70 73 279	P Hedblom	69 68 73 76 286
	M Hallberg	71 69 69 70 279	P Haugsrud	70 72 67 77 286
	J Coceres	71 67 67 74 279	D Robertson	70 73 68 75 286
T17	R Wessels	68 69 70 73 280	M Davis	70 72 70 74 286
	D Gilford	72 71 73 64 280	P Mitchell	73 70 68 75 286
	C Whitelaw	70 71 67 72 280	J Townsend	73 70 69 75 287
T20	P Affleck	72 68 70 71 281	M Tunnicliff	71 72 66 78 287
	P Price	68 71 73 69 281	P Marksaeng	73 70 70 74 287
	M James	71 70 72 68 281	S Torrance	71 72 67 77 287
	P Baker	69 70 72 70 281	R Muntz	69 70 72 76 287
	B May	73 68 67 73 281	A Sherborne	73 69 70 75 287
	A Coltart	67 75 69 70 281	R Burns	71 71 67 79 288
	R Coles	73 70 65 73 281	C Hainline	73 70 71 74 288
	G Orr	71 71 66 73 281	L W Zhang	71 72 75 70 288
	F Jacobson	71 69 67 74 281	P Harrington	72 69 68 79 288
	E Romero	72 67 73 70 282	A Wall	71 68 70 79 288
	G Evans	72 66 72 72 282	P Eales	71 71 68 78 288
	P U Johansson	69 67 71 75 282	T-P Chang	70 73 66 79 288
	J Payne	73 70 68 71 282	T Gogele	73 68 72 75 288
	D Smyth	71 71 68 73 283	S Bottomley	70 72 77 70 289
	P McGinley	72 68 64 79 283	R Cuello	73 70 71 75 289
	J Sandelin	73 68 66 76 283	G Brand Jr	70 72 73 74 289
	J Lomas	72 70 68 73 283	P Sjoland	70 70 69 80 289
	M Jonzon	71 71 70 71 283	I Garbutt	71 70 79 69 289
	A Hunter	69 69 71 74 283	N Joakimides	71 72 72 75 290
	A Forsbrand	69 70 71 73 283	D Tapping	69 71 70 82 292
	J Robson	72 71 70 71 284	P Quirici	71 69 67 85 292
	A Cabrera	70 68 68 78 284	T Sriroj	68 70 73 81 292
	P Broadhurst	72 70 72 70 284	R McFarlane	71 72 73 77 293
	M Reale	69 71 73 71 284	O Karlsson	72 71 71 81 295
	M A Martin	68 71 71 74 284	W Riley	72 71 66 87 296

The 36-hole cut was made at 143 – 1 over par – 83 players qualified.

ROUND BY ROUND LEADERBOARD

FIRST DAY		SECOND DAY	
R Karlsson	6 under	R Karlsson	13 under
I Garrido	5 under	E Els	10 under
A Coltart	5 under	I Garrido	10 under
G Norman	5 under	G Norman	9 under
S Allan	5 under	M Mouland	8 under
J M OLAZABAL	3 under	J M OLAZABAL	8 under
		P U Johansson	8 under
		S Ballesteros	8 under
		D Clarke	8 under

THIRD DAY		FINAL DAY	
R Karlsson	18 under	J M OLAZABAL	19 under
I Garrido	16 under	S Allan	16 under
E Els	15 under	E Els	15 under
J M OLAZABAL	15 under	R Karlsson	15 under
I Woosnam	14 under	I Woosnam	13 under
G Norman	13 under		

PUNTERS' POINTS

- 16/1 Jose Maria Olazabal after finishing T3rd in the Heineken Classic and 2nd in the Greg Norman Invitational returned to the European tour to the course where he made his emotional comeback in 1997 and to a superb victory. His chip in for eagle at the 13th in R4 was the crucial shot. After a bogey at the 16th a birdie-birdie finish clinched his 17th tour win.

- 'Sick players are the ones to watch' was my twelfth tip in EGF 1996. The reasoning is that a player's self-talk tends to become positive as he focuses on overcoming his illness. Well, here Olazabal had a temperature of over 100 degrees for the first couple of days, felt unwell, battled on.....and won!!

- 100/1 player Robert Karlsson, had led from the start. However the 6′ 5″ Swede shot a disappointing 3 over par final round to slip back to finish T3rd. This confirmed his fine 4th place in the 1997 season-ending Volvo Masters.

- On the final day scoring was very difficult in the windy conditions so players with solid scores then showed both skill and temperament.

- Baby-faced Aussie Stephen Allan shot a 68 in R4 to finish 2nd. At the last he played his second shot quickly, found the water and made bogey. Rash maybe, yet it showed a refreshing 'lets-go-for-it' aggression that will win him tournaments.

- Ernie Els seemed to lose his rhythm a little in the winds in the final round. Nevertheless his form figures are now an amazing 3-2-3-W-2!

- Is Seve back, or was this a one-off performance on a course tailor made for him? The 1997 Ryder Cup captain played well to finish T10th and to give him a platform on which to build a successful year.

- Robert Karlsson, Lee Westwood, and Darren Clarke became the first players to avail themselves of a PGA European Tour offer to test professionals' pace of play in practice. It must have worked as they shot 13 under par between them in R1!

- If betting in running please remember the 9th is the hardest hole on the course.
- Among those missing the cut were 28/1 Thomas Bjorn, 33/1 Robert Allenby, 50/1 Costantino Rocca, 66/1 outsiders M A Jimenez and Joakim Haeggman.

1997 RESULT

1	80/1	Richard Green
		(Green won at the first play-off hole)
T2	11/1	Greg Norman
T2	14/1	Ian Woosnam
4	22/1	Bernhard Langer

WINNERS IN THE '90s

1990	Eamonn Darcy
1991	No Tournament (Gulf War)
1992	Seve Ballesteros
1993	Wayne Westner
1994	Ernie Els
1995	Fred Couples
1996	Colin Montgomerie
1997	Richard Green
1998	J M Olazabal

PUNTERS' GUIDE

- This tournament in 1999 will be played for the first time at the Dubai Creek Golf and Yacht Club. The prize fund will increase from this year's £770,000 to £850,000.
- In the last three years an unconsidered Australian outsider has been either first, second or third. A combination of a liking for the heat, an ability to play in the Dubai winds and being sharp from the Aussie tour may explain this trend. So in 1999 consider any big-priced Aussies who have been in form 'down under'.
- Ian Woosnam's recent record is consistent, 5th 1998, T2nd 1997, T7th 1996; although he is usually best priced at 20/1.
- Philip Price with successive top 20 finishes must be noted in match and 3-ball betting.

THE QATAR MASTERS

Date	5th – 8th March
Course	Doha Golf Club
Par	72
Yardage	7,312
First Prize	£100,000
Total Purse	£600,000

With a total yardage of 7,312 yards the Doha Golf Course is very long with the par 5 ninth at 647 yards and the 601-yard par 5 first examples of its length. It was being used for the first time on the European tour.

1998 ODDS

fav	8/1	J M Olazabal (PWW)	40/1	Peter Baker
	10/1	Lee Westwood	50/1	Costantino Rocca
	14/1	Ian Woosnam	66/1	Phillip Price*
	22/1	Darren Clarke	66/1	Patrick Sjoland
	22/1	Ignacio Garrido	66/1	Stephen Allan
	28/1	P U Johansson	66/1	Anders Forsbrand
	33/1	Alexander Cejka	66/1	Jose Coceres
	33/1	Padraig Harrington	66/1	Joakim Haeggman
	33/1	Thomas Bjorn	66/1	M A Jimenez
	33/1	Andrew Coltart	66/1	Paul Broadhurst
	40/1	Retief Goosen	66/1	Sven Struver
	40/1	Paul McGinley	66/1	Clinton Whitelaw
	40/1	Robert Karlsson	66/1	David Howell
	40/1	David Gilford	66/1	Mark James
	40/1	Eduardo Romero	66/1	Seve Ballesteros

30 (!) players were best priced at or under 66/1.

BOOKIES AT ODDS

DYM Philip Price 33/1 Chandlers: 66/1 Tote

Tied second DYM Andrew Sherborne 100/1 Tote: 200/1 Sunderlands

The winner Andrew Coltart, 25/1 or 28/1 across the market, was best priced at Sunderland's double-carpet 33/1.

1998 RESULT

1	33/1	**Andrew Coltart**	**68 70 65 67**	**270**
T2	66/1	**Patrik Sjoland**	**70 66 67 69**	**272**
T2	200/1	**Andrew Sherborne**	**69 64 68 71**	**272**
4	200/1	**Van Phillips**	**70 71 66 66**	**273**
T5	40/1	**Retief Goosen**	**70 72 66 66**	**274**
T5	125/1	**Rolf Munz**	**72 68 66 68**	**274**
T5	80/1	**David Carter**	**69 75 64 66**	**274**

8	P Quirici	69 66 71 70 276		R Karlsson	74 69 70 70 283
T9	R Wessels	69 70 70 68 277		I Garrido	72 71 70 70 283
	D Clarke	73 67 69 68 277		P Walton	71 67 73 72 283
	P U Johansson	72 70 67 68 277		M A Martin	70 70 71 72 283
	I Woosnam	72 65 69 71 277		S Tinning	70 68 72 73 283
T13	J Townsend	69 68 74 67 278		D Cooper	69 71 70 73 283
	A Forsbrand	67 69 72 70 278		M Jonzon	74 67 68 74 283
	M A Jimenez	72 67 69 70 278		T Johnstone	73 71 70 70 283
	S Struver	72 68 68 70 278		P Lawrie	71 72 70 71 284
T17	P Harrington	74 70 67 68 279		W-S Kang	72 71 69 72 284
	A Cabrera	71 70 69 69 279		D Chopra	71 68 72 73 284
	J M Olazabal	71 69 69 70 279		F Jacobson	73 70 68 73 284
	R Drummond	69 70 68 72 279		S Torrance	72 71 68 73 284
T21	A Cejka	72 71 69 68 280		D Thomson	72 72 66 74 284
	M Roe	70 73 68 69 280		P Price	71 72 73 69 285
	I Garbutt	69 71 69 71 280		K Eriksson	72 72 72 69 285
	L Westwood	73 70 66 71 280		E Romero	72 72 71 70 285
	D Howell	73 65 69 73 280		G Orr	76 67 70 72 285
	P McGinley	70 69 68 73 280		J M Singh	74 70 68 73 285
	D Robertson	73 71 70 67 280		S Kjeldsen	75 67 74 70 285
	F Roca	71 72 69 69 280		K Storgaard	72 71 73 70 286
	P Mitchell	72 72 68 69 281		C Rocca	75 68 73 70 286
	M Davis	75 69 67 70 281		S Webster	74 70 68 74 286
	M Reale	69 69 72 71 281		D Smyth	75 69 73 70 287
	P Eales	71 71 68 71 281		R Chapman	72 72 73 70 287
	P Broadhurst	73 67 69 72 281		B May	73 69 71 74 287
	J Van de Velde	73 70 66 72 281		S Cage	72 72 69 74 287
	H P Thul	70 70 72 70 281		R Claydon	73 71 73 71 288
	C Whitelaw	71 70 71 70 281		J Sandelin	72 68 72 77 289
	M Tunnicliff	69 69 73 71 282		M Hallberg	69 75 71 76 291
	S Ballesteros	72 70 68 72 282		J Payne	74 70 75 73 292
	D Gilford	69 71 67 75 282		M Mouland	76 68 78 73 295
	J Haeggman	71 71 71 70 283			

The 36-hole cut was made at 144 – level par – 72 players qualified.

ROUND BY ROUND LEADERBOARD

FIRST ROUND

A Forsbrand	5 under
A COLTART	4 under
M Hallberg	3 under
D Carter	3 under
D Tunnicliff	3 under
M Reale	3 under
D Gilford	3 under
I Garbutt	3 under
P Quirici	3 under
R Wessels	3 under
J Townsend	3 under
D Cooper	3 under
A Sherborne	3 under

SECOND ROUND

A Sherborne	11 under
P Quirici	9 under
A Forsbrand	8 under
P Sjoland	8 under
I Woosnam	7 under
J Townsend	7 under
A COLTART	6 under

THIRD ROUND

A Sherborne	15 under
A COLTART	13 under
P Sjoland	13 under
R Muntz	10 under
I Woosnam	10 under
P Quirici	10 under

FINAL ROUND

A COLTART	18 under
A Sherborne	16 under
P Sjoland	16 under
V Phillips	15 under
R Goosen	14 under
R Muntz	14 under
D Carter	14 under

PUNTERS' POINTS

- Before teeing off for his final round Andrew Coltart learnt that he had finished top of the Australian Order of Merit, earning the 27-year-old Scot places in the British Open, the USPGA and the World Series of Golf.

- Encouraged by that news he played with a relaxed authority to catch Sherborne, overtake him and then to go on to finish a clear and thoroughly deserved winner of his first European tour event.....and it sure won't be his last!

- Short off the tee at around 240 yards 200/1 outsider Andrew Sherborne was always dominated by Coltart in R4. With seventeen pars he could never get 'lift-off' in that final round.

- David Carter, a generous 80/1 with the Tote, played superbly to finish T5th. A tall player, at ease with his new broomstick putter, the 25-year-old is a young player of real promise.

- 26-year-old Swede Patrik Sjoland followed up his superb form of last September and October (consecutive finishes of T4th, T5th, T8th and T4th) with his second top 3 finish of this season. He has a superb temperament, never letting disappointment get to him.

- Retief Goosen's superb finishing 36 holes confirmed what a superb player he is, especially when there is little wind. He must surely play well here again in 1999.

- With six of the first seven players best priced at or over 66/1 this course, with its extremely generous fairways, is always likely to favour the longer-priced players. For example 200/1 Rolf Munz could not post a top 10 finish in 1997 yet here he finished T5th.
- Among those to miss the cut were 33/1 Thomas Bjorn, 40/1 Peter Baker, 50/1 Stephen Allan and 66/1 chances Mark James and Jose Coceres.

1997 RESULT AND WINNERS IN THE '90s

This was the first Qatar Masters.

PUNTERS' GUIDE

- Three pointers emerged from the inaugural Qatar Masters.
  - > Coltart's win was his first on the European tour, and of the first seven players five had never previously won on the tour.
  - > The winner Coltart had been in very consistent form both in Australia and on the European tour.
  - > The first seven players had all made the cut in the Dubai Desert Classic last week.
- So in 1999 give careful consideration to any player seeking his first tour win if he's been in steady cut-making form.

THE MOROCCAN OPEN

Date	12th – 15th March
Course	Golf Royal d'Agadir
Par	72
Yardage	6,657
First Prize	£58,330
Total Purse	£350,000

The Golf Royal d'Agadir course has tight fairways and small sloping greens, so placing a high premium on accuracy. It has five par 5s, the longest being the 530-yard dog-leg opening hole. With comparatively low prize money there was a weak field.

1998 ODDS

fav	12/1	Robert Karlsson	40/1	Jose Coceres
	16/1	Thomas Bjorn	40/1	Tony Johnstone
	16/1	Alexander Cejka	40/1	Rolf Muntz
	22/1	Anders Forsbrand	40/1	Ray Russell
	25/1	Eduardo Romero	40/1	Roger Wessels
	28/1	Costantino Rocca	40/1	Angel Cabrera
	28/1	Mathew Goggin (PWW Aus)	50/1	Thomas Gogele
	28/1	Sven Struver	50/1	Peter Mitchell
	28/1	Greg Chalmers	50/1	Steve Alker
	28/1	Paul Broadhurst	66/1	Daniel Chopra
	33/1	Clinton Whitelaw (DC)	66/1	Stephen Leaney*
	33/1	M A Martin	66/1	Wayne Westner*
	33/1	M A Jimenez	66/1	Mark Roe
	33/1	Seve Ballesteros	66/1	Van Phillips

28 players were best priced at or under 66/1.

BOOKIES AT ODDS

The winner Stephen Leaney was a DYM 33/1 Stan James, Corals: 66/1 Ladbrokes

TYM(!) Wayne Westner 20/1 Stan James: 33/1 Corals: 66/1 Ladbrokes

1998 RESULT

1	66/1	Stephen Leaney	68 67 69 67	271
2 fav	12/1	Robert Karlsson	70 71 67 71	279
3	100/1	Mathias Gronberg	67 74 67 74	282
T4	33/1	M A Martin	69 78 68 69	284
T4	150/1	Mark Davis	71 65 72 76	284

T6	T Gillis	79 64 73 69 285		T Bjorn	70 76 76 72 294
	O Karlsson	72 69 70 74 285		J M Arruti	72 73 69 80 294
	T Johnstone	72 68 73 72 285		E Romero	71 73 75 75 294
T9	R Chapman	72 71 69 74 286		N Henning	76 71 70 78 295
	W Riley	73 69 71 73 286		D Cole	76 71 73 75 295
T11	H P Thul	77 70 70 70 287		E Canonica	71 76 74 74 295
	D Chopra	70 71 74 72 287		P Mitchell	73 71 74 77 295
	B May	69 70 76 72 287		S Alker	74 72 74 76 296
T14	M A Jimenez	82 68 69 69 288		G Owen	74 75 74 73 296
	P Linhart	67 74 75 72 288		R Drummond	79 71 71 75 296
	T Gogele	70 67 74 77 288		A Hunter	76 71 71 79 297
	D Smyth	64 72 77 75 288		F Cea	76 71 74 76 297
18	J Coceres	69 74 76 70 289		R Russell	74 75 74 74 297
T19	F Tarnaud	79 71 70 70 290		J Hawkes	74 76 72 75 297
	P Broadhurst	71 79 70 70 290		S Struver	81 69 77 71 298
	R Jacquelin	74 67 74 75 290		O Edmond	75 70 76 77 298
	D Borrego	69 72 75 74 290		H Nystrom	77 73 74 75 299
	A Cejka	68 70 74 78 290		D A Russell	75 69 76 79 299
T24	M Goggin	77 71 70 73 291		M Olander	70 76 84 70 300
	J Bickerton	76 68 74 73 291		C Hainline	75 73 71 81 300
	A Forsbrand	72 71 71 77 291		A Beal	79 70 80 71 300
	O Eliasson	75 72 71 74 292		F Howley	75 70 77 78 300
	S Talbot	74 74 72 72 292		F Henge	83 67 72 79 301
	A Cabrera	71 75 74 72 292		T V D Walt	77 69 76 80 302
	S Henderson	78 68 74 72 292		S Bennett	75 75 77 75 302
	M Reale	70 75 73 74 292		C Suneson	78 71 78 76 303
	P Golding	71 73 75 73 292		G Hutheon	72 76 80 76 304
	G Chalmers	75 75 70 73 293		G J Brand	77 73 74 82 306
	C Whitelaw	73 71 72 77 293		D Lee	70 80 75 81 306
	S Grappasonni	71 75 78 70 294		M Farry	75 73 83 77 308
	D Edlund	73 74 68 79 294		B Hafthorsson	74 73 85 79 311
	R Burns	68 79 73 74 294			

The 36-hole cut was made at 150 – 6 over par – 70 players qualified.

ROUND BY ROUND LEADERBOARD

FIRST ROUND		SECOND ROUND	
D Smyth	8 under	S LEANEY	9 under
M Gronberg	5 under	M Davis	8 under
P Linhart	5 under	D Smyth	8 under
S LEANEY	4 under	T Gogele	7 under
R Burns	4 under	A Cejka	6 under
A Cejka	4 under	B May	5 under

THIRD ROUND		FINAL ROUND	
S LEANEY	12 under	S LEANEY	17 under
M Gronberg	8 under	R Karlsson	9 under
R Karlsson	8 under	M Gronberg	6 under
M Davis	8 under	M A Martin	4 under
T Gogele	7 under	M Davis	4 under
O Karlsson	7 under		

PLEASE NOTE With the strong gusty winds stopping play on the first day and bad light on the second, the first and second rounds were not fully completed on their scheduled days.

PUNTERS' POINTS

- It was the course wot won it! Yes, just thirteen players beat par so the performances of the first two were very special.
- 66/1 DYM player Stephen Leaney with four sub-70 rounds, played really magnificently throughout. He was controlled, relaxed and refreshingly uncomplicated. A crisp ball striker with a fine putting stroke he proved again here that he merited the 'front runner' symbol given to him last year. He's clearly a tough cookie as he admitted he arrived severely jet-lagged!
- Course specialist Robert Karlsson shot four sub-par rounds to confirm yet again his love affair with this course. "I just love playing here".
- Mark Davis ruined his chances with a 9 on the par 5 tenth in R4. Nevertheless he showed here what a 'streak' player he can be and why he was the top of the putting stats in 1994.
- Blown away by the gusty wind in R1 Miguel Angel Jimenez played the final 54 holes in a brilliant 10 under par to finish T14th. That finish should be noted in 1999.
- Alexander Cejka dropped 5 shots in the four opening holes in R4 as his rhythm and his concentration seemed to go. He may be in need of a break after seven successive tournaments.
- Miguel Martin developed a wicked hook in R2 yet he quickly put it right to finish T4th after going 7 under for the last 36 holes. Let's remember before his injury in 1997 he was in prime form.
- A really gusty wind known as the 'cherki' blew up on the afternoon of the opening round. Steven Richardson started 6-4-6-4-8-7 and was out in 45; Mark Roe opened 7-7, four putting from four feet on the second; Steen Tinning started 7-5-7, and Seve Ballesteros was 13 over par after 12 holes.

The amazing 'unfairness' of this lay in the massive advantage it gave to the early starters on the first day further proving the value of early tee times as emphasised in 'H2WAGB'.

- Among those to miss the cut were 28/1 Costantino Rocca, 40/1 Rolf Munz, 40/1 Roger Wessels and 66/1 Wayne Westner, while 33/1 Seve Ballesteros retired and 66/1 Mark Roe withdrew.

1997 RESULT

1	100/1	Clinton Whitelaw
T2	125/1	Darren Cole
T2	66/1	Roger Chapman
T2	50/1	Wayne Riley

WINNERS IN THE '90s

1992	David Gilford
1993	David Gilford
1994	Anders Forsbrand
1995	Mark James
1996	Peter Hedblom
1997	Clinton Whitelaw
1998	Stephen Leaney

PLEASE NOTE All the tournaments were held at the Golf Royal d'Agadir course, except in 1996 when Royal Dar-Es-Salaam was used.

PUNTERS' GUIDE

- The last two winners have each had three key characteristics
  - > they were DYM players best priced at 125/1 and 66/1
  - > they were in their twenties
  - > they were tournament hardened non Europeans

  So in 1999 carefully examine the credentials of any young Aussie or South African who is a straight hitter and is a DYM player, and so overpriced by at least one firm.
- Robert Karlsson's amazing record here must surely result in a victory one day. He's been 2nd-T6th-3rd-3rd and 4th in five attempts. Even at 12/1 or 14/1 he must be worth an each-way interest in 1999.

THE PORTUGUESE OPEN

Date	19th – 22nd March
Course	Le Meridien Penina Golf Club, Algarve, Portugal
Par	73
Yardage	6,903
First Prize	£58,330
Total Purse	£350,000

This year, the 42nd year of the Portuguese Open, the venue for the sixth time was Le Meridien Penina in the Algarve. It was used for this event in 1982 when Sam Torrance was the winner. With five par 5s (all under 500 yards) the course par was an unusual 73.

1998 ODDS

fav	14/1	Darren Clarke		40/1	Greg Chalmers
	18/1	Ignacio Garrido		40/1	Ray Russell
	25/1	Patrik Sjoland		40/1	David Howell
	28/1	Stephen Leaney (PWW)		50/1	Tony Johnstone
	33/1	Alexander Cejka*		50/1	Mark James
	33/1	David Gilford		50/1	Wayne Riley
	33/1	M A Martin		50/1	Daniel Chopra
	33/1	Eduardo Romero		66/1	Sam Torrance
	33/1	Paul Broadhurst		66/1	Angel Cabrera
	40/1	Jose Coceres		66/1	Mark Davis*
	40/1	David Carter*		66/1	Steve Alker
	40/1	M A Jimenez		66/1	Thomas Gogele
	40/1	Anders Forsbrand		66/1	Peter Mitchell
	40/1	Peter Baker			

27 players were best priced at or under 66/1.

BOOKIES AT ODDS

DYM Tied 2nd Jarmo Sandelin 40/1 Tote, Corals: 80/1 Sunderlands

Tony Johnstone 28/1 Tote, Chandlers, Corals: 50/1 Stan James

DYM David Carter 20/1 Ladbrokes: 40/1 Corals

DYM Alexander Cejka 16/1 Corals, Sunderlands: 33/1 Ladbrokes

DYM Mark Davis 28/1 Stan James: 66/1 Ladbrokes

Winner Peter Mitchell was 66/1 generally, 50/1 Chandlers & Corals: 40/1 Tote

1998 RESULT

1	66/1	**Peter Mitchell**	67 70 67 70	274
T2	80/1	**Jarmo Sandelin**	73 71 64 67	275
T2	33/1	**David Gilford**	70 67 70 68	275
T4	33/1	**Eduardo Romero**	68 75 68 65	276
T4	66/1	**Sam Torrance**	74 66 70 66	276
T4	125/1	**Jonathon Lomas**	71 69 69 67	276

T7	P Baker	72 70 67 68 277		C Clark	74 71 72 70 287
	W Riley	68 66 74 69 277		D Cooper	73 71 73 70 287
9	D Clarke	66 74 69 69 278		S Tinning	72 71 74 70 287
T10	T Johnstone	68 73 70 68 279		P Eales	75 71 72 69 287
	D Carter	73 66 71 69 279		P Lawrie	72 64 69 82 287
T12	R Jacquelin	76 67 70 67 280		J Van de Velde	68 73 74 73 288
	F Cea	71 72 69 68 280		I Pyman	73 71 72 72 288
	A Cejka	72 72 66 70 280		G Evans	74 71 72 71 288
	J M Singh	69 73 68 70 280		C Hainline	77 68 72 71 288
T16	J Bickerton	73 71 70 67 281		S Bennett	74 68 74 73 289
	D Howell	71 72 71 67 281		F Jacobson	72 70 76 71 289
	I Garbutt	72 68 71 70 281		J Rystrom	73 71 74 71 289
T19	F Henge	71 71 71 69 282		G Owen	72 70 76 71 289
	V Phillips	70 74 73 65 282		R Boxall	71 72 72 75 290
	M A Martin	70 72 69 71 282		F Tarnaud	75 69 70 76 290
T22	T Gogele	73 73 68 69 283		S Ballesteros	72 73 69 76 290
	H Nystrom	72 68 73 70 283		J Spence	74 72 72 72 290
	D Hospital	68 75 70 70 283		H Clark	77 67 74 72 290
	A Cabrera	75 68 67 73 283		M A Jimenez	75 71 73 71 290
	S Luna	71 67 71 74 283		A Oldcorn	71 71 74 75 291
	P Hedblom	72 67 75 70 284		J Payne	74 72 71 74 291
	T Gillis	71 74 69 70 284		J Hawkes	74 71 73 72 291
	M James	71 71 72 71 285		R Claydon	75 71 74 71 291
	S Leaney	76 70 71 68 285		J Rask	74 71 72 75 292
	S Alker	74 69 70 72 285		D Thomson	76 67 74 75 292
	R Burns	76 70 68 72 285		D Robertson	73 73 73 73 292
	A Hunter	72 72 73 68 285		R Chapman	72 74 79 67 292
	M Reale	74 69 72 71 286		M Lafeber	73 73 74 73 293
	D Chopra	74 69 71 72 286		J Coceres	69 71 74 80 294
	J Rivero	73 70 71 72 286		O Eliasson	73 71 74 76 294
	D Cole	71 74 71 70 286		A Garrido	72 73 71 79 295
	M Mackenzie	74 70 70 72 286		M Davis	75 71 74 76 296
	P Sjoland	72 72 69 73 286		D Lynn	71 73 74 79 297
	D Smyth	73 68 74 72 287		S Cage	73 70 81 74 298
	J Remesy	70 68 77 72 287			

The 36-hole cut was made at 146 – level par – 75 players qualified.

ROUND BY ROUND LEADERBOARD

FIRST ROUND

D Clarke	7 under
P MITCHELL	6 under
D Hospital	5 under
J Van de Velde	5 under
E Romero	5 under
T Johnstone	5 under
W Riley	5 under

SECOND ROUND

W Riley	12 under
P Lawrie	10 under
P MITCHELL	9 under
D Gilford	9 under
S Luna	8 under
J Remesey	8 under

THIRD ROUND

P MITCHELL	15 under
P Lawrie	14 under
D Gilford	12 under
J Sandelin	11 under
W Riley	11 under
P Baker	10 under
J Lomas	10 under
D Clarke	10 under
S Luna	10 under

FINAL ROUND

P MITCHELL	18 under
J Sandelin	17 under
D Gilford	17 under
E Romero	16 under
S Torrance	16 under
J Lomas	16 under

PUNTERS' POINTS

- So nice guys do come first! Dedicated family man Peter Mitchell shot a superb 6 under par R3 on 'moving day' to lay the platform for a fine 66/1 win, his third on tour. He proved here that when in contention he is well able to take his chance.

- 80/1 DYM Jarmo Sandelin is an aggressive player well able to self destruct (as in R2 recently in the South African PGA when he shot 12 at one hole) or to shoot a low number as he chases victory. His 15 under par for the final two rounds prove what an explosive player he can be.

- Sam Torrance winner here on this course 16 (!) years ago showed that this year, even if it's a non-Ryder Cup year, will see the smokin' Scot notch a few more high finishes. He's now an alcohol-free zone looking like an advert for weight watchers. Rededicated, refocussed, he could yet return to the winners enclosure!

- Paul Lawrie, T2nd after R3 shot 82 (9 over par) in R4 to suggest that he was suffering from a severe case of 'contention rust'.

- Straight-hitting T2nd David Gilford is getting back to his best. The 32-year-old farmer has six tour wins and must always be noted when there is a premium on accuracy.

- Darren Clarke was a deserved favourite having PMAs with the course from his amateur days. A brilliant 66 in R1 gave him the lead and he looked the probable winner until he ordered crab that evening, became very ill, didn't sleep, and did superbly to 'hang in there' in R2. If he plays in this tournament in future you can be sure of two things – he'll play well and he'll give the crab a miss!

- Among those to miss the cut were 18/1 Ignacio Garrido (yet his dad, Antonio made the cut!), 33/1 Paul Broadhurst, and 40/1 chances Greg Chalmers, Ray Russell and Anders Forsbrand.

1997 RESULT

1	125/1	Michael Jonzon
2	66/1	Ignacio Garrido
3	33/1	Paul Broadhurst
T4	25/1	Wayne Riley
T4	18/1	J M Olazabal
T4	150/1	Stephen Allan
T4	40/1	Darren Clarke

WINNERS IN THE '90s

1990	Mike Mclean	Quinta do Lago, Algarve
1991	Steven Richardson	Estela, Rio Alto
1992	Ronan Rafferty	Vila Sol, Vilamoura
1993	David Gilford	Vila Sol, Vilamoura
1994	Philip Price	Penha Longa
1995	Adam Hunter	Penha Longa
1996	Wayne Riley	Aroeira, Lisbon
1997	Michael Jonzon	Aroeira, Lisbon
1998	Peter Mitchell	Le Meridien, Algarve

PUNTERS' GUIDE

- This tournament should carry a punter's wealth warning. Played on three different courses in the last five years it has produced winners at 100/1, 100/1, 40/1, 125/1 and in 1998 at 66/1 to give a five-year average price for the winner of 86/1!!
- There is no discernible pattern regarding the ages of the last five winners with two twenty somethings and three in their thirties including this year's 'old man' Peter Mitchell at 39.
- On recent trends the best advice is to go for an outsider (66/1 or more) who has made the cut in each of his last three tournaments. This formula may give you the 1999 winner just as it would have done in the last two years.

THE CANNES OPEN

Date	16th – 19th April
Course	Royal Mougins Golf Club, Cannes
Par	71
Yardage	6,594
First Prize	£50,000
Total Purse	£300,000

For the fourth successive year the Royal Mougins played host to the Cannes Open. A very short course it places a premium on accuracy rather than length. Knowledge of the undulating greens is a significant advantage.

1998 ODDS

fav	14/1	Andrew Coltart	40/1	Wayne Riley
	20/1	Padraig Harrington	40/1	Peter Mitchell (PWW)
	20/1	David Carter	50/1	Sven Struver
	20/1	David Gilford	50/1	Joakim Haeggman
	25/1	Paul McGinley	50/1	Greg Chalmers
	25/1	Robert Allenby	50/1	Matthew Goggin
	28/1	Paul Broadhurst*	50/1	Jarmo Sandelin
	33/1	Patrik Sjoland	66/1	Jean Van de Velde*
	33/1	Alexander Cejka	66/1	Philip Price
	33/1	David Howell	66/1	M A Jimenez
	33/1	Miguel Martin	66/1	Raymond Russell*
	33/1	Peter Leonard	66/1	Michael Long
	33/1	Greg Turner	66/1	Jonathan Lomas
	40/1	Clinton Whitelaw	66/1	Thomas Gogele

28 players were best priced at or under 66/1.

BOOKIES AT ODDS

DYM Paul Broadhurst 14/1 Ladbrokes: 28/1 Corals

DYM Jean Van de Velde 33/1 Stan James: 66/1 Hills, Ladbrokes, Sunderlands

1996 Winner DYM Raymond Russell 33/1 Ladbrokes, Tote: 66/1 Corals

Winner Thomas Levet was a 'name-your-price' rank outsider.

1998 RESULT

1	150/1	**Thomas Levet**	**69 71 65 73**	**278**
T2	66/1	**Philip Price**	**74 66 72 67**	**279**
T2	50/1	**Sven Struver**	**69 72 69 69**	**279**
T2	33/1	**Greg Turner**	**70 73 67 69**	**279**
T5	40/1	**Clinton Whitelaw**	**72 71 72 65**	**280**
T5	150/1	**Steve Webster**	**70 71 70 69**	**280**

7	R Mc Farlane	76 68 70 67 281	D Lynn	67 75 76 69 287
T8	M Davis	69 69 73 71 282	A Clapp	73 72 71 71 287
	P Lonard	68 71 70 73 282	C Pottier	74 71 72 70 287
	A Sherborne	73 68 68 73 282	J Van de Velde	73 72 72 70 287
T11	M Roe	70 75 70 68 283	P Mitchell	71 74 70 72 287
	J Haeggman	70 73 68 72 283	P Linhart	72 71 69 75 287
	A Cejka	72 73 68 70 283	D Gilford	70 74 74 70 288
	J Remesy	67 74 69 73 283	J Townsend	70 72 72 74 288
	P Lawrie	74 71 67 71 283	P Walton	72 71 73 72 288
T16	M Mouland	71 71 71 71 284	F Tarnaud	70 74 71 73 288
	I Garbutt	74 71 74 65 284	J Lomas	71 70 76 71 288
	M A Martin	69 74 76 65 284	T Gillis	73 67 73 75 288
	M Long	69 72 70 73 284	P Sjoland	72 69 72 76 289
	M Campbell	70 75 72 67 284	A Sandywell	69 74 72 74 289
	E Darcy	71 72 66 75 284	D Montesi (am)	70 73 75 71 289
	A Oldcorn	72 72 70 70 284	R Allenby	67 75 73 75 290
	D Howell	73 70 72 69 284	C V D Velde	71 72 72 75 290
	P Fulke	73 65 71 75 284	D Robertson	73 70 76 72 291
	S Tinning	70 74 69 71 284	S Bennett	72 73 73 73 291
	D Higgins	69 69 75 71 284	S Allan	71 67 72 81 291
	C O'Connor Jr	72 64 75 74 285	W Westner	68 77 76 71 292
	R Jacquelin	69 73 70 73 285	M Farry	70 73 71 78 292
	C Hainline	71 72 71 71 285	J M Singh	67 74 79 72 292
	M A Jimenez	75 69 66 75 285	S Lahary	72 71 77 72 292
	B May	74 71 71 69 285	A Binaghi	71 74 74 74 293
	M Gronberg	73 71 68 74 286	J Robson	71 74 76 72 293
	S Alker	73 71 71 71 286	D Tapping	75 70 76 73 294
	S Luna	69 68 77 72 286	P Edmond	76 69 72 77 294
	O Edmond	72 71 74 69 286	D Chopra	69 73 77 76 295
	G Brand Jr	75 69 71 71 286	R Muntz	74 69 76 79 298

The 36-hole cut was made at 145 – 3 over par – 65 players qualified.

ROUND BY ROUND LEADERBOARD

FIRST ROUND

D Lynn	4 under
R Allenby	4 under
J Remesey	4 under
J M Singh	4 under
W Westner	3 under
P Lonard	3 under
T LEVET	2 under

SECOND ROUND

C O'Connor Jr	6 under
S Luna	5 under
P Fulke	4 under
D Higgins	4 under
S Allan	4 under
M Davis	4 under
T LEVET	2 under

THIRD ROUND

T LEVET	8 under
P Fulke	4 under
P Lonard	4 under
E Darcy	4 under
A Sherborne	4 under
S Allan	3 under
M A Jimenez	3 under
G Turner	3 under
J Remesy	3 under
S Struver	3 under

FINAL ROUND

T LEVET	6 under
S Struver	5 under
G Turner	5 under
P Price	5 under
C Whitelaw	4 under
S Webster	4 under

PUNTERS' POINTS

- A real 'skinner' for the bookies as Thomas Levet, playing on a special exemption because he doesn't have a tour card, held on for a narrow win in his first European PGA event of the year. His four-shot lead going into the final round had vanished before birdies at the 15th and 17th and a nine-foot putt for a bogey at the last gave the 29-year-old Frenchman his maiden tour victory.

- Greg Turner, 13th here last year, made his move over the final two rounds with a tournament best 6 under par. When in contention he's a very gritty player.

- 66/1 Phillip Price has made a fine start to 1998 building on his fine performance when T7th in the individual rankings in the World Cup of Golf last November. He was very well suited by the gusty conditions.

- 150/1 Steve Webster may have finished T5th yet he was the only player to shoot four par or sub-par rounds. Such consistency will place the 22-year-old in contention often in the future.

- Clinton Whitelaw, 6th here last year rushed up the leaderboard on the final day with a 65 to finish T5th although he was never really in contention.

- This tournament's recent reputation as a tournament for outsiders was confirmed when five of the front seven in the market all missed the cut -14/1 favourite Andrew Coltart, 20/1 chances Padraig Harrington and David Carter, 25/1 Paul McGinley and 28/1 Paul Broadhurst. Others to miss the cut were 40/1 Wayne Riley, 50/1 chances Greg Chalmers and Jarmo Sandelin and 66/1 outsiders Thomas Gogele and Raymond Russell.

1997 RESULT

1	100/1	Stuart Cage
T2	20/1	Paul Broadhurst
T2	66/1	David Carter
T4	80/1	Paul Eales
T4	100/1	Jamie Spence

WINNERS IN THE '90s

1990	Mark McNulty	Cannes Mougins
1991	David Feherty	Cannes Mougins
1992	Anders Forsbrand	Cannes Mougins
1993	Rodger Davis	Cannes Mougins
1994	Ian Woosnam	Cannes Mougins
1995	Andre Bossert (36 holes only)	Royal Mougins
1996	Raymond Russell	Royal Mougins
1997	Stuart Cage	Royal Mougins
1998	Thomas Levet	Royal Mougins

PUNTERS' GUIDE

- Of all the transatlantic tournaments the Cannes Open in its four years at the Royal Mougins is now established as THE outsiders' tournament.
  - > It's four winners have all been 100/1+
  - > 77.7% of the players who have finished in the top 4 (or tied 4th) have started at or over 50/1.
  - > Its four winners have all been first-time winners.
- Give careful consideration to any young promising player seeking his maiden tour victory who has played here before and who has an early tee time for his opening round.
- Do note the weather forecast as the gusty winds in 1998 led to a winning score of 278, eight greater than in 1997.

THE PEUGEOT SPANISH OPEN

Date	23rd – 26th April
Course	El Prat, Barcelona
Par	72
Yardage	6,639
First Prize	£91,660
Total Purse	£550,000

El Prat was hosting the Spanish Open for the first time since Seve Ballesteros' victory in 1981. It was last used on the Euro circuit for the 1988 Barcelona Open.

1998 ODDS

fav	8/1	J M Olazabal
	12/1	Bernhard Langer
	14/1	Ian Woosnam
	33/1	Ignacio Garrido
	33/1	Eduardo Romero*
	33/1	Andrew Coltart
	33/1	Alexander Cejka
	40/1	Thomas Bjorn
	40/1	Padraig Harrington
	40/1	M A Martin
	40/1	Greg Turner
	40/1	Robert Karlsson*
	50/1	David Gilford
	50/1	Phillip Price
	50/1	M A Jimenez
	50/1	Robert Allenby*
	50/1	Peter Lonard
	50/1	Peter Baker*
	66/1	David Carter
	66/1	Paul McGinley
	66/1	Sam Torrance
	66/1	Patrik Sjoland
	66/1	Clinton Whitelaw
	66/1	Mark James (DC)
	66/1	Joakim Haeggman
	66/1	David Howell
	66/1	Costantino Rocca
	66/1	Michael Long
	66/1	Jarmo Sandelin
	66/1	Peter Mitchell

30 players were best priced at or under 66/1.

BOOKIES AT ODDS

Tied 4th DYM Eduardo Romero 16/1 Hills: 33/1 Ladbrokes, Chandlers, Sunderlands

DYM Robert Allenby 25/1 Stanleys: 50/1 Chandlers

DYM Peter Baker 25/1 Stan James: 50/1 Hills

DYM Robert Karlsson 20/1 Stanleys: 40/1 Tote

Winner Thomas Bjorn 25/1 Ladbrokes, Stan James, Stanleys: 40/1 Corals, Hills

1998 RESULT

1	40/1	**Thomas Bjorn**	**68 67 66 66**	**267**
T2	80/1	**Greg Chalmers**	**64 66 69 69**	**268**
T2 fav	8/1	**J M Olazabal**	**66 71 64 67**	**268**
T4	33/1	**Eduardo Romero**	**66 67 70 67**	**270**
T4	66/1	**Mark James**	**68 66 70 66**	**270**

6	R Wessels	71 69 66 65	271	
T7	S Allan	66 72 69 65	272	
	M Gronberg	69 67 71 65	272	
	K Tomori	67 67 66 72	272	
10	P Price	67 66 71 69	273	
T11	D Howell	65 68 67 74	274	
	O Karlsson	70 70 67 67	274	
	A Cabrera	67 70 69 68	274	
	G Brand Jr	67 66 73 68	274	
	R Chapman	68 71 66 69	274	
	A Coltart	69 70 68 67	274	
	M A Martin	69 70 70 65	274	
	E Darcy	68 71 65 70	274	
	R Allenby	66 64 70 74	274	
T20	M Tunnicliff	67 69 69 70	275	
	D Chopra	66 72 70 67	275	
	S Torrance	70 69 65 71	275	
	I Giner	67 70 67 71	275	
	P Lawrie	68 66 73 68	275	
	J Townsend	64 69 70 72	275	
	D Carter	68 69 66 73	276	
	M Mackenzie	69 67 74 66	276	
	D Hospital	67 68 72 69	276	
	R Karlsson	72 67 73 64	276	
	P Hedblom	69 67 74 66	276	
	P Sjoland	66 71 69 70	276	
	M A Jimenez	67 67 69 73	276	
	C Hainline	68 71 67 70	276	
	W Riley	73 67 70 67	277	
	I Woosnam	69 70 72 66	277	
	P Mitchell	69 71 71 66	277	
	P Eales	68 72 71 66	277	
	M Roe	69 67 68 73	277	
	S Garcia (am)	66 70 70 71	277	
	K Eriksson	69 71 66 72	278	
	I Garrido	70 66 72 70	278	
	I Pyman	71 68 72 67	278	
	S Luna	68 67 71 72	278	
	J Rivero	71 69 69 69	278	
	M Farry	69 68 69 73	279	
	P Broadhurst	72 67 70 70	279	
	J Haeggman	69 70 70 70	279	
	J Coceres	70 68 69 72	279	
	T Levet	68 71 69 71	279	
	S Leaney	70 69 71 69	279	
	V Phillips	69 71 69 70	279	
	J Remesy	68 69 73 70	280	
	D Edlund	69 70 70 71	280	
	S Grappasonni	70 66 72 72	280	
	M Mouland	72 65 71 72	280	
	J M Lara	69 71 67 73	280	
	K Brink	67 73 71 69	280	
	S Ballesteros	69 71 71 69	280	
	I Garbutt	67 71 71 71	280	
	R Gonzalez	71 68 69 72	280	
	F Cea	70 69 69 72	280	
	J M Carriles	64 70 74 72	280	
	B Dredge	69 68 76 68	281	
	J Van de Velde	65 69 72 75	281	
	J Sandelin	68 71 67 76	282	
	J Lomas	68 70 70 74	282	
	C Whitelaw	68 68 71 75	282	
	D Smyth	69 69 72 73	283	
	G Orr	71 69 73 71	284	
	B Davis	69 71 74 71	285	
	P Baker	69 71 70 76	285	
	J Payne	70 69 72 74	283	
	F Roca	71 68 69 80	288	

The 36-hole cut was made at 140 – 4 under par – 74 players qualified

ROUND BY ROUND LEADERBOARD

FIRST ROUND

G Chalmers	8 under
J Townsend	8 under
J M Carriles	8 under
D Howell	7 under
J Van de Velde	7 under
T BJORN	4 under

SECOND ROUND

R Allenby	14 under
G Chalmers	14 under
J Townsend	11 under
P Price	11 under
E Romero	11 under
D Howell	11 under
G Brand Jr	11 under
T BJORN	9 under

THIRD ROUND

G Chalmers	17 under
K Tomori	16 under
R Allenby	16 under
D Howell	16 under
J M Olazabal	15 under
T BJORN	15 under

FINAL ROUND

T BJORN	21 under
G Chalmers	20 under
J M Olazabal	20 under
E Romero	18 under
M James	18 under

PUNTERS' POINTS

- 'Bjorn again' screamed the headlines as the 27-year-old Dane won for the second time this season. Here he proved two things – first he knows how to win when an opportunity presents itself, and second he goes well fresh as he was playing for the first time after a five-week break.

- 33/1 Eduardo Romero's superb tee-to-green play was the basis of his top position on the leaderboard with six to play. However, bogeys at the 14th and 15th and poor putting from 4 to 6 feet cost the Argentinian a clear winning chance.

- 80/1 Greg Chalmers had led from the first round showing really good form only to find Bjorn just one shot too good. However the 24-year-old Aussie left hander who has already landed the Australian Players Championship at 40/1 has fully justified the "expect him to make a real impact in 1998" comment about him in last year's book.

- Jose Maria Olazabal's superb 13 under par over the final 36 holes was not quite good enough to give the Spaniard his first Spanish Open. "I am furioso," he said!!

- 66/1 Mark James's superb tee-to-green play and improved final-round putting showed that the 44-year-old is still a force to be reckoned with. His T4th finish was a splendid defence of his title.

- Sunderlands enterprisingly opened a book on the Top Spaniard. The result was:- 1. 15/8 fav J M Olazabal: 2. 15/2 2nd fav M A Martin: 3. 66/1 Ivo (who?) Giner.

- Among those missing the cut were 12/1 Bernhard Langer, 33/1 Alexander Cejka, 40/1 chances Padraig Harrington and Greg Turner, 50/1 David Gilford, and 66/1 outsiders Michael Long, Costantino Rocca, and Paul McGinley.

1997 RESULT

1	80/1	Mark James
2 fav	10/1	Greg Norman
T3	40/1	Eduardo Romero
T3	100/1	Jarmo Sandelin

WINNERS IN THE '90s

1990	Rodger Davis
1991	Eduardo Romero
1992	Andrew Sherborne
1993	Joakim Haeggman
1994	Colin Montgomerie
1995	Seve Ballesteros
1996	Padraig Harrington
1997	Mark James
1998	Thomas Bjorn

PUNTERS' GUIDE

- Apart from Seve Ballesteros (winner in 1982, 1985 and 1995) no Spaniard has won this tournament in either the eighties or nineties. Jose Maria Olazabal is determined to win his national title, and although certain to start favourite in 1999 he must be expected to play well.

- Last year's tip was to go for Romero each way. His tournament record (Won 1991, T6th 1995, T4th 1996, T3rd 1997, T4th 1998) is clearly first class and, especially if his putting can improve, he must be expected to go close again in 1999.

THE ITALIAN OPEN

Date	30th April – 3rd May
Course	Castelconturbia, Milan, Italy
Par	72
Yardage	6,826
First Prize	£83,330
Total Purse	£500,000

This tournament is played at different venues throughout Italy each year. This year the Castelconturbia golf course, last used for the 1991 Italian Open, was the venue.

1998 ODDS

fav	8/1	J M Olazabal	50/1	Greg Chalmers
	10/1	Lee Westwood	50/1	Sam Torrance (non-runner)
	20/1	Thomas Bjorn (PWW)	50/1	Angel Cabrera
	20/1	Darren Clarke	50/1	Tony Johnstone
	28/1	Eduardo Romero	66/1	Peter Lonard*
	28/1	Retief Goosen	66/1	Peter Baker
	28/1	Andrew Coltart	66/1	Patrik Sjoland
	40/1	Alexander Cejka	66/1	David Gilford*
	40/1	M A Martin	66/1	Padraig Harrington
	40/1	Mark James	66/1	David Carter
	40/1	Ignacio Garrido	66/1	Stephen Leaney
	40/1	Phillip Price	66/1	Stephen Allan
	40/1	Robert Allenby	66/1	Sven Struver
	40/1	Robert Karlsson	66/1	Mathias Gronberg
	50/1	Greg Turner	66/1	Clinton Whitelaw

30 players were best priced at or under 66/1.

BOOKIES AT ODDS

DYM Peter Lonard 33/1 Stan James: 66/1 Ladbrokes, Sunderlands

DYM David Gilford 33/1 Hills: 66/1 Chandlers, Ladbrokes, Surrey

Winner Patrik Sjoland 40/1 Hills, Ladbrokes: 66/1 Stan James

1998 RESULT

1	66/1	**Patrik Sjoland**	**64 65 66**	**195**
T2 fav	8/1	**J M Olazabal**	**68 65 65**	**198**
T2	80/1	**Joakim Haeggman**	**67 68 63**	**198**
4	20/1	**Thomas Bjorn**	**66 66 68**	**200**
5	66/1	**Peter Baker**	**67 67 67**	**201**

T6	L Westwood	68 67 67 202	M A Martin	72 68 67 207
	B May	69 68 65 202	P Quirici	74 66 67 207
	S Tinning	68 65 69 202	R Muntz	69 71 67 207
	S Struver	67 69 66 202	M Gronberg	70 67 71 208
T10	M James	65 69 69 203	P Harrington	70 69 69 208
	J Van de Velde	67 70 66 203	M Jonzon	74 66 68 208
	D Lynn	71 65 67 203	N Vanhootegem	71 68 69 208
T13	P Price	68 67 69 204	E Darcy	68 70 71 209
	P McGinley	63 72 69 204	A Kankkonen	70 70 69 209
	R Goosen	70 67 67 204	R Coles	71 65 73 209
	G Turner	66 71 67 204	G Evans	69 71 69 209
	J Sandelin	68 70 66 204	M Gates	70 68 72 210
T18	P Broadhurst	68 68 69 205	C V D Velde	73 66 71 210
	G Brand Jr	70 66 69 205	D Carter	68 70 72 210
	A Clapp	72 67 66 205	D Clarke	65 71 74 210
	R Karlsson	67 70 68 205	R Davis	70 70 70 210
	J Townsend	71 66 68 205	E Romero	72 67 71 210
T23	S Grappasonni	68 68 70 206	D Robertson	70 70 70 210
	M Campbell	68 69 69 206	D Edlund	70 70 70 210
	R Allenby	68 71 67 206	M Long	70 70 70 210
	M Florioli	67 70 69 206	S Allan	69 70 72 211
	E Canonica	69 67 70 206	J Spence	68 72 71 211
	A Coltart	70 68 68 206	D Gilford	69 68 74 211
	T Levet	69 69 68 206	S Richardson	72 68 71 211
	R Chapman	68 70 67 206	A Cabrera	73 67 71 211
	P Fulke	67 70 70 207	T Gogele	71 67 74 212
	K Eriksson	66 70 71 207	R Jacquelin	72 67 72 213
	M Farry	68 67 72 207	R Burns	71 66 76 213
	F Henge	68 69 70 207	V Phillips	70 69 74 213
	S Leaney	68 71 68 207	R Rafferty	67 72 76 215
	I Garrido	69 69 69 207	F Bisazza	71 69 75 215
	S Webster	72 66 69 207	M Mackenzie	73 67 75 215
	C Rocca	69 69 69 207	S Henderson	69 69 78 216
	W Westner	69 68 70 207		

The 36-hole cut was made at 140 – 4 under par – 79 players qualified.

ROUND BY ROUND LEADERBOARD

FIRST ROUND		SECOND ROUND	
P McGinley	9 under	P SJOLAND	15 under
P SJOLAND	8 under	T Bjorn	12 under
D Clarke	7 under	S Tinning	11 under
M James	7 under	J M Olazabal	11 under
T Bjorn	6 under	M James	10 under
K Eriksson	6 under	P Baker	10 under
G Turner	6 under		

THIRD AND FINAL ROUND

P SJOLAND	21 under
J M Olazabal	18 under
J Haeggman	18 under
T Bjorn	16 under
P Baker	15 under

- With preferred lies and shortened par 5 holes easily reachable in two shots this rain-reduced tournament on a wet course was a birdie-laden event.

PUNTERS' POINTS

- 66/1 Patrik Sjoland's first tour success, in which he shot just one bogey in a 21-under-par 54-hole victory, was probably based on three factors of interest to golf punters.
  > He had PMAs with the Italian Open – T12th 1997, 2nd 1996.
  > His girlfriend has decided to join him on the tour as his caddie.
  > He was in fine form having made seven cuts in nine starts including two top 3 finishes.
- Jose Maria Olazabal's runners-up spot was his second in successive weeks, and his second successive second in this tournament. He is now top of the European Order of Merit which he is determined to win.
- Joakim Haeggman's "streaking ability" was again shown here with a R4 63 that took the Swede to T2nd.
- Peter Baker's 5th here confirmed the renaissance of the 1993 Ryder Cup hero. It was his fifth top 20 and second top 10 finish this season.
- Punters must note that players who did well in this tournament proved they can handle delays, and cope with many more than 18 holes in a day. These points will be worth noting when similar circumstances recur.
- Among those to miss the cut were :- 40/1 Alexander Cejka, 50/1 Greg Chalmers and 66/1 Peter Lonard. 50/1 Tony Johnstone retired.
- Sam Torrance withdrew before the start with a neck injury.

1997 RESULT

1	14/1	Bernard Langer
2 fav	11/1	J M Olazabal
3	50/1	Darren Clarke
T4	80/1	Philip Walton
T4	150/1	Steve Webster

WINNERS IN THE '90s

1990   Richard Boxall
1991   Craig Parry
1992   Sandy Lyle
1993   Greg Turner
1994   Eduardo Romero
1995   Sam Torrance
1996   Jim Payne
1997   Bernhard Langer
1998   Patrik Sjoland (54 holes)

PUNTERS' GUIDE

With a different course used each year it is difficult to offer any guidelines. However Sjoland's tournament form (T12th 1997: 2nd 1996) suggests that PMAs with the Italian Open may be important. If that is so then the following players must be considered in 1999.

> Sven Struver T6th 1998: T15th 1996
> Jarmo Sandelin T13th 1998: T12th 1997
> Greg Turner T13th 1998: T7th 1996 & 1993 Winner
> Retief Goosen T13th 1998: T17th 1997
> Lee Westwood T6th 1998: T6th 1997: T3rd 1996

THE TURESPANA MASTERS

Date	7th – 10th May
Course	Santa Ponsa 1, Majorca, Spain
Par	72
Yardage	7,155
First Prize	£58,330
Total Purse	£350,000

Played at a different course each year the Santa Ponsa 1 course, last used for the 1993 Balearic Open, was this year's venue.

1998 ODDS

fav	6/1	Bernhard Langer	50/1	Seve Ballesteros
	16/1	M A Martin	50/1	Sergio Garcia*
	18/1	Ignacio Garrido	50/1	Anders Forsbrand
	18/1	Sven Struver	50/1	Steve Alker
	22/1	M A Jimenez	50/1	Matthew Goggin
	25/1	Alexander Cejka	66/1	Michael Long*
	25/1	David Howell	66/1	Roger Wessels*
	28/1	Paul Broadhurst	66/1	Tom Gillis
	40/1	Angel Cabrera	66/1	Mark Davis
	40/1	Peter Mitchell	66/1	Santiago Luna*
	50/1	Jose Coceres*		

21 players were best priced at or under 66/1.

PLEASE NOTE Paul McGinley was a surprise runner so he had not been included in the betting. All bookmakers agreed that he would be treated as a non-runner so if he won the 'winner' would become the runner-up. In the event McGinley finished T3rd. So the tournament had two results – with McGinley (the official result) and without McGinley (the bookmakers' result).

BOOKIES AT ODDS

DYM T3rd (bookmakers' result) Katsuyoshi Tomori 33/1 Hills, 40/1 Tote: 80/1 Corals

DYM T5th (bookmakers' result) Michael Long 33/1 Hills: 66/1 Sunderlands

DYM T5th (bookmakers' result) Santiago Luna 33/1 Stan James, Corals: 66/1 Chandlers

Winner M A Jimenez 16/1 Hills, Ladbrokes, Stanleys, Sunderlands: 22/1 Corals

1998 BOOKMAKERS' RESULT (i.e. without Paul McGinley)

1	22/1	M A Jimenez
2	16/1	M A Martin
3	80/1	Katsuyoshi Tomori
4	125/1	Van Phillips
T5	66/1	Michael Long
T5	66/1	Santiago Luna

1998 OFFICIAL RESULT

1	22/1	M A Jimenez	69 68 70 72	279
2	16/1	M A Martin	67 72 70 72	281
T3	80/1	Katsuyoshi Tomori	74 67 73 68	282
T3	-	Paul McGinley	71 73 67 71	282
5	125/1	Van Phillips	75 69 67 73	284

T6	M Long	71 71 72 71 285		A Forsbrand	72 74 72 76 294
	S Luna	67 70 72 76 285		E Canonica	77 70 72 76 295
T8	A Cabrera	71 69 73 75 288		J M Singh	72 75 74 74 295
	P Broadhurst	71 72 69 76 288		H P Thul	73 73 71 78 295
	M Florioli	72 70 72 74 288		M Gortana	74 72 74 76 296
	M Reale	68 72 70 78 288		P Curry	74 74 72 76 296
T12	A Sandywell	70 74 73 72 289		D Hospital	72 75 74 75 296
	A Beal	72 73 70 74 289		F Valera	75 72 75 74 296
	R Johnson	71 72 72 74 289		S Cage	73 74 75 74 296
T15	D Borrego	70 73 74 73 290		M Blackey	76 72 74 74 296
	A Binaghi	72 76 68 74 290		J Wade	68 75 73 80 296
	G Hutcheon	70 76 70 74 290		R J Derksen	72 76 72 77 297
	D Howell	72 72 72 74 290		B Davis	71 75 75 76 297
T19	M Campbell	74 72 73 72 291		F Roca	72 75 75 75 297
	M Mackenzie	72 71 73 75 291		I Giner	69 77 77 74 297
	J Bickerton	70 72 73 76 291		Y Beamonte	74 72 77 74 297
	F Cea	73 75 66 77 291		B Hafthorsson	72 75 71 79 297
T23	R Wessels	73 75 77 67 292		N Briggs	74 74 76 74 298
	P Mitchell	72 74 72 74 292		A Salto	73 74 73 79 299
	A Hansen	73 71 73 75 292		S Scahill	73 74 75 77 299
	A Wall	70 72 76 74 292		R Quiros (am)	69 76 77 77 299
	J Mellor	72 75 72 74 293		O Eliasson	72 75 78 74 299
	S Bennett	70 74 75 74 293		A McKenna	68 78 72 81 299
	R Jacquelin	71 75 74 73 293		O Edmond	74 74 70 81 299
	S Garcia (am)	70 75 76 72 293		D Edlund	74 74 74 78 300
	D Lee	70 75 73 75 293		G Nicklaus	76 71 76 77 300
	P Linhart	72 73 73 75 293		S Kjeldsen	73 75 76 76 300
	A Clapp	72 71 74 76 293		B Solanes	75 73 77 75 300
	J Rivero	69 70 78 76 293		F de Pablo	75 72 76 78 301
	R Drummond	75 73 71 75 294		J Robson	72 75 77 77 301
	B Langer	72 73 74 75 294		D Westermark	73 75 79 74 301
	G Owen	77 71 72 74 294		P Streeter	73 74 79 76 302
	M Pendaries	72 74 74 74 294		R Gonzalez	75 73 78 76 302
	R Lee	71 75 76 72 294		M Davis	73 75 82 73 303
	T Gillis	76 72 74 72 294		S Richardson	74 74 76 81 305
	J Hawksworth	68 78 76 72 294		M Mouland	74 71 77 85 307
	M Goggin	73 73 77 71 294			

The 36-hole cut was made at 148 – 4 over par – 78 players qualified.

ROUND BY ROUND LEADERBOARD

FIRST ROUND

M A Martin	5 under
S Luna	5 under
M Reale	4 under
A McKenna	4 under
J Wade	4 under
J Hawksworth	4 under
M A JIMENEZ	3 under

SECOND ROUND

S Luna	7 under
M A JIMENEZ	7 under
M A Martin	5 under
J Rivero	5 under
M Reale	4 under
A Cabrera	4 under

THIRD ROUND

M A JIMENEZ	9 under
S Luna	7 under
M A Martin	7 under
M Reale	6 under
P McGinley	5 under
V Phillips	5 under

FINAL ROUND

M A JIMENEZ	9 under
M A Martin	7 under
K Romori	6 under
P McGinley	6 under
V Phillips	4 under

PUNTERS' POINTS

- 'Beware the sick golfer' seems to be the maxim for punters to take from this tournament.
  - \> 16/1 runner up Miguel Angel Martin was taken ill on the eve of the tournament. Doctors found a kidney stone and ordered Martin to drink a lot. After R1 he led the tournament both in shots (just 67) and trips to the loo (5)!!
  - \> The 22/1 winner Miguel Angel Jimenez played through the pain barrier particularly in R2 after the 34-year-old Spaniard had been attended by a doctor because he too had a kidney stone problem. He received an injection on the course in his backside!
- However the player who really got the needle was Santiago Luna who dropped 3 shots in the last 7 holes in R3 after his 3-ball was 'put on the clock'.
- Martin also complained that 'he lost concentration' after a R4 warning for slow play at the 15th. "I am very mad at the timing rule," he said after dropping 2 shots in the last 5 holes.
- The tough course was the real winner as only seven players beat par, and only three (Jimenez, Martin and Long) had four rounds at or under par.
- Young Italian Michele Reale got into real contention here only for a disappointing 78 in R4 to push him back to T8th. The 26-year-old 1997 Challenge tour No.1 will have learned a lot from this experience.
- Paul McGinley played particularly well to put himself in real contention on the final day when he shared the lead with five to play. However, bogeys at the 15th and 16th meant that the 31-year-old Dubliner finished T3rd.
- The importance to a player's on-course performance of his off-field relationships was shown again here with T3rd Katsuyoshi Tomori whose

form (also 7th recently in the Spanish Open) has improved since his wife joined him on tour.

- Among those to miss the cut were 18/1 third favourite Ignacio Garrido, and 50/1 chances Seve Ballesteros and Steve Alker

1997 RESULT

1	12/1	J M Olazabal
2	33/1	Lee Westwood
Te	20/1	Paul Broadhurst
T3	33/1	Eduardo Romero

WINNERS IN THE '90s

1992	Vijay Singh	Paradores Club, Malaga
1993	Andrew Oldcorn	Novo Sancti Petri, Chicarva, Cadiz
1994	Carl Mason	Montecastillo, Jerez
1995	Alexander Cejka	Islantilla, Huelva
1996	Diego Borrego	El Saler, Valencia
1997	J M Olazabal	Maspalomas, Gran Canaria
1998	M A Jimenez	Santa Ponsa 1,Mallorca

PUNTERS' GUIDE

- Two important pointers emerged from the 1998 bookmakers' result
  - > Spanish players were first and second in 1998 following Spanish victories in 1997 and 1996.
  - > DYM players won in 1995, 1996 and filled three of the first five places in 1998. It could be that compilers spend a little less time on this tournament than usual so more DYMs are created.
- So in 1999 carefully consider the Spanish players and any DYMs.

THE BENSON & HEDGES INTERNATIONAL OPEN

Date	14th – 17th May
Course	The Oxfordshire, Thame, Oxon
Par	72
Yardage	7,205
First Prize	£125,000
Total Purse	£750,000

The exposed Oxfordshire course played host to the B& H for the third successive year. This tournament signals the start of the more important, big money European events.

1998 ODDS

jt fav	10/1	J M Olazabal	50/1	Sven Struver
jt fav	10/1	Colin Montgomerie	50/1	Robert Allenby
	12/1	Lee Westwood	50/1	Paul McGinley
	20/1	Bernhard Langer (DC) (non runner)	66/1	Joakim Haeggman
			66/1	David Howell
	20/1	Thomas Bjorn	66/1	Mark James
	22/1	Ian Woosnam	66/1	Greg Turner
	33/1	Darren Clarke	66/1	Peter O'Malley
	33/1	Retief Goosen	66/1	Paul Broadhurst
	40/1	P U Johansson	66/1	Phillip Price
	40/1	Andrew Coltart	66/1	Sam Torrance
	40/1	Patrik Sjoland	66/1	Peter Baker
	50/1	Robert Karlsson	66/1	Padraig Harrington
	50/1	M A Jimenez (PWW)		

26 players were best priced at or under 66/1.

BOOKIES AT ODDS

DYM David Howell 33/1 Ladbrokes: 66/1 Hills
DYM Paul Lawrie 50/1 Chandlers: 100/1 Hills, Ladbrokes
DYM Peter Lonard 50/1 Stan James: 100/1 Chandlers, Corals, Ladbrokes
The winner Darren Clarke 20/1 Chandlers: 33/1 Ladbrokes

1998 RESULT

1	33/1	**Darren Clarke**	**70 69 67 67**	**273**
2	100/1	**Santiago Luna**	**69 71 69 67**	**276**
T3	150/1	**Massimo Florioli**	**68 67 71 71**	**277**
T3	20/1	**Thomas Bjorn**	**68 74 68 67**	**277**
T5 jt fav	10/1	**Colin Montgomerie**	**69 68 69 72**	**278**
T5	33/1	**Retief Goosen**	**71 68 71 68**	**278**

T7	P Sjoland	67 72 68 72 279		F Tarnaud	71 72 69 73 285
	G Turner	72 67 69 71 279		J Lomas	70 72 71 72 285
	R Davis	70 70 70 69 279		M Gronberg	70 74 71 70 285
	M Mouland	70 70 70 69 279		P O'Malley	69 73 73 70 285
T11	G Evans	67 71 69 73 280		B Dredge	68 72 76 69 285
	P Lawrie	67 73 70 70 280		J Rose (am)	72 68 72 74 286
	B Davis	69 70 72 69 280		S Leaney	70 71 71 74 286
	J M Olazabal	72 70 70 68 280		A Coltart –	72 69 71 74 286
T15	P Haugsrud	69 68 71 73 281		D Robertson	67 74 71 74 286
	P Price	69 67 73 72 281		S Struver	70 71 72 73 286
	B May	71 67 71 72 281		D Lynn	69 74 71 73 287
T18	R Claydon	69 73 67 73 282		G Chalmers	71 73 70 73 287
	B Lane	69 66 75 72 282		W Westner	70 72 74 71 287
	S Cage	69 71 71 71 282		D Edlund	74 67 76 70 287
	I Woosnam	71 70 70 71 282		M Hallberg	69 72 71 76 288
	P Mitchell	74 68 69 71 282		D Howell	71 71 70 76 288
	A Sherborne	69 75 70 68 282		R J Derksen	71 69 74 74 288
T24	R Allenby	71 69 69 74 283		M Campbell	72 71 71 74 288
	S Henderson	69 71 70 73 283		S Bennett	73 68 75 72 288
	G Brand Jr	70 71 69 73 283		G Orr	69 74 73 72 288
	D Carter	69 73 68 73 283		D Smyth	69 74 73 72 288
	P Baker	73 66 73 71 283		P Harrington	70 72 74 73 289
	P Affleck	68 73 71 71 283		E Darcy	74 70 70 76 290
	S Kjeldsen	70 71 71 71 283		T Gogele	73 71 70 77 291
	P Fulke	71 72 70 70 283		C V D Velde	70 74 75 72 291
	P McGinley	69 73 73 68 283		A Hunter	72 72 73 75 292
	J Spence	70 69 70 75 284		C Watts	69 74 76 73 292
	P Curry	69 73 68 74 284		C Mason	73 70 73 77 293
	K Tomori	72 70 72 70 284		L Westwood	71 69 77 76 293
	C Suneson	69 73 72 70 284		M Tunnicliff	71 73 74 78 296
	G Owen	73 71 72 68 284		W Riley	71 72 78 76 297
	J Payne	73 69 70 73 285		A Forsbrand	76 68 78 85 307

The 36-hole cut was made at 144 – level par – 70 players qualified.

ROUND BY ROUND LEADERBOARD

FIRST ROUND		**SECOND ROUND**	
D Robertson	5 under	B Lane	9 under
P Lawrie	5 under	M Florioli	9 under
P Sjoland	5 under	P Price	8 under
G Evans	5 under	P Haugsrud	7 under
M Florioli	4 under	C Montgomerie	7 under
P Affleck	4 under	G Evans	6 under
B Dredge	4 under	B May	6 under
T Bjorn	4 under	D CLARKE	5 under
D CLARKE	2 under		

THIRD ROUND		**FINAL ROUND**	
C Montgomerie	10 under	D CLARKE	15 under
D CLARKE	10 under	S Luna	12 under
M Florioli	10 under	M Florioli	11 under
P Sjoland	9 under	T Bjorn	11 under
G Evans	9 under	C Montgomerie	10 under
G Turner	8 under	R Goosen	10 under
P Haugsrud	8 under		

- Thunderstorms delayed play on the Thursday until 1.30 p.m. When play was called off at 8.25 p.m. 78 players had still to complete their opening round.
- On Friday the backlog was almost cleared as only 9 players had still to finish their second round.

PUNTERS' POINTS

- 33/1 Darren Clark was an impressive winner, leaving his playing partner Colin Montgomerie five shots behind after a superb R4 67. The 29-year-old Ryder Cup player was 10 under for the final 36 holes to record his third victory.
- T5th Monty, recent father of his first son, simply could not hole a putt on Sunday, "the worst I have ever putted in a tournament when I have been in contention". He certainly doesn't have PMAs with final rounds on this course – he shot 84 in 1996, and 81 in 1997 when the winds were really blowing!
- Thomas Bjorn maintained his excellent form—"that's the best I have ever played"—to finish T3rd at 20/1. He missed six putts under ten feet in R4.
- Without a tour top 10 before this season 26-year-old Italian Massimo Florioli was T9th in the South African Open, T8th last week in the Turespana Masters and won his biggest-ever cheque here when T3rd at 150/1. Joint leader at halfway he was 9 under for his first two rounds, yet only 2 under for his two final rounds.
- T5th Retief Goosen is one of only two players to have made the top 20 in each of this tournament's three years at the Oxfordshire. Suited by its links type nature he must be a strong fancy in 1999.
- Bernhard Langer could not defend his title because of a neck injury.

- The 17th, a par 5, is the Oxfordshire's signature hole. The players have to decide whether to go over the water to the green in two, or to take the safer route laying up to the right of the lake.
- Sunderlands and Corals showed their usual enterprise. The result of Sunderlands' Top International (excl. Europeans) market was :-

  1   7/2 fav Retief Goosen
  2   11/1   Greg Turner
  3   50/1   Rodger Davis
  4   25/1   Bob May

- Corals opened up a Top Australasian market. The result was

  T1 Rodger Davis 20/1 rank outsider
  T1 Greg Turner 11/2
  3   Robert Allenby 5/1 fav

- Sunderlands and Corals opened up a Top Scandinavian player market. The result was :-

  1   Thomas Bjorn 7/2 fav
  2   Patrik Sjoland 7/1
  3   Pierre Fulke 25/1
  4   Mathias Gronberg 20/1

- Among those missing the cut were 40/1 P U Johansson, 50/1 chances M A Jimenez and Robert Karlsson, and 66/1 outsiders Sam Torrance, Mark James, and Joakim Haeggman.
- 12/1 Lee Westwood withdrew after shooting 77 in R3 when playing with seriously impaired vision. An insect had flown into his eye during the first round!

1997 RESULT

1   11/1 Bernhard Langer
2   16/1 Ian Woosnam
3   125/1 Lee Westwood
4   50/1 Padraig Harrington

WINNERS IN THE '90s

1990 J M Olazabal
1991 Bernhard Langer
1992 Peter Senior
1993 Paul Broadhurst
1994 Seve Ballesteros
1995 Peter O'Malley
1996 Stephen Ames
1997 Bernhard Langer
1998 Darren Clarke

- From 1990-1995 inclusive the B & H was held at St Mellion
- From 1996-1998 inclusive the B & H has used the Oxfordshire course

PUNTERS' GUIDE

- The weather really is the key to the tournament. This is shown by the number of players who beat par: only 5 in 1996 when conditions were dreadful; 16 in 1997 when the winds were blowing; and 52 this year when the sun shone. So in 1999 check the long-range forecast and the barometer in advance.
- This course is in many ways a links course which clearly suits some players.
  > Darren Clarke, winner 1998, T7th 1997
  > Thomas Bjorn, T3rd 1998, 12th 1997
  > Retief Goosen, T5th 1998, top 20s in 1997 and 1996
  > Ian Woosnam, T18th 1998, 2nd 1997, 12th 1996

THE VOLVO PGA CHAMPIONSHIP

Date	22nd – 25th May
Course	West Course, Wentworth
Par	72
Yardage	7,006
First Prize	£200,000
Total Purse	£1.2 million

This is a highly-rated, prestigious tournament starting unusually on a Friday and continuing over the Bank Holiday weekend with the final round on Monday.

1998 ODDS

fav	9/1	Ernie Els	40/1	P U Johansson
	10/1	Colin Montgomerie	40/1	Robert Allenby
	14/1	J M Olazabal	40/1	Greg Turner
	16/1	Lee Westwood	40/1	M A Martin
	20/1	Ian Woosnam (DC)	40/1	Andrew Coltart
	20/1	Thomas Bjorn	66/1	M A Jimenez
	20/1	Darren Clarke (PWW)	66/1	Alexander Cejka
	25/1	Bernhard Langer	66/1	Sven Struver
	28/1	Retief Goosen	66/1	Phillip Price
	40/1	Mark McNulty	66/1	Robert Karlsson
	40/1	Patrik Sjoland	66/1	Paul McGinley
	40/1	Eduardo Romero		

23 players were best priced at or under 66/1.

BOOKIES AT ODDS

DYM Santiago Luna 40/1 Chandlers: 80/1 Ladbrokes, Tote

Winner Colin Montgomerie 8/1 Corals, Stan James, Sunderlands: 10/1 Chandlers, Hills Tote, Stanleys, Surrey

1998 RESULT

1	10/1	Colin Montgomerie	70 70 65 69	274
T2 fav	9/1	Ernie Els	69 69 69 68	275
T2	40/1	Patrik Sjoland	72 71 66 66	275
T2	150/1	Gary Orr	70 69 68 68	275
T5	50/1	Andrew Coltart	72 66 70 68	276
T5	150/1	Peter Lonard	72 65 71 68	276
T5	20/1	Thomas Bjorn	70 69 69 68	276
T5	250/1	Mats Hallberg	68 69 69 70	276
T5	200/1	Dean Robertson	70 69 67 70	276

10	P McGinley	72 69 68 68 277		M McNulty	69 72 72 71 284
T11	G Brand Jr	71 69 72 66 278		P Senior	72 70 69 73 284
	P Price	71 72 68 67 278		M Roe	71 71 69 73 284
	P Harrington	70 69 69 70 278		D Edlund	71 71 74 69 285
	D Gilford	70 69 68 71 278		P Baker	74 69 73 69 285
15	C Rocca	71 70 70 68 279		S Luna	71 71 73 70 285
T16	S Leaney	69 73 71 67 280		C Whitelaw	69 74 72 70 285
	J M Olazabal	72 71 70 67 280		T Gogele	71 71 72 71 285
	S Torrance	70 71 71 68 280		M Mackenzie	68 71 74 72 285
	J Van de Velde	71 71 69 69 280		J Lomas	71 71 71 72 285
	L Westwood	71 71 69 69 280		R Claydon	71 72 70 72 285
T21	P U Johansson	70 71 72 68 281		K Tomori	70 70 72 73 285
	R Karlsson	71 71 71 68 281		A Sherborne	71 70 74 71 286
	R Davis	73 69 69 70 281		B Davis	67 75 72 72 286
	V Phillips	70 73 68 70 281		R Muntz	72 71 71 72 286
	D Howell	68 71 71 71 281		M James	69 73 69 75 286
	W Westner	73 69 68 71 281		S Struver	73 69 75 70 287
	M Florioli	75 68 67 71 281		I Woosnam	73 70 74 70 287
	S Ballesteros	72 71 65 73 281		P Hedblom	70 70 75 72 287
	D Clarke	71 68 75 68 282		S Lyle	69 74 72 72 287
	D Hospital	69 69 74 70 282		E Romero	70 72 70 75 287
	B Langer	69 70 72 71 282		C V D Velde	68 75 76 69 288
	J Coceres	73 69 68 72 282		C Watts	71 69 71 77 288
	F Tarnaud	73 69 72 69 283		R Burns	70 72 74 73 289
	R Wessels	71 71 71 70 283		H Clark	70 73 74 73 290
	M Jonzon	66 70 72 75 283		D Borrego	71 72 74 76 293
	G Turner	70 68 70 75 283		D Tapping	69 74 78 74 295
	T Johnstone	69 73 73 69 284		S Richardson	70 73 74 78 295

The 36-hole cut was made at 143 – 1 under par – 65 players qualified.

WARREN BENNET PLAYED WELL
FROM Q SCHOOL

DAVID CARTER , STEVEN LEANY
PLAYED WELL

ROUND BY ROUND LEADERBOARD

FIRST ROUND		SECOND ROUND	
M Jonzon	6 under	M Jonzon	8 under
B Davis	5 under	P Lonard	7 under
M Mackenzie	4 under	M Hallsberg	7 under
D Howell	4 under	A Coltart	6 under
M Hallberg	4 under	D Hospital	6 under
C Van der Velde	4 under	E Els	6 under
C MONTGOMERIE	2 under	G Turner	6 under
		C MONTGOMERIE	4 under

THIRD ROUND		FINAL ROUND	
C MONTGOMERIE	11 under	C MONTGOMERIE	14 under
D Robertson	10 under	E Els	13 under
M Hallberg	10 under	P Sjoland	13 under
E Els	9 under	G Orr	13 under
G Orr	9 under	A Coltart	12 under
D Gilford	9 under	P Lonard	12 under
		T Bjorn	12 under
		M Hallsberg	12 under
		D Robertson	12 under

PUNTERS' POINTS

- Although never convincing in R4 10/1 Colin Montgomerie landed his 'nappy-factor' victory, his first win in his second tournament after the birth of his first son, Cameron. Watched by his wife Eimear he got up and down from 110 yards to birdie the par 5 final hole, and so avoid a four-man play-off.
- Ernie Els arrived at Wentworth with tendonitis in his right arm, news of a burglary from his South African house, and a touch of jet-lag. Pushing his drives to the right, especially in R2 and R3, he was never at his best. However, his final-hole eagle almost put him in a play-off. With his excellent course record after two successive second places he must have a first-class chance in 1999.
- Spread-betting fans of Monty and Els showed nice profits as City Index gave Els an initial finishing position quote of just 19-22; while IG Index quoted Monty's finishing place as 17-20!
- 20/1 Thomas Bjorn is playing the best golf of his life at present. His form figures now read 1-4-3-5. He must have a leading chance here again in 1999.
- 27-year-old 200/1 rank outsider Dean Robertson had played beautifully in R4 to take the lead at the thirteenth at 14 under. The pressure then told as errant tee shots cost him dearly especially with a double bogey on the 16th. He played the last five holes in 5 under in R3 yet 2 over in R4!
- 150/1 Gary Orr with a fine record here (7th 1996: 12th 1995) took the lead at the tenth at 13 under before wayward tee shots cost him dropped shots at the 11th and 12th. However he recovered to finish T2nd after birdieing the last two, par 5, holes.

- 40/1 Patrik Sjoland continued his fine run of form with a tournament best 12 under for the final 36 holes to finish T2nd. His form figures now read 1-7-2.
- With the final holes, both par 5s, and both reachable in 2 shots this is one of those tournaments were there really is a 'sting in the tail', It makes for rivetting viewing.
- There were a number of speciality markets

Corals' Top Australasian player

1	14/1	Peter Lonard
2	8/1	Stephen Leaney
3	14/1	Rodger Davis

NB Robert Allenby was the unfortunate disqualified 10/3 favourite

Corals' Top Scandinavian player

1	6/1	Patrik Sjoland
T2 fav	11/4	Thomas Bjorn
T2	50/1	Mats Hallberg
T4	5/1	P U Johansson
T4	9/1	Robert Karlsson

Sunderlands Top non-European player

1 fav	9/4	Ernie Els
2	33/1	Peter Lonard
3	33/1	Stephen Leaney
T4	50/1	Wayne Westner
T4	40/1	Rodger Davis

Hills's Top Swedish player

1 jt fav	4/1	Patrik Sjoland
2	25/1	Mats Hallberg
T3 jt fav	4/1	P U Johansson
T3	6/1	Robert Karlsson

- Among those to miss the cut were 28/1 Retief Goosen and 66/1 outsiders Alexander Cejka and M A Jimenez.
- Robert Allenby after scoring a 69 in R1 was disqualified for an incident reported by spectators at the 15th hole. He had taken relief from a path, and instead of dropping within one club length, he dropped within two. As the error came to light after he had signed his card he was disqualified.

1997 RESULT

1	20/1	Ian Woosnam
T2	14/1	Ernie Els
T2	16/1	Nick Faldo
T2	40/1	Darren Clarke

WINNERS IN THE '90s
1990   Mike Harwood
1991   Seve Ballesteros
1992   Tony Johnstone
1993   Bernhard Langer
1994   J M Olazabal
1995   Bernhard Langer
1996   Costantino Rocca
1997   Ian Woosnam
1998   Colin Montgomerie

PUNTERS' GUIDE
- This is very much a course-specialist's tournament with the last six winners all having made or beaten par the previous year.
- The key to Wentworth is accuracy off the tee. Players with driving problems (eg Olazabal in 1998) must be avoided.
- The advice given in the last two volumes to select an experienced quality pro once more paid off with Colin Montgomerie's 10/1 success.
- In the last two years only four players have recorded successive top 20 finishes.
  > Colin Montgomerie W1998: 5th 1997
  > Ernie Els T2nd 1998: 19th 1997
  > Thomas Bjorn T5th 1998: 19th 1997
  > David Gilford T11th 1998: 6th 1997

THE DEUTSCHE BANK – SAP OPEN
TPC OF EUROPE

Date	29th May – 2nd June
Course	Gut Kaden, Hamburg, Germany
Par	72
Yardage	7,029
First Prize	£183,340
Total Purse	£1.1 million

This was the seventh successive year that the Gut Kaden course had played host to a European tour event. It attracted American tour stars Mark O'Meara and Nick Price. The tournament starts on a Friday and finishes on the Monday which is a bank holiday in Germany.

1998 ODDS

fav	8/1	Colin Montgomerie (PWW)	40/1	Robert Allenby
	14/1	J M Olazabal	40/1	P U Johansson
	16/1	Bernhard Langer	40/1	Paul McGinley
	16/1	Thomas Bjorn	50/1	Mark McNulty
	20/1	Darren Clarke	50/1	Phillip Price
	20/1	Nick Price	50/1	Greg Turner
	22/1	Lee Westwood	66/1	Eduardo Romero
	25/1	Mark O'Meara	66/1	David Gilford
	25/1	Ian Woosnam	66/1	Padraig Harrington
	33/1	Patrik Sjoland	66/1	Peter Baker
	33/1	Retief Goosen	66/1	Peter Lonard
	33/1	Andrew Coltart		

23 players were best priced at or under 66/1.

BOOKIES AT ODDS

The winner Lee Westwood 12/1 Victor Chandler: 22/1 Corals

1998 RESULT

1	22/1	Lee Westwood	69 69 61 66	265
2	20/1	Darren Clarke	67 66 65 68	266
3	25/1	Mark O'Meara	67 69 63 70	269
T4	200/1	Philip Walton	69 70 65 67	271
T4	16/1	Bernhard Langer	67 66 70 68	271
T4	100/1	Peter Senior	69 67 64 71	271

T7	J Payne	70 68 69 65 272		P Haugsrud	71 66 67 75 279
	D Howell	69 68 66 69 272		J Spence	67 73 72 68 280
	M A Jimenez	69 69 65 69 272		J Coceres	70 69 72 69 280
T10	C Montgomerie	67 67 72 67 273		D Hospital	72 69 69 70 280
	P Lawrie	68 72 66 67 273		D Gilford	70 71 69 70 280
	B May	67 68 68 70 273		C Watts	73 67 69 71 280
T13	T Bjorn	69 68 71 66 274		M Tunnicliff	70 69 69 72 280
	P Mitchell	66 70 67 71 274		M Mouland	70 69 69 72 280
	J Haeggman	69 70 63 72 274		W Riley	72 69 67 72 280
	P Broadhurst	68 65 65 76 274		K Brink	71 68 72 70 281
T17	G Orr	71 68 69 67 275		D Cooper	72 69 70 70 281
	C Rocca	70 71 66 68 275		R Claydon	71 67 72 71 281
	P Quirici	68 70 67 70 275		D Carter	70 71 69 71 281
	I Woosnam	69 71 64 71 275		P Hedblom	73 68 68 72 281
21	J Van de Velde	67 67 67 74 275		S Webster	72 69 66 74 281
T22	N Price	70 68 68 70 276		P Harrington	69 72 72 69 282
	J M Singh	69 70 67 70 276		A Coltart	68 68 74 72 282
	I Garbutt	70 68 67 71 276		T Gogele	70 68 70 74 282
	R Goosen	68 68 69 71 276		S Luna	72 69 72 70 283
	P McGinley	65 74 66 71 276		P Eales	68 70 73 72 283
	J Sandelin	69 70 71 67 277		T Hennig	73 68 71 71 283
	A Cejka	68 70 70 69 277		D Edlund	67 72 71 73 283
	G Chalmers	67 71 69 70 277		A Hunter	70 69 72 73 284
	J M Olazabal	69 71 67 70 277		D Chopra	72 67 72 73 284
	M Farry	72 66 68 71 277		R Chapman	71 69 71 73 284
	E Canonica	67 71 68 71 277		D Robertson	73 68 70 73 284
	S Henderson	70 66 66 75 277		R Russell	69 69 72 74 284
	P Price	70 71 68 69 278		M Mackenzie	71 68 74 72 285
	P Fulke	72 67 69 70 278		P U Johansson	70 71 72 72 285
	B Davis	69 68 70 71 278		C Hainline	73 68 72 72 285
	K Tomori	68 69 70 71 278		A Oldcorn	70 71 69 75 285
	S Torrance	68 69 69 72 270		G Evans	73 68 72 73 286
	P O'Malley	67 70 71 71 279		R Burns	70 70 73 73 286
	M Roe	68 70 70 71 279		M Davis	70 70 70 76 286
	E Darcy	72 69 67 71 279		S Allan	67 74 67 78 286
	M James	67 68 72 72 279		Y Kaya	72 69 72 74 287
	M Hallberg	70 70 67 72 279		A Wall	71 70 70 76 287
	W Westner	70 66 70 73 279		R Boxall	71 70 72 75 288

The 36-hole cut was made at 141 – 3 under par – 82 players qualified.

ROUND BY ROUND LEADERBOARD

FIRST ROUND

P McGinley	7 under
P Mitchell	6 under
J Spence	5 under
M O'Meara	5 under
E Canonica	5 under
B Langer	5 under
B May	5 under
S Allan	5 under
M Gronberg	5 under
D Edlund	5 under
G Chalmers	5 under
L WESTWOOD	3 under

SECOND ROUND

D Clarke	11 under
B Langer	11 under
P Broadhurst	11 under
C Montgomerie	10 under
J Van de Velde	10 under
M James	9 under
L WESTWOOD	6 under

THIRD ROUND

D Clarke	18 under
P Broadhurst	18 under
L WESTWOOD	17 under
M O'Meara	17 under
P Senior	16 under
J Van de Velde	15 under

FINAL ROUND

L WESTWOOD	23 under
D Clarke	22 under
M O'Meara	19 under
P Walton	17 under
P Senior	17 under
B Langer	17 under

- The second round on Saturday was interrupted by thunderstorms.

PUNTERS' POINTS

- After two weeks suffering from a 'cold' putter Lee Westwood proved once more at Gut Kaden what a superb player he is. With the course defenceless in benign conditions on Sunday he took just 23 putts en route to a brilliant 61. Although his winning margin was a single shot he never actually looked in any real danger coming down the stretch. I wonder when next he'll be allowed to start at 22/1 in a European tournament?

- Darren Clarke, with four birdies in the last five holes, really put pressure on his 'stablemate'. It was the Ulsterman's third successive top 4 finish on this course.

- 25/1 Mark O'Meara's challenge faded after a final-round double bogey on the 11th. Considering the jet lag hit him, especially in R2, he played really well. He may seem quiet yet he's a 100% never give up golfer.

- 80/1 seventh-placed David Howell, a 'stable' companion of Clarke and Westwood, was recording his fifth top 25 finish in his last six starts. He surely falls in the 'winner-about-to-happen' category.

- Starting R4 as joint leader, course specialist Paul Broadhurst suffered a severe bout of 'contention rust' as he shot a 76, the second poorest round of the day!!

- Costantino Rocca, after a very poor start to the season, notched his second successive top 20 finish to signal hopefully that his year is about to begin.

- M A Jimenez showed how much he enjoys warm dry conditions with 65 in R3 and a solid T7th place finish after he missed the cut in last year's windy conditions.
- Among those missing the cut were 33/1 Patrik Sjoland, 40/1 Robert Allenby, 50/1 chances Greg Turner and Mark McNulty, 66/1 Peter Baker and 80/1 outsiders Sven Struver and Ignacio Garrido.

1997 RESULT

1	125/1	Ross McFarlane
T2	125/1	Gordon Brand Jr
T2	100/1	Anders Forsbrand
4	14/1	Darren Clarke

WINNERS IN THE '90s

1992	Bernhard Langer
1993	Sam Torrance
1994	Robert Allenby
1995	Bernhard Langer
1996	Frank Nobilo
1997	Ross McFarlane
1998	Lee Westwood

PUNTERS' GUIDE

- In 1999 this tournament moves south to be staged at St Leon-Rot near Heidelberg. This follows the arrival of the new co-sponsor SAP AG, a German computer software manufacturer.
- As the table shows the weather plays a key role on the Gut Kaden course

	Winning Score	Prices of first three	No of players below par	Weather
1998	265	22/1, 20/1, 25/1	23	Calm
1997	282	125/1, 125/1, 100/1	80	Very blustery

So when next Gut Kaden is used make a careful check on the weather forecast because on the evidence of the last two years the chance of a surprise result increases as the wind increases.

- Gut Kaden is a parkland course and very much one for course specialists with the very best record held by Darren Clarke – 2nd 1998: 4th 1997: 3rd 1996 and 2nd 1992.

THE NATIONAL CAR RENTAL ENGLISH OPEN

Date	4th – 7th June
Course	Marriott Hanbury Manor Hotel, Ware, Herts
Par	72
Yardage	7,016
First Prize	£108,330
Total Purse	£650,000

For the second successive year the English Open was held at the Marriott Hanbury Manor so there was only one year's course form for punters to study.

1998 ODDS

fav	7/1	Colin Montgomerie	50/1	Mark McNulty
	10/1	Lee Westwood (PWW)	50/1	Paul Broadhurst
	14/1	Darren Clarke	50/1	Joakim Haeggman
	16/1	Thomas Bjorn	50/1	M A Jimenez
	33/1	Retief Goosen	50/1	Greg Turner
	33/1	Andrew Coltart	66/1	Mark James
	40/1	Robert Allenby	66/1	Padraig Harrington
	40/1	Patrik Sjoland	66/1	David Gilford
	40/1	P U Johansson (DC)	66/1	Sam Torrance
	40/1	David Howell	66/1	Costantino Rocca*
	40/1	Phillip Price	66/1	Peter Baker
	50/1	Peter Senior	66/1	Peter Mitchell

24 players were best priced at or under 66/1.

BOOKIES AT ODDS

DYM Costantino Rocca 33/1 Chandlers: 66/1 Ladbrokes, Stan James
Winner Lee Westwood 6/1 Stan James: 10/1 Corals

1998 RESULT

1	10/1	Lee Westwood	68 68 67 68	271
T2	200/1	Olle Karlsson	70 70 67 66	273
T2	80/1	Greg Chalmers	70 73 61 69	273
4 fav	7/1	Colin Montgomerie	64 72 69 69	274
5	40/1	Patrik Sjoland	68 67 70 70	275

6	P Price	73 71 67 65 276		M Gronberg	73 70 72 71 286
7	R Allenby	67 71 70 69 277		R Jacquelin	69 71 73 73 286
T8	R Wessels	68 69 70 71 278		R Rafferty	69 72 72 73 286
	J M Singh	71 69 67 71 278		D Howell	74 69 70 73 286
T10	K Storgaard	71 70 72 67 280		T Bjorn	73 70 70 73 286
	C O'Connor Jr	71 70 68 71 280		J Remesy	70 71 71 74 286
	M McNulty	73 68 66 73 280		F Tarnaud	70 66 75 75 286
	S Leaney	66 69 70 75 280		M A Jimenez	68 72 70 76 286
T14	M Campbell	71 72 71 67 281		D Clarke	72 72 75 68 287
	V Phillips	69 72 71 69 281		P Mitchell	70 73 73 71 287
	P Eales	69 72 70 70 281		I Garrido	70 74 71 72 287
	G Evans	70 73 68 70 281		G Owen	72 72 71 72 287
	B May	71 69 69 72 281		S Alker	70 71 73 73 287
	A Coltart	67 72 67 75 281		M Reale	71 71 72 73 287
T20	R Claydon	71 70 72 69 282		P Broadhurst	75 69 70 73 287
	T Gogele	70 73 70 69 282		M Long	71 70 72 74 287
	J Robson	66 73 73 70 282		D Gilford	72 71 76 69 288
	P Baker	69 72 70 71 282		R Muntz	69 72 76 71 288
	N Vanhootegem	66 72 72 72 282		C Hainline	71 69 75 73 288
	P Walton	74 69 70 70 283		S Tinning	74 70 71 73 288
	P Harrington	74 69 70 70 283		S Richardson	70 71 74 74 289
	M Jonzon	72 68 72 71 283		T Gillis	71 73 71 74 289
	I Garbutt	70 72 70 71 283		M Florioli	72 68 74 75 289
	D Cooper	68 76 68 71 283		A Sandywell	74 70 68 77 289
	N Joakimides	65 74 72 72 283		J Townsend	70 73 75 72 290
	S Webster	72 68 70 73 283		W Riley	68 73 76 73 290
	G Orr	75 69 68 72 284		S Allan	73 70 73 74 290
	P Fulke	72 70 69 73 284		I Giner	75 68 73 74 290
	J Rivero	69 73 69 73 284		A Sherborne	72 70 70 78 290
	M Hallberg	72 72 66 74 284		P Curry	73 71 68 78 290
	M Mouland	72 72 72 69 285		C Watts	68 75 74 75 292
	E Darcy	71 72 71 71 285		R Chapman	71 72 73 76 292
	P Affleck	74 65 74 72 285		J Bickerton	74 70 72 76 292
	D Robertson	68 73 71 73 285		H Clark	71 72 74 79 296
	A Wall	75 68 68 74 285		R Davis	73 71 79 77 300

The 36-hole cut was made at 144 – level par – 75 players qualified.

ROUND BY ROUND LEADERBOARD

FIRST ROUND		SECOND ROUND	
C Montgomerie	8 under	P Sjoland	9 under
N Joakimedes	7 under	S Leaney	9 under
N Vanhootegem	6 under	L WESTWOOD	8 under
S Leaney	6 under	C Montgomerie	8 under
J Robson	6 under	F Tarnaud	8 under
R Allenby	5 under	R Wessels	7 under
A Coltart	5 under		
L WESTWOOD	4 under		

THIRD ROUND		FINAL ROUND	
L WESTWOOD	13 under	L WESTWOOD	17 under
G Chalmers	12 under	O Karlsson	15 under
P Sjoland	11 under	G Chalmers	15 under
C Montgomerie	11 under	C Montgomerie	14 under
S Leaney	11 under	P Sjoland	13 under
A Coltart	10 under		

PUNTERS' POINTS

- 10/1 Lee Westwood's win at the Marriott Hanbury Manor course inevitably led to 'Lord of the Manor' headlines. After all, his progress is astonishing.
  - > his ninth career win
  - > his sixth in the last seven months
  - > his fourth on the European tour
  - > his third in the world this year
  - > his second in the last seven days
  - > since winning the Volvo Masters in Spain last November he has won in Japan, Australia, America, and now Britain.

- His last ten rounds have been in the 60s, and he is 40 under for his last two tournaments. "I've got a lot to smile about" – too right he has!

- Greg Chalmers 61 in R3 was followed by three birdies on the first three holes on R4 – 14 under for 21 holes! However the 24-year-old Aussie could not resist Westwood's brilliance and for the second time this season (the Spanish Open was the first) he finished an 80/1 runner-up.

- 200/1 Olle Karlsson had been working very hard over the last couple of months. His reward was a fine 11 under par final 36 holes to finish T2nd.

- 40/1 Philip Price's sixth place is worth noting as the Welshman was notching his ninth top 20 finish in his twelfth tournament. He has made every cut to prove himself a much-improved and truly consistent player.

- Defending champion 40/1 Per-Ulrik Johansson bravely played on when he was clearly still feeling dizzy and unwell. The problem that first surfaced last November in America clearly continues. His form here (75-76) can be ignored.

- Among those to miss the cut were 33/1 Retief Goosen, 40/1 defending champion P U Johansson, 50/1 Greg Turner and 50/1 Joakim Haeggman, and 66/1 outsiders Sam Torrance and Costantino Rocca.

1997 RESULT

1	66/1	P U Johansson
2	200/1	Dennis Edlund
T3	200/1	Jay Townsend
T3	150/1	Steven Webster

WINNERS IN THE '90s

1990	Mark James	The Belfry
1991	David Gilford	The Belfry
1992	Vicente Fernandez	The Belfry
1993	Ian Woosnam	Forest of Arden
1994	Colin Montgomerie	Forest of Arden
1995	Philip Walton	Forest of Arden
1996	Robert Allenby	Forest of Arden
1997	P U Johansson	Hanbury Manor
1998	Lee Westwood	Hanbury Manor

PUNTERS' GUIDE

- This course has top-quality greens which reward the good middle-distance putters (such as Chalmers and Sjoland this year). It also demands accuracy off the tee as the rough can be very unforgiving. It may prove to be a course specialist's track.

  NB. This year's winner Lee Westwood was within ten shots of the winner last year when placed T22nd.

- This year three of the front five players had a win or a second place in one of their last two starts so clearly current form was also an important factor.
- In 1999 it may pay, therefore, to select a player who meets two criteria.
  > A top 25 finish this year.
  > Is in sound current form with a top 10 finish in one of his last two tournaments.
- Only two players have posted successive top 20 finishes in the two years the English Open has been held at the Marriott Hanbury Manor.
  > Colin Montgomerie 4th 1998: T12th 1997
  > Philip Price 6th 1998: T12th 1997.

THE COMPAQ EUROPEAN GRAND PRIX

Date	11th – 14th June
Course	Slaley Hall Golf Club, Hexham, Northumberland
Par	72 This year par was reduced to 69
Yardage	7,073 This year yardage was reduced to 6,392
First Prize	£108,330
Total Purse	£650,000

For the third successive year Slaley Hall was the venue for this tournament which was sponsored for the second successive year by Compaq. As it was the final tournament before the US Open thirteen of the top seventeen European players had left for the States so this was a relatively-weak field.

1998 ODDS

fav	12/1	Patrik Sjoland	50/1	Mark James
	16/1	Andrew Coltart	50/1	Peter Lonard
	16/1	Mark McNulty	50/1	Peter Mitchell
	16/1	Robert Allenby	50/1	Roger Wessels
	20/1	Paul McGinley	50/1	Sam Torrance
	25/1	Stephen Ames	50/1	Peter O'Malley
	28/1	David Gilford	50/1	Sven Struver
	28/1	Phillip Price	66/1	Bob May
	33/1	David Howell	66/1	David Carter
	40/1	Greg Turner	66/1	Jeev Milkha Singh
	40/1	Peter Baker	66/1	Jamie Spence
	40/1	Paul Broadhurst	66/1	Paul Lawrie
	50/1	Gary Orr	66/1	Philip Walton
	50/1	Joakim Haeggman	66/1	Michael Campbell

28 players were best priced at or under 66/1.

BOOKIES AT ODDS

Paul McGinley 11/1 Corals: 20/1 Hills, Chandlers
Philip Price 16/1 Ladbrokes: 28/1 Chandlers

1998 RESULT

The tournament was abandoned on Sunday morning after further heavy rain had left the course completely unplayable.

> At that time only 43 of the 149 players still competing had completed their second round.

As a result all bets were void and stakes would be refunded.

THE SCORES OF THE PLAYERS FOR THEIR COMPLETED ROUNDS AT THE TIME OF ABANDONMENT WERE

Please remember: The par for three holes was reduced so that the par for the course became 69, and the total yardage 6,392.

A Sherborne	67 68 135		F Cea	71 70 141
B Lane	67 68 135		M Reale	70 71 141
J Spence	67 69 136		P O'Malley	73 68 141
G Evans	67 69 136		J Bickerton	72 69 141
M Davis	64 73 137		D Carter	70 72 142
P Sjoland	67 70 137		K Brink	74 68 142
R Chapman	69 69 138		A Stolz	69 73 142
J Sandelin	68 70 138		A Sandywell	70 73 143
K Storgaard	67 72 139		I Pyman	71 72 143
P Quirici	66 73 139		I Giner	70 75 145
D Cole	70 69 139		C Watts	72 73 145
V Phillips	72 67 139		M Molina	71 74 145
R Allenby	69 70 139		J Haeggman	71 74 145
P Broadhurst	69 70 139		G Hutcheon	75 70 145
M Mackenzie	72 68 140		J Wright	71 76 147
M Campbell	68 72 140		S Talbot	71 77 148
S Tinning	67 73 140		M Pinero	74 74 148
H P Thul	68 72 140		G Furey	75 76 151
P Lonard	72 68 140		T Johnstone	76 78 154
A Oldcorn	68 72 140		S Allan	76 79 155
A Beal	69 72 141		D Brunton	80 77 157
R Coles	68 73 141			

THE SCORES OF THE PLAYERS WHO HAD COMPLETED ONLY ONE ROUND WERE:

D Borrego	65	B May	70	P Golding	72
M Hallberg	66	M Tunnicliff	70	R Boxall	72
P Fulke	66	G Nicklaus	70	A Coltart	72
J Robson	66	H Clark	70	G Brand Jr	72
S Struver	66	D Smyth	70	D Lynn	72
D Howell	66	B Davidson	70	S Webster	72
M Lanner	67	H Nystrom	70	B Dredge	72
S Richardson	67	S Ames	70	I Garbutt	72
J Hawksworth	67	D Gilford	70	D Chopra	73
J M Singh	67	J Payne	70	N Joakimides	73
P Hedblom	67	F Henge	70	S Alker	73
M James	67	P Linhart	70	M Lafeber	73
P McGinley	67	B Davis	70	S Henderson	73
W Riley	67	P Mitchell	70	F Howley	73
J Rose (am)	68	G Turner	70	M McNulty	73
C Hainline	68	P Lawrie	70	M Roe	73
A Wall	68	M Archer	70	J Higgins	74

D Edlund	68	R Muntz	70	R J Derksen	74
J Remesy	68	D Cole	70	A Clapp	74
M Long	68	S Field	70	J Townsend	74
S Cage	68	P Affleck	70	M Gronberg	74
E Darcy	68	F Jacobsen	70	I Bolt	74
C Mason	68	S Bennett	71	F Tarnaud	74
M Farry	68	O Sellberg	71	D Thomson	75
R Jacquelin	68	C V D Velde	71	S Ballesteros	75
R Burns	68	P Eales	71	R Russell	75
A Hunter	68	C Suneson	71	S Robinson (am)	75
G Orr	68	R Green	71	N Cheetham	75
N Vanhootegem	69	J Lomas	71	A Hill	75
R Wessels	69	S Torrance	71	D Botes	76
W Westner	69	P Price	71	D Tapping	76
P Haugsrud	69	R McFarlane	71	P Harrison	77
D Robertson	69	P Scott	71	G Owen	77
O Karlsson	69	R Claydon	71	J Kennedy (am)	79
P Baker	69	D Cooper	71	M Jonzon	77 WD
P Walton	69	T Gillis	72	C O'Connor Jr	RET
R Davis	69	S Kjeldsen	72	R Rafferty	RET
M Florioli	69	O Eliasson	72	M Mouland	RET

ROUND BY ROUND LEADERBOARD

FIRST ROUND

M Davis	5 under
D Borrego	4 under
M Hallberg	3 under
P Fulke	3 under
J Robson	3 under
S Struver	3 under
P Quirici	3 under
D Howell	3 under
M Campbell	3 under

SECOND ROUND
(only 43 players completed R2)

A Sherborne	3 under
B Lane	3 under
J Spence	2 under
G Evans	2 under
M Davis	1 under
P Sjoland	1 under

THE LEADERBOARD AT THE TIME OF THE ABANDONMENT

		Holes completed
Diego Borrego	4 under	19
Marc Farry	4 under	34
Andrew Sherborne	3 under	36
Barry Lane	3 under	36

- The first round was completed by Saturday lunchtime.
- When the tournament was abandoned only 43 players had finished their second rounds. A further 106 were either still to tee off, or in play on the waterlogged course.

PUNTERS' POINTS

- The last time a tournament on the European circuit was as badly affected as this one was the BMW International two years ago when Marc Farry finished his first two rounds on time then waited to be declared the winner two days later.

  And who led this rain ruined event at the time of abandonment? Marc Farry, of course!

- Barry Lane's had admitted that "my attitude has been terrible". Here he focussed on solid ball striking to be in contention. A long-hitting player, effective on tough courses in windy conditions, he must be noted here in 1999 if he's then in form.

- This course at over 7,000 yards favours the longer hitters, so do remember outsider Jon Robson in 1999. T6th here in 1997 he shot a fine R1 66 this year. At over 277 yards he's a huge hitter who clearly enjoys Slaley Hall.

1997 RESULT

1 fav	6/1	Colin Montgomerie
2	25/1	Retief Goosen
3	14/1	Lee Westwood
T4	25/1	David Gilford
T4	150/1	Scott Henderson

WINNERS IN THE '90s

1996	Retief Goosen
1997	Colin Montgomerie
1998	Tournament abandoned

PUNTERS' GUIDE

- With three years of course form now available it is clear that Slaley Hall is enjoyed particularly by
  - > Jamie Spence T3 of R2 finishers 1998: T6th 1997: T9th 1996
  - > Gary Evans T3 of R2 finishers 1998: T6th 1997: T4th 1996
  - > Paul McGinley 2 under par R1 1998: T11th 1997: T12th 1996

THE MADEIRA ISLAND OPEN

Date	18th – 21st June
Course	Santo de Serra, Madeira
Par	72
Yardage	6,606
First Prize	£50,000
Total Purse	£300,000

The Santo de Serra course played host to the Madeira Open for the sixth successive year. In two of the previous five years it had been reduced to 54 holes. The course, at 2,300 feet above sea level, is often the victim of very severe winds.

1998 ODDS

fav	12/1	Stephen Ames		50/1	Brian Davis
	20/1	Andrew Sherborne		50/1	Paul Curry
	20/1	Santiago Luna		50/1	Carl Suneson
	22/1	Wayne Westner		66/1	Nik Henning
	25/1	Mathew Goggin		66/1	Tom Gillis
	25/1	Thomas Gogele		66/1	Anthony Wall
	25/1	Katsuyoshi Tomori		66/1	Emanuele Canonica
	33/1	Jeev Milkha Singh		66/1	John Bickerton
	33/1	Michael Campbell		66/1	Alberto Binaghi
	40/1	Daniel Chopra		66/1	Andrew Sandywell
	40/1	Steve Alker		66/1	Francisco Cea
	40/1	Diego Borrego (non runner)		66/1	Michele Reale
	40/1	Paul Affleck		66/1	Miles Tunnicliff
	50/1	Mark Davis		66/1	John Mellor

27 players were best priced at or over 66/1.

BOOKIES AT ODDS

Winner DYM Mats Lanner 40/1 Hills: 80/1 Tote

2nd placed DYM Stephen Scahill 40/1 Ladbrokes: 80/1 Hills, Tote

1998 RESULT

1	80/1	Mats Lanner	70 66 68 73	277
2	80/1	Stephen Scahill	72 61 69 76	278
3	80/1	Andrew Beal	71 68 67 73	279
T4	25/1	Thomas Gogele	68 68 73 73	282
T4	66/1	Francisco Cea	69 69 71 73	282

T6	C Suneson	70 72 69 72 283
	R Sailer	70 68 70 75 283
T8	J Mellor	69 70 73 72 284
	C Cevaer	70 71 69 74 284
T10	K Tomori	70 72 68 76 286
	I Giner	72 67 70 77 286
	T Gillis	70 69 69 78 286
	F Jacobson	71 71 65 79 286
T14	J Bickerton	73 69 74 71 287
	M Lafeber	76 68 71 72 287
	A Hunter	71 72 71 73 287
	R Drummond	71 71 70 75 287
	R Winchester	68 73 69 77 287
T19	M Goggin	73 73 69 73 288
	S Ames	68 78 69 73 288
	P Affleck	76 68 72 72 288
	J Wade	76 70 70 72 288
	R Lee	73 71 70 74 288
	P Linhart	70 69 74 75 288
	M Olander	72 68 73 75 288
	S Alker	71 74 68 75 288
	J Rask	71 69 72 76 288
	G Hutcheon	71 69 71 77 288
	M Campbell	71 67 70 80 288
	S Bennett	72 72 72 73 289
	A Sherborne	74 69 73 73 289
	D Tapping	66 73 73 77 289
	A Stolz	72 69 70 78 289
	J Hawksworth	73 72 72 74 291
	S Watson	74 71 72 74 291
	G J Brand	71 69 73 78 291
	G Nicklaus	72 71 70 78 291
	G Owen	73 72 68 78 291

D Chopra	73 72 67 79 291
S Luna	68 71 72 80 291
O Edmond	73 70 72 77 292
B Nelson	69 76 72 75 292
S Kjeldsen	73 73 71 75 292
J M Singh	75 72 74 71 292
J Remesy	71 76 68 78 293
J L Guepy	70 76 73 74 293
R Moss	71 73 76 73 293
G Emerson	72 71 66 84 293
R Wragg	72 72 73 77 294
G Furey	71 74 69 80 294
P Streeter	75 69 74 77 295
S Bottomley	69 75 74 77 295
D Higgins	73 71 74 77 295
O Eliasson	77 69 74 75 295
D Lee	72 71 71 81 295
C Hainline	72 72 75 77 296
M Reale	72 75 72 77 296
S Hamill	73 74 72 77 296
S Dodd ·	76 71 72 77 296
M Molina	72 73 76 75 296
H Nystrom	73 73 77 73 296
A Sobrinho	73 74 71 79 297
D Lynn	74 69 75 80 298
D Cole	71 72 75 80 298
P Golding	70 73 79 76 298
J Rystrom	74 70 71 83 298
B Davis	73 72 76 79 300
S C Ferriera	74 73 73 80 300
A Wall	72 74 74 81 301
D Silva	71 75 77 78 301
F Howley	73 74 77 80 304

The cut was made at 147 – 3 over par – 70 players qualified

ROUND BY ROUND LEADERBOARD

FIRST ROUND

D Tapping	6 under
S Luna	4 under
T Gogele	4 under
S Ames	4 under
R Winchester	4 under
F Cea	3 under
B Nelson	3 under
S Bottomley	3 under
J Mellor	3 under
M LANNER	2 under

SECOND ROUND

S Scahill	11 under
T Gogele	8 under
M LANNER	8 under
F Cea	6 under
R Sailer	6 under
M Campbell	6 under

THIRD ROUND

S Scahill	14 under
M LANNER	11 under
A Beal	10 under
F Jacobsen	9 under
T Gillis	8 under
M Campbell	8 under
R Sailer	8 under

FINAL ROUND

M LANNER	11 under
S Scahill	10 under
A Beal	9 under
T Gogele	8 under
F Cea	8 under

- There was a near three-hour delay to play on the final day because of low cloud.

PUNTERS' POINTS

- This was the story of a young Kiwi and an older Swede. 28-year-old New Zealand born, London-based Stephen Scahill took the lead after a brilliant 61 in R2, and went into R4 two shots clear of 37-year-old Mats Lanner winner here in 1994.

- However, R4 nerves got to Scahill as he started dropping shots whereas Lanner made pars to lead by the sixth. 80/1 Lanner sealed his win with a sand save on the last. "I'll remember that bunker shot for the rest of my life."

- Scahill had to settle for second place after a 76. He'll surely file that last round in a drawer marked 'learning experience'.

- It was a tough final day when only T14th John Bickerton and T41st Jeev Milkha Singh broke par and experienced Michael Campbell fell out of contention with an 80.

- It may pay to remember that young Australian star Mathew Goggin shot level par on his first visit to Madeira. He will be a player to note here in 1999.

- Amazing but true....on 21st June in the final round of the US Open on the brutal Olympic course more players (six) broke par than in the final round of the Madeira Open (two).

- Among those to miss the cut were 50/1 chances Mark Davis, and Paul Curry, and 66/1 outsiders Alberto Binaghi, Andrew Sandywell, and Emanuele Canonica.

1997 RESULT

1	40/1	Peter Mitchell
2	150/1	Fredrik Jacobsen
3	16/1	Andrew Coltart
4	80/1	Andrew Sherborne

WINNERS IN THE '90s

1993	Mark James	
1994	Mats Lanner	54 holes
1995	Santiago Luna	
1996	Jarmo Sandelin	
1997	Peter Mitchell	54 holes
1998	Mats Lanner	

PUNTERS' GUIDE

Four points to note:-

> The younger players are given a real chance of a first win in this very weak tournament. So it is worth keeping an eye on the latest Challenge Tour form. For example this year second placed 80/1 Stephen Scahill was fresh from a fine T5th in the Austrian Open.

> Nevertheless the advice given here last year to go for an experienced player paid off yet again with 37-year-old Lanner's victory. The average age of the six winners in Madeira is now over 34.

> Please remember this event has a record of bad weather with the 1994 and 1997 tournaments both reduced to three rounds.

> Because of its altitude, the course is 2,300 above sea level, it tends to play short.

THE PEUGEOT FRENCH OPEN

Date	25th – 28th June
Course	National Golf Club, Paris
Par	72
Yardage	7,122
First Prize	£83,330
Total Purse	£500,000

For the eighth successive year the National Golf Club course was the venue for the French Open.

1998 ODDS

fav	7/1	Colin Montgomerie	50/1	Greg Turner*
	14/1	Bernhard Langer	50/1	Thomas Gogele
	20/1	Robert Allenby	66/1	Mathew Goggin*
	20/1	Retief Goosen (DC)	66/1	Sven Struver
	25/1	Eduardo Romero	66/1	Alexander Cejka
	25/1	Andrew Coltart	66/1	Gary Orr
	40/1	David Howell	66/1	Jean Van de Velde
	40/1	Paul Broadhurst	66/1	Katsuyoshi Tomori
	50/1	Peter Lonard	66/1	Santiago Luna
	50/1	M A Jimenez*		

Just 19 players were best priced at or under 66/1.

BOOKIES AT ODDS

DYM T2nd Massimo Florioli 50/1 Chandler, Hills: 125/1 Corals

DYM T2nd Mathew Goggin 33/1 Hills: 66/1 Stan James, Chandlers, Corals

DYM Winner Sam Torrance 40/1 Surrey, Tote: 80/1 Ladbrokes, Sunderlands

A very good tournament for DYM system followers!!

1998 RESULT

1	80/1	Sam Torrance	64 70 72 70	276
T2	125/1	Massimo Florioli	69 67 75 67	278
T2	150/1	Oliver Edmond	70 70 71 67	278
T2	14/1	Bernhard Langer	71 70 68 69	278
T2	66/1	Mathew Goggin	69 70 69 70	278

T6	M Farry	70 67 73 69 279		J L Guepy	75 70 70 70 285
	P Linhart	66 73 70 70 279		W Riley	70 68 76 71 285
T8	S Luna	75 68 67 70 280		C Hainline	71 71 73 70 285
	R Claydon	69 70 70 71 280		A Stolz	74 70 73 69 286
	D Howell	70 69 69 72 280		F Howley	70 72 73 71 286
T11	S Kjeldsen	70 72 75 64 281		A Hunter	71 74 68 73 286
	J Sandelin	74 69 71 67 281		J Spence	72 70 69 75 286
	P Walton	72 73 69 67 281		D Robertson	68 75 74 70 287
	A Cejka	70 69 72 69 281		H P Thul	69 74 74 70 287
	M Campbell	70 67 69 75 281		J Wade	74 71 71 71 287
T16	P McGinley	71 72 72 67 282		M Roe	74 68 70 75 287
	N Joakimides	72 68 73 69 282		R Lee	73 71 74 70 288
	I Garbutt	73 68 72 69 282		S Struver	72 73 73 70 288
	J V D Velde	67 71 73 71 282		G Turner	72 73 72 72 289
	P Broadhurst	73 70 68 71 282		K Tomori	68 73 75 73 289
	R Goosen	70 70 70 72 282		S Webster	70 73 73 73 289
	T Gillis	72 71 66 73 282		D Cole	70 74 72 73 289
T23	A Balicki	72 73 72 66 283		D Borrego	72 72 69 76 289
	C Montgomerie	74 68 73 68 283		S Alker	74 71 77 69 291
	F Cea	75 68 71 69 283		G Evans	72 71 76 72 291
	E Romero	66 75 72 70 283		M Olander	74 71 73 73 291
	A Clapp	72 71 70 70 283		S Bottomley	70 73 72 76 291
	M A Jimenez	72 73 68 70 283		R Boxall	69 72 73 77 291
	R Drummond	70 71 75 68 284		S Field	70 74 78 70 292
	R Jacquelin	73 70 73 68 284		O Eliasson	71 72 78 71 292
	G Nicklaus	69 75 71 69 284		P Golding	72 73 72 75 292
	G J Brand	70 73 71 70 284		J Hawksworth	71 72 72 77 292
	K Eriksson	68 71 74 71 284		J Bickerton	67 77 77 72 293
	P Mitchell	71 74 68 71 284		J Rystrom	72 73 70 78 293
	V Phillips	71 72 69 72 284		D Smyth	69 72 77 76 294
	S Scahill	73 71 68 72 284		R Allenby	70 70 75 79 294
	T Gogele	74 68 69 73 284		O David (am)	74 71 77 79 301
	G Orr	74 70 73 68 285			

The 36-hole cut was made at 145 – 1 over par – 69 players qualified.

ROUND BY ROUND LEADERBOARD

FIRST ROUND		SECOND ROUND	
S TORRANCE	8 under	S TORRANCE	10 under
E Romero	6 under	M Florioli	8 under
P Linhart	6 under	M Campbell	7 under
J Bickerton	5 under	M Farry	7 under
J Van de Velde	5 under	W Riley	6 under
D Robertson	4 under	J Van de Velde	6 under
K Tomori	4 under		
K Eriksson	4 under		

THIRD ROUND		FINAL ROUND	
S TORRANCE	10 under	S TORRANCE	12 under
M Campbell	10 under	M Florioli	10 under
D Howell	8 under	O Edmond	10 under
M Goggin	8 under	B Langer	10 under
T Gillis	7 under	M Goggin	10 under
B Langer	7 under		
P Claydon	7 under		
P Linhart	7 under		

PUNTERS' POINTS

- 80/1 Sam Torrance, the second oldest player in the field, won his first tournament for over three years as, one by one, his young challengers made mistakes while Bernhard Langer left his charge too late.
  > Needing to birdie either of the last two holes Smokin' Sam birdied both, with his seven wood second shot to the 17th a real gem.
  > Now the (almost) 45-year-old Scot may become a contender for the Scotland teams in the Dunhill Cup, and the World Cup and he may even believe he can make the 1999 Ryder Cup side.
- 14/1 Bernhard Langer had putting problems in his early rounds and found that the 7-shot deficit he had to make up from halfway was just too much. With two top 3 finishes in the last three years he can be expected to go close again in 1999.
- Pedro Linhart when in serious contention in the 1996 British Masters shot a R4 78, and he again showed R4 nerves here when he put his second shot in the water at the last to finish T6th.
- Please note the name of Mathew Goggin as I expect he's going to make a real name for himself over the next couple of years. The 1995 Australian amateur champion won the Aussie Tour Championship three months ago and is a player of real promise.
- 26-year-old Italian Massimo Florioli continued his fine 1998 form with his second top 3 finish of the season. Learning fast, he could well land a 'shock' win before the next millenium.
- Colin Montgomerie, having broken a putter earlier in the tournament, finished "a disappointing week" with a R4 68. He will probably be worth opposing

here in 1999 as his recent course record is poor by his standards – T23rd 1998: T11th 1997: Missed cut 1996.

- And finally......what a tournament for DYM followers with three of the front five DYMs!
- I Garrido (81) and S Cage (79) each retired after their first round.
- Among those to miss the cut were 25/1 Andrew Coltart, 50/1 Peter Lonard and 80/1 Jose Coceres. Rolf Muntz retired.

1997 RESULT

1	33/1	Retief Goosen
2	66/1	Jamie Spence
T3	150/1	Martin Gates
T3	100/1	Vanslow Phillips
T3	25/1	Darren Clarke
T3	100/1	Raymond Russell

WINNERS IN THE '90s

1990	Philip Walton
1991	Eduardo Romero
1992	M A Martin
1993	Costantino Rocca
1994	Mark Roe
1995	Paul Broadhurst
1996	Robert Allenby
1997	Retief Goosen
1998	Sam Torrance

PUNTERS' GUIDE

- It is difficult to find any clear recent pattern:
  - > From 1993-1996 an experienced player had come from 'off the pace' to win. However, in the last two years the final round leader has gone onto win.
  - > The formula to select a player who had been placed in the first five in either of the last two years had worked four times in the five years 1993-1997. However it failed in 1998.
- However the last two winners both led after a good first round from an early tee time. With the platform that gave them they had the momentum to go on to win.
- Solid current form has probably been the key factor as the form figures of recent winners show (last tournament on right).

1998	Sam Torrance	16-34-MC
1997	Retief Goosen	2-18-2
1996	Robert Allenby	7-W-DNP-52

- So the best advice is probably to go for a player
  - > Out early with a good tee time
  - > Had made at least two of the last three cuts and posted at least a top 20 finish in those three starts.

THE MURPHY'S IRISH OPEN

Date	2nd – 5th July
Course	Druids Glen, County Wicklow
Par	71
Yardage	7,012
First Prize	£166,660
Total Purse	£1 million

The Druids Glen course can be very demanding, especially if the wind blows. It was the venue for the Irish Open for the third successive year.

1998 ODDS

fav	8/1	Colin Montgomerie (DC2)	33/1	Robert Allenby
	11/1	Ernie Els	50/1	Eduardo Romero
	12/1	Lee Westwood	50/1	David Howell
	16/1	J M Olazabal	50/1	Stephen Ames
	22/1	Darren Clarke	66/1	Sam Torrance*(PWW)
	28/1	Ian Woosnam	66/1	Padraig Harrington
	33/1	Nick Faldo*	66/1	Phillip Price
	33/1	Paul McGinley	66/1	David Gilford
	33/1	Mark McNulty	66/1	Paul Broadhurst
	33/1	Andrew Coltart		

Just 19 players were best priced at or under 66/1.

BOOKIES AT ODDS

DYM Nick Faldo 16/1 Corals: 33/1 Tote

DYM Sam Torrance 33/1 Tote: 66/1 Hills

Winner David Carter 80/1 Tote: 125/1 Chandlers, Corals, Hills, Surrey

1998 RESULT

1	125/1	**David Carter**	**68 72 67 71**	**278**
		(Carter won play-off at first extra hole)		
2 fav	8/1	**Colin Montgomerie**	**65 74 71 68**	**278**
T3	80/1	**Peter Baker**	**69 75 66 70**	**280**
T3	250/1	**John McHenry**	**70 68 70 72**	**280**
5	250/1	**Craig Hainline**	**70 68 72 71**	**281**

T6	G Orr	70 69 72 71 282		D Gilford	73 71 72 76 292
	J Coceres	75 67 70 70 282		K Nolan	71 74 71 76 292
8	P Lonard	69 74 70 70 283		M Jonzon	75 70 72 75 292
T9	S Webster	71 70 70 73 284		S Tinning	75 71 71 75 292
	I Woosnam	73 74 65 72 284		M McNulty	71 74 74 73 292
	I Garbutt	73 69 71 71 284		J Sandelin	69 75 76 72 292
	R Claydon	71 71 73 69 284		J Spence	72 74 74 72 292
	D Cooper	73 70 72 69 284		N Fasth	73 69 75 76 293
	J M Olazabal	73 72 71 68 284		M Roe	74 71 73 75 293
15	L Westwood	70 73 73 69 285		R Green	71 73 75 74 293
T16	S Richardson	68 71 74 73 286		I Garrido	74 69 78 72 293
	P Broadhurst	70 71 72 73 286		S Struver	72 74 75 72 293
	J Payne	71 71 71 73 286		P Affleck	70 77 75 72 294
	P O'Malley	74 70 69 73 286		C Suneson	72 75 74 73 294
	M A Jimenez	71 71 72 72 286		K Tomori	70 73 72 80 295
	B Davis	71 71 73 71 286		D Higgins	75 69 72 79 295
	K Eriksson	71 74 72 69 286		R Chapman	73 72 73 77 295
	P Quirici	72 75 70 69 286		D Robertson	74 72 74 75 295
	B Lane	70 75 62 79 286		C Watts	72 72 77 74 295
T25	M Davis	68 75 72 72 287		R Burns	74 71 73 78 296
	E Darcy	74 72 69 72 287		R Allenby	73 73 77 73 296
	D Lynn	68 76 70 74 288		F Tarnaud	69 74 72 82 297
	N Faldo	75 72 67 74 288		S Garcia	68 73 75 81 297
	T Johnstone	71 67 77 73 288		A Cejka	72 70 77 78 297
	E Romero	74 71 71 72 288		O Edmond	71 71 79 77 298
	A Kankkonen	74 71 73 70 288		F Jacobson	73 70 81 74 298
	S Allan	69 71 78 71 289		S Torrance	71 76 76 76 299
	E Els	71 71 70 78 290		P Price	70 72 81 77 300
	P Senior	75 71 73 71 290		S Ames	68 78 78 76 300
	V Phillips	71 72 71 77 291		N Joakimides	75 72 77 77 301
	G Chalmers	69 75 72 75 291		J Lomas	75 72 74 81 302
	J Rivero	69 75 74 73 291		A Cabrera	75 72 77 79 303
	D Hospital	74 72 74 71 291		A Oldcorn	74 72 80 81 307

The 36-hole cut was made at 147 – 5 over par – 71 players qualified.

ROUND BY ROUND LEADERBOARD

FIRST ROUND		SECOND ROUND	
C Montgomerie	6 under	J McHenry	4 under
S Ames	3 under	C Hainline	4 under
S Garcia (am)	3 under	T Johnstone	4 under
S Richardson	3 under	G Orr	3 under
M Davis	3 under	C Montgomerie	3 under
D Lynn	3 under	S Richardson	3 under
D CARTER	3 under	D CARTER	2 under

THIRD ROUND		FINAL ROUND	
B Lane	6 under	D CARTER	6 under
D CARTER	6 under	C Montgomerie	6 under
J McHenry	5 under	P Baker	4 under
P Baker	3 under	J McHenry	4 under
C Montgomerie	3 under	C Hainline	3 under
C Hainline	3 under		

PUNTERS' POINTS

- 125/1 David Carter's first tour win was truly amazing.
  - > Standing on the thirteenth tee he was 4 ahead. Then a double bogey there and a bogey on the 16th left him to par the final two holes to win.
  - > A fine recovery after a poor tee shot saw him needing par the 17th. Then, after finding the water at the last, he holed a 20-foot putt to bogey the hole and get into a play-off.
  - > On the first extra play-off hole Monty, playing with an injured ankle, drove into the rough, and then overhit a simple chip into the water. Monty conceded the hole to Carter who was on the green in two.
  - > The 25-year-old had won despite his nervousness. However he'd shown a smile when in trouble, and true courage under pressure. He deserved his victory.
- Monty's play-off record continues to be poor – he's now lost all three! However a fully fit Monty is made for this course so expect him to make a really bold show here in 1999 Ryder Cup year.
- Lee Westwood dropped three shots in his last four holes. After finishing 7th and 2nd here in the last two years he too can be expected to do well in 1999.
- 80/1 Peter Baker's T3rd finish here was his fourth top 10 of a consistent season. He could well go on to regain his Ryder Cup place in 1999. Remember his brilliant performance in 1993 at the Belfry?
- Only eight players broke par on this demanding course. So in the three years at Druids Glen par has been broken just 28 times. Monty has broken par each time and now has a superb stroke average of 68.83!

- Corals' Top Irish Player market :-
  1. 33/1   John McHenry
  2. 10/1   Eamonn Darcy
  3. 50/1   Keith Nolan

  2/1 Darren Clarke was the favourite.
- Among those to miss the cut were 22/1 Darren Clarke, 33/1 chances Andrew Coltart and Paul McGinley, 50/1 David Howell and 66/1 Padraig Harrington.

1997 RESULT

1 fav	10/1	Colin Montgomerie
2	25/1	Lee Westwood
3	12/1	Nick Faldo
T4	100/1	Michael Jonzon
T4	16/1	Ian Woosnam

WINNERS IN THE '90s

1990	J M Olazabal
1991	Nick Faldo
1992	Nick Faldo
1993	Nick Faldo
1994	Bernhard Langer
1995	Sam Torrance
1996	Colin Montgomerie
1997	Colin Montgomerie
1998	David Carter

PUNTERS' GUIDE

- This demanding Druids Glen course requires length, and above all accuracy. It will also pay to follow players in future who fitted David Carter's 1998 profile.
  - > A top 20 finish in the previous year here
  - > A top 20 place on the stats for greens in regulation
  - > One of the tour's top 25 for driving distance
- The players with the best records here are
  - > Colin Montgomerie 2nd 1998: W 1997: W 1996
  - > Ian Woosnam T9th 1998: T4th 1997: T17th 1996
  - > Lee Westwood 15th 1998: 2nd 1997: T7th 1996
  - > Jose Maria Olazabal T9th 1998: 6th 1997

THE STANDARD LIFE LOCH LOMOND WORLD INVITATIONAL

Date	8th – 11th July
Course	Loch Lomond GC, Near Glasgow
Par	71
Yardage	7,050
First Prize	£141,660
Total Purse	£850,000

This tournament at this venue was being held for the third successive year. After a mid-September date in 1996 it has been played the week before the British Open in 1997, and again this year.

1998 ODDS

fav	11/1	Colin Montgomerie	50/1	Mark McNulty
	16/1	Tom Lehman (DC)	50/1	Patrik Sjoland
	16/1	Lee Westwood	50/1	Andrew Coltart
	18/1	J M Olazabal	50/1	Eduardo Romero
	25/1	Ian Woosnam	50/1	Peter Baker
	25/1	Thomas Bjorn	66/1	Paul McGinley
	33/1	Stewart Cink	66/1	Stuart Appleby
	33/1	Jesper Parnevik	66/1	David Howell
	40/1	Nick Faldo (non runner)	66/1	Robert Allenby
	50/1	Retief Goosen (non runner)		

Just 19 players were best priced at or under 66/1.

BOOKIES AT ODDS

DYM T2nd Robert Allenby 28/1 Corals: 66/1 Surrey
DYM Jesper Parnevik 16/1 Ladbrokes: 33/1 Stan James
Winner Lee Westwood 11/1 Corals, Surrey: 16/1 Chandlers, Sunderlands

1998 RESULT

1	16/1	Lee Westwood	69 69 68 70	276
T2	25/1	Ian Woosnam	67 73 74 66	280
T2	50/1	Eduardo Romero	71 70 71 68	280
T2	66/1	Robert Allenby	72 72 68 68	280
T2	66/1	David Howell	68 71 70 71	280
T2	200/1	Dennis Edlund	70 69 67 74	280

T7	G Orr	68 72 71 70 281	P Harrington	74 69 77 70 290
	C Montgomerie	72 71 68 70 281	T Levet	74 71 74 71 290
T9	P Broadhurst	69 71 71 71 282	R Damron	70 76 73 71 290
	T Lehman	73 68 69 72 282	G Day	75 71 72 72 290
T11	C Dennis	74 68 71 70 283	D Gilford	74 72 71 73 290
	D Cooper	75 68 67 73 283	R Claydon	74 66 75 75 290
T13	D Robertson	72 72 71 69 284	O Karlsson	74 72 69 75 290
	S Torrance	73 70 72 69 284	G Turner	73 74 73 71 291
	S Cink	70 74 71 69 284	C Rocca	68 74 77 72 291
	M Florioli	73 71 69 71 284	J McHenry	73 71 75 72 291
	C Hainline	75 66 71 72 284	D Carter	72 75 72 72 291
	S Allan	70 68 72 74 284	J Haeggman	73 71 69 78 291
	K Eriksson	73 72 65 74 284	M Lanner	72 72 74 74 292
T20	J Sandelin	75 71 72 67 285	R Chapman	76 70 75 72 293
	P Sjoland	74 73 68 70 285	D Hospital	74 73 73 73 293
	J Spence	70 71 72 72 285	C D Franco	75 72 73 73 293
	A Cejka	71 71 69 74 285	P Eales	76 70 73 74 293
T24	J Payne	74 70 73 70 287	S Struver	74 72 77 71 294
	J Van de Velde	71 72 73 71 287	S Cage	72 75 73 74 294
	P Fulke	75 69 72 71 287	S Garcia (am)	71 71 76 76 294
	S Ames	75 71 70 71 287	A Coltart	71 69 73 81 294
	M A Jimenez	71 70 74 72 287	S Grappasonni	76 69 76 74 295
	S Appleby	73 68 74 72 287	A Cabrera	72 71 76 76 295
	P Baker	73 69 73 72 287	M Gronberg	75 70 76 76 297
	T Gogele	76 69 70 72 287	S Leaney	75 70 75 77 297
	I Garbutt	73 69 72 73 287	R McFarlane	76 69 75 77 297
	T Bjorn	73 72 70 73 288	B Davis	73 74 72 78 297
	P McGinley	72 69 72 75 288	I Garrido	72 73 71 81 297
	J M Olazabal	72 71 69 76 288	G Evans	78 68 73 79 298
	C Watts	74 73 73 69 289	S Luna	74 73 77 75 299
	J Parnevik	71 73 72 73 289	A Oldcorn	71 75 76 77 299
	S Field	75 70 70 74 289	J Coceres	75 72 75 77 299
	R Drummond	71 66 72 80 289		

The 36-hole cut was made at 147 – 5 over par – 71 players qualified.

ROUND BY ROUND LEADERBOARD

FIRST ROUND		SECOND ROUND	
I Woosnam	4 under	R Drummond	5 under
G Orr	3 under	L WESTWOOD	4 under
D Howell	3 under	S Allan	4 under
C Rocca	3 under	D Edlund	3 under
L WESTWOOD	2 under	D Howell	3 under
P Broadhurst	2 under	A Coltart	2 under
		P Broadhurst	2 under
		G Orr	2 under
		I Woosnam	2 under
		R Claydon	2 under

THIRD ROUND		FINAL ROUND	
L WESTWOOD	7 under	L WESTWOOD	8 under
D Edlund	7 under	I Woosnam	4 under
D Howell	4 under	E Romero	4 under
R Drummond	4 under	R Allenby	4 under
D Cooper	3 under	D Howell	4 under
S Allan	3 under	D Edlund	4 under
T Lehman	3 under		
K Eriksson	3 under		

- Play during the third round on Friday was suspended when the persistent rain created waterlogging. The round was however completed that day.

PUNTERS' POINTS

- He's done it again! The Worksop wonder notched his seventh win in nine months with a superb performance. Within 270 days Lee Westwood has won in Spain, America, Japan, Germany, Australia, England and now in Scotland.....as well as in a successful European Ryder Cup team. He's now odds on to win his first European Order of Merit. He's some player!!

- 25/1 Ian Woosnam sadly had a pair of sevens on his card in R3 otherwise he would have posed a real threat. Swinging well he's in fine form....as he usually is at this time of the year.

- If only he could putt.....50/1 Eduardo Romero's consistent and accurate ball striking is often let down by his inability to convert his birdie chances. As a result he may continue to make the frame in the highest company without winning.

- Only four players showed the consistency to shoot four par, or sub-par, rounds. They were Lee Westwood, of course, Eduardo Romero, David Howell and Paul Broadhurst.

- 66/1 David Howell is surely 'a winner about to happen'. Here he will have boosted his confidence with a solid final round as his R4 scoring has been his weakness so far this year.

- Gary Orr shaved the hole a number of times over the last 36 holes. Nevertheless he recorded his second successive top 10 finish and seems to be a player who 'has moved up a gear'. His first win may not be too far away!

- American tour raider 66/1 Stuart Appleby showed in a superb R2 68 when he landed a nice 11/4 bet to win his 3-ball against Colin Montgomerie (71), and Stewart Cink (74). What a fine player he is, especially if the winds blow.
- Final day betting was:-

4/6	Lee Westwood	7 under
5/1	Dennis Edlund	7 under
12/1	Tom Lehman	3 under
14/1	David Howell	4 under
16/1	Colin Montgomerie	2 under
25/1	Ross Drummond	4 under

- Among those to miss the cut were 50/1 Mark McNulty, 80/1 longshots P U Johansson, Robert Karlsson and Phillip Price, and 100/1 outsiders Greg Chalmers and Mark James.
- Steve Webster (81) and Andrew Sherborne (80) both withdrew after their first round.
- Nick Faldo withdrew, just before his tee time, with an elbow tendon injury sustained while practicing.

CORALS SPECIALITY MARKETS
Top American Player
1	Tom Lehman	2/1 fav
2	Clark Dennis	10/1
T3	Stuart Cink	5/1
T3	Craig Hainline	16/1

PLEASE NOTE Sunderlands also quoted this market.
Top Australasian (incl N.Z.) Player
1	Robert Allenby	4/1 fav
2	Stephen Allan	25/1
3	Stuart Appleby	9/2

Top Amateur
| 1 | Sergio Garcia | 13/8 |

beat Justin Rose and Matt Kuchar
Winning Nationality
1st: European 7/4 on
4/1 USA 9/2 Australasian 9/1 ROW
Top Scottish Player
Multi-Sports quoted a 14-runner field with 1/5 odds 1,2,3
T1	Gary Orr	8/1
T1	Colin Montgomerie	5/4 fav
3	Sam Torrance	6/1

1997 RESULT
1	20/1	Tom Lehman
2	10/1	Ernie Els
3	50/1	Retief Goosen
T4	12/1	Greg Norman
T4	200/1	Pierre Fulke

WINNERS IN THE '90s

1996   Thomas Bjorn
1997   Tom Lehman
1998   Lee Westwood

PUNTERS' GUIDE

- In the three years at Loch Lomond the most consistent players have been
  > Robert Allenby T2nd 1998: 13th 1997: 3rd 1996. His stroke average is a superb 69.92.
  > Lee Westwood Won 1998: 22nd 1997: T16th 1996. His stroke average is 70.66.
  Allenby the long-range selection for this tournament in last year's volume obliged when 2nd at 66/1. In 1999 he'll again play well especially if the winds blow.
- Allenby's great friend, American tour player, Stuart Appleby will be an outsider to note in future. He played well this year, especially in R2, on his first visit to Loch Lomond.
- In 1999, with a huge prize in Ryder Cup year, this tournament will have a major impact on the placings for the Ryder Cup team.

THE FOUR FINAL QUALIFYING STAGES FOR THE BRITISH OPEN

Corals' creative compilers, under Jon Wright's leadership, once more showed their skill and enterprise by pricing up the four final 36-hole qualifying stages for the British Open.

Sunday 12th July and Monday 13th July

HESKETH COURSE

fav	11/1	Peter Baker	20/1	Jarmo Sandelin
	12/1	Larry Mize	20/1	Vanslow Phillips
	14/1	Clark Dennis	25/1	Stephen Laycock
	14/1	David Gilford	25/1	Ian Garbutt
	14/1	Harrison Frazar	25/1	Jose Coceres
	16/1	Dudley Hart (non runner)	28/1	Gordon Brand Jr
	18/1	Thomas Gogele	33/1	Bar

Result

1	40/1	Rodger Davis
2	40/1	Gary Evans
T3	33/1	Derrick Cooper
T3	100/1	Richard Bland

HILLSIDE COURSE

fav	10/1	M A Jimenez	25/1	Wayne Westner
	11/1	David Howell	25/1	Ross Drummond
	12/1	Michael Campbell	25/1	Dean Robertson
	14/1	Robert Damron	28/1	Dennis Edlund
	14/1	David Frost	28/1	Paolo Quirici
	16/1	Peter Senior	28/1	Pierre Fulke
	16/1	Sam Torrance (non runner)	28/1	Katsuyoshi Tomori
	20/1	Philip Walton	28/1	Jean Van de Velde
	20/1	Andrew Magee (non runner)	28/1	Barry Lane
	20/1	Len Mattiace	33/1	Bar

Result

1	66/1	Mark Litton
T2	40/1	Justin Rose (am)
T2	14/1	David Frost
T4	100/1	Lee Jones
T4	12/1	Michael Campbell

WEST LANCASHIRE COURSE

fav	7/1	Paul McGinley	22/1	Stephen Scahill
	10/1	Alexander Cejka	25/1	Bob May
	11/1	Peter Lonard	25/1	Craig Hainline
	14/1	Tommy Tolles	28/1	Nico Van Rensburg
	16/1	Steve Webster	28/1	Klas Eriksson
	16/1	Paul Lawrie	28/1	A da Silva

| 20/1 | Jeev Milkha Singh | 28/1 | Jim Carter |
| 20/1 | Jamie Spence | 33/1 | Bar |

Result

T1	16/1	Paul Lawrie
T1	40/1	Des Smyth
3	40/1	Peter Hedblom
T4	50/1	Jeff Remesy
T4	100/1	Bradley Dredge

SOUTHPORT AND AINSDALE COURSE

jt fav	9/1	Bob Tway (non runner)	20/1	Jim Payne
jt fav	9/1	Paul Broadhurst	25/1	Francisco Cea
	12/1	David Carter	28/1	Sven Struver
	14/1	Tim Herron	28/1	Jean Louis Guepy
	16/1	Duffy Waldorf	28/1	Mats Hallberg
	20/1	Massimo Florioli	28/1	Robert Lee
	20/1	Peter Mitchell	33/1	Bar

Result

1	28/1	Jean Louis Guepy
2	33/1	Michael Long
T3	28/1	Sven Struver
T3	33/1	Brian Davis
T3	20/1	Peter Mitchell
T3	28/1	Mats Hallberg

PUNTERS GUIDE

Four key points to note in this market:-

1 Players going out early on the first day have a notable advantage if the forecast points to windy weather from midday onwards.

2 Players travelling straight on after completing four full rounds at Loch Lomond may be tired. However they may be 'in good nick' boosted by the cheque they have just pocketed as the efforts of the following players showed this year

	Loch Lomond	Pre-qual	Course
> Sven Struver	57th	T3rd	Southport and Ainsdale
> Derrick Cooper	11th	T3rd	Hesketh
> Gary Evans	68th	2nd	Hesketh

3 In this particular market there is, of course, no sudden death play-off if two (or more) players are tied after the 36 holes so dead-heat rules then apply to win bets.

4 The build up of pressure over the course of a normal tournament reaching its peak on the back nine in R4 on Sunday is absent here.

THE 127TH BRITISH OPEN

Date	16th – 19th July
Course	Royal Birkdale, Southport, Lancs.
Par	70
Yardage	7,018
First Prize	£300,000
Total Purse	£1.75 million

Please see Part 5.

THE TNT DUTCH OPEN

Date	23rd – 26th July
Course	Hilversum, Utrecht, Holland
Par	71
Yardage	6,635
First Prize	£133,330
Total Purse	£800,000

For the fifth successive year the Dutch Open was held at the Hilversum course.

1998 ODDS

fav	10/1	Lee Westwood	50/1	Paul McGinley
	14/1	Nick Price	50/1	Retief Goosen*
	16/1	John Huston	50/1	Raymond Russell
	20/1	Bernhard Langer	50/1	Andrew Coltart
	22/1	Phil Mickelson	50/1	Greg Turner
	22/1	Darren Clarke	66/1	Justin Rose*
	33/1	David Howell	66/1	Peter O'Malley*
	40/1	Mark McNulty	66/1	David Gilford*
	40/1	Costantino Rocca	66/1	Mark James*
	40/1	Patrik Sjoland	66/1	Sven Struver (DC)*
	50/1	M A Jimenez*	66/1	Gordon Brand Jr
	50/1	Paul Broadhurst*	66/1	Philip Walton
	50/1	Peter Baker	66/1	David Clarter

26 players were best priced at or under 66/1.

BOOKIES AT ODDS

The DYM winner Stephen Leaney 50/1 Tote: 125/1 Corals

1998 RESULT

IAN GARBUTT.

1	125/1	Stephen Leaney	66 63 70 67	266
2	22/1	Darren Clarke	68 69 67 63	267
T3	14/1	Nick Price	68 65 69 66	268
T3	10/1	Lee Westwood	63 66 72 67	268
5	40/1	Costantino Rocca	71 65 69 65	269

6	P Baker	70 68 68 65 271		P McGinley	66 71 71 71 279
T7	I Pyman	73 66 66 68 273		D Howell	71 69 68 71 279
	I Garbutt	68 69 67 69 273		G Turner	71 69 68 71 279
T9	M James	70 69 67 68 274		T Gillis	71 70 67 71 279
	P Sjoland	67 70 66 71 274		P Price	69 72 69 70 280
T11	B Davis	66 72 69 68 275		R Boxall	70 69 69 72 280
	R Jacquelin	68 68 70 69 275		S Struver	65 70 71 74 280
	J Huston	67 69 70 69 275		S Henderson	71 70 68 72 281
	S Tinning	70 67 69 69 275		M Roe	71 68 70 72 281
	J Lomas	65 69 71 70 275		P O'Malley	70 71 67 73 281
	P Walton	68 67 70 70 275		M Reale	72 69 71 70 282
T17	A Coltart	71 68 68 69 276		J Spence	70 70 72 70 282
	G Brand Jr	69 70 68 69 276		J Haeggman	70 68 72 72 282
	P Lonard	69 67 72 69 276		F Cea	70 71 72 70 283
	D Gilford	71 67 68 70 276		K Tomori	71 69 71 72 283
T21	A Oldcorn	69 70 72 66 277		P Harrington	69 72 67 75 283
	M Mouland	70 67 70 70 277		A Sandywell	72 68 72 72 284
	M Long	70 70 67 70 277		M Gronberg	70 70 66 78 284
	P Haugsrud	65 71 71 70 277		S Kjeldsen	72 69 71 73 285
	P Lawrie	67 72 67 71 277		G Evans	70 70 71 74 285
	M A Jimenez	69 66 69 73 277		D Lynn	72 69 74 71 286
	J Van de Velde	69 69 73 67 278		R Wessels	71 69 75 71 286
	M Campbell	73 65 70 70 278		W Riley	71 70 72 73 286
	B Langer	70 65 72 71 278		F Henge	70 69 74 73 286
	M Lanner	69 72 72 66 279		S Ballesteros	68 73 71 74 286
	R J Derksen	70 70 71 68 279		M Florioli	74 67 70 75 286
	P Mitchell	68 71 71 69 279		D Robertson	72 65 73 76 286
	P Fulke	71 66 73 69 279		J Bickerton	69 71 74 73 287
	J Remesy	68 70 71 70 279		M Farry	69 67 77 74 287
	S McAllister	68 68 72 71 279		J Hawksworth	70 70 72 76 288
	K Drink	69 70 69 71 279		R McFarlane	69 72 76 72 289
	M Gortana	67 70 71 71 279			

The 36-hole cut was made at 141 – 1 under par – 68 players qualified.

ROUND BY ROUND LEADERBOARD

FIRST ROUND		SECOND ROUND	
L Westwood	8 under	S LEANEY	13 under
P Haugsrud	6 under	L Westwood	13 under
S Struver	6 under	N Price	9 under
J Lomas	6 under	J Lomas	8 under
P McGinley	5 under	B Langer	7 under
S LEANEY	5 under	S Struver	7 under
B Davis	5 under	M A Jimenez	7 under
		P Walton	7 under
		P Lonard	7 under

THIRD ROUND		FINAL ROUND	
S LEANEY	14 under	S LEANEY	18 under
L Westwood	12 under	D Clarke	17 under
N Price	11 under	N Price	16 under
P Sjoland	10 under	L Westwood	16 under
I Garbutt	9 under	C Rocca	15 under
D Clarke	9 under		
M A Jimenez	9 under		
C Rocca	9 under		

PUNTERS' POINTS

- 125/1 Stephen Leaney fought off the challenge from three of the world's best players to win deservedly his second tournament of the year. Leaney showed here, as he had in his Moroccan success in March, that he is a very controlled, uncomplicated, crisp ball striker who is a fine front runner. He'll win again!!

- 22/1 Darren Clarke, after a pair of missed cuts, played a superbly aggressive final round 63 to almost win the tournament. It was his fourth top 4 finish this season.

- Players who played all four days in the British Open—especially if in contention—rarely do well here. That factor was shown again this year as both Leaney and Clarke had been 'fortunate' enough to miss the Birkdale cut.

- Lee Westwood after a brilliant opening round 63 admitted he was 'drained' after his tiring four days at the British Open. In the end that Birkdale effect probably came into play. However it's proof of his world class that we could be disappointed when he finished T3rd.

- Costantino Rocca is clearly recovering his form. After his T9th finish in the British Open he played really well here, especially over the final 54 holes when he was 15 under par.

- After a poorish quality field last year my Dutch contact Jan Kees Van der Velden, editor in Holland of the Golfers' magazine and Golf Journal, was delighted with the quality of the field under TNT's imaginative sponsorship.

- Raymond Russell has a fine track record here having been 3rd in 1996 and T7th last year for a stroke average of 67.75. However this year, drained after his brilliant T4th in the British Open, he not surprisingly missed the cut. Remember him here in 1999 when he can show once more that Hilversum suits him ideally.

- Among those missing the cut were 22/1 Phil Mickelson, 40/1 Mark McNulty, 50/1 chances Paul Broadhurst and Raymond Russell, and 66/1 'new boy' Justin Rose.
- Retief Goosen (after a 75), Richard Green (after a 79) and Jay Townsend (after an 81) all withdrew after R1.

1997 RESULT

1	100/1	Sven Struver
2	80/1	Russell Claydon
T3	80/1	Roger Chapman
T3	66/1	Angel Cabrera

WINNERS IN THE '90s

1990	Stephen McAllister
1991	Payne Stewart
1992	Bernhard Langer
1993	Colin Montgomerie
1994	M A Jimenez
1995	Scott Hoch
1996	Mark McNulty
1997	Sven Struver
1998	Stephen Leaney

PUNTERS' GUIDE

- In the last two years this tournament has been won by a player at odds of 100/1+ and whose immediate form had not been good. So Hilversum can revive the swing that other courses can't reach.
- Ian Garbutt on his two visits to Hilversum has finished T22nd and T7th for an eight-round stroke average of 69.5. If his putter hots up he could do well here in 1999.
- Do remember to be very wary of players who may be drained after being in contention in the British Open.

THE SCANDINAVIAN MASTERS

Date	30th July – 2nd August
Course	Kungsangen Golf Club, Stockholm
Par	71
Yardage	6,791
First Prize	£133,330
Total Purse	£800,000

This year the Scandinavian Masters moved to the Kungsangen course in Stockholm. The course is one of the flagship courses of the PGA European Tour Courses plc. It was designed by Anders Forsbrand, opened in 1994, and remodelled in recent years.

1998 ODDS

fav	9/1	Colin Montgomerie	50/1	Retief Goosen
	14/1	Jesper Parnevik	50/1	Stephen Leaney (PWW)
	16/1	J M Olazabal	50/1	M A Jimenez*
	16/1	Darren Clarke	50/1	David Howell
	20/1	Thomas Bjorn	66/1	Paul Broadhurst
	28/1	Costantino Rocca	66/1	Ian Garbutt
	33/1	Peter Baker*	66/1	Jarmo Sandelin
	33/1	Patrik Sjoland	66/1	Peter Lonard
	50/1	Sam Torrance	66/1	Paul McGinley
	50/1	David Gilford	66/1	Peter O'Malley
	50/1	Greg Turner	66/1	Philip Walton
	50/1	Andrew Coltart	66/1	Joakim Haeggman (DC)

24 players were best priced at 66/1 or under.

BOOKIES AT ODDS

Winner Jesper Parnevik 10/1 Chandlers, Corals: 14/1 Tote, Sunderlands, Stan James, Hills

1998 RESULT

1	14/1	Jesper Parnevik	67 65 71 70	273
2	16/1	Darren Clarke	67 70 68 71	276
3	200/1	Stephen Field	70 68 70 69	277
T4	100/1	Jean Van de Velde	72 67 70 69	278
T4	125/1	Michael Jonzon	69 65 72 72	278

6	J Rivero	71 73 66 69 279		R Jacquelin	71 69 72 74 286
T7	P Quirici	72 70 66 72 280		S Alker	73 70 71 73 287
	P-U Johansson	69 69 72 70 280		R Goosen	69 75 72 71 287
	M Lanner	69 69 69 73 280		S Struver	72 72 71 72 287
	M Gronberg	68 69 72 71 280		I Garrido	70 75 70 72 287
T11	A Coltart	72 70 68 71 281		E Darcy	70 75 71 71 287
	K Tomori	69 72 68 72 281		A Kankkonen	75 70 73 69 287
	M Davis	72 66 72 71 281		P Eales	71 74 73 69 287
	P Broadhurst	69 68 71 73 281		M Anglert	74 70 71 73 288
	B Davis	65 72 73 71 281		S Luna	74 71 70 73 288
T16	V Phillips	73 70 69 70 282		M Olander	70 75 73 70 288
	P McGinley	73 71 71 67 282		D Edlund	71 74 74 69 288
	C Montgomerie	70 74 69 69 282		T Gogele	72 69 72 75 288
	G Turner	71 73 65 73 282		S Grappasonni	69 74 74 72 289
	G Chalmers	74 70 67 71 282		M Roe	75 69 74 71 289
	T Levet	71 71 69 71 282		M Reale	73 72 72 72 289
	P Fulke	73 68 73 68 282		T Bjorn	76 66 71 76 289
	C Hainline	68 72 68 74 282		D Hospital	69 74 73 74 290
	M Hallberg	70 67 73 72 282		S Lyle	73 72 71 74 290
T25	S Henderson	70 73 69 71 283		M Long	74 71 71 74 290
	S Torrance	72 71 70 70 283		P Lonard	73 69 73 75 290
	D Smyth	71 73 69 70 283		A Hultman (am)	65 76 77 72 290
	H Nystrom	72 70 71 70 283		C Hanell	68 74 78 71 291
	R Muntz	71 70 71 71 283		O Eliasson	71 73 73 74 291
	S Leaney	70 71 68 74 283		D Carter	69 75 74 73 291
	J Sandelin	68 70 74 71 283		B Dredge	73 71 71 76 291
	J Remesy	72 70 71 71 284		P Harrington	72 70 74 75 291
	E Fryatt	70 69 71 74 284		M Campbell	69 73 78 71 291
	D Lynn	74 71 71 69 285		L-W Zhang	68 72 72 79 291
	P Affleck	69 72 74 70 285		A Wall	72 71 76 73 292
	R Boxall	69 72 71 73 285		D Tapping	72 73 73 74 292
	C Rocca	70 71 70 74 285		T Gillis	73 69 74 77 293
	D Howell	67 74 69 75 285		J Payne	73 72 73 76 294
	O Karlsson	71 72 69 74 286		P Sjoland	70 70 72 82 294
	S Kjeldsen	73 71 73 69 286		F Tarnaud	70 74 76 75 295
	K Brink	69 76 66 75 286			

The 36-hole cut was made at 145 – 3 over par – 76 players qualified.

ROUND BY ROUND LEADERBOARD

FIRST ROUND		SECOND ROUND	
B Davis	6 under	J PARNEVIK	10 under
A Hultman	6 under	M Jonzon	8 under
D Clarke	4 under	M Hallberg	5 under
J PARNEVIK	4 under	D Clarke	5 under
D Howell	4 under	B Davis	5 under
		M Gronberg	5 under

THIRD ROUND		FINAL ROUND	
J PARNEVIK	10 under	J PARNEVIK	11 under
D Clarke	8 under	D Clarke	8 under
M Jonzon	7 under	S Field	7 under
M Lanner	6 under	J Van de Velde	6 under
P Quirici	5 under	M Jonzon	6 under
C Hainline	5 under		
S Field	5 under		
P Broadhurst	5 under		

* Play was delayed on the second day by heavy rain.

PUNTERS' POINTS

- 14/1 Jesper Parnevik on home soil is always a player to follow. He's won three times at home on the Challenge tour, and this was his second European tour win in Sweden. Although not at his best, especially on the greens, he deservedly won with a fine front-running performance.

- Darren Clarke was notching his third second place of the year. With his wife expecting their first child there was always doubt about whether he'd finish the tournament. Astonishingly he has still just two victories!

- Punters are often baffled when a player suddenly and inexplicably finds form totally 'out of the blue'. This week 200/1 Stephen Field was the player as the 33-year-old from Barnsley shot four sub-par rounds to pick up a £50,000 cheque.

- Spare a thought for Jose Maria Olazabal who missed the cut at 11 over par. His driving was poor on a course where it was severely punished.

- For the second successive week Justin Rose missed the cut by a shot. He's yet to earn his first playing cheque on the tour.

- In the top Scandinavian player market created by Corals and Sunderlands the result was 1. Jesper Parnevik 4/1 fav, 2nd Michael Jonzon 33/1, T3rd Mats Lanner 25/1, Mathias Gronberg 33/1, and P U Johansson 20/1.

- Among those to miss the cut were 16/1 J M Olazabal, 33/1 DYM Peter Baker, and 66/1 outsiders Ian Garbutt, Philip Walton, and Joakim Haeggman.

- Jamie Spence (after R1 70) and Nicolas Vanhootegem were disqualified. Marc Farry, Jon Robson, Andrew Beal, Adam Hunter, Johan Rystrom, Andrew Oldcorn, Steve Webster, Wayne Riley, Steen Tinning, Derrick Cooper, Andrew Sherborne and 50/1 Miguel Jimenez all retired!!

1997 RESULT

1	80/1	Joakim Haeggman
2	80/1	Ignacio Garrido
T3	150/1	Peter Baker
T3	125/1	Mats Hallberg

WINNERS IN THE '90s

1991	Colin Montgomerie
1992	Nick Faldo
1993	Peter Baker
1994	Vijay Singh
1995	Jesper Parnevik
1996	Lee Westwood
1997	Joakim Haeggman
1998	Jesper Parnevik

PUNTERS' GUIDE

- Three points can be noted:
  - > The roll-call of winners in the nineties is a very impressive one.
  - > The Kungsangen course demands above all accuracy off the tee, so make sure your selection is at ease with his driver.
  - > The common link among the last seven winners is that they all had a top 25 finish in one of their last two starts, and all made the cut last time out.
- In 1999 the tournament will return to the Barseback Golf and Country Club course used in 1992, 1995 and 1997 which will please Peter Baker (T3rd 1997: T2nd 1992) who has a fine record on the Malmo course.

THE GERMAN OPEN

Date	6th – 9th August
Course	Sporting Club Berlin, Berlin
Par	72
Yardage	7,082
First Prize	£116,660
Total Purse	£700,000

This new Nick Faldo designed course was voted best new course in Europe by Golf World magazine and was being used on tour for the first time. It is a links-style course with many undulations and cutely placed deep bunkers with the wind a key factor.

1998 ODDS

fav	13/2	Bernhard Langer	50/1	Katsuyoshi Tomori
	20/1	Paul Broadhurst	66/1	Mathew Goggin*
	20/1	Sam Torrance	66/1	Jarmo Sandelin*
	25/1	Mark James	66/1	Gordon Brand Jr
	25/1	Paul McGinley	66/1	Brian Davis
	33/1	Jean Van de Velde	66/1	Craig Hainline
	40/1	Sven Struver*	66/1	Ian Garbutt
	40/1	Padraig Harrington	66/1	Philip Walton
	40/1	Ignacio Garrido (DC)*	66/1	Phillip Price
	50/1	Thomas Gogele*	66/1	Mats Lanner
	50/1	Michael Jonzon		

21 players were best priced at or under 66/1.

BOOKIES AT ODDS

Winner DYM Stephen Allan 40/1 Hills: 100/1 Corals, Stan James, Stanleys, Surrey

Tied second Ignacio Garrido 16/1 Napoleons: 40/1 Corals, Ladbrokes, Surrey, Tote

1998 RESULT

1	100/1	Stephen Allan	72 71 68 69	280
T2	125/1	Mark Roe	71 70 69 71	281
T2	40/1	Ignacio Garrido	67 72 68 74	281
T2	125/1	Steve Webster	69 73 69 70	281
T2	40/1	Padraig Harrington	73 69 70 69	281

6	S Henderson	72 67 73 71 283	A Wall	74 73 69 74 290
T7	J Wade	73 70 70 71 284	T Gillis	72 70 73 75 290
	D Chopra	75 71 67 71 284	R Claydon	68 73 73 76 290
	P Lawrie	67 73 72 72 284	D Lee	70 73 72 75 290
	K Tomori	72 68 72 72 284	W Riley	76 71 73 71 291
	M Mackenzie	71 75 66 72 284	G J Brand	75 71 72 73 291
	M Campbell	67 70 73 74 284	I Garbutt	72 73 71 75 291
T13	D Edlund	71 74 69 71 285	R Davis	73 74 69 75 291
	M Tunnicliff	73 71 70 71 285	A Kankkonen	71 75 73 73 292
	J Lomas	72 73 69 71 285	R Jacquelin	76 70 72 74 292
	V Phillips	71 68 74 72 285	G Emerson	70 73 74 75 292
	M Goggin	71 72 70 72 285	J McHenry	70 75 71 76 292
	B Langer	74 71 67 73 285	A Oldcorn	74 71 75 73 293
	O Edmond	67 73 70 75 285	M Reale	74 71 74 74 293
T20	S Lyle	73 72 71 70 286	S Torrance	75 71 73 74 293
	E Darcy	77 69 68 72 286	J Sandelin	72 71 74 76 293
	J M Singh	75 68 67 76 286	M Jonzon	71 73 73 76 293
T23	P McGinley	73 73 72 69 287	B Lane	71 73 72 77 293
	S Struver	71 73 70 73 287	A Hunter	73 74 69 77 293
T25	P Broadhurst	72 75 72 69 288	D Botes	70 74 69 80 293
	J Spence	71 72 75 70 288	A Clapp	72 73 74 75 294
	R Karlsson	73 72 73 70 288	B Davis	75 72 71 76 294
	G Brand Jr	71 70 75 72 288	H P Thul	75 70 72 77 294
	T Dier (am)	72 69 75 72 288	J Remesy	76 71 70 77 294
	S Grappasonni	70 74 72 72 288	E Canonica	74 73 76 72 295
	I Pyman	73 69 72 74 288	N Henning	74 73 73 75 295
	D Cooper	72 73 69 74 288	D Hospital	73 72 74 76 295
	O Karlsson	70 75 69 74 288	G Owen	71 74 73 77 295
	P Affleck	70 71 71 76 288	D Higgins	77 70 70 78 295
	M Hallberg	72 73 73 71 289	P Linhart	71 72 73 79 295
	M Gates	73 74 70 72 289	J Hawksworth	73 73 75 75 296
	R Johnson	70 72 74 73 289	G Hutcheon	74 73 71 78 296
	R McFarlane	73 70 73 73 289	K Brink	72 74 75 76 297
	C Hainline	72 74 70 73 289	B Dredge	72 75 74 76 297
	A Beal	69 72 69 79 289	M Farry	74 73 72 78 297
	A Sandywell	69 76 76 69 290	J Van de Velde	71 76 73 78 298
	P Quirici	74 71 72 73 290	P Platz	73 74 73 80 300

ROUND BY ROUND LEADERBOARD

FIRST ROUND		SECOND ROUND	
P Lawrie	5 under	M Campbell	7 under
M Campbell	5 under	S Henderson	5 under
I Garrido	5 under	I Garrido	5 under
O Edmond	5 under	V Phillips	5 under
R Claydon	4 under	K Tomori	4 under
A Beal	3 under	O Edmond	4 under
S Webster	3 under	P Lawrie	4 under
A Sandywell	3 under	S ALLAN	1 under
S ALLAN	level		

THIRD ROUND		FINAL ROUND	
I Garrido	9 under	S ALLAN	8 under
M Roe	6 under	M Roe	7 under
A Beal	6 under	S Webster	7 under
J Singh	6 under	I Garrido	7 under
O Edmond	6 under	P Harrington	7 under
M Campbell	6 under		
S ALLAN	5 under		

PUNTERS' POINTS

- This was a real thriller in the best Agatha Christie tradition. The mystery was not solved until the final curtain as the main suspects Mark Roe (at the 17th) and Padraig Harrington (at the last) dropped shots so that young Aussie Stephen Allan became the winner despite a triple bogey (!) six at the short 13th.

- The 24-year-old Melbourne-born Aussie was runner-up in the amateur German Open in his last year as an amateur, so he certainly had PMAs with the country.

- He now joins the line of hungry young Aussies who join the European tour and go on to success. As a 'breed' they tend to be good wind players, well suited to links conditions and very competitive. Once 'alone' on the tour thousands of miles from home they must sink or swim, and we can be sure this won't be the last Euro success for the new breed of young Aussies.

- 40/1 Padraig Harrington has had a very disappointing season as he has struggled with his long game. However, here he played well until that very last drive in R4.

- Mark Roe, generously priced at 33/1 by Ladbrokes at halfway, missed a few makeable putts on the back nine before his bogey at the penultimate hole cost him his chance. On the 'comeback trail' after personal problems he's now remarried, refocussed and returning to his best form.

- Having finished T24th in the 1995 British Open it was no surprise to find T2nd Steve Webster enjoying this links course. Still only 22 he's going to make a real name for himself over the next few years.

- Defending champion Ignacio Garrido has had a very disappointing season especially with his putter. Starting R4 three shots ahead and the odds-on favourite he lost his rhythm in a disappointing 74. Let's hope he can regain his final-round confidence.

- Among those to miss the cut were 50/1 DYM Thomas Gogele, and 66/1 chances Mats Lanner and Philip Price. 66/1 Philip Walton withdrew.

1997 RESULT

1	66/1	Ignacio Garrido
2	100/1	Russell Claydon
3	50/1	Mark James
T4	100/1	Richard Green
T4 fav	8/1	Bernhard Langer
T4	150/1	Per Haugsrud
T4	200/1	Brian Davis

WINNERS IN THE '90s

1990	Mark McNulty	Hubbelrath
1991	Mark McNulty	Hubbelrath
1992	Vijay Singh	Hubbelrath
1993	Bernhard Langer	Hubbelrath
1994	Colin Montgomerie	Hubbelrath
1995	Colin Montgomerie	Nippenburg
1996	Ian Woosnam	Nippenburg
1997	Ignacio Garrido	Nippenburg
1998	Stephen Allan	Sporting Club, Berlin

PUNTERS' GUIDE

- Two points are worth noting:-
  > Last year's advice stands......"be wary of this tournament unless you're backing players at big prices".

  In the last four years of the 24 players placed in the top 4 (or tied 4th) no fewer than 14 (58.3%) have been best priced at or over 100/1.
  > It is also worth noting that the last two champions have both been first-time winners.

- So in 1999 it may be wise to go for a young, fast-improving 'hungry' player in the "winner about to happen" category with an aptitude for links golf who is at a big price.

THE SMURFIT EUROPEAN OPEN

Date	20th – 23rd August
Course	The K Club, Dublin
Par	72
Yardage	7,179
First Prize	£208,300
Total Purse	£1.25 million

For the fourth successive year the Arnold Palmer designed K Club course at Dublin was the venue for the European Open. This year the course had been 'tightened up' with the fairways being narrowed by up to 13 yards so it would provide a tougher test than in the past. It is hoped that the course will be the venue for the Ryder Cup in 2005.

1998 ODDS

fav	11/1	Colin Montgomerie	50/1	Ignacio Garrido*
	12/1	Lee Westwood	50/1	Retief Goosen
	18/1	Darren Clarke	50/1	Paul Broadhurst
	20/1	Ian Woosnam	50/1	Stephen Ames
	22/1	Bernhard Langer	50/1	Stephen Leaney
	22/1	J M Olazabal	66/1	David Howell
	22/1	P U Johansson (DC2)	66/1	Mark James
	28/1	Costantino Rocca	66/1	M A Jimenez
	28/1	Thomas Bjorn	66/1	Sam Torrance
	40/1	Payne Stewart*	66/1	David Gilford
	40/1	Eduardo Romero	66/1	Stephen Allan
	40/1	Peter Baker	66/1	Alexander Cejka
	40/1	Paul McGinley	66/1	Jarmo Sandelin
	50/1	Padraig Harrington		

27 players were best priced at or under 66/1.

BOOKIES AT ODDS

DYM T2nd Phillip Price 50/1 Hills: 125/1 Corals
Winner Mathias Gronberg 80/1 Corals: 125/1 Sunderlands, Surrey

1998 RESULT

1	125/1	Mathias Gronberg	68 71 67 69	275
T2	66/1	M A Jimenez	73 72 71 69	285
T2	125/1	Phillip Price	72 74 68 71	285
4	18/1	Darren Clarke	69 74 70 73	286
T5	125/1	Angel Cabrera	72 73 75 67	287
T5	100/1	Craig Hainline	71 69 69 78	287

T7	P Broadhurst	72 73 71 72 288		I Garbutt	74 75 73 73 295
	J Van de Velde	78 69 69 72 288		R Boxall	77 72 73 73 295
	B Langer	73 65 75 75 288		J M Olazabal	75 73 75 72 295
T10	C Rocca	72 73 72 72 289		S Grappasonni	74 75 74 72 295
	S Torrance	71 76 70 72 289		G Nicklaus	74 66 77 78 295
	B Lane	75 69 72 73 289		I Woosnam	73 70 72 80 295
	D Gilford	75 74 68 72 289		J Payne	73 72 75 76 296
	P Lawrie	72 72 72 73 289		T Levet	73 76 72 75 296
	J Rivero	72 66 75 76 289		M Davis	73 74 74 75 296
T16	P Haugsrud	72 73 73 72 290		W Westner	75 73 74 74 296
	P Baker	72 76 70 72 290		P Affleck	77 72 74 73 296
	S Luna	72 73 76 69 290		J Spence	75 71 75 76 297
	E Romero	74 73 76 67 290		P Eales	74 75 76 72 297
T20	J Coceres	74 75 69 73 291		S Struver	77 71 75 75 298
	R Wessels	71 71 73 76 291		S Ames	73 76 76 73 298
	P McGinley	72 72 71 76 291		M Mackenzie	71 77 74 77 299
T23	P Harrington	71 74 74 73 292		A Beal	78 70 75 76 299
	J Wade	76 69 76 71 292		K Brink	75 74 75 75 299
	F Tarnaud	73 74 74 71 292		D Edlund	76 73 75 75 299
	J Sandelin	72 77 73 70 292		P Walton	76 71 75 78 300
	T Bjorn	76 70 69 77 292		D McGrane	74 74 76 76 300
	P Fulke	78 71 70 74 293		R Jacquelin	76 73 76 75 300
	G Owen	72 75 73 73 293		D Carter	74 75 77 74 300
	M Tunnicliff	74 74 72 73 293		R Chapman	75 71 77 79 302
	P Hedblom	76 72 72 73 293		D Smyth	73 75 79 75 302
	F Cea	71 75 72 76 294		D Lynn	76 73 78 75 302
	M James	75 71 73 75 294		D Robertson	74 73 77 82 306
	S Leaney	77 70 72 75 294		P Senior	76 73 75 82 306
	S Tinning	73 75 73 73 294		S Kjeldsen	75 74 75 83 307
	S Henderson	75 73 73 73 294		L Westwood	77 71 77Rtd
	I Garrido	77 71 72 75 295			

The 36-hole cut was made at 149 – 5 over par – 67 players qualified.

ROUND BY ROUND LEADERBOARD

FIRST ROUND		SECOND ROUND	
M GRONBERG	4 under	B Langer	6 under
D Clarke	3 under	J Rivero	6 under
R Wessells	1 under	M GRONBERG	5 under
F Cea	1 under	C Hainline	4 under
C Hainline	1 under	G Nicklaus	4 under
P Harrington	1 under	R Wessels	2 under
S Torrance	1 under	D Clarke	1 under
M Mackenzie	1 under	I Woosnam	1 under

THIRD ROUND		FINAL ROUND	
M GRONBERG	10 under	M GRONBERG	13 under
C Hainline	7 under	M A Jimenez	3 under
D Clarke	3 under	P Price	3 under
J Rivero	3 under	D Clarke	2 under
B Langer	3 under	A Cabrera	1 under
P Price	2 under	C Hainline	1 under
P McGinley	1 under		
I Woosnam	1 under		

PUNTERS' POINTS

- For the third successive year Europe's most valuable (non-major) tournament was won by a Swede as Mathias Gronberg strolled unchallenged to a very comfortable 10-shot victory. We now know two things about the 28-year-old winner.

  > He can handle the pressure when ahead. As with his last victory, the 1995 Canon European Masters, he held onto a R3 lead.

  > He is clearly at ease with himself following his American holiday with his US fiancee Tara.

- Darren Clarke—inspired by the 'nappy factor'—was also deeply saddened by the Omagh atrocity which disturbed his concentration, particularly in R3 before and after the one minute's silence. Nevertheless he finished alone in 4th and was top Irish player.

- As already mentioned, the course had been tightened up a lot since last year with most of the fairways narrowed by up to 13 yards. So it was not surprising to see just six players beat par. Punters must remember that this year's form will therefore be more reliable than the previous three years when analysing the 1999 field.

- Paul McGinley is the professional attached to the K Club, and he was consulted over the changes to the course. However, although playing well from tee to green, he was never happy on the greens. Expect him to make a bold bid here in 1999 after three successive top 20s....so long as his putting touch returns.

- Corals created a 16-runner market for the Top USPGA player (i.e. players who played or were invited to play in the USPGA). The result was 1st 9/1

Darren Clarke, 2nd 8/1 Bernhard Langer, 3rd 12/1 Costantino Rocca and 4th 16/1 Eduardo Romero. The place odds were 1/4 1,2,3,4.

- Sunderlands and Corals opened a Top Irish player market in which the front three in the betting finished 1,2,3 with the final result. 1st 15/8 Darren Clarke, 2nd 7/2 Paul McGinley and 3rd 5/1 Padraig Harrington.
- Those missing the cut included 11/1 fav. Colin Montgomerie, 22/1 defending champion P U Johansson, 66/1 Alexander Cejka, and 80/1 outsiders Joakim Haeggman, Greg Chalmers, Peter Lonard and Gordon Brand Jr.
- Van Phillips, Massimi Florioli, Heinz Peter Thul, Niclas Fasth and Oliver Edmond retired.

1997 RESULT

1	40/1	P U Johansson
2	100/1	Peter Baker
T3	20/1	J M Olazabal
T3	40/1	Raymond Russell

WINNERS IN THE '90s

1990	Peter Senior	Sunningdale
1991	Mike Harwood	Walton Heath
1992	Nick Faldo	Sunningdale
1993	Gordon Brand Jr	East Sussex National
1994	David Gilford	East Sussex National
1995	Bernhard Langer	K Club, Dublin
1996	P U Johansson	K Club, Dublin
1997	P U Johansson	K Club, Dublin
1998	M Gronberg	K Club, Dublin

PUNTERS' GUIDE

- It is clear that there are four players well suited to the K Club course

	1998	1997	1996
> Paul Broadhurst	T7th	T10	T6
> Costantino Rocca	T10th	T5	2
> Eduardo Romero	T16th	T10	9
> Per Haugsrud	T16th	T10	T10

- Do make a note of the weather forecast before deciding on an outright selection as if the winds blow, as in R3 this year, the K Club provides a severe test.

THE BMW INTERNATIONAL OPEN

Date	27th – 30th August
Course	Golfclub Munchen, Nord-Eichenried
Par	72
Yardage	6,923
First Prize	£141,330
Total Purse	£850,000

The BMW International was played for the second successive year at the Golfclub Munchen course which was the tournament's venue from 1989-93. It is the flattest course on the European tour which becomes, in essence, almost a putting contest.

1998 ODDS

fav	10/1	Colin Montgomerie	40/1	Peter Baker
	12/1	Darren Clarke	40/1	Paul McGinley
	12/1	Bernhard Langer	50/1	Robert Karlsson (DC)
	22/1	J M Olazabal	50/1	Phillip Price
	22/1	Ian Woosnam	50/1	Sam Torrance
	25/1	Thomas Bjorn	50/1	Mathias Gronberg (PWW)
	25/1	Costantino Rocca	66/1	David Gilford*
	33/1	Eduardo Romero	66/1	David Howell
	33/1	Patrik Sjoland	66/1	Jarmo Sandelin
	33/1	M A Jimenez	66/1	Paul Lawrie*
	40/1	Paul Broadhurst*	66/1	Alexander Cejka

22 players were best priced at or under 66/1.

BOOKIES AT ODDS

The winner Russell Claydon 66/1 Tote: 125/1 Surrey

1998 RESULT

1	125/1	Russell Claydon	66 72 64 68	270
2	125/1	Jamie Spence	68 71 66 66	271
3	125/1	Thomas Gogele	65 71 67 69	272
T4	80/1	Angel Cabrera	69 72 65 67	273
T4	12/1	Bernhard Langer	68 67 67 71	273

T6	A Beal	68 71 66 69 274	G Nicklaus	69 71 68 76 284
	M A Jimenez	69 71 67 67 274	D Howell	69 72 72 71 284
	T Bjorn	64 67 72 71 274	F Jacobson	68 72 73 71 284
	D Cooper	71 66 69 68 274	P Fowler	68 74 72 70 284
	K Tomori	67 70 73 64 274	O Edmond	72 70 69 73 284
11	P Fulke	72 68 70 65 275	A Clapp	68 72 69 75 284
12	D Hospital	70 70 68 68 276	F Cea	70 72 77 66 285
T13	P Eales	68 69 72 68 277	P Broadhurst	70 69 69 77 285
	P Senior	70 71 71 65 277	T Karlsson	72 68 69 76 285
	D Clarke	68 70 67 72 277	E Romero	72 68 73 72 285
T16	M Lanner	70 68 72 68 278	S Tinning	69 72 70 74 285
	S Torrance	69 70 72 67 278	J Bickerton	70 70 74 72 286
T18	S Webster	69 69 72 70 280	A Oldcorn	70 67 72 77 286
	J Van de Velde	69 69 68 74 280	M Reale	67 75 71 73 286
	C Rocca	70 71 71 68 280	M Jonzon	68 74 71 74 287
	J M Olazabal	70 66 73 71 280	F Tarnaud	73 68 74 72 287
	G Chalmers	70 71 66 73 280	D Lynn	69 72 71 75 287
	S Kjeldsen	68 73 71 68 280	M Tunnicliff	71 70 70 76 287
T24	S Luna	70 71 69 71 281	D Borrego	68 69 75 76 288
	S Struver	65 69 74 73 281	P Baker	69 73 73 73 288
	O Karlsson	72 69 74 67 282	G Owen	69 70 76 73 288
	R Jacquelin	73 69 70 70 282	M Long	70 72 73 73 288
	R Chapman	69 72 69 72 282	S Ballesteros	72 66 74 77 289
	M Roe	70 70 70 72 282	J Payne	69 73 73 74 289
	E Darcy	68 71 70 73 282	S Henderson	68 73 77 72 290
	I Garbutt	68 73 72 69 282	D Gilford	70 71 74 75 290
	P Lawrie	70 69 72 71 282	M Gates	73 69 69 79 290
	M Mouland	69 68 72 73 282	M Campbell	71 70 76 74 291
	B May	72 70 69 71 282	R Boxall	72 67 77 75 291
	M Hallberg	70 71 70 71 282	S Field	68 74 77 73 292
	B Davis	71 71 70 71 283	D Tapping	68 73 78 78 297

The 36-hole cut was made at 142 – 2 under par – 67 players qualified.

ROUND BY ROUND LEADERBOARD

FIRST ROUND		SECOND ROUND	
T Bjorn	8 under	T Bjorn	13 under
T Gogele	7 under	S Struver	10 under
S Struver	7 under	B Langer	9 under
R CLAYDON	6 under	J M Olazabal	8 under
M Reale	5 under	T Gogele	8 under
T Dier	5 under	Seven players at	7 under
K Tomori	5 under	R CLAYDON	6 under

THIRD ROUND		FINAL ROUND	
B Langer	14 under	R CLAYDON	18 under
R CLAYDON	14 under	J Spence	17 under
T Gogele	13 under	T Gogele	16 under
T Bjorn	13 under	A Cabrera	15 under
A Beal	11 under	B Langer	15 under
D Clarke	11 under		
J Spence	11 under		

PUNTERS' POINTS

- In Russell Claydon's player profile last year it was suggested that this year "inspired by 'the nappy factor'.....he could well gain his first win, possibly in Germany where his record is particularly good".

  > Here on a course he knew well, having made the cut both in 1993 and 1997, he recorded his first tour win, although punters had been discouraged after he had missed three of the last four cuts.

- 12/1 Bernhard Langer has yet to win this tournament. However in what became a virtual R4 match with Claydon he found the Cambridgeshire man too good, especially on the greens.

- Thomas Gogele had another chance to record his first win here, but his long game was not at its best in R4. However he goes well on this course with a stroke average, in his last twelve rounds here of 68.9.

- On a course where low scoring is standard those with a hot putter inevitably do well, so it was no surprise to see 'off the pace' Jamie Spence shoot 66 in R4 to post a clubhouse target.

- Miguel Angel Jimenez clearly enjoys this tournament. 12th in 1993, 9th 1997 and T6th this year he'll have a real chance here in good weather again in 1999.

- At this time of the year many players are looking to retain their tour card for next year which may explain why so many long priced players play well on a course which does not place a premium on accuracy.

- With course form so important it was disappointing to read in the Racing Post that the course was being used for the second time when it had been the venue from 1989-93 inclusive. The course form point is developed in Punters' Guide.

- Among those missing the cut were 10/1 fav Colin Montgomerie, 22/1 Ian Woosnam (subsequently disqualified), 33/1 Patrik Sjoland, 40/1 Paul

McGinley, 50/1 Phillip Price and 80/1 DYMs Mark James and Mathew Goggin.

1997 RESULT

1	80/1	Robert Karlsson
		(Karlsson won at the third play-off hole)
2	250/1	Carl Watts
3 fav	9/1	Colin Montgomerie
4	200/1	Fabrice Tarnaud

WINNERS IN THE '90s

1990	Paul Azinger	Golfclub Munchen
1991	Sandy Lyle	Golfclub Munchen
1992	Paul Azinger	Golfclub Munchen
1993	Peter Fowler	Golfclub Munchen
1994	Mark McNulty	St Eurach Land-und GC
1995	Frank Nobilo	St Eurach Land-und GC
1996	Marc Farry*	St Eurach Land-und GC
1997	Robert Karlsson	Golfclub Munchen
1998	Russell Claydon	Golfclub Munchen

* Tournament reduced to 36 holes

PUNTERS' GUIDE

- In the last 2 years seven of the nine players who have finished in the first four (or T4th) have been best priced at or over 80/1 with five of them at or over 125/1. So outsiders have an excellent recent record.
- An interesting pointer to the importance of course form is the fact that thirteen players had made the cut here in both 1993 and 1997. They included four of this year's top 6 (or T6th) viz Claydon, Gogele, Langer and Jimenez.

THE CANON EUROPEAN MASTERS

Date	3rd – 6th September
Course	Crans-sur-Sierre, Switzerland
Par	71
Yardage	6,747
First Prize	£133,330
Total Purse	£800,000

Once more this tournament was the first to count for qualification points for the 1999 Ryder Cup.

The course is very picturesque sitting high on an Alpine Plateau. It plays very short as the ball flies through the thin air so it's not surprising to find the course record is just 60!

1998 ODDS

fav	11/1	Colin Montgomerie	50/1	Ignacio Garrido
	14/1	Darren Clarke	66/1	Retief Goosen
	14/1	Lee Westwood	66/1	Peter Lonard
	18/1	Thomas Bjorn	66/1	David Howell
	22/1	J M Olazabal	66/1	Jean Van de Velde
	22/1	Costantino Rocca (DC)	66/1	David Gilford
	33/1	Nick Faldo	66/1	Padraig Harrington
	33/1	Eduardo Romero	66/1	Russell Claydon (PWW)
	40/1	Sam Torrance	66/1	Greg Chalmers
	40/1	Patrik Sjoland	66/1	Jamie Spence
	40/1	Andrew Coltart	66/1	Paul McGinley
	40/1	M A Jimenez	66/1	Katsuyoshi Tomori
	50/1	Stephen Leaney	66/1	Robert Karlsson

26 players were best priced at or under 66/1.

BOOKIES AT ODDS

The winner Sven Struver 50/1 Chandler, Coral, Stan James, Tote 80/1 Ladbrokes

1998 RESULT

1	80/1	Sven Struver	69 63 65 66	263

(Struver won at the first extra play-off)

2	40/1	Patrik Sjoland	65 66 62 70	263
3	14/1	Darren Clarke	64 68 66 67	265
4	22/1	Costantino Rocca	67 66 67 68	268
T5	80/1	Alexander Cejka	70 66 67 66	269
T5	100/1	Gordon Brand Jr	68 68 66 67	269

T7	M A Jimenez	67 69 70 64 270		M Farry	72 67 69 70 278
	J Van de Velde	67 66 72 65 270		I Giner	71 69 68 70 278
	R Karlsson	69 69 66 66 270		R Boxall	70 69 66 73 278
	M Gronberg	69 68 64 69 270		R Coles	68 71 73 67 279
11	S Henderson	68 66 68 69 271		F Cea	68 72 69 70 279
T12	C Montgomerie	70 66 69 67 272		M Mackenzie	70 69 69 71 279
	S Torrance	67 68 70 67 272		P Senior	72 68 68 71 279
	L Westwood	70 68 66 68 272		P Haugsrud	66 71 70 72 279
T15	D Gilford	73 66 67 67 273		L-W Zhang	69 70 68 72 279
	R Jacquelin	70 67 68 68 273		G Nicklaus	70 69 73 68 280
	P Lonard	70 66 67 70 273		J Payne	69 71 71 69 280
T18	S Grappasonni	68 71 65 70 274		P Price	68 70 71 71 280
	C Bovet	68 64 70 72 274		A Sherborne	67 69 72 72 280
T20	M Reale	71 69 70 65 275		G Owen	70 68 69 73 280
	M Lanner	70 67 70 68 275		A Beal	69 70 75 67 281
	E Romero	66 71 70 68 275		S Leaney	74 66 72 69 281
	P Fulke	69 71 67 68 275		J Lomas	69 71 71 70 281
	R Goosen	69 70 67 69 275		S Scahill	71 68 71 71 281
	S Luna	69 67 69 70 275		J Spence	70 69 70 72 281
	M Hallberg	68 71 70 67 276		J M Olazabal	70 70 69 72 281
	R Chapman	72 68 69 67 276		H Clark	70 69 71 72 282
	P Eales	69 67 72 68 276		B Dredge	71 67 72 73 283
	M Roe	67 70 67 72 276		R Wessels	68 72 70 73 283
	S Ballesteros	70 70 70 67 277		M Mouland	70 70 75 69 284
	J Rivero	68 68 73 68 277		M Cunning	71 66 73 74 284
	T Bjorn	69 70 68 70 277		K Tomori	69 68 73 74 284
	G Orr	68 70 68 71 277		G Evans	70 69 70 75 284
	J Sandelin	68 72 66 71 277		A Clapp	73 67 73 72 285
	F Tarnaud	71 66 68 72 277		J M Singh	71 69 75 73 288
	P Harrington	70 69 65 73 277		B Lane	72 68 74 74 288
	A Cabrera	71 68 70 69 278		A Wall	71 68 72 82 293

The 36-hole cut was made at 140 – 2 under par 68 players qualified.

ROUND BY ROUND LEADERBOARD

FIRST ROUND

D Clarke	7 under
P Sjoland	6 under
O Karlsson	5 under
E Romero	5 under
P Haugsrud	5 under
C Rocca	4 under
J Van de Velde	4 under
S Torrance	4 under
M A Jimenez	4 under
A Sherborne	4 under
M Roe	4 under
S STRUVER	2 under

SECOND ROUND

P Sjoland	11 under
D Clarke	10 under
S STRUVER	10 under
C Bovet	10 under
J Van de Velde	9 under
C Rocca	9 under

THIRD ROUND

P Sjoland	20 under
S STRUVER	16 under
D Clarke	15 under
C Rocca	13 under
M Gronberg	12 under
G Brand Jr	11 under
S Henderson	11 under
C Bovet	11 under

FINAL ROUND

S STRUVER	21 under
P Sjoland	21 under
D Clarke	19 under
C Rocca	16 under
A Cejka	15 under
G Brand Jr	15 under

PUNTERS' POINTS

- 80/1 Sven Struver won his third European tournament with a superb final-round display of sound nerve and sound putting. He caught Sjoland, then slipped 3 back and caught him again as the Swede showed signs of final-round nerves.
- In the play-off both played the 18th hole well. However Struver (putting second) holed out to gain a 5-year tour exemption, to take the lead in the Ryder Cup table, and to gain a massive confidence boost.
- In the play-off betting Stan James went 5/6 each of two before money for Struver saw the odds move to 8/11 the German and evens the Swede.
- 40/1 Sjoland, whose sole win was in the rain-reduced 3-round Italian Open in early May, found out what final-round pressure was all about. His fiance Ulrika could not act as his caddie as she was recovering from appendicitis, although she was a spectator.
- 3rd placed Darren Clarke was posting his fifth top 5 of the season. It took him to within £5,500 of Lee Westwood at the top of the Order of Merit.
- T5th Alex Cejka's 14 under par for the final three rounds for the player top of the greens in regulation stats indicated that his putter is at last warming up!
- Robert Karlsson over the last two years (2nd last year, T7th this) has now got a stroke average of 67.125 with all eight rounds in the sixties. The tallest swinger on tour will surely be worth a bet at Crans-Sur-Sierre in 1999!

• Among those to miss the cut were 33/1 Nick Faldo, 40/1 Andrew Coltart, 50/1 Ignacio Garrido, and 66/1 outsiders Russell Claydon (MLD?), David Howell and Greg Chalmers.

1997 RESULT

1	28/1	Costantino Rocca
T2	40/1	Robert Karlsson
T2	125/1	Scott Henderson
T4	150/1	Peter Lonard
T4	80/1	Patrik Sjoland

WINNERS IN THE '90s

1990	Ronan Rafferty
1991	Jeff Hawkes
1992	Jamie Spence
1993	Barry Lane
1994	Eduardo Romero
1995	Mathias Gronberg
1996	Colin Montgomerie
1997	Costantino Rocca
1998	Sven Struver

PUNTERS' GUIDE

• The most consistent players on this course over the last four years have been:
  > Darren Clarke 3rd 1998: 6th 1997: 4th 1996: 6th 1995
  > Costantino Rocca 4th 1998: Won 1997: 2nd 1995
  > Colin Montgomerie T12th 1998: 10th 1997: Won 1996: 11th 1995
  > Jean Van de Velde T7th 1998: Made cut in 1997, 1996 and 1995.

• However with no Ryder Cup points at stake the best value will surely lie with the two Swedes whose chances are shown in their Player Profiles.

THE ONE 2 ONE BRITISH MASTERS

Date	10th – 13th September
Course	Marriott Forest of Arden, Coventry
Par	72
Yardage	7,134
First Prize	£125,000
Total Purse	£750,000

For the second successive year the One 2 One British Masters was played at the Forest of Arden course which had been the venue for the English Open from 1993 – 96 so there was plenty of course form. The course requires length and accuracy off the tee. The greens are very good, helping the best putters.

1998 ODDS

fav	10/1	Colin Montgomerie	50/1	Andrew Coltart
	12/1	Darren Clarke	50/1	Alexander Cejka
	14/1	Lee Westwood	50/1	Peter Baker
	20/1	Thomas Bjorn (non-runner)	50/1	Paul Broadhurst
	28/1	Costantino Rocca	66/1	Padraig Harrington
	28/1	Ian Woosnam	66/1	Greg Turner (DC)*
	33/1	J M Olazabal	66/1	Mathias Gronberg*
	33/1	M A Jimenez	66/1	Ignacio Garrido
	40/1	Eduardo Romero	66/1	Jean Van de Velde
	40/1	P U Johansson	66/1	Peter Lonard
	40/1	Retief Goosen	66/1	Paul McGinley
	40/1	Sam Torrance	66/1	Stephen Leaney*
	50/1	Sven Struver (PWW)	66/1	Angel Cabrera

26 players were best priced at or under 66/1.

BOOKIES AT ODDS

T4th DYM Andrew Oldcorn 100/1 Corals: 200/1 Surrey, Sunderlands

Winner Colin Montgomerie 8/1 Corals: 10/1 Surrey, Tote, Stanley, Stan James, Ladbrokes, Hills

1998 RESULT

1	10/1	**Colin Montgomerie**	70 72 70 69	**281**
T2	125/1	**Pierre Fulke**	71 72 72 67	**282**
T2	40/1	**Eduardo Romero**	70 69 75 68	**282**
T4	200/1	**Andrew Oldcorn**	71 73 71 68	**283**
T4	66/1	**Ignacio Garrido**	70 73 71 69	**283**
T4	125/1	**Paolo Quirici**	68 73 70 72	**283**

7	G Owen	70 71 73 70 284
T8	J Bickerton	70 75 73 67 285
	R Claydon	72 73 68 72 285
	S Torrance	69 72 71 73 285
	D Chopra	71 72 69 73 285
T12	G Chalmers	72 73 74 67 286
	A Kankkonen	71 69 76 70 286
	L Westwood	73 70 73 70 286
	S Kjeldsen	72 71 72 71 286
	I Woosnam	75 66 73 72 286
	S Garcia	71 73 69 73 286
	M Roe	72 69 71 74 286
	M Farry	73 72 67 74 286
T20	P Broadhurst	79 65 74 69 287
	M Lanner	71 73 73 70 287
	M A Jimenez	70 75 72 70 287
	M Campbell	71 69 76 71 287
	P O'Malley	73 71 72 71 287
	C Rocca	71 72 71 73 287
	C Suneson	69 69 75 74 287
	O Karlsson	75 67 71 74 287
	C Hainline	72 71 70 74 287
	D Clarke	67 71 74 75 287
	R Coles	73 72 76 67 288
	P Mitchell	75 70 73 70 288
	M Long	75 69 73 71 288
	R Lee	69 74 73 72 288
	S Luna	70 73 73 72 288
	R Drummond	72 72 69 75 288
	M Gronberg	75 70 75 69 289
	K Storgaard	75 69 75 70 289
	G Hutcheon	72 70 71 76 289
	C Mason	72 73 68 76 289
	T Immelman (am)	71 71 76 72 290
	J Lomas	72 72 74 72 290
	P Haugsrud	72 72 72 74 290
	D Borrego	72 70 73 75 290
	J Coceres	74 70 71 75 290
	A Beal	71 71 74 75 291
	R Chapman	76 69 71 75 291
	M Mouland	72 71 72 76 291
	A Coltart	72 70 72 77 291
	R Boxall	73 70 71 77 291
	I Pyman	76 69 76 71 291
	M Florioli	75 70 75 72 292
	V Phillips	73 72 73 74 292
	T Levet	76 69 73 74 292
	G Orr	71 73 73 75 292
	R Wessels	72 70 73 77 292
	A Cabrera	73 69 71 79 292
	S Allan	71 72 80 70 293
	T Johnstone	73 72 76 72 293
	G Evans	74 71 75 73 293
	S Leaney	74 69 74 76 293
	S Richardson	74 70 73 76 293
	P Baker	72 73 71 77 293
	S Grappasonni	71 72 77 74 294
	S Struver	71 73 76 74 294
	D Howell	72 73 73 76 294
	P U Johansson	72 71 74 77 294
	C Watts	71 74 71 78 294
	P Senior	71 74 74 76 295
	J Payne	74 71 73 77 295
	B Lane	73 72 77 74 296
	J Sandelin	70 69 76 82 297
	S Cage	75 68 83 73 299

The 36-hole cut was made at 145 – 1 over par – 72 players qualified.

ROUND BY ROUND LEADERBOARD

FIRST ROUND		SECOND ROUND	
D Clarke	5 under	D Clarke	6 under
P Quirici	4 under	C Suneson	6 under
S Torrance	3 under	J Sandelin	5 under
C Suneson	3 under	M Campbell	4 under
R Lee	3 under	A Kankkonen	4 under
A Sherborne	3 under	S Torrance	3 under
C MONTGOMERIE	2 under	P Quirici	3 under
		I Woosnam	3 under
		M Roe	3 under
		C MONTGOMERIE	2 under

THIRD ROUND		FINAL ROUND	
P Quirici	5 under	C MONTGOMERIE	7 under
M Farry	4 under	P Fulke	6 under
C MONTGOMERIE	4 under	E Romero	6 under
D Chopra	4 under	A Oldcorn	5 under
M Roe	4 under	I Garrido	5 under
S Torrance	4 under	P Quirici	5 under
D Clarke	4 under		

PUNTERS' POINTS

- Although some way below his best 10/1 favourite Monty came from 'off the pace' on the final day to win after first Pierre Fulke, and then Eduardo Romero had set the clubhouse target.
- Monty enjoys this course particularly as it is close to home. His Forest of Arden record now is surely unsurpassed by any player on any course anywhere – 3 wins, and 2 seconds in five tournaments.
- The wet blustery conditions led to a really bunched field over the last couple of rounds. Players who played well here over the final 36 holes showed not only skill but a whole load of patience – a point we must remember in future.
- Surely 'the winner without a penalty' was Ignacio Garrido who was given a 4-stroke penalty after his caddie inadvertently left an extra club in his bag. Without that the young Spaniard would have been the 2-shot winner.....assuming everything else was unchanged.
- Paolo Quirici, who played well here last year (T15th), is a good player especially in tough conditions, a point noted in his last player profile two years ago. Starting R4 in the lead he did well in the circumstances to shoot par and finish T4th.
- Tee to green Romero and Torrance both looked as good as anyone, yet they could scarcely make a putt.
- The disappointment of the tournament was surely Darren Clarke. Playing well early on (67 – R1) despite a cold, he fell away over the last 36 holes (5 over par!) to bring his recent rich vein of form to an end.

- Jarmo Sandelin, third after R2, showed that patience and course management are not his great strengths as he went 14 over par for the last 36 holes.
- Tucked away in T12th place was Soren Kjeldsen, one of only three players (Monty and Fulke were the others) to have all four rounds at or under par. That was a really praiseworthy effort for the young Dane.
- 100/1 outsider Mark Roe took the lead during R3. However he slipped back to finish T12th. He'll be worth noting here again in 1999 as he has a solid course record including 3rd place here last year.
- Among those missing the cut were 33/1 J M Olazabal, 40/1 Retief Goosen, 50/1 Alexander Cejka and 66/1 outsiders Jean Van de Velde, Padraig Harrington and defending champion Greg Turner.
- Thomas Gogele retired and Paul McGinley withdrew.

1997 RESULT

1	80/1	Greg Turner
2	8/1	Colin Montgomerie
3	100/1	Mark Roe
T4	40/1	Thomas Bjorn
T4	50/1	Raymond Russell

WINNERS IN THE '90s

1990	Mark James	Woburn
1992	Seve Ballesteros	Woburn
1992	Christy O'Connor Jr	Woburn
1993	Peter Baker	Woburn
1994	Ian Woosnam	Woburn
1995	Sam Torrance	Collingtree
1996	Robert Allenby	Collingtree
1997	Greg Turner	Forest of Arden
1998	Colin Montgomerie	Forest of Arden

PUNTERS' GUIDE

> Apart from Monty, five players have finished in the top 20 in each of the last two years.
  * Darren Clarke T20th 1998: T12th 1997
  * Sam Torrance T8th 1998: T6th 1997
  * Mark Roe T12th 1998: 3rd 1997
  * Russell Claydon T8th 1998: T20th 1997
  * Peter O'Malley T20th 1998: T12th 1997
> If in any sort of form in 1999 Monty will surely start as a very short-priced favourite.

THE LANCOME TROPHY

Date	17th – 20th September
Course	St Nom-la-Breteche, Paris
Par	71
Yardage	6,903
First Prize	£133,330
Total Purse	£800,000

With six players (Duval, O'Meara, Parnevik, Couples, Faxon and Faldo) from the American tour there was a very strong field. There was plenty of course form for punters to study as the St Nom-la-Breteche course is the regular home of the Lancome Trophy.

1998 ODDS

fav	10/1	Colin Montgomerie (PWW)	40/1	P U Johansson
	14/1	David Duval	40/1	Patrik Sjoland
	16/1	Mark O'Meara (DC)	50/1	Ignacio Garrido
	16/1	Lee Westwood	50/1	Sam Torrance
	20/1	Jesper Parnevik	50/1	M A Jimenez
	20/1	Fred Couples	66/1	Sven Struver
	22/1	Bernhard Langer	66/1	Nick Faldo*
	28/1	Thomas Bjorn	66/1	Andrew Coltart
	33/1	Ian Woosnam	66/1	Greg Turner
	33/1	Costantino Rocca	66/1	Paul Broadhurst
	40/1	Brad Faxon	66/1	Peter O'Malley
	40/1	Eduardo Romero	66/1	Robert Karlsson

24 players were best priced at or under 66/1.

BOOKIES AT ODDS

Nick Faldo 28/1 Hills: 66/1 Stan James

Winner M A Jimenez 40/1 Corals, Hills Tote: 50/1 Chandlers, Ladbrokes, Stan James

1998 RESULT

1	50/1	M A Jimenez	67 70 67 69	273
T2	14/1	David Duval	69 72 67 67	275
T2	16/1	Mark O'Meara	70 67 69 69	275
T2	150/1	Jarmo Sandelin	68 74 70 63	275
T2	66/1	Greg Turner	67 71 68 69	275

6	N Faldo	70 71 70 65 276		M Campbell	69 72 76 68 285
T7	P O'Malley	68 72 68 69 277		G Evans	71 69 77 68 285
	A Wall	71 70 67 69 277		H Clark	71 72 72 70 285
T9	P U Johansson	75 68 68 68 278		M James	70 68 76 71 285
	F Couples	70 68 70 70 278		C Suneson	72 72 70 71 285
T11	S Torrance	70 73 72 64 279		S Richardson	70 70 71 74 285
	A Cejka	69 69 74 67 279		G Orr	72 69 68 76 285
	G Brand Jr	68 72 69 70 279		P Quirici	73 71 70 72 286
	C Montgomerie	69 68 69 73 279		J Parnevik	73 70 70 73 286
T15	S Grappasonni	74 69 69 68 280		D Cooper	67 72 72 75 286
	R Wessels	73 70 68 69 280		I Pyman	72 69 70 75 286
	P Lonard	71 70 68 71 280		M Long	75 63 78 71 287
T18	F Jacobson	72 70 72 67 281		J Rivero	69 73 71 74 287
	M Hallberg	70 70 73 68 281		E Darcy	67 71 74 75 287
	B Lane	73 69 70 69 281		A Cabrera	70 69 72 76 287
	J Coceres	70 70 71 70 281		M Mouland	71 71 74 72 288
	S Garcia (am)	69 68 73 71 281		F Tarnaud	73 71 71 73 288
	T Levet	72 69 69 71 281		R Davis	72 69 76 71 288
	T Bjorn	74 69 67 71 281		I Giner	74 69 77 69 289
	G Chalmers	72 70 68 71 281		B Davis	70 73 77 69 289
	P Broadhurst	69 71 69 72 281		M Gronberg	69 72 76 72 289
T27	D Gilford	72 69 74 67 282		R Coles	72 71 74 72 289
	O Edmond	74 69 71 68 282		R Goosen	70 73 73 73 289
	M Pendaries	72 69 70 71 282		P Lawrie	72 72 72 73 289
	P Mitchell	69 69 72 72 282		M Farry	68 74 72 75 289
	P McGinley	71 69 70 72 282		R Muntz	73 70 71 75 289
	G Owen	74 70 70 69 283		A Coltart	71 69 73 76 289
	K Tomori	69 70 71 73 283		M Lanner	71 73 78 68 290
	P Walton	73 71 73 67 284		J Payne	71 69 76 74 290
	B Faxon	73 69 73 69 284		R Russell	71 72 73 74 290
	P Sjoland	71 71 72 70 284		A Sherborne	76 68 74 73 291
	B May	69 75 69 71 284		M Jonzon	73 70 78 71 292
	N Vanhootegem	70 72 70 72 284		S Ballesteros	69 73 75 75 292
	O Karlsson	73 71 68 72 284		L Westwood	70 72 73 77 292
	S Allan	67 73 71 73 284			

The 36-hole cut was made at 144 – 2 over par – 75 players qualified.

ROUND BY ROUND LEADERBOARD

FIRST ROUND		SECOND ROUND	
E Darcy	4 under	I Woosnam	7 under
G Turner	4 under	M O'Meara	5 under
M A JIMENEZ	4 under	S Garcia	5 under
S Allan	4 under	M A JIMENEZ	5 under
D Cooper	4 under	C Montgomerie	5 under
J Sandelin	3 under	A Cejka	4 under
M Farry	3 under	P Mitchell	4 under
G Brand Jr	3 under	M Long	4 under
P O'Malley	3 under	E Darcy	4 under
I Woosnam	3 under	G Turner	4 under
		F Couples	4 under
		M James	4 under

THIRD ROUND		FINAL ROUND	
M A JIMENEZ	9 under	M A JIMENEZ	11 under
G Turner	7 under	J Sandelin	9 under
M O'Meara	7 under	D Duval	9 under
C Montgomerie	7 under	M O'Meara	9 under
D Duval	5 under	G Turner	9 under
A Wall	5 under		
P O'Malley	5 under		
F Couples	5 under		

POINTERS' POINTS

- What an amazing finish! First, Jarmo Sandelin, after opening with a bogey, shot a 63 to post a 9 under par clubhouse target. Then the leaders fell away as Duval double-bogeyed and O'Meara bogeyed the final hole. So it was up to Jimenez to par the last, (a par 3) the hardest hole on the course. He pulled his tee shot and a four-way play-off looked likely before the 34-year-old Spaniard chipped in for a birdie 2 to win his fourth European tournament, and his second of the year.

- Having finished T10th in 1996, 2nd in 1994, and with current figures of 2-6-7-20 the 50/1 Spaniard clearly was a player with a chance.

- It was a most encouraging tournament for Nick Faldo as he secured his first Ryder Cup points by finishing sixth. It was the first time he'd been under final round 'pressure' all season.

- Colin Montgomerie's challenge faded as he pulled and hooked off the tee to confirm that his recovery still has some way to go.

- The high finishes of O'Meara, Duval and Couples perhaps gave an early hint of just how difficult the 1999 European Ryder Cup task will be.

- Peter O'Malley, T3rd last year, clearly enjoys this course and posted his second successive top 10 finish here.

- Volatile, impatient, brilliant and with controversy as his companion, Jarmo Sandelin finished second for the second successive year.....and for the second successive year he was involved in controversy.

Last year he accused O'Meara of replacing his ball nearer the hole in a row that rumbled on for months. This year Lee Westwood alleged that Sandelin's ball had moved when he addressed it on Saturday. However the Swede said he hadn't grounded the putter and without any other evidence the case was concluded without a penalty.

- Ian Woosnam had played well from tee to green to be the halfway leader. However his dodgy back then played up again forcing him to withdraw after he shot 77 in R3.

- Among those to miss the cut were 22/1 Bernhard Langer, 33/1 Costantino Rocca, 40/1 Eduardo Romero, 50/1 Ignacio Garrido, 66/1 Sven Struver and 66/1 Robert Karlsson as well as 80/1 outsiders Peter Baker, Mark Roe, Pierre Fulke and Stephen Leaney.

- Raphael Jacquelin was disqualified for dropping his ball in the wrong place after finding water at the 18th during R1. Eduardo Romero made the same error with the resultant penalty causing him to miss the cut for the first time this season.

1997 RESULT

1	33/1	Mark O'Meara
2	80/1	Jarmo Sandelin
T3	9/1	Greg Norman
T3	80/1	Peter O'Malley

WINNERS IN THE '90s

1990	J M Olazabal
1991	Frank Nobilo
1992	Mark Roe
1993	Ian Woosnam
1994	Vijay Singh
1995	Colin Montgomerie
1996	Jesper Parnevik
1997	Mark O'Meara
1998	M A Jimenez

PUNTERS' GUIDE

- In making your selection in 1999 there are three key points to remember.
  > The Lancome trophy is usually won by a proven quality player.
  > In five of the last six years the winner had already recorded a success earlier in the season.
  > If the player has played here before he must have a solid course record.

- In 1999, especially if he's already won earlier in the season, do support Per-Ulrik Johansson (T9th 1998: 18th 1997) who has a stroke average of 69.75 over the last two years. His final 54 holes this year of 9 under par was most impressive and the best in the tournament.

THE LINDE GERMAN MASTERS

Date	24th – 27th September
Course	Gut Larchenhof GC, Cologne, Germany
Par	72
Yardage	7,014
First Prize	£125,000
Total Purse	£1 million

This year the German Masters moved to a new course which had never been used before on the European tour. Jack Nicklaus designed, it had reachable par 5s, and, as usual with his courses, it placed emphasis on course management skills, and tended to favour the 'faders'.

Vijay Singh, Scott Hoch, Brad Faxon and Nick Faldo made this a very strong field.

The tournament is co-sponsored by Bernhard Langer's marketing company.

1998 ODDS

10/1	Colin Montgomerie	40/1	J M Olazabal*
14/1	Darren Clarke	40/1	Patrik Sjoland
16/1	Vijay Singh	40/1	Peter O'Malley
18/1	Bernhard Langer (DC)	50/1	Alexander Cejka
20/1	Scott Hoch	50/1	Paul Broadhurst
20/1	Lee Westwood	50/1	Ignacio Garrido
28/1	Thomas Bjorn	66/1	Jarmo Sandelin*
28/1	M A Jimenez (PWW)	66/1	Sven Struver*
33/1	Nick Faldo	66/1	Retief Goosen
33/1	P U Johansson	66/1	Gordon Brand Jr
33/1	Brad Faxon	66/1	David Gilford
33/1	Costantino Rocca	66/1	Mathias Gronberg
33/1	Sam Torrance	66/1	Paul McGinley
40/1	Greg Turner		

27 players were best priced at or under 66/1.

BOOKIES AT ODDS

J M Olazabal 20/1 Corals: 40/1 Ladbrokes, Stan James, Sunderlands, Surrey
The winner Colin Montgomerie 7/1 Chandler, Corals: 10/1 Surrey

1998 RESULT

1 fav	10/1	**Colin Montgomerie**	**65 68 66 67**	**266**
T2	16/1	**Vijay Singh**	**65 67 69 66**	**265**
T2	80/1	**Robert Karlsson**	**68 65 69 65**	**265**
4	150/1	**Steve Webster**	**68 65 68 67**	**264**
5	33/1	**P U Johansson**	**68 67 67 67**	**263**

T6	L Westwood	66 67 72 66 271		S Struver	66 70 68 73 277
	P McGinley	69 68 67 67 271		M James	69 68 70 71 278
T8	J Sandelin	66 67 74 65 272		R Green	74 68 67 69 278
	J Van de Velde	67 67 70 68 272		P Haugsrud	67 70 69 72 278
	P Harrington	69 64 67 72 272		N Faldo	71 69 70 68 278
T11	G Nicklaus	70 71 67 65 273		P Broadhurst	68 71 71 68 278
	M Farry	68 68 67 70 273		T Gogele	70 68 71 70 279
	R Russell	67 68 68 70 273		V Phillips	65 70 70 74 279
	R Goosen	68 67 67 71 273		P Eales	69 70 70 71 280
T15	K Eriksson	69 71 67 67 274		M Gronberg	71 68 68 73 280
	G Brand Jr	67 70 72 65 274		D Carter	68 70 71 71 280
	B Langer	69 69 68 68 274		C Suneson	68 67 71 74 280
	M Long	71 65 68 70 274		D Gilford	73 68 69 70 280
	R Davis	70 69 63 72 274		S Ballesteros	72 69 69 70 280
	P O'Malley	68 69 65 72 274		M A Jimenez	72 68 72 68 280
T21	P Mitchell	70 68 70 67 275		G Evans	70 67 71 73 281
	M Tunnicliff	68 67 73 67 275		H P Thul	71 71 68 71 281
	J Payne	69 66 71 69 275		S Grappasonni	68 71 71 71 281
	D Clarke	69 70 67 69 275		D Cooper	71 70 70 70 281
	G Turner	68 71 67 69 275		D Hospital	71 71 70 69 281
	J M Olazabal	69 66 70 70 275		J Rivero	69 73 70 69 281
	I Pyman	68 67 69 71 275		S Torrance	71 71 69 72 283
	B Faxon	68 72 68 68 276		R Claydon	74 68 70 71 283
	A Wall	70 68 70 68 276		M Jonzon	73 68 71 71 283
	F Tarnaud	72 70 67 67 276		P Sjoland	73 68 73 69 283
	S Allan	70 68 69 69 276		D Chopra	67 72 71 74 284
	I Garrido	69 70 70 67 276		R Chapman	68 74 71 71 284
	S Henderson	71 71 65 69 276		P Price	69 73 73 69 284
	S Richardson	69 72 69 66 276		F Lubenau	75 67 72 71 285
	S Luna	68 66 71 71 276		P Baker	70 72 71 73 286
	C Rocca	70 68 66 72 276		F Jacobson	72 70 69 76 287
	C Whitelaw	68 70 70 69 277		D Edlund	72 69 71 75 287
	I Garbutt	66 71 69 71 277		D Robertson	73 67 73 75 288
	R Boxall	66 70 69 72 277		J Spence	71 70 77 71 289

ROUND BY ROUND LEADERBOARD

FIRST ROUND

C MONTGOMERIE	7 under
V Singh	7 under
V Phillips	7 under
R Boxall	6 under
S Struver	6 under
L Westwood	6 under
I Garbutt	6 under
J Sandelin	6 under

SECOND ROUND

V Singh	12 under
C MONTGOMERIE	11 under
L Westwood	11 under
S Webster	11 under
P Harrington	11 under
J Sandelin	11 under
R Karlsson	11 under

THIRD ROUND

C MONTGOMERIE	17 under
P Harrington	16 under
V Singh	15 under
S Webster	15 under
P O'Malley	14 under
R Davis	14 under
R Karlsson	14 under
P U Johansson	14 under
R Goosen	14 under

FINAL ROUND

C MONTGOMERIE	22 under
V Singh	21 under
R Karlsson	21 under
S Webster	20 under
P U Johansson	19 under

PUNTERS' POINTS

- Once more, although not at his best, 10/1 Colin Montgomerie showed that he knows how to win. Showing superb course management, he got the par he needed at the last to win and go to the Number 1 position on the Order of Merit.

- US-tour raider 16/1 Vijay Singh found the course suited him. However, three dropped shots on the last two holes in R3 cost him dearly! If he plays here again in 1999 he would have an obvious chance.

- T4th 150/1 Steve Webster is a young player of real promise. He actually led the field during R2 and he will surely have learned a huge amount over the last 36 holes playing in the heat at the top of the leaderboard. He'll surely go on to win golf tournaments.

- It was good to see T8th Padraig Harrington returning to form here. With his long game back in shape he'll be a player to note at nice prices in 1999.

- 80/1 Robert Karlsson's last win was last year in Germany when he was 24 under par in the BMW International. Clearly easy courses in Germany are ideal for the tallest player on the tour.

- Although this course offers more birdies and eagles than a well kept aviary it has a very severe par 4 finishing hole (the hardest on the course) so a player who has set a clubhouse target has a fair chance.

- Among those to miss the cut were 20/1 Scott Hoch, 80/1 Peter Lonard, and 100/1 outsiders David Howell, Paul Lawrie and Mark Roe.

- Thomas Bjorn (70), Alex Cejka (70), Philip Walton (77) all withdrew after R1.

1997 RESULT

1	12/1	Bernhard Langer
2 fav	9/1	Colin Montgomerie
3	28/1	Thomas Bjorn
T4	25/1	Costantino Rocca
T4	20/1	J M Olazabal
T4	50/1	Patrik Sjoland

WINNERS IN THE '90s

1990	Sam Torrance
1991	Bernhard Langer
1992	Barry Lane
1993	Steven Richardson
1994	Seve Ballesteros
1995	Anders Forsbrand
1996	Darren Clarke
1997	Bernhard Langer
1998	Colin Montgomerie
1990 – 1993	Monsheim, Stuttgart
1994 – 1997	Motzener See, Berlin
1998	Gut Larchenhof, Cologne

PUNTERS' GUIDE

With reachable par 5s Gut Larchenhof clearly favours the longer-hitting players. Two players to consider at sensible prices in 1999 would be Retief Goosen (T11th 1998) and Jarmo Sandelin (T8th 1998 after a 65 in R4).

THE BELGACOM OPEN

Date	1st – 4th October
Course	Royal Zoute, Belgium
Par	71
Yardage	6,907
First Prize	£66,660
Total Purse	£400,000

The Royal Zoute course was being used for the first time in over four years. It was last played on the tour in 1992, 1993 and 1994. It is a picturesque links-style course in which sea breezes can play a part.

1998 ODDS

fav	8/1	Lee Westwood	40/1	Padraig Harrington
	14/1	Bernhard Langer (non runner)	40/1	Paul McGinley
	16/1	P U Johansson	40/1	Andrew Coltart
	20/1	Nick Faldo	50/1	Ignacio Garrido
	20/1	J M Olazabal	50/1	Alexander Cejka
	33/1	Greg Turner	50/1	Gordon Brand Jr
	33/1	Robert Karlsson	50/1	Jean Van de Velde
	33/1	Jarmo Sandelin	50/1	Sven Struver
	33/1	Peter O'Malley	66/1	Peter Mitchell
	33/1	Sam Torrance		

Just 19 players were best priced at or under 66/1.

PLEASE NOTE Colin Montgomerie, Darren Clarke, Thomas Bjorn, Steve Webster, MarkRoe, Phillip Price, Jamie Spence and Paul Broadhurst were all late withdrawals.

BOOKIES AT ODDS

Winner Lee Westwood 6/1 Ladbrokes, Stan James: 8/1 Chandlers

1998 RESULT

1 fav	8/1	Lee Westwood	67 68 67 66	268
		(Westwood won at the first extra hole)		
2	150/1	Fredrik Jacobson	65 67 69 67	268
T3	33/1	Robert Karlsson	64 72 68 66	270
T3	33/1	Greg Turner	64 70 67 69	270
T5	66/1	Peter Mitchell	70 68 66 68	272
T5	33/1	Jarmo Sandelin	70 67 66 69	272

T7	M Mouland	71 71 67 64 273		P Baker	68 70 69 72 279
	A Cejka	69 71 67 66 273		P Linhart	71 70 71 68 280
	M Jonzon	70 67 69 67 273		H Clark	71 71 69 69 280
T10	P Affleck	70 70 69 65 274		T Gillis	67 74 67 72 280
	J Haeggman	70 68 69 67 274		D Howell	71 69 74 67 281
	G Brand Jr	71 68 68 67 274		P Walton	73 69 68 71 281
	R Muntz	66 67 73 68 274		W Riley	68 70 69 74 281
	P O'Malley	69 67 69 69 274		S Alker	70 72 71 69 282
	A Wall	69 68 67 70 274		R Chapman	70 68 73 71 282
	P Quirici	67 71 66 70 274		M Farry	72 70 70 70 282
T17	J Rivero	67 71 70 67 275		R Boxall	68 74 69 71 282
	D Robertson	71 68 69 67 275		F Henge	69 73 68 71 282
	J Van de Velde	69 72 67 67 275		C V D Velde	70 71 69 72 282
	M James	68 72 67 68 275		O Edmond	68 72 75 68 283
T21	P Harrington	74 68 67 67 276		I Giner	70 70 73 70 283
	G Evans	71 69 68 68 276		I Garrido	73 67 71 72 283
	R Russell	70 69 69 68 276		A Sherborne	66 71 73 73 283
	P U Johansson	69 67 71 69 276		K Eriksson	73 69 74 68 284
	G Owen	74 62 71 69 276		B Davis	70 71 72 71 284
	R J Derksen	68 70 69 69 276		D Cooper	72 70 71 71 284
	S Struver	67 69 67 73 276		N Vanhootegem	71 70 70 73 284
	O Karlsson	70 69 72 66 277		F Cea	69 72 78 66 285
	A Hunter	69 70 70 68 277		R Davis	70 72 71 72 285
	D Chopra	71 69 70 68 278		S Scahill	71 70 71 73 285
	A Beal	66 71 72 69 278		S Torrance	70 71 70 74 285
	N Faldo	65 72 72 69 278		J Payne	69 73 72 72 286
	V Phillips	64 72 70 72 278		M Mackenzie	69 71 72 74 286
	J M Olazabal	68 71 74 66 279		D De Vooght	70 72 74 72 288
	C Suneson	69 70 72 68 279		P Golding	72 70 73 74 289
	S Bennett	68 71 71 69 279		J Rask	70 70 73 77 291
	R Drummond	68 71 70 70 279			

The 36-hole cut was made at 142 – level par – 67 players qualified.

ROUND BY ROUND LEADERBOARD

FIRST ROUND		SECOND ROUND	
G Turner	7 under	F Jacobsen	10 under
R Karlsson	7 under	R Muntz	9 under
V Phillips	7 under	G Turner	8 under
N Faldo	6 under	L WESTWOOD	7 under
F Jacobsen	6 under	G Owen	6 under
A Sherborne	5 under	V Phillips	6 under
A Beal	5 under	R Karlsson	6 under
R Muntz	5 under	P O'Malley	6 under
L WESTWOOD	4 under	S Struver	6 under
		P U Johansson	6 under

THIRD ROUND		FINAL ROUND	
G Turner	12 under	L WESTWOOD	16 under
F Jacobsen	12 under	F Jacobsen	16 under
L WESTWOOD	11 under	R Karlsson	14 under
S Struver	10 under	G Turner	14 under
J Sandelin	10 under	P Mitchell	12 under
P Quirici	9 under	J Sandelin	12 under
P Mitchell	9 under		
A Wall	9 under		
R Karlsson	9 under		

PUNTERS' POINTS

- Lee Westwood's superb tee-to-green golf formed the basis for this morale-boosting win. He benefited very much from having his coach Peter Cowan with him early in the tournament.

  His great strengths are his brilliant driving, his ability to look forward rather than to dwell on mistakes, and his determination to succeed. Not known as a links player, this will encourage him for the British Open in future years.

- Fredrik Jacobsen needed a top 8 finish here to secure his tour card for next year. He played superbly throughout, even in R4 when the heat was turned up. He clearly enjoys links golf – let's remember for a while his 67 in R1 of this year's British Open made him the clubhouse leader!

- 33/1 Greg Turner is a good links player who plays well at this time of the year. However for the first time in his career he couldn't convert a R3 joint-leader position into a victory.

- 33/1 Robert Karlsson continued his recent rich vein of form here to show that he too is a fine links player. His form figures now are T3rd – 2nd – missed cut – 7th!

- 33/1 Jarmo Sandelin is another player in superb current form. Here T5th, he was posting his third successive top 10 finish. With his length off the tee and a superb putting stroke he just needs to improve his course decision making to become a real star. He could well play in the Ryder Cup.

- The tournament disappointment was surely Nick Faldo. After a morale boosting 65 in R1 and on one of his favourite courses he finished T30th. Nick in the 1999 Ryder Cup team.....perhaps not!
- Among those missing the cut were 40/1 chances Paul McGinley and Andrew Coltart, 80/1 Pierre Fulke and 100/1 outsider DYM Paul Lawrie.

WINNERS IN THE '90s (ON THIS COURSE)

1992	Belgian Open	M A Jimenez
1993	Alfred Dunhill Open	Darren Clarke
1994	Alfred Dunhill Open	Nick Faldo
1998	The Belgacom Open	Lee Westwood

PUNTERS' GUIDE

- The Royal Zoute is a superb links-style golf course. It gives a real chance to those players whose games are suited to links courses.
- In future it will surely pay to remember that Darren Clarke, absent this year, has a fine record here (Won 1993, T9th 1992).
- There are now only two players who have posted three top 20 finishes in the last three tournaments on this course.
  > Greg Turner T3rd 1998: T17th 1994: T10th 1993
  > Gordon Brand Jr T10th 1998: T14th 1994: T4th 1993

THE ALFRED DUNHILL CUP

Date	8th – 11th October	
Course	St Andrews, Scotland	
Par	72	
Yardage	6,933	
Prize Money	£1 million	
Winners	£300,000	£100,000 per player
Runners Up	£150,000	£50,000 per player
Losing S.F.	£95,000	£31,666 per player

The Alfred Dunhill Cup is a team event with an unusual stroke-play match format. Sixteen three-man teams are drawn into four groups and play in a 'round robin' over the first three days with the winners of each group advancing to the semi finals on Sunday morning.

1998 ODDS

9/4	USA (9/4)	20/1	Zimbabwe (16/1)
8/1	South Africa (7/1)	22/1	Argentina (20/1)
9/1	Sweden (11/1)	25/1	New Zealand (25/1)
12/1	Ireland (12/1)	66/1	France (66/1)
12/1*	Australia (10/1)	100/1*	Japan (150/1)
12/1	Scotland (12/1)	400/1*	China (500/1)
14/1	England (20/1)	500/1*	South Korea (500/1)
16/1	Spain (20/1)		
20/1	Germany (25/1)		

NB The prices shown are those after the Wednesday morning draw. The prices in brackets were the best available before the draw.

1998 RESULT

GROUP 1

11/10 USA
3/1 Sweden
6/1 England*
33/1 Japan

DAY ONE

4/11 Sweden beat 4/1 Japan 3-0

8/13 P Sjoland (69) beat H Fijita (77) 3/1
4/6 M Gronberg (78) beat N Serizawa (79) 15/8
4/7 P U Johansson (71) beat K Miyamoto (76) 3/1

1/2 USA beat 9/4 England 3-0

2/1 J Daly (70) beat L Westwood (73) Evens
4/9 T Woods (66) beat D Carter (74) 9/2
4/7 M O'Meara (67) beat P Baker (74) 13/5

DAY TWO

4/6 Sweden beat 6/4 England 3-0

9/4 M Gronberg (72) beat L Westwood (72) 8/13 at the 19th
8/13 P U Johansson (70) beat D Carter (73) 15/8
8/11 P Sjoland (70) beat P Baker (73) 7/4

1/10 USA beat 10/1 Japan 3-0

8/15 J Daly (77) beat N Serizawa (80) 9/2
1/4 T Woods (70) beat K Miyamoto (77) 11/1
3/10 M O'Meara (70) beat H Fujita (75) 11/1

DAY THREE

4/9 USA beat 2/1 Sweden 2½-½

6/4 J Daly (71) beat P U Johansson (72) 10/11
2/5 T Woods (66) beat M Gronberg (73) 4/1
8/11 M O'Meara (68) halved with P Sjoland (68) 7/4

1/3 England beat 11/2 Japan 3-0

4/9 L Westwood (70) beat K Miyamoto (71) 11/2
4/6 P Baker (71) beat H Fujita (73) 10/3
4/5 D Carter (69) beat N Serizawa (75) 3/1

FINAL TABLE

		P	W	L	Games Won
1	USA	3	3	-	8½
2	Sweden	3	2	1	6½
3	England	3	1	2	3
4	Japan	3	0	3	0

GROUP 2

7/4 Ireland
7/4 Scotland
11/4 Spain
66/1 China*

DAY ONE

1/7 Scotland beat 8/1 China 2-1

4/6 G Orr (75) beat Wu Xiang-bing (76) 4/1
2/5 A Coltart (73) beat Cheng Jun (78) 6/1
4/11 C Montgomerie (73) lost to Zhang Lian-Wei (72) 8/1

6/4 Spain beat 5/6 Ireland 2-1

2/1 S Luna (71) lost to D Clarke (71) 4/6 at 22nd hole
11/10 M A Jimenez (70) beat P McGinley (72) 5/4
Evens J M Olazabal (73) beat P Harrington (75) 13/8

DAY TWO

11/1 Scotland beat 5/6 Ireland 2-1

13/8 A Coltart (75) lost to D Clarke (73) 5/6
6/4 G Orr (77) beat P Harrington (78) Evens
8/11 C Montgomerie (72) beat P McGinley (78) 2/1

1/5 Spain beat 5/1 China 2-1

4/9 J M Olazabal (78) lost to Wu Xiang-bing (77) 5/1
4/7 M A Jimenez (76) beat Zhang Lian-Wei (83) 3/1
4/7 S Luna (80) beat Cheng Jun (81) 4/1

DAY THREE

11/10 Spain beat 8/11 Scotland 2-1

4/5 J M Olazabal (68) beat G Orr (71) 7/4
13/8 M A Jimenez (70) beat C Montgomerie (70) 8/11 at the 19th
13/8 S Luna (74) lost to A Coltart (73) 5/6

1/4 Ireland beat 7/1 China 3-0

4/9 D Clarke (71) beat Zhang Lian-Wei (73) 9/2
8/15 P McGinley (74) beat Cheng Jun (78) 4/1
4/5 P Harrington (71) beat Wu Xiang-bing (74) 10/3

FINAL TABLE

		P	W	L	Games Won
1	Spain	3	3	0	6
2	Scotland	3	2	1	5
3	Ireland	3	1	2	5
4	China	3	0	3	2

GROUP 3

6/4 South Africa
11/4 Zimbabwe
9/2 Germany
12/1 France

DAY ONE

2/7 South Africa beat 4/1 France 3-0

4/6 R Goosen (72) beat O Edmond (73) 9/4
4/6 D Frost (70) beat T Levet (75) 9/4
4/7 E Els (69) beat J V D Velde (72) 13/5

Evens Zimbabwe beat 6/5 Germany 3-0

7/4 T Johnstone (69) beat S Struver (76) 8/11
8/13 N Price (72) beat T Gogele (73) 13/5
6/5 M McNulty (73) beat A Cejka (75) 11/8

DAY TWO

7/2 Germany beat 2/7 South Africa 2-1

2/1 T Gogele (78) beat D Frost (78) 8/11 at the 20th
13/8 A Cejka (77) lost to R Goosen (76) 5/6
5/2 S Struver (76) beat E Els (76) 8/15 at the 20th

5/2 France beat 1/3 Zimbabwe 2-1

6/4 J V de Velde (71) beat 21/20 M McNulty (81)
13/8 T Levet (77) beat 4/5 T Johnstone (79)
11/4 O Edmond (78) lost 1/2 to N Price (70)

DAY THREE

8/13 Germany beat 7/4 France 2-1

10/11 T Gogele (69) beat T Levet (72) 13/8
11/8 A Cejka (75) lost to J V de Velde (72) evens
8/11 S Struver (68) beat O Edmond (70) 9/4

4/6 South Africa beat 7/4 Zimbabwe 2-1

1/2 E Els (71) beat T Johnstone (77) 3/1
3/1 D Frost (71) lost to N Price (69) 8/11
10/11 R Goosen (71) beat M McNulty (76) 13/8

FINAL TABLE

		P	W	L	Games Won
1	South Africa	3	2	1	6
2	Germany	3	2	1	4
3	Zimbabwe	3	1	2	5
4	France	3	1	2	3

GROUP 4

11/8 Australia
3/1 Argentina
3/1 New Zealand
66/1 Korea*

DAY ONE

6/1 South Korea beat 1/6 New Zealand 2-1

4/1 S Yong-Jin (75) beat M Long (76) 8/15
7/2 K Wook-Soon (71) beat F Nobilo (75) 8/15
4/1 K Jong-Duck (73) lost to G Turner (70) 4/9

4/6 Australia beat 9/4 Argentina 3-0

4/5 S Appleby (66) beat J Coceres (77) 15/8
Evens C Parry (70) beat A Cabrera (75) 13/8
10/11 S Elkington (70) beat E Romero (70) at the 19th hole

DAY TWO

5/6 New Zealand beat evens Argentina 2-1

11/10 G Turner (75) beat E Romero (disq.) 21/20
Evens F Nobilo (71) beat A Cabrera (77) 11/10
11/8 M Long (81) lost to J Coceres (75) 13/8

1/7 Australia beat 6/1 South Korea 3-0

2/5 C Parry (75) beat S Yong-Jin (75) 7/2 at the 19th
4/7 S Appleby (73) beat K Wook-Soon (77) 7/2
2/5 S Elkington (72) beat K Jong-Duck (77) 4/1

DAY THREE

1/2 Argentina beat 4/1 South Korea 2-1

4/7 E Romero (72) lost to S Yong-Jin (72) 3/1 at the 19th
4/6 A Cabrera (72) beat K Jong-Duck (73) 5/2
21/20 J Coceres (71) beat K Wook-Soon (72) 5/2

3/1 New Zealand beat 4/7 Australia 2-1

11/4 M Long (71) lost to C Parry (72) 8/13
5/4 G Turner (72) beat S Appleby (73) 11/10
15/8 F Nobilo (70) beat S Elkington (74) 4/5

FINAL TABLE

		P	W	L	Games Won
1	Australia	3	2	1	7
2	New Zealand	3	2	1	5
3	Argentina	3	1	2	3
4	S Korea	3	1	2	3

SEMI FINALS

7/4 Spain beat 1/2 USA 2-1
4/5 J Daly (73) beat M A Jimenez (75) 11/8
2/5 T Woods (72) lost to S Luna (71) 3/1
4/7 M O'Meara (76) lost to J M Olazabal (72) 15/8
4/6 South Africa beat 5/4 Australia 2-1
11/10 D Frost (72) beat C Parry (77) evens
Evens R Goosen (71) beat S Appleby (74) 11/10
8/11 E Els (73) lost to S Elkington (72) 11/8

FINAL
4/7 South Africa beat 11/8 Spain 3-0
4/5 R Goosen (72) beat S Luna (73) 6/4
Evens D Frost (78) beat M A Jimenez (78) evens
4/5 E Els (75) beat J M Olazabal (77) 6/4

TOURNAMENT WINNERS IN THE '90s

1990	Ireland beat England	3½-2½
1991	Sweden beat South Africa	2-1
1992	England beat Scotland	3-0
1993	USA beat England	2-1
1994	Canada beat USA	2-1
1995	Scotland beat Zimbabwe	2-1
1996	USA beat New Zealand	2-1
1997	South Africa beat Sweden	2-1
1998	South Africa beat Spain	3-0

TOP INDIVIDUAL POINTS SCORER
IN THE 1998 DUNHILL CUP

Odds	(draw)	Player	Odds	(draw)	Player
6/1 fav	(5/1)	Tiger Woods	33/1	(33/1)	Greg Turner
8/1	(8/1)	Mark O'Meara	33/1	(33/1)	Patrik Sjoland
14/1	(12/1)	Ernie Els	40/1*	(33/1)	Craig Parry
12/1	(14/1)	Colin Montgomerie	40/1*	(33/1)	Retief Goosen
16/1	(16/1)	Lee Westwood	40/1	(33/1)	Stuart Appleby
16/1	(14/1)	Steve Elkington	40/1	(40/1)	M A Jimenez
20/1	(18/1)	Darren Clarke	40/1	(50/1)*	Padraig Harrington
20/1	(20/1)	P U Johansson	50/1	(50/1)	Sven Struver
22/1	(20/1)	Nick Price	50/1	(50/1)	Alex Cejka
28/1	(28/1)	J M Olazabal	50/1	(50/1)	Andrew Coltart
33/1	(33/1)	John Daly	50/1*	(50/1)	Frank Nobilo
33/1	(33/1)	Eduardo Romero	50/1	(50/1)	Paul McGinley
66/1	Bar				

Prices in brackets were those available after the draw.
1/4 odds 1,2,3,4

RESULT

1	Retief Goosen	5 wins	40/1
2	John Daly	4 wins	33/1
T3	M A Jimenez	3 wins	40/1
T3	Greg Turner	3 wins	33/1
T3	Darren Clarke	3 wins	20/1
T3	S Elkington	3 wins	16/1
T3	Nick Price	3 wins	22/1
T3	Craig Parry	3 wins	40/1
T3	Tiger Woods	3 wins	6/1
T3	David Frost	3 wins	66/1*

TOP INDIVIDUAL POINTS SCORER

1997 RESULT
T1 25/1 Retief Goosen 5 pts
T1 16/1 P U Johansson 5 pts
T3 33/1 Frank Nobilo 4 pts
T3 40/1 Joakim Haeggman 4 pts
T3 12/1 Mark O'Meara 4pts

1996 RESULT
1 12/1 S Stricker 5 pts
T2 80/1 Grant Waite 4 pts
T2 80/1 Jarmo Sandelin 4 pts

CORALS' SPECIAL 1998 MARKETS

Which European player will shoot the lowest score on the 1st day?

1	P Sjoland (69)	14/1
2	M A Jimenez (70)	14/1
T3	D Clarke (71)	8/1
T3	S Luna (71)	25/1
T4	P U Johansson (71)	9/1

1/4 odds 1-4

Top European Points Scorer

T1	M A Jimenez	16/1
T1	D Clarke	8/1

What will be the lowest 18 hole score?
64 at 11/4 was the favourite 66 at 6/1 was the winner

What will be the highest 18 hole score?
80 at 10/3 was the favourite
83 at 8/1 was the winner in the wind & rain on day 2

OVERALL PUNTERS' GUIDE

- This is an excellent course, an excellent tournament and an excellent format, making for four days of superb golf. This stroke-play match format means that a match can swing by two, three or even four shots on a hole.
- With its steep bunkers, its infamous 'road hole' (the 17th) and its variable winds the St Andrews course provides a classic test of links golf, which combined with the stroke-play match format made for 'shock' results in individual matches once more this year (Monty's loss to 8/1 Zhang Lian-Wei), and in team matches (South Korea's 2-1 win over 6/1 ON New Zealand).

- Players with proven experience here are worth noting. Craig Parry for instance now has a course record of 9 wins from 11 starts: John Daly has 8 wins from 9 starts: and Retief Goosen has now been the top points scorer in each of the last two years on a run of 10 unbeaten matches.

- In the market for the top individual points scorer it is wise to apply the three-part formula that has been successful over recent years. Go for a player a) who is in a team likely to get at least into the semi-final stage b) who is a long hitter off the tee, and c) who is not the captain.

- This year the world rankings gave an accurate prediction of the draw.

   World Rank 1 plays W.R. 8 in group 1
   W.R. 2 plays W.R. 7 in group 2
   W.R. 3 plays W.R. 6 in group 3
   W.R. 4 plays W.R. 5 in group 4

- In this tournament there are very considerable differences in prices so it really does pay to 'shop around'.

- And almost finally, well done to the Racing Post for highlighting Sky's TV coverage which for the first two days meant that the coverage stopped with key matches still out on the course so recorded programmes could be shown. We all thought that was BBC policy.....so c'mon Sky no repeats of the repeats in 1999 just full coverage.

CISCO WORLD MATCHPLAY CHAMPIONSHIP

Date	15th – 18th October
Course	Wentworth
Par	71
Yardage	7,006
Winner	£170,000
Runner Up	£90,000
Losing S.F	£50,000

Second Round Losers £40,000 (x4) First Round Losers £30,000 (x4)

This well-established tournament has twelve competitors. Eight unseeded players play on the first day for the right to join the four top seeds in the Q.F. stage. All matches are over 36 holes. This year for the first time there was no play-off for third place.

1998 ODDS

7/2	Tiger Woods+		16/1	Steve Stricker
9/2	Ernie Els+		20/1	Darren Clarke
5/1	Vijay Singh+(DC)		33/1	Patrik Sjoland
6/1	Mark O'Meara+		40/1	Ian Woosnam
9/1	Colin Montgomerie		40/1	Thomas Bjorn
14/1	Lee Westwood		50/1	Stuart Appleby

+ *Seeded players*

BOOKIES AT ODDS

P Sjoland 16/1 Tote: 33/1 Corals, Stan James

I Woosnam 16/1 Stanleys: 40/1 Tote

T Bjorn 20/1 Tote: 40/1 Corals, Surrey

1998 RESULT

FIRST ROUND

5/4 P Sjoland beat 8/11 S Stricker by 1 hole
4/7 C Montgomerie beat 2/1 T Bjorn by 4 and 3
4/7 L Westwood beat 7/4 S Appleby by 8 and 7
5/4 I Woosnam beat 5/6 D Clarke by 4 and 3

QUARTER FINAL

8/15 V Singh beat 7/4 P Sjoland by 7 and 6
Evens M O'Meara beat 10/11 C Montgomerie by 5 and 4
11/10 L Westwood beat 8/11 E Els by 2 and 1
2/5 T Woods beat 5/2 I Woosnam at the 37th

SEMI FINAL

Evens M O'Meara beat 11/8 V Singh by 11 and 10 (!)
8/13 T Woods beat 6/5 L Westwood by 5 and 4

FINAL

Evens M O'Meara beat 8/11 T Woods by 1 hole

BETTING IN RUNNING

		Before the Start	QF	SF	Final
1	T Woods	7/2	3/1	9/4	8/11
2	M O'Meara	6/1	7/1	4/1	Evens
3	V Singh	5/1	5/1	9/4	-
4	L Westwood	14/1	8/1	4/1	-
5	E Els	9/2	5/1	-	-
6	C Montgomerie	9/1	7/1	-	-
7	P Sjoland	33/1	18/1*	-	-
8	I Woosnam	40/1	20/1	-	-

PUNTERS' POINTS

- 'Ebony and ivory', Woods and O'Meara, a black guy and a white guy, neighbours and friends, provided a fine example of racial harmony, true sportsmanship and fine golf in a tremendous final.
- In 1999 it will probably pay to oppose Colin Montgomerie who admitted he was tired last year because of the Ryder Cup, and who played poorly in this year's quarter final against O'Meara.
- Three-time champion (1994 – 1996) Ernie Els has now lost his last two matches here. At least in 1999 he won't be involved in the Ryder Cup.

1997 RESULT

Final	V Singh beat E Els 1 up
SFs	E Els beat N Price at the 37th
	V Singh beat B Faxon 4 & 3
3rd Place	B Faxon beat N Price 5 & 4

WINNERS IN THE '90s

1990   Woosnam beat McNulty 4 & 2
1991   Ballesteros beat Price 3 & 2
1992   Faldo beat Sluman 8 & 7
1993   Pavin beat Faldo 1 hole
1994   Els beat Montgomerie 4 & 2
1995   Els beat Elkington 3 & 1
1996   Els beat Singh 3 & 2
1997   Singh beat Els 1 hole
1998   O'Meara beat Woods 1 hole

PUNTERS' GUIDE

- In 1999 this event once more comes a week after the Dunhill Cup, and starts just 18 days after the Ryder Cup so it will be imperative to spot the players who are 'over the top', suffering from M.L.D., or had their swings wrecked in the Dunhill Cup winds at St Andrews. This year, for example, after his four long days helping South Africa last week, it was clear that Ernie Els would be jaded and could be opposed. Each year there are such players, spot them in 1999 and you're quids in!

- In the outright betting it is probably wise to wait for the full draw to assess the players' chances, although the market is usually formed two weeks in advance.

- With the non-seeded players having to play morning and afternoon for four successive days it is not surprising that in the last fourteen years eleven seeds have won.

- However on the second day a 'jaded' seed can be opposed as his non-seeded opponent will be match fit from his opening game.

- I've made the point in Chapter One yet I'll make it again. Isn't it really annoying when you watch the BBC cover this tournament to find it continually interrupted by regular national and regional news bulletins? Also with exclusive coverage they started Saturday's coverage at 12.20 p.m. with highlights at 12.50 a.m. Need I comment?

- This year for the first time there was no 'forecast the finalists' betting. Another reduction in punter choice......surely one of the compilers could have created this market. Let's hope that in 1999 at least one main golfing bookmaker will revive this form of betting.

OPEN NOVOTEL PERRIER

Date	15th – 18th October
Course	Golf du Medoc, Bordeaux, France
Par	71
Yardage	6,909
First Prize	£70,000 Second £50,000 Third £35,000
Total Purse	£350,000

This unusual tournament has 30 pairs competing so there is no halfway cut. The format consists of fourballs on day one, followed by foursomes, greensomes, and on the final day stroke play with both players scores counting. So, in effect, five rounds count.

1998 ODDS

fav 10/1	J Sandelin & O Karlsson	40/1	S Cage & R Russell
12/1	S Ballesteros & M A Jimenez	40/1	M Jonzon & A Forsbrand*(DC)
12/1	J Rivero & S Luna	40/1	B Davis & V Phillips
12/1	P Baker & P Broadhurst	50/1	M Mackenzie & A Sherborne
14/1	J M Olazabal & D Hospital	50/1	J Lomas & S Bottomley
16/1	I Garrido & C Suneson	50/1	J Remesy & R Jacquelin
16/1	P Mitchell & J Spence	50/1	D Edlund & K Eriksson
20/1	M Roe & M Farry	50/1	J Robson & F Jacobson*
22/1	J Payne & P Price	66/1	N Joakamides & C Cevaer*
25/1	M Lanner & P Hedblom	66/1	R McFarlane & D J Russell
25/1	R Chapman & M Mouland	100/1	P Edmond & O Edmond*
25/1	S Garcia & T Immelman*	100/1	C Pottier & M Pendaries
25/1	D Carter & I Pyman	100/1	D Borrego & F Ortiz*
25/1	P Lawrie & S Henderson	125/1	T Levet & B Telleria*
33/1	D Howell & W Riley	200/1	C Ravetto & G Havret*
33/1	R Boxall & D Cooper	200/1	O David & D Montessi*
33/1	G Orr & A Hunter	200/1	S Branger & N Blactot*

All quoted.

1998 RESULT

1 fav	10/1	Jarmo Sandelin/Olle Karlsson	62 68 63 136	329
2	33/1	Richard Boxall/Derrick Cooper	65 69 65 133	332
3	12/1	Seve Ballesteros/Miguel A Jimenez	64 69 67 134	334
4	50/1	Jeff Remesy/Raphael Jacquelin	61 68 68 138	335
T5		J Lomas/S Bottomley	66 67 71 133	337
		P Baker/P Broadhurst	67 68 64 138	337
T7		M Lanner/ P Hedblom	65 70 70 133	338
		S Garcia (am)/T Immelman (am)	64 70 66 138	338
9		J Rivero/S Luna	60 66 71 142	339
T10		P Mitchell/J Spence	67 71 66 137	341
		R McFarlane/D J Russell	63 67 70 141	341
12		D Edlund/K Eriksson	61 72 73 136	342
13		O David (am)/D Montesi (am)	62 70 68 143	343
T14		J Payne/P Price	69 73 64 138	344
		P Edmond/O Edmond	65 72 69 138	344
		I Garrido/C Suneson	62 69 72 141	344
		M Mackenzie/A Sherborne	64 71 68 141	344
18		G Orr/A Hunter	62 70 69 144	345
T19		T Level/B Teilleria	68 70 67 141	346
		J Robson/F Jacobson	64 72 72 138	346
T21		C Pottier/M Pendaries	67 74 68 138	347
		R Chapman/M Mouland	66 69 69 143	347
23		P Lawrie/S Henderson	69 72 69 138	348
T24		D Howell/W Riley	66 74 67 142	349
		D Carter/I Pyman	63 74 71 141	349
		N Joakimides/C Cevaer	60 73 65 151	349
27		B Davis/V Phillips	67 74 73 137	351
28		D Borrego/F Ortiz	66 68 72 147	353
29		J M Olazabal/D Hospital	67 71 73 143	354
T30		M Jonzon/A Forsbrand	67 75 69 144	355
		S Cage/R Russell	66 74 71 144	355
32		C Ravetto (am)/G Havret (am)	69 73 72 144	358
33		S Branger (am)/NBlactot (am)	64 77 72 155	368
34		M Roe/M Farry	66 71WD --	--

ROUND BY ROUND LEADERBOARD

FIRST DAY (fourballs)

Joakimides & Cevaer	11 under
Rivero & Luna	11 under
Edlund & Eriksson	10 under
Remesy & Jacquelin	10 under
Orr & Hunter	9 under
SANDELIN & KARLSSON	9 under
Garrido & Suneson	9 under
David (am) & Montesi (am)	9 under

SECOND DAY (foursomes)

Rivero & Luna	16 under
Remesy & Jacquelin	13 under
SANDELIN & KARLSSON	12 under
McFarlane & Russell	12 under
Garrido & Suneson	11 under
Orr & Hunter	10 under
David (am) & Montesi (am)	10 under

THIRD DAY (greensomes)

SANDELIN & KARLSSON	20 under
Remesy & Jacquelin	16 under
Rivero & Luna	16 under
Joakimedes & Cevaer	15 under
Boxall & Cooper	14 under
Baker & Broadhurst	14 under

FINAL DAY (two single scores)

SANDELIN & KARLSSON	26 under
Boxall & Cooper	23 under
Ballesteros & Jimenez	21 under
Remesy & Jacquelin	20 under
Lomas & Bottomley	18 under
Baker & Broadhurst	18 under

- The first day's play was delayed for 90 minutes because of fog

PUNTERS' POINTS

- For the second successive year the Pairs was won by a Swedish team. It will be interesting to see how they fare if they defend next year as the record of the defending champions is appalling – 1996 winners Lomas & Bottomley were plumb last in 1997, and 1997 winners Forsbrand and Jonzon were T30th (of 33) this year!

- This year's winning score of 329 was the lowest in this event, with Sandelin's extra length a big advantage to the winning Swedes.

- This format is ideal for someone like Seve. His record in this event over the past five years is: T3rd 1994, Won 1995, DNP1996, T3rd 1997, and now T3rd 1998. Trouble is being a 'name' he and his partner are always in the 8/1 to 12/1 range.

- It may be that Peter Baker and Paul Broadhurst will be a partnership to note here in future. T21st in 1997 shooting 357, this year they were 20 shots better in T5th place. Next year......?

- The amateur partnership of Sergio Garcia and Trevor Immelman (T7th) promised much for the future if they stay together. However a Seve Ballesteros and Garcia partnership.....that would be interesting.

1997 RESULT

1	A Forsbrand & M Jonzon
2	S Luna & J Rivero
T3	S Ballesteros & J M Olazabal
T3	M Farry & M Roe
T3	P Hedblom & P Sjoland

1996 RESULT

1	J Lomas & S Bottomley
2	R Boxall & D Cooper
3	W Westner & M Mackenzie
T4	P Broadhurst & R McFarlane
T4	F Lindgren & J Haeggman

PREVIOUS WINNERS

1994 Tournoi Perrier de Paris	P Baker & D J Russell	St Cloud, Paris
1995 Perrier Paris Fourball	S Ballesteros & J M Olazabal	St Cloud, Paris
1996 Novotel Perrier Open	J Lomas & S Bottomley	Golf du Medoc
1997 Novotel Perrier Open	A Forsbrand & M Jonzon	Golf du Medoc
1998 Novotel Perrier Open	O Karlsson & J Sandelin	Golf du Medoc

PUNTERS' GUIDE

- This course is in many ways similar to a Scottish links course with wide fairways surrounded by heathers and gorse. There are just three par 5s.
- With only 30 runners, and bookies still paying one quarter the odds the first four this tournament can offer 'value' opportunities.
- Three pairs with fine recent course records are:-
    > Jonathan Lomas and Steven Bottomley are suited to this links type course. After all they've both posted a top 11 finish in the British Open. Winners in 1996 and T5th this year they clearly are suited here.
    > The French pair Jeff Remesy and Raphael Jacquelin have 'home' advantage. They led into the final round (by 4) last year, and were 4th this year.
    > Richard Boxall and Derrick Cooper have a fine record in foursomes. They were 2nd here in 1996, and were again runners-up this year.

THE VOLVO MASTERS

Date	29th October – 1st November
Course	Montecastillo, Jerez, Spain
Yardage	7,025
Par	72
First Prize	£166,000
Total Purse	£1 million, plus a bonus pool of £700,000

There was a 66-man field for the season-ending Volvo Masters which was played for the second successive year on the Montecastillo course. The tournament would decide whether Lee Westwood, Colin Montgomerie or Darren Clarke would win the Order of Merit.

1998 ODDS

fav	9/1	Colin Montgomerie	50/1	Eduardo Romero
	10/1	Lee Westwood	50/1	Retief Goosen
	11/1	Ernie Els	50/1	Alex Cejka
	22/1	Darren Clarke	66/1	Mark McNulty
	25/1	J M Olazabal	66/1	Jean Van de Velde
	25/1	Ian Woosnam	66/1	Padraig Harrington
	28/1	Patrik Sjoland	66/1	Sven Struver*
	28/1	P U Johansson	66/1	Andrew Coltart
	33/1	Thomas Bjorn	66/1	Ignacio Garrido
	33/1	Robert Karlsson	66/1	Sam Torrance
	33/1	Nick Faldo	80/1	Paul McGinley
	33/1	Bernhard Langer	80/1	Santiago Luna
	40/1	M A Jimenez	80/1	Peter Baker
	40/1	Jarmo Sandelin	80/1	Peter Mitchell
	40/1	Costantino Rocca	80/1	Mark James
	40/1	Greg Turner	80/1	Paul Broadhurst
	50/1	Robert Allenby	80/1	Stephen Leaney
	50/1	Peter O'Malley	80/1	Gordon Brand Jr

28 players were best priced at or under 66/1
36 players were best priced at or under 80/1

BOOKIES AT ODDS

Sven Struver 33/1 Hills: 66/1 Tote

Winner Darren Clarke 16/1 Corals, Sunderlands: 22/1 Chandlers

1998 RESULT

1	22/1	Darren Clarke	67 73 68 63	271
2	66/1	Andrew Coltart	69 73 65 66	273
3 fav	9/1	Colin Montgomerie	70 67 69 68	274
T4	80/1	Peter Baker	69 72 67 67	275
T4	50/1	Peter O'Malley	67 71 67 70	275

6	B Langer	72 69 67 68	276		C Rocca	71 75 72 71	289
7	J M Olazabal	68 70 70 70	278		M Roe	73 69 75 72	289
T8	R Allenby	69 73 70 67	279		M McNulty	73 70 74 72	289
	S Torrance	72 69 69 69	279		J Spence	69 74 72 74	289
	C Hainline	73 70 67 69	279		N Faldo	71 73 70 75	289
	E Els	70 71 68 70	279		S Allan	74 72 73 71	290
T12	P Lonard	68 66 75 71	280		I Woosnam	74 71 74 71	290
	A Cejka	67 73 69 71	280		R Claydon	72 71 75 72	290
	S Leaney	71 70 68 71	280		D Gilford	69 73 75 73	290
	L Westwood	70 68 67 75	280		P Price	71 72 74 73	290
T16	M A Jimenez	71 72 69 69	281		S Ballesteros	72 72 71 75	290
	P Harrington	70 69 70 72	281		T Bjorn	72 67 75 76	290
	M Gronberg	73 67 68 73	281		I Garbutt	72 73 68 77	290
T19	K Tomori	72 71 70 69	282		R Goosen	75 68 79 69	291
	G Chalmers	67 75 70 70	282		P U Johansson	71 75 73 72	291
	P McGinley	68 72 69 73	282		P Sjoland	72 72 73 74	291
	G Brand Jr	67 74 68 73	282		G Orr	69 75 72 75	291
23	J Sandelin	67 71 73 72	283		D Howell	72 71 72 76	291
T24	S Luna	69 72 72 71	284		P Broadhurst	72 75 71 74	292
	J Van de Velde	75 69 68 72	284		S Struver	72 71 71 78	292
	R Karlsson	72 77 68 68	285		M Hallberg	73 72 73 76	294
	A Cabrera	70 69 74 72	285		M Lanner	77 72 69 76	294
	G Turner	73 72 68 72	285		T Gogele	72 74 69 79	294
	E Romero	75 73 69 69	286		O Karlsson	75 75 74 71	295
	V Phillips	73 71 71 71	286		P Fulke	69 74 75 78	296
	R Wessels	71 71 72 72	286		M Harwood	74 74 73 77	298
	S Webster	70 75 67 74	286		T Johnstone	72 72 74 80	298
	P Mitchell	72 70 68 76	286		I Garrido	72 76 73 78	299
	M Florioli	74 73 69 71	287		D Carter	77 76 69 78	300
	P Quirici	72 74 73 69	288		J Cheng	73 70 84 85	312

ROUND BY ROUND LEADERBOARD

FIRST ROUND		SECOND ROUND	
A Cejka	5 under	P Lonard	10 under
P O'Malley	5 under	C Montgomerie	7 under
G Chalmers	5 under	L Westwood	6 under
J Sandelin	5 under	J M Olazabal	6 under
D CLARKE	5 under	J Sandelin	6 under
P McGinley	4 under	P O'Malley	6 under
J M Olazabal	4 under	D CLARKE	4 under
P Lonard	4 under		

THIRD ROUND		FINAL ROUND	
P O'Malley	11 under	D CLARKE	17 under
L Westwood	11 under	A Coltart	15 under
C Montgomerie	10 under	C Montgomerie	14 under
A Coltart	9 under	P O'Malley	13 under
J M Olazabal	8 under	P Baker	13 under
P Baker	8 under		
B Langer	8 under		
D CLARKE	8 under		
M Gronberg	8 under		

PUNTERS' POINTS

- The Nappy Factor rules OK! After holing the putt to win the tournament Darren Clarke held his 13-week-old son Tyrone – it was an emotional moment as, tears in his eyes, he knew he'd won his first tournament as a dad!

- Lee Westwood's challenge for the Order of Merit was lost, mainly on the greens, in a very disappointing 75 in R4.

- The most interesting punter point from Montecastillo 1998 may be the performance of T4th Peter Baker. He has worked hard, with coach Bill Ferguson, to improve his putting and chipping. 1999 may very well see Baker's re-emergence as a really top player.

- Andrew Coltart, a stablemate of Westwood and Clarke, has always had a fine swing and here his new blade putter was the secret of his superb form. Like Baker he must be expected to do really well in 1999.

- One point for punters to note here was to avoid the temptation to bet on news of injured players. There were a number of players who did not play in the Pro-Am and one of them, Padraig Harrington, had a strained wrist. Paired with Romero in a match bet Ladbrokes punters rushed in to back Romero to beat the injured player....the bet lost as Harrington finished T16th!

- Monty did what Monty had to do.....just enough to record his SIXTH successive Order of Merit triumph. This really is some achievement and I'd be very surprised if it is ever beaten.

- On this course, with reachable par 5s, it really is possible for a player to shoot a 63 or 64, and so come from 'off the pace' to win in R4. So be wary of taking short prices about tournament leaders in 'betting in running'!

1997 RESULT

1	25/1	Lee Westwood
2	33/1	Padraig Harrington
3	18/1	J M Olazabal
4	66/1	Robert Karlsson

WINNERS IN THE '90s

1990	Mike Harwood
1991	Rodger Davis
1992	Sandy Lyle
1993	Colin Montgomerie
1994	Bernhard Langer
1995	Alex Cejka
1996	Mark McNulty
1997	Lee Westwood
1998	Darren Clarke

PUNTERS' GUIDE

- This Jack Nicklaus course has wide, forgiving fairways and large greens. The wind can play a part here as it did in 1997. Length off the tee, accurate iron play and an ability to play in breezy conditions are the main requirements.

- With Montecastillo the venue once more in 1999 punters have two consecutive years' form to study. Only three players have posted successive top 10 finishes. They are

  > Colin Montgomerie 23 under par for 7 rounds. 3rd 1998: 8th 1997
  > Peter O'Malley 23 under par for 7 rounds. T4th 1998: T5th 1997
  > J M Olazabal 22 under par for 7 rounds. T7th 1998: 3rd 1997

TOUR FORM 1998 Part 4
AMERICAN

THE AMERICAN MONEY LIST

Date	From 8th January in California to the 1st November in Georgia
Courses	Assorted
Par	70 – 72
Yardage	Various
First Prize	The US tour's Number 1

Similar to the European Order of Merit in that the US Money list is a monetary league table of the dollar earnings of all the US tour players over the full American season.

1998 ODDS

fav	11/4	Tiger Woods	40/1	Colin Montgomerie*
	9/1	Davis Love III	40/1	Vijay Singh
	14/1	Phil Mickelson	40/1	Fred Couples
	16/1	David Duval	40/1	Steve Elkington
	16/1	Ernie Els	40/1	Nick Faldo
	16/1	Justin Leonard	50/1	Jesper Parnevik
	18/1	Tom Lehman	66/1	Loren Roberts*
	20/1	Greg Norman*	66/1	Mark Calcavecchia
	25/1	Nick Price	66/1	Brad Faxon*
	25/1	Jim Furyk	66/1	Steve Jones*
	25/1	Scott Hoch	66/1	Stewart Cink
	40/1	Lee Janzen	66/1	Jeff Maggert
	40/1	Mark O'Meara		

25 players were best priced at or under 66/1.

BOOKIES AT ODDS

David Duval 10/1 Ladbrokes, Stanleys, Sunderlands: 16/1 Tote

1998 RESULT

1	16/1	David Duival
2	40/1	Vijay Singh
3	25/1	Jim Furyk
4 fav	11/4	Tiger Woods

PUNTERS' POINTS

- In the last two years three players (similar to Monty, Clarke and Westwood on the European O/M) have finished in the top 4 in each year.

  > Tiger Woods 4th 11/4 1998: W 10/1 1997
  > Jim Furyk 3rd 25/1 1998: 4th 80/1 1997
  > David Duval W 16/1 1998: 2nd 33/1 1997

- The interesting feature over the last five years has been the successful progress of the younger players as shown in this table.

Year	Average age of the first 3 on US Money List
1998	29.66
1997	25.33
1996	31.66
1995	32.66
1994	39.00

1997 RESULT

1	10/1	Tiger Woods
2	33/1	David Duval
3	16/1	Davis Love III
4	80/1	Jim Furyk

1996 RESULT

1	33/1	Tom Lehman
2	33/1	Phil Mickelson
3	80/1	Mark Brooks
4	100/1	Steve Stricker

WINNERS' IN THE '90s

1990	Greg Norman
1991	Corey Pavin
1992	Fred Couples
1993	Nick Price
1994	Nick Price
1995	Greg Norman
1996	Tom Lehman
1997	Tiger Woods
1998	David Duval

PUNTERS' GUIDE

The book's Money list record really is very good:-

1996	Tom Lehman	W 33/1
1997	Steve Stricker	Lost. Changed clubs and lost form
1998	David Duval	W 16/1
	Jim Furyk	3rd 25/1

So a £10 each-way bet on those four would have yielded a nice (pre-tax) clear profit of £645. Bookmakers will therefore be cautious in laying the 1999 selection so this time, unusually, I shall wait till all the prices are known, so the selection will be given on my Timeform Sportsview Line (0897 22 33 11) on TUESDAY, 5TH JANUARY AT 10.00 A.M. (Calls cost £1.50 per minute, maximum duration 4 minutes).

Top 5 finishes on the USPGA Tour

1	2	3	4	5
Mercedes Championship				
14/1 P Mickelson	11/2 T Woods	-	16/1 N Price	-
	25/1 M O'Meara		33/1 J Cook	
Bob Hope Chrysler Classic				
22/1 F Couples	200/1 B Lietzke	50/1 A Magee	14/1 D Duval	-
			28/1 S Jones	
Phoenix Open				
33/1 J Parnevik	150/1 T Armour III	-	-	-
	200/1 S Pate			
	125/1 B Geiberger			
	66/1 T Watson			
AT&T Pebble Beach				
22/1 P Mickelson	250/1 T Pernice Jr	40/1 J Furyk	-	-
		125/1 P Azinger		
		250/1 J P Hayes		
Buick Invitational				
150/1 S Simpson	100/1 S Kendall	13/2 T Woods	-	-
		14/1 D Love		
		150/1 K Sutherland		
Hawaiian Open				
50/1 J Huston	22/1 T Watson	125/1 T Dodds	150/1 G Kraft	-
			200/1 B Quigley	
			150/1 M Reid	
Tucson Chrysler Classic				
20/1 D Duval	33/1 J Leonard	-	100/1 T Herron	-
	125/1 D Toms		150/1 S Lowery	
Nissan Open				
100/1 B Mayfair	5/1 T Woods	125/1 S Ames	50/1 P Stewart	-
			66/1 J Daly	
Doral Ryder Open				
80/1 M Bradley	66/1 B Mayfair	-	33/1 V Singh	-
	66/1 J Huston		150/1 M Brisky	
			50/1 S Cink	
Honda Classic				
40/1 M Calcavecchia	25/1 V Singh	20/1 C Montgomerie	50/1 J Daly	-
			80/1 J Maggert	
			66/1 S Appleby	
Bay Hill Invitational				
20/1 E Els	66/1 J Maggert	-	40/1 M Calcavecchia	-
	100/1 B Estes		40/1 B Langer	

Players Championship

50/1 J Leonard	33/1 T Lehman 200/1 G Day	-	40/1 M Calcavecchia	50/1 L Westwood 40/1 S Hoch 200/1 L Mattiace

Freeport McDermott Classic

20/1 L Westwood	200/1 S Flesch	50/1 G Day 150/1 M Wiebe 80/1 S Lowery 150/1 J Carter	-	-

US MASTERS

66/1 M O'Meara	33/1 D Duval 40/1 F Couples	-	50/1 J Furyk	150/1 P Azinger

MCI Classic

20/1 D Love III	80/1 G Day	66/1 P Stewart 20/1 P Mickelson	-	200/1 F Allem

Greater Greensboro Classic

125/1 T Dodds	125/1 S Verplank	28/1 B Estes	150/1 N Lancaster	50/1 F Nobilo

Shell Houston Open

11/1 D Duval	20/1 J Maggert	14/1 F Couples	28/1 L Janzen 66/1 D Hart	-

Bell South Classic

15/2 T Woods	200/1 J D Blake	200/1 E Toledo 80/1 S Flesch	-	150/1 S Verplank 125/1 B Glasson 80/1 B Tway 50/1 S Cink 50/1 J Huston

Byron Nelson Classic

66/1 J Cook	50/1 H Sutton 22/1 F Couples 150/1 H Frazar	-	-	80/1 S Stricker

Mastercard Colonial

66/1 T Watson	125/1 J Furyk	66/1 J Sluman	100/1 H Frazar	33/1 J Cook

The Memorial

25/1 F Couples	125/1 A Magee	14/1 D Duval	22/1 J Furyk	20/1 D Love III 150/1 B Chamblee

Kemper Open

100/1 S Appleby	18/1 S Hoch	20/1 M O'Meara 125/1 B Fabel 80/1 C Dennis 150/1 T Tolles 100/1 F Funk	-	-

Buick Classic

250/1 J P Hayes	20/1 J Furyk	28/1 T Lehman	200/1 B Fleisher	25/1 J Maggert 200/1 T Byrum

US OPEN

66/1 L Janzen	80/1 P Stewart	66/1 B Tway	66/1 N Price	80/1 S Stricker
				20/1 T Lehman

Western Open

125/1 J Durant	50/1 V Singh	100/1 D Hart	-	33/1 S Stricker
		33/1 L Janzen		125/1 G Kraft

Greater Hartford Open

200/1 O Browne	200/1 L Mize	-	100/1 D Waldorf	-
	20/1 S Cink		50/1 F Funk	
			150/1 D Tewell	

Quad City Classic

20/1 S Jones	66/1 S Gump	20/1 K Perry	66/1 D Toms	50/1 B Fabel
				20/1 F Funk
				33/1 S McCarron
				80/1 D A Weibring

Deposit Guaranty Classic

12/1 F Funk	200/1 T Loustalot	-	-	100/1 P H Horgan III
	150/1 F Langholm			80/1 J Magines
	66/1 P Goydos			

THE BRITISH OPEN

40/1 M O'Meara	250/1 B Watts	12/1 T Woods	200/1 R Russell	-
			500/1 J Rose	
			28/1 J Furyk	
			50/1 J Parnevik	

CVS Charity Classic

125/1 S Pate	16/1 S Hoch	-	125/1 N Henke	-
	150/1 B Hughes		125/1 M Heinen	
			125/1 W Wood	

Fedex St Jude Classic

16/1 N Price	66/1 J Sluman	66/1 G Day	66/1 B Estes	500/1 T Conley

Buiok Open

125/1 B Mayfair	66/1 S Verplank	100/1 A Magee	500/1 E Booker	-
			11/2 T Woods	

THE USPGA

50/1 V Singh	66/1 S Stricker	100/1 S Elkington	20/1 N Price	-
			33/1 M O'Meara	
			100/1 F Lickliter	

Sprint Championship

33/1 V Singh	200/1 W Wood	-	8/1 T Woods	150/1 R Mediate
	18/1 P Mickelson			

NEC World Series

20/1 D Duval	12/1 P Mickelson	14/1 D Love III	40/1 J Cook	50/1 L Roberts
				7/1 T Woods

Greater Vancouver Open

40/1 B Chamblee	20/1 P Stewart	150/1 L Porter	125/1 B Claar	100/1 O Uresti
				150/1 H Royer
				20/1 J Maggert
				80/1 M Weir
				25/1 R Cochran
				25/1 B Estes

Greater Milwaukee Open

33/1 J Sluman	16/1 S Stricker	33/1 M Calcavecchia	-	-
		100/1 N Henke		
		80/1 C Perry		

Canadian Open

66/1 B Andrade	150/1 B Friend	150/1 M Hulbert	40/1 H Sutton	-
			125/1 B Hughes	
			50/1 G Day	

BC Open

25/1 C Perry	80/1 P Jacobsen	50/1 N Henke	150/1 C Byrum	-
			40/1 R Allenby	
			100/1 T Tryba	

Texas Open

33/1 H Sutton	16/1 J Leonard	-	200/1 M Reid	-
	50/1 J Haas		100/1 S Lowery	
			28/1 A Magee	
			20/1 L Roberts	

Buick Challenge

33/1 S Elkington	28/1 F Funk	40/1 B Glasson	125/1 J L Lewis	100/1 S Kendall

Michelob Championship

9/1 D Duval	200/1 P Tataurangi	150/1 B Cheesman	40/1 P Stewart	-
			100/1 B Hughes	

Las Vegas

33/1 J Furyk	25/1 M Calcavecchia	80/1 S Verplank	50/1 B Tway	12/1 D Love III

National Car Rental Golf Classic at Disney

50/1 J Huston	14/1 D Love	100/1 B Geiberger	50/1 J Parnevik	-
			150/1 R Mediate	
			200/1 T Purtzer	

The Tour Championship

40/1 H Sutton	20/1 V Singh	18/1 J Furyk	-	25/1 S Stricker
		33/1 J Parnevik		25/1 J Leonard
				66/1 S Verplank

THE MERCEDES CHAMPIONSHIP

Date	8th – 11th January
Course	La Costa, Carlsbad, California
Par	72
Yardage	7,022
First Prize	$216,000
Total Purse	$1.2 million

This tournament is open only to players who were US tour winners in 1997. So with Bill Glasson unfit, 30 players teed off. There were ten foreign born players, and ten players in their twenties. Overall the 30 players had won 20 majors between them.

1998 ODDS

fav	11/2	Tiger Woods (DC)	33/1	John Cook
	11/1	Davis Love III	33/1	Frank Nobilo
	12/1	Ernie Els	40/1	Loren Roberts
	14/1	David Duval	40/1	Steve Jones
	14/1	Phil Mickelson	40/1	Stewart Cink
	16/1	Nick Price	50/1	Scott McCarron
	16/1	Greg Norman	50/1	Paul Stankowski
	22/1	Justin Leonard	50/1	Stuart Appleby
	22/1	Scott Hoch	66/1	Jeff Sluman
	25/1	Steve Elkington	66/1	Tim Herron
	25/1	Mark O'Meara	80/1	David Frost*
	28/1	Vijay Singh	80/1	Phil Blackmar
	33/1	Nick Faldo	100/1	David Toms*
	33/1	Mark Calcavecchia	150/1	Billy Ray Brown
	33/1	Brad Faxon	150/1	Gabriel Hjerstedt

ALL QUOTED
25 players were priced at or under 66/1.

BOOKIES AT ODDS

Greg Norman 9/1 Corals: 16/1 City Index
Steve Elkington 14/1 Hills: 25/1 Stanleys, Surrey
Nick Faldo 20/1 City Index, Hills, Stan James: 33/1 Sunderlands
Steve Jones 22/1 Chandlers: 40/1 Stan James, Sunderlands
The winner Phil Mickelson 12/1 Hills: 14/1 generally.

1998 RESULT

1	14/1	Phil Mickelson	68 67 68 68	271
T2 fav	11/2	Tiger Woods	72 67 69 64	272
T2	25/1	Mark O'Meara	71 70 67 64	272
T4	16/1	Nick Price	66 70 69 70	275
T4	33/1	John Cook	65 70 70 70	275

T6	M Calcavecchia	70 74 66 67 277		T19	J Sluman	70 75 71 68 284
	S Cink	71 67 71 68 277			S Elkington	72 73 71 68 284
	G Hjerstedt	69 68 69 71 277			S Hoch	70 70 69 75 284
	D Duval	68 70 66 73 277		T22	D Toms	73 75 70 67 285
T10	E Els	67 71 71 69 278			N Faldo	71 75 70 69 285
	F Nobilo	67 69 70 72 278			B Faxon	72 72 70 71 285
12	S McCarron	70 71 70 68 279		T25	P Blackmar	73 69 73 71 286
T13	S Jones	69 71 72 68 280			J Leonard	73 73 69 71 286
	V Singh	75 72 67 66 280		27	G Norman	73 72 73 70 388
	P Stankowski	69 72 69 70 280		28	B R Brown	69 74 71 75 289
	L Roberts	70 72 68 70 280		29	T Herron	74 75 68 73 290
	D Love III	70 72 67 71 280		30	S Appleby	77 72 73 72 294
18	D Frost	74 72 68 68 282				

PUNTERS' POINTS

- What a cracking tournament to start the year. 14/1 Phil Mickelson, the only player to shoot four sub-70 rounds took a two-shot lead up the 18th in the final round, made bogey and won. Although Tiger Woods led at the twelfth in the final round, Mickelson quickly regained the lead and never lost it again.

- However the great sight, and I mean great sight, of the final day was watching the 2-ball of Tiger Woods and Mark O'Meara. One in his forties, one in his twenties: one white, one black; both friends and neighbours! ......and both shot 64.

- After a poor start Tiger Woods finished like an express train. That improvement may have been related to the fact that he had switched from Mizuno to Titleist irons. It is hoped the change will give him greater control of his wedge shots and improve his performance in cross winds.

- Greg Norman once more proved that this is simply not his tournament, and not his coast. His 27th place meant that anyone following the advice in last year's player profile to oppose him in match bets and on spread betting terms will have made huge profits.

- 16/1 Nick Price's performance was really eye catching. A winner of the Sun City Million in December, here he played very well to finish T4th. Back to his best he's set for a good season.

- 14/1 David Duval's 73 in R4 brought memories of his final round fade outs early last year. It will be interesting to see if his confidence is affected....I doubt it as he now knows (and has proved it three times) that he's a winner.

- 150/1 Gabriel Hjerstedt was the 'surprise' package of the tournament. His recovery shots kept his score going to give him a T6th finish. However, I don't think he'll be a player to follow this year.

- Finally, congratulations to Victor Chandlers for paying one-quarter the odds on the 5th place. It proved costly as Nick Price (16/1) and John Cook (33/1) were both well supported each way.

ROUND BY ROUND LEADERBOARD

FIRST ROUND		SECOND ROUND	
J Cook	7 under	P MICKELSON	9 under
N Price	6 under	J Cook	9 under
E Els	5 under	F Nobilo	8 under
F Nobilo	5 under	N Price	8 under
D Duval	4 under	G Hjerstedt	7 under
P MICKELSON	4 under	D Duval	6 under
		E Els	6 under
		S Cink	6 under

THIRD ROUND		FINAL ROUND	
P MICKELSON	13 under	P MICKELSON	17 under
D Duval	12 under	T Woods	16 under
N Price	11 under	M O'Meara	16 under
J Cook	11 under	N Price	13 under
F Nobilo	10 under	J Cook	13 under
G Hjerstedt	10 under		

PLEASE NOTE Only 4 players completed play on the second day due to heavy rain which first delayed and later halted play.

1997 RESULT

1	12/1	Tiger Woods

(Woods won at the first play-off hole)

2	12/1	Tom Lehman
3	125/1	Guy Boros
T4	80/1	Paul Goydos
T4	14/1	Fred Couples

WINNERS IN THE '90s

1990	Paul Azinger	1995	Steve Elkington
1991	Tom Kite	1996	Mark O'Meara
1992	Steve Elkington	1997	Tiger Woods
1993	Davis Love III	1998	Phil Mickelson
1994	Phil Mickelson		

PUNTERS' GUIDE

- With only thirty or so 'runners' this event offers punters a real chance especially if they can bet each way on the fifth place.
- It is essential to back only players who are proven early-season performers.
- In 1999 the tournament moves from its 'home' in Carlsbad, California to the island of Maui, Hawaii previous home of the Kapalua International.
- The change of venue will suit Davis Love III and Fred Couples who are both two-time winners of the Kapalua and will have PMA-based confidence going into the 1999 Mercedes.

THE BOB HOPE CHRYSLER CLASSIC

Date	14th – 18th January			
Courses	Bermuda Dunes	Indian Wells	La Quinta	PGA West
Par	72	72	72	72
Yardage	6,927	6,478	6,901	6,894
First Prize	$414,000			
Total Purse	$2.3 million			

Held in California, this is an unusual tournament as for the first four days each pro plays with a different amateur threesome on each of the courses, after which the cut is made. Of the 128 pros the top 70 (plus ties) go forward to play the final day, without the amateurs, on one of the courses selected by rotation – this year it was held at Bermuda Dunes.

1998 ODDS

fav	14/1	David Duval	40/1	Paul Stankowski
	16/1	Mark O'Meara	50/1	Chris Smith
	16/1	John Cook (DC)	50/1	Andrew Magee
	20/1	Jim Furyk	50/1	Jeff Sluman
	20/1	Scott Hoch	66/1	Steve Stricker
	20/1	Jesper Parnevik	66/1	Tom Byrum
	20/1	Mark Calcavecchia	66/1	Jay Haas*
	22/1	Fred Couples	66/1	Grant Waite
	28/1	Steve Jones	66/1	Kenny Perry
	33/1	Lee Janzen	66/1	Fred Funk*
	33/1	Loren Roberts	66/1	Bob Estes
	33/1	Stuart Cink	66/1	Gabriel Hjerstedt
	40/1	Tommy Tolles	66/1	Steve Lowery

26 players were best priced at or under 66/1.

BOOKIES AT ODDS

Jay Haas 66/1 Ladbrokes: 33/1 Hills

Fred Funk 66/1 Chandler, Corals: 33/1 Tote, Ladbrokes, Surrey

The winner Fred Couples was biggest with City Index at 22/1 when the general quote was 20/1, although Corals and Sunderlands went just 16/1.

1998 RESULT

1	22/1	**Fred Couples**	**64 70 66 66 66**	**332**
		(Couples won at the first play-off hole)		
2	200/1	**Bruce Lietzke**	**65 65 71 62 69**	**332**
3	50/1	**Andrew Magee**	**63 68 64 68 70**	**333**
T4	14/1	**David Duval**	**65 67 68 67 68**	**335**
T4	28/1	**Steve Jones**	**66 70 65 65 69**	**335**

T6	S Cink	65 67 67 68 69 336		J Kelly	70 68 70 64 73 345
	M O'Meara	67 67 65 68 69 336		T Tryba	67 70 70 71 67 345
T8	S Kendall	69 66 69 68 67 339		S Flesch	67 69 70 72 67 345
	F Zoeller	66 69 68 66 70 339		J Ozaki	67 68 70 73 66 345
T10	K Triplett	71 67 69 66 67 340		S Gump	66 68 70 71 71 346
	P Stankowski	69 69 65 70 67 340		L Rinker	70 71 67 68 70 346
	J Huston	67 70 67 68 68 340		F Funk	71 74 65 66 70 346
	B Fabel	64 70 66 69 71 340		D Martin	69 67 69 69 72 346
	M Wiebe	73 65 66 66 70 340		C Pavin	70 71 68 69 68 346
	B Tway	65 68 67 69 71 340		R Cochran	73 67 69 69 68 346
T16	R Fehr	71 66 68 69 67 341		P H Horgan III	68 65 69 73 72 347
	P Jordan	65 72 72 64 68 341		M Christie	69 69 67 71 71 347
	C Perry	69 70 70 64 68 341		D Forsman	67 74 67 69 70 347
T19	B McCallister	66 67 73 69 67 342		H Sutton	68 66 71 71 72 348
	L Roberts	70 68 66 68 70 342		C Smith	67 71 70 68 72 348
	B Estes	68 68 67 67 72 342		L Janzen	69 67 71 69 72 348
	D Toms	66 71 66 67 72 342		J Haas	66 71 71 70 70 348
	M Calcavecchia	69 67 70 65 71 342		L Nelson	71 71 69 67 70 348
T24	S Lowery	64 71 70 70 68 343		D Hammond	70 70 68 70 70 348
	P Azinger	69 69 67 70 68 343		S Pate	70 69 69 70 70 348
	O Uresti	73 65 66 71 68 343		L Porter	68 69 68 71 73 349
	G Day	68 67 67 71 70 343		J Sluman	72 65 71 69 72 349
	P Goydos	68 67 72 63 73 343		F Langham	66 70 69 72 72 349
	D Stockton Jr	67 70 71 67 69 344		L Mattiace	69 67 73 69 71 349
	S Stricker	69 70 68 67 70 344		Lee Rinker	72 73 67 67 70 349
	N Lancaster	66 71 68 70 69 344		B Geiberger	69 71 70 69 71 350
	J D Blake	70 71 68 67 68 344		T Tolles	67 72 65 67 80 351
	S Appleby	70 70 69 67 68 344		B Gilder	72 68 69 70 72 351
	L Mize	69 69 69 70 67 344		F Lickliter	69 69 69 71 74 352
	S Verplank	73 68 70 64 70 345		B Kamm	69 74 69 67 73 352
	R Damron	68 73 68 65 71 345		J Parnevik	71 70 68 68 76 353
	C Stadler	73 64 70 67 71 345		C DiMarco	72 70 70 67 74 353
	B Cheesman	72 68 64 69 72 345			

ROUND BY ROUND LEADERBOARD

FIRST ROUND		SECOND ROUND	
A Magee	9 under	B Lietzke	14 under
B Fabel	8 under	A Magee	13 under
S Lowery	8 under	D Duval	12 under
F COUPLES	8 under	S Cink	12 under
D Duval	7 under	B Tway	11 under
B Lietzke	7 under	B McCallister	11 under
P Jordan	7 under	P H Horgan III	11 under
S Cink	7 under	F COUPLES	10 under
W Wood	7 under		
B Tway	7 under		

THIRD ROUND		FOURTH ROUND	
A Magee	21 under	B Lietzke	25 under
S Cink	17 under	A Magee	25 under
M O'Meara	17 under	F COUPLES	22 under
F COUPLES	16 under	S Jones	22 under
B Tway	16 under	S Cink	21 under
D Duval	16 under	M O'Meara	21 under
B Fabel	16 under	D Duval	21 under

FINAL ROUND	
F COUPLES	28 under
B Lietzke	28 under
A Magee	27 under
D Duval	25 under
S Jones	25 under

PUNTERS' POINTS

- 16/1 Fred Couples' victory came at a point when his career was said to be at a cross roads. In 1997 his new girlfriend was diagnosed to have breast cancer and he ended the year nursing his father who died in November.
- However, here in the relaxed Pro-Am atmosphere he loves, with his back in good shape, he came from behind to land his thirteenth tour victory after a play-off. Boom-Boom is back!
- 46-year-old 200/1 outsider Bruce Lietzke nearly brought a huge smile to the bookies' faces. The part-time golfer and avid fisherman had won the Shark Shoot Out (with Scott McCarron at 25/1) before Xmas, and had a proven Bob Hope record (2nd as long ago as 1977 and a top 15 as recently as 1996) so his fine form was not a complete surprise although it was only his second official tour event in eight months!!
- Stan James went 8/11 Couples evens Lietzke for the play-off.
- After missing a 6 footer to win Lietzke could not match Couples' birdie in the play-off on the par 5 18th.
- 50/1 third-placed Andrew Magee playing for the first time since the Mexican Open, could not quite regain his earlier form on the final day. Nevertheless

he'd played really well and clearly merited the F, S and g symbols given to him last year.

- David Duval 2nd here in 1995, his rookie year, once more played consistently to finish T4th, and will surely be a factor here again in the future.
- And so too will straight hitting Stewart Cink who in just two tournaments here has finished T6th 1998, and T9th in 1997.
- Only four players posted five sub-70 rounds – they were Duval, Cink, O'Meara and noticeably 33-year-old Skip Kendall who was building on his best-ever season last year.
- Players to miss the 72-hole cut included defending champion 16/1 John Cook, 20/1 Jim Furyk, 20/1 Scott Hoch and 66/1 chances Kenny Perry, Gabriel Hjerstedt, and Grant Waite.

1997 RESULT

1	33/1	John Cook
2	40/1	Mark Calcavecchia
3	50/1	Jesper Parnevik
4	25/1	Mark O'Meara

WINNERS IN THE '90s

1990	Peter Jacobsen
1991	Corey Pavin
1992	John Cook
1993	Tom Kite
1994	Scott Hoch
1995	Kenny Perry
1996	Mark Brooks
1997	John Cook
1998	Fred Couples

PUNTERS' GUIDE

- This decade there have been three keys to finding the winner.
  - > Be a proven winner in their thirties – each of the winners this decade (other than Tom Kite) have been in this category

		Age	Previous US tour wins
1990	Peter Jacobsen	35	3
1991	Corey Pavin	32	7
1992	John Cook	34	3
1993	Tom Kite	43	17
1994	Scott Hoch	38	4
1995	Kenny Perry	34	2
1996	Mark Brooks	34	4
1997	John Cook	39	8
1998	Fred Couples	38	12

  - > Be proven in 90-hole events – the other on the tour is the Las Vegas International.

> Have a track record in celebrity tournaments, such as the AT&T and the Walt Disney Classic, showing they can handle the 'razzmatazz' of such events.

- However in 1999 two younger players must also be noted:-
  > Stewart Cink 25 years old; T6th 1997 and T9th 1996 and
  > David Duval 27 years old; T4th 1997 and 2nd 1995

THE PHOENIX OPEN

Date	22nd – 25th January
Course	Scottsdale, Arizona
Par	71
Yardage	6,992 yards
First Prize	$360,000
Total Purse	$2 million

This well-established tournament has been held at Scottsdale, Arizona since 1987. So punters have plenty of solid course form to study.

1998 ODDS

fav	12/1	Phil Mickelson	33/1	Vijay Singh
	14/1	David Duval	40/1	Andrew Magee
	14/1	Nick Price	50/1	Bob Tway
	14/1	Steve Jones (DC)	50/1	Paul Stankowski
	18/1	Tom Lehman	50/1	Scott McCarron
	20/1	Mark Calcavecchia	66/1	Bruce Lietzke
	28/1	Justin Leonard	66/1	Tommy Tolles*
	33/1	Jesper Parnevik	66/1	Jeff Maggert*
	33/1	Jim Furyk	66/1	Tom Watson
	33/1	Stewart Cink	66/1	Chris Smith
	33/1	Scott Hoch	66/1	Steve Lowery
	33/1	Frank Nobilo	66/1	Steve Stricker
	33/1	Lee Janzen		

25 players were best priced at or under 66/1.

BOOKIES AT ODDS

Justin Leonard 18/1 Hills, Stan James: 28/1 Corals

Vijay Singh 20/1 Chandlers, Tote: 33/1 Hills

Andrew Magee 25/1 Chandler: 40/1 Hills, Ladbrokes

Winner Jesper Parnevik, 20/1 Stan James: 33/1 Surrey, Tote, Ladbrokes, Chandlers

1998 RESULT

Pos	Odds	Player	Scores	Total
1	33/1	Jesper Parnevik	68 68 66 67	269
T2	150/1	Tommy Armour III	68 70 70 64	272
T2	200/1	Steve Pate	69 69 70 64	272
T2	125/1	Brent Geiberger	64 70 72 66	272
T2	66/1	Tom Watson	68 70 68 66	272

Pos	Player	Scores	Total
T6	B Andrade	69 67 71 67	274
	G Day	68 70 69 67	274
T8	J Huston	73 67 68 67	275
	D Hart	70 68 69 68	275
	S McCarron	67 70 70 68	275
	F Lickliter	72 67 66 70	275
T12	J Daly	70 70 66 71	277
	P Stankowski	70 67 67 73	277
T14	T Lehman	71 68 72 67	278
	F Nobilo	69 69 71 69	278
	N Henke	69 71 69 69	278
	L Rinker	65 72 71 70	278
	M Hulbert	63 72 73 70	278
	S Kendall	73 67 67 71	278
	L Janzen	71 68 67 72	278
	S Verplank	73 63 66 76	278
T22	D Sutherland	72 68 70 69	279
	O Browne	70 68 73 68	279
	S Stricker	64 71 73 71	279
	N Price	67 72 68 72	279
	V Singh	69 65 71 74	279
	K Gibson	67 66 76 71	280
	J D Blake	70 69 70 71	280
	K Perry	70 70 72 68	280
	J Leonard	67 71 70 72	280
	P Goydos	71 71 70 68	280
	D Duval	65 70 72 73	280
	R Damron	71 71 71 67	280
	F Funk	72 70 68 71	281
	C Smith	72 69 68 72	281
	R Fehr	67 71 74 69	281
	D Toms	72 67 69 73	281
	C Perry	69 72 72 68	281
	L Mize	69 68 69 75	281
	S Jones	65 69 71 76	281
	J Furyk	72 68 71 71	282
	M Carnevale	69 70 72 71	282
	B Mayfair	72 68 72 70	282
	J Kaye	72 67 73 70	282
	R Cochran	72 70 70 70	282
	D Waldorf	68 70 69 75	282
	M Brooks	71 70 69 73	283
	T Byrum	71 71 69 72	283
	R Mediate	70 72 69 72	283
	C DiMarco	72 69 72 70	283
	K Sutherland	71 67 74 72	284
	D Forsman	68 73 72 71	284
	S Simpson	70 70 74 70	284
	B Estes	73 69 72 70	284
	J Maggert	69 71 71 74	285
	D Martin	72 68 74 71	285
	L Mattiace	70 71 73 71	285
	P Mickelson	68 71 72 75	286
	B Chamblee	69 72 70 75	286
	P Blackmar	71 69 72 74	286
	D Barron	67 70 76 73	286
	A Magee	70 71 75 70	286
	D Hammond	72 70 74 70	286
	M Springer	69 73 69 76	287
	D Edwards	68 73 73 73	287
	D Pooley	68 71 72 77	288
	D Ogrin	70 72 72 75	289
	S Flesch	68 73 77 71	289
	Lee Rinker	69 73 74 74	290
	S Appleby	73 69 75 73	290
	T Tryba	71 69 75 77	292
	W Levi	74 68 77 75	294

ROUND BY ROUND LEADERBOARD

FIRST ROUND		SECOND ROUND	
M Hulbert	8 under	K Gibson	9 under
S Stricker	7 under	S Jones	8 under
B Geiberger	7 under	V Singh	8 under
S Jones	6 under	D Duval	7 under
D Duval	6 under	S Stricker	7 under
L Rinker	6 under	M Hulbert	7 under
J PARNEVIK	3 under	J PARNEVIK	6 under

THIRD ROUND		FINAL ROUND	
J PARNEVIK	11 under	J PARNEVIK	15 under
S Verplank	11 under	T Armour III	12 under
P Stankowski	9 under	S Pate	12 under
F Lickliter	8 under	B Geiberger	12 under
S Jones	8 under	T Watson	12 under
V Singh	8 under		

- The start of the first round was delayed thirty minutes due to frost. Play therefore ended slightly early on that opening day because of darkness with five players still to complete their rounds.

PUNTERS' POINTS

- With six wins worldwide and five second places in 1997 Jesper Parnevik, at 33/1, finally broke through here to land his first (and it sure won't be his last) American tournament victory on the course where he finished second last year.
- Final-day tension certainly took its toll.
  > Brent Geiberger was joint leader at 13 under when he stood on the 17th tee and promptly drove into the water.
  > Steve Pate made a bogey on the last hole.
  > Scott Verplank went into the final round as the joint leader only to shoot a 76 and finish T14th!
- Tom Watson's fine performance in finishing T2nd at 66/1 could be very significant as his putting was really good: "I putted like I did when I was 25 years old. I'm following through on my putts and I'm not stopping on impact."
- In future it may be worth noting that three players finished very strongly.
  > John Huston 11 under over the last three rounds finished T8th
  > Dudley Hart 8 under over the last three rounds finished T8th
  > Glen Day 7 under over the last three rounds finished T6th
- It was good to see John Daly on the comeback trail again. Cheered onto every tee and onto every green 'the Wild Thing' finished a very respectable T12th and looked focussed. Let's hope he can conquer his inner demons.
- Among those to miss the cut were 20/1 Mark Calcavecchia, 33/1 Stewart Cink, 50/1 Bob Tway, 66/1 Tommy Tolles and 100/1 outsiders Kirk Triplett, Grant Waite and Hal Sutton.

1997 RESULT

1	20/1	Steve Jones
2	33/1	Jesper Parnevik
3	33/1	Nick Price
T4	50/1	Kenny Perry
T4	25/1	Mark Calcavecchia
T4	100/1	Rick Fehr

WINNERS IN THE '90s

1990	Tommy Armour III
1991	Nolan Henke
1992	Mark Calcavecchia
1993	Lee Janzen
1994	Bill Glasson
1995	Vijay Singh
1996	Phil Mickelson
1997	Steve Jones
1998	Jesper Parnevik

PUNTERS' GUIDE

- This tournament should carry a punters' wealth warning. In the last six years 31 players have finished in the top 4 (or T4th), 8 were over 100/1, and 12 were 66/1 or 80/1. So two thirds (20 from 31) were 66/1 plus!

- Apart from Jesper Parnevik the only player to have posted top 10 finishes in each of the last two years is the long hitting Scott McCarron (T8th 1998: T7th 1997). He must have a leading chance in 1999.

- Course form is a major factor in this tournament as the last four winners' records show.

Year	Winner	Previous Course form
1998	Jesper Parnevik	2nd 1997
1997	Steve Jones	T10th 1996
1996	Phil Mickelson	T8th 1994
1995	Vijay Singh	Top 20 1994

THE AT&T PEBBLE BEACH NATIONAL PRO-AM

Date 29th January – 1st February

Course	Pebble Beach	Spyglass Hill	Poppy Hills
Par	72	72	72
Yardage	6,799	6,859	6,861
First Prize	$360,000		
Total Purse	$2 million		

This unique tournament, held in California, is played on three different courses over the first three days, before the cut is made after the third round. However on the final day the leading amateurs continue to play on.

1998 ODDS

fav	5/1	Tiger Woods		40/1	Steve Elkington
	14/1	Mark O'Meara (DC)		40/1	Tom Watson*
	16/1	Davis Love III		40/1	Paul Stankowski
	16/1	David Duval		40/1	Billy Andrade
	22/1	Phil Mickelson		50/1	John Cook
	25/1	Tom Lehman		50/1	Scott McCarron
	25/1	Jesper Parnevik		50/1	Stewart Cink
	33/1	Justin Leonard		66/1	Andrew Magee
	33/1	Vijay Singh		66/1	Jeff Maggert
	40/1	Jim Furyk		66/1	Payne Stewart*
	40/1	Brad Faxon			

21 players were best priced at or under 66/1.

BOOKIES AT ODDS

DYM Tom Watson 20/1 Corals: 40/1 Surrey

DYM Payne Stewart 33/1 Corals: 66/1 Hills, Surrey

Winner Phil Mickelson 14/1 Ladbrokes, Hills, Stan James: 22/1 Corals

ROUND BY ROUND LEADERBOARD

FIRST ROUND		SECOND ROUND	
T Lehman	8 under	T Watson	10 under
P MICKELSON	7 under	T Herron	10 under
J Parnevik	5 under	P MICKELSON	9 under
D Toms	5 under	T Lehman	9 under
T Pernice Jr	5 under	P Azinger	8 under
F Allem	5 under	J Furyk	8 under
P Azinger	5 under	D Love III	8 under
T Watson	5 under	C Smith	8 under
		T Pernice Jr	8 under

THIRD and FINAL ROUND

- Heavy rain and hail caused a four-hour delay on the first day with players completing only nine holes. On the second day the first round was completed.

- The second round was completed on Saturday.

- It was decided that Sunday's third round would complete the tournament and as each player would then have completed each course the result would be official.

  However although some players played a few holes the play was abandoned as the courses, especially the greens were waterlogged.

- The third round was to be completed on Monday with only the professionals playing. However the weather prevented any further play so the tour announced that the third round would be restarted and completed on 17th August.

  This decision particularly helped the players (like Tom Watson) who had not started the third round too well and penalised the likes of Tim Herron who had begun that round with a birdie or two.

17TH AUGUST

The tournament was concluded on Monday, 17th August the day following Vijay Singh's 50/1 USPGA victory.

The betting then was

fav 6/1	Phil Mickelson	9 under	Pebble Beach
13/2	Tom Lehman	9 under	Spyglass Hill
7/1	Tom Watson	10 under	Poppy Hill
9/1	Davis Love III	8 under	Poppy Hill
9/1	Tim Herron	10 under	Spyglass Hill
9/1	Jim Furyk	8 under	Pebble Beach
12/1	Jay Haas	9 under	Spyglass Hill
16/1	Paul Azinger	8 under	Poppy Hill
25/1	Chris Smith	8 under	Poppy Hill
28/1	Tom Pernice Jr	8 under	Poppy Hill
40/1	Steve Elkington*	6 under	Poppy Hill
40/1	J P Hayes	7 under	Poppy Hill
50/1	Bar		

1998 RESULT

1	22/1	Phil Mickelson (6/1)	65 70 67	202
2	250/1	Tom Pernice Jr (28/1)	67 69 67	203
T3	40/1	Jim Furyk (9/1)	69 67 68	204
T3	125/1	Paul Azinger (16/1)	67 69 68	204
T3	250/1	J P Hayes (40/1)	70 67 67	204

T6	J Haas	68 67 70 205		N Lancaster	71 70 72 213
	F Zoeller	70 70 65 205		J Carter	69 72 72 213
	S Elkington	70 68 67 205		L Rinker	74 69 70 213
T9	T Watson	67 67 72 206		D Hart	71 68 74 213
	C Smith	69 67 70 206		J Estes	71 73 69 213
	B Gilder	68 70 68 206		M Reid	70 70 74 214
	T Lehman	64 71 71 206		O Browne	70 71 73 214
T13	T Dodds	69 69 69 207		S Kendall	73 70 71 214
	D Toms	67 71 69 207		S McCarron	69 72 73 214
	P Jordan	70 69 68 207		D Frost	71 74 69 214
	S McRoy	71 69 67 207		O Uresti	74 70 70 214
	K Triplett	70 68 69 207		W Levi	69 74 71 214
	J Gallagher	68 71 68 207		T Armour III	69 72 73 214
T19	T Herron	68 66 74 208		B Estes	72 71 72 215
	J Parnevik	67 72 69 208		D Forsman	69 74 72 215
	P Stewart	71 70 67 208		J Johnston	75 71 69 215
T22	M Brooks	68 72 69 209		J Daly	70 71 74 215
	D Love III	68 68 73 209		B Henninger	71 71 73 215
	G Day	70 71 68 209		M Wurtz	70 72 73 215
T25	J Sluman	71 70 69 210		K Perry	73 72 70 215
	S Skinner	70 71 69 210		W Austin	76 68 70 216
	T Tolles	73 71 66 210		J Delsing	76 71 69 216
	Joe Ozaki	71 69 70 210		B Fleisher	69 74 73 216
	R Mediate	70 68 72 210		C Barlow	70 75 71 216
	S Gump	73 70 67 210		B Cheesman	72 74 70 216
	H Frazar	71 67 72 210		E Toledo	71 72 73 216
	S Cink	70 69 71 210		K Gibson	72 74 70 216
	C Stadler	70 68 72 210		G Kraft	72 73 71 216
	C Dennis	76 71 63 210		B Wadkins	72 72 72 216
	S Randolph	72 72 66 210		B Andrade	72 72 73 217
	D Martin	72 68 70 210		J Adams	69 74 74 217
	T Purtzer	71 70 70 211		M Wiebe	75 70 72 217
	L Mattiace	72 68 71 211		A Magee	73 71 73 217
	C Rose	75 70 66 211		D Pride	75 70 72 217
	T Loustalot	73 69 69 211		P Tataurangi	70 76 71 217
	F Langham	73 70 68 211		W Wood	70 75 73 218
	L Porter	70 68 73 211		M Weir	69 75 74 218
	R Friend	69 73 69 211		I Gooch	70 71 77 218
	B Bates	70 71 70 211		F Lickliter	74 73 71 218
	D Hammond	72 70 70 212		G Stubblefield	73 76 69 218
	K Jones	73 68 71 212		K Wenthworth	70 71 77 218
	C Pavin	71 70 71 212		J Pate	70 72 76 218
	F Allem	67 73 72 212		K Nolan	73 70 75 218
	P Jacobsen	68 70 74 212		C Perry	71 76 72 219
	P H Horgan III	68 76 68 212		G Sauers	71 72 76 219
	J Riegger	72 69 71 212		B Porter	73 75 71 219

G Hallberg	68 71 73 212		L Rinker	72 74 73 219
J Leonard	68 73 71 212		L Hinkle	73 73 74 220
B R Brown	72 70 70 212		B Quigley	70 74 76 220
M Small	74 70 68 212		I Steel	72 74 74 220
K Sutherland	72 69 72 213		M Springer	68 73 79 220
J McGovern	72 71 70 213		R Maltbie	74 71 76 221
D Sutherland	70 74 69 213		S Jurgensen	77 69 75 221
S Flesch	73 68 72 213		S Schneiter	73 77 72 222
M Brisky	72 69 72 213		V Veazey	73 75 74 222
J Cook	71 71 71 213		T Conley	72 76 74 222
R Coughlan	70 70 73 213		S McMichael	76 70 77 223
B Kamm	70 72 71 213		M Soli	75 79 71 225
J Johnson	71 70 72 213		D Pohl	77 73 77 227
B Faxon	72 68 73 213		G Burns	79 77 77 233

PUNTERS' POINTS

- In this much-delayed event Phil Mickelson's round of 67 at Pebble Beach earned him his 13th win on the USPGA tour. He also became the fifth multiple winner on the tour this year.

  > Needing a birdie at the par 5 last to win he reached the green in two then two putted for victory.

- Tom Pernice Jr. had shot a 79 in R4 when in contention in the Kemper Open. Here he took his final-day chance to shoot a 67 at Poppy Hills and earn his biggest-ever cheque and secure his tour card for 1999.

- After two successive missed cuts Jim Furyk will have had his confidence restored to some extent after his final round 68 took him into T3rd place. However he has still to win this season.

- J P Hayes had won his first tournament, the Buick Classic, since the AT&T started, so he returned to the final day a more self-assured player than when he left it. He shot an excellent 67 to post another high finish.

- The final-round disappointments were:-

  > Tom Watson with a 72 at Poppy Hills to finish T9th.

  > Final-day leader Tim Herron at Spyglass Hill with a 74 to finish T19th.

  > Final-day second favourite Tom Lehman finished T9th after a 71 at Spyglass Hill.

  > Davis Love III who shot a 73 at Poppy Hills to finish T22nd.

1997 RESULT

1	22/1	Mark O'Meara
T2 jt fav	14/1	Tiger Woods
T2	50/1	David Duval
4	40/1	Jim Furyk

WINNERS IN THE '90s

1990	Mark O'Meara
1991	Paul Azinger
1992	Mark O'Meara
1992	Brett Ogle
1994	Johnny Miller
1995	Peter Jacobsen
1996	Void
1997	Mark O'Meara
1998	Phil Mickelson

PUNTERS' GUIDE

- There are three guidelines for this unique tournament. Your player
  - > Should have a sound record in this unusual celebrity studded event.
  - > A proven ability to handle the windy conditions that can occur at Pebble Beach
  - > Should have experience on his side. Six of the last eight winners have been thirty one or over, with three of the last four in their forties.
- Paul Azinger (T3rd 1998: T7th 1997 and winner in 1991) meets all the criteria and must have a leading chance in 1999.

THE BUICK INVITATIONAL

Date	5th – 8th February
Course	Torrey Pines, California
Par	North Course South Course
	72 72
Yardage	6,592
First Prize	$378,000
Total Purse	$2.1 million

Held at Torrey Pines since 1968 there is plenty of course form available to punters. This year there were twelve previous winners in the 156-man field.

1998 ODDS

fav	13/2	Tiger Woods		40/1	Billy Andrade
	12/1	Phil Mickelson		50/1	Scott McCarron
	14/1	Davis Love III		50/1	Payne Stewart
	20/1	Fred Couples		66/1	Steve Stricker
	20/1	Mark O'Meara (DC)		66/1	Andrew Magee
	20/1	David Duval		66/1	Tim Herron*
	20/1	Jesper Parnevik		66/1	Jay Haas*
	28/1	Lee Janzen		66/1	Chris Smith
	33/1	Justin Leonard		66/1	Steve Lowery
	33/1	Stewart Cink		66/1	Craig Stadler*
	33/1	Mark Calcavecchia*		66/1	Bob Tway
	40/1	Brad Faxon			

23 players were best priced at or under 66/1.

BOOKIES AT ODDS

Mark Calcavecchia 16/1 Ladbrokes, Tote: 33/1 Chandlers

Jay Haas 28/1 Tote: 66/1 Ladbrokes, City Index

Craig Stadler 28/1 Tote, Chandlers: 66/1 Ladbrokes

Tim Herron 33/1 Chandlers: 66/1 Sunderlands

Winner DYM Scott Simpson 66/1 Chandlers, Corals: 150/1 Hills, Surrey

Second-placed DYM Skip Kendall 50/1 Chandlers, Corals: 100/1 Stan James, Stanleys, City Index

1998 RESULT

1	150/1	Scott Simpson	69 71 64	204
		(Simpson won at the first play-off hole)		
2	100/1	Skip Kendall	71 63 70	204
T3 fav	13/2	Tiger Woods	71 66 68	205
T3	14/1	Davis Love III	62 73 70	205
T3	150/1	Kevin Sutherland	68 67 70	205

T6	T Armour III	67 73 66 206		B Wadkins	65 73 73 211
	B Geiberger	67 72 67 206		B Mayfair	76 66 69 211
	R Cochran	67 70 69 206		S McCarron	68 69 74 211
	J L Lewis	70 67 69 206		S Stricker	70 66 75 211
	S McRoy	70 66 70 206		D Waldorf	71 71 69 211
	S Jurgensen	63 73 70 206		S Lyle	69 71 72 212
	S Pate	67 65 74 206		Larry Rinker	71 68 73 212
T13	B Gilder	72 67 68 207		S Gump	69 70 73 212
	C Stadler	69 70 68 207		P Mickelson	70 69 73 212
	S Cink	65 72 70 207		G Day	70 68 74 212
T16	J Daly	70 70 68 208		D Ogrin	68 70 74 212
	D Martin	65 71 72 208		J Durant	68 70 74 212
	R Damron	68 67 73 208		A Magee	68 74 70 212
	J Sanday	63 72 73 208		J Gallagher	71 69 73 213
	J Sluman	67 69 72 208		M Calcavecchia	69 72 72 213
	B Tway	63 72 73 208		M O'Meara	71 70 72 213
T22	P Stewart	66 72 71 209		M Springer	68 73 72 213
	L Janzen	70 71 68 209		F Zoeller	63 75 75 213
	T Dodds	66 72 71 209		G Twiggs	67 74 72 213
	K Gibson	72 65 72 209		P Azinger	66 72 75 213
	T Kite	65 70 74 209		D Forsman	71 71 71 213
	P Goydos	67 73 70 210		P Jacobsen	69 73 71 213
	R W Eaks	65 75 70 210		R Mediate	68 74 71 213
	B Estes	66 73 71 210		M Bradley	69 71 74 214
	T Pernice Jr	71 69 70 210		J McGovern	74 68 72 214
	M Standly	70 71 69 210		D Stockton Jr	73 69 72 214
	J D Blake	70 71 69 210		J Adams	71 71 72 214
	S Skinner	69 73 68 210		V Veazey	71 71 72 214
	B McCallister	73 69 68 210		C Perry	65 75 75 215
	L Porter	69 70 72 211		J Riegger	69 71 75 215
	J Kelly	67 73 71 211		K Triplett	71 70 74 215
	D A Weibring	67 73 71 211		L Mattiace	71 71 73 215
	R Fehr	69 71 71 211		E Toledo	68 72 76 216
	L Clements	66 73 72 211		F Lickliter	69 72 75 216
	B Henninger	73 66 72 211		J Haas	70 72 74 216
	O Uresti	68 71 72 211		D Barr	71 71 74 216
	S Flesch	72 67 72 211		B Bates	71 71 75 217
	N Lancaster	67 71 73 211		D Edwards	75 67 78 220

ROUND BY ROUND LEADERBOARD

FIRST ROUND		SECOND ROUND	
D Love III	10 under	S Pate	12 under
F Zoeller	9 under	S Kendall	10 under
B Tway	9 under	K Sutherland	9 under
S Jurgenson	9 under	D Love III	9 under
J Sanday	9 under	J Sanday	9 under
T Kite	9 under	B Tway	9 under
S SIMPSON	2 under	T Kite	9 under
		R Damron	9 under
		S SIMPSON	4 under

WHEN PLAY RESUMED ON SUNDAY DURING THE THIRD AND FINAL ROUND

	Holes Played	
S SIMPSON	15	11 under
B Tway	9	11 under
S Pate	8	11 under
K Sutherland	8	11 under
B Geiberger	15	10 under
S McRoy	11	10 under
R Cochran	13	10 under
S Jurgensen	10	10 under
D Love III	9	10 under
J Sanday	10	10 under
T Woods	12	9 under

THIRD AND FINAL ROUND

S SIMPSON	12 under
S Kendall	12 under
T Woods	11 under
D Love III	11 under
K Sutherland	11 under

- Play was suspended during the second day with the second round completed on Saturday. The third round was then started, however rain again caused a suspension of play.
- So the final day started with the third round still incomplete with sixteen players within two shots off the leaders.
- Given the weather forecast on the Sunday it was decided that the tournament would be reduced to 54 holes.

PUNTERS' POINTS

- For the second successive week the famous El Nino storms rolled in off the Pacific Ocean to force another rain-shortened tournament.
- On the Sunday Scott Simpson posted a clubhouse target of 12 under par and then watched "as those guys out there can't make any birdies. I dodged a lot of bullets today".
  - > Tiger Woods's charge was too late. Needing an eagle at the last he made birdie.
  - > Davis Love III dropped vital shots at the 14th and 16th.
  - > Steve Pate suffering from 'contention rust' slipped to T6th with a 74.

> Kevin Sutherland could not make a birdie after bogeying the 13th.

● In form (8-14), and 9th here last year, 100/1 DYM player Skip Kendall was the one to force the play-off. However Simpson's first-extra-hole birdie beat him. While father-to-be Kendall still seeks his first win it was Simpson's seventh victory.

● San Diegan born Simpson no longer lives in California. However his local course knowledge and the calming influence of his caddie, the San Diego Chargers' quarterback Stan Humphries, took him to that nice cheque ($378,000) and that seventh win.

● Simpson's form last year had been so poor that he had to use a one-time exemption given to the top 50 career money winners to retain his tour card for 1998.

● In the last two years five players have posted successive top 20 finishes in this event – Scott Simpson (W-T16), Skip Kendall (2-T9), Craig Stadler (T13-T2), and 1986 winner Bob Tway (T16-T11).

● After the R1 3-ball of Davis Love III (62), Bob Tway (63), and Payne Stewart (66) had finished 25 (!) under par Stewart observed that "when guys are playing well they feed off each other".

● Eight of the market leaders missed the cut. They were 20/1 shots Fred Couples, David Duval and Jesper Parnevik, 33/1 Justin Leonard, 40/1 chances Brad Faxon and Billy Andrade, and 66/1 outsiders Chris Smith and Steve Lowery.

1997 RESULT

1	12/1	Mark O'Meara
T2	125/1	David Ogrin
T2	80/1	Duffy Waldorf
T2	25/1	Lee Janzen
T2	20/1	Jesper Parnevik
T2	80/1	Mike Hulbert
T2	33/1	Craig Stadler
T2	125/1	Donnie Hammond

WINNERS IN THE '90s

1990	Dan Forsman
1991	Jay Don Blake
1992	Steve Pate (3 rounds only)
1993	Phil Mickelson
1994	Craig Stadler
1995	Peter Jacobsen
1996	Davis Love III
1997	Mark O'Meara
1998	Scott Simpson (3 rounds only)

PUNTERS' GUIDE

- The results in recent years make interesting reading:-

			Previous Year's Finish
1998	Scott Simpson	San Diegan	T16th
1997	Mark O'Meara	-	T3rd
1996	Davis Love III	-	T12th
1994	Craig Stadler	San Diegan	T9th
1993	Phil Mickelson	San Diegan	-
1992	Steve Pate	-	Winner in 1988

- This is very much a tournament for Californian-born course specialists. One player who will fit the bill in 1999 is Californian Brent Geiberger (T6th 1998: T25th 1997) who has solid course form.
- If betting in running do remember that the North course in 1998 played 2.25 shots easier than the longer South course.

THE HAWAIIAN OPEN

Date	12th – 15th February
Course	Waialae C.C., Honolulu
Par	72
Yardage	6,975
First Prize	$324,000
Total Purse	$1.8 million

This long-established tournament is always held at the Waialae Club so there is plenty of course form for punters to study.

1998 ODDS

fav	8/1	Tom Lehman	50/1	Skip Kendall*	
	12/1	Jim Furyk	50/1	Paul Goydos*	
	14/1	Fred Couples	50/1	Scott Simpson (PWW)*	
	18/1	Steve Jones	50/1	John Huston	
	20/1	Paul Stankowski (DC)	66/1	Jeff Maggert*	
	20/1	Loren Roberts	66/1	Tim Herron	
	22/1	Tom Watson	66/1	Duffy Waldorf	
	28/1	Craig Stadler	66/1	David Ogrin	
	33/1	Paul Azinger	66/1	Jeff Sluman*	
	40/1	Steve Stricker	66/1	Russ Cochran*	
	40/1	Brent Geiberger			

21 players were best priced at or under 66/1 including 6 DYMs.

BOOKIES AT ODDS

DYM Jeff Sluman 33/1 Chandlers, Ladbrokes, Stanleys: 66/1 City Index

DYM Russ Cochran 28/1 Chandlers: 66/1 Hills

Winner: John Huston was 40/1 or 50/1 throughout the market

1998 RESULT

1	50/1	John Huston	63 65 66 66	260
2	22/1	Tom Watson	67 64 70 66	267
3	125/1	Trevor Dodds	65 70 65 68	268
T4	150/1	Mike Reid	65 68 69 67	269
T4	200/1	Brett Quigley	68 68 67 66	269
T4	150/1	Greg Kraft	69 67 63 70	269

T7	R W Eaks	72 63 70 65 270	B Fabel	71 68 66 71 276
	S Stricker	66 67 68 69 270	K Clearwater	67 65 73 71 276
	O Browne	67 66 66 71 270	K Gibson	68 68 65 75 276
	F Lickliter	68 64 66 72 270	I Steel	71 68 67 70 276
T11	P Jacobsen	69 68 67 67 271	L Roberts	68 69 71 68 276
	L Mize	71 66 66 68 271	W Austin	65 72 67 73 277
	S Jones	68 70 67 66 271	J Ozaki	71 68 66 72 277
	D Waldorf	68 66 67 70 271	T Simpson	70 68 64 75 277
	B Chamblee	68 67 66 70 271	D Stockton Jr	70 67 69 71 277
T16	R Cochran	70 67 67 68 272	L Mattiace	70 67 70 70 277
	K Perry	67 67 68 70 272	R Coughlan	72 65 71 69 277
	J D Blake	70 67 65 70 272	J Gallagher	67 70 72 68 277
	S Kendall	67 63 70 72 272	C Dennis	67 70 72 68 277
	R Gamez	68 67 65 72 272	T Smith	71 68 66 73 278
T21	K Cotner	70 67 67 69 273	K Jones	69 69 68 72 278
	J Furyk	69 68 67 69 273	B R Brown	69 65 72 72 278
	B Geiberger	68 70 66 69 273	P Stankowski	67 71 69 71 278
	C Stadler	69 65 69 70 273	S Skinner	69 67 72 70 278
	T Armour III	67 67 71 68 273	B McCallister	69 69 70 70 278
	M Weir	68 71 68 66 273	J Johnston	72 67 71 68 278
	E Toledo	69 68 67 70 274	C Pavin	71 67 69 72 279
	B Henninger	67 67 70 70 274	D Barron	69 70 71 69 279
	J Maggert	65 69 69 71 274	J Carter	70 69 71 69 279
	C Strange	65 67 71 71 274	J Delsing	68 70 74 68 280
	H Royer, III	67 65 72 70 274	C Barlow	67 70 73 70 280
	P H Horgan III	67 68 68 71 274	M Carnevale	68 70 67 76 281
	D Ogrin	63 69 73 69 274	S Flesch	68 69 71 73 281
	T Byrum	64 68 69 73 274	T Lehman	71 68 72 70 281
	B Mayfair	69 67 68 71 275	J Morse	70 68 70 73 281
	F Couples	70 69 65 71 274	G Sauers	68 70 70 73 281
	T Herron	66 71 68 70 275	M Springer	69 70 71 71 281
	V Veazey	70 69 66 70 275	F Allem	66 68 76 71 281
	H Twitty	70 69 70 66 275	G Hallberg	68 71 71 72 282
	J McGovern	67 70 67 72 276	G Hnatiuk	71 64 71 77 283
	D Pooley	70 65 69 72 276	D Ishii	65 69 74 75 283
	O Uresti	68 67 69 72 276	S McRoy	68 71 70 75 284
	P Goydos	66 68 69 73 276		

ROUND BY ROUND LEADERBOARD

FIRST ROUND		SECOND ROUND	
J HUSTON	9 under	J HUSTON	16 under
D Ogrin	9 under	S Kendall	14 under
T Byrum	8 under	T Watson	13 under
D Ishii	7 under	K Clearwater	12 under
M Reid	7 under	F Lickliter	12 under
C Strange	7 under	C Strange	12 under
W Austin	7 under	D Ogrin	12 under
J Maggert	7 under	T Byrum	12 under
T Dodds	7 under	H Royer	12 under

THIRD ROUND		FINAL ROUND	
J HUSTON	22 under	J HUSTON	28 under
F Lickliter	18 under	T Watson	21 under
G Kraft	17 under	T Dodds	20 under
O Browne	17 under	M Reid	19 under
T Dodds	16 under	B Quigley	19 under
R Gamez	16 under	G Kraft	19 under
S Kendall	16 under		

PUNTERS' POINTS

- In almost windless, and warm conditions, with little rough due to a lack of rain, the course was defenceless against the top American pros with last-placed Spike McRoy finishing 4 under par!
- John Huston, after a poor year in 1997, retained his tour card in 1998 through a one-time use of an exemption as top 50 career money winning player. Following Scott Simpson's win last week after using the same exemption, it proved the importance of the incentive to retain the tour card on ability alone that has inspired both players this year.
- With 31 birdies, and a final 28 under par total 50/1 John Huston's first win outside Florida was a real record-breaker. Huston has always been a 'streak' player – however this was his first 72-hole streak!!
- The importance of the impetus that a player can get from a fast start off an early tee time was well illustrated here by Huston's R1 63 when in the third group out from the first tee, and Tony Watson's R2 64 when in the fifth group out.
- Tom Watson's improved putting was the basis for his second successive second-placed finish. His accurate ball striking and now a smooth putting stroke will surely see him in regular contention in 1998.
- These generally windless and warm conditions encouraged really low scoring, so reducing the comparative advantage of the 'wind' players such as course specialist Paul Azinger who missed the cut by 6 shots.
- Mike 'Radar' Reid, T2nd here at 200/1 in 1997, was again 'in the frame' at huge odds when T4th at 150/1.
- 28-year-old Brett Quigley posted his best ever tour finish. He will take confidence from four sub-70 rounds and a 66 in R4.

• Among those to miss the cut were 33/1 Paul Azinger, 50/1 Scott Simpson (who suffered MLD after last week's win) and 66/1 Jeff Sluman.

1997 RESULT

1	50/1	Paul Stankowski
		(Stankowski won at the 4th extra hole)
T2	18/1	Jim Furyk
T2	200/1	Mike Reid
T4	66/1	Donnie Hammond
T4	50/1	Jay Don Blake

WINNERS IN THE '90s

1990	David Ishii
1991	Lanny Wadkins
1992	John Cook
1993	Howard Twitty
1994	Brett Ogle
1995	John Morse
1996	Jim Furyk
1997	Paul Stankowski
1998	John Huston

PUNTERS' GUIDE

• In 1999 the Sony Open in Hawaii held in the second week of the season will be the new title for this event. It will still be held on the Waialee course.

• With hardly a breath of wind in a record-breaking tournament this year 'normal' breezy Hawaiian conditions might return in 1999. If they do then remember that Paul Azinger in his last seven starts at Waialee has a superb record (six top 10s including three top 4s).

THE TUCSON CHRYSLER CLASSIC

Date	19th – 22nd February
Course	Tucson National, Arizona
Par	72
Yardage	7,148
First Prize	$360,000
Total Purse	$1.5 million

For the second successive year this tournament was played solely on the Tucson National course. It has an extremely difficult final hole – at 465 yards with water right and left it is a challenge to any player needing a par to win.

1998 ODDS

fav	12/1	Phil Mickelson	40/1	Steve Stricker
	16/1	Steve Jones	50/1	John Huston (PWW)
	20/1	David Duval	50/1	Jeff Maggert
	20/1	Tom Lehman	50/1	Andrew Magee
	20/1	Lee Janzen	50/1	Jeff Sluman (DC)
	28/1	Nick Faldo	50/1	Bob Tway
	33/1	Paul Stankowski	50/1	Payne Stewart
	33/1	Justin Leonard	50/1	Russ Cochran
	33/1	John Cook	66/1	Paul Goydos
	33/1	Jim Furyk	66/1	Billy Andrade
	33/1	Loren Roberts	66/1	Bob Estes
	33/1	Scott Hoch	66/1	Brent Geiberger*
	40/1	Mark Calcavecchia		

25 players were best priced at or under 66/1.

BOOKIES AT ODDS

DYM Brent Geiberger 33/1 Chandlers: 66/1 Stanleys

T2nd David Toms 66/1 generally: 125/1 Surrey

T4th DYM Tim Herron 50/1 Tote: 100/1 Ladbrokes

Winner David Duval was 16/1, 18/1, or 20/1 throughout the market

1998 RESULT

1	20/1	David Duval	66 62 68 73	269
T2	33/1	Justin Leonard	65 70 68 70	273
T2	125/1	David Toms	70 67 68 68	273
T4	100/1	Tim Herron	69 70 67 69	275
T4	150/1	Steve Lowery	68 70 68 69	275

T6	B Tway	70 68 71 67	276
	A Magee	69 68 72 67	276
	T Lehman	66 71 69 70	276
T9	S Pate	70 66 72 69	277
	J Furyk	69 70 68 70	277
	T Tolles	69 70 68 70	277
	J Sindelar	72 70 66 69	277
	S Hoch	69 66 71 71	277
T14	M Standly	70 67 72 69	278
	G Hnatiuk	68 74 67 69	278
	R Damron	69 72 68 69	278
	S Lyle	69 69 70 70	278
T18	J Kelly	72 69 70 68	279
	P Stewart	69 70 70 70	279
	J Daly	70 70 69 70	279
	M Reid	71 71 72 65	279
T22	R Cochran	69 71 70 70	280
	S Stricker	73 68 68 71	280
	R Mediate	73 67 67 73	280
T25	D Martin	70 72 69 70	281
	B Estes	72 70 70 69	281
	D Sutherland	67 72 73 69	281
	J Huston	72 66 71 72	281
	B Mayfair	71 69 69 72	281
	D Ogrin	70 69 67 75	281
	G Waite	71 69 72 70	282
	K Perry	71 69 72 70	282
	T Tryba	70 69 72 71	282
	N Henke	69 70 73 70	282
	J Kern	68 72 70 72	282
	C Strange	70 71 69 72	282
	J D Blake	69 72 69 72	282
	D Hart	72 70 71 69	282
	M Bradley	70 73 70 69	282
	M Calcavecchia	68 71 70 73	282
	T Dodds	68 72 74 68	282
	F Allem	71 71 72 68	282
	P Goydos	71 72 65 74	282
	S Verplank	73 70 67 73	283
	L Mattiace	72 69 72 70	283
	M Brisky	72 69 73 69	283
	P H Horgan III	72 71 71 69	283
	Lee Rinker	74 69 68 73	284
	C Hanell	69 72 71 72	284
	R Black	73 69 70 72	284
	J Kaye	67 74 69 74	284
	M Hulbert	70 73 70 71	284
	M Brooks	71 68 69 76	284
	D Rummells	69 72 71 73	285
	K Sutherland	72 70 71 72	285
	Y Mizumaki	72 71 70 72	285
	W Wood	73 68 73 71	285
	J Adams	71 69 74 71	285
	D Edwards	70 73 70 73	286
	J Sluman	73 70 70 73	286
	R Coughlan	73 69 72 72	286
	B Andrade	69 74 71 72	286
	B Cheesman	72 71 71 72	286
	S Jones	68 71 76 71	286
	J Gallagher Jr	70 71 72 74	287
	D Forsman	73 68 74 72	287
	N Faldo	70 73 72 72	287
	K Nolan	69 70 77 71	287
	B Geiberger	69 70 75 74	288
	J L Lewis	72 71 75 70	288
	J McGovern	68 74 71 76	289
	L Roberts	70 73 73 73	289
	B Lietzke	69 74 73 74	290
	J Cook	70 73 75 72	290
	J Delsing	67 72 74 78	291
	O Uresti	71 72 73 75	291
	K Triplett	72 70 72 79	293

ROUND BY ROUND LEADERBOARD

FIRST ROUND		SECOND ROUND	
J Leonard	7 under	D DUVAL	16 under
T Lehman	6 under	J Leonard	9 under
D DUVAL	6 under	S Pate	8 under
J Kaye	5 under	T Lehman	7 under
D Sutherland	5 under	D Toms	7 under
J Delsing	5 under	A Magee	7 under

THIRD ROUND		FINAL ROUND	
D DUVAL	20 under	D DUVAL	19 under
J Leonard	13 under	J Leonard	15 under
D Toms	11 under	D Toms	15 under
D Ogrin	10 under	T Herron	13 under
T Herron	10 under	S Lowery	13 under
S Lowery	10 under		
T Lehman	10 under		
S Hoch	10 under		

PLEASE NOTE The inevitable El Nino-driven heavy rains drenched the course on the Friday afternoon. R2 therefore had to be completed early on Saturday.

PUNTERS' POINTS

- 20/1 David Duval dominated this tournament after shooting 62 in R2. With a 9-shot lead after 42 holes, he still looked a 'certainty' when starting the final round 7 shots clear.

  However, he drove out of bounds at the 13th, Leonard birdied, Duval took triple bogey and, whoops, the lead was just one. Then they were level after Duval bogeyed the 14th. Could Duval come back? Would his one-time doubts about his final round 'bottle' return?

- However the 26-year-old Florida resident chipped in on the 15th to regain the lead and a brilliant final-hole birdie sealed it. It was his fourth win since October, and it sure won't be his last! It moved him to the Number 1 position on the US Money list.

- 33/1 Justin Leonard is rarely at his best early in the season. However here he played well enough to win most tournaments yet had to settle for second place.

- It is worth noting that David Toms won the final day 3-ball, outscoring both Duval and Leonard. His sound form here could be expected as he had led into the final round in this tournament in 1996, finished 3rd in 1992, and entered the week T6th on the 'Putting Leaders' table.

- Tim Herron played really well yet could scarcely hole a putt on the final day. A much-underrated player who has always shown good form in February and March, he is often available at 'value' odds. Here he was a DYM player thanks to Ladbrokes' 100/1.

- The aggressive Steve Lowery also played consistently well on a course suited to his game. If the course is set up similarly in 1999 then he must enter into calculations.

- Among those to miss the cut were 12/1 fav Phil Mickelson, 20/1 Lee Janzen, 33/1 Paul Stankowski, and 50/1 Jeff Maggert.

1997 RESULT

1	100/1	Jeff Sluman
2	16/1	Steve Jones
3	66/1	Brad Bryant
4	33/1	Paul Stankowski

WINNERS IN THE '90s

1990	Robert Gamez
1991	Phil Mickelson
1992	Lee Janzen
1993	Larry Mize
1994	Andrew Magee
1995	Phil Mickelson
1996	Phil Mickelson
1997	Jeff Sluman
1998	David Duval

PUNTERS' GUIDE

- It must be remembered that there was really no rough on this course this year so that there was little penalty for inaccuracy. This is shown by the fact that Duval only hit three out of every five fairways. The flat greens also were not a severe test of putting.

   If this course set-up continues in 1999 it will probably be a recipe for a close finish with outsiders well to the top of the leaderboard. Of the nine players who have finished in the top 4 in the last two years four have been 100/1 or more, and one 66/1.

- Only three players have posted top 20 finishes in each of the two years (1997 & 1998) this tournament has solely used the Tucson National course – Andrew Magee (T6th 1998: T10th 1997), Bob Tway (T6th 1998: T17th 1997), and Jerry Kelly (T18th 1998: T10th 1997).

- This year's winner, David Duval, finished within 7 shots of the lead in 1997. On that form it may be wise to start your search for the 1999 winner with the eight players who finished within 7 shots of this year's winner.

THE NISSAN OPEN

Date	26th February – 1st March
Course	Valencia C.C., California
Par	71
Yardage	7,038
First Prize	$378,000
Total Purse	$2.1 million

For the first time since 1983 the Nissan Open moved from its traditional venue, the Riviera Country Club, to the Valencia Club.

1998 ODDS

fav	5/1	Tiger Woods		50/1	Bob Tway
	20/1	Phil Mickelson		50/1	Craig Stadler
	20/1	Justin Leonard		50/1	Scott McCarron
	20/1	Tom Lehman		50/1	Payne Stewart
	20/1	Fred Couples		50/1	Steve Pate
	25/1	Scott Hoch		50/1	Skip Kendall
	33/1	Steve Jones		66/1	Brent Geiberger*
	33/1	Nick Faldo (DC)		66/1	John Daly
	40/1	John Cook		66/1	Russ Cochran
	40/1	Frank Nobilo		66/1	Steve Lowery
	40/1	Andrew Magee		66/1	David Toms
	50/1	Loren Roberts		66/1	Bob Estes

24 players were best priced at or under 66/1.

BOOKIES AT ODDS

DYM Brent Geiberger 33/1 Chandlers: 66/1 Corals, Stanleys, Sunderlands

Winner Billy Mayfair 66/1 Hills, Stan James, Stanleys: 100/1 City Index, Corals, Ladbrokes

1998 RESULT

1	100/1	Billy Mayfair	65 71 69 67	272
		(Mayfair won at the first play-off hole)		
2 fav	5/1	Tiger Woods	68 73 65 66	272
3	125/1	Stephen Ames	66 71 70 68	275
T4	50/1	Payne Stewart	70 67 69 70	276
T4	66/1	John Daly	73 71 66 66	276

T6	J Gallagher	69 71 68 69 277		M Standly	67 73 73 74 287
	B Estes	69 70 67 71 277		R Coughlan	71 72 73 71 287
	S Hoch	67 71 68 71 277		N Faldo	73 70 73 71 287
	T Armour III	69 68 67 73 277		H Frazar	73 71 72 71 287
T10	B Cheesman	72 73 67 66 278		B.Friend	71 74 71 71 287
	S Verplank	68 72 70 68 278		Larry Rinker	69 75 68 75 287
	J Haas	73 70 67 68 278		C DiMarco	69 72 76 70 287
T13	H Sutton	72 69 66 72 279		W Wood	71 75 72 69 287
	S Kendall	69 73 64 73 279		P H Horgan III	68 78 72 69 287
T15	L Roberts	68 73 72 67 280		A Magee	69 75 71 73 288
	B Wadkins	69 72 70 69 280		K Fukabori	67 74 75 72 288
	K Triplett	74 69 68 69 280		P Mickelson	67 76 74 71 288
	F Funk	71 70 70 69 280		N Fasth	73 70 75 70 288
	K Sutherland	70 73 67 70 280		R Gamez	72 72 70 75 289
T20	B Chamblee	73 70 70 69 282		J Daley	69 72 75 73 289
	F Lickliter	71 71 70 70 282		D A Weibring	73 73 72 71 289
	J Kelly	68 71 71 72 282		I Steel	72 72 73 73 290
	J Carter	71 68 71 72 282		D Paulson	75 71 71 73 290
T24	T Pernice Jr	71 74 70 68 283		K Jones	75 68 75 72 290
	G Hill	71 74 67 71 283		B Fabel	74 72 72 72 290
	M Bradley	71 71 70 71 283		F Zoeller	72 74 73 71 290
	B Quigley	69 70 69 75 283		S Maruyama	67 79 75 69 290
	R Fehr	71 67 70 75 283		S Skinner	71 72 73 75 291
	S Simpson	70 73 70 71 284		F Couples	70 73 74 74 291
	M Springer	70 73 70 71 284		B Bates	69 75 71 77 292
	D Forsman	71 74 71 68 284		B Geiberger	70 71 74 77 292
	T Kite	68 75 69 72 284		C Barlow	73 73 72 74 292
	M Wiebe	68 72 69 75 284		K Gibson	74 71 71 77 293
	D Barron	75 71 68 71 285		T Schulz	73 72 75 73 293
	O Uresti	73 73 69 70 285		D Waldorf	72 73 76 72 293
	L Rinker	70 73 71 72 286		L Porter	75 71 75 72 293
	J Cook	70 71 72 73 286		B McCallister	72 72 72 78 294
	T Lehman	73 71 68 74 286		M Reid	70 74 76 74 294
	C Rose	71 75 70 70 286		G Day	72 74 79 69 294
	S Jones	71 72 74 69 286		K Wentworth	72 72 74 77 295
	J Kaye	74 68 75 69 286		K Conant	74 72 74 82 302
	N Lancaster	72 71 78 65 286			

ROUND BY ROUND LEADERBOARD

FIRST ROUND		SECOND ROUND	
B MAYFAIR	6 under	B MAYFAIR	6 under
S Ames	5 under	P Stewart	5 under
M Standly	4 under	T Armour III	5 under
P Mickelson	4 under	S Ames	5 under
S Hoch	4 under	R Fehr	4 under
S Maruyama	4 under	S Hoch	4 under
K Fukabori	4 under		

THIRD ROUND		FINAL ROUND	
T Armour III	9 under	B MAYFAIR	12 under
B MAYFAIR	8 under	T Woods	12 under
T Woods	7 under	S Ames	9 under
S Kendal	7 under	P Stewart	8 under
B Estes	7 under	J Daly	8 under
S Hoch	7 under		
P Stewart	7 under		

PUNTERS' POINTS

- Needing a birdie at the par 5 final hole to force a play-off with Tiger Woods Billy Mayfair found the front bunker in two. However he wasn't Number 1 for sand saves in 1995 for nothing and he splashed out to 4 feet and holed the putt.

   Then in the play-off he played immaculate straight golf to once more shoot birdie while Woods once more went right off the tee and could only make par.

- Stan James's odds for the play-off makes interesting reading

Tiger Woods   4/9   1/2   8/15   4/7
Billy Mayfair   13/8   6/4   11/8   5/4

The money was for Mayfair because backers who were already on Woods hedged, and also because at 13/8 Mayfair's composure suggested he was a 'value' price.

- Stephen Ames earned his US tour card with a most impressive T3rd at Q. School where he was the only player to shoot six rounds of 70 or under. Here he was also impressive in finishing 3rd at 125/1. A naturally-talented player, 5th in the 1997 British Open, he is a player of real quality who must be expected to have a good year.

- With his best finish since winning the British Open 66/1 T4th John Daly showed here that 'the Wild Thing' is back. His form figures are now MC-12-16-8-5 and he is 32 under par for his last four tournaments. However as his scores have come down his weight has gone up. Let's hope he finds the salad bar!

- Tournament leader going into the last round, the pressure got to Tommy Armour. Playing very well is one thing yet winning is another. Sadly he was my 125/1 outsider!

- Among those to miss the cut were 20/1 Justin Leonard, 50/1 chances Bob Tway and tournament specialist Craig Stadler, and 66/1 outsiders Steve Lowery and David Toms.
- 40/1 Frank Nobilo withdrew after 76 in R1.

1997 RESULT

1	20/1	Nick Faldo
2	28/1	Craig Stadler
3	40/1	Scott Hoch
T4	125/1	Tom Purtzer
T4	66/1	Fred Funk

WINNERS IN THE '90s

1990	Fred Couples
1991	Ted Schulz
1992	Fred Couples
1993	Tom Kite (3 rounds only)
1994	Corey Pavin
1995	Corey Pavin
1996	Craig Stadler
1997	Nick Faldo
1998	Billy Mayfair

PUNTERS' GUIDE

- In 1999 the Nissan Open will probably return to its traditional home at the Riviera Country Club. So once more punters will be able to use the mass of course form available.
- So, after missing the cut in 1998 at Valencia, we can expect a bold showing from Craig Stadler who simply loves Riviera – his last three starts there in this event have been 2nd 28/1, won 33/1 and 4th 50/1.

THE DORAL RYDER OPEN

Date	5th – 8th March
Course	Doral Resort and C C, Miami, Florida
Par	72
Yardage	7,125
First Prize	$360,000
Total Purse	$2 million

This course was subject to a major redesign before the 1997 tournament. It created thirty-four new bunkers some with very very steep faces. The final hole, the 443-yard par 4, is one of the toughest on the US tour.

1998 ODDS

fav	13/2	Tiger Woods		40/1	Stewart Cink
	14/1	Greg Norman		50/1	Nick Faldo
	16/1	David Duval		66/1	Brad Faxon
	16/1	Nick Price		66/1	Bill Glasson
	20/1	Davis Love III		66/1	Bob Tway
	25/1	Colin Montgomerie		66/1	Mark Calcavecchia
	33/1	Bernhard Langer		66/1	John Cook
	33/1	Scott Hoch		66/1	Tim Herron
	33/1	Jesper Parnevik		66/1	Billy Mayfair (PWW)
	33/1	Vijay Singh		66/1	John Huston
	40/1	Steve Elkington (DC)		66/1	Tommy Armour
	40/1	Justin Leonard*		66/1	Skip Kendall
	40/1	Jim Furyk		66/1	Jay Haas
	40/1	Steve Stricker			

27 players were best priced at or under 66/1.

BOOKIES AT ODDS

DYM Justin Leonard 18/1 Hills: 40/1 Corals

Winner DYM Michael Bradley 40/1 City Index, Hills, Ladbrokes: 80/1 Corals

1998 RESULT

1	80/1	Michael Bradley	71 66 70 71 278
T2	66/1	Billy Mayfair	72 70 68 69 279
T2	66/1	John Huston	70 69 73 67 279
T4	33/1	Vijay Singh	71 68 72 70 281
T4	150/1	Mike Brisky	68 71 71 71 281
T4	50/1	Stewart Cink	70 68 71 72 281

T7	D Love III	73 72 70 67 282	
	S Hoch	72 66 74 70 282	
T9	T Herron	70 67 76 70 283	
	J Furyk	77 62 73 71 283	
	L Mattiace	73 67 72 71 283	
	J Cook	71 66 74 72 283	
	B Tway	68 71 72 72 283	
	T Woods	70 69 71 73 283	
T15	D Hart	71 70 73 71 285	
	T Tryba	71 70 73 71 285	
	L Rinker	71 72 71 71 285	
	P Azinger	73 71 69 72 285	
	Ray Floyd	71 68 73 73 285	
	P H Horgan III	71 70 70 74 285	
T21	R Black	68 71 74 73 286	
	B Langer	70 70 73 73 286	
T23	O Browne	73 70 75 69 287	
	N Lancaster	70 71 76 70 287	
	F Funk	72 73 71 71 287	
	D Duval	70 72 73 72 287	
	T Tolles	69 72 72 74 287	
	J Sindelar	71 69 72 75 287	
	R Mediate	71 67 73 76 287	
	D Martin	69 71 77 71 288	
	M Calcavecchia	68 75 73 72 288	
	S Appleby	70 74 72 72 288	
	B McCallister	74 70 72 72 288	
	B Friend	72 71 71 74 288	
	J Parnevik	75 69 70 74 288	
	N Price	71 70 77 71 289	
	H Sutton	69 74 74 72 289	
	J Sluman	76 68 73 72 289	
	B Wadkins	75 70 70 74 289	
	J Haas	72 68 73 76 289	
	M Christie	71 71 75 73 290	

N Henke	72 70 75 73 290
L Porter	69 71 76 74 290
A Bean	70 74 71 75 290
C Strange	68 71 75 76 290
K Perry	70 71 77 73 291
L Rinker	73 70 75 73 291
C Di Marco	73 71 74 73 291
M Weir	71 69 77 74 291
J Carter	69 72 76 74 291
C Rose	73 71 73 74 291
H Frazar	71 72 73 75 291
R W Eaks	73 71 77 71 292
Jeff Gallagher	74 67 79 72 292
C Perry	72 69 77 74 292
S Gump	73 72 72 75 292
S Skinner	71 72 73 76 292
J Morse	70 71 76 76 293
B Gilder	70 73 74 76 293
N Faldo	72 70 74 77 293
J Nicklaus	70 74 72 77 293
K Gibson	76 67 78 73 294
G Waite	76 69 75 74 294
R Coughlan	74 68 77 75 294
B Lietzke	71 74 73 76 294
K Jones	72 70 78 75 295
W Grady	73 71 77 75 296
D Sutherland	76 66 78 76 296
Ed Fiori	74 70 76 76 296
S Lyle	71 74 74 78 297
G Hill	74 71 76 77 298
S Stricker	77 68 75 78 298
C Smith	74 70 74 80 298
M S Filippo	71 72 76 80 299
F Lickliter	76 69 79 79 303

ROUND BY ROUND LEADERBOARD

FIRST ROUND		SECOND ROUND	
M Brisky	4 under	T Herron	7 under
R Black	4 under	M BRADLEY	7 under
M Calcavecchia	4 under	J Cook	7 under
B Tway	4 under	S Hoch	6 under
C Strange	4 under	R Mediate	6 under
T Tolles	3 under	S Cink	6 under
L Porter	3 under		
H Sutton	3 under		
J Carter	3 under		
D Martin	3 under		
M BRADLEY	1 under		

THIRD ROUND		FINAL ROUND	
M BRADLEY	9 under	M BRADLEY	10 under
S Cink	7 under	J Huston	9 under
B Mayfair	6 under	B Mayfair	9 under
M Brisky	6 under	V Singh	7 under
T Woods	6 under	M Brisky	7 under
P Horgan	5 under	S Cink	7 under
B Tway	5 under		
V Singh	5 under		
R Mediate	5 under		
J Cook	5 under		

PUNTERS' POINTS

- Course specialist Floridian DYM player Michael Bradley priced by Corals at a staggering 80/1 cost the Barking firm a reported £35,000. Bradley must be noted after this win for one key reason – he sure can handle disappointment. Told before the tournament that he had a herniated disc problem, he then lost the lead when missing an eight-inch putt on the eleventh green in R4. However, he played the last tough seven holes in 1 under par to gain a really merited victory.

- Nothing succeeds like success.....just ask Billy Mayfair. Drawing enormous confidence from last week's win, here he went very close indeed to becoming the tour player to follow a West Coast victory with one on the East Coast. Momentum rules O.K.!

- John Huston's fine effort in finishing T2nd at 66/1 in his home state in a tournament he won in 1994 took him to the Number 1 position on the Money list. His brilliant short game has now been matched by accuracy off tee and fairway. He's now 2nd on the Total Driving stats and 5th for Greens In Regulation.

- Tiger Woods 'win or bust' approach showed at the very last hole. On one of the tour's toughest holes he gambled, found the water, and shot double bogey. The lesson for punters may be that if you fancy Tiger to do well back him win only.....after all he sure ain't interested in coming second!

- T4th Stewart Cink played well. His accuracy and strong all-round game (he's now 6th on the All Round stats) will surely see him win again.
- T4th Vijay Singh was let down by his putter. His consistency in this tournament is truly impressive – four consecutive top 20 finishes with sixteen par or sub-par rounds since 1995.
- T4th 150/1 Mike Brisky (T14 1996: T17 1997) was recording his third successive top 20 in this event. Florida resident Mike must be noted particularly in 3-ball and match betting in 1999, especially as he's now shot twelve successive par or sub-par rounds.
- Did I believe my ears? Steve Livingstone on SKY TV described Vijay Singh, who was making his fiftieth successive cut, as "one of the tour's regular grinders...." With twenty-two worldwide wins Singh sure is some grinder!!
- Among those to miss the cut were course specialist 14/1 Greg Norman, 25/1 Colin Montgomerie on his 1998 US tour debut, 40/1 Justin Leonard and 40/1 defending champion Steve Elkington, and 66/1 outsiders Brad Faxon and Skip Kendall.

1997 RESULT

1	50/1	Steve Elkington
T2	125/1	Larry Nelson
T2	18/1	Nick Price
4	50/1	David Duval

WINNERS IN THE '90s

1990	Greg Norman
1991	Rocco Mediate
1992	Ray Floyd
1993	Greg Norman
1994	John Huston
1995	Nick Faldo
1996	Greg Norman
1997	Steve Elkington
1998	Michael Bradley

PUNTERS' GUIDE

- Winners over the last six years have shown two key characteristics
  - > They have posted a top 20 finish in one of the previous two years. Indeed the last four winners have finished in the top 10 in one of the previous two tournaments.
  - > They were Florida residents.
- Best recent course records are held by Michael Bradley (W 1998: T18 1997: T2 1996), Stewart Cink (T4 1998: T20 1997), Mike Brisky (T4 1998: 17 1997: T14 1996) and Vijay Singh (T4 1998: after three successive top twenties).

THE HONDA CLASSIC

Date	12th – 15th March
Course	Heron Bay, Coral Springs, Florida
Par	72
Yardage	7,268
First Prize	$324,000
Total Purse	$1.8 million

The Honda Classic was held at the Mark McCumber designed Heron Bay course for the second successive year.

1998 ODDS

fav	10/1	Ernie Els	40/1	Tim Herron
	20/1	Colin Montgomerie	40/1	Steve Elkington
	25/1	Jim Furyk	50/1	Paul Stankowski
	25/1	Vijay Singh	50/1	Andrew Magee
	25/1	Stewart Cink	50/1	John Daly
	25/1	John Huston	66/1	Bob Estes*
	25/1	Lee Janzen	66/1	Stuart Appleby (DC)*
	25/1	Mark O'Meara	66/1	Craig Stadler
	28/1	Payne Stewart	66/1	Tommy Tolles*
	28/1	Jesper Parnevik	66/1	Craig Parry
	33/1	Bernhard Langer	66/1	David Frost
	33/1	Tom Watson	66/1	Skip Kendall
	40/1	Mark Calcavecchia	66/1	Mike Brisky

26 players were best priced at or under 66/1.

BOOKIES AT ODDS

DYM Defending champion and T4th Stuart Appleby 33/1 Hills: 66/1 City Index

DYM Bob Estes 33/1 Sunderlands: 66/1 Tote

DYM Tommy Tolles 33/1 Surrey: 66/1 Ladbrokes, City Index

DYM Jeff Maggert 40/1 Corals: 80/1 Stanleys, Sunderlands, Tote

Winner Mark Calcavecchia 25/1 Stanleys, City Index: 33/1 generally, was 40/1 with Ladbrokes, Sunderlands and Surrey

1998 RESULT

1	40/1	Mark Calcavecchia	70 67 68 65	270
2	25/1	Vijay Singh	70 68 68 67	273
3	20/1	Colin Montgomerie	69 69 71 66	275
T4	50/1	John Daly	68 76 68 64	276
T4	80/1	Jeff Maggert	67 68 76 65	276
T4	66/1	Stuart Appleby	70 67 72 67	276

T7	C Stadler	73 66 71 68 278		M Springer	73 69 73 68 283
	B Friend	70 70 70 68 278		B Bates	73 70 72 68 283
	B Geiberger	70 68 71 69 278		J McGovern	74 69 72 68 283
	B Estes	70 69 70 69 278		D Hammond	70 70 74 69 283
	K Sutherland	70 68 70 70 278		D Ogrin	75 69 68 71 283
T12	S Cink	68 70 74 67 279		R Mediate	73 69 69 72 283
	R W Eaks	73 68 70 68 279		O Browne	72 72 67 72 283
	J Furyk	72 70 69 68 279		J Sindelar	71 71 75 67 284
T15	L Mize	74 69 71 66 280		C Rose	73 71 71 69 284
	S Flesch	72 71 70 67 280		F Zoeller	71 69 73 71 284
	G Waite	71 70 71 68 280		T Herron	73 71 69 71 284
	B Cheesman	70 68 74 68 280		T Tryba	75 68 69 72 284
	B Henninger	73 69 69 69 280		J Gallagher Jr	71 73 74 67 285
	L Janzen	70 66 73 71 280		P Stankowski	74 70 72 69 285
	S Pate	69 70 70 71 280		J Durant	75 69 71 70 285
T22	A Magee	73 70 72 66 281		P Stewart	76 66 71 72 285
	D Sutherland	71 72 71 67 281		G Sauers	76 66 71 72 285
	R Cochran	76 67 71 67 281		D Rummells	74 67 76 69 286
	C DiMarco	72 69 71 69 281		S Ames	72 71 73 70 286
	M O'Meara	75 66 69 71 281		S McRoy	75 67 73 71 286
	J Kelly	70 68 71 72 281		P Jordan	74 70 71 71 286
	B Langer	70 69 70 72 281		R Howison	70 71 71 74 286
	T Tolles	70 73 65 73 281		S Jurgensen	73 71 75 68 287
	D Martin	73 69 73 67 282		K Nolan	72 72 73 70 287
	P Goydos	75 68 71 68 282		N Henke	71 72 73 71 287
	C Perry	72 70 71 69 282		J Morse	74 70 72 71 287
	D Hart	73 71 69 69 282		P Blackmar	71 71 68 77 287
	H Frazar	71 71 70 70 282		B Kamm	71 72 75 70 288
	B Wadkins	75 69 68 70 282		G Hill	71 73 73 72 289
	J Huston	73 71 68 70 282		K Jones	73 68 76 73 290
	E Toledo	75 68 68 71 282		H Royer III	74 69 74 73 290
	T Watson	70 73 67 72 282		J Gallagher	73 71 71 75 290
	L Mattiace	70 72 73 68 283			

ROUND BY ROUND LEADERBOARD

FIRST ROUND		SECOND ROUND	
J Maggert	5 under	J Maggert	9 under
J Daly	4 under	L Janzen	8 under
S Cink	4 under	S Appleby	7 under
S Pate	3 under	M CALCAVECCHIA	7 under
C Montgomerie	3 under	S Cink	6 under
M CALCAVECCHIA	2 under	C Montgomerie	6 under
15 other players at	2 under	J Kelly	6 under
		B Geiberger	6 under
		V Singh	6 under
		K Sutherland	6 under

THIRD ROUND		FINAL ROUND	
M CALCAVECCHIA	11 under	M CALCAVECCHIA	18 under
V Singh	10 under	V Singh	15 under
T Tolles	8 under	C Montgomerie	13 under
K Sutherland	8 under	J Daly	12 under
B Langer	7 under	J Maggert	12 under
B Estes	7 under	S Appleby	12 under
S Pate	7 under		
J Kelly	7 under		
B Geiberger	7 under		
C Montgomerie	7 under		
S Appleby	7 under		
L Janzen	7 under		

PUNTERS' POINTS

- 40/1 Calcavecchia made his Mark once more with a very convincing 3-shot victory, his ninth on the tour. His victory highlighted two points of real punter interest.

  > Tenth in the rankings for final-round scoring in 1997 he shot a brilliant 7 under par 65 in R4 to clinch victory here.

  > He lives just 40 minutes from the course. Relaxed he played superb golf especially on the Sunday when his family were all present.

- Although Vijay Singh took the lead once during R4 this was the tournament Calc won rather than the one Singh lost. The tall Fijian putted well thanks to his new caddie, Dave Renwick, who has started to line up his putts. Caddies are often overlooked by golf punters yet Renwick looks to be the ideal man for Singh. It could become a world class pairing!

- Colin Montgomerie played very well although (as usual?) he was let down by his putting, especially in R3. However playing on the back of a domestic burglary and severe press criticism in America this 3rd place proved the Scot's true grit!

- What a delight to see John Daly playing superb golf, especially in that last-round 64. Yet why did the Racing Post make him their headline selection at 50/1 but in their spread-betting advice we were told it was too risky to 'sell' his finishing position of 34th? If he had a real chance of winning he must surely have been expected to be in the top 34.

- Some golfers are really very predictable and Jeff Maggert is one of them. In the lead after R2 he shot a 76 to slip down the field; then relaxed and out of contention he shot a brilliant final-round 65 to finish T4th. Like some racehorses he must come from well off the pace and get his head up on the line if he's ever to win again.
- Stuart Appleby much prefers the Bermuda grass greens of Florida to the bent grass found in California in the early-season West coast tournaments. His putting improved here to place him T4th at 66/1 as he put up a fine defence of his championship.
- With less wind than last year the scoring was slightly lower than in 1997.
- Among those to miss the cut were 10/1 favourite Ernie Els, 28/1 Jesper Parnevik, 40/1 Steve Elkington and 66/1 outsiders Craig Parry, Mike Brisky, Skip Kendall, David Frost and course designer Mark McCumber.

1997 RESULT

1	125/1	Stuart Appleby
T2	50/1	Michael Bradley
T2	40/1	Payne Stewart
T2	16/1	Colin Montgomerie

WINNERS IN THE '90s

1990	John Huston
1991	Steve Pate
1992	Corey Pavin
1993	Fred Couples
1994	Nick Price
1995	Mark O'Meara
1996	Tim Herron
1997	Stuart Appleby
1998	Mark Calcavecchia

PUNTERS' GUIDE

- Heron Bay is a relatively flat course with over a hundred large unlipped bunkers. Unusually it demands an ability to play longer distance shots from sand.
- The best records on this course are held by Stuart Appleby (T4th 1998: Won 1997), Colin Montgomerie (3rd 1998; 4th 1997), Brent Geiberger (T7th 1998: T20th 1997) and Lee Janzen (T15th 1998: T14th 1997).
- It is worth noting that the top 3 this year all played last year and all made the cut then.

		1997 Finish
1	Mark Calcavecchia	T37th
2	Vijay Singh	T30th
3	Colin Montgomerie	4th

THE BAY HILL INVITATIONAL

Date   19th – 22nd March
Course   Bay Hill Club, Orlando, Florida
Par   72
Yardage   7,114
First Prize $360,000
Total Purse $2 million

Played at Bay Hill since 1979 there is clearly plenty of course form. As usual there was a strong field as the star players prepared for next week's fifth major, the Players' Championship.

1998 ODDS

fav	6/1	Tiger Woods	40/1	Mark Calcavecchia (PWW)
	18/1	Davis Love III	50/1	Lee Janzen
	20/1	Ernie Els	50/1	Justin Leonard
	25/1	Colin Montgomerie	50/1	Lee Westwood
	25/1	Phil Mickelson (DC)	50/1	Stuart Appleby
	28/1	Nick Price	50/1	Billy Mayfair
	28/1	Tom Lehman	50/1	John Huston
	33/1	Vijay Singh	50/1	Loren Roberts
	33/1	Mark O'Meara	50/1	Steve Jones
	40/1	Bernhard Langer	50/1	Tom Watson
	40/1	Fred Couples	66/1	Nick Faldo
	40/1	John Daly	66/1	Michael Bradley
	40/1	Jim Furyk	66/1	Ian Woosnam
	40/1	Stewart Cink	66/1	Jeff Maggert
	40/1	Scott Hoch	66/1	Brad Faxon

30 players were best priced at or under 66/1.

BOOKIES AT ODDS

Defending champion Phil Mickelson 18/1 Stan James: 25/1 Chandlers, City Index, Ladbrokes

Vijay Singh 20/1 Ladbrokes, Tote: 33/1 Hills, Stanleys

Tied 2nd DYM Bob Estes 40/1 Sunderlands: 100/1 Ladbrokes

Winner Ernie Els 12/1 Hills, 14/1 Stan James, Tote, Corals: 16/1 Stanleys, Ladbrokes: 20/1 City Index

1998 RESULT

1	20/1	Ernie Els	67 69 65 73	274
T2	66/1	Jeff Maggert	70 71 69 68	278
T2	100/1	Bob Estes	69 71 67 71	278
T4	40/1	Bernhard Langer	68 73 69 69	279
T4	40/1	Mark Calcavecchia	70 69 69 71	279

T6	C Parry	70 71 70 69 280	D Forsman	71 73 73 71 288
	S Stricker	67 72 68 73 280	F Couples	70 74 71 73 288
T8	J Furyk	70 72 69 70 281	R Damron	65 74 74 75 288
	C Montgomerie	71 68 73 69 281	F Zoeller	73 71 70 74 288
T10	C Stadler	70 73 70 70 283	S Hoch	72 67 73 76 288
	A Magee	69 74 70 70 283	M Reid	72 71 71 75 289
	S Ames	69 74 73 67 283	S Kendall	72 70 72 75 289
T13	G Waite	71 70 74 69 284	J Sindelar	74 69 69 77 289
	G Kraft	71 70 70 73 284	B Faxon	70 72 71 76 289
	L Westwood	70 69 69 76 284	P Goydos	69 74 74 72 289
	T Woods	64 70 73 77 284	S Cink	72 68 74 75 289
	D Toms	70 72 69 74 285	J Leonard	73 70 76 71 290
	R Cochran	70 74 67 74 285	J Haas	68 74 75 73 290
	J D Blake	69 75 71 70 285	B Quigley	70 74 71 75 290
	D Martin	71 73 70 71 285	K Triplett	70 74 74 73 291
	D Love III	68 66 75 76 285	J Delsing	69 71 75 76 291
T22	S Lowery	69 74 70 73 286	R Fehr	68 72 75 76 291
	T Lehman	70 71 71 74 286	S Verplank	71 73 72 75 291
	K Sutherland	69 72 72 73 286	S McCarron	70 73 75 74 292
	V Singh	68 72 71 75 286	P Harrington	71 73 76 75 295
	L Rinker	73 70 69 75 287	R Mediate	69 75 73 78 295
	T Kite	75 69 70 73 287	R Gamez	74 69 78 76 297
	S Pate	69 75 71 72 287	J Daly	68 75 70 85 298
	T Watson	71 72 70 75 288	M Brisky	74 69 79 78 300
	O Browne	71 73 71 73 288	F Lickliter	72 72 78 83 305

ROUND BY ROUND LEADERBOARD

FIRST ROUND		SECOND ROUND	
T Woods	8 under	T Woods	10 under
R Damron	7 under	D Love III	10 under
S Stricker	5 under	E ELS	8 under
E ELS	5 under	S Hoch	5 under
J Daly	4 under	C Montgomerie	5 under
R Fehr	4 under	L Westwood	5 under
J Haas	4 under	R Damron	5 under
V Singh	4 under	S Stricker	5 under
D Love III	4 under	M Calcavecchia	5 under
B Langer	4 under		

THIRD ROUND		FINAL ROUND	
E ELS	15 under	E ELS	14 under
B Estes	9 under	J Maggert	10 under
S Stricker	9 under	B Estes	10 under
T Woods	9 under	B Langer	9 under
M Calcavecchia	8 under	M Calcavecchia	9 under
L Westwood	8 under		

- Rain ruined the first day with only 8 players completing their first round and 43 players unable to start their round. The first round was completed on Friday when there were further rain delays.
- The first two rounds were completed on Saturday leaving a demanding 36 holes to be played on Sunday.

PUNTERS' POINTS

- 22nd March 1998 was Mothers' day awash with cards of love.....while over at Bay Hill Big Ernie made Love fade and gave the father and mother of a beating to Tiger Woods.
- With 36 holes to be played the three leaders 5/4 fav Tiger Woods (10 under), 5/2 Davis Love III (10 under), and 4/1 Ernie Els (8 under) were paired together for the full day. The result was to give the tall South African a huge psychological boost as
  > Love shot 75-76 to finish T13th.
  > Woods went 6 over par for the day and shot 77 (!) in R4 – the poorest finish of his professional career.
  > Els played brilliantly in R3 to shoot 65 and go on to a convincing 4-shot win.
  > Over those final 36 holes Els had beaten Love by 13, and Woods by 12.
- It was Els's first win in his adopted state of Florida. Tom Watson, Jay Haas, Steve Jones and Scott Hoch are among the top US players who have yet to win on Florida's Bermuda grass.
- It is worth noting that Els was winning on the back of last week's missed cut in the Honda Classic. The last time Ernie missed a cut was last June and he then went onto win his next two tournaments!!

- John Daly's comeback train hit the buffers big time at the par 5 sixth hole in R4. Big John going for the green in 2 with his driver found the water, then with a 3 wood he found the water again......and again and again and again and again.....with more hits than the Beatles he took an 18!!!
- Jeff Maggert's consistency continued here as the 34-year-old finished strongly on the final day to record his eleventh (!!) 2nd-placed finish since his only win, in the 1993 Walt Disney Classic.
- It is worth noting the players who played the final 36 holes particularly well. So when, in future, a similar situation arises we know which players have proven mentally and physically toughest when facing two rounds on the final day

	Final 36 holes under Par	Both R3 + R4 under Par
Ernie Els	6 under	No
Jeff Maggert	7 under	Yes
Bob Estes	6 under	Yes
Bernhard Langer	6 under	Yes
Craig Parry	5 under	Yes
Jim Furyk	5 under	Yes
Mark Calcavecchia	4 under	Yes
Craig Stadler	4 under	Yes
Andrew Magee	4 under	Yes
Jay Don Blake	3 under	Yes
Doug Martin	3 under	Yes

- 21 players 'made' the cut, qualified for prize money, yet did not play the final 36 holes on the Sunday. They included 25/1 defending champion Phil Mickelson, 50/1 Lee Janzen, 66/1 Nick (he was 14/1 jt fav last year) Faldo, and 80/1 DYM outsider Payne Stewart.
- Those missing the cut completely included 28/1 Nick Price, 33/1 Mark O'Meara and 50/1 chances John Huston, and Steve Jones. Loren Roberts after 75 in R1 withdrew, and so did Michael Bradley when 3 over par after three rounds.
- In the Top Non-American market the leading players were

  5/1 Ernie Els
  5/1 Colin Montgomerie
  6/1 Vijay Singh
  8/1 Nick Price
  9/1 Bernhard Langer
  12/1 Stuart Appleby (last year's 22/1 winner of this section)
  12/1 Lee Westwood
  16/1 Nick Faldo
  25/1 Frank Nobilo
  25/1 Craig Parry
  25/1 Retief Goosen
  33/1 Bar   1/4 odds 1,2,3,4

  The result was   1.   5/1   Ernie Els
                   2.   9/1   Bernhard Langer
                   3.   25/1 Craig Parry
                   4.   5/1   Colin Montgomerie

- The European tour players' results were

Retief Goosen	Missed cut
Colin Montgomerie	T8th
Nick Faldo	made cut yet did not play Sunday
Ian Woosnam	missed cut
Padraig Harrington	T50th
Lee Westwood	T13th
Bernhard Langer	T4th

- Corals other special markets were:-

EURO RYDER		THE MAJOR MEN	
5/2	C Montgomerie	2/1	T Woods
7/2	N Faldo	7/2	Els – Won
7/2	B Langer – Won	4/1	D Love III
4/1	I Woosnam	5/1	T Lehman
4/1	L Westwood	5/1	N Price

1997 PGA WINNERS

5/2	F Couples
11/4	M Calcavecchia – Won
9/2	J Huston
9/2	M Bradley
9/2	B Mayfair

1997 RESULT

1	28/1	Phil Mickelson
2	66/1	Stuart Appleby
T3	150/1	Omar Uresti
T3	33/1	Mark O'Meara
T3	33/1	Payne Stewart

WINNERS IN THE '90s

1990	Robert Gamez
1991	Andrew Magee (3 rounds)
1992	Fred Couples
1993	Ben Crenshaw
1994	Loren Roberts
1995	Loren Roberts
1996	Paul Goydos
1997	Phil Mickelson
1998	Ernie Els

PUNTERS' GUIDE

- If the evidence of the last two years is any guide then Bay Hill course form can be safely ignored.

1998 winner Ernie Els course form figures MC/42/42/MC
1997 winner Phil Mickelson course form figures -/MC/MC

- Current form seems to be the key:-
  - > In the last two years nine of the ten players in the top 5 places had posted at least a top 15 finish in one of his last three tournaments.
  - > The winner of the previous week's Honda Classic in 1997 was 2nd here at 66/1 and in 1998 T4th at 40/1.
  - > In each of the last two years the front four in the Honda Classic have provided two of the first five in the Bay Hill Invitational.

THE PLAYERS CHAMPIONSHIP

Date   26th – 29th March
Course   Sawgrass, Ponte Vedra, Florida
Par   72
Yardage   6,896
First Prize $720,000
Total Purse $2.3 million

This is the first really big tournament of the year Stateside. Known as 'the fifth major' it always attracts a truly top-class field. It completes the 'Florida Swing' and has been held at Sawgrass since 1982. Its signature hole is the 132-yard par 3 seventeenth on an island green surrounded by water.

1998 ODDS

fav	9/1	Tiger Woods	40/1	Scott Hoch
	12/1	Ernie Els (PWW)	40/1	Fred Couples
	18/1	Colin Montgomerie	50/1	Stewart Cink
	22/1	Davis Love III	50/1	Lee Westwood
	25/1	David Duval	50/1	Jesper Parnevik
	25/1	Greg Norman (non runner)	50/1	Justin Leonard
	33/1	Phil Mickelson	50/1	Jeff Maggert
	33/1	Bernhard Langer	50/1	Tom Watson
	33/1	Jim Furyk	66/1	Mark O'Meara
	33/1	Tom Lehman	66/1	Lee Janzen
	33/1	Vijay Singh	66/1	John Daly
	33/1	Nick Price	66/1	Steve Stricker
	40/1	J M Olazabal	66/1	John Huston
	40/1	Mark Calcavecchia	66/1	John Cook

28 players were best priced at or under 66/1.

BOOKIES AT ODDS

Davis Love 14/1 Corals, Sunderlands: 22/1 Hills

Tied 5th DYM Len Mattiace 100/1 Tote: 200/1 Surrey

Justin Leonard was 50/1 with all ten bookmakers in the Racing Post Pricewise column.

1998 RESULT

1	50/1	Justin Leonard	72 69 70 67	278
T2	33/1	Tom Lehman	72 70 70 68	280
T2	200/1	Glen Day	66 73 70 71	280
4	40/1	Mark Calcavecchia	69 75 68 69	281
T5	50/1	Lee Westwood	74 71 68 69	282
T5	40/1	Scott Hoch	73 69 70 70	282
T5	200/1	Len Mattiace	69 71 72 70	282

T8	P Stewart	72 71 75 65 283		S McCarron	72 72 71 75 290
	N Price	71 72 70 70 283		B Chamblee	72 73 76 70 291
	P Mickelson	69 73 70 71 283		S Cink	71 73 74 73 291
	E Els	71 72 70 71 284		M O'Meara	70 75 72 74 291
	S Verplank	71 71 72 70 284		B Mayfair	69 75 69 78 291
T13	J Cook	71 73 71 70 285		B Estes	72 70 74 75 291
	B Lietzke	69 70 74 72 285		S Pate	71 71 74 75 291
	L Janzen	70 67 69 79 285		K Sutherland	72 70 73 76 291
T16	J Daly	71 70 76 69 286		F Couples	67 73 73 78 291
	D Sutherland	72 73 69 72 286		D Frost	69 71 73 78 291
T18	B Tway	72 71 75 69 287		S Stricker	74 72 76 70 292
	H Sutton	74 69 74 70 287		M Bradley	74 72 76 70 292
	D Barron	71 72 74 70 287		J Maggert	69 71 76 76 292
	D Duval	69 77 70 71 287		S Gump	72 68 76 77 293
	N Faldo	75 69 70 73 287		P U Johansson	69 74 78 72 293
	J Ozaki	69 68 76 74 287		V Singh	72 71 75 75 293
	O Uresti	72 71 70 74 287		D Love III	73 72 69 80 294
T25	Lee Rinker	72 73 72 71 288		P Goydos	72 70 80 72 294
	T Kite	72 66 78 72 288		N Henke	69 73 77 75 294
	J Parnevik	72 72 72 72 288		R Mediate	67 73 77 77 294
	J M Olazabal	72 74 70 72 288		T Tryba	70 74 72 79 295
	D Hart	74 70 71 73 288		J Sindelar	73 69 81 72 295
	S Jones	71 71 73 73 288		F Nobilo	72 72 75 77 296
	L Mize	73 73 73 70 289		R Gamez	74 72 77 73 296
	T Armour III	71 75 71 72 289		G Waite	76 70 75 75 296
	J Kelly	68 71 77 73 289		B Henninger	73 72 73 79 297
	C Stadler	71 70 72 76 289		P Blackmar	72 74 76 75 297
	B Andrade	70 74 75 71 290		S Kendall	74 72 73 79 298
	J Furyk	70 75 73 72 290		D Hammond	71 75 72 81 299
	T Woods	72 73 73 72 290		F Funk	73 73 75 78 299
	B Faxon	71 73 72 74 290		M Wiebe	76 69 76 79 300
	T Watson	71 74 71 74 290		Larry Rinker	78 67 81 74 300
	K Triplett	71 71 73 75 290			

ROUND BY ROUND LEADERBOARD

FIRST ROUND		SECOND ROUND	
G Day	6 under	L Janzen	7 under
F Couples	5 under	Joe Ozaki	7 under
R Mediate	5 under	T Kite	6 under
J Kelly	4 under	G Day	5 under
12 players at	3 under	J Kelly	5 under
J LEONARD	level	B Lietzke	5 under
		J LEONARD	3 under

THIRD ROUND		FINAL ROUND	
L Janzen	10 under	J LEONARD	10 under
G Day	7 under	T Lehman	8 under
J LEONARD	5 under	G Day	8 under
M Calcavecchia	4 under	M Calcavecchia	7 under
P Mickelson	4 under	L Westwood	6 under
T Lehman	4 under	S Hoch	6 under
S Hoch	4 under	L Mattiace	6 under
L Mattiace	4 under		

PUNTERS' POINTS

- Coming down 'the stretch' it soon became clear that the ability, experience and temperament of British Open champion Justin Leonard would triumph.
  - > Glen Day's swing quickened a little as he could not sustain his challenge when the pressure was really turned on.
  - > Len Mattiace, after taking the lead at the 12th, bogeyed the 13th and although recovering well his chance sank with an horrendous quintuple bogey 8 (!!) at the par 3 17th, to go from 10 under par to 5 under par!
  - > Leonard, on the other hand, shot four birdies in the first five holes on the back nine to come (as in the British Open) from 'off the pace' to win.
- Justin Leonard, with his fourth win, confirmed what a fine R4 player he is when in serious contention. Only 25 years old he's got a massive future!
- Who would have guessed it? Going into R4 Lee Janzen was a proven last-round tough guy, a confirmed winner, was successful here in 1995, and he had a 3-shot lead over Day, and a 5-shot advantage over Leonard. He then misses the first four fairways, shoots 79 and inflicts G.B.H. on the wallets of punters who tried to buy money with 'the Big three' at 4/1 or 5/1 ON!
- Lee Westwood confirmed here what a superb player he is in finishing T5th at 50/1. He was top European player at 7/1, and top non-American at 16/1 and in those categories he will always be worth noting in future. His greatest asset is probably his temperament......if only Monty could buy it!
- Colin Montgomerie, as stressed in last year's volume, finds it very difficult to handle disappointment. So in R2 one dropped shot followed another as he dropped 4 shots in three holes from the 15th to miss the cut on a course on which he'd played so well before.

- On Sunday there were two markets, one with, the other without Janzen.

With Janzen

L Janzen	4/9	
G Day	10/1	
J Leonard	12/1	Won
Bar	14/1	

Without Janzen

9/2	G Day	7 under	T2nd
11/2	J Leonard	5 under	Won
9/1	P Mickelson	4 under	
9/1	M Calcavecchia	4 under	4th
9/1	T Lehman	4 under	T2nd
10/1	S Hoch	4 under	
14/1	Bar six		

- This decade the winner had always been a player placed in the first three, or tied for third after the first round.

  1998 broke that mould!

After	R1	R2	R3
> Justin Leonard	T44th	T13th	3rd

- > The first three after R1 were

  1st Glen Day who finished T2nd
  T2nd Fred Couples who finished T42nd
  T2nd Rocco Mediate who finished T57th

- There were a number of specialist markets

To be top European golfer

		Made Cut
Colin Montgomerie	3/1	No
Bernhard Langer	9/2	No
J M Olazabal	11/2	Yes
Lee Westwood	7/1	Yes
Jesper Parnevik	9/1	Yes
Ian Woosnam	12/1	W/D
Nick Faldo	12/1	Yes
Darren Clarke	16/1	No
P U Johansson	25/1	Yes
Costantino Rocca	33/1	No
Sandy Lyle	40/1	No
Gabriel Hjerstedt	50/1	No

The result was:-
1. 7/1 Lee Westwood 6 under
2. 12/1 Nick Faldo 1 under
3. 11/2 J M Olazabal even

To be top non-American

Ernie Els	5/1	
Colin Montgomerie	6/1	
Greg Norman	9/1	(non-runner)
Bernhard Langer	10/1	
J M Olazabal	12/1	
Vijay Singh	14/1	
Nick Price	14/1	
Lee Westwood	16/1	
Jesper Parnevik	20/1	
Ian Woosnam	25/1	(W/D after R1)
Nick Faldo	33/1	
Stuart Appleby	40/1	*

The result was:-
1. 16/1 Lee Westwood 6 under
2. 14/1 Nick Price 5 under
3. 5/1 Ernie Els 4 under
4. 33/1 Nick Faldo 1 under

Craig Parry	40/1 *
Darren Clarke	40/1
Frank Nobilo	40/1
'Jumbo' Ozaki	66/1

Corals created two Eurostar bets

Eurostar one:

20/1 (backed into 10/1) that Darren Clarke, Bernhard Langer, Colin Montgomerie, Lee Westwood and P U Johansson all make the cut.

Result Corals 1 Punters NIL: Clarke, Langer and Monty all missed the cut.

Eurostar two:

25/1 that Nick Faldo, J M Olazabal, Jesper Parnevik, Ian Woosnam and Costantino Rocca all make the cut.

Result Woosnam withdrew, Rocca missed the cut and punters missed a pay-out! Corals 2 Punters Nil.

Winning Nationality

4/9 an American Won
5/1 a European
7/1 an Australasian
8/1 an African
50/1 an Asian

- Birdies, eagles and now at Sawgrass seagulls! Steve Lowery on Friday played a fine six iron to the heart of the dreaded 17th green. Along came a seagull wondering....."I don't remember laying this one"....and proceeded to move the ball along the green before picking it up in its beak and dropping it in the water....enter rules official stage right!

- Greg Norman withdrew before the start with a shoulder injury. He was replaced by the 1997 USPGA Q. School Number 1 Scott Verplank. Ian Woosnam, 5 over par after 12 holes also withdrew with a back injury.

- Among those to miss the cut were 18/1 Colin Montgomerie, 33/1 Bernhard Langer and 66/1 John Huston. Jay Don Blake and Paul Stankowski retired and Dan Forsman withdrew.

1997 RESULT

1	40/1	Steve Elkington
2	50/1	Scott Hoch
3	66/1	Loren Roberts
4	80/1	Brad Faxon
5	100/1	Billy Andrade

WINNERS IN THE '90s

1990	Jodie Mudd
1991	Steve Elkington
1992	Davis Love III
1993	Nick Price
1994	Greg Norman
1995	Lee Janzen
1996	Fred Couples
1997	Steve Elkington
1998	Justin Leonard

PUNTERS' GUIDE

- The best course records over the last two years are held by Tom Lehman, T14th 1995, T8th 1996, T6th 1997, T2nd 1998; and Scott Hoch, T19th 1996, 2nd 1997, and T5th 1998. They can be followed in match bets, in outright betting or on the spreads.

- This is very much a tournament for proven winners. Every Players' Champion this decade had won before. As Day and Mattiace discovered this year, the back nine at Sawgrass is not the ideal finish as you try for your first win.

- It will also be worth consulting the US tour stats. Justin Leonard (78.3%) was 6th for Driving Accuracy, so vital on this course.

- So the amended guidelines would be to go for a player with five key characteristics

  > a proven winner

  > made the Sawgrass cut the previous year

  > the player shows patience

  > has a high ranking for driving accuracy

  > has made the cut in his last tournament

- If 'betting in running' do remember the easiest hole is the par 5 sixteenth at 497 yards and it's then followed by the treacherous par 3 seventeenth variously described as a 'bugga of a hole' (Frank Nobilo) or 'a monster' (Nick Faldo).

- One final thought – the course set up and the fast, dry conditions brought chipping and pitching back into play instead of the usual American target golf. So perhaps it wasn't a coincidence that the last two British Open champions, Justin Leonard (1997) and Tom Lehman (1996) finished first and T2nd.

THE FREEPORT McDERMOTT CLASSIC

Date	2nd – 5th April
Course	English Turn, New Orleans, Louisiana
Par	72
Yardage	7,116
First Prize	$306,000
Total Purse	$1.6 million

The English Turn course played host for the tenth successive year to the 'Freeport', which once more gave players a final opportunity to secure the final place for next week's US Masters by winning here.

1998 ODDS

14/1	Davis Love III	40/1	Bob Tway
14/1	Tom Lehman	40/1	Steve Elkington
16/1	Scott Hoch	50/1	Glen Day
20/1	Lee Westwood	50/1	Craig Parry
25/1	Jesper Parnevik	50/1	Ian Woosnam
25/1	J M Olazabal*	66/1	Joe Ozaki
33/1	Scott McCarron	66/1	Len Mattiace
33/1	Bob Estes	66/1	Russ Cochran
33/1	Brad Faxon (DC)	66/1	Kirk Triplett
33/1	John Cook*	66/1	Scott Verplank
40/1	Tommy Tolles		

Just 21 players were best priced at or under 66/1.

BOOKIES AT ODDS

DYM J M Olazabal 12/1 Ladbrokes: 25/1 Surrey

DYM John Cook 16/1 Ladbrokes: 33/1 Hills, Surrey, Tote

QYM second placed Steve Flesch 33/1 Ladbrokes: 125/1 Corals: 200/1 elsewhere

DYM tied third Steve Lowery 33/1 Hills: 80/1 Tote

DYM tied third Jim Carter 66/1 Hills: 150/1 Sunderlands

Winner Lee Westwood 12/1 Corals, Chandlers: 20/1 Tote

1998 RESULT

1	20/1	Lee Westwood	69 68 67 69	273
2	200/1	Steve Flesch	66 68 71 71	276
T3	150/1	Jim Carter	68 69 71 71	279
T3	150/1	Mark Wiebe	69 68 71 71	279
T3	50/1	Glen Day	64 75 69 71	279
T3	80/1	Steve Lowery	72 66 70 71	279

7	D Waldorf	67 69 70 74 280
T8	L Rinker	71 70 73 68 282
	B Estes	70 71 72 69 282
	I Woosnam	70 70 71 71 282
	T Dodds	67 72 71 72 282
T12	P H Horgan III	70 68 76 69 283
	S Hoch	74 69 70 70 283
	R Damron	73 71 68 71 283
	Jeff Gallagher	68 69 73 73 283
	J Parnevik	71 71 69 72 283
	J Ozaki	69 67 72 75 283
	P Tataurangi	71 67 70 75 283
T19	L Mattiace	71 67 76 70 284
	M Weir	72 71 73 68 284
	J M Olazabal	72 69 73 70 284
	M Brooks	73 70 71 70 284
	F Langham	73 70 69 72 284
	E Toledo	72 72 68 72 284
	P Azinger	69 74 68 73 284
	R Black	72 67 70 75 284
	C Perry	72 70 71 72 285
	B McCallister	67 73 71 74 285
	D Love III	72 72 66 75 285
	D Barron	73 68 74 71 286
	D A Weibring	67 74 75 70 286
	N Fasth	67 75 72 72 286
	R Friend	71 70 72 73 286
	P Blackmar	70 72 71 73 286
	N Lancaster	68 72 72 74 286
	R W Eaks	71 69 75 73 288
	K Gibson	67 75 72 74 288
	D Forsman	72 68 76 72 288
	B R Brown	72 72 73 71 288
	M Wurtz	69 75 74 70 288
	O Uresti	71 72 70 75 288
	H Frazar	70 69 76 74 289
	W Wood	72 71 73 73 289

B Henninger	68 73 73 75 289
B Wadkins	71 69 74 75 289
J Delsing	66 73 78 72 289
S Jurgensen	70 72 76 71 289
P Jordan	71 69 78 71 289
D Toms	70 70 80 69 289
J Johnston	71 69 80 69 289
B Tway	69 74 72 75 290
J P Hayes	70 70 75 75 290
T Pernice Jr	70 73 73 74 290
S Gump	68 73 73 76 290
F Lickliter	67 74 75 74 290
T Armour III	67 74 75 75 291
C Rocca	73 71 74 73 291
M Heinen	70 72 78 71 291
B Bates	72 71 73 76 292
L Porter	71 73 73 75 292
D Hammond	69 75 74 74 292
G Kraft	70 74 75 73 292
S McRoy	70 70 80 72 292
C Dennis	69 70 75 79 293
T Tryba	71 71 74 77 293
B Fleisher	76 68 74 75 293
J Adams	73 68 77 75 293
B Faxon	72 72 76 73 293
R Cochran	68 72 76 78 294
T Tolles	68 74 72 80 294
T Conley	73 70 75 76 294
S Elkington	71 70 79 74 294
F Allem	74 69 80 71 294
S Verplank	70 71 80 74 295
S Skinner	71 71 74 80 296
K Jones	74 70 76 76 296
B Fabel	75 69 77 75 296
T Simpson	73 71 74 79 297
J Riegger	70 73 76 78 297
C Barlow	72 70 80 75 297

ROUND BY ROUND LEADERBOARD

FIRST ROUND		SECOND ROUND	
G Day	8 under	S Flesch	10 under
J Delsing	6 under	J Ozaki	8 under
S Flesch	6 under	D Waldorf	8 under
T Armour III	5 under	M Wiebe	7 under
F Lickliter	5 under	J Carter	7 under
D A Weibring	5 under	Jeff Gallagher	7 under
D Waldorf	5 under	L WESTWOOD	7 under
N Fasth	5 under		
B McCallister	5 under		
K Gibson	5 under		
T Dodds	5 under		
L WESTWOOD	3 under		

THIRD ROUND		FINAL ROUND	
L WESTWOOD	12 under	L WESTOOD	15 under
S Flesch	11 under	S Flesch	12 under
D Waldorf	10 under	J Carter	9 under
G Day	8 under	M Wiebe	9 under
S Lowery	8 under	G Day	9 under
J Ozaki	8 under	S Lowery	9 under
M Wiebe	8 under		
P Tataurangi	8 under		
J Carter	8 under		

PUNTERS' POINTS

- 20/1 Lee Westwood's impressive first US tour win meant that he had won on all the World's four tours in the last six months. This success also took the 24-year-old Ryder Cup player to Number 14 in the World rankings.

  > Westwood has a fine all-round game, being particularly long off the tee. However, his greatest asset is his cool temperament which he showed again here, notably after calling a penalty on himself for double hitting a chip at the 14th hole on the final day.

  > His convincing win brought his odds for next week's US Masters tumbling down from 40/1 to 16/1 third favourite.

- Steve Flesch was "unquoted even at 200/1 in Life and Racing Post betting lists" (Sporting Life, Tuesday 7.4.98). This was particularly surprising as he was 33/1 with Ladbrokes and, after I tipped him, he was backed from 125/1 to 66/1 at Corals.

  The 30-year-old left hander, winner of last year's Nike tour championship, Number 1 on the USPGA tour stats for Greens In Regulation having made six out of eight cuts, and second on the Nike tour last weekend, clearly had a real chance.

  His performance shows the importance to punters of keeping an eye out for the 'New Nike Kids on the Block!'

- 150/1 Mark Wiebe has been suffering from the 'yips' and was out of form after finishing plumb last, last week. So his performance in finishing T3rd shows just how unpredictable golf form can be. However, the 40-year-old was T10th here in 1995.

- However 80/1 DYM player Steve Lowery's fine effort was predictable. It was his third successive top 7 finish in this tournament in which he has now replaced Mike Standly as the course specialist.

- Glen Day confirmed here that he really is an improved player. Following last week's fine T2nd in the Players' Championship he took full advantage of his R1 early tee time to shoot an opening 64 and lay the foundation for another top 3 finish.

- Final day betting was:-

12 under	Lee Westwood	5/6	WON
11 under	Steve Flesch	10/3	2nd
10 under	Duffy Waldorf	5/1	
8 under	Glen Day	20/1	T3rd
8 under	Steve Lowery	20/1	T3rd
8 under	Mark Wiebe	25/1	T3rd
8 under	Jim Carter	28/1	T3rd
6 under	Davis Love III	25/1	

- With this tournament providing a final opportunity for players to secure a place in the US Masters it is interesting to note that there were just three players priced at or under 50/1 who had that Augusta incentive – they were T3rd Glen Day, T8th Bob Estes, and Craig Parry who missed the cut.

- This Jack Nicklaus designed course, with generous fairways and small fast greens, demands length off the tee and precise iron play. It sure can jump up and bite as Scott Verplank (with an eleven!) and Fulton Allem (with a thirteen) discovered at the 15th in R3.

  The toughest hole is the 18th where a par 4 is a real bonus, with water left and deep-lipped bunkers right it is a very very tough final hole.

- Amongst those to miss the cut were 14/1 jt favourite Tom Lehman, 33/1 chances John Cook and Scott McCarron. One-time course specialist 125/1 DYM Mike Standly missed the cut for the second time in the last three years.

1997 RESULT

1	28/1	Brad Faxon
T2	100/1	Bill Glasson
T2	33/1	Jesper Parnevik
T4	50/1	Kirk Triplett
T4	50/1	Scott McCarron

WINNERS IN THE '90s

1990	David Frost
1991	Ian Woosnam
1992	Chip Beck
1993	Mike Standly
1994	Ben Crenshaw
1995	Davis Love III
1996	Scott McCarron
1997	Brad Faxon
1998	Lee Westwood

PUNTERS' GUIDE

- In 1999 this tournament is retitled the Entergy Classic, and moves from early April (before the US Masters) to early May. It will still be played on the English Turn course.
- With its move from being the final tournament before the US Masters there will presumably be less of a European challlenge in future.
- The course specialist in recent years has been Steve Lowery with three successive top 7 finishes, including T3rd at 80/1 this year.

THE US MASTERS

Date	9th – 12th April
Course	Augusta National, Augusta, Georgia
Par	72
Yardage	6,925
First Prize	£576,000
Total Purse	$3 million

Please see Part 5.

THE MCI CLASSIC

Date	16th – 19th April
Course	Hilton Head, South Carolina
Par	71
Yardage	6,916
First Prize	$342,000
Total Purse	$1.9 million

This tournament has been played every year, since its inception in 1969, at the Harbour Town Course at Hilton Head.

1998 ODDS

12/1	Ernie Els	50/1	Bob Estes
18/1	David Duval (non runner)	50/1	Lee Janzen*
20/1	Justin Leonard	50/1	Brad Faxon
20/1	Phil Mickelson	50/1	Nick Faldo
20/1	Davis Love III	50/1	Tom Watson
25/1	Scott Hoch	66/1	Steve Jones*
28/1	Jim Furyk	66/1	Bob Tway
28/1	Nick Price (DC)	66/1	Michael Bradley
33/1	Tom Lehman	66/1	Jay Haas*
33/1	Mark O'Meara (PWW)	66/1	John Huston*
40/1	John Daly	66/1	Steve Stricker
40/1	Vijay Singh	66/1	Paul Azinger*
40/1	Jesper Parnevik	66/1	Payne Stewart*
50/1	Jeff Maggert	66/1	Darren Clarke
50/1	John Cook	66/1	P U Johansson

There were 30 players best priced at or under 66/1.

BOOKIES AT ODDS

- There were six DYM players among the front thirty in the market – all created by the extraordinarily poor prices offered by the Tote!
  Lee Janzen 25/1 Tote: 50/1 Chandlers
  Steve Jones 33/1 Tote: 66/1 Sunderlands
  Jay Haas 33/1 Tote: 66/1 Hills, Ladbrokes
  John Huston 33/1 Tote: 66/1 Corals, Sunderlands
  Paul Azinger 33/1 Tote: 66/1 generally
  T3rd Payne Stewart 28/1 Tote: 66/1 City Index
- The winner Davis Love III 12/1 at Corals and Ladbrokes was 20/1 with City Index.

1998 RESULT

1	20/1	Davis Love III	67 68 68 65	266
2	80/1	Glen Day	67 67 72 67	273
T3	66/1	Payne Stewart	69 71 64 72	276
T3	20/1	Phil Mickelson	67 71 65 73	276
5	200/1	Fulton Allem	68 71 68 70	277

T6	F Lickliter	67 66 75 70 278	M Brooks	72 72 71 71 286
	J Sindelar	69 67 70 72 278	S Kendall	71 72 71 72 286
	N Price	67 69 70 72 278	B Andrade	72 71 71 72 286
	D Tewell	66 73 67 72 278	M Bradley	73 68 72 73 286
T10	E Els	73 68 70 68 279	D Ogrin	70 72 74 71 287
	L Mize	69 70 70 70 279	R Damron	72 71 72 72 287
	K Perry	74 68 66 71 279	C Strange	70 74 71 72 287
	J Huston	66 73 67 73 279	D Frost	69 71 74 73 287
T14	T Lehman	70 73 69 68 280	M Standly	70 72 71 74 287
	B Faxon	70 71 69 70 280	P Jordan	72 72 69 74 287
	R Mediate	68 69 70 73 280	B Fabel	70 73 74 71 288
	B Estes	68 68 71 73 280	J Carter	72 71 73 72 288
T18	R Fehr	69 73 72 67 281	C Rose	72 72 70 74 288
	J Parnevik	68 71 73 69 281	J Leonard	71 72 69 76 288
	B Tway	69 73 69 70 281	F Nobilo	68 68 74 78 288
	L Janzen	71 66 72 72 281	T Herron	71 69 70 78 288
	M Brisky	70 71 67 73 281	S McRoy	71 71 74 73 289
	L Mattiace	69 67 69 76 281	O Uresti	70 74 72 73 289
T24	M O'Meara	70 73 69 70 282	D Edwards	70 71 73 75 289
	N Lancaster	68 72 71 71 282	J Cook	68 72 74 75 289
	T Armour III	74 70 67 71 282	B Henninger	69 75 70 75 289
	F Funk	73 70 67 72 282	P H Horgan III	69 71 73 76 289
	R W Eaks	68 69 72 73 282	P U Johansson	71 71 71 76 289
	J Haas	66 66 76 74 282	D A Weibring	72 70 71 76 289
	V Singh	68 72 68 74 282	D Hart	72 72 68 77 289
	S Hoch	69 70 76 68 283	H Sutton	72 67 77 74 290
	D Pooley	73 70 69 71 283	B R Brown	72 71 72 75 290
	S Gump	72 72 66 73 283	K Gibson	67 72 74 77 290
	T Watson	71 71 72 70 284	R Cochran	72 70 76 73 291
	S Lowery	69 72 72 71 284	T Tryba	72 72 76 71 291
	J Sluman	72 71 69 72 284	L Clements	73 71 72 75 291
	D Martin	72 71 68 73 284	H Royer III	71 71 72 77 291
	S Pate	69 70 69 76 284	G Sauers	70 70 73 78 291
	B McCallister	73 69 70 73 285	J Furyk	73 71 76 72 292
	B Geiberger	72 72 68 73 285	J Mahaffey	70 73 77 72 292
	B Mayfair	73 71 67 74 285	D Barron	71 73 74 75 293
	F Zoeller	71 73 67 74 285	B Friend	69 74 75 76 294
	J Kelly	70 70 70 75 285	N Henke	72 70 75 78 295
	B Wadkins	71 70 69 75 285	N Faldo	70 74 73 83 300
	D Clarke	72 71 72 71 286		

ROUND BY ROUND LEADERBOARD

FIRST ROUND		SECOND ROUND	
J Huston	5 under	J Haas	10 under
D Tewell	5 under	F Lickliter	9 under
J Haas	5 under	G Day	8 under
G Day	4 under	D LOVE III	7 under
P Mickelson	4 under	L Mattiace	6 under
D LOVE III	4 under	B Estes	6 under
K Gibson	4 under	F Nobilo	6 under
N Price	4 under	N Price	6 under
F Lickliter	4 under	J Sindelar	6 under

THIRD ROUND		FINAL ROUND	
D LOVE III	12 under	D LOVE III	18 under
P Mickelson	10 under	G Day	11 under
P Stewart	9 under	P Stewart	8 under
L Mattiace	8 under	P Mickelson	8 under
D Tewell	7 under	F Allem	7 under
J Sindelar	7 under		
J Huston	7 under		
N Price	7 under		
G Day	7 under		

PUNTERS' POINTS

- Davis Love III's fourth win in this tournament was further confirmation that this is a course-specialist's track. Although it was his fifth successive tournament, and his R4 scoring had been poor in recent weeks, Love clearly loves Hilton Head! PMAs rule, OK!

- Runner-up Glen Day, marked up at a huge 80/1 by City Index, was recording his third successive top 3 finish – a truly astonishing achievement on such a competitive tour.

- T3rd Payne Stewart disappointed in R4 yet the 41-year-old with the trademark plus–fours had won here twice before.

- The other T3rd Phil Mickelson found that his often magical short game deserted him as the par 3s wrecked his chances.

- The finishing positions of those who finished in the top 10 at Augusta is interesting.

	Augusta	Hilton Head
Mark O'Meara	Won	T24th
David Duval	T2	DNP. Late withdrawal
Jim Furyk	4th	T79th
Paul Azinger	5th	W/D after R1
Darren Clarke	T8th	T45th
Justin Leonard	T8th	T56th

- Going into the final round the odds were:-

Davis Love III	5/6	12 under
Phil Mickelson	5/2	10 under
Payne Stewart	7/1	9 under
Nick Price	16/1	7 under
Len Mattiace	16/1	8 under
Glen Day	25/1	7 under

- Nick Faldo's final round 83 was his worst in 219 US tournaments. Nick finished plumb last. Faldo finished as a significant force?......
- One interesting market point: the first four in the betting were all best priced by spread firm City Index. Not only was their 20/1 Love the market best, their 80/1 about runner-up Glen Day made the in form 32-year-old a DYM. Let's hope I.G. and Sporting Index start to offer conventional odds, too!
- 84 players made the cut, however among those to miss it were 40/1 John Daly (15 over par!!), 66/1 Steve Stricker, 80/1 Andrew Magee and 125/1 DYM Stuart Appleby. Paul Azinger (back injury) withdrew after R1, while Steve Jones was disqualified for refusing to sign his card after a ten over par 81 in R2!

1997 RESULT

1	18/1	Nick Price
T2	33/1	Jesper Parnevik
T2	40/1	Brad Faxon
T4 fav	16/1	Tom Lehman
T4	125/1	Lennie Clements
T4	150/1	Hal Sutton

WINNERS IN THE '90s

1990	Payne Stewart
1991	Davis Love III
1992	Davis Love III
1993	David Edwards
1994	Hale Irwin
1995	Bob Tway
1996	Loren Roberts
1997	Nick Price
1998	Davis Love III

PUNTERS' GUIDE

- Hilton Head is a very flat course with few, if huge, bunkers. It has small relatively flat greens with reasonably wide fairways. It favours experienced players who are crisp accurate ball strikers.
- Davis Love III's fourth MCI Classic win with two-time winner Payne Stewart T3rd confirmed this tournament as one for course specialists.
- As the tournament is usually held the week after the US Masters do remember 'The Law of Hilton Head' which states that 'you must not back

any player who was in serious contention at Augusta as they will be suffering from MLD'.

- However on spread-betting terms you can profitably oppose Augusta contenders who are now hit by the fatigue factor.
- The pattern of results this decade suggest you go for a player
  > of experience, the last five winners' average age is 39.
  > who (if he played in the US Masters) made the cut yet was never in serious contention at Augusta the previous week.
  > with a solid track record in this course-specialists' event.

THE GREATER GREENSBORO OPEN

Date	23rd – 26th April
Course	Forest Hills GC, Greensboro, North Carolina
Par	72
Yardage	7,062
First Prize	$396,000
Total Purse	$2 million

This tournament had been held at Forest Hills since 1977 so there was plenty of course form for punters to study.

1998 ODDS

fav	11/1	Phil Mickelson	50/1	Frank Nobilo (DC)
	14/1	Mark O'Meara	50/1	David Frost
	16/1	Jim Furyk	66/1	Craig Parry
	25/1	Brad Faxon	66/1	Steve Lowery
	28/1	Bob Estes	66/1	Duffy Waldorf
	28/1	Steve Elkington	66/1	Billy Mayfair*
	33/1	Jeff Maggert	66/1	Tom Kite
	40/1	John Daly	66/1	Steve Flesch*
	40/1	Michael Bradley	66/1	Len Mattiace*
	50/1	Steve Stricker	66/1	Robert Damron
	50/1	Rocco Mediate		

Just 21 players were best priced at or under 66/1.

BOOKIES AT ODDS

DYM Steve Flesch 25/1 Ladbrokes: 66/1 Chandlers

DYM Len Mattiace 33/1 Ladbrokes: 66/1 Stanleys

DYM Billy Mayfair 33/1 Ladbrokes: 66/1 Sunderlands

Winner Trevor Dodds 80/1 City Index, Corals: 125/1 Hills, Stanleys, Surrey

1998 RESULT

1	125/1	Trevor Dodds	68 69 70 69	276
		(Dodds won at the first play-off hole)		
2	125/1	Scott Verplank	67 71 66 72	276
3	28/1	Bob Estes	67 65 72 73	277
4	150/1	Neal Lancaster	70 67 70 71	278
5	50/1	Frank Nobilo	71 65 71 72	279

T6	P Mickelson	74 65 71 70 280		J Riegger	72 70 76 69 287
	F Funk	72 69 67 72 280		J Johnston	69 69 74 75 287
T8	M Bradley	69 71 72 69 281		K Gibson	70 69 73 75 287
	L Clements	68 68 72 73 281		L Mattiace	71 71 70 75 287
	H Sutton	65 67 74 75 283		J P Hayes	71 72 69 75 287
T11	J Furyk	70 67 73 72 282		C Rose	73 70 69 75 287
	D Hart	68 68 74 72 282		J Durant	72 71 75 70 288
	J Kelly	70 68 68 76 282		S Lowery	75 68 72 73 288
	T Tryba	71 67 67 77 282		G Kraft	69 71 74 74 288
	S Kendall	68 73 63 78 282		D Tewell	71 71 72 74 288
T16	J Estes	70 70 75 68 283		G Hnatiuk	69 73 72 74 288
	M Hulbert	69 73 72 69 283		D Stockton	70 71 72 75 288
	H Frazar	71 71 71 70 283		G Hjertstedt	70 70 71 77 288
	C Dennis	69 70 73 71 283		J Adams	71 71 74 73 289
	J Maggert	71 69 71 72 283		T Loustalot	70 73 73 73 289
	T Herron	71 69 71 72 283		R Coughlan	74 68 73 74 289
	J Maginnes	68 72 70 73 283		B Quigley	69 69 76 75 289
T23	B Bates	71 72 71 70 284		S Skinner	72 69 73 75 289
	D Toms	70 70 73 71 284		M Wurtz	70 70 73 76 289
	S Flesch	71 70 71 72 284		F Allem	69 74 69 77 289
	S Appleby	70 69 70 75 284		Jeff Gallagher	74 69 73 74 290
	F Zoeller	67 73 69 75 284		B Cheesman	70 71 74 75 290
	B Faxon	67 70 71 76 284		P O'Malley	70 72 73 75 290
	D Hammond	69 70 69 76 284		K Wentworth	69 71 74 76 290
	M Standly	69 71 75 70 285		R Gamez	71 72 71 76 290
	B Wadkins	69 71 74 72 285		T Byrum	70 70 76 75 291
	R Black	71 69 73 72 285		J Kaye	69 74 73 75 291
	G Hill	71 71 69 74 285		T Kite	70 69 76 76 291
	D Edwards	69 69 72 75 285		B Mayfair	70 69 75 77 291
	S Elkington	71 71 67 76 285		J Carter	71 70 73 77 291
	D Frost	66 75 68 76 285		R Damron	70 73 75 74 292
	S Ames	71 70 66 78 285		J Daley	73 69 75 75 292
	R Mediate	68 72 74 72 286		B Henninger	76 67 75 75 293
	B Andrade	73 69 71 73 286		G Boros	73 70 73 77 293
	L Rinker	70 69 72 75 286		J Daly	72 70 76 79 297
	C Perry	66 75 68 77 286		S Stricker	72 71 74 81 298

ROUND BY ROUND LEADERBOARD

FIRST DAY		SECOND DAY	
H Sutton	7 under	B Estes	12 under
C Perry	6 under	H Sutton	12 under
D Frost	6 under	D Hart	8 under
B Faxon	5 under	L Clements	8 under
S Verplank	5 under	F Nobilo	8 under
B Estes	5 under	J Furyk	7 under
F Zoeller	5 under	T DODDS	7 under
T DODDS	4 under	B Faxon	7 under
		N Lancaster	7 under

THIRD DAY		FINAL DAY	
B Estes	12 under	T DODDS	12 under
S Kendall	12 under	S Verplank	12 under
S Verplank	12 under	B Estes	11 under
T Tryba	11 under	N Lancaster	10 under
J Kelly	10 under	F Nobilo	9 under
H Sutton	10 under		
T DODDS	9 under		

PUNTERS' POINTS

- A dream result for the bookmakers as two rank outsiders fought out a play-off. Even then the outsider won as Stan James made Scott Verplank the 8/11 favourite with Trevor Dodds even money.

- Last summer Trevor Dodds had surgery and radiation treatment for testicular cancer. This year he hadn't shown any real form having missed four cuts in his last five starts. Nevertheless here he showed real final-day guts to put himself in with a real chance. He birdied the tough final hole for the fourth successive day.

- Scott Verplank, the US Amateur Champion won the 1985 Western Open as an amateur. However, elbow injuries and diabetes subsequently stopped him from reaching the top golfing honours. However he took top spot in Q. School last November and here he played very well indeed to make the final-hole birdie he needed to force a play-off. However he found the rough from the tee in the play-off to finish second.

- 28/1 Bob Estes was in the lead and looking all over the winner until he bogeyed both the last two holes to finish a morale-sapping 3rd. It will be very interesting to see how he reacts to this.

- Frank Nobilo made a stout defence of his title although he never quite got to the leaders. He is clearly regaining his best form.

- Neal Lancaster was born and lives at Smithfield just a couple of hours' drive from the course. A real 'streak' player, who was T4th in the 1995 US Open, he actually had 24 birdies in the tournament – that is one every third hole on average!

- Among those missing the cut were 14/1 Mark O'Meara, 66/1 outsiders Craig Parry and Duffy Waldorf and 80/1 Kirk Triplett (3rd last year).

1997 RESULT

1	80/1	Frank Nobilo
2	20/1	Brad Faxon
3	66/1	Kirk Triplett
T4	66/1	Billy Andrade
T4	100/1	Robert Damron

WINNERS IN THE '90s

1990	Steve Elkington
1991	Mark Brooks
1992	Davis Love III
1993	Rocco Mediate
1994	Mike Springer
1995	Jim Gallagher Jr
1996	Mark O'Meara
1997	Frank Nobilo
1998	Trevor Dodds

PUNTERS' GUIDE

- In the last five years the Greater Greensboro has proved to be an outsiders' paradise. In those five years of the 21 players in the top 4 (or T4th).

  > 16 (76%) have been priced at or over 50/1.

  > 11 (52%) have been priced at or over 80/1, with at least two each year.

  > 8 (38%) have been priced at or over 100/1.

- With punishing rough the course favours straight-hitting, solid ball-striking players. It can result in poor scoring from players who become inaccurate and low scores from those who are straight and whose putter is hot.

  As a result on the final day players can come from 'off the pace' to win.

  Seven times in the last nine years the winner has started the final round no higher than T7th.

- If he's showing up well in the driving accuracy stats next year a player to consider would be Dudley Hart (T3rd 1993: T8th 1994 and T11th 1998) as an outsider in an outsiders' tournament.

°THE SHELL HOUSTON OPEN

Date	30th April – 3rd May
Course	The Woodlands, Houston, Texas
Par	72
Yardage	7,062
First Prize	$360,000
Total Purse	$1.9 million

Played at the tough Woodlands course since 1975 this tournament has produced five first-time winners this decade.

1998 ODDS

fav	11/1	David Duval	40/1	John Cook
	12/1	Phil Mickelson	40/1	John Huston*
	14/1	Fred Couples	40/1	Fred Funk*
	16/1	Scott Hoch	50/1	Steve Flesch
	20/1	Jeff Maggert	50/1	Scott McCarron
	25/1	Payne Stewart	50/1	Hal Sutton
	28/1	Lee Janzen	66/1	Tom Kite
	28/1	Steve Elkington	66/1	Dudley Hart
	33/1	Jay Haas		

Just 17 players were best priced at or under 66/1.

BOOKIES AT ODDS

DYM John Huston 20/1 Ladbrokes: 40/1 Hills

DYM Fred Funk 20/1 Stanleys: 40/1 Ladbrokes, Tote

Winner David Duval 8/1 Ladbrokes, City Index: 11/1 Tote

1998 RESULT

1	11/1	David Duval	69 70 73 64	276
2	20/1	Jeff Maggert	71 71 64 71	277
3	14/1	Fred Couples	72 68 70 68	278
T4	28/1	Lee Janzen	69 69 71 70	279
T4	66/1	Dudley Hart	70 72 70 67	279

T6	J Kelly	71 71 70 68 280		D A Weibring	75 69 71 72 287
	D Stockton	74 71 67 68 280		P O'Malley	70 70 74 73 287
	H Sutton	70 73 69 68 280		T Kite	69 75 69 74 287
	D Forsman	68 70 68 74 280		P Jacobsen	75 70 72 71 288
10	S Ames	72 68 71 70 281		D Barr	72 73 72 71 288
11	S Kendall	73 72 70 67 282		S Skinner	74 71 71 72 288
T12	S Flesch	75 71 69 68 283		J P Hayes	70 75 74 70 289
	S Hoch	66 76 73 68 283		K Nolan	70 76 72 71 289
	J Huston	71 69 73 70 283		P Stankowski	70 75 74 70 289
	J Durant	70 72 71 70 283		D Barron	75 70 72 72 289
	F Langham	66 74 71 72 283		B McCallister	71 71 74 73 289
T17	B Lietzke	67 76 72 69 284		P Stewart	71 74 74 71 290
	J Gallagher	74 72 68 70 284		G Kraft	70 75 73 72 290
	O Browne	69 77 68 70 284		R Coughlan	72 73 73 72 290
	G Waite	73 72 69 70 284		J McGovern	73 73 71 73 290
	M Hulbert	67 73 71 73 284		R Thompson	73 72 72 73 290
T22	B Gage	71 73 74 67 285		R Fehr	71 70 71 78 290
	P Tataurangi	70 73 74 68 285		J Mahaffey	73 73 76 69 291
	D Sutherland	73 69 74 69 285		Joe Daley	72 74 73 72 291
	C Rose	76 70 70 69 285		B Quigley	74 70 75 72 291
	M Sullivan	70 72 74 69 285		J Sindelar	73 72 73 73 291
	B Bates	71 71 73 70 285		J Carter	74 71 73 73 291
	G Boros	67 76 72 70 285		L Rinker	69 76 72 74 291
	D Hammond	68 76 69 72 285		C Parry	72 72 75 73 292
	P Mickelson	71 75 72 68 286		D Martin	72 74 72 74 292
	C Perry	76 69 72 69 286		M Standly	72 74 75 72 293
	W Wood	70 75 72 69 286		J Delsing	67 73 78 75 293
	O Uresti	74 72 69 71 286		G Hjertstedt	72 73 71 77 293
	K Gibson	72 71 71 72 286		L Wadkins	68 76 76 74 294
	P Jordan	73 71 70 72 286		F Funk	72 74 73 75 294
	D Tewell	68 75 75 69 287		B Hughes	70 76 73 77 296
	B Gilder	72 72 74 69 287		Z Zorkic	72 74 74 77 297
	K Perry	71 71 75 70 287			
	B Chamblee	74 72 70 71 287			

ROUND BY ROUND LEADERBOARD

FIRST ROUND		SECOND ROUND	
S Hoch	6 under	D Forsman	6 under
F Langham	6 under	L Janzen	6 under
M Hulbert	5 under	D DUVAL	5 under
J Delsing	5 under	S Ames	4 under
G Boros	5 under	F Couples	4 under
B Lietzke	5 under	J Huston	4 under
D DUVAL	3 under	M Hulbert	4 under
		J Delsing	4 under
		P O'Malley	4 under
		F Langham	4 under

THIRD ROUND		FINAL ROUND	
J Maggert	10 under	D DUVAL	12 under
D Forsman	10 under	J Maggert	11 under
L Janzen	7 under	F Couples	10 under
F Couples	6 under	L Janzen	9 under
S Ames	5 under	D Hart	9 under
F Langham	5 under		
M Hulbert	5 under		
D DUVAL	4 under		

- On the second day there was a strong swirling wind which was a severe handicap to those players who had a late tee time on that day.

PUNTERS' POINTS

- Starting the final day 6 shots off the pace David Duval made his confident putting and huge, accurate length tell with eagles at the par 5 13th and 15th, and a birdie at the par 3 16th. This shot him up to 12 under par to set a clubhouse target after a brilliant R4 64. It was his fifth win in his last twelve starts!

- Jeff Maggert led after R3 for the eighth time.....and failed to win for the eighth time, as he recorded his eleventh 2nd place since his sole victory in 1993, and his third 2nd place in this tournament in the last five years!!!

  His R4 play was rather tentative and defensive, lacking the positive confidence he showed in a superb 64 in R3.

- Fred Couples lives in Dallas and drew huge galleries as, like Duval, he brought his US Masters form to the Woodlands to finish 3rd after three birdies in the last four holes.

- The final-day disappointment was the spectacle of Lee Janzen on the back nine. He led the tournament with five holes to play before nervously dropping 3 shots to finish a sad T4th.

- Dan Forsman, who also led this tournament into the final round in 1987 when he finished T13th, again showed the pressures of the final day to shoot 74 to finish T6th.

- T4th 66/1 Dudley Hart (T9th for Driving Accuracy and T12th for Greens In Regulation this season) made his accuracy tell here. He's an underrated player who can play tough courses well.
- This is a tough course with the par 3 8th and 9th the toughest holes while the par 5 13th and 15th offer birdie and eagle opportunities.

   As in all Texas tournaments the wind can blow, especially late in the day.
- The final-day betting was

10 under	Jeff Maggert	11/8
10 under	Dan Forsman	3/1
7 under	Lee Janzen	13/2
6 under	Fred Couples	13/2
4 under	David Duval	20/1 – won

   However with Ladbrokes, Corals, and Hills going 1/4 odds 1,2,3 why did Stan James offer a paltry 1/5 odds?
- With four of the first five players among the top 8 in the market golf punters could feel a return to sanity after Dodds' 125/1 win last week!
- Among those to miss the cut were 28/1 Steve Elkington, 33/1 Jay Haas, 40/1 John Cook, 50/1 Scott McCarron and last year's play-off players 80/1 Phil Blackmar and 100/1 Kevin Sutherland.

1997 RESULT

1	100/1	Phil Blackmar
		(Blackmar won at the first play-off hole)
2	150/1	Kevin Sutherland
3	16/1	Steve Elkington
T4	100/1	Hal Sutton
T4	20/1	Scott Hoch

WINNERS IN THE '90s

1990	Tony Sils
1991	Fulton Allem
1992	Fred Funk
1993	Jim McGovern
1994	Mike Heinen
1995	Payne Stewart
1996	Mark Brooks
1997	Phil Blackmar
1998	David Duval

PUNTERS' GUIDE

- The players with the best recent course records are
  > Jeff Maggert with three 2nds in the last five years
  > Scott Hoch T12th 1998: T4th 1997: 2nd 1995
  > David Duval winner 1998: 15th 1997: 3rd 1996.
- The last 4 winners had all shown solid course form

	Previous Year	Two Years Earlier
> 1998 winner David Duval	15	3
> 1997 winner Phil Blackmar	19	48
> 1996 winner Mark Brooks	32	75
> 1995 winner Payne Stewart	DNP	T3

- The importance of going for players with a proven record of accuracy was shown by the positions on the US tour stats of the front players this year
  > David Duval   10th   Greens In Regulation
  > Jeff Maggert   2nd   Driving Accuracy
  > Fred Couples   6th   Greens In Regulation
  > Dudley Hart   12th   Greens In Regulation: T9th Driving Accuracy
  > Lee Janzen   11th   Greens In Regulation
- So the advice must be to select a player with proven course form who is in the top 20 for Greens In Regulation.

THE BELL SOUTH CLASSIC

Date	7th – 10th May
Course	Sugarloaf TPC, Duluth, Georgia
Par	72
Yardage	7,259
First Prize	$324,000
Total Purse	$1.8 million

The Greg Norman designed Sugar Loaf course, just north of Atlanta, Georgia, hosted the Bell South Classic for the second successive year. So the 1997 result was the only course form available.

1998 ODDS

fav	15/2	Tiger Woods	50/1	John Huston*
	9/1	David Duval (PWW)	50/1	Glen Day
	14/1	Davis Love III (non runner)	50/1	Brad Faxon
	25/1	Nick Price	50/1	Hal Sutton
	28/1	Tom Lehman	50/1	John Daly
	28/1	Mark Calcavecchia	66/1	Jay Haas
	33/1	Bob Estes	66/1	Scott McCarron* (DC)
	40/1	Lee Janzen	66/1	David Toms
	40/1	Stewart Cink	66/1	Steve Elkington

18 players were best priced at or under 66/1.

PLEASE NOTE Davis Love III, 14/1 third favourite, was a very late pre-tournament withdrawal, so punters benefited as golf does not have a Rule 4.

BOOKIES AT ODDS

T5th DYM John Huston 25/1 Ladbrokes: 50/1 Hills

T3rd DYM Steve Flesch 33/1 City Index: 80/1 Chandlers, Hills

T5th TYM Scott Verplank 50/1 Stan James: 150/1 Surrey

T5th TYM Bill Glasson 40/1 Stan James: 125/1 City Index

D. PAULSON 4X SUB 70 ROUNDS

A MAGEE QUALITY PLAYED WELL

1998 RESULT

1 fav	15/2	Tiger Woods	69 67 63 72	271
2	200/1	Jay Don Blake	67 68 67 70	272
T3	200/1	Esteban Toledo	66 75 66 67	274
T3	80/1	Steve Flesch	66 71 68 69	274
T5	150/1	Scott Verplank	67 74 69 65	275
T5	125/1	Bill Glasson	68 73 68 66	275
T5	80/1	Bob Tway X	73 69 66 67	275
T5	50/1	John Huston	68 68 71 68	275
T5	50/1	Stewart Cink	67 71 65 72	275

T10	T Dodds	71 67 72 66 276
	C Dennis	72 65 71 68 276
T12	G Waite	68 70 72 67 277
	C Rose	70 70 69 68 277
T14	D Duval	67 73 73 65 278
	L Janzen	71 69 68 70 278
	J Kelly	68 71 69 70 278
	C Parry	69 66 72 71 278
18	G Hnatiuk	67 69 70 73 279
T19	B Wadkins	70 72 69 69 280
	B Estes	69 74 66 71 280
	S Ames	70 69 70 71 280
	S McRoy	68 68 72 72 280
	S Gump	70 70 68 72 280
T24	J Gallagher	74 70 68 69 281
	G Kraft	71 71 69 70 281
	H Sutton	67 72 70 72 281
	D Pride	71 73 67 71 282
	L Mize	70 72 69 71 282
	J Daley	68 74 69 71 282
	N Price	73 70 69 71 283
	G Day	72 72 68 71 283
	S Pate	72 68 74 69 283
	F Langham	71 69 70 73 283
	T Herron	68 69 77 69 283
	P Goydos	71 70 67 75 283
	M Hulbert	73 70 68 73 284
	K Perry	71 71 71 71 284
	B Henninger	71 72 68 73 284
	T Pernice Jr	69 71 73 71 284
	J Johnston	70 69 74 71 284
	S McCarron	71 73 69 71 284

M Kuchar (am)	70 69 71 74 284
R Gamez	74 68 68 74 284
F Lickliter	67 76 71 70 284
T Lehman	72 72 70 70 284
G Hill	71 69 69 75 284
B Friend	74 70 69 72 285
R Cochran	73 71 71 70 285
H Irwin	72 70 74 69 285
C Barlow	70 69 71 76 286
D Forsman	70 69 76 71 286
S Stricker	70 73 66 77 286
J Haas	71 71 74 70 286
J L Lewis	69 73 74 70 286
B Cheesman	70 74 73 69 286
Jeff Gallagher	72 67 67 80 286
A Magee	73 68 73 73 287
J Sluman	71 70 74 72 287
B Gage	73 69 71 76 289
G Sauers	71 72 67 79 289
M Calcavecchia	65 75 76 73 289
P Stankowski	71 73 74 71 289
B Faxon	72 70 75 73 290
R Mediate	72 72 73 73 290
K Jones	70 72 73 76 291
B Andrade	70 74 72 75 291
B Chamblee	73 69 75 74 291
R Freeman	69 72 73 79 293
G Hallberg	73 71 76 73 293
S Jurgensen	70 72 74 78 294
B Bates	70 74 76 75 295
N Henke	72 69 76 80 297
M Carnevale	72 72 79 76 299

ROUND BY ROUND LEADERBOARD

FIRST ROUND		SECOND ROUND	
M Calcavecchia	7 under	C Parry	9 under
S Flesch	6 under	J D Blake	9 under
E Toledo	6 under	T WOODS	8 under
D Duval	5 under	J Huston	8 under
S Verplank	5 under	S McRoy	8 under
G Hnatiuk	5 under	G Hnatiuk	8 under
T WOODS	3 under		

THIRD ROUND		FINAL ROUND	
T WOODS	17 under	T WOODS	17 under
J D Blake	14 under	J D Blake	16 under
S Cink	13 under	E Toledo	14 under
S Flesch	11 under	S Flesch	14 under
Jeff Gallagher	10 under	B Tway	13 under
G Hnatiuk	10 under	S Verplank	13 under
		B Glasson	13 under
		S Cink	13 under
		J Huston	13 under

- The opening two days were both rain shortened with 78 players on each day still to complete their rounds.

PUNTERS' POINTS

- The tip in last year's volume to back Tiger Woods.when he's fresh from a break, on a par 72 long course with four par 5s and if his Dad was in good health, paid off here. Fresh, in his first tournament since the US Masters, Tiger recorded his first USPGA tour win of 1998 despite shooting a poor final round 72 in ideal conditions. His ability to hole out for par from missable distances was crucial.

- Tiger Woods's finishing-position quotes with the spread firms were 16-19 with Ladbrokes, and IG Index, and 14-17 with Sporting Index, so providing Tiger punters with a real profitable opportunity in a tournament tailor made for his game.

- Jay Don Blake, who was second in this tournament in 1992, has clearly recovered from a herniated disc in his lower back. Punters who tried to 'buy money' by punting on Woods in the final day 3-ball found that Blake had defeated them. A fine putter, he burnt the edge of the hole many times in R4 and for me he was an unlucky loser.

- Stewart Cink's putter let him down on Sunday especially on the par 3 eleventh when Tiger got up and down from up on a rock while Cink missed from 4 feet. He lives in Atlanta so this is very much his home tournament.

- Bob Tway was very impressive with a 67 in R4. He clearly enjoys this course having made the top 20 last year and finishing T5th this time. Keep him on the right side here in 1999.

- Left hander Steve Flesch continues to impress both by his swing and by his temperament. This was his second top 3 finish in five weeks!

- Scott Verplank's superb R4 65 was conclusive proof that the 33-year-old is now well over all his various injuries. He's now in the top 20 for both greens in regulation and putting.

- In 1999 do please pay special attention to the 608-yard par 5 tenth which Tiger Woods this year reached in two after a 280 yard 2 iron; and also to the par 4 thirteenth which is short enough for the long drivers to reach from the tee as Scott McCarron did when winning in 1997.

- Among those to miss the cut were 50/1 John Daly, 66/1 David Toms, 80/1 outsiders Stuart Appleby and Skip Kendall, and 100/1 chances Tommy Tolles (DYM), Fred Funk (DYM), Kelly Gibson and Donnie Hammond.

1997 RESULT

1	50/1	Scott McCarron
T2	25/1	Lee Janzen
T2	28/1	David Duval
T2	150/1	Brian Henninger

WINNERS IN THE '90s

1990	Wayne Levi
1991	Corey Pavin
1992	Tom Kite
1993	Nolan Henke
1994	John Daly
1995	Mark Calcavecchia
1996	Paul Stankowski
1997	Scott McCarron
1998	Tiger Woods

- 1990-1996 inclusive the tournament was held at the Atlanta Country Club, Marietta, Georgia.

PUNTERS' GUIDE

- For the second time in its two-year history on this course the Bell South Classic was won by a very long-hitting player. However we must remember that going into this tournament.

  > Jay Don Blake, 2nd at 200/1, was T118th for driving distance at 261.9 yards.

  > Esteban Toledo, T3rd also at 200/1, was 139th (of 153) for driving distance at 258.9 yards.

- Accuracy, as shown by the Greens In Regulation stats, may be more significant as six of the eleven players in the top 10 (or T10th) were in the top 20 for G.I.R. going into this tournament.

- Just three players have finished in the top 20 in both of the Sugarloaf years

  > David Duval T14th 1998: T22nd 1997

  > Bob Tway T5th 1998: T19th 1997

  > Bill Glasson T5th 1998: T19th 1997

- In 1999 the tournament moves to early April and will be the final tournament before the US Masters.

THE BYRON NELSON CLASSIC

Date	14th – 17th May	
Courses	TPC at Four Seasons Resort, Irving, Texas	
	Las Colinas	Cottonwood Valley
Par	70	70
Yardage	6,924	6,846
First Prize	$450,000	
Total Purse	$2.5 million	

Each of the two courses is used for the first two days. After the halfway cut the final two rounds are played at the Las Colinas course. The Cottonwood course is normally the easier course by about a shot.

1998 ODDS

fav	6/1	Tiger Woods (PWW+DC)	50/1	Bob Tway
	10/1	Ernie Els	50/1	Hal Sutton
	20/1	Phil Mickelson	50/1	Payne Stewart
	22/1	Fred Couples	66/1	Steve Jones
	28/1	Justin Leonard	66/1	Frank Nobilo
	28/1	Nick Price	66/1	John Cook
	33/1	Tom Lehman	66/1	Jay Don Blake
	33/1	Jim Furyk	66/1	Loren Roberts
	33/1	Stewart Cink	66/1	Scott Verplank
	40/1	Mark O'Meara	66/1	Michael Bradley
	40/1	Jeff Maggert	66/1	Glen Day
	40/1	Mark Calcavecchia	66/1	Tom Watson
	40/1	Steve Flesch	66/1	Steve Elkington
	50/1	Bob Estes		

27 players were best priced at or under 66/1.

BOOKIES AT ODDS

Hal Sutton 28/1 Chandlers: 50/1 City Index

The winner John Cook 40/1 Stan James: 66/1 Chandlers, City Index, Ladbrokes, Sunderlands

1998 RESULT

1	66/1	John Cook	66 68 66 65	265
T2	50/1	Hal Sutton	66 65 68 69	268
T2	22/1	Fred Couples	66 67 63 72	268
T2	150/1	Harrison Frazar	64 68 66 70	268
5	80/1	Steve Stricker	67 72 65 65	269

T6	S McCarron	66 72 68 64 270		G Hill	70 69 71 67 277
	P Mickelson	66 68 69 67 270		B Crenshaw	70 69 70 68 277
	B Friend	63 70 68 69 270		R W Eaks	66 73 69 69 277
T9	T Herron	69 69 67 66 271		L Mize	69 69 70 69 277
	C Dennis	67 72 63 69 271		D Martin	69 68 70 70 277
	J Carter	68 68 66 69 271		T Watson	64 70 72 71 277
T12	T Woods	65 71 69 67 272		S Gump	65 70 69 73 277
	B Estes	66 68 70 68 272		T Dodds	68 71 65 73 277
	J Sluman	67 67 69 69 272		T Byrum	68 71 70 69 278
T15	P Blackmar	69 69 69 66 273		V Veazey	69 70 69 70 278
	K Triplett	69 70 67 67 273		W Wood	69 68 70 71 278
	M O'Meara	67 69 69 68 273		R Mediate	67 70 70 71 278
	J Furyk	66 70 68 69 273		C Stadler	71 67 69 71 278
T19	P Tataurangi	70 68 68 68 274		R Black	73 66 66 73 278
	B Tway	70 66 69 69 274		J Maggert	69 70 71 69 279
	P Jacobsen	70 68 67 69 274		C Perry	67 70 73 69 279
	T Tryba	66 68 70 70 274		M Hulbert	71 68 69 71 279
	J D Blake	67 68 69 70 274		D Pooley	67 71 70 71 279
	P Stewart	68 67 68 71 274		L Rinker	69 68 69 73 279
T25	S Jones	69 70 69 67 275		K Perry	67 72 66 74 279
	B Fabel	70 69 68 68 275		B Bates	65 74 70 71 280
	D Forsman	67 71 69 68 275		F Lickliter	65 72 72 71 280
	G Hjertstedt	70 66 70 69 275		C Barlow	69 68 72 71 280
	S Flesch	71 66 69 69 275		E Els	69 69 71 71 280
	C Pavin	70 67 69 69 275		F Allem	69 70 69 72 280
	R Cochran	68 67 70 70 275		P Goydos	72 66 69 73 280
	T Kite	69 70 66 70 275		N Henke	75 64 70 72 281
	T Armour III	67 72 66 70 275		M Springer	71 68 71 72 282
	G Day	68 70 67 70 275		T Pernice Jr	73 66 71 72 282
	M Heinen	70 69 70 67 276		G Hnatiuk	68 69 72 73 282
	L Mattiace	71 66 70 69 276		J McGovern	71 67 71 73 282
	D Hammond	66 70 70 70 276		D Frost	68 71 74 72 285
	B McCallister	65 72 69 70 276		D Ogrin	67 72 72 74 285
	J Leonard	68 69 69 70 276		R Coughlan	70 68 74 73 285
	C DiMarco	67 71 68 70 276		O Uresti	69 68 79 71 287
	R Damron	68 65 72 71 276		J Daly	67 71 70 79 287
	E Toledo	72 67 66 71 276		Jeff Gallagher	69 69 74 76 288

ROUND BY ROUND LEADERBOARD

FIRST ROUND		SECOND ROUND	
B Friend (T)	7 under	H Sutton	9 under
T Watson (C)	6 under	H Frazar	8 under
H Frazar (C)	6 under	F Couples	7 under
B McCallister (C)	5 under	R Damron	7 under
T Woods (C)	5 under	B Friend	7 under
S Gump (C)	5 under	B Estes	6 under
F Lickliter (C)	5 under	J Sluman	6 under
B Bates (T)	5 under	T Tryba	6 under
J COOK (T)	4 under	P Mickelson	6 under
		T Watson	6 under
		J COOK	6 under

THIRD ROUND		FINAL ROUND	
F Couples	14 under	J COOK	15 under
H Frazar	12 under	H Sutton	12 under
H Sutton	11 under	F Couples	12 under
J COOK	10 under	H Frazar	12 under
B Friend	9 under	S Stricker	11 under
J Carter	8 under		
C Dennis	8 under		

(T) after a player indicates he played the TPC at Las Colinas
(C) after a player indicates he played the Cottonwood Valley course

PUNTERS' POINTS

- 40-year-old 66/1 outsider John Cook showed in his tenth USPGA tour win the qualities that have served him so well – straight hitting, a cool temperament and, crucially, a shrewd strategic approach when it matters. Here in R4 he edged ever closer to the R3 leader Fred Couples until as co-leader standing on the par 3 17th tee Cook aimed left hoping to two putt and make par. He did just that. By contrast joint leader Couples, playing in the pair behind Cook, boldly went for the pin, found the water then three putted for a triple bogey six. The better strategist John Cook had won!

- Throughout his final round 'Boom-Boom' had lacked accuracy off the tee and sharpness with his irons. This was the second tournament, the other was the US Masters, that he has lost when in front on the back nine.

- 50/1 Hal Sutton, the each-way tip for this tournament in his Player Profile last year kept up his superb form This was his third top 10 in his last four tournaments.....if only his putting was in the same class as his iron play he'd be virtually unbeatable.

- At last he's back! Two time 1996 winner 31-year-old Steve Stricker was posting his first top 5 finish since the Tour Championship in 1996.

- 6/1 favourite and defending champion Tiger Woods was never at his best. This tournament does not really play to his long-hitting strengths....he's always best with four par 5s on longer courses. He'll be opposable here again in 1999.

- 150/1 T2nd Harrison Frazar was a creditable 13th in 1997 as a rookie on the Nike tour when he won the South Carolina Classic. He had already shown fine form with a superb top 20 in the Greater Greensboro Open. Here in his own backyard as a guy living in Dallas where he was born he'll always remember Sunday, 17th May 1998 – the day he beat another Dallas resident, Fred Couples, by 2 shots in their R4 last out 2-ball.

- T15th Jim Furyk was posting his third top 15 finish in his last four tournaments. It may be best to make money from him by selling his finishing position on the spreads rather than by backing him each way on conventional terms. Here Sporting Index's finishing position quote was 26-29 so giving a nice 11 pt profit.

- Two points to note about this two-course format tournament.

  > The importance of an early first-day tee time on either course is reduced as half the field is on the other course.

  > Cottonwood Valley plays about one shot easier than Las Colinas – a point to remember in outright betting after R1.

- If there's to be a 59 shot on the USPGA tour it could well be here on the Cottonwood Valley course where Scott Gump went out in 29 this year in R1!

- Among those to miss the cut were 28/1 Nick Price, 33/1 chances Stewart Cink and Tom Lehman, 40/1 Mark Calcavecchia and 66/1 outsiders Frank Nobilo and Loren Roberts.

1997 RESULT

1 fav	6/1	Tiger Woods
2	150/1	Lee Rinker
T3	66/1	Tom Watson
T3	150/1	Dan Forsman

WINNERS IN THE '90s

1990	Payne Stewart
1991	Nick Price
1992	Billy Ray Brown
1993	Scott Simpson
1994	Neil Lancaster
1995	Ernie Els
1996	Phil Mickelson
1997	Tiger Woods
1998	John Cook

PUNTERS' GUIDE

- In the last five years twenty-three players have finished in the top 4 (or T4th).
  > Nine (39%) have been 100/1 plus
  > Fifteen (65%) have been 66/1 plus

So this is clearly a tournament in which big-priced outsiders regularly do well.

- Over the last three years the best tournament records are held by
  > Hal Sutton T2nd 1998: T12th 1997: T10th 1996
  > Phil Mickelson T6th 1998: T12th 1997: Won 1996
- In 1999 Jim Furyk must have an outstanding chance. His stroke average over the last three years is 67.8.

THE MASTERCARD COLONIAL CLASSIC

Date	21st – 24th May
Course	Colonial Country Club, Fort Worth, Texas
Par	70
Yardage	7,010
First Prize	$414,000
Total Purse	$2.3 million

The winner of this prestigious tournament has his name enscribed on a plaque on the Wall of Champions. It is a tournament always played at the Colonial Country Club course. It is the last of the three tournaments on 'the Texas trail'.

1998 ODDS

fav	12/1	David Duval	40/1	Jeff Maggert
	16/1	Phil Mickelson	40/1	Mark Calcavecchia
	16/1	Davis Love III	40/1	Vijay Singh
	20/1	Fred Couples	40/1	Bob Tway
	22/1	Justin Leonard	40/1	John Huston
	25/1	Jim Furyk	40/1	Steve Flesch
	28/1	Scott Hoch	50/1	Payne Stewart
	33/1	John Cook (PWW)	66/1	Bill Glasson
	33/1	Lee Janzen	66/1	David Frost (DC)
	33/1	Nick Price	66/1	Nick Faldo
	40/1	Brad Faxon	66/1	Steve Jones
	40/1	Stewart Cink	66/1	Tom Watson
	40/1	Bob Estes	66/1	Jeff Sluman*
	66/1	Glen Day		

27 players were best priced at 66/1 or under.

BOOKIES AT ODDS

DYM third placed Jeff Sluman 33/1 Chandler: 66/1 Sunderlands, Ladbrokes, Stan James, Stanleys

DYM fourth placed Harrison Frazar 50/1 Hills, City Index: 100/1 Ladbrokes

Winner Tom Watson 40/1 Tote, Hills, Stan James: 66/1 Corals, Ladbrokes, Stanleys, Sunderlands

1998 RESULT

1	66/1	Tom Watson	68 66 65 66	265
2	25/1	Jim Furyk	66 67 66 68	267
3	66/1	Jeff Sluman	67 67 66 69	269
4	100/1	Harrison Frazar	64 67 68 71	270
5	33/1	John Cook	68 66 69 68	271

T6	T Gallagher	69 69 68 66 272		J Sindelar	69 70 74 67 280
	K Perry	68 65 69 70 272		M Wiebe	71 70 71 68 280
T8	J Leonard	70 70 67 66 273		G Day	72 66 71 71 280
	B Henninger	70 66 68 69 273		D Edwards	72 69 68 71 280
T10	D Forsman	69 67 71 67 274		C Pavin	73 66 69 72 280
	S Flesch	68 66 72 68 274		S Cink	68 72 67 73 280
	C Parry	68 69 69 68 274		D Ogrin	71 64 71 74 280
	S Appleby	68 69 69 68 274		B Geiberger	70 69 67 74 280
T14	D Frost	68 69 69 69 275		M Calcavecchia	68 65 70 77 280
	M Brisky	70 70 66 69 275		P Jacobsen	69 70 71 71 281
	C Dennis	68 68 68 71 275		R Fehr	70 69 70 72 281
	D Duval	66 70 68 71 275		D Hart	68 72 69 72 281
T18	S Kendall	68 71 69 68 276		D Pohl	70 66 77 69 282
	F Couples	72 69 67 68 276		K Sutherland	69 71 73 69 282
	J Maggert	69 72 67 68 276		G Hjertstedt	70 69 73 70 282
	L Wadkins	66 71 70 69 276		B Chamblee	68 69 75 70 282
	D Martin	67 69 70 70 276		J D Blake	72 68 72 70 282
	P Stewart	68 72 66 70 276		G Boros	68 73 71 70 282
	K Triplett	69 68 68 71 276		B McCallister	69 71 71 71 282
	S Hoch	67 73 66 70 276		L Rinker	69 68 74 71 282
	J Huston	70 69 66 71 276		M Brooks	71 70 70 71 282
	S McCarron	70 67 67 72 276		F Allem	69 69 72 72 282
	R Mediate	67 68 67 74 276		B Fabel	67 68 71 76 282
	N Faldo	72 69 70 66 277		T Kite	69 70 74 70 283
	F Funk	75 65 68 69 277		J Carter	67 72 71 73 283
	T Armour III	70 65 72 70 277		G Waite	69 72 69 73 283
	B Lietzke	67 69 67 74 277		D Stockton	71 69 75 69 284
	F Nobilo	69 68 73 68 278		R W Eaks	67 73 74 71 285
	J Kelly	67 69 71 71 278		S Lowery	70 69 75 72 286
	S Jones	69 69 72 69 279		C Stadler	71 70 71 74 286
	S Verplank	70 69 71 69 279		R Damron	74 66 70 76 286
	B Tway	67 71 72 69 279		D Toms	71 69 76 71 287
	L Mattiace	71 69 70 69 279		B Andrade	71 69 77 71 288
	N Price	71 69 68 71 279		N Lancaster	69 71 73 75 288
	P Blackmar	66 68 72 73 279			

ROUND BY ROUND LEADERBOARD

FIRST ROUND

H Frazar	6 under
P Blackmar	4 under
J Furyk	4 under
L Wadkins	4 under
D Duval	4 under
J Kelly	3 under
S Hoch	3 under
B Tway	3 under
B Estes	3 under
J Carter	3 under
R Mediate	3 under
B Fabel	3 under
D Martin	3 under
B Lietzke	3 under
J Sluman	3 under
R W Eaks	3 under
T WATSON	2 under

SECOND ROUND

H Frazar	9 under
M Calcavecchia	7 under
K Perry	7 under
J Furyk	7 under
S Flesch	6 under
J Sluman	6 under
T WATSON	6 under
P Blackmar	6 under
J Cook	6 under

THIRD ROUND

T WATSON	11 under
H Frazar	11 under
J Furyk	11 under
J Sluman	10 under
R Mediate	8 under
K Perry	8 under

FINAL ROUND

T WATSON	15 under
J Furyk	13 under
J Sluman	11 under
H Frazar	10 under
J Cook	9 under

PUNTERS' POINTS

- 66/1 Tom Watson played superbly to notch win number 34. The key was a magnificent fairway bunker shot on the ninth in R4, with the ball below his feet he hit it 140 yards, holed the 6-foot putt for birdie to take the lead. He then went into cruise control, hitting the ball beautifully. He went on to win comfortably.

- Jim Furyk played very steady golf. However he could never match Watson's superb R4 performance. Nevertheless the 28-year-old with the quirky swing, who was 8th here last year, will surely play well here again in 1999.

- T8th Justin Leonard could never get into contention. However he has now played The Colonial four times and has never finished lower than thirteenth. A Texan with a fine course record he could be the player in 1999 to break the stranglehold of the older players on this tournament.

- Texan 100/1 DYM Harrison Frazar followed up his superb 2nd place last week with a fine first 54 holes to go into R4 as joint leader. However on Sunday he played poorly off both tee and fairway. Looking very uncomfortable he could have shot 80, however he holed countless single putts to save par and so finish alone in 4th place.

- Jeff Sluman with solid course form figures of 13-2-23 played consistently to finish a fine third at 66/1. IG Index quoted his finishing position as 31-34 so giving spread betting sellers of the 40-year-old a nice 28 pt profit.
- Nick Faldo's R4 66 was his lowest round of the year so far and this was his first 1998 tournament in which he's shot two sub-70 rounds.
- Among those to miss the cut were 16/1 Phil Mickelson (10 over!), 33/1 Lee Janzen, 40/1 chances Bob Estes, Brad Faxon, Vijay Singh. 66/1 Bill Glasson withdrew after a R1 74.

1997 RESULT

1	100/1	David Frost
T2	22/1	Brad Faxon
T2	100/1	David Ogrin
T4 fav	4/1	Tiger Woods
T4	100/1	Paul Goydos

WINNERS IN THE '90s

		Age
1990	Ben Crenshaw	38
1991	Tom Purtzer	39
1992	Bruce Lietzke	40
1993	Fulton Allem	35
1994	Nick Price	37
1995	Tom Lehman	36
1996	Corey Pavin	36
1997	David Frost	37
1998	Tom Watson	48 (!)

PUNTERS' GUIDE

- This course with just two par 5s, tight fairways and small greens suits accurate shot makers rather than the younger longer hitters.
- Let's be clear...experienced pros do best as the ages of the winners this decade clearly show :-
  > Every winner was in his thirties or forties.
  > The youngest winner was 35.
  > The winners' average age was 38.4.
- However two younger players with fine records here are :-
  > Jim Furyk 2nd 1998: 8th 1997
  > Justin Leonard T8th 1998: 13th 1997: 10th 1996: 5th 1995.
- No player has led the tournament from the start and gone on to win, to record a wire-to-wire victory, this decade.

THE MEMORIAL

Date	28th -31st May
Course	Muirfield Village, Dublin, Ohio
Par	72
Yardage	7,163
First Prize	$396,000
Total Purse	$2.2 million

This is a very prestigious tournament with a select field of 108. It is played in the North East, in the State of Ohio on the Jack Nicklaus designed Muirfield Village course.

1998 ODDS

fav	8/1	Tiger Woods	50/1	David Frost
	14/1	Ernie Els	50/1	John Huston
	14/1	David Duval	50/1	Jesper Parnevik
	20/1	Davis Love III	50/1	Vijay Singh (DC)
	22/1	Jim Furyk	50/1	Payne Stewart
	25/1	Fred Couples	50/1	Steve Flesch
	25/1	Justin Leonard	66/1	Steve Stricker
	28/1	Phil Mickelson	66/1	Stewart Cink*
	33/1	Scott Hoch	66/1	Bob Estes
	33/1	John Cook	66/1	Brad Faxon
	40/1	Lee Janzen	66/1	Bob Tway
	40/1	Mark Calcavecchia	66/1	Frank Nobilo
	40/1	Tom Lehman	66/1	Jeff Sluman*
	50/1	Jeff Maggert	66/1	Scott McCarron

28 players were best priced at or under 66/1.

BOOKIES AT ODDS

DYM Jeff Sluman 33/1 Chandlers: 66/1 Ladbrokes, Stan James

DYM Stewart Cink 33/1 City Index, Hills, 66/1 Corals, Stan James, Sunderlands:

Winner Fred Couples 20/1 generally available: 25/1 Stanleys, Sunderlands

1998 RESULT

1	25/1	Fred Couples	68 67 67 69	271
2	125/1	Andrew Magee	67 71 68 69	275
3	14/1	David Duval	74 66 67 69	276
4	22/1	Jim Furyk	74 68 67 68	277
T5	20/1	Davis Love III	66 73 66 73	278
T5	150/1	Brandel Chamblee	71 72 66 69	278

T7	T Herron	72 72 67 68 279		S Verplank	72 70 71 72 285
	M Calcavecchia	68 69 72 70 279		H Frazar	68 69 75 73 285
	T Tryba	67 71 68 73 279		E Fryatt	73 70 69 73 285
	E Els	67 72 67 73 279		T Dodds	66 72 72 75 285
T11	C Stadler	67 73 70 70 280		G Kraft	67 74 76 69 286
	J Parnevik	73 71 66 70 280		K Perry	71 69 76 70 286
	R Damron	70 70 69 71 280		B Estes	72 68 74 72 286
	G Day	73 71 65 71 280		J Sindelar	66 72 73 75 286
	T Lehman	68 70 70 72 280		B Geiberger	69 70 76 72 287
T16	F Nobilo	71 72 69 69 281		M Brooks	68 75 72 72 287
	B Tway	70 73 68 70 281		B Elder	70 72 70 75 287
	J Leonard	69 70 71 71 281		D Pooley	71 73 73 71 288
	N Lancaster	73 69 68 71 281		T Woods	70 74 71 73 288
	K Triplett	67 71 70 73 281		D Toms	72 73 70 73 288
	C Perry	71 69 68 73 281		D Tewell	73 67 74 74 288
	B Wadkins	71 72 65 73 281		B Faxon	74 71 69 74 288
T23	S Lowery	73 71 71 67 282		P Blackmar	73 69 71 75 288
	D Forsman	69 75 68 70 282		J Gallagher	71 74 68 75 288
	J Haas	69 76 67 70 282		Joe Ozaki	75 70 72 72 289
	M Wiebe	72 70 68 72 282		E Toledo	73 70 73 73 289
	B Quigley	69 69 70 74 282		J Carter	74 71 69 75 289
	B Fabel	71 71 70 71 283		M Hulbert	70 75 70 75 290
	S Jones	68 71 72 72 283		G Hjertstedt	69 75 70 76 290
	L Mize	72 70 66 75 283		F Lickliter	72 70 69 79 290
	B Mayfair	72 73 68 71 284		J Maggert	75 69 74 73 291
	L Janzen	68 74 70 72 284		D Edwards	74 69 72 76 291
	S Stricker	71 72 68 73 284		K Sutherland	70 73 70 78 291
	N Faldo	71 70 69 74 284		S Pate	66 74 73 79 292
	J Cook	74 68 68 74 284		V Singh	73 70 76 74 293
	L Mattiace	68 67 73 76 284		D Ogrin	74 70 70 79 293
	J Huston	69 75 65 75 284		J Sluman	73 70 75 77 295
	F Funk	75 69 70 71 285		P Stewart	67 72 74 83 296
	S Cink	75 69 70 71 285			

ROUND BY ROUND LEADERBOARD

FIRST ROUND		SECOND ROUND	
D Love III	6 under	F COUPLES	9 under
J Sindelar	6 under	L Mattiace	9 under
T Dodds	6 under	H Frazar	7 under
S Pate	6 under	M Calcavecchia	7 under
A Magee	5 under	T Tryba	6 under
P Stewart	5 under	J Sindelar	6 under
E Els	5 under	T Lehman	6 under
T Tryba	5 under	K Triplett	6 under
K Triplett	5 under	A Magee	6 under
C Stadler	5 under	T Dodds	6 under
G Kraft	5 under		
F COUPLES	4 under		

THIRD ROUND		FINAL ROUND	
F COUPLES	14 under	F COUPLES	17 under
D Love III	11 under	A Magee	13 under
E Els	10 under	D Duval	12 under
A Magee	10 under	J Furyk	11 under
T Tryba	10 under	D Love III	10 under
D Duval	9 under	B Chamblee	10 under

- There was a 2½ hour delay during the second round and two weather delays during the final round.

PUNTERS' POINTS

- Fred Couples does not usually play here because the damp climate is not good for his dodgy back. However, he had shown his ability here earlier this decade when T3 in 1990, and T4 in 1993.
  - > Having lost final-day leads recently in the US Masters and the Byron Nelson here Couples played a solid final round to record his second win of the season, and the fourteenth of his career.
  - > 17 under par for the tournament, the key to his success was undoubtedly the par 5s for which he was 12 under par.
- 20/1 Davis Love III, Couples' partner in the Ryder Cup, World Cup and President's Cup, partnered Fred in R4. However he lost his rhythm and showed poor course management on his way to a disappointing 73 to slip back to finish T5th.
- 14/1 David Duval had three disaster holes in the tournament which cost him 6 shots. However, generally he played really well to post his third top 3 finish in the last four years.
- 22/1 Jim Furyk shot a quadruple bogey at the par 3 sixteenth in R1 and had to play 'catch up' over the later rounds. T2nd here last year he must have a leading chance again in 1999.
- 125/1 Andrew Magee, "is a quality player who I believe can win again in 1998". The 36-year-old Arizona resident justified that confidence, shown in

his player profile last year, with a fine display after a spell of poor recent form.

- Tiger Woods has now played the Memorial twice. T51st on level par this year, and next to last last year, he has beaten par just twice in his seven rounds and has still to shoot a sub-70 round.
- 25-year-old Robert Damron was born in Kentucky, the adjacent southern state to Ohio, and he clearly enjoys this difficult course. In just two starts he was T21st in 1997 and T11th this year, and his seven rounds (stroke average 70.28) have all been under par. He's one to note for 1999.
- Among those to miss the cut were, 28/1 Phil Mickelson, 33/1 Scott Hoch, 50/1 chances Steve Flesch and course specialist David Frost, 66/1 Scott McCarron and jet-lagged European raider Robert Karlsson. Glen Hnatiuk withdrew after a R1 73.

1997 RESULT

1	50/1	Vijay Singh
T2	12/1	Greg Norman
T2	40/1	Jim Furyk
T4	40/1	Lee Janzen
T4	40/1	Scott Hoch
T4	66/1	Tommy Tolles

WINNERS IN THE '90s

		Age
1990	Greg Norman	35
1991	Kenny Perry	30
1992	David Edwards	36
1993	Paul Azinger	33
1994	Tom Lehman	35
1995	Greg Norman	40
1996	Tom Watson	46
1997	Vijay Singh	34
1998	Fred Couples	38

PUNTERS' GUIDE

- As the table shows experienced pros have won throughout the nineties with the average winning age 36.3.
- Last year's advice to go for 'straight hitting guys in their thirties' paid off with Couples' 1998 win.
- However the two younger players with superb recent Memorial records are:
  > David Duval 3rd 1998: 17th 1997: 2nd 1996 and 2nd 1995.
  > Jim Furyk 4th 1998: T2nd 1997
- With the tournament regularly interrupted by bad weather a good player with an early opening-round tee time can have an advantage.

THE KEMPER OPEN

Date	4th – 7th June
Course	Avenel, Potomac, Maryland
Par	71
Yardage	7,005
First Prize	$360,000
Total Purse	$2 million

The Kemper Open has been held at Avenel since 1987 so there were eleven successive years of course form available to punters.

1998 ODDS

fav	10/1	Justin Leonard (DC)	40/1	Vijay Singh
	16/1	Tom Lehman	50/1	Jay Haas
	18/1	Scott Hoch	50/1	Craig Parry
	20/1	Mark O'Meara	50/1	Steve Elkington
	20/1	Lee Janzen	50/1	Dan Forsman
	33/1	Jesper Parnevik	66/1	Andrew Magee*
	33/1	Steve Stricker	66/1	John Daly
	33/1	Hal Sutton	66/1	Loren Roberts
	33/1	Steve Flesch	66/1	Jay Don Blake
	40/1	Tim Herron	66/1	Kirk Triplett
	40/1	Brad Faxon		

21 players were best priced at or under 66/1.

BOOKIES AT ODDS

DYM Andrew Magee 25/1 Chandlers: 66/1 Corals

Tied third DYM Fred Funk 50/1 Hills: 100/1 Chandlers

Tied third DYM Tommy Tolles 66/1 Chandlers, Hills, Stanleys: 150/1 Corals

The winner Stuart Appleby 66/1 generally: 100/1 City Index

1998 RESULT

1	100/1	Stuart Appleby	70 63 69 72	274
2	18/1	Scott Hoch	69 68 68 70	275
T3	20/1	Mark O'Meara	68 70 71 69	278
T3	125/1	Brad Febel	69 66 70 73	278
T3	80/1	Clark Dennis	70 65 70 73	278
T3	150/1	Tommy Tolles	70 68 66 74	278
T3	100/1	Fred Funk	64 66 71 77	278

T8	S Stricker	70 69 71 69 279	Lee Rinker	71 71 74 70 286
	C Parry	67 66 76 70 279	J Haas	69 72 73 72 286
	H Sutton	69 69 69 72 279	F Langham	74 68 72 72 286
T11	S Flesch	69 68 74 69 280	P H Horgan III	74 68 72 72 286
	B McCallister	70 71 70 69 280	J Kaye	70 71 72 73 286
13	D Hart	69 71 71 70 281	G Hnatiuk	74 67 72 73 286
T14	C Barlow	71 71 73 67 282	J Sindelar	71 71 71 73 286
	L Mize	75 67 72 68 282	B Elder	71 63 78 74 286
	K Perry	70 68 74 70 282	M Weir	67 69 73 77 286
	J Adams	71 69 72 70 282	M Muehr	70 69 70 77 286
	R Black	68 68 72 74 282	T Pernice Jr	69 70 68 79 286
	W Wood	73 66 70 73 282	D Hammond	70 69 74 74 287
	C DiMarco	68 65 70 79 282	B Quigley	68 69 73 77 287
T21	L Janzen	71 64 79 69 283	W Austin	68 69 73 77 287
	L Roberts	71 69 70 73 283	B R Brown	69 73 76 70 288
	J Durant	69 66 74 74 283	D Barr	70 68 77 73 288
	J D Blake	68 70 70 75 283	J Johnston	68 70 76 74 288
T25	L Porter	72 68 76 68 284	K Gibson	71 68 70 79 288
	J McGovern	70 70 73 71 284	J Parnevik	69 71 75 74 289
	J Kelly	69 72 72 71 284	T Byrum	71 70 74 74 289
	B Cheesman	72 70 70 72 284	Joe Daley	72 70 72 75 289
	J Leonard	68 67 76 73 284	M Small	68 71 74 76 289
	E Toledo	69 69 71 75 284	D Barron	70 72 69 78 289
	J Ozaki	71 68 70 75 284	T Lehman	71 66 77 76 290
	S Simpson	71 68 70 75 284	B Kamm	69 66 78 77 290
	C Perry	65 74 70 75 284	S Gump	73 69 71 77 290
	S Lyle	70 68 70 76 284	H Royer	71 70 76 74 291
	D Forsman	68 69 70 77 284	B Wadkins	73 69 74 76 292
	M Springer	71 70 75 69 285	D Edwards	70 68 75 79 292
	B Fleisher	72 70 74 69 285	O Browne	69 73 73 78 293
	J L Lewis	67 74 73 71 285	P Jordan	70 70 72 81 293
	T Armour III	67 70 76 72 285	M Reid	71 70 78 75 294
	T Dodds	69 70 74 72 285	G Kraft	72 66 74 83 295
	B Geiberger	69 69 73 74 285	W Grady	69 72 81 75 297
	V Singh	70 72 75 69 286		

ROUND BY ROUND LEADERBOARD

FIRST ROUND		SECOND ROUND	
F Funk	7 under	F Funk	12 under
C Perry	6 under	C Parry	9 under
M Weir	4 under	S APPLEBY	9 under
J L Lewis	4 under	C DiMarco	9 under
T Armour III	4 under	B Elder	8 under
C Parry	4 under	B Fabel	7 under
S APPLEBY	1 under	B Kamm	7 under
		J Durant	7 under
		J Leonard	7 under

THIRD ROUND		FINAL ROUND	
F Funk	12 under	S APPLEBY	10 under
S APPLEBY	11 under	S Hoch	9 under
C DiMarco	10 under	M O'Meara	6 under
T Tolles	9 under	B Fabel	6 under
S Hoch	8 under	C Dennis	6 under
C Dennis	8 under	T Tolles	6 under
B Fabel	8 under	F Funk	6 under

PLEASE NOTE This year the players had to contend with windy conditions in R3, and very windy conditions in R4. Judgement of distance, club selection and judging the pace of the hardening greens made scoring difficult particularly on the final day.

PUNTERS' POINTS

- 100/1 Stuart Appleby, although he'd missed seven cuts in his last nine tournaments, showed here why I'd given him the G + Y symbols last year. A superb wind player he had the guts to face the gusts! Watched by his wife he needed to par the last two holes in really tough windy conditions to win, and he did so most impressively.

  > Twice a winner on the NIKE tour this was his second win on the full tour.....and it won't be his last. When he's in contention he knows how to win....so let's remember that in 1999.

- Poor old (he's 41) Fred Funk. He literally carried a white flag up the 18th to signal his poor R4 form. He'd led from the start. However, his demise was shown by the fact that in R1 he took just 31 for the front nine whereas on Sunday he took 42!! His straight-hitting game was not suited by the windy conditions in the last two days.

- Mr Consistency 18/1 Scott Hoch, kept up his superb recent Kemper record to notch his 122nd career top 10, his 12th runners-up spot, and his 43rd top 3 finish! It was his third top 3 Kemper finish in the last six years – a 50% strike rate!

- Chris DiMarco found himself in contention in R4. However his high ball hitting and unusual putting grip were taken apart by the wind as the 29-year-old shot 79.

- T3rd Mark O'Meara was recording his third top 4 finish here in the last four years.
- Spare a thought for Sandy Lyle! Standing on the par 3 17th tee in R4 he was 5 under par heading for a huge cheque – then whoops he found the water twice, took a quintuple bogey eight and finished T25th!!
- Woody Austin had the USPGA tour's first 1998 albatross on the par 5 sixth hole in R1. The same hole also yielded an albatross to Mark Brooks here back in 1991. Watch for hole No. 6 in 1999!!
- Russ Cochran, Guy Boros, and Richard Coughlan withdrew after R1, and Michael Bradley after R2 with a recurrence of back trouble.
- Among those to miss the cut were 40/1 chances Tim Herron and Brad Faxon, 50/1 Steve Elkington, and 66/1 outsiders Kirk Triplett and Andrew Magee. European raider Robert Karlsson and course specialist and 1993 winner Grant Waite also missed the cut.

1997 RESULT

1	40/1	Justin Leonard
2	150/1	Mark Wiebe
T3 fav	9/1	Greg Norman
T3	14/1	Nick Price
T3	20/1	Nick Faldo
T3	250/1	Mike Springer

WINNERS IN THE '90s

		Age
1990	Gil Morgan	43
1991	Billy Andrade	27
1992	Bill Glasson	32
1993	Grant Waite	28
1994	Mark Brooks	33
1995	Lee Janzen	30
1996	Steve Stricker	29
1997	Justin Leonard	26
1998	Stuart Appleby	27

PUNTERS' GUIDE

Year	Winner	Course Form	Current Form	Age
1998	S Appleby	8-14	MC-10-MC	27
1997	J Leonard	4-13	27-13-46	26
1996	S Stricker	MC-DNP	3-DNP-76	29
1995	L Janzen	7-4	18-MC-19	30
1994	M Brooks	6-DNP	8-7-42	33

NB latest form shown on the right.

From the above a clear formula emerges for pinpointing the winner of the Kemper Open in 1999.

> The player must have shot a top 20 finish, or top 10 finish in one of the last two years on the course.

> He must be in solid current form with a top 20 finish in one of his last two starts.

> He will probably be in his late twenties. The average age of the winners over the last five years is just 29 (that is also the average over the last eight years).

THE BUICK CLASSIC

Date	11th – 14th June
Course	Westchester, Rye, New York
Par	71
Yardage	6,779
First Prize	$324,000
Total Purse	$1.8 million

This year the Buick Classic reverted to its position as the final tournament before the US Open. In the past it has provided a fine guide to the season's second major because the Westchester course set up, like the US Open, favours accuracy off the tee and the fairway.

1998 ODDS

fav	6/1	Ernie Els (DC)	50/1	Brad Faxon*
	14/1	Davis Love III	50/1	Darren Clarke
	20/1	Jim Furyk	50/1	Frank Nobilo
	20/1	Lee Westwood	50/1	Stewart Cink*
	25/1	Jeff Maggert	50/1	Craig Parry
	28/1	Tom Lehman	50/1	Steve Jones
	33/1	Bernhard Langer	66/1	Bob Tway
	33/1	Hal Sutton	66/1	Craig Stadler
	33/1	J M Olazabal	66/1	Fred Funk
	33/1	Mark Calcavecchia	66/1	Ian Woosnam
	40/1	Vijay Singh	66/1	Bob Tway
	40/1	Jesper Parnevik		

23 players were best priced at or below 66/1.

BOOKIES AT ODDS

Third placed Tom Lehman 16/1 Ladbrokes: 28/1 Sunderlands

The winner J P Hayes was a complete 'skinner' for the bookmakers.

1998 RESULT

1	250/1	**J P Hayes**	**66 67 68**	**201**
		(Hayes won at the first play-off hole)		
2	20/1	**Jim Furyk**	**70 63 68**	**201**
3	28/1	**Tom Lehman**	**67 72 65**	**204**
4	200/1	**Bruce Fleisher**	**68 68 69**	**205**
T5	200/1	**Tom Byrum**	**69 71 66**	**206**
T5	25/1	**Jeff Maggert**	**68 71 67**	**206**

T7	B Tway	66 70 71 207		R Damron	69 71 74 214
	K Sutherland	64 70 73 207		C Parry	74 72 68 214
9	S Lowery	66 72 70 208		S Cink	74 69 72 215
T10	C Perry	72 69 68 209		N Faldo	74 70 71 215
	J Parnevik	69 67 73 209		L Westwood	68 74 73 215
T12	G Kraft	69 73 68 210		D Kestner	74 71 70 215
	C Stadler	72 70 68 210		J Riegger	72 73 70 215
	B Faxon	72 69 69 210		P Goydos	66 74 75 215
	H Royer	68 72 70 210		S Jurgensen	70 76 69 215
	J Ozaki	70 70 70 210		W Grady	71 72 73 216
T17	O Uresti	72 71 68 211		T Loustalot	73 70 73 216
	M Standly	69 75 67 211		M Sullivan	72 71 73 216
	Lee Rinker	73 69 69 211		B McCallister	70 73 73 216
	J Sindelar	74 71 66 211		S Simpson	73 70 73 216
	M Wurtz	68 73 70 211		P Tataurangi	72 72 72 216
	D Love III	73 68 70 211		J Kaye	75 70 71 216
	M Calcavecchia	67 71 73 211		K Jones	74 72 70 216
T24	S Jones	70 73 69 212		O Browne	73 73 70 216
	D Clarke	73 71 68 212		N Henke	75 71 71 217
	P Azinger	72 73 67 212		G Hallberg	75 69 73 217
	J M Olazabal	73 72 67 212		M Carnevale	72 73 72 217
	B Kamm	71 70 71 212		J Durant	74 71 72 217
	V Singh	71 70 71 212		B Crenshaw	72 69 76 217
	K Fergus	68 73 71 212		C Smith	77 69 72 218
	B Claar	71 75 66 212		B Quigley	72 73 73 218
	J Gallagher	71 72 70 213		D Hammond	72 73 73 218
	D Sutherland	68 75 70 213		B Gilder	71 75 72 218
	W Wood	71 73 69 213		R Gage	73 73 73 219
	B Bates	72 70 71 213		J Estes	69 75 75 219
	B Friend	72 70 71 213		J Gallagher	73 73 73 219
	S Elkington	72 73 68 213		F Langham	71 75 73 219
	M Brooks	72 68 73 213		G Hnatiuk	73 72 75 220
	L Porter	68 72 73 213		L Mattiace	71 74 75 220
	T Tryba	74 72 67 213		F Lickliter	75 70 76 221
	F Nobilo	74 69 71 214		T Conley	73 73 76 222
	S Gump	73 71 70 214		G Hjertstedt	70 76 77 223
	G Hill	73 69 72 214		M Brisky	73 73 81 227
	B Andrade	74 66 74 214			

ROUND BY ROUND LEADERBOARD

FIRST ROUND
K Sutherland	7 under
S Lowery	5 under
B Tway	5 under
J P Hayes	5 under
P Goydos	5 under
T Lehman	4 under
M Calcavecchia	4 under

SECOND ROUND
J Furyk	9 under
J P Hayes	9 under
K Sutherland	8 under
B Fleisher	6 under
B Tway	6 under
J Parnevik	6 under

THIRD AND FINAL ROUND
J P Hayes	12 under
J Furyk	12 under
T Lehman	9 under
B Fleisher	8 under
J Maggert	7 under
T Byrum	7 under

PLEASE NOTE Heavy rain prevented the second round from being fully completed until Sunday morning. The third and final round was then played.

This was the 12th US tournament this year to be affected by either torrential rain, high winds, lightning, fog or even frost.

PUNTERS' POINTS

- "It's an incredible feeling of satisfaction that I could play like that under the circumstances," J P Hayes said after his amazing 250/1 victory was followed by cheers from the bookmakers and tears from myself.

  > He started the final day with 5 holes of his second round to play and a couple of shots behind Furyk. Over those holes he made a couple of birdies so that he started the third and final round level with, and playing alongside Jim Furyk.

  > At the last hole Furyk made eagle to Hayes's birdie to force a play-off which Hayes won after Furyk had driven into the rough!

- 250/1 J P who? had won, much to Corals' relief as the Barking firm's top price 20/1 about Furyk had been eagerly snapped up!

- So the jury is now out on Furyk's nerve, although it will be wise to remember that he did eagle that final regulation hole to force the play-off. In his last three tournaments Furyk has finished 2nd, 4th and now 2nd again. It was his fifth 2nd place since 1997.

- The key point for punters to come from this tournament was the vital importance of tee times.

  Early tee times are nearly always desirable and to do well in this event this year they were compulsory!

  The early first-day players actually got the better of the weather conditions during both the first rounds. The R1 tee times of the first six players show the point really clearly.

  > J P Hayes 12th group out in the morning from 10th tee

> Jim Furyk 5th group out in the morning from 10th tee
> Tom Lehman 5th group out in the morning from 10th tee
> Bruce Fleisher 2nd group out in the morning from 10th tee
> Jeff Maggert 3rd group out in the morning from 1st tee
> Tom Byrum 1st group out in the morning from 10th tee

• Bookmakers had a smile on their faces as early as halfway through the first day when the heavily-backed 6/1 favourite Ernie Els withdrew with back problems halfway through his opening round.

• This was the third tournament of 1998 to be shortened to 54 holes because of rain following the AT&T Pebble Beach National Pro-Am and the Buick Invitational.

• Among those to miss the cut were 33/1 Hal Sutton, 50/1 Bernhard Langer, 66/1 chances Jeff Sluman and Ian Woosnam and 80/1 DYM Harrison Frazar.

• Fred Funk withdrew after 74 in R1.

1997 RESULT

1	9/1	Ernie Els
2	40/1	Jeff Maggert
T3	25/1	Jim Furyk
T3	125/1	Robert Damron

WINNERS IN THE '90s

1990	Hale Irwin
1991	Billy Andrade
1992	David Frost
1993	Vijay Singh
1994	Lee Janzen
1995	Vijay Singh
1996	Ernie Els (by 8 shots!)
1997	Ernie Els
1998	J P Hayes (reduced to 54 holes)

PUNTERS' GUIDE

• This is very much a course specialists tournament which, in 1999, is scheduled for the week following the US Open.

The course specialists are

> Ernie Els w/d 1998: Won 1997: Won 1996: 4th 1995: 2nd 1994
> Jeff Maggert T5th 1998: 2nd 1997: T2nd 1996: DNP 1995: 8th 1994
> Tom Lehman 3rd 1998: DNP 1997: 2nd 1996: 15th 1995

All three players have Westchester stroke averages over the last four years below 70!

THE US OPEN CHAMPIONSHIP

Date	18th – 21st June
Course	Olympic GC (Lake Course) San Francisco, California
Par	70
Yardage	6,797
First Prize	$535,000
Total Purse	$3 million

Please see Part 5.

THE MOTOROLA WESTERN OPEN

Date   25th – 28th June
Course   Cog Hill, Lemont, Illinois
Par   72
Yardage   7,040
First Prize $360,000
Total Purse $2 million

For the ninth successive year the bunker-strewn Cog Hill course played host to the Western Open.

1998 ODDS

fav	15/2	Tiger Woods (DC)	40/1	John Cook
	18/1	Jim Furyk	40/1	John Huston
	20/1	Justin Leonard	50/1	Jeff Sluman
	20/1	Nick Price	50/1	Loren Roberts
	25/1	Phil Mickelson	50/1	Vijay Singh
	28/1	Mark O'Meara	50/1	Stuart Appleby*
	33/1	Lee Janzen (PWW)*	50/1	Steve Flesch
	33/1	Steve Stricker	66/1	Hal Sutton
	33/1	Scott Hoch*	66/1	Glen Day
	40/1	Bob Tway	66/1	Frank Nobilo*
	40/1	Mark Calcavecchia		
	40/1	Payne Stewart*		

22 players were best priced at or under 66/1

BOOKIES AT ODDS

Last week's US Open winner DYM Lee Janzen 14/1 Surrey: 33/1 Chandlers
Winner Joe Durant 80/1 Surrey, Tote: 125/1 Chandler, Sunderlands

1998 RESULT

1	125/1	**Joe Durant**	**68 67 70 66**	**271**
2	50/1	**Vijay Singh**	**68 68 65 72**	**273**
T3	100/1	**Dudley Hart**	**74 70 70 63**	**277**
T3	33/1	**Lee Janzen**	**68 69 69 71**	**277**
T5	33/1	**Steve Stricker**	**71 69 67 71**	**278**
T5	125/1	**Greg Kraft**	**67 70 66 75**	**278**

T7	J Furyk	72 71 68 68 279		K Sutherland	73 73 71 70 287
	S Hoch	71 67 70 71 279		S Simpson	75 71 71 70 287
T9	S Verplank	75 71 68 67 281		B Tway	73 69 72 73 287
	C Dennis	71 69 73 68 281		L Rinker	73 69 73 73 288
	H Frazar	74 70 69 68 281		J Huston	74 69 71 74 288
	J Leonard	72 72 69 68 281		D Hammond	72 74 72 71 289
	D Forsman	74 71 68 68 281		D Martin	77 68 72 72 289
	T Woods	76 67 69 69 281		N Lancaster	72 71 73 73 289
	S Appleby	73 71 68 69 281		D Toms	72 74 69 74 289
	Joe Ozaki	71 69 68 73 281		B Wadkins	72 69 72 76 289
T17	F Lickliter	75 68 72 67 282		C Smith	75 71 74 70 290
	S Kendall	70 69 74 69 282		J L Lewis	74 70 75 71 290
	T Armour III	72 69 69 72 282		B Kamm	72 72 73 73 290
T20	D Waldorf	74 70 71 68 283		L Mize	74 71 70 75 290
	R Damron	74 71 68 70 283		H Royer	72 74 75 70 291
T22	T Byrum	70 71 75 68 284		D Green (am)	75 70 75 71 291
	N Price	72 74 69 69 284		B Fleisher	75 67 76 73 291
	S Gump	71 72 71 70 284		M Reid	74 69 74 74 291
	H Sutton	76 69 69 70 284		F Langham	74 70 72 75 291
	L Roberts	72 73 68 71 284		J Delsing	73 72 71 75 291
	C Perry	73 69 69 73 284		P Stewart	72 74 69 76 291
	M Wiebe	74 70 67 73 284		J McGovern	69 72 73 77 291
	T Conley	71 70 69 74 284		D Barron	74 71 79 69 293
	S Flesch	69 70 70 75 284		D Ogrin	73 69 78 73 293
	J P Hayes	72 72 73 68 285		B Mayfair	71 74 74 74 293
	T Herron	70 70 74 71 285		B Estes	72 73 74 74 293
	C Rose	74 66 72 73 285		L Mattiace	73 72 74 74 293
	T Tryba	70 72 70 73 285		N Henke	72 73 71 77 293
	B Chamblee	76 70 72 68 286		T Pernice Jr	73 69 79 73 294
	J Sluman	74 66 76 70 286		B Fabel	74 70 76 74 294
	T Dodds	75 69 72 70 286		J Carter	75 71 74 74 294
	D Frost	72 69 74 71 286		W Grady	78 68 77 73 296
	R W Eaks	73 73 69 71 286		D Rummells	76 68 77 75 296
	P Mickelson	77 69 69 71 286		R Mediate	72 74 74 76 296
	J Sindelar	73 72 68 73 286		J Morse	73 69 76 78 296
	T Tolles	73 70 74 70 287		G Hill	72 72 73 82 299

ROUND BY ROUND LEADERBOARD

FIRST ROUND		SECOND ROUND	
G Kraft	5 under	J DURANT	9 under
J DURANT	4 under	V Singh	8 under
V Singh	4 under	L Janzen	7 under
L Janzen	4 under	G Kraft	7 under
J McGovern	3 under	S Hoch	6 under
S Flesch	3 under	S Flesch	5 under
		S Kendall	5 under

THIRD ROUND		FINAL ROUND	
V Singh	15 under	J DURANT	17 under
G Kraft	13 under	V Singh	15 under
J DURANT	11 under	D Hart	11 under
L Janzen	10 under	L Janzen	11 under
S Stricker	9 under	S Stricker	10 under
Joe Ozaki	8 under	G Kraft	10 under
S Hoch	8 under		

PUNTERS' POINTS

- What a difference a year makes! Last year, starting the final round 4 shots off the pace, Joe Durant shot a 78. This year, again 4 shots behind, he shot a 66....to record his first-ever tour victory at 125/1.

  A friend of the recent shock Buick Classic winner, J P Hayes, Durant took IBC to overtake Singh and win. His game is based on his driving, shown by the fact that he entered this event 2nd on tour for driving accuracy at 80%!

  However the key to his success was his R4 putting as he holed putts of over eight feet for seven of his nine birdies.

- Vijay Singh revelled in the incredible heat and using a cross-handed putting stroke he built a lead that made him 9/4 on to win entering the final round. However, his par round was not good enough.

- Last week's US winner Lee Janzen was generally expected to suffer MLD here. In fact he was relaxed and confident playing well to finish T3rd at 33/1, the price at which Chandlers opposed him.

- On the final day Dudley Hart had nine birdies to tie the course record of 63 held by John Adams (R3, 1993) and Jeff Sluman (R3, 1992).

- Defending champion Tiger Woods never really got into serious contention. However he did finish T9th and did feel that his putting was getting 'very close'.

- The high temperatures and ideal scoring conditions resulted in six players finishing at 10 under par, or better – the highest number since 1993!

- Among those to miss the cut were 28/1 Mark O'Meara, 40/1 John Cook and 66/1 Glen Day and Frank Nobilo.

1997 RESULT

1 fav	8/1	Tiger Woods
2	40/1	Frank Nobilo
T3	100/1	Jeff Sluman
T3	20/1	Justin Leonard
T3	100/1	Steve Lowery

WINNERS IN THE '90s

1990 Wayne Levi
1991 Russ Cochran
1992 Ben Crenshaw
1993 Nick Price
1994 Nick Price
1995 Billy Mayfair
1996 Steve Stricker
1997 Tiger Woods
1998 Joe Durant

PUNTERS' GUIDE

- The last four years suggest punters can adopt a bold approach.
  - > 10 out of the 21 players in the top 4 have been best priced at or over 80/1.
  - > 18 out of those 21 players (85.7%) have been 40/1 or more.
- The best recent course records are held by
  - > Justin Leonard T9th 1998: 3rd 1997: 8th 1996: 2nd 1995
  - > Stuart Appleby T9th 1998: 7th 1997
  - > Steve Stricker T5th 1998: 28th 1997: Won 1996
  - > Tiger Woods T9th 1998: Won 1997

THE GREATER HARTFORD OPEN

Date	2nd – 5th July
Course	River Highlands, Cromwell, Connecticut
Par	70
Yardage	6,860
First Prize	$360,000
Total Purse	$2 million

The GHO was being held at the River Highlands course for the eighth successive year.

1998 ODDS

fav	9/1	David Duval	50/1	Fred Funk
	14/1	Justin Leonard	50/1	Joe Durant (PWW)
	16/1	Scott Hoch	66/1	Tom Byrum*
	20/1	Stewart Cink (DC)	66/1	Greg Kraft
	20/1	Vijay Singh	66/1	Harrison Frazar*
	28/1	Mark Calcavecchia	66/1	Tim Herron*
	33/1	Bob Estes	66/1	Clark Dennis*
	33/1	Brad Faxon	66/1	Jay Haas
	33/1	Steve Flesch	66/1	John Daly
	50/1	David Frost	66/1	Paul Azinger*
	50/1	Kenny Perry	66/1	Scott McCarron
	50/1	Dudley Hart (non runner)		

23 players were best priced at or over 66/1.

BOOKIES AT ODDS

The winner DYM Olin Browne 80/1 Tote, Surrey: 200/1 Stanleys.

1998 RESULT

1	200/1	**Olin Browne**	67 66 66 67	266
		(Browne won at first extra hole)		
T2	200/1	**Larry Mize**	68 63 66 69	266
T2	20/1	**Stewart Cink**	67 65 67 67	266
T4	100/1	**Duffy Waldorf**	70 67 64 66	267
T4	50/1	**Fred Funk**	70 66 65 66	267
T4	150/1	**Doug Tewell**	66 66 68 67	267

T7	D Duval	68 65 66 69 268	T Herron	67 70 67 72 276
	S Hoch	65 68 64 71 268	J Haas	71 66 67 72 276
T9	J Sindelar	69 66 69 65 269	G Kraft	69 67 67 73 276
	L Mattiace	67 69 66 67 269	A Magee	71 65 67 73 276
	K Perry	65 69 67 68 269	S Gump	68 62 72 74 276
T12	V Singh	68 67 73 72 270	D Stockton Jr	68 69 70 70 277
	M Brooks	69 65 67 69 270	B Fleisher	69 70 68 70 277
T14	M Springer	71 67 68 65 271	J Kaye	67 66 73 71 277
	B Andrade	68 69 66 68 271	C Smith	68 68 70 71 277
T16	J Durant	70 68 69 65 272	P Azinger	66 72 68 71 277
	M Calcavecchia	70 69 64 69 272	N Henke	69 69 68 71 277
	W Wood	70 66 64 72 272	M Carnevale	69 70 67 71 277
	G Waite	68 64 65 75 272	P Morgan	64 71 69 73 277
T20	D Toms	72 66 70 65 273	O Uresti	67 64 72 74 277
	J Carter	68 71 67 67 273	B Faxon	68 70 74 66 278
	G Sauers	71 65 68 69 273	J Johnston	67 70 71 70 278
	J Riegger	67 70 67 69 273	G Boros	70 68 70 70 278
	N Lancaster	71 63 69 70 273	J J Henry	68 71 69 70 278
T25	F Zoeller	69 68 68 69 274	H Frazar	66 67 73 72 278
	S Flesch	71 66 67 70 274	D Martin	69 68 69 72 278
	B Bates	69 68 67 70 274	J Estes	67 70 69 72 278
	D Hammond	67 70 67 70 274	E Toledo	69 68 71 71 279
	K Sutherland	66 67 69 72 274	L Clements	74 65 69 71 279
	C DiMarco	70 64 68 72 274	K Jones	72 67 70 71 280
	S McRoy	66 72 69 68 275	C Barlow	72 67 70 71 280
	K Triplett	72 67 67 69 275	B Gage	72 66 70 72 280
	K Fergus	69 68 68 70 275	B Geiberger	67 71 68 74 280
	L Porter	69 70 66 70 275	J Daley	70 69 67 74 280
	J Leonard	70 68 66 71 275	F Lickliter	69 69 74 69 281
	G Hnatiuk	70 68 70 68 276	R Coughlan	69 70 69 73 281
	J Gallagher	68 67 72 69 276	G Hallberg	72 67 72 71 282
	B Henninger	68 69 70 69 276	T Tryba	68 70 70 74 282
	V Veazey	74 65 68 69 276	B McCallister	73 66 69 74 282
	J L Lewis	69 67 69 71 276	K Wentworth	69 70 72 72 283
	B Wadkins	73 65 67 71 276	J Daly	71 68 70 76 285

ROUND BY ROUND LEADERBOARD

FIRST ROUND		SECOND ROUND	
P Morgan	6 under	S Gump	14 under
K Perry	5 under	O Uresti	13 under
S Hoch	5 under	L Mize	13 under
K Sutherland	4 under	G Waite	12 under
B Fabel	4 under	D Tewell	12 under
S McRoy	4 under	S Cink	12 under
H Frazar	4 under	O BROWNE	7 under
P Azinger	4 under		
D Tewell	4 under		
O BROWNE	3 under		

FIRST ROUND		FINAL ROUND	
S Hoch	13 under	O BROWNE	14 under
L Mize	13 under	L Mize	14 under
G Waite	13 under	S Cink	14 under
O BROWNE	11 under	D Waldorf	13 under
D Duval	11 under	F Funk	13 under
S Cink	11 under	D Tewell	13 under

PUNTERS' POINTS

- There was a three-way play-off between the tournaments defending champion, Stewart Cink, a former US Masters champ Larry Mize and Olin Browne who chipped in from 35 feet on the first play-off hole to notch his first USPGA tour win at 39 years of age.
- Having missed the cut both in his last tournament and on this course last year Browne's win was a good result for the bookies. However driving accuracy is the key to this course and he was T16th in that category on the stats.

  He deserved his success after showing superb resilience to fight back after a double bogey on the tough tenth hole when in a share of the lead in R4.
- Larry Mize incredibly lost a 4-shot lead over the final four holes. However top marks to the 39-year-old who applauded as Browne chipped in for victory just as Mize himself had done so memorably in 1987 to snatch the US Masters from Greg Norman.
- Stewart Cink made a tremendous defence of his title. In the last two years here his stroke average is a truly amazing 66.62!
- Scott Gump (R2-62), and Vijay Singh (R4-62) both equalled the course record. However Vijay's 28 for the back nine on Sunday was the lowest ever!
- Caddies count – Mike Harmon, Olin Browne's caddie was enjoying his third success here this decade. The others were in 1992 and 1996.
- If betting in running do remember the par 4 tenth hole is the toughest on the course.
- Among those missing the cut were 50/1 David Frost, 66/1 chances Tom Byrum, Clark Dennis, and Scott McCarron and 100/1 outsiders 1996 champion D A Weibring, Steve Lowery and Brad Fabel.

1997 RESULT

1	40/1	Stewart Cink
T2	80/1	Tom Byrum
T2	80/1	Brandel Chamblee
T2	33/1	Jeff Maggert

WINNERS IN THE '90s

		Age
1990	Wayne Levi	38
1991	Billy Ray Brown	28
1992	Lanny Wadkins	42
1993	Nick Price	36
1994	David Frost	34
1995	Greg Norman	40
1996	D A Weibring	43
1997	Stewart Cink	24
1998	Olin Browne	39

PUNTERS' GUIDE

- There are four key pointers for punters trying to solve the GHO puzzle in 1999.

  > The average age of the winners in this decade is exactly 36. Experienced players have tended to win, although Stewart Cink's 1997 victory was an exception.

  > Of the 19 players who have finished 4th (or T4th) in the last four years 13 (68.4%) have been best priced at or over 66/1.

  > The key to River Highlands is driving accuracy rather than length.
  The 1998 winner Olin Browne was in the top 20 for driving accuracy yet was T112th for driving distance, while Larry Mize was Number 1 for driving accuracy yet T119th for driving distance.

  > Early tee times are nearly always an advantage. The three players in the 1998 play-off all were no later than the fourth group out in R1.

THE QUAD CITY CLASSIC

Date	9th – 12th July
Course	Oakwood, Coal Valley, Illinois
Par	70
Yardage	6,796
First Prize	$279,000
Total Purse	$1.55 million

Played at the Oakwood course since 1975 there is a large volume of course form for punters to study. Coinciding once more with the Loch Lomond Invitational the week before the British Open there was, once more, a weak field for this event.

1998 ODDS

jt fav	20/1	Fred Funk	50/1	Greg Kraft
jt fav	20/1	Steve Flesch	50/1	Brad Fabel*
jt fav	20/1	Kenny Perry	50/1	Grant Waite
jt fav	20/1	Steve Jones	50/1	Joey Sindelar
	22/1	Hal Sutton	66/1	Frank Lickliter*
	25/1	Jeff Sluman*	66/1	Scott Gump*
	33/1	Scott Verplank	66/1	Brandell Chamblee*
	33/1	Scott McCarron	66/1	David Toms (DC)*
	40/1	John Daly*	66/1	Jim Carter*
	40/1	Olin Browne (PWW)	66/1	Paul Stankowski*
	40/1	Chris Perry*	66/1	Skip Kendall*
	40/1	Russ Cochran		

23 players were best priced at or under 66/1.

BOOKIES AT ODDS

- Of the 74 players quoted in RACING POST'S Pricewise column 38 (51.35%) were DYMs. Last year there were 44%!!

Second placed DYM Scott Gump 33/1 Hills: 66/1 Stan James

Fourth placed DYM David Toms 25/1 Ladbrokes: 66/1 Stan James, Stanley

T5th placed DYM Brad Fabel 25/1 Hills, Stan James: 50/1 Corals

Winner Steve Jones 12/1 Tote, Corals: 20/1 Hills, Stanleys.

1998 RESULT

1 jt fav	20/1	**Steve Jones**	**64 65 68 66**	**263**
2	66/1	**Scott Gump**	**65 67 64 68**	**264**
3 jt fav	20/1	**Kenny Perry**	**65 65 67 68**	**265**
4	66/1	**David Toms**	**65 65 65 71**	**266**
T5 jt fav	20/1	**Fred Funk**	**66 70 65 66**	**267**
T5	50/1	**Brad Fabel**	**68 66 65 68**	**267**
T5	33/1	**Scott McCarron**	**67 66 66 68**	**267**
T5	80/1	**D A Weibring**	**64 68 65 70**	**267**

T9	S Verplank	67 66 71 64 268	B Gage	65 69 71 68 273
	H Sutton	64 68 71 65 268	S Flesch	66 69 70 68 273
	D Stockton	64 71 68 65 268	H Royer	66 69 69 69 273
	R Cochran	65 66 70 67 268	K Clearwater	66 69 69 69 273
T13	T Pernice Jr	67 71 68 63 269	B Fleisher	70 67 67 69 273
	J Carter	67 67 68 67 269	T Conley	72 63 68 70 273
	P Goydos	67 68 66 68 269	B Cheesman	68 66 67 72 273
	F Lickliter	65 64 68 72 269	K Gibson	67 68 72 67 274
T17	B Quigley	68 68 69 65 270	P Jacobsen	70 66 69 69 274
	C Byrum	63 69 72 66 270	B Clampett	66 70 68 70 274
	J Morse	66 66 72 66 270	S Kendall	69 66 68 71 274
	B Bates	71 67 66 66 270	J Estes	69 64 69 72 274
	D Barron	65 72 66 67 270	D Barr	66 66 70 72 274
	S Utley	67 67 68 68 270	C Perry	66 70 66 72 274
	A Bean	66 68 68 68 270	D Martin	71 66 68 74 274
	D Forsman	67 69 66 68 270	M Brisky	70 67 69 69 275
	M Springer	66 67 68 69 270	S Micheel	70 68 68 69 275
	B Claar	70 66 64 70 270	J Daley	68 66 71 70 275
	M Carnevale	67 67 66 70 270	F Langham	69 68 68 70 275
	N Henke	65 67 67 71 270	C Smith	68 70 70 68 276
	R Freeman	69 67 71 64 271	C Martin	66 68 73 69 276
	L Clements	65 71 70 65 271	T Loustalot	69 69 68 70 276
	O Uresti	65 70 68 68 271	G Hnatiuk	65 67 72 72 276
	P H Horgan III	65 66 71 69 271	O Browne	69 69 72 67 277
	D Sutherland	66 67 69 69 271	J Delsing	66 71 71 69 277
	M Wiebe	70 65 67 69 271	P Tataurangi	72 66 69 70 277
	R Coughlan	65 71 72 64 272	B Henninger	66 69 70 72 277
	M Hulbert	70 68 70 64 272	K Fergus	67 68 69 73 277
	M Weir	69 68 69 66 272	D Ogrin	67 68 69 73 277
	M Small	66 70 69 67 272	T Sills	67 71 71 69 278
	D Tewell	65 71 67 69 272	B Jaeckel	69 68 72 69 278
	J Sluman	70 68 65 69 272	D Edwards	67 68 71 72 278
	G Sauers	66 70 71 66 273	M Smith	69 68 73 69 279
	J McGovern	68 70 69 66 273	W Grady	69 67 72 71 279
	G Boros	68 68 70 67 273	D Peoples	66 72 72 71 281
	K Wentworth	69 69 68 67 273	W Wood	69 67 74 71 281
	G Kraft	67 71 68 67 273	J Renner	72 66 75 71 284
	J Riegger	65 68 72 68 273		

ROUND BY ROUND LEADERBOARD

FIRST ROUND

C Byrum	7 under
S JONES	6 under
H Sutton	6 under
D A Weibring	6 under
D Stockton Jr	6 under

SECOND ROUND

F Lickliter	11 under
S JONES	11 under
K Perry	10 under
D Toms	10 under
P H Horgan III	9 under
R Cochran	9 under

THIRD ROUND

D Toms	15 under
S Gump	14 under
D A Weibring	13 under
K Perry	13 under
F Lickliter	13 under
S JONES	13 under

FINAL ROUND

S JONES	17 under
S Gump	16 under
K Perry	15 under
D Toms	14 under
F Funk	13 under
B Fabel	13 under
S McCarron	13 under
D A Weibring	13 under

PUNTERS' POINTS

- With three of the four 20/1 joint favourites in the front five, which also included three DYM players, punters had a good tournament.
- 20/1 Steve Jones won his eighth USPGA title thanks to superb putting in the final round. This was his fourth win in the last three seasons so he's clearly a player to note. His accuracy will often put him into contention, so when his putter's 'hot' he wins.
- 66/1 Scott Gump belied his 144th place in the final round scoring averages with a gutsy 68 on Sunday to go very close to being yet another USPGA tour first time winner.
- 20/1 Kenny Perry loves the midsummer heat and proved once more his liking for Coal Valley with a very consistent performance to finish third.
- Defending champion David Toms put up a fine defence of his title. However a double bogey on the 16th in R4 finished his challenge.
- Among those missing the cut were 40/1 DYM John Daly, 50/1 Grant Waite, 66/1 outsiders Steve Pate and Paul Stankowski, 80/1 DYM Steve Lowery, and 100/1 DYM Jim Gallagher Jr.

1997 RESULT

1	50/1	David Toms
T2	50/1	Robert Gamez
T2	100/1	Brandel Chamblee
T2	125/1	Jimmy Johnston

WINNERS IN THE '90s

1990	Joey Sindelar
1991	D A Weibring
1992	David Frost
1993	David Frost
1994	Mark McCumber
1995	D A Weibring
1996	Ed Fiori
1997	David Toms
1998	Steve Jones

PUNTERS' GUIDE

- Experienced players clearly have done best on this course with the average winning age in the '90s being 36.

   In 1999 this tournament will be retitled the John Deere Classic. However, the Oakwood course will continue to be used. So all the years of course form can still be studied.

- Three players with solid recent form are:
  > Scott Verplank with three successive top 10s.
  > Frank Lickliter T13th 1998 and T5th 1997.
  > D A Weibring, three-time winner here in 1977, 1991 and 1995 and 2nd in 1993.

- Experienced players do best with the average winning age this decade 36.

- This decade this has not been a course for first-time winners.

THE DEPOSIT GUARANTY GOLF CLASSIC

Date   16th – 19th July
Course   Annandale, Madison, Mississippi
Par   72
Yardage   7,157
First Prize $216,000
Total Purse $1.2 million

This tournament, held at the same time as the British Open, offers the 'lesser lights' a chance to shine. For the fifth successive year the Jack Nicklaus designed Annandale course was the venue.

1998 ODDS

fav	12/1	Fred Funk	50/1	Grant Waite*	
	14/1	Hal Sutton	50/1	Brian Henninger*	
	18/1	Scott Verplank (non runner)	66/1	Chris di Marco*	
	25/1	David Toms	66/1	Paul Goydos*	
	25/1	Kirk Triplett	66/1	Mike Springer*	
	28/1	Chris Perry	66/1	Neal Lancaster	
	33/1	Russ Cochran	66/1	Paul Stankowski*	
	33/1	Greg Kraft	66/1	Brian Claar	
	40/1	Steve Lowery*	66/1	Willie Wood*	
	40/1	David Ogrin*	66/1	Mark Carnevale	
	50/1	Tommy Armour*	66/1	Jerry Kelly	

21 players were best priced at or under 66/1.

BOOKIES AT ODDS

Ten DYMs among the twenty-one players priced at or below 66/1 shows that some compilers did not do their homework, or/and were too busy in British Open week.

Tied 2nd Paul Goydos, 25/1 Stan James, Surrey: 66/1 Ladbrokes, Tote

Winner Fred Funk 10/1 Hills: 12/1 Ladbrokes, Stan James, Tote, Surrey

1998 RESULT

1	12/1	Fred Funk	69 64 69 68	270
T2	200/1	Tim Loustalot	69 69 68 66	272
T2	150/1	Franklin Laugham	67 67 70 68	272
T2	66/1	Paul Goydos	66 66 72 68	272
T5	100/1	P H Morgan	76 66 66 65	273
T5	80/1	John Maginnes	70 71 66 66	273

T7	K Triplett	68 72 68 66 274		B Fabel	68 71 75 67 281
	J Kelly	70 66 70 68 274		R Zokol	68 72 73 68 281
	C Smith	66 68 71 69 274		M Donald	70 72 71 68 281
	A Doyle	67 69 69 69 274		L Porter	69 73 71 68 281
T11	B Bates	69 70 70 66 275		G Boros	68 70 74 69 281
	J Delsing	67 73 69 66 275		B Claar	69 69 74 69 281
	G Waite	68 70 67 70 275		R Crowder	69 74 68 70 281
T14	H Sutton	69 71 66 70 276		K Gibson	75 66 66 74 281
	T Conley	69 69 67 71 276		D Mast	74 68 73 67 282
	D Tewell	66 66 72 72 276		M Dawson	72 70 70 70 282
	M Brisky	68 68 66 74 276		S McRoy	70 69 72 71 282
T18	J Kaye	67 70 72 68 277		L Gooch	71 70 69 72 282
	P Stankowski	74 67 67 69 277		J Adams	71 68 68 75 282
	B Henninger	66 70 69 72 277		W Wood	71 72 70 70 283
T21	K Wentworth	74 65 71 68 278		G Kraft	71 70 70 72 283
	R Freeman	73 67 70 68 278		C Byrum	65 73 71 74 283
	R Coughlan	74 69 67 68 278		D Toms	74 69 74 67 284
	E Toledo	71 66 72 69 278		J L Lewis	71 70 69 74 284
	D Ogrin	75 68 66 69 278		B Hughes	70 70 70 74 284
	K Fergus	69 68 69 72 278		M Springer	70 72 68 74 284
	S Randolph	74 66 72 67 279		C Barlow	71 71 71 72 285
	S Lowery	71 68 71 69 279		G Sauers	71 70 71 73 285
	S Skinner	72 67 71 69 279		T Sills	69 73 75 69 286
	M Carnevale	70 67 72 70 279		J O'Keefe	73 70 75 68 286
	S Pate	71 66 71 71 279		T Tyner	71 72 72 71 296
	D Stockton Jr	72 70 66 71 279		B Lohr	69 72 75 71 287
	B R Brown	70 72 66 71 279		K Jones	70 73 71 73 287
	M Heinen	69 70 68 72 279		G Powers	69 67 77 74 287
	M Weir	68 74 73 65 280		B McCallister	72 70 71 74 287
	D Dunakey	72 68 70 70 280		D Halldorson	73 69 75 71 288
	J Riegger	72 65 71 72 280		H Royer III	68 74 73 73 288
	C DiMarco	70 69 69 72 280		T Smith	73 70 76 71 290
	N Lancaster	72 71 72 66 281		B Henry	73 70 79 79 301

ROUND BY ROUND LEADERBOARD

FIRST ROUND		SECOND ROUND	
C Byrum	7 under	D Tewell	12 under
B Henninger	6 under	P Goydos	12 under
P Goydos	6 under	F FUNK	11 under
D Tewell	6 under	C Smith	10 under
C Smith	6 under	F Langham	10 under
F Langham	5 under	J Kelly	8 under
J Kaye	5 under	M Brisky	8 under
J Delsing	5 under	G Powers	8 under
A Doyle	5 under	B Henninger	8 under
F FUNK	3 under		

THIRD ROUND		FINAL ROUND	
M Brisky	14 under	F FUNK	18 under
F FUNK	14 under	T Loustalot	16 under
F Langham	12 under	F Langham	16 under
P Goydos	12 under	P Goydos	16 under
D Tewell	12 under	P H Horgan III	15 under
G Waite	11 under	J Maginnes	15 under
T Conley	11 under		
A Doyle	11 under		
B Henninger	11 under		
C Smith	11 under		

PUNTERS' POINTS

- Let's be clear.....this was the tournament 150/1 Franklin Langham lost as the 30-year-old blew a 4-shot lead on the back nine in R4 to let in Fred Funk who recorded his fifth USPGA win.

- This is Funk's time of the year as he has now won four of his five tournaments in or after July!

- 'Unknown' 200/1 Tim Loustalot is a former Nike Tour player, who regained his tour card at Q School last November. His good form here came 'out of the blue' as his previous best finish on tour had been 32nd in 1995.

- This will be a tournament to forget for 33-year-old Mike Brisky. Third last year and starting the final round sharing the lead with Funk he shot a 74 (only two players in the whole field shot a bigger score) to finish a very disappointing T14th.

- P H Horgan III's amazing 19 under par for the final 54 holes was easily the best in the field (4 better than Funk, for example). With three Nike tour wins under his belt he'll be looking to this event in 1999 for his breakthrough win on the main tour.

- Among those to miss the cut were 80/1 David Edwards, 100/1 DYM Brett Quigley, 100/1 TYM Steve Jurgenson, 100/1 DYM Omar Uresti, and 100/1 DYM Mike Standly.

1997 RESULT

1	100/1	Billy Ray Brown
2	100/1	Mike Standly
3	80/1	Mike Brisky
T4	100/1	Blaine McCallister
T4	250/1	Brian Rowell
T4	25/1	Steve Lowery
T4	100/1	Steve Jurgenson
T4	100/1	Brian Claar
T4	50/1	Mike Springer

WINNERS IN THE '90s

1990	Gene Sauers
1991	Larry Silveira
1992	Richard Zokol
1993	Greg Kraft
1994	Brian Henninger
1995	Ed Dougherty
1996	Willie Wood
1997	Billy Ray Brown
1998	Fred Funk

PUNTERS' GUIDE

- The Annandale course demands accuracy rather than length and Funk's win proved the point. He entered the tournament the No. 2 player on the Driving Accuracy stats.
- The last four winners have all been experienced players.
- The most consistent course records in recent years are held by:-
  > Kirk Triplett T7th 1998: 13th 1997: 2nd 1996: 4th 1995
  > Robin Freeman T21st 1998: 19th 1997: 9th 1996
  > Brian Henninger T18th 1998: 10th 1997: 16th 1996: W 1994.
  > David Ogrin T21st 1998: T13th 1997: T5th 1996.

THE CVS CHARITY CLASSIC

Date	23rd – 26th July
Course	Pleasant Valley GC, Sutton, Massachusetts
Par	71
Yardage	7,110
First Prize	$270,000
Total Purse	$1.5 million

This year this tournament returned to its customary position as the first after the British Open. There was plenty of Pleasant Valley course form for punters to study.

1998 ODDS

fav	11/1	Jim Furyk	50/1	Chris Smith
	16/1	Scott Hoch	50/1	Greg Kraft
	16/1	Fred Funk	50/1	Brian Henninger
	16/1	Kenny Perry	66/1	Joey Sindelar
	20/1	Loren Roberts (DC)	66/1	Tom Byrum
	20/1	Brad Faxon	66/1	Clark Dennis*
	25/1	John Cook	66/1	Jo Durant*
	40/1	Steve Flesch	66/1	Scott Gump
	40/1	Paul Azinger	66/1	Tommy Tolles*
	50/1	Jeff Sluman*	66/1	Billy Andrade
	50/1	Craig Parry	66/1	Chris Perry*

22 players were best priced at or under 66/1.

BOOKIES AT ODDS

Winner DYM Steve Pate 50/1 Tote: 125/1 Corals, Ladbrokes

1998 RESULT

1	125/1	Steve Pate	70 65 67 67	269
T2	16/1	Scott Hoch	68 68 69 65	270
T2	150/1	Bradley Hughes	68 69 67 66	270
T4	125/1	Nolan Henke	69 65 70 67	271
T4	125/1	Mike Heinen	74 65 65 67	271
T4	125/1	Willie Wood	64 69 68 70	271

T7	E Toledo	69 71 68 64 272		D Pride	71 67 71 71 280
	L Roberts	71 70 65 66 272		N Fasth	69 71 69 71 280
	M Wiebe	69 67 68 68 272		B Claar	69 69 70 72 280
	B Glasson	69 68 67 68 272		D Martin	68 69 71 72 280
	D Stockton	67 68 66 71 272		B Kamm	69 71 66 74 280
T12	Larry Rinker	67 69 71 66 273		R Mediate	69 72 73 67 281
	P Azinger	68 65 71 69 273		C DiMarco	71 70 70 70 281
	S Flesch	66 70 67 70 273		G Kraft	70 70 68 73 281
T15	K Gibson	71 68 67 68 274		R Black	71 70 73 68 282
	J Cook	70 66 69 69 274		P Morgan	70 71 71 70 282
	F Lickliter	71 69 64 70 274		J Durant	69 71 71 71 282
	O Browne	70 68 65 71 274		J Sluman	67 72 71 72 282
T19	S Gump	73 68 66 68 275		C Byrum	71 69 70 72 282
	B Henninger	71 66 69 69 275		I Steel	68 72 70 72 282
	O Uresti	67 72 66 70 275		F Quinn	70 71 69 72 282
	S Lowery	69 67 68 71 275		S Skinner	70 70 74 69 283
T23	C Parry	69 71 68 68 276		R Zokol	68 70 76 69 283
	M Springer	65 67 72 72 276		G Waite	72 69 69 73 283
T25	C Perry	68 71 69 69 277		D Mast	72 69 69 73 283
	J McGovern	70 70 67 70 277		W Grady	72 66 76 70 284
	F Funk	70 66 70 71 277		A Doyle	70 69 73 72 284
	P H Horgan III	64 72 67 74 277		K Sutherland	71 70 70 73 284
	G Hallberg	69 69 71 69 278		A Bean	70 67 71 76 284
	Lee Rinker	67 67 73 71 278		P Jacobsen	69 69 72 75 285
	K Fergus	67 70 70 71 278		M Donald	67 74 75 70 286
	B McCallister	71 69 67 71 278		J Sindelar	72 69 75 70 286
	J Maginnes	67 69 69 73 278		L T Broeck	67 69 75 75 286
	C Smith	71 70 70 68 279		M Pfeil	69 70 77 71 287
	P Tataurangi	71 66 72 70 279		Jeff Gallagher	69 71 73 74 287
	G Boros	67 70 72 70 279		B Fleisher	69 72 69 77 287
	F Zoeller	68 65 74 72 279		D Rummells	73 68 73 74 288
	D A Weibring	67 71 69 72 279		J Driscoll (am)	70 70 72 76 288
	R Freeman	70 71 66 72 279		D Pooley	71 69 73 76 289
	B Faxon	68 67 69 75 279		S Jurgensen	72 69 69 80 290
	L Clements	73 68 70 69 280		G Sauers	71 70 72 78 291
	P Jordan	70 71 70 69 280		L Hinkle	74 66 77 75 292
	B Quigley	71 69 69 71 280			

ROUND BY ROUND LEADERBOARD

FIRST ROUND		SECOND ROUND	
W Wood	7 under	M Springer	10 under
M Springer	6 under	W Wood	9 under
P H Horgan III	6 under	F Zoeller	9 under
S Flesch	5 under	P Azinger	9 under
D Stockton Jr	4 under	N Henke	8 under
Lee Rinker	4 under	Lee Rinker	8 under
Larry Rinker	4 under	S PATE	7 under
9 others at	4 under		
S PATE	1 under		

THIRD ROUND		FINAL ROUND	
D Stockton Jr	12 under	S PATE	15 under
W Wood	12 under	S Hoch	14 under
S PATE	11 under	B Hughes	14 under
O Browne	10 under	N Henke	13 under
P H Horgan III	10 under	M Heinen	13 under
S Flesch	10 under	W Wood	13 under

- Play was suspended on the first day because of bad light with 63 players still to complete their first round.

PUNTERS' POINTS

- Steve Pate had hinted at a return to his best form when T2nd in the Phoenix Open back in January, and again in the US Open when although finishing T32nd he was T2nd on the putting stats.
  - > Here the 37-year-old proved once more that a player with a proven winning record on the 'comeback trail' after injury must be noted. He had broken his right hand and wrist in a road accident in January 1996. This was the first time that right hand had lifted a winning trophy since the 1992 Buick Invitational.
- Scott Hoch, playing at Pleasant Valley for the first time since 1982, showed that course form is not a necessary condition for success. A brilliant R4 65 took the controversial 42-year-old to T2nd place.
- It was noticeable that the three players who had slogged through the four rounds of the British Open did not play too well.
  - > Jim Furyk T4th in the Open was 11/1 jt favourite here and he missed the weekend after seventeen successive cuts!
  - > Brad Faxon finished T34th and was never in contention.
  - > Loren Roberts started poorly (71-70) feeling Birkdale's after effects before finishing better than anyone else over the final 36 holes (11 under par) to end in T7th place.
- Steve Pate's success was another victory for the DYM system and it followed the 125/1 win of DYM Stephen Leaney in the Dutch Open a few hours earlier to give a transatlantic DYM double of a mere 15,875-1!

- The rainy, windy, stormy conditions on the first morning made an early R1 tee time a big disadvantage as, for example, Kenny Perry (75 in R1) found to his cost.
- Among those missing the cut were 11/1 fav Jim Furyk, 16/1 jt second fav Kenny Perry, and 66/1 Billy Andrade. Clark Dennis withdrew after a first round 75.

1997 RESULT

1	18/1	Loren Roberts
2	40/1	Bill Glasson
3	125/1	Peter Jacobsen
4	100/1	Chris Smith

WINNERS IN THE '90s

1990	Morris Hatalsky
1991	Bruce Fleisher
1992	Brad Faxon
1993	Paul Azinger
1994	Kenny Perry
1995	Fred Funk
1996	John Cook
1997	Loren Roberts
1998	Steve Pate

PUNTERS' GUIDE

- One astonishing fact.....in the last six years 57% of the players finishing 4th or T4th (ie 19 out of 33) have been priced at or over 100/1!!
- Unfortunately for punters the five-foot putt of Dave Stockton Jr on the final green signalled the end of Pleasant Valley as a USPGA tour venue.

THE FEDEX ST. JUDE CLASSIC

Date	30th July – 2nd August
Course	TPC at Southwind, Memphis, Tennessee
Par	71
Yardage	7,006
First Prize	$324,000
Total Purse	$1.8 million

The Southwind course played host to the St Jude Classic for the tenth successive year.

1998 ODDS

jt fav	16/1	Nick Price	50/1	Craig Parry
jt fav	16/1	Scott Hoch	50/1	Paul Azinger
jt fav	16/1	Justin Leonard	66/1	Paul Goydos
jt fav	16/1	Davis Love III	66/1	Dudley Hart
	20/1	Lee Janzen	66/1	David Toms
	25/1	John Cook	66/1	Kirk Triplett
	33/1	Jeff Maggert	66/1	Glen Day
	33/1	Steve Flesch	66/1	Bob Estes*
	40/1	Hal Sutton	66/1	Michael Bradley*
	40/1	Loren Roberts*	66/1	Jay Haas*
	40/1	Kenny Perry	66/1	Jeff Sluman
	40/1	Bob Tway		

23 players were best priced at or under 66/1.

BOOKIES AT ODDS

DYM Loren Roberts 20/1 Corals: 40/1 Hills
4th placed DYM Bob Estes 33/1 Hills: 66/1 Surrey
Winner Nick Price 10/1 Stan James: 16/1 Stanleys

1998 RESULT

1 fav	16/1	Nick Price	65 67 70 66	268
		(Price won at the second play-off hole)		
2	66/1	Jeff Sluman	70 67 66 65	268
3	66/1	Glen Day	69 64 72 65	270
4	66/1	Bob Estes	68 67 67 69	271
5	500/1	Tim Conley	68 68 67 69	272

6	P Goydos	72 66 69 67 274		P H Horgan III	67 70 75 70 282
T7	R Damron	68 74 66 67 275		J McGovern	70 72 70 70 282
	J Haas	70 67 70 68 275		B Hughes	68 71 72 71 282
	K Triplett	68 70 69 68 275		S Micheel	69 71 71 71 282
	P Azinger	65 69 69 72 275		D Pride	74 68 68 72 282
11	S Hoch	66 68 74 68 276		D Hart	67 74 68 73 282
T12	L Porter	73 69 69 66 277		S Kendall	71 69 67 75 282
	M Bradley	70 69 71 67 277		R Black	70 69 76 68 283
	B Cheesman	73 65 72 67 277		D Hammond	66 69 79 69 283
	N Lancaster	67 65 77 68 277		R Tryba	73 67 73 70 283
	T Herron	72 66 71 68 277		M Small	72 67 72 72 283
	S Verplank	69 70 67 71 277		P Stankowski	73 69 69 72 283
	J Durant	71 67 67 72 277		B Andrade	71 70 69 73 283
	K Wentworth	67 70 67 73 277		J Kaye	71 70 76 67 284
T20	D Ogrin	74 67 70 67 278		B Henninger	71 70 74 69 284
	O Uresti	69 68 72 69 278		L Roberts	68 73 72 71 284
	M Hulbert	70 70 69 69 278		B Quigley	72 69 72 71 284
	R Mediate	69 72 67 70 278		Lee Rinker	72 69 71 72 284
	K Sutherland	67 70 70 71 278		J D Blake	69 69 71 75 284
	Larry Rinker	67 69 71 71 278		M Reid	70 72 75 68 285
	J Riegger	69 68 76 66 279		K Clearwater	68 73 73 71 285
	B Chamblee	67 72 74 66 279		W Wood	73 69 72 71 285
	E Toledo	69 70 73 67 279		G Boros	72 70 71 72 285
	L Janzen	69 73 70 67 279		D Sutherland	75 67 69 74 285
	C DiMarco	72 70 68 69 279		B Tway	69 69 71 76 285
	M Wiebe	70 69 69 71 279		C Dennis	71 69 75 71 286
	M Carnevale	66 71 76 67 280		J Johnston	71 70 72 73 286
	B Fleisher	74 66 71 69 280		J P Hayes	74 68 70 74 286
	R Cochran	65 70 75 70 280		J Kelly	71 69 75 72 287
	B McCallister	70 71 68 71 280		D Gossett (amat)	66 70 74 77 287
	H Sutton	69 70 68 73 280		D Martin	74 68 72 74 288
	C Smith	70 70 74 67 281		D Toms	72 69 76 72 289
	C Rose	73 66 72 70 281		R Coughlan	73 68 75 73 289
	J Delsing	72 70 69 70 281		L Mize	71 71 75 72 289
	M Weir	69 71 70 71 281		M Standly	71 71 74 77 293
	B Friend	69 70 71 71 281		M Christie	70 69 82 76 297
	B Bates	73 65 71 72 281			

ROUND BY ROUND LEADERBOARD

FIRST ROUND		SECOND ROUND	
N PRICE	6 under	N PRICE	10 under
P Azinger	6 under	N Lancaster	10 under
R Cochran	6 under	G Day	9 under
M Carnevale	5 under	S Hoch	8 under
D Gossett	5 under	P Azinger	8 under
D Hammond	5 under	D Hammond	7 under
S Hoch	5 under	B Estes	7 under
		R Cochran	7 under

THIRD ROUND		FINAL ROUND	
N PRICE	11 under	N PRICE	16 under
B Estes	11 under	J Sluman	16 under
J Sluman	10 under	G Day	14 under
T Conley	10 under	B Estes	13 under
P Azinger	10 under	T Conley	12 under
K Wentworth	9 under		

PUNTERS' POINTS

- Nick Price sure is a tough cookie! After a really tough test in the British Open (T29th incl. an 82 in R3), he went straight on to finish T3rd in the Dutch Open, and then straight on to this tournament. However, in fine form, with his putter working on a course where he shot four sub-70 rounds last year, he deserved his win.

- However, it took a long putt on the second play-off hole to beat 66/1 Jeff Sluman's challenge. It was Slu's second top 3 finish of the season.

- Bob Estes' very consistent season continued with a fine 4th place at 66/1. It was the 32-year-old Texan's third top 4 finish this year. His stroke average is now 68.7 over the last four years here!

- Another really consistent performer this year is Glen Day who was recording his fourth top 4 finish of the season.

- Congratulations to Corals. When they discovered that Nick Price was to be a runner they introduced him as 11/1 jt favourite. However they extended the odds of six other players. Contrast that with Stan James who simply added Nick Price to their list as 10/1 jt favourite without extending any other odds at all.

- Among those to miss the cut were 16/1 jt favourites Davis Love III and Justin Leonard, 25/1 John Cook, 33/1 chances Jeff Maggert and Steve Flesch and 40/1 Kenny Perry, so six of the front twelve in the market failed to make the weekend.

1997 RESULT

1	10/1	Greg Norman
2	100/1	Dudley Hart
T3	50/1	Craig Parry
T3	66/1	Robert Damron

WINNERS IN THE '90s

1990 Tom Kite
1991 Fred Couples
1992 Jay Haas
1993 Nick Price
1994 Dicky Pride
1995 Jim Gallagher Jr
1996 John Cook
1997 Greg Norman
1998 Nick Price

PUNTERS' GUIDE

- As pointed out here last year, the winner has nearly always played well with a high finish the previous year. The recent record illustrates the point.

		Age	Previous Year's finish
1998	Nick Price	41	T5th
1997	Dudley Hart (1)		21st
1996	John Cook	38	T5th
1995	Jim Gallagher Jr	34	T10th
1994	Dicky Pride	25	-
1993	Nick Price	36	T13th
1992	Jay Haas	38	T3rd

(1) The winner, Greg Norman, had not played in the tournament in recent years so the runner-up, Dudley Hart, is included here. Norman was 42 when he won.

- The course has Zoysia-grass (Z-grass) fairways. It's much thicker and sturdier than the usual Bermuda grass and, as a result, the ball sits up and can be swept rather than propelled after taking a divot. This generally favours the older players. The average age of the last seven winners is therefore perhaps not surprisingly 36.28.

- Two younger players with solid recent records here are :-

> Robert Damron T7th 2998: T33rd 1997

> Michael Bradley T12th 1998: T5th 1997: 7th 1996

THE BUICK OPEN

Date	6th – 9th August
Course	Warwick Hills, Grand Blanc, Michigan
Par	72
Yardage	7,105
First Prize	$324,000
Total Purse	$1.8 million

The Warwick Hills course has been the venue for the Buick Open ever since 1978.

1998 ODDS

fav	11/2	Tiger Woods	40/1	Bob Tway
	20/1	Justin Leonard	50/1	Jeff Sluman*
	22/1	Vijay Singh (DC)	50/1	Hal Sutton
	28/1	Steve Stricker*	50/1	Jay Haas
	33/1	Fred Funk	66/1	Paul Goydos*
	33/1	John Huston	66/1	Russ Cochran*
	33/1	John Cook	66/1	Scott McCarron
	40/1	Stewart Cink	66/1	Steve Pate
	40/1	Brad Faxon	66/1	Scott Verplank*
	40/1	Glen Day		

Just 19 players were best priced at or under 66/1.

BOOKIES AT ODDS

Third placed DYM Andrew Magee 40/1 Stan James: 100/1 Stanleys, Corals
2nd placed DYM Scott Verplank 33/1 Ladbrokes: 66/1 Hills, Napoleons
The winner DYM Billy Mayfair 50/1 Stan James: 125/1 Sunderlands

1998 RESULT

1	125/1	Billy Mayfair	70 69 65 67	271
2	66/1	Scott Verplank	71 67 71 64	273
3	100/1	Andrew Magee	69 71 70 64	274
T4	500/1	Eric Booker	71 68 70 66	275
T4 fav	11/2	Tiger Woods	71 67 69 68	275

T6	J Sindelar	69 71 72 64 276		B McCallister	70 70 72 71 283
	S Stricker	69 67 68 72 276		C Strange	71 71 70 71 283
T8	Jeff Gallagher	70 70 71 66 277		T Tryba	69 71 71 72 283
	B Chamblee	65 68 72 72 277		J Delsing	73 68 70 72 283
	V Singh	66 70 69 72 277		D Berganio Jr	69 71 71 72 283
	P Blackmar	67 68 70 72 277		F Langham	71 70 70 72 283
T12	D Hart	66 69 75 68 278		G Day	69 72 70 72 283
	H Sutton	70 67 70 71 278		C DiMarco	67 73 69 74 283
	K Jones	67 67 73 71 278		P Jordan	72 69 75 68 284
T15	S Cink	70 70 71 68 279		S Elkington	70 72 73 69 284
	J Sluman	68 69 72 70 279		L Porter	70 72 72 70 284
	G Hallberg	66 73 70 70 279		J P Hayes	67 72 73 72 284
	B Tway	67 73 69 70 279		J Acosta Jr	68 73 71 72 284
	P Goydos	68 73 68 70 279		P Tataurangi	74 68 70 72 284
	S McCarron	67 71 70 71 279		L Mattiace	72 70 68 74 284
	F Funk	70 69 68 72 279		D A Weibring	70 72 74 69 285
	D Ogrin	70 70 67 72 279		Joe Ozaki	70 70 74 71 285
T23	J L Lewis	65 76 72 67 280		S Hebert	73 69 73 70 285
	J Riegger	68 74 70 68 280		D Pooley	71 70 72 72 285
	C Perry	67 72 72 69 280		H Royer	72 69 72 72 285
	C Rose	67 73 70 70 280		J Roth	73 69 71 72 285
	D Martin	69 72 69 70 280		J D Blake	72 68 72 73 285
	J Cook	69 70 70 71 280		M Standly	69 70 73 73 285
	J Carter	74 66 72 69 281		B Fleisher	71 71 69 74 285
	R Mediate	68 70 73 70 281		L Rinker	70 70 76 70 286
	D Hammond	71 71 67 72 281		D Edwards	72 69 75 70 286
	B Geiberger	68 70 69 74 281		A Bean	72 70 72 72 286
	W Austin	69 69 69 74 281		C Barlow	68 71 74 73 286
	J Kaye	70 71 66 74 281		H Frazar	71 71 71 73 286
	B Hughes	69 73 65 74 281		N Henke	69 72 74 72 287
	D Barron	72 69 74 67 282		B R Brown	75 67 71 74 287
	S Kendall	70 72 71 69 282		T Armour III	70 71 76 71 288
	J McGovern	69 73 71 69 282		J Johnston	69 72 72 75 288
	D Waldorf	72 70 73 68 283		M Brooks	70 71 77 71 289
	P Stankowski	68 73 72 70 283		F Zoeller	73 67 77 77 294

ROUND BY ROUND LEADERBOARD

FIRST ROUND		SECOND ROUND	
J L Lewis	7 under	B Chamblee	11 under
B Chamblee	7 under	K Jones	10 under
V Singh	6 under	D Hart	9 under
D Hart	6 under	P Blackmar	9 under
G Hallberg	6 under	V Singh	8 under
8 players at	5 under	S Stricker	8 under
B MAYFAIR	2 under	B MAYFAIR	5 under

THIRD ROUND		FINAL ROUND	
B MAYFAIR	12 under	B MAYFAIR	17 under
S Stricker	12 under	S Verplank	15 under
V Singh	11 under	A Magee	14 under
P Blackmar	11 under	E Booker	13 under
B Chamblee	11 under	T Woods	13 under
B Hughes	9 under		
J Kaye	9 under		
D Ogrin	9 under		
F Funk	9 under		
W Austin	9 under		
T Woods	9 under		
B Geiberger	9 under		
H Sutton	9 under		
K Jones	9 under		

PUNTERS' POINTS

- 125/1 Billy Mayfair may have an odd-looking putting stroke yet the 32-year-old sure knows how to win. Here he was securing his fifth tour win, and his second of this year. His bogey-free final round showed that when in contention punters must keep him on their side.

- The big Sunday disappointment was surely Steve Stricker who shot a really poor 72 to lose not only a winning opportunity, but to finish T6th.

- 66/1 Scott Verplank's final-round 64 catapulted him into 2nd place. "I really had nothing to lose and I kind of played that way."

- Tiger Woods was an absurdly-short 11/2, as he used Warwick Hills as a warm-up for the final major. "All parts of my game are really starting to fall into place, so I'm glad I played."

- Punters should remember that with receptive rain-softened greens and 'lift, clean and place' on the fairways the scope for low scoring was high, as three 64s (Verplank, Magee, and Sindelar) in the final round showed.

- 35-year-old T4th Eric Booker had been in good form on the Nike tour where he won the Lehigh Valley Open six weeks ago after a R4 65. Here a fine final-round 66 showed once more that he can handle the last day pressure.

- Four poor final-round performances by Jonathan Kaye, Bradley Hughes, Brent Geiberger, and Woody Austin (who all shot 74s) when in contention should be noted for future R4 2-ball betting.

- DYM system fans will be smiling with the first three all DYMs, and with a 100/1 DYM success in the German Open as well there was a transatlantic DYM double for the second time in three weeks!
- Among those to miss the cut were 20/1 Justin Leonard, 33/1 John Huston, 40/1 Brad Faxon, 50/1 Jay Haas, 66/1 outsiders Russ Cochran, Steve Pate and 80/1 chances Robert Allenby David Frost and Robert Damron.

1997 RESULT

1	33/1	Vijay Singh
T2	66/1	Tom Byrum
T2	80/1	Russ Cochran
T2	9/1	Ernie Els
T2	125/1	Brad Fabel
T2	125/1	Joe Ozaki
T2	125/1	Curtis Strange

WINNERS IN THE '90s

1990	Chip Beck
1991	Brad Faxon
1992	Dan Forsman
1993	Larry Mize
1994	Fred Couples
1995	Woody Austin
1996	Justin Leonard
1997	Vijay Singh
1998	Billy Mayfair

PUNTERS' GUIDE

- Three points are worth noting.
  - > Warwick Hills's wide open fairways provide a comparative advantage for those players who are not the most accurate off the tee. Often the tournament becomes virtually a 'pitch and putt' contest.
  - > In the last 24 tournaments there have been 10 first-time winners.
  - > In the last couple of years eleven players have finished in the top 4 (or T4th), and seven of them have been priced at or over 100/1.

THE 80TH USPGA CHAMPIONSHIP

Date	13th – 16th August
Course	Sahalee C.C., Redmond, Washington
Par	71
Yardage	6,906
First Prize	$470,000
Total Purse	$2.6 million

Please see Part 5.

THE SPRINT INTERNATIONAL

Date	20th – 23rd August
Course	Castle Pines, Castle Rock, Colorado
Par	72
Yardage	7,559
First Prize	$360,000
Total Purse	$2 million

This unusual tournament awards points as follows:- Albatross + 8, Eagle +5, Birdie +2, par zero, Bogey -1, Double bogey or worse -3. Points accumulate over all four rounds with the field cut to the lowest 70 players and ties for Saturday's round, and to the lowest 36 and ties for Sunday's final round.

In the thin desert air in Colorado the ball probably travels an extra 10-15% at the 6,200 foot Castle Pines, which is the longest course on the tour.

1998 ODDS

fav	8/1	Tiger Woods	40/1	Billy Mayfair*
	16/1	Nick Price	50/1	Bob Tway
	16/1	Ernie Els	50/1	Stewart Cink
	18/1	Phil Mickelson (DC)	50/1	Steve Flesch
	18/1	Davis Love III	66/1	Paul Goydos
	20/1	David Duval	66/1	Kenny Perry*
	28/1	Jim Furyk	66/1	Jay Haas
	33/1	Vijay Singh (PWW)	66/1	Andrew Magee
	33/1	Tom Lehman	66/1	Frank Lickliter
	33/1	Lee Janzen	66/1	Bob Estes
	40/1	Steve Elkington	66/1	Mark Calcavecchia
	40/1	Brad Faxon	66/1	Scott Verplank
	40/1	Jesper Parnevik		

25 players were best priced at or under 66/1.

BOOKIES AT ODDS

DYM Tied 2nd Willie Wood 100/1 Corals: 200/1 Surrey
Winner Vijay Singh 20/1 Chandler: 33/1 Ladbrokes, Stanleys

1998 RESULT

1	33/1	**Vijay Singh**		**15 12 6 14**		**47**
T2	200/1	**Willie Wood**		**9 8 15 9**		**41**
T2	18/1	**Phil Mickelson**		**8 5 16 12**		**41**
4 fav	8/1	**Tiger Woods**		**14 3 14 7**		**38**
5	150/1	**Rocco Mediate**		**7 9 14 7**		**37**

T6	B Tway	4 9 7 16	36		B Mayfair	5 3 14 4	26
	B Faxon	3 9 11 13	36		D Love III	13 7 5 1	26
	B Jobe	13 9 5 9	36	26	J Carter	15 4 1 5	25
	S Flesch	12 11 5 8	36		G Turner	4 5 12 4	25
10	S Elkington	9 8 8 10	35		J Haas	2 6 14 3	25
11	D Toms	7 4 7 16	34		M Reid	9 1 8 5	23
12	B Chamblee	6 11 2 14	33		J Riegger	11 1 7 4	23
T13	J Parnevik	5 16 3 8	32		S Appleby	3 11 8 1	23
	P Jacobsen	2 12 11 7	32		E Toledo	-2 14 7 3	22
T15	A Magee	10 6 2 13	31		K Jones	7 7 6 2	22
	K Triplett	11 0 14 6	31		O Browne	4 4 13 1	22
17	T Pernice Jr	4 10 6 10	30		D Hart	4 9 5 2	20
18	D Sutherland	13 9 1 6	29		J Sindelar	9 6 4 1	20
19	C Perry	8 3 7 10	28		R Allenby	0 12 10 -3	19
20	S Jones	10 -2 11 8	27		M Brooks	9 4 13 -7	19
T21	M Weir	12 -3 9 8	26		A Bean	-3 12 11 -2	18
	Larry Rinker	4 10 5 7	26		C Dennis	3 11 5 -3	16
	S Cink	6 8 7 5	26		N Lancaster	2 7 9 -5	13

The following players played on Saturday but failed to qualify for the final day

B Gilder	8 4 5	17		C Parry	7 2 4	13
B Wadkins	6 7 4	17		J Furyk	9 4 0	13
M Springer	8 5 4	17		S Verplank	12 1 0	13
S Pate	7 3 7	17		T Loustalot	1 8 3	12
C Pavin	13 1 3	17		P Stankowski	9 3 -1	11
E Els	6 9 2	17		B Kamm	5 5 1	11
C Barlow	8 7 2	17		L Janzen	5 3 3	11
J D Blake	8 1 8	17		C Rose	2 6 3	11
T Dodds	12 1 3	16		R Fehr	5 5 0	10
G Hnatiuk	3 8 5	16		F Nobilo	5 3 2	10
S Gump	8 2 6	16		T Kite	4 5 0	9
B Bates	4 8 3	15		K Sutherland	8 6 -5	9
B Henninger	10 9 -4	15		J McGovern	12 -3 0	9
C Stadler	9 -1 7	15		N Price	4 4 0	8
R Damron	4 8 2	14		P Tataurangi	6 3 -2	7
K Perry	5 4 5	14		T Herron	9 2 -5	6
K Wentworth	5 3 6	14				

DAILY LEADERBOARD

FIRST ROUND

V SINGH	15 points
J Carter	15 points
T Woods	14 points
C Pavin	13 points
D Sutherland	13 points
D Love III	13 points
B Jobe	13 points

SECOND ROUND

V SINGH	27 points
S Flesch	23 points
B Jobe	22 points
J Parnevik	21 points
D Love III	20 points
B Henninger	19 points
W Wood	17 points
T Woods	17 points
S Elkington	17 points

THIRD ROUND

V SINGH	33 points
W Wood	32 points
T Wood	31 points
R Mediate	30 points
P Mickelson	29 points
S Flesch	28 points
B Jobe	27 points

FINAL ROUND

V SINGH	47 points
W Wood	41 points
P Mickelson	41 points
T Woods	38 points
R Mediate	37 points

- On the first day play was delayed for 2 hours 40 minutes due to lightning then eventually suspended with 45 players still out on the course.
- For the second successive day the tournament was suspended on Friday due to lightning strikes in the area.

PUNTERS' POINTS

- "Winning a major like that, I just wanted to get back on the golf course and play again....I don't worry about the bad shots, I just think about where I'm going to hit the ball. The feeling is good, and you've got to ride it while you can."

  Vijay sure did ride his feeling to record a highly impressive front running victory.
- Pursued all the way by the brilliant putting of Willie Wood, 33/1 Singh clinched victory with an eagle at the par 5 17th hole. Vijay's back-to-back victories were based on his new found confident touch with his putter.
- Defending champion Phil Mickelson finished eagle-birdie to tie for 2nd place. After winning $450K at Pebble Beach on Monday plus a $100K bonus as the Number 1 on the West Coast he pocketed $176K here to earn over $626K in six days. You can't live on it but it's a start!!
- Japanese tour player Brandt Jobe lives next to the course, although "right now Japan is my home." His strong performance here, finishing T6th, following Brian Watts's excellent British Open, shows how important it is for punters to keep an eye on the Japanese tour players and results.
- The adapted Stableford scoring system certainly helped Tiger Woods who shot four eagles. However he'd have finished 18th, rather than 4th on normal scoring. This was his first Sprint so if he returns in 1999 he'll have an obvious chance after this year's 'failure'.

- It was a shock to see Ernie Els fail to make the final day here. In the previous three years he had figures of 7th-19th-2nd and averaged 27.6 points. Big Ernie can be expected to do well here again in 1999.
- One point to remember: 2-ball betting on the final day really can be profitable because tied matches are unlikely due to the scoring system. This year only one of the fourteen Sunday 2-ball pairs priced up was tied. So punters have a virtual two-outcome contest in which to pick the winner.
- Among the players who did not make the first cut were 20/1 David Duval, 33/1 Tom Lehman, and 66/1 chances Paul Goydos, Frank Lickliter, Mark Calcavecchia, and Bob Estes.

1997 RESULT

1	33/1	Phil Mickelson
2	66/1	Stuart Appleby
3	125/1	Skip Kendall
4	125/1	Dudley Hart

WINNERS IN THE '90s

1990	Davis Love III	
1991	J M Olazabal	
1992	Brad Faxon	
1993	Phil Mickelson	
1994	Steve Lowery	
1995	Lee Janzen	34 pts
1996	Clarence Rose	31 pts
1997	Phil Mickelson	48 pts
1998	Vijay Singh	47 pts

PUNTERS' GUIDE

- Short-hitting players who are in hot putting form do well here, as Willie Wood did this year. Nevertheless the long hitters with an ability to reach the par 5s in two and give themselves eagle (5 point!) putts do have an advantage.
- I suggest you go for a player with four key characteristics.
  > he's in solid current form
  > he's a long hitter, preferably in the top 20 for driving distance and certainly 275 yards or longer off the tee
  > he's in the top 20 for total eagles
  > he's proven on the course
- Only three players have made it to the last day in each of the last three years. They are :-

	1998	1997	1996	Av.pts 1996-98
> Phil Mickelson	41	48	21	36.6
> Brad Faxon	36	25	31	30.6
> Andrew Magee	31	27	22	26.6

- In 1999 Steve Flesch T6th this year on his first appearance must go well again. In 1998 he entered the Sprint 11th for birdies per round, T12th for total eagles, T9th for driving distance, T6th for R4 scoring and 2nd for greens in regulation.......With his 1998 experience behind him, especially of club selection, he must have a real chance.

THE NEC WORLD SERIES OF GOLF

Date	27th – 30th August
Course	Firestone C.C., Akron, Ohio
Par	70
Yardage	7,149
First Prize	$405,000
Total Purse	$2.25 million

This was the 23rd and final staging of this prestigious tournament which is open only to players who have won specific tournaments on the World's five tours. There is no halfway cut so all competitors receive a cheque, with the winner gaining a 10-year tour exemption. The course rewards accuracy. However with seven very long par 4s the longer hitters have an advantage.

1998 ODDS

fav	7/1	Tiger Woods	80/1	Jo Durant
	12/1	Vijay Singh	80/1	Tim Herron
	12/1	Phil Mickelson	80/1	Brandt Jobe
	14/1	Nick Price	80/1	Michael Bradley
	14/1	Davis Love III	100/1	Craig Parry
	18/1	Ernie Els	100/1	Olin Browne
	18/1	Fred Couples	100/1	Trevor Dodds
	20/1	Mark O'Meara	125/1	Bradley Hughes
	20/1	David Duval	125/1	P U Johansson
	33/1	Billy Mayfair	125/1	Shigeki Maruyama
	33/1	Scott Hoch	125/1	Steve Pate
	33/1	Jesper Parnevik	125/1	Brian Watts
	33/1	Lee Janzen	150/1	Andrew Coltart
	33/1	Justin Leonard	150/1	Scott Simpson
	40/1	John Cook	150/1	Greg Turner
	40/1	Fred Funk	150/1	J P Hayes
	40/1	John Huston	150/1	David Carter
	40/1	Mark Calcavecchia	200/1	M Kusakabe
	50/1	Steve Jones	200/1	S Yokota
	50/1	Loren Roberts	250/1	G Hjertstedt
	66/1	Bill Glasson	250/1	T Johnstone
	80/1	Stuart Appleby	300/1	B Zabriski

ALL QUOTED

BOOKIES AT ODDS
Winner David Duval 12/1 Hills: 20/1 Sunderlands
T4th John Cook 25/1 Corals, Stanleys: 40/1 Napoleons

1998 RESULT

1	20/1	**David Duval**	69 66 66 68	**269**
2	12/1	**Phil Mickelson**	66 71 66 68	**271**
3	14/1	**Davis Love III**	71 69 67 65	**272**
4	40/1	**John Cook**	71 69 62 71	**273**
T5	50/1	**Loren Roberts**	72 67 69 67	**275**
T5 fav	7/1	**Tiger Woods**	67 68 70 70	**275**

T7	J Durant	73 67 70 66 276	J Huston	70 71 70 74 285
	M O'Meara	72 67 65 72 276	F Couples	72 73 65 75 285
T9	S Hoch	70 69 71 69 279	G Turner	68 77 71 70 286
	C Parry	67 68 72 72 279	B Watts	68 72 70 76 286
T11	B Glasson	71 71 68 70 280	J Leonard	68 71 74 74 287
	S Maruyama	75 68 65 72 280	A Coltart	70 73 69 75 287
	J Parnevik	71 70 66 73 280	P U Johansson	73 69 75 72 289
T14	S Pate	72 71 69 69 281	F Funk	70 71 71 79 291
	V Singh	71 68 71 71 281	B Hughes	72 71 72 77 292
	M Calcavecchia	70 70 69 72 281	D Carter	77 73 72 74 296
	S Yokota	68 72 69 72 281	G Hjertstedt	77 74 73 72 296
	B Jobe	70 71 67 73 281	T Dodds	72 74 73 77 296
19	E Els	69 74 72 67 282	M Kusakabe	75 68 77 76 296
20	B Mayfair	72 74 68 69 283	M Bradley	75 75 75 72 297
T21	S Appleby	73 71 72 68 284	J P Hayes	77 70 81 72 300
	S Jones	73 69 73 69 284	S Simpson	76 75 78 73 302
	N Price	76 70 68 70 284	T Johnstone	79 76 73 75 303
T24	T Herron	68 76 71 70 285	B Zabriski	77 75 79 73 304
	O Browne	73 68 72 72 285		

ROUND BY ROUND LEADERBOARD

FIRST ROUND

P Mickelson	4 under
T Woods	3 under
C Parry	3 under
T Herron	2 under
S Yokota	2 under
G Turner	2 under
B Watts	2 under
J Leonard	2 under
D DUVAL	1 under

SECOND ROUND

D DUVAL	5 under
T Woods	5 under
C Parry	5 under
P Mickelson	3 under
L Roberts	1 under
V Singh	1 under
M O'Meara	1 under
S Hoch	1 under
J Leonard	1 under

THIRD ROUND

D DUVAL	9 under
J Cook	8 under
P Mickelson	7 under
M O'Meara	6 under
T Woods	5 under
J Parnevik	3 under
D Love III	3 under
C Parry	3 under

FINAL ROUND

D DUVAL	11 under
P Mickelson	9 under
D Love III	8 under
J Cook	7 under
L Roberts	5 under
T Woods	5 under

PUNTERS' POINTS

- David Duval was winning for the sixth time over the last eleven months and for the third time this year. Here he showed fine character with a superb front-running performance in which he showed a fine short game whenever his driving or approach play let him down.
  - > Playing on the back of two successive missed cuts he was as big as 20/1 in a place.
- 12/1 Phil Mickelson's confidence is very very high after his record earnings last week so it was no surprise to see him record his fourth successive top 4 finish in this event.
- Make a note of Davis Love III here next year. His final 54 holes here were 12 under par to give him a stroke average here over the last 3 years of 69.41!
- Tiger Woods 'failed' again in T5th place. However in his eight rounds here he's only been over par once. 1999 will surely see a big challenge from the tiger.
- John Cook, 3rd last year, looked the value each-way bet and so it proved. Born in Ohio, raised in Akron, with his dad the tournament manager, he simply loves this course. In R3 he almost shot a 59. He could never recapture that in R4 to finish 4th.
- Lee Janzen was disqualified for waiting too long for a putt on the 17th to drop in R1. He was placed last.
- Congratulations to Sunderlands for creating two special markets.

The results were:

To be Top American			To be Top Non-American		
1	12/1	David Duval	1	22/1	Craig Parry
2	11/2	Phil Mickelson	T2	25/1	Shigeki Maruyama
3	8/1	Davis Love III	T2	6/1	Jesper Parnevik
4	18/1	John Cook			

1997 RESULT

1	12/1	Greg Norman
2	16/1	Phil Mickelson
T3	50/1	John Cook
T3 fav	7/1	Tiger Woods
T3	66/1	Fred Funk

WINNERS IN THE '90s

1990	J M Olazabal
1991	Tom Purtzer
1992	Craig Stadler
1993	Fulton Allem
1994	J M Olazabal
1995	Greg Norman
1996	Phil Mickelson
1997	Greg Norman
1998	David Duval

PUNTERS' GUIDE

- This is the last year the NEC World Series of Golf will be played. Next year the NEC Invitational will be played August 26-29 at Firestone Country Club. The field will be comprised mainly of members of the current Ryder Cup and Presidents Cup teams. The tournament is part of the World Golf Championships series.

- One player certain to be in the 1999 field will be Phil Mickelson whose recent form here is 'simply the best!' He has finished 2nd 1998: 2nd 1997: Won 1996: 4th 1995 and his sixteen-round stroke average for those four years is 68.8. Keep him on your side here in 1999!

THE GREATER VANCOUVER OPEN

Date	27th – 30th August
Course	Northview C.C., Ridge Course
Par	71
Yardage	6,832
First Prize	$270,000
Total Purse	$1.5 million

For the third successive year the Northview course provided a big chance for all those players who did not qualify for the NEC World Series of Golf.

1998 ODDS

jt fav	14/1	Steve Flesch	40/1	Brandel Chamblee
jt fav	14/1	Andrew Magee	40/1	Scott McCarron
	16/1	Stewart Cink	50/1	David Ogrin
	20/1	Hal Sutton	66/1	Steve Lowery
	20/1	Jeff Maggert	66/1	David Frost*
	20/1	Payne Stewart	66/1	Frank Nobilo
	25/1	Russ Cochran	66/1	Scott Gump
	25/1	Bob Estes	66/1	Chris Smith
	33/1	Glen Day	66/1	Jim Carter
	40/1	Robert Allenby	66/1	Greg Kraft
	40/1	Willie Wood	66/1	Brian Henninger

22 players were best priced at or under 66/1.

BOOKIES AT ODDS

The winner Brandel Chamblee 25/1 Tote: 40/1 Chandlers, Hills, Stanleys

1998 RESULT

1	40/1	Brandel Chamblee	67 64 68 66	265
2	20/1	Payne Stewart	64 69 65 70	268
3	150/1	Lee Porter	67 67 71 66	271
4	125/1	Brian Claar	68 68 69 67	272
T5	100/1	Omar Uresti	71 68 68 66	273
T5	150/1	Hugh Royer	67 68 70 68	273
T5	20/1	Jeff Maggert	68 67 70 68	273
T5	80/1	Mike Weir	70 66 68 69	273
T5	25/1	Russ Cochran	71 67 66 69	273
T5	25/1	Bob Estes	67 70 67 69	273

T11	B Friend	69 68 69 68 274		Jeff Gallagher	73 67 69 71 280
	P Stankowski	67 73 65 69 274		G Kraft	67 70 74 69 280
	T Pernice Jr	70 66 67 71 274		P Devenport	73 66 69 73 281
	B Geiberger	71 66 66 71 274		D Edwards	71 69 68 73 281
T15	T Tryba	68 69 71 67 275		P O'Malley	72 68 66 75 281
	K Gibson	68 72 67 68 275		P Tataurangi	71 66 69 75 281
	E Toledo	69 71 67 68 275		E Booker	69 72 71 69 281
	J Maginnes	66 71 68 70 275		F Langham	67 70 71 74 282
	H Sutton	71 68 65 71 275		K Green	71 70 68 73 282
T20	J Carter	68 71 69 68 276		P Jonas	70 71 72 69 282
	F Zoeller	70 69 69 68 276		S Skinner	69 68 70 76 283
	M Springer	68 71 68 69 276		R Coughlan	69 66 73 75 283
	C Barlow	68 70 69 69 276		D Frost	71 67 71 74 283
	K Sutherland	71 69 69 67 276		G Boros	67 67 72 77 283
	D Stockton	72 69 68 67 276		I Leggatt	70 70 71 72 283
	K Wentworth	69 68 68 71 276		S Gump	70 71 70 72 283
	T Byrum	68 68 68 72 276		D Mijovic	69 71 74 69 283
T28	J Estes	67 70 71 69 277		S Cink	71 69 74 69 283
	J Riegger	71 66 71 69 277		T Conley	70 69 70 75 284
	M Hulbert	69 70 68 70 277		M Reid	70 67 72 75 284
	P Jacobsen	70 67 70 70 277		R Black	70 70 69 75 284
	R Zokol	69 69 71 68 277		D Sunderland	70 69 71 74 284
	G Day	67 70 69 71 277		T Loustalot	69 72 73 70 284
	R Allenby	71 66 68 72 277		B Bates	68 73 75 68 284
	C DiMarco	68 63 72 74 277		J Adams	71 70 71 74 286
	H Frazar	68 66 69 74 277		J Thorpe	69 72 73 72 286
	Larry Rinker	68 66 69 74 277		F Nobilo	68 71 72 76 287
	D Ogrin	70 69 69 70 278		A Magee	67 71 75 74 287
	D Martin	67 68 73 70 278		J Hobby	67 67 75 79 288
	S Flesch	69 69 70 71 279		P H Horgan III	70 67 74 77 288
	C Smith	72 65 70 72 279		S Jurgensen	68 73 74 73 288
	B Cheesman	72 66 68 73 279		D Tewell	71 70 71 77 289
	G Hallberg	71 69 72 67 279		R Stewart	70 71 72 76 289
	M Wiebe	70 67 71 72 280		K Clearwater	69 71 73 79 292
	M Carnevale	71 67 69 73 280		D Rummells	71 69 73 DQ.

ROUND BY ROUND LEADERBOARD

FIRST ROUND		SECOND ROUND	
P Stewart	7 under	B CHAMBLEE	11 under
J Maginnes	6 under	C DiMarco	11 under
D Martin	4 under	P Stewart	9 under
G Boros	4 under	Larry Rinker	8 under
A Magee	4 under	J Hobby	8 under
P Stankowski	4 under	G Boros	8 under
H Royer	4 under	H Frazar	8 under
F Langham	4 under	L Porter	8 under
G Day	4 under		
J Estes	4 under		
G Kraft	4 under		
J Hobby	4 under		
L Porter	4 under		
B CHAMBLEE	4 under		

THIRD ROUND		FINAL ROUND	
P Stewart	15 under	B CHAMBLEE	19 under
B CHAMBLEE	14 under	P Stewart	16 under
B Geiberger	10 under	L Porter	13 under
T Pernice Jr	10 under	B Claar	12 under
H Frazar	10 under	O Uresti	11 under
Larry Rinker	10 under	H Royer	11 under
C DiMarco	10 under	J Maggert	11 under
		M Weir	11 under
		R Cochran	11 under
		B Estes	11 under

PUNTERS' POINTS

- Brandel Chamblee became the second first-time winner in this tournament's three-year history. Starting R4 a shot behind 9/4 on favourite Payne Stewart he played superbly to win.
- 20/1 Payne Stewart started R4 125th on the final-round scoring averages compared to Chamblee's 21st position, so Stewart's failure was not a surprise. Indeed it was his twenty-third 2nd place of his career for the 41-year-old who last won in 1995.
- Another point for punters – Stewart had a poor 71 here last year in R4 too so he went into this final round with negative memories.
- Lee Porter, who had showed up well in the first rounds of the US Open and finished strongly in the St Jude Classic, recorded his best-ever finish when T3rd following a 66 in R4.
- 4th placed Brian Claar was Rookie of the Year back in 1986. However he didn't even merit a player profile in last year's book as his form had been so poor. He had made the cut here in both 1996 and 1997.

- Three players have now showed first-class course form.
  - \> Russ Cochran T5th 1998: 4th 1997: T5th 1996
  - \> Bob Estes T5th 1998: 3rd 1997
  - \> Mike Weir T5th 1998: T5th 1996
- Make a note of any player coming to the GVO with his confidence boosted by a high finish in the Sprint International. Brandel Chamblee and Mike Weir must have felt good coming into the GVO this year after their 12th- and 21st-place finishes in the Sprint last week. In 1999 the GVO takes place a fortnight after the Sprint.
- Of the front twenty-two in the market only 40/1 Willie Wood and 50/1 Scott McCarron failed to make the cut.

1997 RESULT

1	20/1	Mark Calcavecchia
2	40/1	Andrew Magee
3	50/1	Bob Estes
4	33/1	Russ Cochran

WINNERS IN THE '90s

1996	Guy Boros
1997	Mark Calcavecchia
1998	Brandel Chamblee

PUNTERS' GUIDE

- After three years of tournament form on the same course three key points stand out.
  - \> In 1997 two of the first four had been in the top 10 in 1996. In 1998 three of the top 10 had been in the top 10 in 1997.
  - \> The form figures of the three winners were
    1996 Guy Boros 59-69-MC-71
    1997 Mark Calcavecchia 10-5-25-23
    1998 Brandel Chamblee 26-8-12
  - \> Guy Boros (1996) and Brandel Chamblee (1998) were both first-time winners.
- So when making your selection in 1999 consider any in-form player who finished in the top 20 this year, and who will be looking for his maiden tour win.

THE GREATER MILWAUKEE OPEN

Date	3rd – 6th September
Course	Brown Deer Park, Milwaukee
Par	71
Yardage	6,739
First Prize	$324,000
Total Purse	$1.8 million

The short course at Brown Deer Park was the venue for the GMO for the fifth successive year. The course unusually has five par 3s.

1998 ODDS

jt fav	14/1	Vijay Singh	33/1	Fred Funk
jt fav	14/1	Scott Hoch (DC)	33/1	Jeff Sluman
jt fav	14/1	Loren Roberts	40/1	Jo Durant
	16/1	Steve Stricker	50/1	Russ Cochran
	16/1	John Cook	66/1	Paul Goydos
	22/1	Bob Estes	66/1	Jay Haas*
	25/1	Andrew Magee	66/1	Frank Lickliter*
	25/1	Steve Flesch	66/1	David Toms
	33/1	Bill Glasson*	66/1	Tom Pernice Jr
	33/1	Mark Calcavecchia	66/1	Skip Kendall*

Only 20 players were best priced at or under 66/1.

BOOKIES AT ODDS

Winner Jeff Sluman 25/1 Chandler: 33/1 Ladbrokes, Stanley, Tote, Stan James, Sunderlands

1998 RESULT

1	33/1	Jeff Sluman	68 66 63 68	265
2	16/1	Steve Stricker	68 63 67 68	266
T3	33/1	Mark Calcavecchia	66 64 69 69	268
T3	100/1	Nolan Henke	70 62 67 69	268
T3	80/1	Chris Perry	68 62 67 71	268

6	D Barron	67 67 68 67 269	K Green	71 68 66 72 277
T7	F Funk	68 70 65 67 270	L Roberts	62 70 72 73 277
	M Carnevale	66 66 69 69 270	J L Lewis	74 63 64 76 277
T9	T Byrum	67 68 69 67 271	P Jordan	71 67 73 67 278
	G Hjertstedt	66 67 69 69 271	C Beck	69 68 73 68 278
	B Andrade	74 64 65 68 271	V Singh	67 70 71 70 278
	K Wentworth	68 65 68 70 271	M Brisky	68 68 71 71 278
13	B Kamm	70 66 67 69 272	B McCallister	72 65 70 71 278
T14	W Austin	68 68 69 68 273	W Wood	70 65 74 70 279
	K Sutherland	69 66 69 69 273	J D Blake	65 71 72 71 279
	T Armour III	68 68 66 71 273	J McGovern	67 67 72 73 279
	D Ogrin	69 64 68 72 273	S Hoch	70 67 69 73 279
T18	T Pernice Jr	68 67 73 66 274	B Bates	72 67 66 74 279
	J Cook	67 71 69 67 274	Larry Rinker	72 67 71 70 280
	D Edwards	67 69 70 68 274	G Hnatiuk	74 65 70 71 280
	J P Hayes	68 70 68 68 274	P Goydos	69 69 70 72 280
	J Maginnes	67 65 68 74 274	B Cheesman	67 69 72 72 280
T23	S Kendall	68 71 71 65 275	D Halldorson	68 68 69 75 280
	D Sutherland	71 68 70 66 275	B Fleisher	70 69 72 70 281
	D Toms	67 69 71 68 275	R Gamez	67 71 74 69 281
	J Delsing	68 68 70 69 275	J Kelly	72 67 71 71 281
	D Waldorf	68 67 70 70 275	J Johnston	70 68 72 71 281
	L Porter	66 68 71 70 275	B Glasson	67 70 71 73 281
	B Claar	66 70 69 70 275	K Fergus	68 69 71 73 281
	S Skinner	71 66 67 71 275	B Wadkins	70 68 73 71 282
	K Jones	69 69 70 68 276	B Gilder	70 65 74 73 282
	K Gibson	71 65 70 70 276	C Rose	70 69 71 73 283
	C DiMarco	67 69 70 70 276	J Durant	71 68 70 74 283
	M Hulbert	67 69 69 71 276	J Estes	71 66 72 74 283
	M Reid	69 70 68 70 277	J Daley	70 69 75 72 286
	M Springer	66 72 69 70 277	O Uresti	70 67 72 77 286
	B Hughes	71 66 70 70 277	I Steel	70 67 79 72 288
	A Bean	69 68 70 70 277		

ROUND BY ROUND LEADERBOARD

FIRST ROUND		SECOND ROUND	
L Roberts	9 under	M Calcavecchia	12 under
J D Blake	6 under	C Perry	12 under
M Calcavecchia	5 under	S Stricker	11 under
B Claar	5 under	M Carnevale	10 under
L Porter	5 under	N Henke	10 under
M Carnevale	5 under	L Roberts	10 under
M Springer	5 under	J Maginnes	10 under
G Hjertstedt	5 under	J SLUMAN	8 under
J SLUMAN	3 under		

THIRD ROUND		FINAL ROUND	
J SLUMAN	16 under	J SLUMAN	19 under
C Perry	16 under	S Stricker	18 under
S Stricker	15 under	M Calcavecchia	16 under
N Henke	14 under	C Perry	16 under
M Calcavecchia	14 under	N Henke	16 under
J Maginnes	13 under		

PUNTERS' POINTS

- 'The nappy factor' rules OK! Jeff Sluman, who became a first-time dad four and a half months ago, played well to hold off the challenge of the 'local boy' Steve Stricker who himself became a first-time dad on Monday so missing the Pro-Am as he arrived late.

- This course favours the accurate player who has experience of the Brown Deer Park course first used in 1994. This year with recent rain thickening the rough there was an even greater premium on accuracy.

- 33/1 Jeff Sluman was winning his third tournament on a course tailor-made for his game where he'd finished 3rd in 1995. Living in Chicago, Illinois he'll be a player to note for the 1999 USPGA played in his own backyard and let's remember he's already won it once!

- 16/1 Steve Stricker, despite his late arrival, made a really brave effort to land the one non-major tournament he rates above all others. His stroke average here over the last three years is now an unrivalled 67.08!!

- 80/1 T3rd Chris Perry showed here in R4 that he prefers to play for a big cheque rather than going for a win, and he showed real nerves at the last hole. A consistent player, on this evidence if he's to win he'll have to come from 'off the pace'.

- "The GMO was the first tournament I played in on the tour. I have always enjoyed coming here. I have been trying to win it for a long time." So T3rd 33/1 Mark Calcavecchia will be worth noting here in future.

- On the Sunday when nearly all the leading players beat par it is worth noting those that didn't – Chris Perry (71), John Maginnes (74), David Ogrin (72), and after being the tournament's lowest scorer in R2 and 3 at 15 under par for those 36 holes J L Lewis shot 76 in R4!

- In-form Vijay Singh played the course for the first time. He looked a player to oppose on a track that did not play to his strengths and so it proved as the Fijian finished 13 shots back in T42nd place.
- Among those to miss the cut were five of the front 20 in the market, namely 22/1 Bob Estes, 25/1 Steve Flesch, 50/1 Russ Cochran and 66/1 chances Jay Haas and Frank Lickliter.

1997 RESULT

1 jt fav	16/1	Scott Hoch
T2 jt fav	16/1	Loren Roberts
T2	80/1	David Sutherland
4	125/1	Tom Pernice Jr

WINNERS IN THE '90s

1990	Jim Gallagher Jr	Tuckaway GC
1991	Mark Brooks	Tuickaway GC
1992	Richard Zokol	Tuckaway GC
1993	Billy Mayfair	Tuckaway GC
1994	Mike Springer	Brown Deer Park
1995	Scott Hoch	Brown Deer Park
1996	Loren Roberts	Brown Deer Park
1997	Scott Hoch	Brown Deer Park
1998	Jeff Sluman	Brown Deer Park

PUNTERS' GUIDE

- In 1999 the GMO will be played the week before the US Open when it will be worth noting Billy Andrade who is the only player (apart from Steve Stricker) with three successive top 20 finishes here. The course suits his game, his final 54 holes this year (16 under par) was the best in the whole tournament, and he was 100/1!

THE BELL CANADIAN OPEN

Date	10th – 13th September
Course	Glen Abbey Golf Club, Oakville, Ontario
Par	72
Yardage	7,112
First Prize	$396,000
Total Purse	$2.2 million

After moving last year to Quebec the Canadian Open returned to the Glen Abbey course which had been its home throughout the nineties, so there was plenty of course form to go on.

This course, typical of Jack Nicklaus designed courses, has fast undulating greens and tends to favour faders (left to right players) of the ball as five of its six doglegs go left to right.

1998 ODDS

fav	12/1	Ernie Els	33/1	Bob Tway
	16/1	Vijay Singh	50/1	Glen Day
	20/1	Jim Furyk	50/1	Steve Flesch*
	20/1	Tom Lehman (late withdrawal)	50/1	Paul Azinger
	25/1	Mark Calcavecchia	66/1	Billy Andrade
	25/1	Steve Elkington (late withdrawal)	66/1	Scott Verplank
	33/1	Steve Jones (DC)	66/1	Robert Allenby
	33/1	Jeff Sluman (PWW)	66/1	Tom Byrum
	33/1	Billy Mayfair	66/1	Nolan Henke
	33/1	Andrew Magee	66/1	Frank Lickliter
	33/1	Brad Faxon	66/1	Tim Herron
	33/1	Hal Sutton		

23 players were best priced at or under 66/1.

BOOKIES AT ODDS

The winner Billy Andrade 50/1 Hills, Stan James: 66/1 Chandlers, Corals, Tote, Stanleys

1998 RESULT

1	66/1	Billy Andrade	68 69 69 69	275
		(Andrade won at the first play-off hole)		
2	150/1	Bob Friend	69 67 68 71	275
3	150/1	Mike Hulbert	72 70 66 68	276
T4	40/1	Hal Sutton	71 69 67 73	280
T4	125/1	Bradley Hughes	73 72 69 66	280
T4	50/1	Glen Day	74 71 64 71	280

T7	M Standly	72 71 71 67 281	K Gibson	68 72 71 76 287
	S Lyle	75 70 66 70 281	J Sluman	69 77 72 70 288
T9	J Delsing	76 68 68 70 282	P H Horgan III	71 72 73 72 288
	M Small	68 71 71 72 282	N Lancaster	75 71 70 72 288
	C DiMarco	73 65 71 73 282	D Hart	68 74 72 74 288
	S Verplank	68 71 71 72 282	P Blackmar	69 71 76 73 289
T13	T Loustalot	73 70 72 68 283	T Pernice Jr	72 73 70 74 289
	R Coughlan	70 75 70 68 283	B Fabel	72 74 68 75 289
	M Calcavecchia	73 69 72 69 283	T Tolles	72 71 70 76 289
	A Magee	73 70 70 70 283	P Azinger	72 70 76 72 290
	S Ames	71 73 68 71 283	F Nobilo	72 74 71 73 290
	S Jones	74 69 69 71 283	B Henninger	70 70 76 74 290
	F Zoeller	69 76 67 71 283	K Jones	75 71 70 74 290
	A Chinner	76 70 66 71 283	D McKenzie	74 69 72 75 290
	J Sindelar	71 73 65 74 283	B Fleisher	74 70 74 73 291
T22	B Faxon	74 68 72 70 284	D Barron	72 71 74 74 291
	V Singh	74 70 69 71 284	T Conley	72 71 73 75 291
	J Furyk	71 72 69 72 284	S McCarron	75 70 74 73 292
T25	T Herron	68 75 71 71 285	P Tataurangi	69 75 74 74 292
	D Martin	74 69 71 71 285	M Wiebe	72 71 74 75 292
	R Damron	71 67 75 72 285	Larry Rinker	71 71 73 77 292
	T Dodds	72 69 72 72 285	T Byrum	75 71 69 77 292
	B Tway	72 69 72 72 285	C Barlow	71 72 69 80 292
	K Fergus	71 72 70 72 285	D Barr	71 75 70 77 293
	M Bradley	75 70 68 72 285	J L Lewis	72 70 69 82 293
	P Jacobsen	73 68 71 73 285	T Purtzer	70 75 75 74 294
	D Edwards	69 71 72 73 285	S Lowery	76 69 75 74 294
	F Langham	72 74 67 73 286	P Jonas	76 70 72 76 294
	S McRoy	72 72 67 75 286	D Edwards	74 71 72 77 294
	G Hnatiuk	70 74 71 72 287	D Halldorson	75 71 69 79 294
	T Armour III	70 75 70 72 287	G Waite	75 71 68 80 294
	B Gilder	70 71 72 74 287	G Hill	70 76 72 78 296
	K Sutherland	71 71 71 74 287	P Devenport	75 71 71 79 296
	C Smith	66 77 70 74 287	I Steel	73 72 72 80 297
	L Mattiace	70 73 69 75 287		

ROUND BY ROUND LEADERBOARD

FIRST ROUND		SECOND ROUND	
C Smith	6 under	B Friend	8 under
B ANDRADE	4 under	B ANDRADE	7 under
D Hart	4 under	R Damron	6 under
M Small	4 under	C DiMarco	6 under
T Herron	4 under	S Verplank	5 under
S Verplank	4 under	M Small	5 under
K Gibson	4 under		

THIRD ROUND		FINAL ROUND	
B Friend	12 under	B ANDRADE	13 under
B ANDRADE	10 under	B Friend	13 under
H Sutton	9 under	M Hulbert	12 under
M Hulbert	8 under	H Sutton	8 under
C DiMarco	7 under	B Hughes	8 under
G Day	7 under	G Day	8 under
J Sindelar	7 under		

PUNTERS' POINTS

- 66/1 'fader' Billy Andrade fulfilled the criteria both of course form (T12th here in 1996 when Glen Abbey was last used) and current form (a tournament-best 16 under par for the last 54 holes last week).

  It was his third win and on each occasion he has entered the final day trailing.

- 150/1 Bob Friend was very nearly the bookies' friend. However he did not play the play-off hole (the par 5 18th) at all well, finding the water with his second shot. Nevertheless after a year when he'd made only ten from twenty-four cuts he had played very well to post his third top 10 of the year.

- 40/1 Hal Sutton has a superb course record. However the absence of any real wind did not help his low ball striking in R4 as he slipped to finish T4th after putting poorly.

- 150/1 Mike Hulbert, after missing the cut here on his last three visits, caught fire and finished with three birdies to finish third. Let's remember this guy actually putted one handed for some months just three years ago.

- Poor final round performances from players 'in contention' included J L Lewis (again) 82 (!), Kelly Gibson 76, Craig Barlow 80 and Spike McRoy 75.

- It was pleasing to see long-hitting Chris Smith play so well in his first round 66. However his 77 in R2 showed that he is still to find the consistency he showed last year when he was King of the Nike tour.

- Among those to miss the cut were 12/1 fav Ernie Els, 33/1 Billy Mayfair, 50/1 Steve Flesch and 66/1 chances Frank Lickliter and Robert Allenby.

- 20/1 Tom Lehman was a late withdrawal with a shoulder problem.

1997 RESULT

1	66/1	Steve Jones
2	10/1	Greg Norman
3	150/1	Phil Tataurangi
T4	100/1	David Ogrin
T4	125/1	Frank Lickliter

WINNERS IN THE '90s

1990	Wayne Levi	Glen Abbey
1991	Nick Price	Glen Abbey
1992	Greg Norman	Glen Abbey
1993	David Frost	Glen Abbey
1994	Nick Price	Glen Abbey
1995	Mark O'Meara	Glen Abbey
1996	Dudley Hart	Glen Abbey (54 holes)
1997	Steve Jones	Royal Montreal
1998	Billy Andrade	Glen Abbey

PUNTERS' GUIDE

> Of the sixteen players in the top 4 (or T4) in the last three years ten (62.5%) have been 100/1 plus.

> Round one leader Chris Smith maintained the disappointing record of fast starters in this event. It is now 21 years since a first-round leader has won.

> In making your selection it is probably wise to look for a player with three key characteristics
  * his 'natural' shot is a fade
  * he has at least one win under his belt
  * he is proven on this tough, often wind-ravaged, course.

> There are only two players who have posted top 20 finishes on each of the last three occasions that Glen Abbey has hosted the Canadian Open

	1998	1996	1995
* Joey Sindelar	T13	T7	T14
* Andrew Magee	T13	T15	T5

> My idea of the 1999 winner can be found in his player profile.

THE B C OPEN

Date	17th – 20th September
Course	En Joie, New York
Par	72
Yardage	7,073
First Prize	$270,000
Total Purse	$1.5 million

This tournament, started in 1971, has always been played on the En Joie course. Last year changes to the course were made with half the greens raised, made larger and more undulating. The par was then increased from 71 to 72.

1998 ODDS

fav	11/1	Jim Furyk	50/1	Dan Forsman
	16/1	Fred Funk	50/1	Steve Pate
	16/1	Stewart Cink	50/1	Brian Claar
	22/1	Paul Azinger	66/1	Skip Kendall*
	25/1	Chris Perry	66/1	Chris DiMarco*
	33/1	Billy Andrade* (PWW)	66/1	Kelly Gibson*
	33/1	Joey Sindelar	66/1	Frank Lickliter*
	40/1	Mike Hulbert	66/1	Jim Carter
	40/1	Michael Bradley	66/1	Phil Blackmar*
	40/1	Bradley Hughes	66/1	Stephen Ames
	40/1	Robert Allenby	66/1	Chris Smith
	50/1	Nolan Henke		

23 players were best priced at or under 66/1.

BOOKIES AT ODDS

Last week's winner Billy Andrade 12/1 jt second fav, Chandlers: 33/1 Ladbrokes

DYM second placed Peter Jacobsen 40/1 Chandlers, Stan James: 80/1 Sunderlands

DYM Tied 4th Ted Tryba 40/1 Stanleys: 100/1 Hills

Winner Chris Perry 16/1 Ladbrokes: 25/1 Chandlers, Corals, Surrey, Stan James.

1998 RESULT

1	25/1	Chris Perry	67 70 69 67	273
2	80/1	Peter Jacobsen	68 70 71 67	276
3	50/1	Nolan Henke	69 69 67 72	277
T4	150/1	Curt Byrum	71 73 69 65	278
T4	40/1	Robert Allenby	69 70 71 68	278
T4	100/1	Ted Tryba	72 69 67 70	278

T7	M Weir	71 68 69 71 279		G Waite	69 75 72 69 285
	D Barron	67 71 70 71 279		T Dodds	72 71 73 69 285
T9	B Quigley	72 71 69 68 280		P Blackmar	75 69 71 70 285
	S Kendall	71 69 70 70 280		G Twiggs	73 70 72 70 285
	C DiMarco	66 70 72 72 280		B McCallister	72 71 70 72 285
	B Henninger	69 69 70 72 280		J Carter	73 69 71 72 285
	R W Eaks	73 65 69 73 280		G Hjertstedt	73 70 66 76 285
	R Coughlan	69 71 67 73 280		H Royer	73 71 74 68 286
	B Fleisher	69 72 63 76 280		D Hammond	69 73 72 72 286
T16	B Andrade	70 70 73 68 281		J McGovern	75 65 72 74 286
	F Wadsworth	72 71 69 69 281		I Steel	72 71 68 75 286
	C Rose	71 68 70 72 281		J Kaye	71 73 71 72 287
	F Funk	71 67 71 72 281		S Utley	70 73 71 73 287
T20	G Hallberg	74 68 70 70 282		J Maginnes	74 70 69 74 287
	P Tataurangi	68 70 73 71 282		K Gibson	72 72 74 70 288
	S Skinner	69 74 67 72 282		S Sykora	74 69 73 72 288
	M Springer	71 71 67 73 282		S Lowery	71 71 73 73 288
	D Barr	70 65 73 74 282		D Mast	73 70 68 77 288
T25	S Pate	70 71 73 69 283		B Kamm	67 73 79 70 289
	D Waldorf	72 71 69 71 283		S Ames	72 71 77 69 289
	M Carnevale	72 70 70 71 283		B Friend	72 71 74 72 289
	M Small	71 70 70 72 283		M Pfeil	69 72 75 73 289
	Lee Rinker	72 69 70 72 283		C Pavin	71 70 73 75 289
	J Furyk	70 72 69 72 283		R Black	75 69 69 76 289
	F Langham	72 71 68 72 283		B Elder	75 68 73 74 290
	S Lyle	68 72 69 74 283		J J Henry	71 70 72 77 290
	M Standly	72 71 74 67 284		D Pohl	71 73 76 71 291
	B Cheesman	70 73 71 70 284		T Tolles	69 74 80 69 292
	M Heinen	72 70 72 70 284		K Fergus	71 73 74 74 292
	P H Horgan III	73 70 70 71 284		D Martin	70 74 74 75 293
	E Herrera	70 71 71 72 284		J Riegger	71 72 74 76 293
	T Loustalot	69 73 69 73 284		B Cole	71 71 74 78 294
	M Hulbert	69 73 68 74 284		D Forsman	71 67 76 WD

ROUND BY ROUND LEADERBOARD

FIRST ROUND		SECOND ROUND	
C DiMarco	6 under	D Barr	9 under
B Kamm	5 under	C DiMarco	8 under
D Barron	5 under	C PERRY	7 under
C PERRY	5 under	N Henke	6 under
P Tataurangi	4 under	F Funk	6 under
P Jacobsen	4 under	P Jacobsen	6 under
S Lyle	4 under	R W Eaks	6 under
		P Tataurangi	6 under
		B Henninger	6 under
		D Barron	6 under
		D Forsman	6 under

THIRD ROUND		FOURTH ROUND	
B Fleisher	12 under	C PERRY	15 under
N Henke	11 under	P Jacobsen	12 under
C PERRY	10 under	N Henke	11 under
R Coughlan	9 under	C Byrum	10 under
R W Eaks	9 under	R Allenby	10 under
C DiMarco	8 under	T Tryba	10 under
T Tryba	8 under		
M Weir	8 under		
D Barron	8 under		
B Henninger	8 under		
D Barr	8 under		

- 22 players could not complete their second round on Friday because of fog.

PUNTERS' POINTS

- "Chris Perry is a player to note in 1998 especially in a tournament like this when 'the big guns' are not playing", and how last year's Punters' Point was proved here when he got his first win in his 378th tournament.

- He had seemed the classic case of a solid, top 20 type pro who can't make it to the winning line. However 3rd in the Greater Milwaukee Open two weeks ago, and 2nd here last year, this was to be his tournament after a superb 67 in his final round.

- Perry had started his final round 123rd in the R4 scoring averages. However learning how to handle the pressures when in contention can take players some time (remember Duval?). On this occasion he had built up sufficient deposits of experience in his learning bank that he was able to draw on them when he needed to.

- 50/1 Nolan Henke chalked up his third top 4 finish in his last five starts yet could not match Perry's steadiness in that final round.

- Bruce Fleisher is looking forward to his 50th birthday cake, and to playing with the roundbellies on the Seniors tour. He illustrated a key point for punters to remember – that it is very difficult, if not impossible, to follow one really low round with another. After his amazing 63 in R3 (only 22 putts) he shot a 76 in R4.

- One player who'll be available at 100/1 in future will be Brett Quigley. This very promising 29-year-old is having his best-ever year, and his T9th finish (8 under for the last 54 holes) suggests he could surprise here next year.

- Once more 30-year-old Chris DiMarco featured high on the leaderboard, and once more he couldn't break par on Sunday. However he can take heart from Chris Perry who had learnt over the years how to handle the pressure on a Sunday.

- Among those to miss the cut were 16/1 Stewart Cink, 22/1 Paul Azinger, 33/1 Joey Sindelar, 40/1 Bradley Hughes and 50/1 Brian Claar.

- Michael Bradley after a 76, and Guy Boros after a 77, withdrew after their opening rounds.

1997 RESULT

1	200/1	Gabriel Hjerstedt
T2	80/1	Lee Rinker
T2	80/1	Chris Perry
T2	25/1	Andrew Magee

WINNERS IN THE '90s

1990	Nolan Henke
1991	Fred Couples
1992	John Daly
1993	Blaine McCallister
1994	Mike Sullivan
1995	Hal Sutton
1996	Fred Funk
1997	Gabriel Hjerstedt
1998	Chris Perry

PUNTERS' GUIDE

- In 1999 the BC Open will be played the week before the Ryder Cup so it will once more give a real chance to the 'second and third division' players.

- If there is to be a first-time winner, for the third successive year, it could be Skip Kendall who was T9th in 1998, made the cut in 1997, and was T7th in 1995.

- Only three players have posted successive top 20 finishes in the last two years – the winner Chris Perry, Bruce Fleisher who'll be 50 in November 1998 and Billy Andrade.

  > Andrade was playing on the back of last week's win, so he did well to finish T16th which after his T12th in 1997 gave him a stroke average in those eight rounds of 70. He'll be a player to note here in 1999.

THE WESTIN TEXAS OPEN

Course	LaCantera GC, San Antonio, Texas
Date	24th – 27th September
Par	72
Yardage	6,889
First Prize	$306,000
Total Purse	$1.7 million

The LaCantera course was the venue for the Texas Open for the fourth successive year.

1998 ODDS

fav	16/1	Justin Leonard	40/1	Bob Estes
	18/1	Steve Jones	40/1	John Huston*
	20/1	Loren Roberts	50/1	Kenny Perry*
	22/1	Fred Funk	50/1	David Ogrin
	25/1	Jeff Maggert	50/1	Duffy Waldorf
	28/1	Andrew Magee	50/1	Jay Haas
	33/1	Robert Allenby	50/1	Tom Byrum
	33/1	Glen Day	50/1	Steve Flesch
	33/1	Hal Sutton*	66/1	Paul Goydos
	33/1	Stewart Cink	66/1	Brandel Chamblee*
	33/1	Bob Tway	66/1	Ted Tryba
	33/1	Bill Glasson	66/1	Brent Geiberger
	40/1	Tim Herron (DC)		

26 players were best priced at or below 66/1.

BOOKIES AT ODDS

The winner was the DYM Hal Sutton 16/1 Stanleys: 33/1 Hills

1998 RESULT

1	33/1	Hal Sutton	67 68 67 68	270
T2	16/1	Justin Leonard	67 67 69 68	271
T2	50/1	Jay Haas	70 69 64 68	271
T4	200/1	Mike Reid	70 69 72 62	273
T4	100/1	Steve Lowery	70 70 69 64	273
T4	28/1	Andrew Magee	68 72 67 66	273
T4	20/1	Loren Roberts	67 68 71 67	273

T8	J Maggert	71 68 69 66 274		D A Weibring	65 74 74 68 281
	S Gump	68 70 65 71 274		L Mattiace	71 71 71 68 281
10	C Pavin	71 68 67 69 275		D Tewell	73 69 71 68 281
T11	M Springer	70 71 71 64 276		J McGovern	66 73 73 69 281
	S Jones	68 71 70 67 276		T Loustalot	71 70 70 70 281
	T Tryba	71 68 70 67 276		T Byrum	72 68 70 71 281
	J Carter	73 67 69 67 276		S Flesch	72 69 69 71 281
	B Estes	68 67 73 68 276		M Carnevale	73 68 68 72 281
	T Armour III	69 67 71 69 276		J Gallagher Jr	69 71 73 69 282
	B Glasson	68 70 69 69 276		B Tway	71 70 72 69 282
	C Dennis	71 69 67 69 276		V Veazey	73 69 70 70 282
	S Cink	67 70 69 70 276		M Wurtz	69 69 73 71 282
T20	J L Lewis	69 69 73 66 277		D Hammond	71 71 69 71 282
	F Funk	73 69 67 68 277		D Waldorf	70 69 70 73 282
	G Hallberg	71 68 68 70 277		J J Henry	71 71 74 67 283
	J Riegger	70 69 68 70 277		B Bates	73 68 74 68 283
	F Lickliter	72 68 66 71 277		K Green	68 71 73 71 283
T25	B Hughes	73 67 71 67 278		D Martin	69 72 71 71 283
	D Forsman	68 72 70 68 278		B Wadkins	73 69 69 72 283
	J Maginnes	67 67 73 71 278		C Rose	71 71 74 68 284
	R Black	68 70 68 72 278		J P Hayes	67 75 73 69 284
	M Small	67 70 68 73 278		C Smith	69 72 74 69 284
	B Fabel	71 64 70 73 278		C Barlow	67 71 72 74 284
	Larry Rinker	71 69 71 68 279		B Cheesman	72 70 74 69 285
	J Estes	72 70 68 69 279		G Gregory	69 73 72 71 285
	Lee Rinker	70 71 69 69 279		G Kraft	70 72 69 74 285
	B McCallister	67 70 71 71 279		K Jones	70 69 71 75 285
	R Zokol	69 70 69 71 279		S Jurgensen	72 70 67 76 285
	J Delsing	70 68 69 72 279		H Frazar	78 74 75 69 286
	R Allenby	70 71 72 67 280		D Pohl	72 69 74 71 286
	B Chamblee	67 72 72 69 280		B Quigley	68 70 73 75 286
	E Toledo	69 72 70 69 280		C Byrum	70 71 70 75 286
	J Huston	73 69 69 69 280		M Brisky	68 74 72 73 287
	M Weir	70 70 70 70 280		L Mize	73 68 72 74 287
	D Ogrin	72 65 70 73 280		P H Horgan III	70 71 71 75 287
	P Jordan	69 72 66 73 280		D Rummells	70 71 73 75 289
	D Frost	72 64 70 74 280			

ROUND BY ROUND LEADERBOARD

FIRST ROUND		SECOND ROUND	
D A Weibring	7 under	J Leonard	10 under
J McGovern	6 under	J Maginnes	10 under
H SUTTON	5 under	H SUTTON	9 under
B Chamblee	5 under	B Fabel	9 under
J P Hayes	5 under	L Roberts	9 under
S Cink	5 under	B Estes	9 under
L Roberts	5 under	T Armour III	8 under
B McCallister	5 under	D Frost	8 under
M Small	5 under		
J Leonard	5 under		
C Barlow	5 under		
J Maginnes	5 under		

THIRD ROUND		FINAL ROUND	
H SUTTON	14 under	H SUTTON	18 under
J Leonard	13 under	J Leonard	17 under
S Gump	13 under	J Haas	17 under
J Haas	13 under	M Reid	15 under
M Small	12 under	S Lowery	15 under
B Fabel	12 under	A Magee	15 under
		L Roberts	15 under

PUNTERS' POINTS

- Another clear triumph for the DYM system as 33/1 Hal Sutton played superb consistent golf to land his first win since 1995 and his ninth in all.

  He was in form (15th, 4th on his last two outings), he had the incentive of securing a place in the very lucrative Tour Championship, and was highly ranked in driving accuracy (T4th) and greens in regulation (4th), and as his putter worked well he held on to win.

- 16/1 Justin Leonard finished bogey – bogey to give Sutton his chance. The young Texan's course form is now an impressive 2nd – 11th – 2nd in three appearances

- 50/1 Jay Haas nearly notched his first win since he won this event in 1993 on a different course. 2nd here in 1996 this course is clearly suited to his game. He'll be worth noting here, especially in match bets, next year.

- Steve Lowery's ability to shoot very low when 'off the pace' was again shown here with a 64 in R4. His course form figures are now T4th – 14th – 22nd for a stroke average of 69.66 over the last three years.

- Poor final rounds under pressure from Ronnie Black (72), Brad Fabel (73), and Mike Small (73) can be noted for future R4 2-ball betting.

- To steal a football cliché this was a tournament of two halves for John Maginnes. He was 10 under for the first 36 holes and level par for the last 36!

- The Texans in the field had the following finishes:-
  > Justin Leonard (Dallas) T2nd
  > Tommy Armour (Dallas) T11th
  > Bob Estes (Austin) T11th
  > David Frost (Dallas) T31st
  > Blaine McCallister (Fort Stockton) T31st
- Among those to miss the cut were defending champion 40/1 Tim Herron, 50/1 DYM Kenny Perry, 66/1 chances Russ Cochran and Brent Geiberger, and 80/1 Brian Henninger.

1997 RESULT

1	50/1	Tim Herron
T2	100/1	Brent Geiberger
T2	125/1	Rick Fehr
4	100/1	Duffy Waldorf

WINNERS IN THE '90s

1990	Mark O'Meara	
1991	Blaine McCallister	
1992	Nick Price	
1993	Jay Haas	
1994	Bob Estes	
1995	Duffy Waldorf	LaCantera GC
1996	David Ogrin	LaCantera GC
1997	Tim Herron	LaCantera GC
1998	Hal Sutton	LaCantera GC

PUNTERS' GUIDE

- This hilly course is physically demanding, and it is interesting that of the eleven players who finished in the top 5 (or T5th) in the last two years no less than eight were fresh after a break of at least a week.
- Last year Justin Leonard's chance was highlighted, and he finished T2nd at 16/1. This time I suggest Bill Glasson, who was an eye-catching T11th this year after four rounds at or below 70. His player profile develops the point.

THE BUICK CHALLENGE

Date   1st – 4th October
Course   Callaway Gardens, Pine Mountain, Georgia
Par   72
Yardage   7,057
First Prize $270,000
Total Purse $1.5 million

This Buick sponsored tournament was being held for the eighth successive year at the Callaway Gardens resort course. The tournament has been weather reduced in three of the last six years.

1998 ODDS

fav	12/1	David Duval	40/1	Jeff Sluman
	14/1	Davis Love III (DC)	40/1	Bill Glasson
	20/1	Vijay Singh	50/1	Bob Tway
	25/1	Jim Furyk	50/1	Jay Haas
	25/1	Stewart Cink	50/1	Glen Day
	25/1	Justin Leonard	50/1	Chris Perry
	28/1	Hal Sutton (PWW)	50/1	Andrew Magee
	28/1	Loren Roberts	50/1	Payne Stewart
	28/1	Fred Funk	50/1	Bob Estes
	33/1	Mark Calcavecchia	66/1	Billy Mayfair*
	33/1	Steve Elkington	66/1	Billy Andrade*
	33/1	Scott Hoch	66/1	Brandel Chamblee
	40/1	Jeff Maggert		

25 players were best priced at or under 66/1.

BOOKIES AT ODDS

Winner Steve Elkington 22/1 Chandlers: 33/1 Sunderlands

1998 RESULT

1	33/1	Steve Elkington	66 70 66 65	267
		(Elkington won at the first play-off hole)		
2	28/1	Fred Funk	63 67 68 69	267
3	40/1	Bill Glasson	69 65 65 69	268
4	125/1	J L Lewis	66 69 66 68	269
5	100/1	Skip Kendall	71 70 67 63	271

T6	D Duval	66 68 70 69 273		R Fehr	68 68 72 72 280
	S Flesch	67 66 69 71 273		B Quigley	69 68 71 72 280
T8	J Maggert	69 69 69 67 274		C Strange	70 70 68 72 280
	C Perry	70 68 69 67 274		G Waite	69 69 70 72 280
	B Bates	71 69 67 67 274		G Hnatiuk	69 70 73 68 280
	H Sutton	72 66 67 69 274		C Pavin	68 71 71 71 281
	J Carter	63 71 69 71 274		O Uresti	69 70 72 70 281
	N Lancaster	70 67 66 71 274		D Sutherland	68 72 72 69 281
T14	P Stewart	70 67 71 67 275		G Hallberg	71 70 73 67 281
	D Love III	69 70 70 66 275		R Cochran	64 71 73 74 282
	T Herron	66 74 68 67 275		L Roberts	69 71 69 73 282
	L Mize	70 71 67 67 275		S McCarron	70 71 69 72 282
	K Wentworth	68 71 68 68 275		F Langham	66 72 72 72 282
	B Andrade	71 67 67 70 275		R Gamez	72 69 71 70 282
T20	B Tway	71 67 69 69 276		D Pride	71 68 73 70 282
	D Peoples	71 68 68 69 276		S Gump	70 71 72 69 282
	F Lickliter	66 71 69 70 276		C Dennis	69 70 74 69 282
	J P Hayes	68 70 67 71 276		T Byrum	65 73 75 69 282
T24	B Chamblee	67 68 73 69 277		J Sluman	71 70 74 67 282
	J Leonard	67 73 71 66 277		V Singh	69 70 70 74 283
	S Ames	68 68 70 71 277		M Brooks	70 71 70 72 283
	M Bradley	70 69 71 68 278		J McGovern	69 71 72 71 283
	B Gilder	71 67 69 71 278		M Kuchar (am)	72 67 73 71 283
	D A Weibring	68 65 71 74 278		H Frazar	69 72 72 70 283
	C Rose	70 71 68 70 279		D Pooley	71 69 71 73 284
	D Ogrin	70 67 71 71 279		M Springer	69 69 73 73 284
	B Geiberger	68 69 72 70 279		S Hoch	70 70 72 72 284
	M Small	70 69 71 69 279		M Calcavecchia	68 73 74 70 285
	M Reid	71 69 68 71 279		D Forsman	71 70 72 73 286
	B Mayfair	69 71 68 71 279		T Tolles	67 74 73 72 286
	M Brisky	72 69 67 71 279		P Tataurangi	72 69 75 71 287
	K Triplett	70 68 73 68 279		G Boros	72 68 78 72 290
	G Day	71 70 65 73 279		I Steel	73 68 81 77 299

ROUND BY ROUND LEADERBOARD

FIRST ROUND

F Funk	9 under
J Carter	9 under
R Cochran	8 under
T Byrum	7 under
T Herron	6 under
S ELKINGTON	6 under
D Duval	6 under
F Langham	6 under
F Lickliter	6 under
J L Lewis	6 under

SECOND ROUND

F Funk	14 under
D A Weibring	11 under
S Flesch	11 under
B Glasson	10 under
D Duval	10 under
J Carter	10 under
S ELKINGTON	8 under

THIRD ROUND

F Funk	18 under
B Glasson	17 under
J L Lewis	15 under
S ELKINGTON	14 under
S Flesch	14 under
J Carter	14 under
N Lancaster	14 under

FINAL ROUND

S ELKINGTON	21 under
F Funk	21 under
B Glasson	20 under
J L Lewis	19 under
S Kendall	17 under

PUNTERS' POINTS

- "I love coming here, I know how to play this course." He sure did, as the Elk caught the front-running Fred Funk over the closing holes to force a play-off, and then to win at the first extra hole.
- 33/1 Elkington, fresh from a break, was scoring his ninth US triumph after a season dogged by ill health and injury. He's certain to win many more tournaments so long as he stays fit.
- 28/1 Fred Funk got off to a flier with 63 in R1 and looked to be the all-the-way winner, on one of his favourite courses, until 'The Elk' struck. Funk is a much-underrated player who is always suited by a straight-hitter's course such as this.
- 40/1 3rd Bill Glasson is surely a player to note in 1999. He played very steadily here yet could not quite find the magic needed to win on Sunday.
- The surprise of R3 was the 3/1 3-ball win of J L Lewis over Funk and Glasson. After poor final rounds in recent tournaments 38-year-old Lewis kept his nerve to post his best-ever finish.
- Jim Carter clearly enjoys Callaway Gardens 20th in 1996, 9th in 1997 he was T8th this year after a 63 in R1. His ten rounds in the last three years have all been under par for an impressive stroke average of 68.9. Every year at least one 100/1+ outsider 'makes the frame' perhaps it will be JC in 1999.
- Among those to miss the cut were 25/1 chances Jim Furyk and Stewart Cink, 50/1 Andrew Magee and Bob Estes, and 80/1 outsiders Scott Verplank, Nolan Henke, Steve Lowery and Tom Watson.

1997 RESULT

1	16/1	Davis Love III
2	25/1	Stewart Cink
T3	100/1	Steve Lowery
T3	80/1	Hal Sutton

WINNERS IN THE '90s

1990	Kenny Knox
1991	David Peoples
1992	Gary Hallberg
1993	John Inman
1994	Steve Elkington
1995	Fred Funk
1996	Michael Bradley
1997	Davis Love III
1998	Steve Elkington

PUNTERS' GUIDE

> The tree-lined fairways and well-protected greens place a premium on accuracy so this is very much a track for the straight hitters.

> This tournament has been weather reduced in three of the last six years. This makes it particularly important for your outright seleection to have an early tee time as Funk (63 in R1) had (fifth group out) this year.

> Davis Love III will have a major chance here in 1999 if he's not suffering MLD after a US Ryder Cup victory. He won in 1997, was second in 1996, and was T14th this year as defending champion. He loves the course and knows the Bermuda greens really well.

> So too does Georgia-born Stewart Cink. 2nd in 1997, 9th in 1996, he shot a 64 in R2 here last year and should be prominent next year, especially if he has an early tee time.

> In the last six years of the 29 players in the first four (or T4th) eleven (38%) have started at or over 100/1.

THE MICHELOB CHAMPIONSHIP

Date   8th – 11th October
Course   Kingsmill, Virginia
Par   71
Yardage   6,797
First Prize $324,000
Total Purse $1.8 million

The Kingsmill course has been the venue for this tournament since 1981. Known as the Anheuser-Busch Golf Classic up to 1995, it was retitled the Michelob Championship in 1996. The course has just three par 5s, all of which are reachable. It suits the straight-hitting players.

1998 ODDS

fav	9/1	David Duval (DC)	40/1	Chris Perry
	16/1	Fred Funk	40/1	Billy Andrade
	20/1	Scott Hoch	40/1	Brad Faxon
	25/1	Tom Lehman	40/1	Payne Stewart
	25/1	Justin Leonard	50/1	Ted Tryba
	25/1	John Cook	50/1	Robert Allenby
	28/1	Hal Sutton	50/1	Bob Estes
	33/1	Lee Janzen	50/1	Skip Kendall*
	33/1	Jim Furyk	66/1	Jeff Sluman*
	33/1	Steve Jones	66/1	Billy Mayfair*
	33/1	Loren Roberts	66/1	Michael Bradley

22 players were best priced at or under 66/1.

BOOKIES AT ODDS

Winner David Duval 13/2 Chandlers: 9/1 Stanleys

1998 RESULT

1	9/1	David Duval	65 67 68 68	268
2	200/1	Phil Tataurangi	65 68 69 69	271
3	150/1	Barry Cheesman	69 68 69 66	272
T4	40/1	Payne Stewart	70 67 67 69	273
T4	100/1	Bradley Hughes	68 67 69 69	273

T6	B Mayfair	67 70 70 68 275		J Kaye	69 68 72 74 283
	J Huston	69 70 68 68 275		K Sutherland	73 68 72 70 283
	F Lickliter	66 67 70 72 275		J Furyk	70 71 72 70 283
	G Hallberg	68 67 66 74 275		D Waldorf	70 72 69 73 284
T10	J Sluman	68 72 71 66 277		B Quigley	73 69 71 71 284
	T Armour III	70 71 70 66 277		N Lancaster	71 69 73 71 284
	C Pavin	67 70 70 70 277		F Funk	73 68 73 70 284
T13	B Bates	67 70 73 68 278		L Clements	71 71 70 73 285
	J L Lewis	69 67 70 72 278		M Springer	69 71 72 73 285
	L Roberts	69 69 68 72 278		G Hnatiuk	73 65 70 77 285
	K Wentworth	67 70 69 72 278		J Morse	69 72 72 72 285
T17	B Fleisher	69 70 70 70 279		S Kendall	69 72 73 71 285
	R Allenby	69 70 70 70 279		D Peoples	68 72 77 68 285
	M Brooks	68 71 69 71 279		C Campbell	71 69 71 75 286
	S Pate	66 69 72 72 279		H Frazar	68 68 73 77 286
	J Sindelar	68 69 70 72 279		T Byrum	69 72 72 73 286
T22	K Jones	70 71 71 68 280		P Goydos	72 70 72 72 286
	S Hoch	69 69 70 72 280		L Janzen	71 70 73 72 286
	B Gilder	72 68 68 72 280		T Tolles	72 67 68 80 287
T25	J Maginnes	70 70 71 70 281		P Blackmar	69 70 72 77 288
	S Verplank	71 71 70 69 281		C Smith	70 71 75 72 288
	J Leonard	68 69 73 71 281		M Bradley	71 69 77 71 288
	R Black	70 70 70 71 281		K Triplett	67 68 74 80 289
	J D Blake	72 68 70 71 281		J Riegger	73 67 74 75 289
	S Cink	71 71 67 72 281		B Estes	69 73 74 73 289
	T Lehman	71 67 70 73 281		F Langham	71 70 76 72 289
	G Boros	69 67 71 74 281		L Wadkins	73 69 76 71 289
	V Veazey	70 68 73 71 282		S Hart	69 72 77 71 289
	L Mize	71 71 68 72 282		M Weir	67 73 74 76 290
	B Andrade	67 70 75 70 282		G Waite	69 68 78 75 290
	L Porter	70 72 71 69 282		K Fergus	73 67 72 79 291
	Larry Rinker	70 69 69 74 282		C Strange	66 74 77 74 291
	B Claar	67 68 80 67 282		G Hill	68 74 74 76 292
	R Coughlan	70 72 70 71 283		D Stockton	69 72 73 81 295
	C Perry	69 71 72 71 283		S Skinner	71 70 76 82 299

ROUND BY ROUND LEADERBOARD

FIRST ROUND

D DUVAL	7 under
P Tataurangi	7 under
C Strange	6 under
F Lickliter	6 under
S Pate	6 under

SECOND ROUND

D DUVAL	10 under
P Tataurangi	9 under
F Lickliter	9 under
S Pate	7 under
G Hallberg	7 under
B Hughes	7 under
B Claar	7 under
K Triplett	7 under

THIRD ROUND

D DUVAL	13 under
G Hallberg	12 under
P Tataurangi	11 under
F Lickliter	10 under
P Stewart	9 under
B Hughes	9 under

FINAL ROUND

D DUVAL	16 under
P Tataurangi	13 under
B Cheesman	12 under
P Stewart	11 under
B Hughes	11 under

PUNTERS' POINTS

- 9/1 Duval's superb win from the front here as defending champion was his seventh in twelve months and confirmed him as golf's Mr October. He's now won four of his last five October tournaments.

  "If this is some type of dream, I certainly don't want to wake up anytime soon." Other members of the 'wide-awake club' will be pleased they backed him to win the money list for which he's now the runaway leader.

- Phil Tataurangi played really well alongside Duval to post his best-ever finish and so retain his tour card. "I dare say he played a better round of golf than me today with all that riding on his shoulders," was Duval's fair comment.

- Barry Cheesman, too, had a card-saving final round 66 to finish clear 3rd. The finishes of Cheesman and Tataurangi should alert us to the chances of those players who need a big finish to retain their card for the following season.

- Payne Stewart shot his twelfth consecutive sub-par round on Sunday. However the guy in the plus fours hasn't won now since 1995!

- Bradley Hughes, Number 1 on the total driving stats, will be a player to note here next year. 36th last season on his first time on this course he improved by 11 shots this year to finish T4th.

- Among those missing the cut were 25/1 John Cook, 28/1 Hal Sutton, 33/1 Steve Jones and 40/1 Brad Faxon.

1997 RESULT

1	40/1	David Duval
		(Duval won at the first play-off hole)
T2	100/1	Grant Waite
T2	100/1	Duffy Waldorf
4	40/1	Fred Funk

WINNERS IN THE '90s

1990	Larry Wadkins
1991	Mike Hulbert
1992	David Peoples
1993	Jim Gallagher Jr
1994	Mark McCumber
1995	Ted Tryba
1996	Scott Hoch
1997	David Duval
1998	David Duval

PUNTERS' GUIDE

- Since this tournament was moved from July to its new spot near the end of the season of the nine players in the top 4 (or T4th) five have started at or over 100/1. This may be because of the extra incentive lesser-known players have at this late stage to retain their card.

- In 1999 it will be worth remembering that Jeff Sluman has had three successive high finishes here (T10th 1998: T11th 1997: T8th 1995) for a stroke average of 69.33.

- This year Fred Funk may have been suffering from MLD after last week's play-off defeat. In 1999 it will be worth remembering that from 1995 through to 1997 he was T8th-T3rd-4th for a stroke average of 68.5.

- It may be that course specialist Scott Hoch (T22nd 1998) is not to be followed here in future as the weather is colder than it was when he played the course so well in the July heat in 1996 when he won, and 1995 when third.

THE LAS VEGAS INVITATIONAL

Date	14th – 18th October		
Courses	Summerlin	Desert Inn	Las Vegas
Par	72	72	72
Yardage	7,243	7.200	7,164
First Prize	$360,000		
Total Purse	$2 million		

The Las Vegas is a five-round 90-hole tournament. The first three rounds follow a Pro-Am format with one round at each of the three courses. The final two rounds are held at the Summerlin course.

1998 ODDS

fav	12/1	Davis Love III	40/1	Stewart Cink
	14/1	Fred Couples	40/1	Billy Mayfair
	20/1	Phil Mickelson*	50/1	Bob Tway
	25/1	Bill Glasson (DC)	50/1	Glen Day
	25/1	Mark Calcavecchia	50/1	Billy Andrade
	25/1	Tom Lehman	50/1	Andrew Magee
	28/1	Justin Leonard	66/1	Chris Perry
	28/1	John Cook	66/1	Bob Estes
	33/1	Jim Furyk	66/1	Frank Lickliter
	33/1	Steve Jones	66/1	Bradley Hughes
	33/1	Lee Janzen	66/1	Steve Flesch
	40/1	Hal Sutton		

23 players were best priced at or under 66/1.

BOOKIES AT ODDS

Phil Mickelson 10/1 Ladbrokes, Corals: 20/1 Hills

Winner Jim Furyk 20/1 Ladbrokes: 33/1 Hills, Surrey

1998 RESULT

1	33/1	Jim Furyk	67 68 69 63 68	335
2	25/1	Mark Calcavecchia	65 71 69 65 66	336
3	80/1	Scott Verplank	67 68 69 67 67	338
4	50/1	Bob Tway	68 65 69 72 65	339
5 fav	12/1	Davis Love III	70 66 68 70 66	340

T6	P Stankowski	67 71 68 70 65 341	D Ogrin	67 66 71 76 71 351
	J Leonard	70 66 71 66 68 341	J Cook	69 69 70 71 72 351
T8	R Fehr	69 65 71 69 68 342	K Perry	72 70 69 69 71 351
	K Triplett	70 65 72 66 69 342	B Glasson	69 65 76 69 72 351
T10	K Wentworth	71 70 68 67 67 343	S McRoy	68 68 73 74 69 352
	B Chamblee	69 68 70 68 68 343	M Standly	70 69 73 70 70 352
T12	R Damron	65 68 72 72 67 344	D Barron	66 71 74 71 70 352
	T Byrum	67 70 70 70 67 344	D Hammond	68 71 71 70 72 352
	S Pate	70 72 68 66 68 344	B Bates	73 65 75 66 73 352
15	T Pernice Jr	66 75 70 66 68 345	K Sutherland	72 70 71 65 74 352
T16	S Cink	72 65 74 71 64 346	M Brooks	73 68 73 69 70 353
	D A Weibring	69 69 72 67 69 346	J D Blake	71 69 71 70 72 353
	L Porter	69 65 71 70 71 346	J Gallagher	74 69 71 68 72 354
	B May	69 65 72 67 73 346	C Beck	67 68 78 69 72 354
T20	P Azinger	66 68 79 68 66 347	T Lehman	69 72 72 68 73 354
	R Mediate	68 69 74 68 68 347	D Hart	66 72 70 73 73 354
T22	A Magee	68 71 73 72 64 348	D Pooley	67 70 74 70 73 354
	F Couples	71 70 73 66 68 348	M Carnevale	71 69 70 70 74 354
	J Sindelar	69 71 71 68 69 348	J Daly	68 70 72 67 77 354
	M Springer	71 68 71 68 70 348	D Sutherland	67 71 76 72 69 355
	B Geiberger	67 70 72 68 71 348	J L Lewis	68 74 71 71 72 356
	S Jones	68 69 72 72 68 349	T Loustalot	73 69 72 68 74 356
	K Gibson	72 65 75 66 71 349	D Barr	69 70 74 73 71 357
	P Goydos	70 69 72 67 71 349	B Henninger	66 72 75 73 71 357
	L Janzen	67 71 74 66 71 349	C Pavin	69 70 75 69 74 357
	C Stadler	68 71 72 67 71 349	R Coughlan	68 70 75 71 74 358
	C Perry	68 69 72 72 69 350	D Waldorf	66 70 76 73 73 358
	B McCallister	72 69 69 71 69 350	T Conley	68 69 75 71 75 358
	B Estes	68 70 73 68 71 350	E Toledo	68 70 71 78 72 359
	N Henke	69 67 71 69 74 350	J Kelly	71 72 70 70 77 360
	S Kendall	70 70 71 73 67 351	B Andrade	68 69 76 76 72 361
	Larry Rinker	68 72 71 73 67 351	G Waite	67 70 77 73 74 361
	B Gilder	72 68 71 72 68 351	K Jones	71 68 73 74 77 363
	R W Eaks	67 72 70 72 70 351	M Hulbert	69 70 75 73 78 365
	J Gallagher	69 69 72 70 71 351		

ROUND BY ROUND LEADERBOARD

FIRST DAY

M Calcavecchia	7 under
R Damron	7 under
D Waldorf	6 under
B Henninger	6 under
D Barron	6 under
T Pernice Jr	6 under
P Azinger	6 under
T Armour III	6 under
D Hart	6 under
J FURYK	5 under

SECOND DAY

D Ogrin	11 under
R Damron	11 under
B Tway	11 under
P Azinger	10 under
B May	10 under
L Porter	10 under
R Fehr	10 under
B Glasson	10 under
J FURYK	9 under

THIRD DAY

B Tway	14 under
D Ogrin	12 under
D Love III	12 under
J FURYK	12 under
S Verplank	12 under
R Fehr	11 under
M Calcavecchia	11 under
R Damron	11 under
L Porter	11 under

FOURTH DAY

J FURYK	21 under
M Calcavecchia	18 under
S Verplank	17 under
J Leonard	15 under
K Triplett	15 under
B May	15 under

FINAL DAY

J FURYK	25 under
M Calcavecchia	24 under
S Verplank	22 under
B Tway	21 under
D Love III	20 under

PUNTERS' POINTS

- 33/1 Jim Furyk has been the 'Mr Consistency' of US golf. However he hadn't won since early 1996. He put that right here in the tournament that brought him his first win in 1995. It was his 24th (!) top 10 finish in the last two years.

- 25/1 Mark Calcavecchia is a 90-hole tournament specialist. This was his fourth top 4 finish in his last five five-round events – that's some record.

- Stewart Cink is showing good form in the 90-hole tournaments. T6th in this year's Bob Hope he can build on his top 20 position here, especially that eye-catching 64 at Summerlin on Sunday.

- Rick Fehr has a useful record here (T8th 1998: 5th 1996: 10th 1995) and he's shot a course record 62 on the main Summerlin course. So in early 3-ball betting and as a possible long shot keep him in mind....his middle name's Elliott, too!

- Kirk Triplett has yet to win. However if he is to tiptoe into the winners enclosure from off the pace it could well be in this event (T8th 1998: 10th 1995).

- The guy in his forties who had a top 20 finish here and could be the best 100/1 outsider in 1999 can be found in his player profile.
- Among those to miss the cut 20/1 Phil Mickelson, 40/1 Billy Mayfair, 40/1 Hal Sutton, 66/1 Frank Lickliter and 80/1 outsiders Jim Carter and Michael Bradley.
- Glen Day (75), Bradley Hughes (74), Dan Forsman (73 & 72) and Fulton Allem (76 & 74) all withdrew: Jonathan Kaye was disqualified.

1997 RESULT

1	66/1	Bill Glasson
T2	125/1	David Edwards
T2	150/1	Billy Mayfair
T4	40/1	Mark Calcavecchia
T4	66/1	Duffy Waldorf

WINNERS IN THE '90s

1990	Bob Tway
1991	Andrew Magee
1992	John Cook
1993	Davis Love III
1994	Bruce Lietzke
1995	Jim Furyk
1996	Tiger Woods
1997	Bill Glasson
1998	Jim Furyk

PUNTERS' GUIDE

- This is very much a course-specialists' event. This year, for example, the first 5 included three previous winners as well as Mark Calcavecchia who had been in the top 4 in both previous years.
- Best recent records are held by:
  Jim Furyk Winner in 1998 and 1995: 22nd 1996 and 19th 1997
  Davis Love III Winner in 1993, 7th 1995, 2nd 1996, 5th 1998
  Mark Calcavecchia 2nd 1998: T4th 1997: T3rd 1996
- At this time of the year do study the Money list positions, and make a special note of any player who is around 30th as he'll have a special incentive to do well because he wants to clinch a top 30 spot, and so a place in the mega-dollar season ending Tour Championship. This year this applied to previous course winner Bob Tway who was 30th on the Money list!

THE NATIONAL CAR RENTAL CLASSIC AT WALT DISNEY

Date	22nd – 25th October	
Course	Magnolia	Palm Lake
Par	72	72
Yardage	7,190	6,957
First Prize	$360,000	
Total Purse	$2 million	

The Disney Classic is still a Pro-Am, but the format was changed this year. Instead of one pro with three amateurs for three rounds over three courses, two pros were paired with two amateurs at the Magnolia and Palm courses for the first two rounds, and the weekend played on Magnolia, the toughest of the Disney-resort courses.

1998 ODDS

fav	8/1	David Duval (DC)		50/1	Stewart Cink
	9/1	Tiger Woods		50/1	Jesper Parnevik*
	14/1	Davis Love III		50/1	John Huston*
	25/1	Payne Stewart		50/1	Glen Day
	25/1	Mark O'Meara		50/1	Loren Roberts
	33/1	Phil Mickelson		50/1	Fred Funk
	33/1	Vijay Singh		50/1	Bob Tway
	33/1	Tom Lehman		50/1	Jeff Sluman
	40/1	Jeff Maggert		50/1	Andrew Magee
	40/1	John Cook		66/1	Chris Perry
	40/1	Bill Glasson		66/1	Brad Faxon
	40/1	Scott Hoch			

23 players were best priced at or under 66/1.

BOOKIES AT ODDS

Winner DYM John Huston 25/1 Ladbrokes: 50/1 Chandlers

T4th DYM Jesper Parnevik 25/1 Ladbrokes: 50/1 Chandlers

1998 RESULT

1	50/1	John Huston	67 70 69 66	272
2	14/1	Davis Love III	73 64 65 71	273
3	100/1	Brent Geiberger	72 70 68 65	275
T4	200/1	Tom Purtzer	69 68 72 67	276
T4	150/1	Rocco Mediate	67 70 71 68	276
T4	50/1	Jesper Parnevik	66 72 69 69	276

T7	N Henke	69 70 72 66 277		B Tway	71 67 73 72 283
	T Woods	66 73 68 70 277		T Dodds	71 70 71 71 283
	F Funk	72 67 68 70 277		P Goydos	68 71 71 73 283
	D Martin	69 68 68 72 277		S Kendall	69 69 71 74 283
11	G Day	70 67 68 73 278		L Nelson	67 76 66 74 283
T12	Larry Rinker	69 75 67 68 279		D Duval	68 72 68 75 283
	P Jordan	70 72 68 69 279		B Friend	72 71 73 67 283
	V Singh	69 71 69 70 279		B McCallister	71 73 73 66 283
T15	T Tryba	72 72 67 69 280		J Haas	68 72 72 72 284
	T Lehman	72 72 66 70 280		S Flesch	70 72 71 71 284
	J L Lewis	69 72 68 71 280		S Cink	70 70 68 76 284
	T Tolles	71 70 68 71 280		D Sutherland	73 71 68 73 285
T19	D Barron	69 71 71 70 281		S McRoy	69 74 69 73 285
	B Chamblee	68 71 72 70 281		J Sluman	70 72 71 72 285
	J Cook	70 73 69 69 281		J Gallagher	71 73 70 72 286
	R Coughlan	73 68 70 70 281		B Glasson	74 69 72 71 286
	T Pernice Jr	70 70 70 71 281		L Roberts	71 70 75 70 286
	G Hnatiuk	68 72 70 71 281		C Dennis	69 71 72 75 287
	J Sindelar	71 72 70 68 281		K Triplett	71 73 70 73 287
	M Brooks	69 69 70 73 281		C Smith	71 70 73 73 287
T27	B Henninger	70 73 68 71 282		M Wiebe	70 74 71 72 287
	M Brisky	69 72 70 71 282		P Blackmar	69 72 72 75 288
	B Bates	72 71 69 70 282		M Weir	72 71 71 74 288
	R Fehr	72 69 71 70 282		D Waldorf	63 78 73 74 288
	R Damron	72 71 68 71 282		O Uresti	71 70 75 72 288
	B Quigley	72 69 71 70 282		M O'Meara	71 71 75 71 288
	E Toledo	71 73 67 71 282		F Nobilo	73 71 75 69 288
	R Gamez	70 69 73 70 282		S Lyle	71 72 70 76 289
	P H Horgan III	73 71 69 69 282		M Carnevale	72 72 70 75 289
	D Ogrin	71 70 69 72 282		J Durant	71 71 72 75 289
	B Andrade	71 69 70 72 282		T Conley	73 69 72 75 289
	J Riegger	69 69 71 73 282		B Cheesman	73 71 73 73 290
	J Carter	70 72 67 73 282		K Gibson	69 72 74 76 291
	C Rose	69 69 70 74 282		B Faxon	76 67 71 79 293
	L Mattiace	66 72 70 74 282		F Allem	71 72 74 78 295
	F Langham	70 74 71 67 282			

ROUND BY ROUND LEADERBOARD

FIRST DAY		SECOND DAY	
D Waldorf	9 under	T Purtzer	7 under
T Woods	6 under	R Mediate	7 under
J Parnevik	6 under	D Martin	7 under
L Mattiace	6 under	D Love III	7 under
J HUSTON	5 under	G Day	7 under
L Nelson	5 under	J HUSTON	7 under
R Mediate	5 under		

THIRD DAY		FINAL DAY	
D Love III	14 under	J HUSTON	16 under
D Martin	11 under	D Love III	15 under
G Day	11 under	B Geiberger	13 under
J HUSTON	10 under	T Purtzer	12 under
T Woods	9 under	R Mediate	12 under
F Funk	9 under	J Parnevik	12 under
J Parnevik	9 under		

PUNTERS' POINTS

- He'd done it before and he's done it again! Back in 1992 John Huston shot a low final round to win 'The Disney' and this year, coming from 4 shots back he did the same, shooting a 66 to win his second Disney, and his second tournament of the season.
- On the comeback trail this year he said his 1998 success has been due to "...determination. You feel like you have to prove yourself again. I think that had a lot to do with it."
- Davis Love III let a 4-shot lead go. This confirmed that, despite winning 13 tournaments, he's had a number of disappointing final rounds in 1998.
- Brent Geiberger's scoring got lower each round to enable the West Coast long-hitting 30-year-old to finish 3rd. In two seasons on tour he's now posted three top 3 finishes. A player to note!
- Tiger Woods 'failed' again, in T7th place. That gave him his seventh straight top 10 finish, and his 13th for the year.
- Tournament specialist Payne Stewart missed the cut. Surely we can expect the guy with plus fours to get back to his normal Disney form in 1999. (Winner 1983: 2nd 1996: 4th 1992 and Magnolia course record holder).
- What a triumph for the DYM system with the only two DYMs among those best priced at or under 66/1, finishing 4th at 50/1 and first at 50/1!
- Among those missing the 36-hole cut were 25/1 Payne Stewart, 33/1 Phil Mickelson, 40/1 chances Jeff Maggert and Scott Hoch, and 66/1 Chris Perry. John Daly after 76 in R1 withdrew.

1997 RESULT

1	25/1	David Duval
		(Duval won at the first extra play-off hole)
2	200/1	Dan Forsman
T3	100/1	Ted Tryba
T3	125/1	Len Mattiace
5	100/1	Paul Goydos

WINNERS IN THE '90s

1990 Tim Simpson
1991 Mark O'Meara
1992 John Huston
1993 Jeff Maggert
1994 Rich Fehr
1995 Brad Bryant
1996 Tiger Woods
1997 David Duval
1998 John Huston

PUNTERS' GUIDE

- If you fancy a real long shot well take heart.....in the last four years of the 20 players who have finished in the first 4 (or T4th) 10 have started at or over 100/1!

  With this tournament in 1999 coming at the end of a long, hard Ryder Cup season it could well produce a 100/1 winner.

- The latest result of recent winners suggests that you must select an in-form player.

  1998 John Huston 6th
  1997 David Duval Won
  1996 Tiger Woods 3rd
  1995 Brad Bryant 12th
  1994 Rich Fehr 31st
  1993 Jeff Maggert 14th

- Accuracy to the greens was the key to Huston's success. He hit 65 (of 72) greens, and hit every green in R4. So in 1999 make sure your selection is in the top 30 for greens in regulation.

- In 1999 go for a player who fulfils the following criteria:-

  > Lives in Florida
  > Is a long hitter ie. in the top 30 for Driving Distance
  > Is accurate to the greens ie. in the top 30 for Greens in Regulation.

  Long-hitting, accurate, Florida-based players (like Huston, Duval and Woods, the last three winners) are usually successful.

THE TOUR CHAMPIONSHIP

Date   29th October – 1st November
Course   East Lake Golf Club, Atlanta, Georgia
Yardage   7,108
Par   70
First Prize $720,000
Total Purse $4 million

This is the multi-dollar tournament open to the top 30 on the Money list. With no halfway cut all the players are guaranteed a large cheque.

1998 ODDS

fav	15/2	Tiger Woods	33/1	Phil Mickelson
	8/1	David Duval (DC)	40/1	Fred Funk
	12/1	Davis Love III	40/1	Lee Janzen
	18/1	Mark O'Meara	40/1	Jeff Maggert
	18/1	Jim Furyk	40/1	Scott Hoch
	20/1	Vijay Singh	40/1	Bob Tway
	22/1	Fred Couples*	40/1	Hal Sutton
	22/1	Nick Price	50/1	Billy Mayfair
	25/1	Steve Stricker	50/1	Glen Day
	25/1	Justin Leonard	50/1	Payne Stewart
	33/1	Mark Calcavecchia	50/1	Jeff Sluman
	33/1	Jim Huston (PWW)	66/1	Scott Verplank
	33/1	Tom Lehman	80/1	Andrew Magee*
	33/1	Jesper Parnevik	80/1	Tom Watson*
	33/1	John Cook	100/1	Bob Estes*

All quoted.

BOOKIES AT ODDS

Winner Hal Sutton 25/1 Hills: 40/1 general

1998 RESULT

1	40/1	**Hal Sutton**	69 67 68 70	274
		(Sutton won at the first extra hole)		
2	20/1	**Vijay Singh**	63 70 70 71	274
T3	18/1	**Jim Furyk**	67 68 69 71	275
T3	33/1	**Jesper Parnevik**	70 70 67 68	275
T5	25/1	**Steve Stricker**	69 71 71 69	280
T5	25/1	**Justin Leonard**	68 72 68 72	280
T5	66/1	**Scott Verplank**	70 70 71 69	280

T8	D Duval	75 69 69 68 281		20	T Woods	75 76 69 69 289
	D Love III	70 71 70 70 281		T21	A Magee	73 73 75 69 290
	B Tway	71 70 70 70 281			S Hoch	73 71 74 72 290
T11	J Huston	72 72 70 68 282			J Cook	73 75 71 71 290
	J Sluman	68 72 71 71 282		T24	L Janzen	77 72 71 71 291
T13	B Mayfair	66 77 71 69 283			P Stewart	69 72 76 74 291
	M O'Meara	71 70 71 71 283			F Funk	73 68 74 76 291
15	T Lehman	67 70 75 72 284			F Couples	73 67 75 76 291
16	J Maggert	73 70 71 71 285		28	B Estes	71 76 74 71 292
17	P Mickelson	73 74 69 70 286		29	M Calcavecchia	73 73 73 75 294
T18	T Watson	73 71 69 74 287		30	N Price	74 76 72 75 297
	G Day	73 70 69 75 287				

ROUND BY ROUND LEADERBOARD

FIRST ROUND
V Singh	7 under
B Mayfair	4 under
T Lehman	3 under
J Furyk	3 under
J Sluman	2 under
J Leonard	2 under
H SUTTON	1 under

SECOND ROUND
V Singh	7 under
J Furyk	5 under
H SUTTON	4 under
T Lehman	3 under
F Couples	level
S Verplank	level
S Stricker	level
J Parnevik	level
J Sluman	level
J Leonard	level

THIRD ROUND
V Singh	7 under
H SUTTON	6 under
J Furyk	6 under
J Parnevik	3 under
J Leonard	2 under
B Tway	1 over
S Stricker	1 over
D Love III	1 over
S Verplank	1 over

FINAL ROUND
H SUTTON	6 under
V Singh	6 under
J Furyk	5 under
J Parnevik	5 under
S Stricker	level
S Verplank	level
J Leonard	level

PUNTERS' POINTS

- Hal Sutton's 40/1 triumph may have come on the back of two missed cuts but he had won this year and shown up well on all leading stats (except for sand saves). So it was the sign of a very good player that his bunker play was brilliant over the back nine in R4 as he got up and down from the bunker at the last to beat Singh who had led from the start until that very hole.
- That devilish par 3 18th was the first extra hole and Sutton made birdie to win. His triumph proved once more that players on the comeback trail have that extra drive (please see Part Two).
- However in 1999 Sutton may not follow his twin triumphs of 1998 as his wife is expecting twins in February, and he plans to play less as a result.
- Jim Furyk was posting his second successive top 3 finish in this event. Also, for the second successive year he was placed in the top 4 on the Money list – 4th in 1997, he was 3rd this year.
- 66/1 Scott Verplank's fine performance (T5th) must be noted for 1999. He is surely a player on the comeback trail in 'the winner about to happen' category.
- Jesper Parnevik is another player who showed here that he must be followed in 1999. It is really only his medium-length putting that is holding him back from moving right up the world rankings.
- Tiger Woods found this narrow track did not really suit him; and Davis Love III despite knowing the course well could never get into real contention.
- Set up very much like a US Open course the form here should be referred to when that major comes around again in June 1999.
- 'You can't win a tournament on the first day, yet you sure can lose one' is a golfing truism.
  Tiger Woods (75), David Duval (75) certainly 'lost' it on day one and Vijay Singh (63) posted his only sub-par round and (in a sense) nearly won it on that Thursday.

1997 RESULT

1	20/1	David Duval
2	25/1	Jim Furyk
3	16/1	Davis Love III
T4	40/1	Mark Calcavecchia
T4	40/1	Bill Glasson

WINNERS IN THE '90s

1990	Jodie Mudd
1991	Craig Stadler
1992	Paul Azinger
1993	Jim Gallagher Jr
1994	Mark McCumber
1995	Billy Mayfair
1996	Tom Lehman
1997	David Duval
1998	Hal Sutton

PUNTERS' GUIDE

- With six play-offs in its twelve-year history perhaps the bet will be to see if a bookie anywhere will offer you odds against for extra holes in 1999.
- The two players with the most consistent top-5 form in this event over the last three years have been.
  > Jim Furyk 18/1 T3rd 1988: 25/1 2nd 1997
  > Steve Stricker 25/1 T5th 1998: 20/1 3rd 1996

THE 62ND US MASTERS

Date	9th – 12th April
Course	Augusta National, Augusta, Georgia
Par	72
Yardage	6,925
First Prize	$576,000
Total Purse	$3 million

The season's first major is the only one held on the same course each year. With generous fairways and lightning fast slopy greens the course favours precise iron play and good putting although with no rough it places little penalty on wayward driving. There was a field of 87. Loren Roberts was a non-runner who after 'a bad sneeze' broke a rib!

1998 ODDS

fav	11/2	Tiger Woods (DC)		40/1	John Daly
	11/1	Ernie Els		40/1	Nick Faldo
	18/1	Lee Westwood (PWW)		50/1	Vijay Singh
	22/1	Davis Love III		50/1	Jim Furyk
	25/1	Tom Lehman		66/1	Jesper Parnevik*
	25/1	Greg Norman		66/1	Lee Janzen
	25/1	Justin Leonard		66/1	Mark O'Meara
	25/1	Phil Mickelson		66/1	Tom Watson
	28/1	Colin Montgomerie		66/1	Stewart Cink
	28/1	Nick Price		66/1	Ian Woosnam
	33/1	J M Olazabal		80/1	John Cook
	33/1	David Duval		80/1	Brad Faxon
	40/1	Fred Couples		80/1	John Huston*
	40/1	Scott Hoch		80/1	Frank Nobilo
	40/1	Bernhard Langer		80/1	Jeff Maggert
	40/1	Mark Calcavecchia		80/1	Steve Elkington

32 players were priced at or under 80/1 compared to 39 (1997), 36 (1996) and 37 in 1995.

Prices shown were the best available on Wednesday morning.

BOOKIES AT ODDS

DYM Jesper Parnevik 33/1 Corals: 66/1 Chandler

Augusta specialist DYM John Huston 40/1 Ladbrokes: 80/1 Sunderlands

Headline selection in both the Sporting Life and Racing Post Tiger Woods was backed from a best priced 11/2 to 9/2, 4/1 and even 7/2 at City Index.

Winner Mark O'Meara was 50/1 generally with Hills's 40/1 the lowest, and Chandlers' 66/1 the top quote.

1998 RESULT

1	66/1	Mark O'Meara	74 70 68 67	279
T2	33/1	David Duval	71 68 74 67	280
T2	40/1	Fred Couples	69 70 71 70	280
4	50/1	Jim Furyk	76 70 67 68	281
5	150/1	Paul Azinger	71 72 69 70	282

T6	D Toms	75 72 72 64 283			D Frost	72 73 74 71 290
	J Nicklaus	73 72 70 68 283			B Faxon	73 74 71 72 290
T8	J Leonard	74 73 69 69 285		29	M Bradley	73 74 72 72 291
	D Clarke	76 73 67 69 285		30	S Elkington	75 75 71 71 292
	C Montgomerie	71 75 69 70 285		T31	J Parnevik	75 73 73 72 293
	T Woods	71 72 72 70 285			A Magee	74 72 74 73 293
T12	P Johansson	74 75 67 70 286		T33	P Blackmar	71 78 75 70 294
	J Haas	72 71 71 72 286			L Janzen	76 74 72 72 294
	J Olazabal	70 73 71 72 286			F Zoeller	71 74 75 74 294
	P Mickelson	74 69 69 74 286			J Daly	77 71 71 75 294
T16	M Calcavecchia	74 74 69 70 287			D Love III	74 75 67 78 294
	I Woosnam	74 71 72 70 287		38	T Kite	73 74 74 74 295
	S McCarron	73 71 72 71 287		T39	B Langer	75 73 74 74 296
	E Els	75 70 70 72 287			P Stankowski	70 80 72 74 296
	S Hoch	70 71 73 73 287		T41	C Pavin	73 77 72 75 297
T21	W Wood	74 74 70 70 288			C Stadler	79 68 73 77 297
	M Kuchar (am)	72 76 68 72 288		43	J Cook	75 73 74 76 298
T23	S Cink	74 76 69 70 289		44	L Westwood	74 76 72 78 300
	J Huston	77 71 70 71 289		45	J Kribel (am)	74 76 76 75 301
	J Maggert	72 73 72 72 289		46	G Player	77 72 78 75 302
T26	S Jones	75 70 75 70 290				

The following players missed the cut

T Watson	78 73 151		S Maruyama	74 80 154
T Herron	76 75 151		B Crenshaw	83 72 155
B Mayfair	76 75 151		D Ogrin	77 78 155
B R Brown	76 75 151		T Lehman	80 76 156
N Price	75 76 151		M Brooks	80 76 156
T Tolles	75 76 151		V Singh	76 80 156
S Lyle	74 77 151		I Garrido	85 72 157
R Floyd	74 77 151		S Simpson	79 78 157
N Faldo	72 79 151		G Hjertstedt	79 78 157
M 'Joe' Ozaki	75 77 152		C Watson (am)	79 78 157
B Tway	74 78 152		F Funk	79 78 157
L Mize	73 79 152		S Ballesteros	78 79 157
O Browne	72 80 152		T Clark	80 78 158
C Rocca	81 72 153		G Brewer	72 86 158
F Nobilo	77 76 153		T Aaron	81 79 160
B Andrade	75 78 153		K Bakst (am)	82 78 160
B Hughes	75 78 153		B Glasson	82 79 161
J Sluman	78 76 154		C Coody	79 85 164
S Appleby	77 77 154		A Palmer	79 87 166
G Norman	76 78 154		B Casper	81 86 167

ROUND BY ROUND LEADERBOARD

FIRST ROUND		SECOND ROUND	
F Couples	3 under	D Duval	5 under
P Stankowski	2 under	F Couples	5 under
S Hoch	2 under	S Hoch	3 under
J M Olazabal	2 under	P Mickelson	1 under
F Zoeller	1 under	J Haas	1 under
P Blackmar	1 under	P Azinger	1 under
C Montgomerie	1 under	T Woods	1 under
T Woods	1 under	J M Olazabal	1 under
P Azinger	1 under	M O'MEARA	level
M O'MEARA	2 over		

THIRD ROUND		FINAL ROUND	
F Couples	6 under	M O'MEARA	9 under
M O'MEARA	4 under	D Duval	8 under
P Azinger	4 under	F Couples	8 under
P Mickelson	4 under	J Furyk	7 under
J Furyk	3 under	P Azinger	6 under
D Duval	3 under		

- Thunderstorms delayed play by 90 minutes, at the start of the first day. As a result ten players had still to finish their round when darkness prevented any further play. Gusty winds of 25-30 mph made conditions very difficult on the opening day, when only one player broke seventy!

ROUND BY ROUND OUTRIGHT BETTING

AFTER FIRST DAY			AFTER SECOND ROUND		
Tiger Woods	5/2	-1	D Duval	7/2	-5
Fred Couples	12/1	-3	F Couples	5/1	-5
J M Olazabal	12/1	-2	T Woods	10/3	-1
Colin Montgomerie	14/1	-1	S Hoch	10/1	-3
Scott Hoch	16/1	-2	P Mickelson	12/1	-1
David Duval	16/1	-1 (3 holes to play)	J M Olazabal	16/1	-1
MARK O'MEARA	25/1	+2	E Els	20/1	+1
			J Haas	33/1	-1
			P Azinger	33/1	-1
			M O'MEARA	33/1	level

FINAL DAY BETTING

F Couples	15/8	-6	T2nd	E Els	16/1	-1	
P Mickelson	5/1	-4		J M Olazabal	20/1	-2	
M O'MEARA	8/1	-4	Won	S Hoch	25/1	-2	
T Woods	9/1	-1		C Montgomerie	25/1	-1	
D Duval	12/1	-3	T2nd	J Haas	40/1	-2	
J Furyk	14/1	-3		J Haas	40/1	-2	
P Azinger	16/1	-4		D Love III	40/1	Even	

PUNTERS POINTS

- Just when we thought that top class golf had become a game for the younger players here we found that experience was the key factor.
  - > 41-year-old Mark O'Meara had tiptoed through the field almost unnoticed to put himself into contention on the back nine on Sunday. His birdie-birdie finish gave him his first major win at his 57th attempt.
  - > 58-year-old Jack Nicklaus' astonishing performance in finishing T6th, the dead-heat winner on Surrey's handicap and the 5/2 4-stroke winner of his Sunday 2-ball with Ernie Els confirmed that, as Ernie said, "he is an unbelievable man – the greatest there ever was."
  - > 63-year-old Gary Player became the oldest player ever to make the cut....even if he finished plumb last.
- So the conventional wisdom that experience, especially Augusta experience, counts at Augusta returns after it was blown away by Tiger Woods 1997 triumph.

  The ability to think your way round and manage your game well is once more accepted as a key ingredient for success.
- As Steve Elkington observed, "it's not power out there on Sunday. It's experience and emotion, and he's [O'Meara] the king of that".
- Fred Couples lost the lead on the par 5 thirteenth after a hook from the tee and an iron shot into the water cost him a double-bogey seven. Back in it after an eagle on the par 5 fifteenth Fred's play-off hopes sank with O'Meara's putt on the final green.
- David Duval lost the lead with a bogey at the sixteenth and must have expected a play-off until O'Meara birdied the last. "I started three behind, I shot 67 and gave myself a chance. I should be patting myself on the back, but I'm not." He's some player!
- Jim Furyk found water on the 15th to lose his chance. Nevertheless his final round 68, and his 9 under par for the last 36 holes (equalled only by O'Meara) gave him his fourth successive top 6 major finish. He is a superb young player with iron nerves!
- The current and course form of the front five make interesting reading, with the latest figures on the right.

		Current Form	Course Form
1.	Mark O'Meara	MC.42.DNP	31.18.30
T2	Fred Couples	29.42.DNP	10.15.7
T2	David Duval	-.18.DNP	-.18.MC
4	Jim Furyk	12.8.35.DNP	-.29.29
5.	Paul Azinger	MC.MC.19	17.18.28

- 150/1 Paul Azinger had played well here over the last three years (T28th -T18th – T17th) when not fully fit. So he was an outsider with a chance. A fine wind player he played particularly well in the gusty conditions in R1.
- The massive gamble on Tiger Woods failed as the 1997 winner could never find the crisp accuracy with his irons that had set up so many birdie/eagle chances twelve months earlier. Nevertheless an out-of-form Tiger shot four par or sub-par rounds to finish T8th.....Watch for him in 1999!

- 32-year-old Scot McCarron has now played in just three US Masters finishing T10th (1996), T30th (1997), and T16th (1998).

  He has proven bottle (8th in R4 scoring in 1997) and the length to attack the par 5s – he'll be an outsider to note in 1999.
- If you are 'betting to running' it is worth remembering that any player who has played the first six holes has already played four of the five toughest holes, and he has five of the six easiest to come.

Hole No.	Par	Rank *from 1 most difficult to 18 least difficult*			
1	4	1	10	4	8
2	5	17	11	4	9
3	4	5	12	3	2
4	3	3	13	5	18
5	4	10	14	4	6
6	3	4	15	5	13
7	4	15	16	3	7
8	5	16	17	4	12
9	4	14	18	4	11

1997 RESULT

1 jt fav	16/1	Tiger Woods
2	125/1	Tom Kite
3	80/1	Tommy Tolles
4	66/1	Tom Watson
T5	100/1	Costantino Rocca
T5	66/1	Paul Stankowski

WINNERS IN THE '90s

1990	Nick Faldo
1991	Ian Woosnam
1992	Fred Couples
1993	Bernhard Langer
1994	J M Olazabal
1995	Ben Crenshaw
1996	Nick Faldo
1997	Tiger Woods
1998	Mark O'Meara

PUNTERS' GUIDE

- If you fancy an outsider for the 1999 US Masters take heart – this decade 43 players have finished in the top 4, or tied for 4th, with 20 (46%) of them priced at or over 66/1.
- Two shorter-priced players who can be expected to play well in 1999 will be
  > Justin Leonard, 6 under par for the last 36 holes in 1998 to finish T8th after he finished T7th in 1997.
  > Tiger Woods runaway 1997 winner, and T8th in 1998 when his iron play in particular was below par.

TOP AMERICAN PLAYER

1998 ODDS

fav	3/1	Tiger Woods		40/1	Lee Janzen
	14/1	Davis Love III		40/1	John Huston
	14/1	Tom Lehman		50/1	Jeff Maggert*
	14/1	Phil Mickelson		50/1	Brad Faxon
	16/1	Justin Leonard		50/1	Steve Jones
	20/1	David Duval		50/1	John Cook
	20/1	Mark Calcavecchia		66/1	Tom Kite
	20/1	John Daly		66/1	Craig Stadler
	22/1	Fred Couples		66/1	Tommy Tolles
	28/1	Scott Hoch		66/1	Jay Haas
	28/1	Jim Furyk		66/1	Andrew Magee
	33/1	Mark O'Meara		66/1	Michael Bradley
	40/1	Tom Watson		66/1	Scott McCarron
	40/1	Stewart Cink		80/1	Bar

BOOKIES AT ODDS

DYM Jeff Maggert 25/1 Hills: 50/1 Corals, Ladbrokes.

1998 RESULT

1	33/1	Mark O'Meara
T2	20/1	David Duval
T2	22/1	Fred Couples
4	28/1	Jim Furyk

1997 RESULT

1	16/1	Phil Mickelson
T2	33/1	Scott Hoch
T2	100/1	Duffy Waldorf
T4	40/1	Jeff Maggert
T4	14/1	Corey Pavin
T4	14/1	Davis Love III

PUNTERS' GUIDE

• If you expect a strong challenge from the Rest of the World and European players then it is wise to back your American fancy in this special market.

TOP NON AMERICAN PLAYER

1998 ODDS

fav	9/2	Ernie Els		20/1	Jesper Parnevik
	8/1	Lee Westwood		25/1	Ian Woosnam
	10/1	Greg Norman		33/1	Steve Elkington
	10/1	Nick Price		33/1	Frank Nobilo
	11/1	Colin Montgomerie		40/1	David Frost
	12/1	J M Olazabal		40/1	Stuart Appleby
	12/1	Bernhard Langer		50/1	P U Johansson*
	14/1	Vijay Singh		50/1	Darren Clarke

| 18/1 | Nick Faldo | 50/1 | Ignacio Garrido |
| | | 66/1 | Bar   1/4 odds 1.2.3.4. |

BOOKIES AT ODDS
DYM P U Johansson 20/1 Stanleys: 50/1 Corals DYM
Jumbo Ozaki 40/1 Corals: 100/1 Ladbrokes

1998 RESULT			**1997 RESULT**		
T1	50/1	Darren Clarke	1	40/1	Costantino Rocca
T1	11/1	Colin Montgomerie	2	18/1	Bernhard Langer
T3	50/1	P U Johansson	T3	100/1	P U Johansson
T3	12/1	J M Olazabal	T3	12/1	Steve Elkington

PUNTERS' GUIDE
• This market over the last two years has been dominated by the Europeans. With the decline of Greg Norman and the poor Augusta records of Singh and Price this market can offer the best value about the European players.
• P U Johansson, T3rd 50/1 1998 and T3rd 100/1 1997, may still be on offer at 28/1+ in 1999.

TOP EUROPEAN PLAYER

1998 ODDS
fav	4/1	Lee Westwood	
	6/1	Colin Montgomerie	
	7/1	Bernhard Langer	
	8/1	J M Olazabal	
	9/1	Nick Faldo	
	11/1	Jesper Parnevik	
	16/1	Ian Woosnam	
	25/1	Darren Clarke	
	33/1	P U Johansson*	
	33/1	Ignacio Garrido*	
	40/1	Seve Ballesteros*	
	40/1	Costantino Rocca*	
	66/1	Sandy Lyle*	
	66/1	Gabriel Hjerstedt*	1/4 odds 1.2.3.

BOOKIES AT ODDS
• Corals quoted the biggest odds about each of the last six in the betting so making each of them a DYM player.

1998 RESULT			**1997 RESULT**		
T1	25/1	Darren Clarke	1	22/1	Costantino Rocca
T1	6/1	Colin Montgomerie	2	15/2	Bernhard Langer
T3	33/1	P U Johansson	T3	5/1	J M Olazabal
T3	8/1	J M Olazabal	T3	66/1	P U Johansson

PUNTERS' GUIDE

- P U Johansson also has a fine record in this market in the US Masters – T3rd 66/1 1997, and T3rd 1998. He can be expected to go close again in 1999 although 16/1 maybe the best price then.

TOP REST OF THE WORLD PLAYER
(i.e. excluding American and European players)

1998 ODDS

fav	3/1	Ernie Els	
	6/1	Greg Norman	
	6/1	Nick Price	
	7/1	Vijay Singh	
	14/1	Steve Elkington	
	14/1	Frank Nobilo	
	16/1	David Frost	
	16/1	Stuart Appleby	
	25/1	Retief Goosen	
	28/1	Jumbo Ozaki	
	33/1	Bradley Hughes	
	33/1	Shigeki Maruyama	1/4 odds 1.2.3.

BOOKIES AT ODDS

There was remarkable uniformity in both the rank order and the odds in this 12-runner field.

1998 RESULT

1	3/1	E Els
2	16/1	D Frost
3	14/1	S Elkington
	only 3 finished!	

PUNTERS' GUIDE

- If this market is continued the player to follow, if he plays, will be David Frost who has been placed in this category in each of the last three years.

SPECIALITY BETS

- As always Corals created speciality markets.

> WINNING NATIONALITY

8/15 American   Won
10/3 European
6/1 Rest of World
11/1 Australasian (incl. Fiji)

> WINNING SCORE

279 – 9 under par – 12/1
NB 13 under par was the 9/2 favourite.

> GROUPS OF PLAYERS TO MAKE THE CUT:-

Eurostar One 10/1 (from 16/1)
Seve Ballesteros
Nick Faldo
Ignacio Garrido
J M Olazabal

Bet lost

American Express One 9/2
Fred Couples
Lee Janzen
Paul Azinger
Brad Faxon

Bet won

Eurostar Two 8/1 (from 14/1)
Darren Clarke
Colin Montgomerie
Costantino Rocca
Lee Westwood

Bet lost

American Express Two 9/4
Mark Calcavecchia
Loren Roberts (non-runner)
John Huston
John Cook

Bet won

Eurostar Three 8/1 (from 20/1)
P U Johansson
Ian Woosnam
Bernhard Langer
Sandy Lyle

Bet lost

American Express Three 4/1
John Daly
Tom Watson
Tom Lehman
Jeff Maggert

Bet lost

- Surrey once more created a handicap with the market ranging from the tournament favourite Tiger Woods off scratch to the rank outsiders with an 11½-stroke start.

With 1/4 odds the first five the result was:-

T1 Mark O'Meara (+7)
T1 Paul Azinger (+10)
T1 Jack Nicklaus (+11)
4   David Toms (+10)
5   Fred Couples (+6)

SPREAD BETTING ON THE US MASTERS

US MASTERS FINISHING POSITIONS

	City	Hills	I.G.	Lads	Sporting	Finishing Position
T Woods	14-17	15-18	13-16	13-16	13-16	T8
E Els	17-20	18-21	17-20	17-20	17-20	T16
L Westwood	20-23	22-25	19-22	21-24	21-24	44
D Love III	24-27	22-25	22-25	23-26	24-27	T33
M Calcavecchia	-	-	22-25	23-26	24-27	T16
J M Olazabal	24-27	24-27	25-28	24-27	24-27	T12
T Lehman	24-27	-	24-27	25-28	24-27	MC
P Mickelson	-	-	25-28	25-28	24-27	T12
J Leonard	25-28	25-28	24-27	25-28	25-28	T8
S Hoch	-	-	25-28	25-28	26-29	T16
F Couples	-	-	26-29	27-30	26-29	T2
D Duval	-	-	26-29	27-30	26-29	T2
J Furyk	-	-	27-30	27-30	-	4
C Montgomerie	27-30	27-30	27-30	28-31	29-32	T8
T Watson	-	-	28-31	28-31	27-30	MC
G Norman	-	-	28-31	28-31	28-31	MC
J Daly	27-30	29-32	28-31	28-31	29-32	T33
N Price	28-31	-	29-32	29-32	28-31	MC

Max. Make-up 50

A WEALTH WARNING TO SPREAD BETTORS

Sporting Index quoted Tiger Woods to beat US amateur champion Matt Kuchar by 3.6-4.4 shots on the opening day. Press comment encouraged spread backers to snap up Tiger at 4.4.

On the day Woods shot 71, Kuchar 72, the bet made-up at just 1 shot with Tiger's buyers suffering a 3.4 points loss.

Trying to buy money 'on the obvious' in spread betting is not a wise policy!

THE 98TH US OPEN

Date	18th – 21st June
Course	Olympic GC, (Lake Course), San Francisco, California
Par	70
Yardage	6,797
First Prize	$535,000
Total Purse	$3 million

The Olympic course followed the usual US Open set up with very narrow fairways, particularly severe rough and lightning-fast, undulating greens. However it provided an even tougher test than usual because (a) the greens were small, and (b) the bunkers had fluffy sand into which the ball could easily become buried.

1998 ODDS

fav	9/1	Tiger Woods	66/1	Bernhard Langer
	12/1	Colin Montgomerie	66/1	Lee Janzen
	14/1	David Duval	66/1	Vijay Singh
	16/1	Ernie Els (DC)	66/1	Nick Price*
	20/1	Tom Lehman	66/1	Stewart Cink
	20/1	Fred Couples	66/1	John Huston
	22/1	Jim Furyk	66/1	Bob Tway
	22/1	Davis Love III	80/1	Ian Woosnam
	25/1	Lee Westwood	80/1	Thomas Bjorn
	28/1	Justin Leonard	80/1	Frank Nobilo
	33/1	Phil Mickelson	80/1	Steve Stricker
	40/1	Mark O'Meara	80/1	Payne Stewart
	40/1	J M Olazabal	80/1	Brad Faxon
	40/1	Scott Hoch	80/1	Darren Clarke
	50/1	Jesper Parnevik	80/1	Nick Faldo
	50/1	Mark Calcavecchia	80/1	Jay Haas
	50/1	Jeff Maggert	80/1	Steve Jones
	50/1	Tom Watson	80/1	Stuart Appleby
	66/1	John Cook		

Thirty seven players were best priced at or under 80/1.
There were 32 in 1997, 37 in 1996 and 38 in 1995.

BOOKIES AT ODDS

Fourth placed DYM Nick Price 33/1 Sunderlands: 66/1 Chandlers

The winner Lee Janzen 40/1 Hills, Ladbrokes: 66/1 Chandlers

1998 RESULT

1	66/1	Lee Janzen	73 66 73 68	280
2	80/1	Payne Stewart	66 71 70 74	281
3	66/1	Bob Tway	68 70 73 73	284
4	66/1	Nick Price	73 68 71 73	285
T5	80/1	Steve Stricker	73 71 69 73	286
T5	20/1	Tom Lehman	68 75 68 75	286

T7	D Duval	75 68 75 69 287		S Pate	72 75 73 73 293
	L Westwood	72 74 70 71 287		B Zabriski	74 71 74 74 293
	J Maggert	69 69 75 74 287		J Durant	68 73 76 76 293
T10	J Sluman	72 74 74 68 288		J Huston	73 72 72 76 293
	P Mickelson	71 73 74 70 288		C DiMarco	71 71 74 77 293
	S Appleby	73 74 70 71 288		L Porter	72 67 76 78 293
	S Cink	73 68 73 74 288	T40	J Leonard	71 75 77 71 294
T14	P Azinger	75 72 77 65 289		S McCarron	72 73 77 72 294
	J Parnevik	69 74 76 70 289		F Nobilo	76 67 76 75 294
	M Kuchar (am)	70 69 76 74 289	T43	D Clarke	74 72 77 72 295
	J Furyk	74 73 68 74 289		T Kite	70 75 76 74 295
T18	C Montgomerie	70 74 77 69 290		J Acosta Jr	73 72 76 74 295
	L Roberts	71 76 71 72 290		J Sindelar	71 75 75 74 295
	T Woods	74 72 71 73 290		O Browne	73 70 77 75 295
	F Lickliter	73 71 72 74 290		J Nicklaus	73 74 73 75 295
	J M Olazabal	68 77 71 74 290	T49	E Els	75 70 75 76 296
T23	M Casey	74 71 74 72 291		M Reid	76 70 73 77 296
	G Day	73 72 71 75 291		S Verplank	74 72 73 77 296
	D A Weibring	72 72 75 73 292		B Faxon	73 68 76 79 296
	P U Johansson	71 75 73 73 292	T53	J Johnson	74 73 79 71 297
	E Romero	72 70 76 74 292		F Couples	72 75 79 71 297
	V Singh	73 72 73 74 292		T Herron	75 72 77 73 297
	C Perry	74 71 72 75 292		J Daly	69 75 75 78 297
	T Bjorn	72 75 70 75 292	57	M Brooks	75 71 76 76 298
	M Carnevale	67 73 74 78 292	58	S Simpson	72 71 78 79 300
T32	M O'Meara	70 76 78 69 293	59	R Walcher	77 70 77 79 303
	P Harrington	73 72 76 72 293	60	T Sipula	75 71 78 81 305

The following players missed the cut

The cut was made at 147 – 7 over par. 60 players qualified.

D Gilchrist	74 74 148		T Straub	74 78 152
C Pavin	76 72 148		T Sutter	79 73 152
B Andrade	74 74 148		K Triplett	73 79 152
P Simpson (am)	76 72 148		R Deruntz	75 77 152
J Haas	76 72 148		B Chamblee	76 77 153
G Fieger	76 72 148		B Langer	75 78 153
B Geiberger	71 77 148		K Sutherland	77 76 153
G Waite	77 71 148		M Brisky	74 79 153
L Patrick	72 76 148		G Willis	83 70 153
A Magee	70 78 148		J Gore	77 76 153
H Irwin	80 68 148		D Love III	78 75 153
T Watson	73 75 148		P Jordan	81 72 153
J Cook	75 73 148		M Small	76 77 153
R Goosen	74 74 148		J Allen	76 78 154
B Fabel	75 73 148		I Garrido	76 78 154
O Uresti	78 71 149		J Estes	77 77 154
D Martin	74 75 149		R Karlsson	78 76 154
S Jones	72 77 149		S Bertsch	77 77 154
N Faldo	77 72 149		P Parker	75 79 154
B Baird	75 74 149		M Lonardi	76 78 154
E Fryatt	73 76 149		C Rocca	71 83 154
D Eger (am)	78 71 149		P Moss	76 78 154
S Hoch	74 75 149		C Strange	77 78 155
P Stankowski	76 73 149		R Palmer (am)	82 73 155
Jumbo Ozaki	78 71 149		C Beck	78 77 155
G Hallberg	77 72 149		T Oh	74 81 155
K Wentworth	76 73 149		W Weston	79 76 155
C Kaufman	77 72 149		R Gehr	73 82 155
D Kirkpatrick	78 72 150		R Todd	80 76 156
T Dodds	74 76 150		G Boros	77 79 156
S Elkington	77 73 150		C Tidland	76 80 156
D Ogrin	70 80 150		G March	76 81 157
C Chernock	73 77 150		M Burke Jr	81 76 157
M Wilson	74 76 150		J Kribel (am)	83 75 158
W Wood	74 76 150		J Thorsen	77 81 158
C Rose	75 75 150		B Wetterich	78 80 158
S Randolph	80 70 150		K Peyreferry	80 79 159
J Green	76 74 150		G Larson	80 79 159
M Calcavecchia	74 76 150		B Crenshaw	82 78 160
P Tataurangi	77 73 150		H Twitty	79 81 160
G Clough	78 73 151		A Morin	80 82 162
D Pooley	74 77 151		J Johnston	84 78 162
I Woosnam	72 79 151		R Rangel	82 80 162
F Zoeller	75 76 151		J McMillian	82 81 163
D Mast	76 76 152		T Anderson	84 80 164
G Marsh	75 77 152		A Stills	85 81 166
V Taylor (am)	76 76 152		R Ames	86 81 167

Withdrawn: T Tolles (bad back)
D Hart (wrist injury)

ROUND BY ROUND LEADERBOARD

FIRST ROUND		SECOND ROUND	
P Stewart	4 under	P Stewart	3 under
M Carnevale	3 under	J Maggert	2 under
J Durant	2 under	B Tway	2 under
T Lehman	2 under	M Kuchar	1 under
J M Olazabal	2 under	L Porter	1 under
B Tway	1 under	L JANZEN	1 under
J Maggert	1 under	M Carnevale	level
J Daly	1 under		
J Parnevik	1 under		
L JANZEN	3 over		

THIRD ROUND		FINAL ROUND	
P Stewart	3 under	L JANZEN	level
T Lehman	1 over	P Stewart	1 over
B Tway	1 over	B Tway	4 over
N Price	2 over	N Price	5 over
L JANZEN	2 over	S Stricker	6 over
S Stricker	3 over	T Lehman	6 over
J Maggert	3 over		

- In R1 9 players broke par
- In R2 9 players broke par
- In R3 3 players broke par
- In R4 6 players broke par

CORALS' FINAL DAY BETTING WAS

With P Stewart			Without P Stewart		
4/7	P Stewart	3 under	11/4	T Lehman	1 over
5/1	T Lehman	1 over	5/1	B Tway	1 over
8/1	B Tway	1 over	11/2	N Price	2 over
11/1	N Price	2 over	13/2	L Janzen	2 over
12/1	L Janzen	2 over	9/1	J Maggert	3 over
			12/1	S Stricker	3 over

Result			Result		
1	12/1	L Janzen	1	13/2	L Janzen
2	4/7	P Stewart	2	5/1	B Tway
3	8/1	B Tway	3	11/2	N Price

1/5 odds 1,2,3   1/4 odds 1,2,3

The winner, Lee Janzen's odds through the tournament were:

Pretournament	After R1	After R2	After R3
66/1	80/1	8/1	12/1

PUNTERS' POINTS

- 16/1 Lee Janzen won his second US Open after a brilliant final round 68. 7 shots behind Payne Stewart after two holes in R4 he clawed his way back with a fine exhibition of iron play and putting. Ultimately it was Janzen's nerve and accuracy (he topped the Greens In Regulation stats) that won the day.

  After playing poorly when in the lead in the final rounds of both the Players Championship and the Shell Houston Open here he showed he prefers playing 'catch-up' rather than 'front running'.

- Through the first three days 80/1 Payne Stewart appeared to have every piece of luck possible. Although he had 'front run' to his 1991 Open success he found this time that the strain of 'front running' was too much. He is the top player on tour currently for the number of consecutive cuts made – he's now made the last twenty.

- Colin Montgomerie had a troubled tournament as he was heckled by the galleries. If only he could be seen to inject some humour into his responses he could perhaps turn the galleries against the heckler rather than against himself.

- Monty was Top Euro in each of the last two years. However, this time Lee Westwood took the honour at 9/2. Joint Number 1 for Driving Accuracy in the tournament 'the Worksop Wonder' finished a very creditable T7th.

- Tiger Woods's aggression cost him dearly on the greens where he twice four putted. This tournament, with its emphasis on accuracy rather than power and patience rather than aggression, is not designed for this Tiger. However his suspect back did not give him any problems.

- Fourth-placed 66/1 Nick Price, second in Greens In Regulation, proved here that if he can regain his putting touch he will once more win golf tournaments.

- The amateur Matt Kuchar, after a fine effort in the US Masters, followed up here with another first-class performance to finish T14th. Fresh faced with an apparently permanent smile, this guy seems to have a Westwood-like temperament to match his undoubted skill.

- Tom Lehman's US Open record shows incredible consistency – T5th 1998: 3rd 1997: T2nd 1996: 3rd 1995. However his apparent inability to vary from his stock shot, a draw, is a handicap and so is his putting touch under pressure. However selling his finishing position on the spreads has been a guaranteed winner in recent years.

1997 RESULT

1	25/1	Ernie Els
2	20/1	Colin Montgomerie
3	25/1	Tom Lehman
4	150/1	Jeff Maggert
T5	125/1	Bob Tway
T5	200/1	Olin Browne
T5	66/1	Jim Furyk
T5	66/1	Tommy Tolles
T5	125/1	Jay Haas

WINNERS IN THE '90s

1990 Hale Irwin
1991 Payne Stewart
1992 Tom Kite
1993 Lee Janzen
1994 Ernie Els
1995 Corey Pavin
1996 Steve Jones
1997 Ernie Els
1998 Lee Janzen

PUNTERS' GUIDE

- The US Open may move venue each year yet the course set up is always the same.
  - > Severe penal rough off the fairways and around the greens
  - > Lightning fast slopy greens
  - > Narrow fairways
- So a player must have
  - > Patience and a cool temperament.
  - > A good putting touch.
  - > The accuracy to regularly hit the fairways and greens.
- The US stats are of great help here. For example with our Masters' degree in Hindsight it's worth noting that Lee Janzen was T10th for Greens In Regulation and in the top 20 (18th) for putting so the stats highlighted his chance.
- Some players find the US Open unsuited to their particular talents. Brad Faxon, for example, has only once posted a US Open top 50 finish, and Tiger Woods is never value at 6/1 – 9/1 on a course with just two par 5s that demands patience rather than aggression.
- Payne Stewart's final-round defeat maintained the poor record of R3 leaders. In the last 34 US Opens only twelve third-round leaders have gone on to win. So there is a 64.71% probability, equivalent to odds of (approx) 8/15 on, that the leader on Sunday morning will not win. So the advice once more is to go for a player from 'off the pace' on that final day.

TOP AMERICAN PLAYER

1998 ODDS

13/2	Tiger Woods	28/1	Mark O'Meara*
10/1	David Duval	33/1	Jeff Maggert
14/1	Fred Couples	33/1	Lee Janzen
14/1	Tom Lehman	33/1	Bob Tway
14/1	Jim Furyk	33/1	Mark Calcavecchia
16/1	Davis Love III	40/1	John Cook
20/1	Justin Leonard	40/1	Stewart Cink
22/1	Phil Mickelson	40/1	Payne Stewart
22/1	Scott Hoch	40/1	Steve Stricker
28/1	Tom Watson	50/1	Bar

BOOKIES AT ODDS

DYM Mark O'Meara 14/1 Sunderlands: 28/1 Ladbrokes

1998 RESULT

1	33/1	Lee Janzen
2	40/1	Payne Stewart
3	33/1	Bob Tway
T4	40/1	Steve Stricker
T4	14/1	Tom Lehman

PUNTERS' GUIDE

- This market is worth playing IF you expect Rest of the World and European players to be in contention because a bet on the top American may be a winner when the player does not win the tournament eg. Lehman was 3rd in the 1997 US Open yet was the 14/1 winner in the top American market.
- Bob Tway has been T3rd 66/1 and 3rd 33/1 in the last two years. His straight hitting is well suited to this event.

1997 RESULT

1	14/1	Tom Lehman
2	80/1	Jeff Maggert
T3	66/1	Bob Tway
T3	40/1	Jim Furyk
T3	40/1	Tommy Tolles
T3	80/1	Jay Haas
T3	125/1	Olin Browne

TOP EUROPEAN PLAYER

1998 ODDS

11/4	Colin Montgomerie	16/1	Ian Woosnam
9/2	Lee Westwood	33/1	P U Johansson
8/1	J M Olazabal	40/1	Padraig Harrington
10/1	Jesper Parnevik	50/1	Robert Karlsson
12/1	Bernhard Langer	50/1	Costantino Rocca*
16/1	Thomas Bjorn	66/1	Ignacio Garrido
16/1	Nick Faldo	150/1	Ed Fryatt
16/1	Darren Clarke		

BOOKIES AT ODDS

Colin Montgomerie 15/8 Chandlers: 11/4 Tote
DYM Costantino Rocca 18/1 Chandlers: 50/1 Ladbrokes

1998 RESULT

1	9/2	Lee Westwood
2	10/1	Jesper Parnevik
T3	8/1	J M Olazabal
T3 fav	11/4	Colin Montgomerie

PUNTERS' GUIDE

- Westwood, Monty and Olazabal have finished in the top 3 in each of the last two years.
- Westwood will surely by vying with Monty for favouritism in 1999.

1997 RESULT

1	7/2	Colin Montgomerie
2	8/1	J M Olazabal
3	16/1	Lee Westwood

TOP NON AMERICAN PLAYER

1998 ODDS

fav	4/1	Colin Montgomerie	28/1	Frank Nobilo
	11/2	Ernie Els	33/1	Vijay Singh*
	7/1	Lee Westwood	33/1	Thomas Bjorn
	14/1	J M Olazabal	33/1	Stuart Appleby*
	14/1	Nick Price	33/1	Darren Clarke
	16/1	Jesper Parnevik	40/1	Steve Elkington*
	20/1	Nick Faldo	50/1	Retief Goosen
	20/1	Bernhard Langer	50/1	Trevor Dodds
	28/1	Ian Woosnam	50/1	P U Johansson

BOOKIES AT ODDS

DYM Vijay Singh 12/1 Stanleys: 33/1 Ladbrokes

Third placed DYM Stuart Appleby 16/1 Stanleys: 33/1 Ladbrokes

DYM Steve Elkington 20/1 Corals, Stanleys: 40/1 Ladbrokes

1998 RESULT

1	14/1	Nick Price
2	7/1	Lee Westwood
3	33/1	Stuart Appleby
4	16/1	Jesper Parnevik

PUNTERS' GUIDE

- It makes good sense to play this market if you expect the Americans to do well yet fancy a ROW player to put up a good performance.

   This year, for example, Stuart Appleby was T10th in the tournament yet was a nice 33/1 each-way winning bet in this market.

SPECIALITY BETS

ON THE HANDICAP

Surrey's handicap: 66/1 the field.

Players were rated from Tiger Woods on scratch to outsiders at +9 who were 125/1 plus in the outright betting.

Paying one quarter the odds the first five the result was

T1	L Janzen	(+6½)
T1	P Stewart	(+7½)
3	B Tway	(+8)
T4	N Price	(+6)
T4	S Stricker	(+7)

The 1997 Surrey handicap result was

1	J Maggert	(+9)
T2	E Els	(+3½)

T2	C Montgomerie	(+4½)
T4	B Tway	(+9)
T4	O Browne	(+9)
T4	J Haas	(+9)

CORALS' HALFWAY CUT SPECIALS

Corals created six groups of players who all had to make the cut for the bet to win!

Eurostar One 7/1 C Rocca, I Woosnam, C Montgomerie, N Faldo

Result BET LOST

Eurostar Two 6/1 P Harrington, B Langer, L Westwood, T Bjorn

Result BET LOST

Eurostar Three 12/1 P U Johansson, R Karlsson, J M Olazabal, D Clarke

Result BET LOST

American Express One 4/1 M Calcavecchia, M Brooks, S Cink, T Lehman

Result BET LOST

American Express Two 5/1 J Daly, T Herron, J Cook, J Furyk

Result BET LOST

American Express Three 5/1 C Pavin, J Huston, B Faxon, D Love III

Result BET LOST

Final Score Jon Wright, Corals' senior compiler, 6 Punters 0!!

THE 127TH BRITISH OPEN

Date	16th – 19th July
Course	Royal Birkdale, Southport, Lancs
Par	70
Yardage	7,018
First Prize	£300,000
Total Purse	£1.75 million

The British Open returned to Royal Birkdale where it was last held in 1991 when Ian Baker Finch was the 50/1 winner.

Each year this, the most prestigious of all the majors, is held on a different links course. It therefore provides a very different test compared to the US Majors.

1998 ODDS

fav	12/1	Tiger Woods		50/1	Lee Janzen
	14/1	Lee Westwood (PWW)		50/1	Ian Woosnam
	16/1	Colin Montgomerie		50/1	Scott Hoch
	16/1	Ernie Els		66/1	Darren Clarke*
	25/1	David Duval		66/1	Vijay Singh*
	25/1	Fred Couples		66/1	Mark Calcavecchia
	25/1	Tom Lehman		66/1	Payne Stewart
	28/1	Jim Furyk		66/1	Tom Watson
	33/1	Justin Leonard (DC)		66/1	Jeff Maggert
	33/1	J M Olazabal		66/1	Thomas Bjorn*
	33/1	Davis Love III		80/1	Frank Nobilo
	40/1	Nick Price		80/1	Brad Faxon
	40/1	Phil Mickelson		80/1	Steve Jones (PWW)
	40/1	Mark O'Meara*		80/1	Robert Allenby
	40/1	Jesper Parnevik*		80/1	Bernhard Langer*

25 players were best priced at 66/1 or less. (29 in 1997 and 30 in 1996).
30 players were best priced at 80/1 or less. (34 in 1997 and 35 in 1996).

BOOKIES AT ODDS

DYM T4th Jesper Parnevik 25/1 Stanleys: 50/1 Chandlers

Winner DYM Mark O'Meara 20/1 Bernstein: 40/1 Corals, Hills, Stan James, Sunderlands

1998 RESULT

1	40/1	Mark O'Meara	72 68 72 68	280

(O'Meara won the 4-hole play-off by 2 shots)

2	250/1	Brian Watts	68 69 73 70	280
3 jt fav	12/1	Tiger Woods	65 73 77 66	281
T4	200/1	Raymond Russell	68 73 75 66	282
T4	500/1	Justin Rose (am)	72 66 75 69	282
T4	50/1	Jesper Parnevik	68 72 72 70	282
T4	28/1	Jim Furyk	70 70 72 70	282

8	D Love III	67 73 77 68 285		R Davis	76 70 78 71 295
T9	C Rocca	72 74 70 70 286		D Frost	72 73 78 72 295
	T Bjorn	68 71 76 71 286		D Carter	71 75 76 73 295
T11	D Duval	70 71 75 71 287		P Stewart	71 71 78 75 295
	B Faxon	67 74 74 72 287		N Faldo	72 73 75 75 295
	J Huston	65 77 73 72 287		A Coltart	68 77 75 75 295
14	G Brand Jnr	71 70 76 71 288		K Tomori	75 71 70 79 295
T15	J M Olazabal	73 72 75 69 289	T52	B Jobe	70 73 82 71 296
	P Baker	69 72 77 71 289		L Mize	70 75 79 72 296
	D Smyth	74 69 75 71 289		S Stricker	70 72 80 74 296
	G Turner	68 75 75 71 289		B Mayfair	72 73 77 74 296
T19	R Allenby	67 76 78 69 290		F Minoza	69 75 76 76 296
	C Strange	73 73 74 70 290	T57	J Leonard	73 73 82 69 297
	V Singh	67 74 78 71 290		T Dodds	73 71 81 72 297
	M James	71 74 74 71 290		I Garrido	71 74 80 72 297
	S Lyle	71 72 75 72 290		S Jones	73 72 79 73 297
T24	L Janzen	72 69 80 70 291		G Chalmers	71 75 77 74 297
	S Torrance	69 77 75 70 291		I Woosnam	72 74 76 75 297
	P O'Malley	71 71 78 71 291		E Romero	71 70 79 77 297
	S Ames	68 72 79 72 291	T64	L Westwood	71 71 78 78 298
	B Estes	72 70 76 73 291		C Franco	71 73 76 78 298
T29	S Dunlap	72 69 80 71 292	T66	S Cink	71 73 83 72 299
	N Price	66 72 82 72 292		M Campbell	73 73 80 73 299
	S Garcia (am)	69 75 76 72 292		D De Vooght (am)	70 76 80 73 299
	E Els	72 74 74 72 292		M Long	70 74 78 77 299
	L Roberts	66 76 76 74 292		M Brooks	71 73 75 80 299
	S Maruyama	70 73 75 74 292		F Couples	66 74 78 81 299
T35	S Struver	75 70 80 68 293	72	A Clapp	72 74 81 73 300
	S Luna	70 72 80 71 293	73	G Evans	69 74 84 74 301
	M Calcavecchia	69 77 73 74 293	74	B May	70 73 85 75 303
	J Haeggman	71 74 78 71 294	75	A McLardy	72 74 80 78 304
	S Tinning	69 76 77 72 294	76	F Jacobson	67 78 81 79 305
	P Sjoland	72 72 77 73 294	77	K Hosokawa	72 73 81 80 306
	Joe Ozaki	72 73 76 73 294	78	R Giles	72 74 83 78 307
	T Kite	72 69 79 74 294	79	P Mickelson	71 74 85 78 308
	P Walton	68 76 74 76 294	80	A Oldcorn	75 71 84 79 309
T44	D Howell	68 77 79 71 295	81	D Hart	73 72 85 80 310

The following players missed the cut

T Levet	72 75 147		M Kuchar (am)	75 75 150
B Davis	72 75 147		S Hoch	73 77 150
J Maggert	73 74 147		C Pavin	74 76 150
P Price	72 75 147		P U Johansson	74 76 150
C Parry	73 74 147		K Ju Choi	70 80 150
B Lane	72 75 147		L Jones	73 77 150
K Fukabori	70 77 147		S Kendall	74 77 151
C Montgomerie	73 74 147		S Leaney	75 76 151
B Tway	68 79 147		J Daly	73 78 151
T Johnstone	73 74 147		G Player	77 74 151
P McGinley	72 75 147		M McGuire	74 77 151
C Suneson	77 70 147		M McNulty	73 78 151
P Mitchell	76 72 148		H Clark	73 79 152
J Durant	74 74 148		S Allan	72 80 152
Y Mizumaki	71 77 148		R Drummond	74 78 152
G Day	75 73 148		S Young	74 78 152
P Senior	71 77 148		F Henge	75 77 152
S McCarthy (am)	73 75 148		F Nobilo	76 77 153
S Ballesteros	73 75 148		A Magee	75 78 153
T Taniguchi	71 77 148		R Claydon	74 79 153
D Clarke	73 75 148		M Hallberg	77 77 154
B Langer	74 75 149		D Lee	76 78 154
D Cooper	72 77 149		S Armstrong	76 78 154
P Lawrie	73 76 149		R Karlsson	72 82 154
R Bland	71 78 149		B Crenshaw	76 78 154
T Watson	73 76 149		G Spring	74 80 154
J P Hayes	70 79 149		S Alker	73 81 154
P Azinger	76 73 149		M Litton	75 80 155
P Harrington	73 76 149		T Suzuki	78 77 155
G Brown	74 75 149		G Orr	78 78 156
G Dodd	70 79 149		B Dredge	78 78 156
R Goosen	74 76 150		S Appleby	76 80 156
T Lehman	71 79 150		G Hutcheon	73 83 156
D Shacklady	76 74 150		S Henderson	77 80 157
J Lovell	72 78 150		P Hedblom	76 82 158
J L Guepy	74 76 150		J Remesy	77 82 159

The 36-hole cut was made at 146 – 6 over par – 81 players qualified.

- The most notable cut missers were 16/1 Colin Montgomerie, 25/1 Tom Lehman, 50/1 Scott Hoch, 66/1 Darren Clarke, 66/1 Jeff Maggert and 80/1 outsiders Bernhard Langer and Frank Nobilo
- 125/1 Steve Elkington withdrew after 75 in R1. 100/1 M A Jimenez was disqualified after scoring 151 in the first 2 rounds.

ROUND BY ROUND LEADERBOARD

FIRST ROUND

T Woods	5 under
J Huston	5 under
F Couples	4 under
N Price	4 under
L Roberts	4 under
F Jacobsen	3 under
B Faxon	3 under
D Love III	3 under
V Singh	3 under
R Allenby	3 under
M O'MEARA	2 over

SECOND ROUND

B Watts	3 under
J Rose	2 under
T Woods	2 under
N Price	2 under
T Bjorn	1 under
D Love III	level
F Couples	level
M O'MEARA	level
S Ames	level
J Furyk	level
J Parnevik	level

THIRD ROUND

B Watts	level
J Parnevik	2 over
J Furyk	2 over
M O'MEARA	2 over
J Rose	3 over
J Huston	5 over
B Faxon	5 over
T Bjorn	5 over
T Woods	5 over

FINAL ROUND

M O'MEARA	level
B Watts	level
T Woods	1 over
R Russell	2 over
J Rose	2 over
J Parnevik	2 over
J Furyk	2 over

The weather was

Thursday Warm and sunny with little wind
Friday Very wet in the morning. Dry with strong winds in the afternoon. Play suspended because of the wind at 5.27 p.m. All rounds were completed later.
Saturday With very strong winds conditions were extremely testing all day.
Sunday Early rain. Gentle breeze compared to Saturday.

PUNTERS' POINTS

• What a superb tournament! A blooming Rose, a Tiger on the prowl, O'Meara making his Mark with an 'unknown' American from Japan....Watts going on? Yes it really was rivetting stuff.

• In the end the best player did win as 40/1 O'Meara used his strategic ability, course knowledge and a huge slice of luck (at the sixth in R3 when he 'lost' his ball in a bush yet was allowed a free drop) to beat Brian Watts comfortably in a play-off.

• Brian Watts had shown a lovely rhythm and real composure throughout. His sand save on the final hole to force a play-off was well merited. Unable to secure a USPGA tour card he has been playing very well in Japan where in eight tournaments he'd had four top 3 finishes including a win.

• O'Meara showed that an experienced player high on confidence can break the apparent rule that says that in modern times it is very unlikely that a player can win two majors in the same year.

- Mark O'Meara's odds during the tournament were

before R1	after R1	after R2	after R3	before P/off
40/1	100/1	14/1	4/1	4/6

- When will Tiger learn the art of lag putting? His aggression on the greens cost him the Championship as he regularly hit his putts 5 – 6 feet past and then missed the return putt, especially on the final day. As I said in last year's volume, I wonder whether his caddie Fluff could be more influential in tempering the young man's more reckless excesses.

- Nevertheless Woods highlighted a key difference between himself and the ultra-consistent Jim Furyk. When needed Tiger has that electric ability 'to make things happen' as he clearly relishes a challenge whereas Furyk seems unable to 'go up a gear' in that final lap. Indeed Furyk's putting over the back nine looked edgy.

- If he can temper his aggression on the greens Tiger will surely be a factor in this tournament in future years as he is clearly learning links golf quickly, and what's more relishing its challenge. However he must try more to think his way out of trouble, rather than hit his way, out in future.

- Of course, the headlines were all for Justin Rose who played superbly with a real charm and a smile that was a joy to watch. His chip in on the 72nd hole was a fitting reward for the 17-year-old.

  However let's be clear....the challenge now will be to handle the absurdly-excessive media hype. He'll do very well to secure his card for next season and I wouldn't be surprised to see him miss the cut in this week's Dutch Open now he's turned professional.

- Spare a thought for Jesper Parnevik. The 33-year-old Swede has now played in six British Opens and has been 2nd twice and 4th once. So a top 4 strike rate of 50% proves that his game is well suited to links golf.

- 16/1 Colin Montgomerie showed once more how unsuited his game, and indeed his temperament, is to links golf.

  His full record for a player of his ability is truly poor – in ten starts he has missed six cuts with only one top 20 finish, in 1994 when he finished 8th. If the winds blow at Carnoustie in 1999 he can be opposed again in spread betting.

- Shigeki Maruyama was the Japanese player noted in last year's volume. He is a superb putter and a fine links golfer. This year he rewarded punters with a nice 3/1 (!) 3-ball success in R1, and he was the top Japanese player at 9/4. Keep him on the right side again in 1999!

- 14/1 Lee Westwood stood to win a $1 million bonus if he was to win the British Open on the back of his splendid Loch Lomond triumph. However, he was never remotely in contention. He may have a magnificent temperament and a superb all-round game, however he is human and looked rather jaded. Carnoustie in 1999 will probably be a very different story.

- The stroke average in the wind–blown R3 was over 77 so we will do well to remember the players who then went round in 74 or less. They were:-

  > 70 C Rocca, K Tomori
  > 72 M O'Meara, J Furyk, J Parnevik
  > 73 B Watts, J Huston, M Calcavecchia

> 74 C Strange, M James, B Faxon, P Walton, E Els
- The value of the DYM system was illustrated here once more as the winner 40/1 Mark O'Meara and the T4th 40/1 Jesper Parnevik were the only DYMs best priced at or under 50/1.

1997 RESULT

1	50/1	Justin Leonard
T2	50/1	Jesper Parnevik
T2	66/1	Darren Clarke
4	66/1	Jim Furyk
T5	150/1	Stephen Ames
T5	100/1	Padraig Harrington

1996 RESULT

1	40/1	Tom Lehman
T2	16/1	Ernie Els
T2	110/1	Mark McCumber
4 fav	12/1	Nick Faldo
T5	80/1	Jeff Maggert
T5	66/1	Mark Brooks

WINNERS IN THE '90s

1990	Nick Faldo
1991	Ian Baker-Finch
1992	Nick Faldo
1993	Greg Norman
1994	Nick Price
1995	John Daly
1996	Tom Lehman
1997	Justin Leonard
1998	Mark O'Meara

PUNTERS' GUIDE

- The usual pattern of the winners in the nineties was broken by Mark O'Meara.
  > He was the first player over 40 to win this decade.
  > He was successful on the back of form figures of 3-32-MC. So he became only the second player this decade to win without a top 10, or top 20, finish in his last tournament.
- When Carnoustie, the 1999 venue, was last used on the European tour for the 1996 Scottish Open (please see Elliott's Golf Form 1997 p. 123+) Lee Westwood played superbly to finish T4th playing particularly well in the wind especially on the final day. Expect 'the Worksop Wonder' to be high on the Carnoustie leaderboards in the 1999 British Open.

TOP AMERICAN PLAYER

1998 ODDS

fav	6/1	Tiger Woods	33/1	Payne Stewart
	9/1	David Duval	33/1	Jeff Maggert
	12/1	Fred Couples	33/1	Scott Hoch
	14/1	Jim Furyk	33/1	Lee Janzen*
	14/1	Tom Lehman	40/1	Stewart Cink*
	16/1	Justin Leonard	40/1	Steve Stricker*
	20/1	Davis Love III	40/1	Steve Jones
	22/1	Mark O'Meara	40/1	Brad Faxon
	22/1	Phil Mickelson	40/1	Bob Tway
	33/1	Tom Watson	50/1	John Huston
	33/1	Mark Calcavecchia	80/1	Bar

BOOKIES AT ODDS

DYM Stewart Cink 20/1 Ladbrokes: 40/1 Chandlers
DYM Steve Stricker 20/1 Ladbrokes: 40/1 Hills

1998 RESULT

1	22/1	Mark O'Meara
2	150/1	Brian Watts
3	6/1	Tiger Woods
4	14/1	Jim Furyk

PUNTERS' POINTS

- Jim Furyk 4th 14/1 1998, 2nd 20/1 1997 has the best recent record in this submarket.

1997 RESULT

1	25/1	Justin Leonard
2	20/1	Jim Furyk
3	22/1	Fred Couples
T4	66/1	Tom Kite
T4	50/1	Mark Calcavecchia
T4	40/1	Tom Watson

1996 RESULT

1	20/1	Tom Lehman
2	50/1	Mark McCumber
T3	33/1	Mark Brooks
T3	33/1	Jeff Maggert

PUNTERS' GUIDE

- In 1999 at Carnoustie keep an eye out for the Texan Bob Estes.
  - > In the Scottish Open at Carnoustie in 1996 he finished T11th and was the 11/1 winner of the Top American market.
  - > In 1995 at 66/1 he was T3rd in this market at the British Open when it was last played in Scotland.

  He'll be a big price in 1999 to be Top American and worth an each-way bet, assuming he qualifies.

TOP BRITISH (incl IRISH) PLAYERS

1998 ODDS

jt fav	11/4	Lee Westwood	33/1	Paul McGinley
jt fav	11/4	Colin Montgomerie	33/1	David Carter
	8/1	Ian Woosnam	33/1	Sam Torrance
	11/1	Darren Clarke	40/1	David Howell*
	20/1	Nick Faldo	40/1	Mark James
	25/1	Andrew Coltart	50/1	Sandy Lyle
	28/1	Phillip Price	66/1	Derrick Cooper
	33/1	Peter Baker	66/1	Philip Walton
	33/1	Padraig Harrington	66/1	Paul Lawrie
	33/1	Gary Orr	80/1	Bar

BOOKIES AT ODDS

DYM David Howell 16/1 Chandlers, Stanleys, Tote: 40/1 Jennings

1998 RESULT

T1	100/1	Raymond Russell
T1	250/1	Justin Rose
3	100/1	Gordon Brand Jr
T4	33/1	Peter Baker
T4	100/1	Des Smyth

PUNTERS' POINTS

- Colin Montgomerie's name and reputation puts him at the head of the market. Nevertheless in the last six years (when T3rd at 6/1 in 1994) he's only been placed once in this section.

1997 RESULT

1	12/1	Darren Clarke
2	33/1	Padraig Harrington
3	11/1	Lee Westwood
4	25/1	Mark James

1996 RESULT

1	7/2	Nick Faldo
2	40/1	Darren Clarke
3	50/1	Paul McGinley
T4	66/1	Padraig Harrington
T4	500/1	Michael Welch

PUNTERS' GUIDE

- Andrew Coltart, a fine player in windy conditions, was second at Carnoustie in the 1996 Scottish Open and he could reward each-way support in this market in 1999.

TOP AUSTRALASIAN PLAYER (incl. FIJI)

1998 ODDS

fav	9/2	Vijay Singh	20/1	Greg Chalmers
	7/1	Frank Nobilo	20/1	Stephen Leaney
	7/1	Stuart Appleby	22/1	Stephen Allan
	10/1	Robert Allenby	22/1	Michael Campbell
	14/1	Craig Parry	25/1	Rodger Davis
	14/1	Steve Elkington	33/1	Steve Alker
	14/1	Greg Turner	33/1	Michael Long
	14/1	Peter O'Malley	50/1	Bar
	20/1	Peter Senior		

BOOKIES AT ODDS

DYM Robert Allenby 5/1 Sunderlands, Corals: 10/1 Hills

1998 RESULT

1	14/1	Greg Turner
T2	10/1	Robert Allenby
T2 fav	9/2	Vijay Singh

1997 RESULT

1	28/1	Peter O'Malley
2	7/1	Frank Nobilo
3	14/1	Robert Allenby

1996 RESULT

1T fav	3/1	Greg Norman
1T	18/1	Greg Turner
3	7/1	Frank Nobilo

PUNTERS' GUIDE

- It is worth noting that Greg Turner has won this category twice (14/1 1998: 18/1 (dh) 1996) in the last three years and he was also top Australasian at Carnoustie in 1996 in the Scottish Open. He'll be worth an interest in 1999.

TOP EUROPEAN PLAYER

1998 ODDS

9/2	Lee Westwood	14/1	Bernhard Langer
9/2	Colin Montgomerie	20/1	Nick Faldo
12/1	J M Olazabal	25/1	Costantino Rocca
14/1	Ian Woosnam	28/1	Patrik Sjoland
14/1	Darren Clarke	33/1	Andrew Coltart
14/1	Jesper Parnevik	33/1	Paul McGinley
14/1	Thomas Bjorn	33/1	David Howell
		40/1	Bar

BOOKIES AT ODDS

DYM J M Olazabal 6/1 Ladbrokes: 12/1 Jennings

1998 RESULT

T1	150/1	Raymond Russell
T1	100/1	Justin Rose
T1	14/1	Jesper Parnevik
T4	25/1	Costantino Rocca
T4	14/1	Thomas Bjorn

PUNTERS' GUIDE

• Raymond Russell is a fine player who could go well again at Carnoustie in 1999 in this section – although he won't be 150/1 then!!

TOP REST OF THE WORLD
(without EUROPEANS and AMERICANS)

1998 ODDS

10/3	Ernie Els		20/1	Craig Parry
11/2	Nick Price		20/1	Stephen Ames
11/1	Vijay Singh		28/1	Retief Goosen
20/1	Robert Allenby		33/1	Steve Elkington*
20/1	Stuart Appleby		33/1	Peter O'Malley
20/1	Eduardo Romero		33/1	Shigeki Maruyama
20/1	Frank Nobilo		40/1	Bar
20/1	Mark McNulty			

BOOKIES AT ODDS

DYM Vijay Singh 5/1 Ladbrokes: 11/1 Chandlers
DYM Robert Allenby 10/1 Stanleys: 20/1 Ladbrokes

1998 RESULT

1	40/1	Greg Turner
T2	20/1	Robert Allenby
T2	11/1	Vijay Singh
T4	33/1	Peter O'Malley
T4	20/1	Stephen Ames

PUNTERS' GUIDE

• Keep an eye on the opening prices in this market as 'value', such as this year's 20/1 Robert Allenby, can be found. He must be considered again in 1999.

THE TOP AFRICAN PLAYER (created by Corals)

1998 ODDS

fav	1/1	Ernie Els	12/1	David Frost

10/3	Nick Price	18/1	Tony Johnstone
7/1	Retief Goosen	66/1	Andrew McLardy
7/1	Mark McNulty	80/1	Gary Player
12/1	Trevor Dodds	1/3 odds 1.2.	

1998 RESULT

T1	10/3	Nick Price
T1	1/1	Ernie Els

PUNTERS' GUIDE

If Ernie's fit and well he will surely win in 1999 after Nick Price's poor finish at Royal Birkdale this year.

TOP JAPANESE PLAYER (created by Hills)

1998 ODDS

fav	9/4	Shigeki Maruyama	7/1	Yoshinori Mizumaki
	7/2	Joe Ozaki	9/1	Keiichiro Fukabori
	9/2	Katsuyoshi Tomori	14/1	Kazuhiko Hosokawa
	13/2	Toru Suzuki	14/1	Toru Taniguchi
1/5 odds 1.2.3.				

1998 RESULT

1	9/4	Shigeki Maruyama
2	7/2	Joe Ozaki
3	9/2	Katsuyoshi Tomori

PUNTERS' GUIDE

Maruyama's British Open record in the last three years make him a worthy favourite in this market

SPECIALITY BETS

TOP AMATEUR

1998 ODDS

Matt Kuchar	6/4
Sergio Garcia	13/8
Justin Rose	7/2
S McCarthy	16/1
Didier De Vooght	20/1

Result Winner was 7/2 Justin Rose.

NATIONALITY OF THE WINNER (created by Corals)

8/11	American
2/1	European
7/1	African

12/1   Australasian

Result Winner 8/11 American

SURREY RACING 'ON THE HANDICAP' 66/1 THE FIELD

As usual Surrey Racing gave all players a handicap from Tiger Woods and Colin Montgomerie (?) on scratch to rank outsiders getting 9½ shots.

The result was:-

1.   Brian Watts (+9½)
2.   Raymond Russell (+9½)
3.   Justin Rose (+9½)
4.   Mark O'Meara (+4½)

PUNTERS' GUIDE

The winners' handicaps in recent years have been 1994 + 9: 1995 + 9: 1996 + 8: 1997 + 9 and now 1998 + 9½.

The motto seems clear – go for players who are outsiders in the outright betting with at least an 8-point handicap.

THE 80TH USPGA CHAMPIONSHIP

Date   13th – 16th August
Course   Sahalee C.C., Redmond, Washington
Par   70
Yardage   6,906
First Prize $470,000
Total Purse $2.6 million

Sahalee is a tree-lined tough course demanding accuracy rather than length off the tee. The huge cedar trees which fill the course provided narrow tunnels through which the players had to drive. The large bentgrass greens were tricky to read. With two par 5s there was an overall par of 70.

1998 ODDS

fav	9/1	Tiger Woods	50/1	Vijay Singh
	14/1	David Duval	66/1	Steve Stricker*
	20/1	Ernie Els	66/1	Stewart Cink
	20/1	Nick Price	66/1	Mark Calcavecchia
	22/1	Colin Montgomerie	66/1	J M Olazabal
	25/1	Lee Westwood	66/1	Payne Stewart
	25/1	Jim Furyk	66/1	John Huston
	28/1	Davis Love III (DC)	66/1	Jeff Maggert
	28/1	Fred Couples	66/1	John Cook
	33/1	Mark O'Meara	80/1	Fred Funk
	33/1	Tom Lehman	80/1	Nick Faldo
	40/1	Lee Janzen	80/1	Brad Faxon
	40/1	Jesper Parnevik	80/1	Steve Jones
	40/1	Justin Leonard	80/1	Tom Watson
	40/1	Scott Hoch	80/1	Ian Woosnam
	50/1	Phil Mickelson	80/1	Billy Mayfair (PWW)

25 (26 last year) players were best priced at or under 66/1. 32 (36 last year) players were best priced at or under 80/1.

BOOKIES AT ODDS

- Second placed DYM Steve Stricker 33/1 Corals: 66/1 Chandlers, Hills, Stan James
- Winner Vijay Singh 28/1 Jennings: 50/1 Chandlers

1998 RESULT

1	50/1	Vijay Singh	70 66 67 68	271
2	66/1	Steve Stricker	69 68 66 70	273
3	100/1	Steve Elkington	69 69 69 67	274
T4	20/1	Nick Price	70 73 68 65	276
T4	33/1	Mark O'Meara	69 70 69 68	276
T4	100/1	Frank Lickliter	68 71 69 68	276

T7	B Mayfair	73 67 67 70 277		J Durant	75 68 74 70 287
	D Love III	70 68 69 70 277		C Franco	71 70 73 73 287
9	J Cook	71 68 70 69 278	T44	P H Horgan III	71 71 72 74 288
T10	K Perry	69 72 70 68 279		M Calcavecchia	70 73 71 74 288
	T Woods	66 72 70 71 279		D Hart	70 75 69 74 288
	S Kendall	72 68 68 71 279		K Sutherland	74 71 71 72 288
T13	J Huston	70 71 68 71 280		C Montgomerie	70 67 77 74 288
	R Allenby	72 68 69 71 280		J Ozaki	73 71 75 69 288
	S Flesch	75 69 67 69 280		J Maggert	71 73 73 71 288
	F Couples	74 71 67 68 280		S Lowery	76 69 72 71 288
	B Tway	69 76 67 68 280		D Ogrin	73 72 71 72 288
	P Azinger	68 73 70 69 280		B Andrade	68 77 68 75 288
	B Glasson	68 74 69 69 280	T54	S Verplank	71 71 71 76 289
	B Faxon	70 68 74 68 280		N Faldo	73 71 72 73 289
T21	A Magee	70 68 72 71 281	T56	J Carter	71 73 72 74 290
	E Els	72 72 71 66 281		M Brooks	72 73 72 73 290
T23	S Gump	68 69 72 73 282		B Watts	72 73 72 73 290
	P U Johansson	69 74 71 68 282		T Tryba	70 74 76 70 290
	F Funk	70 71 71 70 282		D Frost	70 69 76 75 290
	G Kraft	71 73 65 73 282		J D Blake	70 72 73 75 290
T27	H Sutton	72 68 72 71 283	T62	O Browne	73 71 71 76 291
	J Sluman	71 73 70 69 283		T Dodds	69 75 75 72 291
T29	G Day	68 71 75 70 284		T Byrum	72 71 74 74 291
	T Lehman	71 71 70 72 284	T65	R Karlsson	71 73 75 73 292
	I Woosnam	70 75 67 72 284		S Maruyama	68 77 73 74 292
	L Rinker	70 70 71 73 284		L Roberts	72 71 74 75 292
	S Hoch	72 69 70 73 284	68	S Leaney	72 70 72 79 293
T34	R Cochran	69 71 70 75 285	69	A Coltart	70 75 75 74 294
	B Estes	68 76 69 72 285	70	D Sutherland	77 68 77 73 295
	P Goydos	70 70 72 73 285	T71	B Geiberger	73 70 79 74 296
	P Mickelson	70 70 79 67 285		C Parry	70 75 74 77 296
T38	C Stadler	69 74 71 72 286		B Fabel	73 72 73 78 296
	D Waldorf	74 70 70 72 286	74	C Perry	73 71 75 78 297
	J Sindelar	71 71 75 70 287	75	T Herron	73 70 79 76 298
	J Haas	72 72 73 69 287			

The following players missed the cut:-

R Thompson	73 73 146		K Stauffer	74 76 150
L Mize	75 71 146		J Schuman	71 79 150
P Stankowski	72 74 146		J P Hayes	74 76 150
J Parnevik	70 76 146		N Lancaster	75 75 150
L Mattiace	71 75 146		P Stewart	76 74 150
B Crenshaw	70 76 146		C Pavin	71 79 150
J Furyk	72 74 146		K Triplett	73 77 150
R Mediate	75 72 147		B Boyd	77 74 151

C Rocca	73 74 147		R McDougal	77 74 151
G Fieger	74 73 147		S Pate	72 79 151
T Armour III	78 69 147		B Ford	72 79 151
S Cink	73 74 147		J Daly	80 72 152
J Leonard	70 77 147		R Damron	74 78 152
M Wiebe	75 72 147		T Tolles	80 72 152
S McCarron	69 78 147		G Turner	72 80 152
R Goosen	73 74 147		S Williams	78 74 152
C Dennis	73 74 147		F Nobilo	75 78 153
H Frazar	69 78 147		B Zabriski	79 74 153
S Simpson	70 78 148		P Lonard	72 81 153
E Romero	70 78 148		P Sjoland	74 79 153
G Chalmers	75 73 148		J Thomsen	78 76 154
M Ozaki	74 74 148		P Blackmar	79 75 154
T Bjorn	75 73 148		T Smith	77 77 154
B Jobe	70 78 148		D Duval	76 78 154
I Garrido	73 75 148		G Hjertstedt	76 78 154
M Mielke	74 74 148		K Kimball	80 75 155
E Terasa	72 76 148		C Tucker	78 78 156
M Burke	75 73 148		A Geiberger	81 77 158
D Toms	72 76 148		W Grady	76 82 158
T Watson	72 76 148		B Godd	84 74 158
L Janzen	76 72 148		W Frantz	81 77 158
S Kepler	73 76 149		G Waite	79 79 158
J Overton	77 72 149		R Stelten	78 81 159
J M Olazabal	75 74 149		K Schall	79 80 159
B Gaus	72 77 149		J Lankford	78 81 159
L Westwood	74 76 150		P Earnest	85 82 167
T Kite	73 77 150		Wd. J Kelly (went home to
S Appleby	77 73 150		become a dad!)

- The most significant cut-missers were 14/1 2nd fav David Duval, 25/1 chances Jim Furyk (!) and Lee Westwood, 40/1 Jesper Parnevik, Justin Leonard and Lee Janzen, and 66/1 outsiders Payne Stewart and Stewart Cink.

ROUND BY ROUND LEADERBOARD

FIRST ROUND

T Woods	4 under
G Day	2 under
B Estes	2 under
F Lickliter	2 under
P Azinger	2 under
B Glasson	2 under
S Maruyama	2 under
C Stadler	2 under
B Andrade	2 under
S Gump	2 under
V SINGH	level

SECOND ROUND

V SINGH	4 under
C Montgomerie	3 under
S Gump	3 under
S Stricker	3 under
S Elkington	2 under
A Magee	2 under
B Faxon	2 under
T Woods	2 under
D Love III	2 under

THIRD ROUND

V SINGH	7 under
S Stricker	7 under
B Mayfair	3 under
S Elkington	3 under
D Love III	3 under
M O'Meara	2 under
S Kendall	2 under
T Woods	2 under
F Lickliter	2 under

FINAL ROUND

V SINGH	9 under
S Stricker	7 under
S Elkington	6 under
N Price	4 under
M O'Meara	4 under
F Lickliter	4 under

FINAL DAY BETTING

		Par	Finish
6/4	Vijay Singh	7 under	W
13/8	Steve Stricker	7 under	2nd
10/1	Tiger Woods	2 under	-
11/1	Davis Love III	3 under	-
16/1	Billy Mayfair	3 under	-
16/1	Mark O'Meara	2 under	T4th
16/1	Steve Elkington	3 under	3rd
40/1	Bar		

VIJAY SINGH'S ODDS THROUGH THE TOURNAMENT

At the start	After R1	After R2	After R3
50/1	25/1	11/2	6/4

PUNTERS' POINTS

- In my four Golf Form books only one player has been in every one of my annual lists of players to follow – Vijay Singh, and here he won his first Major in the tournament nominated for him in last year's volume.

  > On the final day he could use his experience as World Matchplay champion in what became a virtual match against 31-year-old American Steve Stricker.

> He rode his luck with favourable bounces down the stretch, yet in the end was a worthy 2-shot winner.

> Vijay's win may have been his first yet it completed a remarkable hat-trick for his caddie Dave Renwick who had previously won majors with Jose Maria Olazabal and Steve Elkington.

- Steve Stricker had let a winning opportunity go last week and was 159th for final-round scoring so it was little surprise to see him start nervously. However, he showed a lot of courage with his recovery shots to 'hang on in there' to finish in second place. Wife Nicki, his former caddie, is about to give birth so expect the 'nappy factor' to work in Steve's favour in 1999.

- Steve Elkington has had all manner of ailments, viruses, allergies and trapped nerves in a season in which he has rarely played. However he simply loves this tournament and this sweet-swinging Aussie must be noted here in future. In the last seven USPGAs he's now posted one win, two thirds, a seventh and two top 20s. If he's fit in 1999 remember him in the top Australasian and Rest of the World markets and also on the spreads.

- Mark O'Meara's gallant attempt to equal Ben Hogan's record of three majors in the same year didn't quite come off. So many of us have noted the beneficial effect he has had on Tiger Woods when in fact it could well be that the truth is the other way round and that Tiger's tough competitive streak has actually made its Mark on O'Meara!

- Tiger himself 'failed' again finishing T10th. Yet his major finishes 8th – 18th – 3rd – 10th make him the only player to have four top 20 finishes. Expect him to do even better in 1999.......so long as his Dad stays well and he cures the pullhook that ruined his chances here.

- The enigma of Colin Montgomerie continues. At halfway just a shot off the lead and appearing relaxed he promptly shot a 77 in R3 eventually to finish T44th!

- Having finished T8th two years ago Per-Ulrik Johansson once more played well to finish as the top European at a massive 33/1 (!). With his ability to move the ball both ways, if he stays fit he will become a major contender in future years.

- Like Monty, Phil Mickelson 'blew' his chance in R3 with a 79, and like Monty it may well be that the burden of expectations is getting to him.

- John Huston finished T13th so that he made the cut in every major with a record of 23rd – 32nd – 11th and now 13th. That's very solid, consistent, all-round play.

1997 RESULT

1	40/1	Davis Love III
2	28/1	Justin Leonard
3	80/1	Jeff Maggert
4	66/1	Lee Janzen

1996 RESULT

1	40/1	Mark Brooks
(Brooks won at the first extra hole)		
2	80/1	Kenny Perry
T3	100/1	Tommy Tolles
T3	40/1	Steve Elkington

WINNERS IN THE '90s

1990	Wayne Grady
1991	John Daly
1992	Nick Price
1993	Paul Azinger
1994	Nick Price
1995	Steve Elkington
1996	Mark Brooks
1997	Davis Love III
1998	Vijay Singh

PUNTERS' GUIDE

- In this section last year the formula for finding the winner was given and Vijay Singh was specifically named.

  The formula again is to go for a player with three key characteristics:-

  > He is an experienced pro in his thirties.

  > He is seeking his first major win.

  > His recent form figures show he is in good current form.

- Vijay Singh was the ELEVENTH first-time major winner in the last thirteen years, and the ELEVENTH in his thirties in the same period. His form figures were 2-12-18-8.

TOP AMERICAN PLAYER

1998 ODDS

fav	11/2	Tiger Woods	40/1	Steve Stricker
	10/1	David Duval	50/1	Brad Faxon
	14/1	Jim Furyk	50/1	Billy Mayfair
	20/1	Davis Love III	50/1	Bob Tway
	20/1	Mark O'Meara	50/1	Fred Funk
	20/1	Fred Couples	50/1	Scott Verplank
	20/1	Tom Lehman	50/1	Tom Watson
	25/1	Lee Janzen	50/1	Loren Roberts
	25/1	Scott Hoch	66/1	Jeff Sluman*
	28/1	Justin Leonard	66/1	Steve Flesch
	28/1	Phil Mickelson	66/1	Bob Estes
	33/1	Jeff Maggert	66/1	Steve Jones
	40/1	Mark Calcavecchia	66/1	Paul Azinger*
	40/1	Stewart Cink	66/1	Glen Day
	40/1	John Cook	66/1	Hal Sutton*
	40/1	John Huston	66/1	Scott McCarron
	40/1	Payne Stewart	80/1	Bar

1998 RESULT

1	40/1	Steve Stricker
T2	20/1	Mark O'Meara
T2	80/1	Frank Lickliter
T4	50/1	Billy Mayfair
T4	20/1	Davis Love III

PUNTERS' POINTS

- This year with three non-Americans in the first six this market was a wise choice for punters who fancied American players.

1997 RESULT

1	22/1	Davis Love III
2	20/1	Justin Leonard
3	50/1	Jeff Maggert
4	40/1	Lee Janzen

1996 RESULT

1	20/1	Mark Brooks
2	50/1	Kenny Perry
3	80/1	Tommy Tolles
4	25/1	Justin Leonard

PUNTERS' GUIDE

- Davis Love III (W22/1 1997: T4 20/1 1998) has the best recent record in this market.
- If you expect European, Australasian or South African players to do well then it is always wise to back your top US fancy in this category.

TOP EUROPEAN PLAYER

1998 ODDS

jt fav	7/2	Lee Westwood	25/1	Patrik Sjoland
jt fav	7/2	Colin Montgomerie	28/1	Costantino Rocca
	6/1	Jesper Parnevik	33/1	Andrew Coltart
	12/1	J M Olazabal	33/1	Ignacio Garrido
	14/1	Ian Woosnam	33/1	P U Johansson*
	16/1	Nick Faldo	66/1	Robert Karlsson*
	18/1	Thomas Bjorn	66/1	Gabriel Hjerstedt*

BOOKIES AT ODDS

Winner DYM P U Johansson 14/1 Chandlers: 33/1 Stanleys (!), 25/1 Hills, Ladbrokes

1998 RESULT

1	33/1	Per-Ulrik Johansson
2	14/1	Ian Woosnam
3 jt fav	7/2	Colin Montgomerie

PUNTERS' POINTS

- For the fourth successive year Nick Faldo did not make the frame.

1997 RESULT

1	7/2	Colin Montgomerie
2	7/1	Bernhard Langer
3	14/1	Lee Westwood

1996 RESULT

1	20/1	Jesper Parnevik
2	40/1	P U Johansson
3	40/1	M A Jimenez

PUNTERS' GUIDE

- What a value bet! P U Johansson's 33/1 win proved what excellent value golf betting can provide and what massive 'ricks' compilers can make.

  Having been one of the front three Europeans in the last six US Majors and clearly in form and fit again after finishing 7th in the Scandinavian Masters, Johansson at 33/1 in a 14-runner race was surely a candidate for 'value of year'.

EUROPEAN TOUR PLAYERS' PERFORMANCES

Made the cut		Missed the cut (the cut was made at 145)	
T23	P U Johansson	J Parnevik	146
T29	Ian Woosnam	C Rocca	147
T44	Colin Montgomerie	R Goosen	147
T54	Nick Faldo	E Romero	148
T65	Robert Karlsson	T Bjorn	148
69	Andrew Coltart	I Garrido	148
		J M Olazabal	149
		L Westwood	150
		P Sjoland	153

TOP REST OF THE WORLD PLAYER

1998 ODDS

jt fav	3/1	Nick Price	33/1	Joe Ozaki
jt fav	3/1	Ernie Els	33/1	Trevor Dodds
	8/1	Vijay Singh	33/1	Retief Goosen
	14/1	Stuart Appleby	33/1	Shigeki Maruyama
	20/1	Craig Parry	40/1	Greg Chalmers
	22/1	Robert Allenby	40/1	Eduardo Romero
	22/1	Steve Elkington	40/1	Greg Turner
	22/1	Frank Nobilo	40/1	Grant Waite
	25/1	David Frost	50/1	Bar
	33/1	Stephen Leaney		

1998 RESULT

1	8/1	Vijay Singh
2	22/1	Steve Elkington
3 jt fav	3/1	Nick Price

PUNTERS' POINTS

Singh won there for the second successive year with Nick Price making the frame once more.

1997 RESULT

T1	11/1	Vijay Singh
T1	13/2	Nick Price
T1	4/1	Greg Norman

PUNTERS' GUIDE

"I feel very comfortable at this tournament," and when you look at Steve Elkington's outright placings (3rd 1998: T3rd 1996: W 1995: T7th 1994) in recent years you can see why. He must be the long-range selection for 1999 in this category.

TOP AUSTRALASIAN PLAYER

Corals created this market

jt fav	4/1	Craig Parry	
jt fav	4/1	Stuart Appleby	
	11/2	Steve Elkington	
	15/2	Robert Allenby	
	15/2	Frank Nobilo	
	10/1	Stephen Leaney	
	10/1	Greg Turner	
	10/1	Grant Waite	
	12/1	Greg Chalmers	
	12/1	Peter Lonard	
	20/1	Wayne Grady	1/4 1.2.3.

1998 RESULT

1	11/2	Steve Elkington
2	15/2	Robert Allenby
3	10/1	Stephen Leaney

PUNTERS' GUIDE

If Greg Norman returns in 1999 he may well be favourite in this market so making USPGA specialist Steve Elkington a superb each-way bet if he is fully fit.

SPECIALITY BETS
ON THE HANDICAP
As usual Surrey went 66/1 the field 'on the handicap'.
The result was:-

1	V Singh	+6
2	S Elkington	+8
3	F Lickliter	+9½
4	S Stricker	+6

CORALS' MARKETS TO MAKE THE CUT
Corals created six groups of players. To win all the players in the group had to make the cut.

5/1 EUROSTAR ONE
L Westwood
N Faldo
A Coltart
J Parnevik

5/2 AMERICAN EXPRESS ONE
D Duval
J Leonard
J Maggert
M O'Meara

14/1 EUROSTAR TWO
C Montgomerie
R Karlsson
T Bjorn
I Woosnam

10/3 AMERICAN EXPRESS TWO
L Janzen
S Hoch
D Love III
J Cook

14/1 EUROSTAR THREE
P Sjoland
C Rocca
J M Olazabal
P U Johansson

4/1 AMERICAN EXPRESS THREE
S Stricker
B Faxon
J Huston
S Cink

Jon Wright 6 Punters Nil as once more each group had at least one player who missed the cut.

Golf Form Symbols

Seventeen symbols and letters are used to indicate features about different players.

💡	Nappy factor
☀	Player at his best in sunny, dry conditions
⛈	Indicates a very good player in bad weather
🐎	Proven front runner well able to take a lead and go on to win a tournament
🍾	Player has appeared to lack 'bottle' in a tournament in the last year or two
🎂	Player has a significant birthday i.e. 29 or 39; 30 or 40
A	Player who is still an amateur, or has turned professional in the past year
CT	Players on the 'comeback trail' after illness, or after a winless spell
D	Disappointing in 1998
F	Player who plays particularly well when fresh after a break
G	Almost certain to go on to win important tournaments
g	Likely to go on to win important tournaments
M	Player with the ability to win a Major for the first time in the next year or two
Pb	Probably past his best
S	Streak player capable of low scores when 'on fire'
Y	Young player, under 30, of real promise and potential
y	Young player, under 30, of some promise and potential

These symbols are used for players on both the European and USPGA tours.

THE EUROPEAN TOUR PLAYERS

Paul Affleck
Steve Alker
Stephen Allan
Peter Baker
Seve Ballesteros
Andrew Beal
Warren Bennett
John Bickerton
Thomas Bjorn
Diego Borrego
Richard Boxall
Gordon Brand Jr
Paul Broadhurst
Stuart Cage
Angel Cabrera
Michael Campbell
David Carter
Francisco Cea
Alexander Cejka
Greg Chalmers
Roger Chapman
Daniel Chopra
Darren Clarke
Russell Claydon
Jose Coceres
Andrew Coltart
Derrick Cooper
Eamon Darcy
Brian Davis
Mark Davis
Rodger Davis
Paul Eales
Denis Edlund
Olivier Edmond
Klas Eriksson
Gary Evans
Nick Faldo MBE
Marc Farry
Stephen Field
Massimo Florioli
Anders Forsbrand
Pierre Fulke
Ian Garbutt
Sergio Garcia
Ignacio Garrido

David Gilford
Tom Gillis
Thomas Gogele
Mathew Goggin
Retief Goosen
Silvio Grappasonni
Mathias Gronberg
Joakim Haeggman
Craig Hainline
Mats Hallberg
Padraig Harrington
Per Haugsrud
Scott Henderson
Domingo Hospital
David Howell
Fredrik Jacobson
Raphael Jacquelin
Mark James
Miguel Angel Jimenez
Per-Ulrik Johansson
Tony Johnstone
Michael Jonzon
Olle Karlsson
Robert Karlsson
Soren Kjeldsen
Barry Lane
Bernhard Langer
Mats Lanner
Paul Lawrie
Stephen Leaney
Thomas Levet
Jonathan Lomas
Peter Lonard
Michael Long
Santiago Luna
Malcolm Mackenzie
Miguel Angel Martin
Bob May
Paul McGinley
John McHenry
Mark McNulty
Peter Mitchell
Colin Montgomerie MBE
Mark Mouland
Rolf Muntz

Jose Maria Olazabal
Andrew Oldcorn
Peter O'Malley
Gary Orr
Greg Owen
Jesper Parnevik
Jim Payne
Van Phillips
Phillip Price
Iain Pyman
Paulo Quirici
Michele Reale
Wayne Riley
Jose Rivero
Dean Robertson
Jon Robson
Costantino Rocca
Mark Roe
Eduardo Romero
Raymond Russell
Justin Rose
Jarmo Sandelin
Peter Senior
Jeev Milkha Singh
Andrew Sherborne
Patrik Sjoland
Des Smyth
Jamie Spence
Sven Struver
Fabrice Tarnaud
Steen Tinning
Katsuyoshi Tomori
Sam Torrance MBE
Jay Townsend
Greg Turner
Miles Tunnicliff
Jean Van de Velde
Anthony Wall
Philip Walton
Steve Webster
Roger Wessels
Wayne Westner
Lee Westwood
Clinton Whitelaw
Ian Woosnam MBE

EUROPEAN TOUR PLAYERS

PAUL AFFLECK

Paul broke into the top 100 on the O/M for the first time, in his 'nappy factor' year 1995 when he was 73rd. Since then he's posted just two top 10s – both in the Madeira Open.

In 1998 the 32-year-old Welshman had three top 25 finishes – in the Dubai Desert Classic (T20th), the Benson and Hedges (T24th) and yes, you've guessed it, the Madeira Open (T19th) before he saved his card with a fine performance in the Belgacom Open (T10th after 65 in R4).

Seems unable to breakaway from the lower reaches of the O/M where there is the annual worry of retaining your card.

Represented Wales in the Dunhill Cup in 1995 and 1996. 106th on the O/M.

➤ Worth noting in 3-ball betting in the early rounds of the South African PGA after his 67 to take the lead in R1 there in 1998.

➤ His best chance in 1999 will definitely be in the Madeira Open (T19th 1998: T9th 1997: 2nd 1996). If he gets an early R1 tee time have a little each way on the Welshman.

STEVE ALKER

27-year-old Kiwi who turned pro in 1995. He made his breakthrough in October 1996 when he won the Queensland Open on the Australasian tour. He followed this up in 1997 with a 33/1 victory in the Ford Australian Open, and a 2nd place (after a play-off) in the Canon Challenge.

Represented New Zealand in the Dunhill Cup in 1997 winning three of his four matches.

In 1998 in a disappointing rookie year on the European tour he posted just one top 20 finish – when T19th in the weak field for the Madeira Open. 138th on O/M.

➤ Short off the tee, his strength is around the greens where he makes better chips than Harry Ramsden. Needs to improve his iron play.

➤ With two wins on the Australasian tour in his first two years as a pro this guy can play.

➤ With Frank Nobilo and Greg Turner to inspire him he may still make a mark in Europe.

STEPHEN ALLAN   G Y

This 25-year-old baby-faced Aussie from Melbourne impressed in 1997, his rookie year with six top 20 finishes including a T4th in the Portuguese Open. He ended that year 82nd on the O/M.

In 1998 he was T2nd at 33/1 in the Australian PGA before he started his 'second season' on the European tour.

He was impressive when 2nd at 200/1 in the Dubai Desert Classic (68 in R4). He also posted high finishes in the Spanish Open (7th, 65 in R4) and the Loch Lomond Invitational (T13th), where he was second-best Australasian player at 25/1.

Last year his profile said, "....his career has real momentum so a 'shock' success in 1998 would be no surprise" and that success came in August in the German Open when he was the 100/1 winner after shooting 69 in R4.

Missed the cut in his second British Open as he had done, as an amateur, in 1996.

Finished 1998 16th on the O/M.

➤ Having improved every year and merited the gy symbols he was awarded last year expect his progress to continue in 1999.

➤ Must be noted for the tournaments 'down under' in January and February. He finished T2nd at 28/1 in the Ford Championship, the first event on the 1998/99 Australasian O/M.

➤ A fine wind player who is well suited to links style courses such as the one at the Sporting Club, Berlin where he won.

PETER BAKER   G

Rookie of the year in 1987, winner of the Benson and Hedges in 1988, dual winner and Ryder Cup star in 1993 when he won 4 points from five games, his future seemed completely assured.

However from 7th in the O/M the 31-year-old Wolves fan slipped to 55th (1994), 25th (1995), and 32nd (1996) in the following years. Towards the end of 1997 he showed signs of improved form when T3rd at 150/1 in the Scandinavian Masters, T11th in the German Masters, and T9th in the Oki Pro-Am to finish 24th on the O/M.

In 1998 his improved form continued with high finishes in the Johnnie Walker Classic (T14th although 75 in R4), the Dubai Desert Classic (T20th), the English Open (T20th), the Loch Lomond (T24th) and the European Open (T16th).

His best finishes were in the Heineken Classic (T3rd) the rain-reduced Italian Open (5th), the Irish Open (T3rd at 80/1) and the Dutch Open (6th).

Played well in the British Open to finish T15th. Played in the Dunhill Cup for the second time in October, winning one of his three matches. Finished a fine T4th in the Volvo Masters to give him a real confidence boost.

His strength has been his accuracy to the greens. He is working hard with coach Bill Ferguson to improve his chipping and putting.

Finished 1998 12th in the O/M.

➤ He is now surely a player in 'the winner about to happen' category who can be expected to post a victory or two in 1999.

➤ After a six-year gap he can be expected to make the 1999 Ryder Cup team for which his opening quote was 2/1.

➤ Now that his long game is back in top shape he can be followed when there is a premium on accuracy, as in the Irish Open (T3rd 1997) and the Dutch Open (6th 1997).

SEVE BALLESTEROS   Pb D

The legendary charismatic Spaniard who steered Europe to its 1997 Ryder Cup victory is now, let's face it, a shadow of his former self.

I first gave him the PB symbol three years ago and he's not won since. Sure, he retains much of his magical ability on and around the greens, and is still the world's best player from car parks, tree trunks and assorted jungle. Trouble is, his erratic play off the tee gives him plenty of practice.

In 1998 hints of form were shown in the Dubai Desert Classic (T10th), and the Volvo PGA (T21st after 65 in R3). Alongside Jimenez was 3rd in the Novotel Perrier Pairs. Ended the season top of the putts per green in regulation stats. 108th on O/M.

➤ He retains the PB symbol.

➤ It is very very difficult to see him winning his 49th (!) European tour title.

➤ The way to profit from Seve is to oppose him in 3-ball betting whenever the course places any sort of premium on accuracy. You've then got a virtual two-runner race.

➤ He's been 3rd in each of the last two Novotel Perrier Pairs as the format suits his game.

➤ The men in the white coats are still looking for the punters who backed him at 16/1 to make the 1999 Ryder Cup team.

ANDREW BEAL

The 33-year-old makes his appearance in these Player Profiles for the first time. He should write about the Qualifying school as he'd been to ten in a row from 1988-1997,

However 1998 really has been different as he's posted three high finishes in the Turespana Masters (T12th), the Madeira Open (3rd 80/1) and the BMW International (T6th after 69 in R4).

As a result he's secured his 1999 tour card and can give Q. school a miss. 83rd on O/M.

It may well be that he is more relaxed now having been married in May. Wife expecting a baby at the end of October so 1999, all being well, will be his 'nappy factor' year.

➤ If his strength has been his putting his achilles heel had been his final round scoring until his fine effort in the BMW International.

➤ Like a team getting promotion to the Premier League his goal will be consolidation, i.e. retention of his card.

➤ His best chance will surely lie in the weakly-contested Madeira Open where he posted his best-ever finish when 3rd this year.

WARREN BENNETT

The 27-year-old guy from Watford had a glittering amateur record. Indeed in 1994 Sir Michael Bonallack predicted he'd win the British Open within ten years. Sadly Warren turned out to be the Justin Rose of his day!

However 1998 has seen Warren comeback with a vengeance. He has been in simply brilliant form on the challenge tour to end the year Number 1 on its Order of Merit after he recorded five wins with victories in France (twice), Slovenia, Russia and notably in the Tour Championship at the East Sussex National. In a spell in July and August he won four times in five weeks.

He has now won seven times on the Challenge tour.

He is now over the neck problems that had prevented him from playing three weeks in a row. Plays best when in continuous week-to-week tournament play.
➤ The form from the East Sussex National Course on the Challenge tour has proved extremely good with recent winners, Bjorn, Edlund and Chalmers all making a big mark on the full tour.
➤ In 1999 expect to see Bennett, now he's fully fit, with renewed confidence, and with his elder brother Jason as his full-time caddie, make a real impact.

JOHN BICKERTON

The 29-year-old from Redditch had four high finishes on the main tour in 1998 – the Portuguese Open (T16th), the Turespana Masters (T19th), the Madeira Open (T14th) and the One 2 One British Masters (T8th after a 67 in R4 from an early tee time).

He also played successfully on the 1998 Challenge tour with the highlights being a 2nd place in the Tour Championship on the East Sussex National (10 under – he finished 68 – 65), and a third place in the Finnish Masters and the Audi Quattro Trophy in Germany.
➤ A fine bunker player, he shows up well in the sand save stats.
➤ Consolidation will be the aim in 1999 with the Madeira Open (T14th 1998) offering him his best opportunity of his first tour success.

THOMAS BJORN   G Y

The 27-year-old Dane laid a solid foundation for his career in 1995 when he won four times on the Challenge tour to end that season easily the top player on that tour's Order of Merit.

In 1996, his rookie year, he posted his first success when he won the Loch Lomond Invitational at 80/1, and with five other top 10s finished 10th in the O/M.

In 1997 he continued his progress with punter-friendly top 5 finishes in the Data Dimension Pro-Am (3rd), the BMW International (5th), the British Masters (T4th) and the German Masters (3rd).

He qualified for the Ryder Cup team that retained the trophy at Valderrama. He halved his singles with Justin Leonard, and with Woosnam he won in the fourballs to have an unbeaten record.

In 1998 his momentum was maintained with two wins. He was the 33/1 winner of the Heineken Classic when, in his victory speech, he thanked 2nd-placed Woosy (his Ryder Cup partner) for looking after him over the last six holes.

He also won the Spanish Open at 40/1, although he never actually led until the 70th hole.

He also had punter-friendly finishes in the rain-reduced Italian Open (4th at 20/1), the Benson and Hedges (T3rd at 20/1) and the Volvo PGA (T5th).

He also had high finishes in the Deutsche Bank Open (T13th), the British Open (T9th), the BMW International (T6th after having a 3-shot lead at halfway), the European Open (T23rd after a 77 (!) in R4) and the Lancome Trophy (T18th).

In the Johnnie Walker Classic he was R1 joint leader then he got food poisoning, shot 81 and missed the cut.

25th in the US Open. He missed the cut in the USPGA.

Led the British Open briefly in R3 before finishing T9th.

He was not invited to the US Masters!

Beaten by Monty in R1 of the World Match play in October after doctors told him not to play.

He has huge length which helps to set up birdie and eagle chances on par 5s. Tends to draw the ball.

He's been troubled with a neck injury and back problems during the second half of this season. 6th on the O/M.

➤ A player with proven bottle who has won from 'off the pace' and from the front. "After the Ryder Cup I am not scared of anybody. I don't get intimidated."

➤ 6/1 ON to make the 1999 Ryder Cup side.

➤ With three wins in three years as well as seven top 5 finishes he's clearly a player who must be considered whenever he plays.

➤ He is similar to Tiger Woods in that he has huge length, so he's best on courses with four par 5s, and he's very aggressive on the greens. He'll often send a putt racing 4 to 5 feet past the hole. When he makes the return putts, as in the 1998 Heineken Classic, he wins, when he doesn't, as in the 1998 BMW International, he loses!

➤ If his neck injury does not re-occur he can be expected to be in contention a number of times in 1999, and to turn at least one of them into another victory, perhaps in the Benson and Hedges (T3rd 1998: 12th 1997) or the Dubai Desert Classic (T7th 1996) both on long courses, over 7000 yards, with four par 5s.

DIEGO BORREGO **D**

The breakthrough for 26-year-old Diego came in his seventh tournament in 1996 when he was the 80/1 winner of the Turespana Masters beating Tony Johnstone in a play-off. Having led from the start it was a fine, front-running performance.

He ended 1996 30th on the O/M.

He had a disappointing 1997 finishing 117th on the O/M with only two high finishes – in the Turespana Masters (7th as defending champion) and the Moroccan Open (T10th).

His decline continued in 1998 with the Turespana Masters (T15th) and the Moroccan Open (T21st) his best finishes. However he was unlucky in the cancelled Compaq European Grand Prix when after 19 holes he was joint leader.

The two-year exemption for his tournament win ends on 31.12.98 so he will have to go to Q school to secure his card for 1999.

➤ Unquestionably he enjoys the Turespana Masters (T15th 1998: 7th 1997: Won 1996) in which he can be noted in 3-ball betting and as an outsider in the outright market.

RICHARD BOXALL **D**

'Boxie' joined the tour in 1983 and has kept his card ever since. His best year was 1990 when he finished in the top 20 on the O/M (he was 17th) after a win in the Italian Open, plus two second places.

Broke his left leg in 1991 after 45 holes when in contention for the British Open.

Since then he's posted eight top 10s, with a 2nd place in the 1994 Spanish Open his best finish.

In recent years he's been 57th (1994), 58th (1995), 67th (1996) and 65th (1997) on the O/M.

However in 1998 the 37-year-old from Camberley has struggled to retain his card.

He found some form in the second half of the season but he couldn't post a top 20 finish and must now go to Q school. 121st on O/M.

With Derrick Cooper was 2nd in the Novotel Perrier Pairs in October

He has joined the BBC commentary team in 1998.

➤ He would be an outsider with a real 'squeak' in the Dutch Open (T5th 1997: T7th 1995: T10th 1994) where he's had three top 10s in the last five years.

➤ Last year's advice was to "make a note of Boxall when he partners Derrick Cooper in foursomes competitions", and I hope you did when in October they were 2nd (for the second time in three years) at 33/1 in the Novotel Perriers Pairs. They can be supported there again in 1999.

GORDON BRAND JR

'Junior' may have won eight European tournaments and played in two Ryder Cups (1987 and 1989) yet he has won only once this decade and that was back in 1993.

His poorest-ever year was when he was 88th in the 1995 O/M.

In 1997 he returned to a 'natural' style of playing, notching three top 15 finishes to end the year 49th on the O/M.

In 1998 he had high finishes in the Spanish Open (T11th after a poor 73 in R4), the Italian Open (T18th), the Volvo PGA (T11th from 'off the pace' after a 66 in R4), the Dutch Open (T17th), the Canon European Masters (T5th at 100/1), the Lancome Trophy (T11th), the German Masters (T15th after 65 in R4), the Belgacom Open (T10th) and the Volvo Masters (T19th).

He proved his quality when 14th in the British Open, just 8 shots off the winner.

He was 40 in August 1998. 39th on the O/M.

➤ He is a magnificent bad-weather player as he showed in the winds when T2nd in the 1997 Deutsche Bank Open and in his last victory in the 1993 European Open.

➤ Very competitive, he enjoys the challenge when near the top of a leaderboard.

➤ Whenever the rains rain and the winds blow he can be followed in 3-ball betting and 'in running' in the outright market.

➤ His last three top 3 finishes were preceded by a missed cut or a poor finish, so he can suddenly find his form.

PAUL BROADHURST

33-year-old 'Broady' joined the tour in 1989 and has almost always finished in the top 50 on the O/M. He lost his way in 1994 when 131st on the O/M but bounced back in 1995 with his fourth, and last tour win – the French Open.

He was 18th on the O/M in 1995, 9th in 1996 and 25th last year.

In 1998 he posted a whole series of high finishes although he could never make a top 4 cheque.

His top 10s were in the Turespana Masters (T8th), the Loch Lomond Invitational (T9th with all rounds at or below par) and the European Open (T7th).

His other high finishes were in the Heineken Classic (T11th), the Moroccan Open (T19th – chance destroyed by a 79 in R2), the rain-reduced Italian Open (T18th), the French Open (T16th), the Irish Open (T16th), the Scandinavian Masters (T11th), the Deutsche Bank Open (T13th – after being R3 leader), the One 2 One British Masters (T20th after a 69 in R4) and the Lancome Trophy (T18th).

Mainly a right-left player. He shows well up very well on the 1998 putting stats. Uses coach Bill Ferguson. 35th on O/M.

➤ His only Ryder Cup appearance was in 1991. He's 11/4 to get back in the team although I doubt he'll make it.

➤ In both the 1997 Portuguese Open (73 in R4) and the 1998 Deutsche Bank Open (his 76 in R4 was the second worst of the final day) he has put in a poor final round when in contention so there must be some doubts about his ability to win for the fifth time.

➤ 'Broady' has a very consistent record in the Lancome Trophy (T18th 1998: 10th 1996: 8th 1995) where he can be noted in 3-ball and match betting.

➤ He can be followed in match bets in two tournaments – the Loch Lomond Invitational, where in the last two years he finished T9th (1998) and T6th (1997) with all eight rounds under par, and the European Open at the tough K Club course where his four-year record is 7th (1998), 10th (1997), 6th (1996) and 23rd (1995) and his stroke average 71.06.

STUART CAGE

There was real momentum behind the 25-year-old guy from Leeds as he entered 1998. He'd been English Amateur Champion in 1992 and a Walker Cup player a year later.

He was eighth on the Challenge tour in 1994 thus securing his 1995 tour card.

He had two top 4 finishes in 1995 ending the year 42nd on the O/M, and another top 4 in the 1996 Lancome Trophy ending the season 61st on the O/M.

Then the breakthrough came in April 1997 when he was the superb front-running 100/1 winner of the Cannes Open.

Since then he's struggled and this year he's posted just one high finish when T18th in the Benson and Hedges International.

His Cannes victory secured a two-year tour exemption so he retains his card for 1999.

➤ He's certainly crossed the thin line between success and failure over the past eighteen months.

➤ It will be no surprise to see him post high finishes again in 1999 when he knows his exemption expires because he is fundamentally a fine player.

ANGEL CABRERA G Y

'Pato' is the 29-year-old Argentinean who uses his one-time sponsor Eduardo Romero as his role model.

Joined the tour in 1996 when he finished 72nd on the O/M thanks to a 2nd place in the Oki Pro-Am which secured his 1997 card.

Made a very big impression in 1997 with five top 10s to end the year 38th on the O/M. He also played for Argentina in the Dunhill Cup and won all his three matches.

In 1998 he posted high finishes in the Qatar Masters (T17th), the Portuguese Open (T22nd), the Spanish Open (T11th) and the Turespana Masters (T8th after 75 in R4).

His best finishes were in August when T5th in the European Open (never in contention 67 in R4) and T4th at 125/1 in the BMW International.

Had a disappointing Dunhill Cup at St Andrews this time, winning only one of his three matches.

He is enormously long off the tee but he must improve his driving accuracy on a consistent basis. 45th on the O/M.

➤ Make no mistake this guy can play and will surely go on to win tournaments. He deserves the G and Y symbols. He's probably at his best in warm, sunny conditions.

➤ Has posted high finishes on a tight course (T3rd 1997 Dutch Open), on a links course (1997 Dunhill Cup Pl 3 W3) and on a wide-open 'putting contest' course (T4th 1998 BMW International) so he's a versatile player.

➤ Worth a bet for the 1999 Qatar Masters at the massively-long 7,300-yard Doha course where he posted a top 20 finish with four sub-par rounds this year. The course's length and the heat suit him ideally.

MICHAEL CAMPBELL  G CT

"My world fell apart after I led at St Andrews (1995 British Open) with a round to play. I was thinking about holding the Claret jug and making my victory speech and it got away from me."

Since that fateful day when he finished T3rd in the British Open the 29-year-old Kiwi has really struggled.

From the dizzy heights of 5th in the 1995 O/M he slipped to 120th in 1996, and 133rd a year later with just one top 10 in those two years.

"I'm fit again and my new coach Jonathan Yarwood has got my swing back to where it was," and in 1998 the first steps on the comeback trail were taken with high finishes in the Cannes Open (T16th after a 67 in R4), the Turespana Masters (T19th), the English Open (T14th after 67 in R4), the Madeira Open (T19th – 80 in R4!), the French Open (T11th – R3 joint leader then 75 in R4), the German Open (T7th – 74 in R4) and in the One 2 One British Masters (T20th). T66th in the British Open

Became a first-time father in August. He'll be 30 in February 1999. 81st on the O/M.

➤ In 1999 he'll be firmly on the comeback trail, inspired by the 'nappy factor' and over the 'dodgy' age of 29.

➤ He simply loves playing in wind and rain, so do take advantage in 3-ball betting if there's a bad-weather tournament.

➤ A clear pattern emerged this year in which he shot very good final rounds when 'off the pace', yet collapsed (three times) when in with a real chance in the final round, so sadly he must be awarded the bottle.

➤ He can be expected to play well in the Heineken Classic in late January on the windy Vines course where he's done well in the past (T4th after R2 1997: T4th 1995: T9th 1994). Worth noting there as a possible bet in running if 'off the pace'.

DAVID CARTER   g y

South African born 26-year-old David lives in Chesterfield wondering why the spire's so crooked!

He was the Number 1 player at Q School in late 1994 to earn his card for the tour the following year in which he ended 92nd on the O/M.

In 1996 he showed real promise when 33rd on the O/M.

Before the 1997 season started, his confidence was boosted after he was 2nd in the Mauritius Open. He then won his first tournament, the 1996 Indian PGA after a seven-hole play off.

In 1997 he again finished 33rd on the O/M with his best finish being a 2nd place (for the second successive year) in the Cannes Open.

However two days before the 1997 Dubai Desert Classic he felt ill, collapsed unconscious and subsequently underwent brain surgery. He had seen death's door but fortunately it had stayed firmly shut!

In 1998 it became fairytale stuff after he recorded his first win when he beat Monty in a play-off to land the Irish Open in July at 125/1. He had dropped 4 shots in the last six holes, yet once in the play-off he kept his nerve to deservedly win.

"When you almost die, to come back and play golf and to win is an unbelievable feeling.....I never stopped believing in myself." Indeed his happy countenance after the closing holes led one reader to write to nominate him for the 1998 Smile Award which he won, as you can see in Chapter One.

In 1998 he also had high finishes in the Qatar Masters (T5th), the Dubai Desert Classic (T13th), the Portuguese Open (T10th) and the Benson and Hedges (T24th).

Finished T44th in the British Open, and 35th (of 44) in the World Series of Golf yet he still won over $19,000!

Made his Dunhill Cup debut in October winning one of his three matches.

His dad plays on the Seniors tour.

His accuracy from tee to green is his strength with his putting open to considerable improvement. 19th on the O/M.

➤ Having survived in '97 and won in '98 he will be hoping to progress in '99 and perhaps make the Ryder Cup team for which Corals gave him a 5/2 opening quote.

➤ His tee-to-green play was first class in the 1998 Heineken Classic. However he three putted thirteen times and when you remember he was only 12 shots back had his putter behaved half decently he'd have been in the top 4. Unexposed in this event he'll be worth a penny or two in 1999 when 80/1+ should be available.

➤ He has real PMAs with the Cannes Open after he was 2nd on his 'comeback' in 1997 and also 2nd in 1996.

FRANCISCO CEA

y ☀

The 24-year-old from Malaga makes his first Player Profile.
Earned his 1998 tour card through Q. school. He has posted four high finishes
– in the Portuguese Open (T12th), the Turespana Masters (T19th) and the
French Open (T23rd), and his highest place was when he finished T4th at 66/1
in the Madeira Open.
Finished 109th on the O/M.

➤ A promising young player, Cea's best chance will surely come in the weak
contest for the Madeira Open in which he finished T4th this year.

➤ However history could repeat itself! In 1995 a 24-year-old from Malaga called
Diego Borrego won the Turespana Masters, and in 1999 another 24-year-old
from Malaga called Francisco Cea (T19th 1998: T16th 1997) would have a
very real chance.

ALEX CEJKA

G Y  CT

This 28-year-old lover of fast cars came to real prominence in 1995 when
he won three tournaments including the prestigious Volvo Masters. He ended
the year 6th on the O/M.

He widened his horizons the following year by playing a lot in America and
in only eleven European events. He made the cut in every major including a
T11th in the British Open.

In 1997 he had six top 20 finishes to end the year 59th on the O/M. This
year he's played consistently without posting a top 3 finish. His best
performances being in the Johnnie Walker Classic (T4th), the Heineken Classic
(T25th), the South African Open (T9th), the Dubai Desert Classic (9th after a
69 in R4), the Qatar Masters (T21st), the Moroccan Open (T21st), the
Portuguese Open (T12th), the Cannes Open (T11th), the French Open (T11th),
the Loch Lomond Invitational (T20th), the Canon European Masters (T5th), the
Lancome Trophy (T11th), the Belgacom Open (T7th) and the Volvo Masters
(T12th).

Played superbly in late 1997 in the World Cup of Golf to finish 2nd in the
individual placings at 50/1.

Can occasionally seem to lose concentration, as in the early holes in R4 of
this year's Moroccan Open.

In the Dunhill Cup in October he lost all his three matches.

Became a father of a son in May 1998. Tour Number 1 for greens in
regulation. 34th on O/M.

➤ His stats tell the story so well. He hit the greens in regulation consistently
and then missed the putts with a Faldo-like frequency.

➤ Cejka is a very good player with a proven ability to turn 'being in contention'
into wins. Inspired by 'the nappy factor' in 1999 expect him to resume winning
ways in 1999 as he is a well-travelled, very experienced, proven player in
'the winner about to happen' category.

➤ Once his putter warms up he'll surely win and then could reward those
who've taken the 7/2 for him to make the Ryder Cup team.

GREG CHALMERS   g y S

I was very impressed with this guy's 1997 Challenge tour record of seven top 10s in 18 starts, and particularly by his victory in the Challenge Tour Championship.

Having earned his 1998 card "Expect him to make a real impact in 1998" was the first comment in last year's Player Profile for this 25-year-old Aussie left hander and that's exactly what he did.

He won the Australian Players Championship in December 1997 at 40/1, was T2nd in the Victorian Open and T3rd at 16/1 in the Australian tour championship to finish 3rd on the Australasian O/M.

On the European tour he was twice runner up – in the Spanish Open at 80/1, when after a fine front running performance he was pipped by Bjorn, and in the English Open when T2nd at 80/1 after a brilliant 61 in R3.

He also had high finishes in the Heineken Classic (T8th), the South African Open (T17th including a ten at one hole in R3), the South African PGA (T16th), the Scandinavian Masters (T16th), the BMW International (T18th – fell away in R4), the One 2 One British Masters (T12th after a 67 in R4), the Lancome Trophy (T18th) and the Volvo Masters (T19th).

T57th British Open. A brilliant putter who can turn poor/ordinary approach play into birdies.

He's going to the American Q School to try to earn his US 1999 tour card. 25th on O/M.

➤ He has four wins in Australia and one on the Challenge tour, so with his brilliant putting it is possible that in 1999 he'll secure his first European win.

➤ A streak player capable of shooting really low numbers. He could have shot 59 (not 61) in R3 of the English Open had he birdied any two of the last four holes.

➤ Worth noting for the early-season Heineken Classic (T8th 1998: T11th 1997). He's a more confident player now than when just 4 shots back from the winner this year.

➤ Can be noted for the British Masters where the greens suit his putting brilliance as he showed with a final round 67 to finish T12th in 1998.

ROGER CHAPMAN   D S 🎂

Chapman, Roger not Jeremy, is a record holder – he's won more money on the European tour than any other non-winner! Sadly for the 39-year-old, who was born in Kenya and lives in Windlesham, another season has passed without a victory. Indeed he couldn't add to his six runner-up finishes.

He had three high finishes – in the Spanish Open (T11th), the rain-reduced Italian Open (T23rd) and the Moroccan Open (T9th after a 7 at the 15th in R4!).

His best-ever British Open finish was T12th in 1991 yet this year he was a star.......as a commentator.

He'll be blowing the candles out on his 40th birthday cake on May day 1999.

At his best he's a straight-hitting, consistent, non-winning, money-making pro who developed a reputation for nervy final rounds. He's a classic case of a player who's most comfortable when 'off the pace'.

➤ It's very difficult to see him winning on a tour that now has so many promising young players, a new crop of Aussies, and the return of Parnevik and Faldo.
➤ Worth noting in match bets and early-round 3-ball betting on the Royal d'Agadir course home of the Moroccan Open (T9th 1998).

DANIEL CHOPRA   D

25-year-old Swede who was a very creditable 36th on the O/M in 1996 after posting four top 10 finishes. He followed up in 1997 with one top 10 and five top 20s to be 51st on the O/M.

In 1997 he was T2nd on the Australasian tour in the Victorian Open.

However in 1998 on the European tour he's had only a few high finishes when T11th in the Moroccan Open, T20th in the Spanish Open, T7th in the German Open and T8th in the British Masters. His long game has not enabled him to hit sufficient greens in regulation.

Raised in Delhi, he lives in Sweden where he was born of a Swedish mother and Indian father.

Finished 96th on the O/M.

➤ Although a dual winner on the Challenge Tour and a five-time winner on the Asian tour, 'Dan the man' has shown real R4 nerves when in contention on the European tour in the 1996 Madeira Open, the 1997 European and Dutch Opens and in R4 in the 1998 British Masters.

➤ "I like the Australian courses," so it's worth keeping him in mind, when in form, particularly in the early-round 3-ball betting at his favourite courses – the Vines (home of the Heineken Classic) and Melbourne (home of the Victorian Open where he was T2nd last season).

DARREN CLARKE   G M

What a year it's been for Darren! Another win on the European tour, the joy of becoming a first-time dad to his son Tyrone in his new home, and the deep personal upset at the tragedy of Omagh.

He had entered 1998 having finished 8th and 4th in the O/M in the previous two years. However although he had thirty-nine top 10s only two had been victories – the 1993 Alfred Dunhill Open and the 1996 German Masters.

In 1998 in Europe he had high finishes in the Dubai Desert Classic (T13th), the Qatar Masters (T9th) and the Portuguese Open (T9th after his chance was ruined by food poisoning), before he won the Benson and Hedges at 33/1.

Went on to be 2nd at 20/1 in the Deutsche Bank Open, 2nd at 22/1 in the Dutch Open, 2nd at 16/1 in the Scandinavian Masters, 4th at 18/1 in the European Open and 3rd at 16/1 in the Canon European Masters.

Finished 13th in the BMW International and T20th in the British Masters.

In America he was T8th in the US Masters after shooting 8 under for the last 36 holes: T43rd in the US Open: he missed the USPGA to be with his new son (and what a refreshing priority that showed!).

Missed the cut in the British Open.

However two contrasting events affected him deeply – the first was the birth of his son Tyrone in August. "My perspective on life now is completely changed. I've got a beautiful wife and son now at home who are much more important than my golf. That takes the pressure off and let's me go and play and accept whatever happens." Darren's words fully proved the nappy factor's influence! The other was the Omagh outrage which deeply affected Darren who was born in Dungannon and called his son Tyrone. Indeed he set about organising a Pro-Am for 14th September at Portmarnock which raised over £330,000. That was a big cheque raised by a big man with a big heart!

In the Dunhill Cup he won all his three matches for Ireland. He was below his best when easily beaten by Woosnam in R1 of the World Matchplay in October. Ended the season with a truly-brilliant victory in the Volvo Masters after a magnificent 63 in R4. As a result he was 2nd on the O/M.

Long off the tee, Darren has a fine all-round game. However his achilles heel is clearly his putting, especially from within six feet. I am convinced that it is this flaw rather than any lack of bottle that explains his amazing record of eight 2nds yet only four wins.

➤ 1999 will be his first full 'nappy factor' year, his first full year as a 30-year-old and it's also Ryder Cup year. He will therefore have every incentive to do well. He will probably win again.....and again.....if that putting weakness can be corrected.

➤ 8/1 on was his initial quote to retain his Ryder Cup place.

➤ He has an outstanding record in two tournaments in which he can be followed with confidence.

* The European Open (4th 1998: 2nd 1997: 2nd 1996) at Dublin's K Club.
* The Canon European Masters (3rd 1998: 6th 1997: 4th 1996: 6th 1995) in which he will be a must in match betting and worth an interest on the spreads

RUSSELL CLAYDON   S

A year to remember for the popular 16 stone plus former amateur champion even if it was a year to forget for Spurs, his favourite team. Spurs had problems with Sugar and Gross while Russell had no problems being gross, partly because of sugar!

After six European 2nd places the big moment, his first win, arrived in the BMW International at 125/1 in August when he kept his nerve in what developed into a match-play situation with the home favourite Bernhard Langer. It was a hugely-popular win for a hugely-popular huge guy.

His other high finishes were when T18th in the Benson and Hedges, T20th in the English Open, T8th in the French, T9th in the Irish Open and T8th in the One 2 One British Masters.

It really is refreshing to see a guy who is really comfortable just being himself. It seems reasonable to believe that he is now even more relaxed and at ease with himself after the birth in 1997 of his first child, Alex.

He missed the cut in the British Open.

Finished 22nd on the O/M.

➤ He retains his streaker symbol as he can shoot really-low numbers when his putter's hot.

➤ His win came on the back of three missed cuts in his previous four outings, so he can clearly strike form at any time.

➤ Last year his Player Profile was spot on – "In 1998, inspired by the 'nappy factor'....he could well gain his first win, possibly in Germany where his record is particularly good," so let's see if we can follow that!

➤ In 1999 he'll be worth noting in match bets and in the outright betting for the English Open as he's one of only three players to have recorded successive top 20 finishes in the English Open at the Hanbury Manor course – seven of his eight rounds there have been under par and his stroke average is a tasty 69.5.

➤ Just the sort of patient player to support for the British Masters (T8th 1998: T20th 1997).

➤ 6/1 to make the Ryder Cup team. I doubt it but if he did Roly-poly Russell against the Red-shirted Tiger......what a thought!

JOSE COCERES

After finishing 29th on the O/M in 1993 he was 68th in 1994 and 46th in 1995 before he had his best year in 1996 with five top 10s, shooting up to 24th in the O/M.

He maintained the progress in 1997 with seven top 10s including four 5th places.

However he slipped back in 1998 with only a few high finishes – in the Dubai Desert Classic (T13th), the Moroccan Open (T18th), the Irish Open (T6th after going 6 under par for the last 54 holes), the European Open (T20th) and the Lancome Trophy (T18th).

Representing Argentina in the Dunhill Cup he won two of his three matches in October

The 35-year-old Argentinean's disappointing year has been caused mainly by his putter.

Finished 66th on the O/M.

➤ He is a low ball striker with a lot of patience so he can be backed with confidence in blustery weather.

➤ In the 1999 European Open if there are really blustery conditions forecast for all four days remember Coceres – he played a fine 69 there in R3 this year in the wind.

➤ His straight hitting has led to high finishes in the Dutch Open (T5th 1997) and the Irish Open (T6th 1998) in the last two years, so keep Jose in mind on those tight tracks in 1999.

ANDREW COLTART G Y

The 28-year-old Scot joined the tour in 1993, lost his card that year, and since rejoining it in 1994 via the Q School his career has blossomed. He had finished 42nd (1994), 28th (1995), 7th (1996) and 46th (1997) on the O/M. Although he had six top 3 finishes as he entered 1998 he was still looking for his first European tour success.

And 1998 has proved the 'breakthrough' year for this member of the Chubby Chandler stable. He ended 1997 high on confidence after winning the Australian PGA Championship (for the second time) and finishing T2nd in the New Zealand Open in December when he stayed with Greg Turner's family.

He had high finishes in the Johnnie Walker Classic (T4th at 50/1), the Heineken Classic (T15th after a quadruple bogey at the par 3 fourth in R4), the Australian Masters (T7th) and the Dubai Desert Classic (T20th).

He did not contest the final Australian tournament that would determine whether he stayed in the Number 1 position on that tour's Order of Merit. However he received the news that he was the Aussie Number 1 during the Qatar Masters. Playing with a relaxed authority he secured his first European tour victory at 33/1.

He later had high finishes in the Spanish Open (T11th), the Italian Open (T23rd), the Volvo PGA (T5th after an eagle at the last hole), the English Open (T14th), the Dutch Open (T17th) and the Scandinavian Masters (T11th).

He was T44th in the British Open: T69th in the USPGA.

Finished 30th (of 44) in the World Series of Golf.

Won two of his three matches for Scotland in the Dunhill Cup. Ended the season with a highly encouraging 2nd in the Volvo Masters after 66 in R4.

Had his favourite putter and driver stolen en route to the Cannes Open.

Due to get married on 28th November. 9th on the O/M.

➤ His first European victory, second Aussie triumph and Number 1 position on the Australian Order of Merit are based on a more relaxed frame of mind. He is now about to be married and, with the help of sports psychologist John Allsop, he has stopped getting down on himself.

➤ However poor putting (R4 of the English Open) and occasional very wayward rounds (82 in R2 of the Irish Open: 81 in R4 of the Loch Lomond) show that he is still a little way from playing really consistent golf.

➤ He is a fine player in bad weather and on links courses (2nd in dreadful conditions in the 1996 Scottish Open), so if there's poor weather at Carnoustie for the 1999 British Open he'd be in with a chance.

➤ Last year his profile said that "this guy will go on to win golf tournaments" and he's done just that. With greater confidence and a more relaxed mental approach he will surely win again, possibly in the Volvo PGA (T5th 1998) on a course suited to his straight hitting.

DERRICK COOPER

The 42-year-old veteran may have won only one tournament, back in 1988, yet he always secures his card for the following season.

In 1998 he had high finishes in the English Open (T25th), the Irish Open (T9th), the Loch Lomond Invitational (T11th) and the BMW International (T6th) to once more ensure his playing privileges for 1999.

Finished 1998 77th on the O/M.

➤ He offers serious, and I mean serious, betting opportunities for any punter in the wide-awake club who has a barometer! His stocky build and excellent iron play make him a really superb player in very windy conditions when he can be on offer at real 'value' prices especially in 3-ball betting.

➤ If the winds are forecast for the Benson and Hedges at the exposed Oxfordshire course follow Cooper in 3-ball and match betting, and as a big-priced outsider – remember last time it really blew there he was 3rd in 1996 at 150/1, when only five players broke par!

➤ Must be supported in October in the Novotel Perrier Pairs when partnering his great buddy, Richard Boxall (2nd 33/1, 1998: 2nd 40/1 1996).

EAMONN DARCY

The 46-year-old four-time Ryder Cupper from County Wicklow has four European tour wins and eleven others worldwide. However back problems combined with being in his mid forties has meant that he's been hovering in the lower reaches of the O/M in 1996 (97th) and 1997 (100th).

In 1998 he had high finishes in the Cannes Open (T16th – T2nd after R3), the Spanish Open (T11th), the Irish Open (T25th) and the German Open (T20th). He was joint R1 leader in the Lancome Trophy.

Suffers from back trouble. Deeply affected by the death of Darren, the 17-year-old son of his best mate Christy O'Connor, in mid season. 102nd on O/M.

➤ Without a top 10 finish in any of the last three years Darcy cannot be recommended for outright betting.

➤ He's the course professional attached to the Druids Glen course, home of the Irish Open. So he can be considered there in the market to be the top Irish Player (2nd 10/1 1998).

➤ In 3-ball betting he's not a player to be opposed lightly in windy conditions.

BRIAN DAVIS   g y

This promising 24-year-old Londoner had a memorable start to 1998, his second season on tour, when he contracted chickenpox after missing the cut in the Dubai Desert Classic. Really ill for seven weeks – "I looked like the Elephant Man" – he bounced back with sufficient success to secure his 1999 tour card after four high finishes in the Benson and Hedges (T11th), the Irish Open (T16th), the Dutch Open (T11th) and the Scandinavian Masters (T11th).

This followed his excellent rookie year in 1997 when he was 53rd on the O/M after three top 10s – Italian Open (T6th), the German Open (T4th) and the European Open (T5th).

A former England amateur international at all levels he has made a fine start to his professional career in his first two seasons.

➤ Finished 79th on the O/M.

➤ Further consolidation in Ryder Cup year can be expected.

➤ Although his accuracy stats are not good, his high finishes in 1998 were on straight hitters' tracks in the Irish Open, Dutch Open and Scandinavian Masters.

➤ He deserves the g and y symbols after the bright start he's made to his tour career.

MARK DAVIS

The Essex 34-year-old has two wins – both in the Austrian Open in 1991 and 1993.

Finished 73rd (1993), 31st (1994), 81st (1995) and 51st (1996) on the O/M. However 1997 was very disappointing with just one top 20 finish in his worst-ever season, he finished 145th on the O/M.

In 1998 having secured his card via Q School, he posted high finishes in the Moroccan Open (T4th at 150/1 after 76 in R4), the Cannes Open (T8th), the Irish Open (T25th) and the Scandinavian Masters (T11th).

Played well especially in R1 (64) of the Compaq European Grand Prix. His putting is his strength and his inaccuracy off the tee his weakness. 98th on O/M.

➤ He was the tour's top putter in 1994 and has the ability to pop up at the top of the leaderboard during a tournament. However after the 1998 Moroccan Open there must be a doubt if he can force a victory, especially in Ryder Cup year.

➤ Worth noting, especially in the early-round 3-ball betting, in the Portuguese Open where his recent tournament record is very good – T15th 1997, T2nd 1996, T10th 1995.

RODGER DAVIS

47-year-old Aussie from Sydney who has been on the European tour since 1977. He gave up the game in the 80's to focus on business interests which failed. Since his 'comeback' he's won six times on the European tour, the last the 1993 Cannes Open.

He now has nineteen international victories and seven in Europe.

He was T2nd in the 1987 British Open.

However in 1995 (129th), 1996 (130th) and 1997 (101st) he couldn't make the top 100 on the O/M, posting only one top 10 in those three years.

In 1998 he played well in the Benson and Hedges to finish T7th after all four rounds were at or under 70. He followed up with a T21st in the Volvo PGA. Late in September he was T15th in the German Masters (65 in R3).

Prequalified for the British Open finishing T44th. 101st on O/M.

➤ With only two top 10s in the last four years he's obviously not one for the outright markets.

➤ Clearly, at 47, he's past his prime. However he is still a fine player in windy conditions and he does present a possible betting opportunity because he can be considered in the Top Australian market for two tournaments:-

* the Volvo PGA: 3rd top Aussie at 14/1 in 1998 in a tournament in which this decade he's made seven of nine cuts, including when T4th (1990) and T8th (1991).

* the Benson and Hedges: he was T1st at 20/1 in the 1998 top Aussie market.

PAUL EALES

Paul has now completed six full years on tour. He has one win, the Extremadura Open, in 1994 when he had his highest order of merit finish when he was 35th.

More recently he has struggled with only one top 10, when T4th at 80/1 in the 1997 Cannes Open, in the last two years.

In 1998 his high finishes came when he was T14th in the English Open, and T13th in the BMW International won by his friend Russell Claydon.

Although an accurate driver he lacks length, and he must improve his putting. 95th on O/M.

➤ A thorough professional in every way. However with only one top 3 finish in the last four years he is not one for outright betting.
➤ A fine player in windy conditions.
➤ His best chance will surely be on the Royal Mougins course, home of the Cannes Open, which places an emphasis on accuracy rather than length. T4th in 1997 he could be fancied there in 1999 if his putting touch returns.

DENIS EDLUND

After playing the Challenge tour from 1989-1996 the 33-year-old Swede won back-to-back tournaments on the Challenge tour to secure his 1997 card as the No. 2 player on that tour.

In 1997, his rookie year, he finished 41st on the money list thanks mainly to a fine 2nd place in the English Open.

In 1998 he found his form 'out of the blue' when T2nd at 200/1 in the Loch Lomond Invitational to secure his card.

His other high finish was when T13th in the German Open.

Finished the year 70th on the O/M.

➤ In his two years he has shown that he is an inconsistent player who can suddenly get into contention and post a high finish.
➤ With six challenge tour wins and impressive when chasing home Johansson (English Open 1997) and Westwood (Loch Lomond 1998) he could land a shock win 'out of the blue' in 1999 – if so it will probably be in the twelve-week period from mid May to early August when he's been at his best in the last two years.

OLIVIER EDMOND

28-year-old Frenchman makes his first appearance in these pages.

He secured his 1998 card via the Q school and retained it for 1999 after a fine 2nd place in the French Open in late June thanks to a 67 in R4 when coming from behind.

His other high finish was when T13th in the German Open where he shot a disappointing 75 in R4 when in contention.

His poor stats for driving accuracy and putting clearly point to the areas of his game that have often been in 'intensive care'.

Made his debut for France in October in the Dunhill Cup. Sadly however he lost all his three matches. 93rd on O/M.

➤ To retain his card in Ryder Cup year will be an achievement in itself.
➤ On the evidence of this rookie year he is clearly best when coming from 'off the pace' and can be opposed in R4 2-ball betting if in serious contention.

KLAS ERIKSSON

27-year-old Swede who made an impact in 1994, his rookie year, when he was 45th on the O/M thanks mainly to a 2nd place in the Czech Open.

He struggled with wrist and back problems in 1995 when 123rd on the O/M, and in 1996 he had the putting 'yips' and only secured his card late in the season thanks to a 5th place in the Oki Pro-Am.

In 1997 he had four top 20 finishes but could not post a top 10.

In 1998 he has had high finishes in the Irish Open (T16th), the Loch Lomond Invitational (T13th) and the German Masters (T15th after a 67 in R4).

He was in contention after a 66 in R1 of the rain-reduced Italian Open then fell away.

A very long hitter. 119th on O/M so Q. School beckons.

➤ Without a top 10 in the last two years it's not very easy to see Eriksson winning again. However his long hitting is suited to the course used for the German Masters.

➤ Worth noting in match bets and 3-ball betting for the Irish Open which is the only tournament in which he's shown consistent form (T16th 1998: T15th 1997).

GARY EVANS

29-year-old who had a superb rookie season in 1992 (35th O/M) after an outstanding amateur career.

However major problems with his left wrist stopped his progress. Despite surgery his career has been stalled. Finished 1996 95th and 1997 99th on the O/M to retain his card. In 1998 he was ill with a stomach virus early in the season. His best finishes were in the Benson and Hedges (T11th), the English Open (T14th) and the Belgacom Open (T21st).

He prequalified for the British Open. He made the cut and his wife presented him with their second baby daughter. He finished T73rd. 94th on O/M.

➤ There is one tournament in which 'the nappy factor' inspired Evans must be backed – it's the Compaq European Grand Prix on a course he loves and in which his record is first class – T4th 1996, 6th 1997 and T3rd of the R2 finishers in the cancelled tournament in 1998. If 80/1 is available again in 1999 get on each way – Evans above it's a good wager!

➤ He was 4th in the Volvo PGA at Wentworth in his rookie year (1992). With such PMAs he can be noted there in 3-ball betting.

NICK FALDO MBE   Pb D

41-year-old Nicholas Alexander is returning to the European tour in 1998 after playing most of his golf in the States in recent years. He joined the US tour in 1995 winning the Doral Ryder Open in his first year when he was 19th on the money list.

In 1996 he scored that memorable win, over Greg Norman, in the US Masters on his way to finishing 12th on the money list.

In 1997 he won the Nissan Open at 20/1 on a course ideal for his game. He also had a high finish in the Kemper Open (T3rd). However there were worrying signs for Nick as the year progressed.

In the 1997 majors he missed the cut in the US Masters (as defending champion) and the USPGA, and was only T47th in the US Open and T51st in the British Open.

He ended the year 58th on the Money list.

In 1998 the decline in his form, noticeable at the end of the previous year, continued for the first nine months.

His T18th in the Players Championship was his only US top 20 finish, and his R4 of 83 at Hilton Head in the MCI Classic in April was the worst score he'd ever posted in America.

He missed the cut in the US Masters (for the second successive year) and the US Open; in the British Open, although he made his 23rd successive cut he finished T44th. He was 54th in the USPGA.

Showed highly encouraging form in mid September when 6th in the Lancome Trophy (after 65 in R4). However in the Belgacom Open after 65 in R1 he finished a disappointing T30th.

He has six major triumphs – the US Masters in 1989, 1990 and 1996, and the British Open in 1987, 1990 and 1992.

He has three other US tour wins, and a further total of thirty worldwide.

His recent play has led to the phrase 'he's shaved the hole again' becoming almost a soundbite as putt after putt look in and stay above ground.

➤ Although his major problem has been on the greens his poor putting has clearly affected his confidence and the rest of his game.

➤ "I'll try to do both tours. It's a lot of golf and a long season but the goal is to make the (European) team as quickly as possible, and then decide what to do after that".

➤ Nick has been a truly superb player with a magnificent individual and Ryder Cup record. However any objective analysis of his performances over the last two seasons must show that he is 'over the top' – an example of a once great player who is clearly in decline and so must be given the PB symbol.

➤ For a player who gears everything to his play in the majors his recent performances speak volumes about his decline – in the last nine majors he missed four cuts and has not posted a top 40 finish!

➤ As I explained fully earlier in Part Two I do NOT expect him to line up for the Ryder Cup team in 1999. Indeed I expect his failure to secure automatic selection will lead to massive media hype and pressure on Mark James to offer him a wild card which I do not expect him to do. So the 13/8 on for Nick to make the team looks a poor bet indeed. At one time he'd have been a 'no offers thank you' certainty!

➤ However if there is one European tournament to get Nick back into the winner's enclosure it must surely be the 1999 Volvo PGA at Wentworth. In twenty starts from 1977 he's been in the top 10 fourteen times, won it four times, missed only one cut, and on his last two efforts was 2nd in both 1997 and 1996.

MARC FARRY

Punters did not find it Farry funny when Marc won the rain-reduced two-round 1996 BMW International at 100/1. Yet for the 39-year-old Frenchman it was easily his best finish and hoisted him to 53rd on the O/M.

In 1997 top 10s in the Johnnie Walker Classic (T7th) and the Heineken Classic (T3rd) secured his tour card as he ended the year 81st on the O/M.

In 1998 he had three high finishes – the French Open (T6th), the One 2 One British Masters (T12th – slipped back after sharing lead in R4) and the German Masters (T11th).

He was 4 under par and T1st in the Compaq European Grand Prix after 34 holes when the tournament was cancelled.

Has had real putting difficulties in 1998. Has had back problems.

Finished 87th on the O/M.

➤ Has PMAs with the BMW International (T12th 1997: W 1996: T7th 1995) and can be noted there in match and 3-ball betting.

➤ Probably at his very best in high temperatures – it was 44°C when he was T3rd in the 1997 Heineken Classic.

STEPHEN FIELD

This 33-year-old guy from Barnsley finished 1996 (114th) and 1997 (112th) just high enough on the O/M to secure his tour card without ever recording a top 3 finish.

However in 1998 he was 3rd at 200/1 in the Scandinavian Masters virtually to secure his card for 1999. It was a completely unexpected piece of form.

There were no other high finishes in 1998.

Finished the year 105th on the O/M.

➤ With only one piece of isolated form Stephen sadly does not provide punters with a Field of Dreams!

MASSIMO FLORIOLI   G Y

Inspired by fellow Italian and Ryder Cup star Costantino Rocca he has made a real impact in 1998 – his second full year on tour (he finished 114th in 1997's O/M).

His high finishes were in the South African Open (T9th), the Italian Open (T23rd), the Turespana Masters (T8th), the Volvo PGA (T21st) and the Loch Lomond Invitational (T13th).

However he had two really big pay days when T3rd at 150/1 in the Benson and Hedges having been joint leader at halfway; and when T2nd at 125/1, after a 67 in R4 when 'off the pace', in the French Open.

He has two challenge tour victories. 49th on O/M.

➤ A promising and rapidly-improving young player he deserves the G and Y symbols.

➤ He is still getting used to the pressure of being 'in serious contention'

➤ in the Benson and Hedges he was 9 under par for R1 and R2: 2 under for R3 and R4.

-in the French Open when 2nd at halfway he shot 75 in R3. So he may prove to be a player best when coming from 'off the pace'

➤ He may well take advantage of an early-season opportunity in the Turespana Masters (T8th 1998: T11th 1997).

ANDERS FORSBRAND   Pb D

37-year-old 'grand pappy' of Swedish golf who now lives in Marbella. A winner of six European tour events and seven other tournaments, the indications now are that Anders is past his peak.

In 1998 he had a few high finishes – in the South African PGA (8th), the Qatar Masters (T13th) and the Moroccan Open (T24th – after 77 in R4).

However he had plenty of rounds to forget, including the Benson and Hedges (R3 and R4 = 163) and Loch Lomond where his halfway score was 172!!

Won the 1997 Open Novotel Paris tournament with Michael Jonzon. As defending champions in 1998 they finished T30th of 34!

His putting can still be good but his long game is now a shadow of what it was when he finished 4th on the O/M in 1992 after two wins and twelve other top 10s! 137th on O/M.

➤ This season his driving has often made Seve's look straight! So like the Spaniard he's awarded the Pb symbol.

PIERRE FULKE

27-year-old Swede who joined the tour in 1993 via the Challenge tour. His best year by far was 1994 when he made 80% of his cuts and had six top 10s, including a 2nd place in the Canon European Masters, to finish 23rd on the O/M.

In 1998 he had high finishes in the Benson and Hedges (T24th), the Loch Lomond Invitational (T24th), the Scandinavian Masters (T16th), the BMW International (T11th after 65 in R4 when 'off the pace'), the Cannes Open (T16th after a poor 75 in R4), the Canon European Masters (T20th) and especially in the One 2 One British Masters (T2nd after a 67 in R4 from 'off the pace').

Very accurate off the tee. He was Number 1 on the tour for driving accuracy. Finished 1998 42nd on the O/M.

➤ He has disappointed on two occasions when he's been in contention (Loch Lomond 1997 R4 – 73 and Cannes Open 1998 R4 – 75). So he's proving to be an 'off the pacer'.

➤ Can be opposed in final-round 2-ball betting if in serious contention.

➤ His best chance will be when coming from 'off the pace', probably in the Cannes Open (T16th 1998: 5th 1994: T3rd 1993) on a course that suits him because it rewards accuracy rather than length. He lives nearby in Monte Carlo.

IAN GARBUTT   G Y

Quietly and almost unnoticed this 26-year-old Doncaster guy has laid a really solid foundation for what could well prove to be a successful and punter-friendly year in 1999.

In 1996 he won the UAP Grand Final to finish in first place on the Challenge tour.

In 1997 he finished 85th on the money list with four top 20 finishes.

In 1998 he has hit a really consistent vein of form. After a hole in one in R3 of the Heineken Classic he won $100,000 in gaming chips which he cashed in!!

He had high finishes in the Qatar Masters (T21st), the Portuguese Open (T16th – four sub-par rounds), the Cannes Open (T16th – after 65 in R4), the Deutsche Bank Open (T22nd), the English Open (T25th), the French Open (T16th), the Irish Open (T9th), the Loch Lomond Invitational (T24th) and the Dutch Open (T7th).

Picked up an ankle injury in September.

A member of the Chubby Chandler stable he'll be hoping to emulate Lee Westwood and Darren Clarke.

Finished 1998 52nd on the O/M.

➤ His great strength is his accuracy off the tee and fairway (as shown by his stats) which has been the basis for his consistency. To convert top 20s to top 10s and to his first win he must improve his putting. In the belief that he will do so and post his first win in 1999 he's given the G and Y symbols.

➤ He's 6/1 to make the 1999 Ryder Cup team.

➤ He must be backed for the 1999 Dutch Open on the tight Hilversum course – in the last two years he's finished 22nd and 7th, played every round below par and has a stroke average of 68.87!!

➤ Worth an each-way interest in the Irish Open where accuracy is very important and where he was a fine T9th this year just six behind the winner.

SERGIO GARCIA   G Y A

Sergio is the 18-year-old Spanish 'wonderkid' who is going to make a massive impact on European golf over the next few years. Given the nickname 'El Nino' he has been hailed by Seve Ballesteros as "Europe's Tiger Woods".

He is the son of the Madrid Club pro and at college in the States.

He was off scratch at 13 and incredibly at 14 years of age he played in the 1995 Mediterranean Open and made the cut!

He is hugely long off the tee, has a good short game, is very fit and very competitive.

In 1997 he won fifteen amateur titles, and in 1998 he led the Monterrey Open on the Nike tour in the States before finishing 19th. He was T3rd on the Nike Greensboro Open later in the season. In the autumn he played in the Catalonian Open, a Spanish PGA event, shot three successive 64s to be the first amateur ever to win the tournament.

He was T34th in the Spanish Open when he was warned for slow play, T27th in the Turespana Masters and T18th in the Lancome Trophy.

He won the British Amateur Championship with ease in early June.

He made the cut at Loch Lomond (T57th) and in the Irish Open (T60th), although his finish (R3 – 75 and R4 – 81) was poor. Played well in the British Masters to finish T12th.

Finished T29th in the British Open.

➤ Believe me, this guy is going to be one mega star. He has all the golfing and personal qualities needed to emulate the 'greats' of the European tour.

➤ Expect him to turn pro after he plays in the 1999 US Masters, and do watch for the media to 'discover' him suddenly in the New Year.

➤ With the new World Championship tournaments (for which he's ineligible) counting for Ryder Cup points, and without him being able to earn any points until he turns pro in mid April he won't make the 1999 side, but he'll sure play in 2001!

➤ Having built up experience both in America and in Europe on the professional circuits he should find the transition to the pro ranks one that he takes in his stride.

➤ A certain future winner, a certain future Ryder Cup player and, yes, a certain future winner of a major.....this guy is going to be one very, very big star!!

IGNACIO GARRIDO ☼ D CT G Y

The 26-year-old Spaniard was the 'surprise' player of 1997 when he won the German Open from the front at 66/1 and was 2nd in the Portuguese Open, the Scandinavian Masters and the Czech Open. As a result he made the Ryder Cup team – halving three matches and losing his singles to Tom Lehman 7 and 6.

In last year's profile I said that he 'must guard against mental let down in 1998'. Sadly MLD did set in.

Although 3rd at 40/1 in the individual ranking in the World Cup of Golf in late 1997 and posting high early-season finishes in the South African Open (T7th) and the Dubai Desert Classic (T6th – after 76 in R4) he had a poor year.

He missed the cut in the US Masters (after shooting 85 in R1, including an 11 at the 15th), the US Open and the USPGA. T57th in the British Open.

His high finishes came later in the season when as defending champion in the German Open he threw away a winning chance after a 74 in R4 to finish T2nd at 40/1. In September he finished T4th at 50/1 in the British Masters after incurring a 4-shot penalty because he had an extra club in his bag. His caddie's error probably cost him the tournament. Played very poorly in the Volvo Masters.

At his very best in very warm weather. A martial arts student. 40th (!) on O/M.

➤ We must remember he is still a young man and having tasted the heights of the Ryder Cup, he'll be ultra determined to regain his form in 1999.

➤ He's 3/1 to retain his Ryder Cup place.

➤ Expect him to bounce back in 1999, although his poor final rounds in the Dubai Desert Classic and the German Open suggest he may have high finishes rather than wins.

DAVID GILFORD CT 🏇

The 33-year-old Crewe farmer won six times between 1991 and 1994. However in four years since then he has not added to his earlier triumphs.

In 1996 (59th) and 1997 (31st) he had his lowest O/M positions since he started winning.

In 1998 he had high finishes in the Dubai Desert Classic (T17th after 64 in R4), the Portuguese Open (T2nd on a course requiring accuracy), the Volvo PGA (T11th), the Dutch Open (T17th), the European Open (T10th) and the Canon European Masters (T15th).

He is a straight hitter whose weakness has been his short game where his chipping and pitching have been his achilles heel.

He's a proven front runner. 48th on O/M.

➤ His best chances will probably be in
  * the Volvo PGA (T11th 1998: 6th 1997) where he's one of only four players to post successive top 20 finishes.
  * the European Open (T10th 1998) where the tightening of the course has placed a premium on accuracy which is his strong suit.

➤ He played in the Ryder Cup in 1991 and 1995 and is 4/1 to play in it again in 1999.

➤ Can be followed in match bets whenever there is a premium on accuracy.

TOM GILLIS

30-year-old American player from Michigan who earned his 1998 tour card via Q school.

Made a good impression with high finishes in the Moroccan Open (T6th – 10 under par final three rounds), the Madeira Open (T10th – after a 78 in R4) and the French Open (T16th – after 73 in R4).

Finished 1998 116th on the O/M.

➤ His disappointing final round in the Madeira Open is an obvious concern. However 'on a learning curve' he could turn that experience to his advantage, so remember him in 3-ball betting, and as an outright each-way bet for the 1999 Madeira Open.

THOMAS GOGELE   g y

The 28-year-old German has a progressive record in his mid twenties – 75th in the O/M in 1996, 58th in 1997, he again improved his position in 1998.

He had three top 10s prior to 1998, in the 1996 German Open (T2nd) and in 1997 in the Madeira Open (8th) and the Dubai Desert Classic (5th).

He had top 10s in 1998 in the Heineken Classic (7th), the South African Open (T9th), the Madeira Open (T4th at 25/1) and the BMW International (3rd at 125/1).

Other high finishes included the Moroccan Open (T14th after a 77 in R4), the Portuguese Open (T22nd), the English Open (T20th) and the Loch Lomond Invitational (T24th).

Representing Germany in the Dunhill Cup he won two of his three matches. 46th on the O/M.

➤ He is an improving progressive player, however his 1998 scoring when in contention suggest he's more of an 'off the pacer' than a front runner.
* South African Open R1 + R2 6 under: R3 + R4 1 over
* Moroccan Open R1 + R2 7 under: R3 + R4 7 over
* Madeira Open R1 + R2 8 under: R3 + R4 2 over
➤ The weakly-contested Madeira Open (T4th 1998: 8th 1997: 12th 1996) will provide a very real winning opportunity in a Ryder Cup year.
➤ "I enjoy playing on home soil," so he can be followed as an outsider in the outright market and in early-round 3-ball betting in the BMW International. He loves the Golfclub Munchen course where he had an impressive stroke average of 68.9 in 1998 when 3rd.

MATHEW GOGGIN   g y

24-year-old from Tasmania who was the Australian Amateur champion in 1995 and played his first year on the European tour in 1997. However, although he had high finishes in the South African PGA (8th) and the Canon European Masters (12th) he made only five other cuts in 22 starts and had to return to Q School.

Since then he's made a real impact with three superb finishes on the Australasian tour when 2nd in the Australian Masters, T3rd in the Canon Challenge and the 25/1 winner of the Tour Championship in March.

On the European tour he had high finishes in the Moroccan Open (T24th after 77 in R1), the Madeira Open (T19th) and the German Open (T13th).

Finished 3rd in the Challenge Tour championship at East Sussex National in August.

His big finish came when he was T2nd at 66/1 in the French Open. 117th on O/M.

➤ He has been inconsistent on the European tour. However he has won on the Aussie tour, twice on the Challenge tour and he was the Aussie Amateur champ, so inspired by the examples of Richard Green, Greg Chalmers, Stephen Allan and Stephen Leaney expect him to make a real impact in 1999.

➤ Level par when T19th on his first visit to the Madeira Open in 1998 he must be fancied when he returns there in 1999.

➤ After his devastating form early in 1998 watch out for him in the Australian Masters (2nd 1998), the Canon Challenge (T3rd 1998) in February and as defending champion in the Australian tour championship in early March.

RETIEF GOOSEN

The 29-year-old South African joined the tour fully in 1993 after finishing the Number 1 player on the 1992 Q School.

On the Order of Merit he was 44th (1993), 39th (1994), 94th (1995) and 25th (1996), with his first win coming in the Slaley Hall Northumberland Challenge in 1996.

In 1997 he showed further improvement with a second victory in the French Open at 33/1 together with three top 4 finishes in the South African PGA (T4th), the Compaq European Grand Prix (2nd) and the Loch Lomond Invitational (3rd).

He ended the year winning all five matches in the Dunhill Cup to be T1st at 25/1 in the individual top scorer betting as he helped South Africa to victory. After all that, plus a 10th place in the British Open, I made him a confident each-way bet for the 1998 European Order of Merit......and he has let us down!

In 1998 he started brightly with really-high finishes in the Johnnie Walker Classic (3rd at 40/1), the South African PGA (3rd 33/1), the Qatar Masters (T5th 40/1), the Italian Open (T13th) and the Benson and Hedges (T5th).

However his normally well-grooved swing was in difficulties through the summer. He finished T22nd in the Deutsche Bank Open and T16th in the French Open.

Later he was T20th in the Canon European Masters and T11th in the German Masters.

In America he missed the cut in the Bay Hill Invitational, the Players Championship and the US Masters (going well till a 10 wrecked his card in R2).

Played brilliantly in the Dunhill Cup in helping South Africa to retain the trophy. For the second successive year he won all his five matches to be the top individual scorer at 40/1.

He has huge length off the tee although not always accurate. His medium length putting has been his weakness in the past. 33rd on O/M.

➤ He must be noted in the three tournaments in which he has shown up so well in recent years on courses over 7000 yards long.

 * the South African PGA (3rd 1998: 4th 1997)

* the Benson and Hedges (3 successive top 20s including T5th 1998)
* the French Open (T16th 1998: W 1997)

➤ Retief must be a banker each-way bet in the Qatar Masters. 12 under par for the last 36 holes in 1998 when T5th, the combination of a 7,300 plus yard course and guaranteed sunshine provide an ideal mix for the South African who will then have just celebrated his 30th birthday.

➤ His game is clearly well suited to the Gut Larchenhof course used for the German Masters. T11th in 1998 he must have a real chance there in 1999.

➤ His inconsistency makes him a player to avoid in match betting, and to oppose when on tight, shorter courses unsuited to his game.

➤ He'll sure be looking forward to the British Open at St Andrews in 2000. If his 6 – 9 foot putting there improved then with his tee-to-green play so brilliant he'd have a serious chance.

SILVIO GRAPPASONNI

Silvio is a 36-year-old Monte Carlo resident who was born in Como, Italy.

His best year on tour was in 1995 when he was 67th on the O/M. In 1998 he again struggled with his only high finishes in the Italian Open (T23rd), the Canon European Masters (T18th) and the Lancome Trophy (T15th).

He has represented Italy in both the World Cup and Dunhill Cup.

Very short off the tee at 260 yards, he is a reasonably accurate player. However his putting really has been poor.

He has won four times on the Challenge tour, three in Italy. 11th on O/M.

➤ To date in over 200 tournaments he's yet to win or finish in the first three, and he's posted only eight top 10s.

➤ The Canon European Masters with its forgiving fairways and thin atmosphere obviously suit his game (T18th 1998: T21st 1997).

➤ For a player of his ranking his performances in the Lancome Trophy are extremely good. He's had three successive top 15 finishes (T15th 1998: T11th 1997: T15th 1996), and his R2 scoring in the last three years (69-69-67) is impressive. Make a note of Silvio in the 3-ball betting and if a bookie would give you match bet against a 100/1 rag he'd be a real steal!

MATHIAS GRONBERG　　　　F 🐎

In his rookie year 1994, the 28-year-old Swede got his name noticed when T2nd in the Madeira Open in a season when he finished 86th in the O/M.

His first victory came in his second year when he won the Canon European Masters and ended the year 22nd on the O/M.

In 1996 he had four top 10s to finish 71st before his form dipped in 1997 as he ended the year 108th on the O/M without a top 10 finish.

However 1998 saw a renaissance in his form with high finishes in the South African PGA (9th), the Moroccan Open (3rd at 100/1), the Spanish Open (7th), the Scandinavian Masters (T7th when he was T3rd at 33/1 in the top Scandinavian player betting) and the Canon European Masters (T7th).

In the European Open at the K Club he simply ran away from his field to win comfortably by 10 (!) shots at 125/1. His victory came after he had spent two weeks on holiday in the States with his American fiancee, Tara.

"Since I got engaged I have stayed calm and been in harmony with my golf more."

Won two of his three matches in the Dunhill Cup on his debut. Finished T16th in the Volvo Masters. 10th on O/M.

➤ His two wins have come in the period from mid August to mid September so it may be he's always going to be his best in late summer/early autumn.

➤ His 1998 win after that two-week break shows he goes well when fresh and relaxed.

➤ One point to note is that he was R3 leader for both his tour wins so the next time he's leading going into Sunday he will be confident and he'll then be worth a bet in running.

➤ Worth an interest in the Canon European Masters – it's his time of the year, and he's a fine recent record in this event – T7th 1998: 12th 1997: made cut 1996: Won 1995 – with a four-year stroke average of 68.56.

JOAKIM HAEGGMAN

With so many talented young Swedes coming off the production line Haeggman, the first Swedish Ryder Cup player in 1993, seems to be an old man – yet he's just 29 years old.

He's won twice – the Spanish Open (1993), and the Scandinavian Masters (from the front in 1997). His best year was 1993 when he had eleven top 10s as well as his first win to finish 15th on the O/M,

Since then he's been 25th (1994), 40th (1995), 60th (1996) and 19th (1997). Brilliant in the Dunhill Cup for Sweden in October 1997 – he won four and lost one as Sweden finished 2nd. In late 1997 he tried for his US tour card but missed out by a single shot.

In 1998 he had high finishes in the Cannes Open (T11th), the Italian Open (T2nd), the Deutsche Bank Open (T13th) and the Belgacom Open (T10th).

His 35th place in the British Open was his highest-ever finish in that major. 67th on O/M.

➤ He's an inconsistent streak player as shown in the 1997 Cannes Open when he shot 83 – 63 to make the cut! His capacity to shoot low was shown by rounds of 63 twice in 1998 – the Italian Open (R3) and the Deutsche Bank Open (R3) – so he retains the 'streaker' symbol!

So be wary of opposing him in early-round 3-ball betting because of this streakiness.

➤ His inaccuracy off tee and fairway is reflected in his stats so he can be opposed when there is a premium on accuracy.

CRAIG HAINLINE

28-year-old American who finished 10th on the 1997 Challenge tour, when he won once, to earn his 1998 tour card.

He's had a satisfactory first year with high finishes in the Irish Open (5th), the Loch Lomond Invitational (T13th – where he was T3rd at 16/1 as top American player), the Scandinavian Masters (T16th), the European Open (T15th after a 78 in R4), the One 2 One British Masters (T20th after 74 in R4) and the Volvo Masters (T8th).

A good iron player. His strength is his accuracy, his weakness is his putting. At his best when there is a premium on accuracy and the wind is blowing. 41st on O/M.

➤ When he won the 1997 Perrier European Pro-Am on the Challenge tour he came from 'off the pace' with a 64 in R4, and in the 1998 European Open he started R4 4 shots clear in 2nd place, shot 78, and finished T15th. Similarly when starting R4 2 strokes back he shot 74 to finish T20th in the 1998 One 2 One British Masters. Such evidence suggests he's an 'off the pacer' not a front runner.

➤ He'll have PMAs with Ireland after his two successful visits there this year so remember him in the early-round 3-ball betting in the Irish Open and the European Open, especially if the winds blow. Coming from Wichita he's used to playing when there are really windy conditions.

MATS HALLBERG

The 33-year-old Swede has struggled to make any significant impact on the European tour with 76th (1997) his best O/M finish.

In 1998 he had high finishes in the Dubai Desert Classic (T13th), the Volvo PGA (a fine 5th), the Scandinavian Masters (T16th) and the Lancome Trophy (T18th).

He missed the cut in the British Open.

Finished 1998 61st on the O/M.

➤ He has posted one punter-friendly top 5 finish in each of the last three years – 1996 Scottish Open (3rd), the 1997 Scandinavian Masters (T3rd) and the 1998 Volvo PGA (5th).

➤ However it's best to remember him in 3-ball betting when there are really wild blustery conditions as he self confessedly enjoys playing when the winds howl, as they did in the 1996 Scottish Open when he was a brilliant 3rd.

PADRAIG HARRINGTON g y

Padraig (Pordrig) is a 27-year-old Dublin guy who made a very big impact in his first two years on tour.

In 1996 he ended his 'rookie' year 11th on the O/M after winning the Spanish Open and notching seven other top 10s.

In 1997 he kept up that good work when he was 8th on the O/M after eight more top 10 finishes.

In late 1997, alongside Paul McGinley, he won the World Cup of Golf for Ireland at 16/1.

In 1998 he started well with high finishes in the Johnnie Walker Classic (T8th – 3rd at halfway), the Heineken Classic (T3rd), the Qatar Masters (T17th), the Volvo PGA (T11th) and the English Open (T25th) and he was a creditable T32nd in the US Open after missing the cut in the Irish Open and the British Open at a time when he was having trouble with his long game.

He hit form in the German Open when T2nd at 40/1, although he bogeyed the final hole. Played well to be T8th in the German Masters in September.

Played well over last 54 holes in the Belgacom Open to finish T21st. T16th in the Volvo Masters.

Won only one of his three matches in the Dunhill Cup in October. Finished 29th on the O/M.

➤ Once he can get his long game back to its 1996/97 level he will once more be a real player to note as his short game, his temperament and his ambition are first class.

➤ He's a fine links player as he proved when T5th in the 1997 British Open. If he's in steady form he can be backed each way at Carnoustie in 1999 in the 'top Brit' market in which he's been in top 4 twice in the last three years.

➤ Worth an interest in windy conditions in tournaments in Australia, particularly in the Heineken Classic (T3rd 1998 after 66 in R4 and T11th 1997 after a course record 63 in R2).

➤ 11/4 to make the 1999 Ryder Cup team.

PER HAUGSRUD

The 33-year-old Norwegian is struggling to make an impact with gaining his card his annual pre-occupation.

80th on the O/M in 1996 and 96th the following year. His highest finish has been T3rd in the 1994 Scandinavian Masters.

In 1998 he had three high finishes in the Benson and Hedges (T15th), the Dutch Open (T21st) and the European Open (T16th).

He finished the year 97th on the O/M.

➤ The way to profit from Haugsrud is to back him in 3-ball and 2-ball betting in the European Open in which he has such a consistent record (T16th 1998: T10th 1997: T10th 1996). It's the PER-fect way to follow him and real value bets can be found.

SCOTT HENDERSON

42nd on the O/M when Rookie of the Year in 1997 in which he was T2nd in the European Masters, T4th in the Compaq European Grand Prix and T9th in the Deutsche Bank Open.

In 1998 he consolidated with top 30 finishes in the Benson and Hedges (T24th), the Deutsche Bank Open (T27th after 75 in R4) and the Scandinavian Masters (T25th).

However his best performances were in the German Open (6th) and the Canon European Masters (11th).

Finished the year 68th on the O/M.

➤ From Aberdeen, he is well suited by links-type courses such as the Sporting Club, Berlin, home of the German Open where he was 6th this year.

➤ Must be noted for the Canon European Masters (11th 1998: T2nd 1997) in which he has a two-year stroke average of 67.25, with seven of his eight rounds in the '60s.

➤ Having shot 73 in R3 of the 1997 Canon European Masters when the halfway leader, and that 75 in R4 in the 1998 Deutsche Bank Open he may well be best when coming from 'off the pace'.

DOMINGO HOSPITAL

The 40-year-old Spaniard who lives in Switzerland joined the tour in 1993 as a 34-year-old golden oldie, and has kept his card since with three top 3 finishes, four other top 10s yet no wins.

In 1998 however he had a disappointing year with a top 25 finish in the Portuguese Open, and a solid 12th in the BMW International (after an off the pace 68 in R4).

Finished the year 107th on the O/M.

➤ When in 1997 he led the star-studded Dubai Desert Classic by 2 shots, he said he couldn't win, and of course he didn't − he finished T20th. With that mental approach I really can't see him winning a 72-hole tournament. However a rain-reduced 36-hole event could fall into his lap.

➤ He can be noted in the 3-ball betting in the BMW International (12th 1998: 22nd 1997) and in the Canon European Masters on a course which he knows so well as a local Swiss resident.

DAVID HOWELL   G Y

It's easy to forget that this Swindon born lad is still just 23.

He joined the tour in 1996 and after three top 4 finishes ended the year 54th on the O/M. He maintained his progress in 1997 with three top 10s including two top 5 finishes.

In late 1997 he finished T2nd at 25/1 in the Hassan Trophy in Morocco.

In early 1998 his name seemed to be a fixture in the higher reaches of the leaderboard as he posted a series of high finishes in the Heineken Classic (T8th), the South African Open (T9th), the Qatar Masters (T21st), the Portuguese Open (T16th), the Cannes Open (T16th), the Spanish Open (T11th), the Turespana Masters (T15th), the Volvo PGA (T21st), the Deutsche Bank Open (T7th), the French Open (T8th) and when T2nd in the Loch Lomond Invitational.

However his season's turning point was surely the British Open. He led briefly early in R2 before finishing T44th. However his swing had been ravaged in the Birkdale breezes. He then had a disappointing second half to the season.

Finished the season 32nd on the O/M.

Tends to move the ball right to left.

A member of the highly successful Chubby Chandler stable, his coach is Peter Cowen.

➤ A highly talented, progressive, consistent and level-headed player. However to win tournaments he must improve both his putting, for which he seems to have little feel, and his R4 scoring which has been nervy on occasions (eg 1998 Spanish Open 74 in R4).

➤ Clearly he's in 'the winner about to happen category', and with seven top 5 finishes in the last three years (including the close season) he must always be considered.

➤ Worth noting in match bets in the South African Open (T9th 1998: 4th 1996).

➤ A very versatile player who has played really well in every continent in every month of the year, and on a number of different types of courses.

➤ I expect he'll win in 1999 probably when the 'really big guns' are absent, and as he has signed a contract to represent the Le Meridien Algarve resort he'll be especially keen to do well in Portugal, so let's take the hint and back him for the 1999 Portuguese Open (T16th 1998).

➤ Corals fancy him to make the Ryder Cup team, quoting him at just 15/8.

FREDRIK JACOBSON

24-year-old Jacobson earned his 1997 tour card via the Challenge tour.

In 1997 he was 84th on the M/L. He had two top 10s, in the Spanish Open (T8th) and when 2nd in the Madeira Open.

In 1998 he was T10th in the Madeira Open, T20th in the Dubai Desert Classic and had a moment of glory when he shot 67 in R1 of the British Open on his way to finishing T76th.

In October in the Belgacom Open he needed a top 8 finish to secure his card and he played brilliantly to finish 2nd after losing to a long Lee Westwood putt in a play-off

75th on O/M.

➤ Clearly he must have a real chance in the Madeira Open after successive top 10 finishes (T10th 1998: 2nd 1997).

➤ His performance in the Belgacom Open and R1 of the British Open show that links courses suit his game.

RAPHAEL JACQUELIN   g y

This 24-year-old French guy earned his 1998 tour card after a highly successful year on the Challenge tour in which he won three times ending the year 4th on the Challenge tour O/M.

In October 1997, with Jeff Remesey, he finished T6th in the Novotel Perrier Pairs in which he played extremely well.

In 1998 he has consolidated and retained his card with high finishes in the South African PGA (T23rd), the Moroccan Open (T21st), the Portuguese Open (T12th – after shooting 15 under par for last 54 holes), the Dutch Open (T11th after four sub-par rounds) and the Canon European Masters (T15th). Finished 4th at 50/1 with Jeff Remesey, in the Novotel Perrier Pairs.

88th on O/M.

➤ He must be noted for three tournaments:

* The Cannes Open is a tournament won by outsiders with course experience and his form figures there in the last three years of T27th: 54th: T32nd suggest Jacquelin will be worth an each-way interest at 100/1+ in 1999.

* The Canon European Masters is held at the Crans-Sur-Sierre course on which he won in 1997 on the Challenge tour (over 36 holes) and on which he was T15th in 1998. Jacquelin would be a 1999 outsider with a real chance high up in the Swiss Alps.

* In the last two years he and fellow Frenchman Jeff Remesey have played very well in the Novotel Perrier Pairs. They had a 4-shot lead going into the last day in 1997 before finishing 6th, and this year they were 4th at 50/1. They will be a genuine value each-way value bet in this tournament in 1999.

MARK JAMES

The 45-year-old Manchester-born, Ilkley-based player has eighteen European wins, his last being the 1997 Spanish Open. He has enjoyed a really successful playing career with his crowning glory being his appointment as the 1999 European Ryder Cup captain.

In 1998 he had high finishes in the Dubai Desert Classic (T20th), the Portuguese Open (top 30) and as defending champion he was T4th at 66/1 in the Spanish Open.

Further big cheques came his way in the Italian Open (T10th), the Dutch Open (T9th), and the Belgacom Open (T17th).

Once more he played well in the British Open to finish T19th.

He still refuses to play the US Open – a fact that the American media may use against him once the Ryder Cup temperature rises.

A superb iron player. His strength is his accuracy, his weakness his putting. 58th on O/M.

➤ As Ryder Cup captain and with so many hungrier young players it's difficult to see him winning in 1999.

➤ However he is a brilliant player in wind, and on links courses. His British Open record this decade is superbly consistent – from 1990 it reads T31st: T26th: MC: T27th: T4th: T8th: T22nd: T20 and T19th. So he must be noted on the spreads for the 1999 British Open.

➤ In conventional markets for the British Open remember him for match betting and 'value' 3-ball betting, especially if the winds really get up at Carnoustie when he can also be backed in the top Brit market in which he's been in the top 4 three times in the last five years including a 25/1 win in 1994.

➤ His team is as big as 5/2 with Corals to beat the USA. It's a long way off, but it's most likely that when the Ryder Cup shoot out starts 'Jessie' James will be gunned down!

MIGUEL ANGEL JIMENEZ G

The 34-year-old Spaniard is a highly experienced player who came into 1998 on the back of the Ryder Cup triumph at Valderrama when he had acted as Seve's right-hand man.

He started a really successful year when he landed the Turespana Masters at 22/1. During it he proved the validity of the old saying, 'beware the sick golfer', as he had to have an injection on the course, during R3, for his gallstone problems.

He also had high finishes in the Qatar Masters (T13th), the Moroccan Open (T14th), the Deutsche Bank Open (T7th including 65 in R3), the French Open (T23rd), the Irish Open (T16th), the Loch Lomond Invitational (T24th) and the Dutch Open (T21st).

He was disqualified after R2 of the British Open when he would have missed the cut anyway.

Then from mid August he hit real form when in five successive weeks he was T2nd at 66/1 in the European Open, T6th in the BMW International, T7th in the Canon European Masters and T20th in the One 2 One British Masters before he was the 50/1 winner of the Lancome Trophy. It was his fifth European tour win (if you include the 1988 Lyon Open) and his second of the year. He showed there that he had the nerve to win in the very best company.

Played very well in the Dunhill Cup to help Spain to reach the final. He won three of his five matches.

3rd in the Novotel Perrier Pairs playing with Ballesteros. T16th in the Volvo Masters.

Finished 4th on the O/M.

➤ An accurate player who is really at his best in warm, dry, humid conditions as he showed in the Deutsche Bank Open when he missed the cut in windy conditions in 1997 yet was T7th in warm weather this year.

➤ He can be backed when 'off the pace' in final rounds of tournaments in 3-ball betting when he can shoot very low (eg. 63 in 1997 BMW International: 69 in 1998 European Open: 64 in 1998 Canon European Masters) and rapidly climb the leaderboard.

➤ He can be noted in match bets for the Canon European Masters (T7th 1998: T8th 1996).

➤ On the last three occasions the BMW International has been held at the Eichenried course (1993,1997 and 1998) he has a stroke average of 68.25 with finishes of T6th 1998: 9th 1997 and 12th 1993. He must be worth an each-way interest there in 1999.

➤ Will be worth a bet 'in running' before the final round in the Canon European Masters or the BMW International if within four or five shots of the lead.

➤ Finished the year 3rd in the Ryder Cup points table, and as his world ranking will get him an entry to the World Golf tournament in February (which counts for Ryder Cup points) he must have a bright chance of playing in the Ryder Cup.

PER-ULRIK JOHANSSON G M

This is the guy who wore his cap back to front so that now the manufacturers make them back to front so he now wears them the right way round. If that's not clear check out the headgear of the 32-year-old Swede next time he's on telly.

Since joining the tour in 1991 he had always been in the top 50 on the O/M. He was Rookie of the Year in 1991 when 23rd on the O/M after winning the Belgian Open.

He went on to post four more victories in the Czech Open (1994), the European Open (1996), English Open and European Open, as defending champion (1997).

He ended 1997 after those two victories 11th on the O/M.

In late 1997 he pulled out of the US tour Q school with unexplained dizzy spells. Whether or not it was stress related was never discovered. He was never apparently in the best of health until the second half of 1998.

On the European tour he was T9th in the Qatar Masters and T21st in the Volvo PGA, before as defending champion his dizziness re-occurred as he missed the cut in the English Open.

First showed better form and renewed health in the Scandinavian Masters (T7th), missed the cut as double defending champion in the European Open after an 83 in R1, was T9th in the Lancome Trophy, 5th in the German Masters and T21st in the Belgacom Open.

He was T12th in the US Masters: T25th in the US Open: missed the cut in the British Open and T23rd in the USPGA.

Represented Sweden in the Dunhill Cup at St Andrews. He played very well to shoot all three rounds at, or under, par to win two of his three games. Played poorly in the Volvo Masters. 55th on O/M.

➤ Able to move the ball both ways, he now has a fine all-round game. If he stays healthy (without recurrence of his dizzy spells) he'll surely go on to win many more tournaments.

➤ If he can stay healthy I regard this guy as an absolute certainty to make the Ryder Cup for the third successive time. His opening quote of 13/8 went very quickly as 4/5 became the offer.

➤ Last year I suggested he should be avoided immediately on returning from America and he proved the point when on returning from the USPGA he shot 83 in R1 of the European Open.

➤ In the US Masters and the USPGA he simply must be followed in the betting to be the top European player. His record in that market in those events in recent years is

    US Masters   T3rd 33/1 1998: T3rd 66/1 1997, and
    USPGA   W 33/1 1998: 2nd 40/1 1996

➤ Indeed he could even force a place in the top 5 in the US Masters. After all Costantino Rocca did just that in 1997 when T5th, and Johansson is a better player now than the Italian was then. So come Augusta a place-only bet and a wager in the top Euro betting could prove a PER of profitable bets on JOHANSSON.

➤ With the 1999 European Open held midway between the British Open and the USPGA it will give Johansson a chance to reproduce the excellent form that secured his wins there in 1996 and 1997.

➤ Could well surprise by winning a major over the next few years with the British Open at St Andrews giving him a first rate opportunity in the year 2000.

➤ Taking a chance on his health he'd be worth an each-way bet for the 1999 O/M, especially as he'll play in the New World Golf events.

TONY JOHNSTONE

The Zimbabwean born 42 years ago started 1998 without a win on the European tour since 1992, without a win in South Africa since 1994 and with the Pb symbol I gave him last year when it seemed fair to conclude that he was 'over the top'.

He gave us his answer clearly early in 1998 when he gave up caffeine (no more coffee or chocolates), to improve his sight after he saw an eye specialist. He then won the South African PGA as a 100/1 DYM player in February. He felt that he lacked the length for success but his fine short game and excellent course management brought him his victory.

He went on to post top 10s in the Moroccan Open (T6th where in R2 he holed a brilliant 40-yard bunker shot for an eagle at the 15th) and the Portuguese Open.

Troubled with a hand injury in June. Johnstone is a truly brilliant bunker player and was Number 1 on the European tour for sand saves in 1998.

Missed the cut in the British Open for the fifth time in a row.

Played poorly in the World Series of Golf when 42nd of 44. Won one of his three matches in the Dunhill Cup.

➤ His high 1998 finishes, including his win, were based on much-improved putting. Nevertheless I still can't see him winning again on the continent of Europe with there being so many keen, hungry young players aiming for success in Ryder Cup year.

➤ He can be noted for the 1999 Moroccan Open (T6th 1998: T10th 1997), especially in match betting.

MICHAEL JONZON

He joined the tour in 1995 and finished a very creditable 36th on the O/M in his first year thanks mainly to a T2nd in the Dutch Open and three other top 10s.

In 1996 he slipped back to 107th on the O/M with just one top 10 before in 1997 he recorded his first win in the Portuguese Open in March. He ended the season 45th on the O/M with only one other top 10 finish (T4th Irish Open).

He won the Novotel Perriers Pairs in October 1997 with Forsbrand.

In 1998 he had a top 25 in the English Open (T25th) before he finished T4th at 100/1 in the Scandinavian Masters to retain his card. Showed nerves when he was the halfway leader in the Volvo PGA after which he then shot 72 – 74 to finish T33rd. Finished T7th in the Belgacom Open.

Inaccuracy off the tee has been his major 1998 problem.

Finished 1998 71st on the O/M.

➤ He'll probably pop up in the top 5 at a big price in 1999 in one of the lesser tournaments as in each of his four years on tour he has had at least one top 4 finish (as well as his 1997 victory) and they have usually come when there has been a premium on accuracy.

OLLE KARLSSON

The 29-year-old Swede joined the tour in 1993 when he was 56th in the O/M. A car accident in early 1994 ruined that season although he bounced back in 1995 when 51st on the O/M with high finishes in the Madeira Open (T4th), the Andalucian Open (T5th) and the Jersey Open (T3rd).

In 1996 he had only one high finish, when T3rd at 100/1 in the Johnnie Walker Classic to end the year 88th.

Last year he played only a handful of tournaments before he had surgery in October to repair tendons in his left thumb which had troubled him for three years.

In 1998 he played on a medical exemption and secured his tour card when a fine T2nd at 200/1 in the English Open in the first week of June. He shot 67 (R3) and 66 (R4).

His other high finishes were in the Moroccan Open (T6th), the Spanish Open (T11th) and the One 2 One British Masters (T20th).

With Jarmo Sandelin won the Novotel Perrier Pairs in October at 10/1. 56th on O/M.

➤ Inaccuracy off the tee became a problem in the second half of the season. A determined, hard-working player with a much-improved swing. He is a fine bunker player.
➤ If he is to win it will probably be when he comes from 'off the pace' as in the 1998 English Open because he has shown signs of nerves when in contention as in the 1996 Portuguese Open (77 in R4) and the 1998 Moroccan Open (74 in R4).
➤ The Moroccan Open (T6th 1998) will provide an early opportunity for Olle to prove to himself that he has fully rediscovered his driving accuracy.

ROBERT KARLSSON

Jan Robert is the tallest swinger on the tour. He joined the tour as a 21-year-old in 1991 and since then he has won twice – the Turespana Open (1995) and the BMW International (1997) – as well as notching eight other top 3 finishes.

1997 was his best year when he finished 10th on the O/M. His only poor year came in 1996 ("I lost myself") when trying to change his swing.

In 1998 he had high finishes in the Heineken Classic (T20th), the Dubai Desert Classic (T3rd after leading throughout before a 75 in R4), the Moroccan Open (2nd at 12/1), the rain-reduced Italian Open (T18th), the Volvo PGA (T21st), the Canon European Masters (T7th), the German Masters (T2nd at 21 under par) and the Belgacom Open (T3rd).

Missed the cut in the US and British Opens and finished T65th in the USPGA.

Went to the States for the Memorial tournament. His flight was delayed (a bit fell off the plane, honest it did!), he arrived jet-lagged and missed the cut.

Unusually for a tall guy he is a fine player in windy conditions and a very good putter.

Very hard-working player who practises a lot. 17th on O/M.
➤ The 29-year-old can be followed with real confidence in the Moroccan Open. "I just get a good feeling when I come here." In six successive starts he's been in the top 4 five times although he's yet to win.
➤ He'll be 30 on 3rd September 1999 and he could well celebrate by winning the Canon European Masters. In the last two years he has finished T7th (1998) and 2nd (1997), shot eight rounds in the sixties and recorded a stroke average of a staggering 67.125. Karlsson is a must bet for the 1999 Canon European Masters!
➤ His last victory was on the easy course in the BMW International (24 under par) and his latest big finish was on the easy course used for the German Masters (21 under when 2nd) so his game is clearly suited to easy courses, especially in Germany, so follow him in the 1999 BMW International and German Masters.
➤ 4/1 to make the 1999 Ryder Cup team.

SOREN KJELDSEN

The young Dane joined the tour via the 1997 Q School. He posted three high finishes in the Benson and Hedges (T24th), the French Open (T11th) and the BMW International (T19th) before he virtually secured his card with a fine performance when T12th in the One 2 One British Masters in September. He was the only player (outside the first two) in the entire tournament to shoot all four rounds at or under par.

Accuracy off the tee is his main strength. 115th on O/M, he retains his card.

➤ Second seasons are always difficult. Nevertheless he showed in the British Masters patience, an ability to play in wind and rain, and consistent application.

➤ That British Masters performance suggests he can be noted in 3-ball betting when conditions are tough, the weather is blustery and patience is the order of the day.

BARRY LANE

After winning the $1 million Anderson Consulting World Championship in 1995 four-time European winner and 1993 Ryder Cup player, Barry Lane decided to change his swing.

Since then his form has deserted him. He finished 1996 76th, and 1997 83rd on the O/M with just three top 10s in that time.

In 1998 he was the halfway leader in the Benson and Hedges before he shot 75 – 72 to finish T18th. In the Irish Open he was joint leader after R3 before a 79 (!) in R4 finished his chance. Finished well to be T18th in the Lancome Trophy.

Played well in the European Open to be T10th and in the Compaq European Grand Prix he was joint leader in the clubhouse when that tournament was cancelled.

He has worked hard with his coach Scott Cranfield using old videos of his earlier wins to recreate the successes of the early nineties.

His great strength is his length and his proven ability in really windy conditions. 110th on O/M.

➤ After his collapses in the Benson and Hedges and the Irish Open this year he is awarded the bottle. His best chances of winning will be when coming from 'off the pace', or more likely if he is in the lead when bad weather stops a tournament.

➤ He talks about positive thinking yet it seems that he may not fully understand the nature of the mental skills necessary, or the mental 'drills' necessary to act and believe positive rather than just to talk and speak positive.

➤ There are two tournaments in which to back Barry

* the Compaq European Grand Prix (clubhouse leader 1998: T19th 1997) on a course suited to his long game.
* the European Open (T10th 1998: 14th 1996: 2nd 1995) especially if the winds blow.

BERNHARD LANGER   Pb

The amazingly-consistent German player is now a 41-year-old veteran.

He ended 1997 2nd on the O/M and a successful member (three points from four games, including his singles win) of the successful 1997 Ryder Cup team.

As he started 1998 he had won 37, yes 37, times on the European tour with six others worldwide, and on the European tour his astonishing consistency was shown by the fact that he had made the cut in 86.7% of his 300-plus tournaments!

He had also won at least twice in every year of this decade apart from his 'annus horribilus' of 1996.

So by his own standards 1998 has not been a typical year.

He had two high finishes on the European tour when T11th in the Heineken Classic and T4th in the South African Open before he played in America on the 'Florida Swing'.

He was T21st in the Doral Ryder Open, T22nd in the Honda Classic and T4th at 40/1 in the Bay Hill Invitational he missed the cut in the Players Championship then he was T39th in the US Masters.

He has had intermittent neck problems since May.

He later had top 4 finishes in the Deutsche Bank Open (T4th at 16/1), the French Open (T2nd at 14/1) and the BMW International (T4th at 12/1).

He was disappointing when a never-in-contention T13th in the German Open. Suffering from a bad back and a dodgy putter he was a candidate for worst value of the year as 13/2 favourite. Also a disappointing T15th in the German Masters – the tournament his company sponsors. Encouraging 6th in the Volvo Masters.

Missed the cuts in the British Open, the US Open and the USPGA. T39th in the US Masters. 18th on O/M.

➤ His great strengths have been his iron play and his mental toughness. However, although his change of clubs at the beginning of the year clearly had an effect, it may just be that we are seeing the start of the decline of a legend. With neck and back problems, the greater length of his younger opponents, and the return of his putting problems it seems that we are coming to the end of an era when Langer was always in the top 4 on the O/M after posting at least two victories per season. As a result he's awarded the Pb symbol.

➤ This decade he's been in the top 4 on the Order of Merit seven times in nine years. However he's no longer an each-way steal in that market in which he can now be opposed.

➤ He can be safely opposed in the US Open where this decade in nine starts he's missed six cuts and hasn't posted a top 20 finish.

➤ 4-1 ON to make the Ryder Cup team. The question will be whether he's given a wild card if he doesn't secure automatic qualification.

MATS LANNER

The 37-year-old Swede started 1998 with one tour stroke-play win in the 1994 Madeira Open, and a best-ever year in 1987 when aided by the 'nappy factor' he was 19th on the O/M.

In 1998 he again won the Madeira Open as an 80/1 DYM player in June.

He also had high finishes in the Scandinavian Masters (T7th where he was T3rd at 25/1 in the Top Scandinavian player market), the BMW International (T16th), the Canon European Masters (T20th), and the One 2 One British Masters (T20th).

Won on the Challenge tour in October. 59th on O/M.

➤ The best way to profit from Mats in 1999 will be in the Canon European Masters (T20th 1998: T10th 1996: T9th 1995). With indifferent greens and wide fairways he would be a 100/1 outsider with a real squeak!

➤ Beware of backing Lanner to retain his Madeira Open title. As defending champion at just 20/1 in 1995 he missed the cut by 9 (!) shots so he will be worth opposing in match bets and on the spreads as defending champ in 1999.

PAUL LAWRIE

Paul is a 29-year-old guy from Aberdeen who has shown improved form over the last three years.

He joined the tour in 1992 and kept his card in each of his first four years when he was 83rd (1992), 57th (1993), 76th (1994) and 107th (1995) on the O/M, posting two top 10s every year.

He won his first tournament, the weather-reduced 1996 Catalan Open in his 'nappy factor' year, when he was 21st on the O/M.

In 1997 he had seven top 20s including T8th in the Lancome Trophy with four par, or sub-par rounds.

In 1998 he posted high finishes in the Cannes Open (T11th), the Spanish Open (T21st), the Benson and Hedges (T11th), the Deutsche Bank Open (T10th), the Dutch Open (T21st), the German Open (T7th) and the European Open (T10th).

He'll be 30 on New Year's Day 1999. 62nd on O/M.

➤ He is a very good player in windy conditions and on links courses (T6th 1993 British Open), so he can be noted for the German Open at the Sporting Club Berlin (T7th 1998) where the links-type course suits him well.

➤ Worth noting as a big-priced outsider for the Benson and Hedges (T11th 1998: T6th 1996) where his game is suited to the course and the windy conditions.

➤ If he's to gain his first 72-hole tournament win he'll have to improve a lot on his performance in the 1998 Portuguese Open when he entered R4 in 2nd place only to shoot an 82 and finish T41st!

➤ If the winds blow for the British Open at Carnoustie this 30-year-old from East Scotland will be worth noting in match and 3-ball betting. He's had one top 10 and two top 25s in the Open in the last seven years.

STEPHEN LEANEY   G

Last year I noted that this 29-year-old Aussie was "a proven winner with real bottle who could well make his mark on the European tour", and that's precisely what he's done in 1998.

Was 4th in the Australian Open and 6th in the Victorian Open on the Australasian tour.

He was T8th in the Johnnie Walker Classic before he put up a brilliant performance to win the Moroccan Open from the front in March as a 66/1 DYM player.

He had other high finishes in the Portuguese Open (top 30), the Volvo PGA (T16th) and the English Open (T10th) before he notched his second victory of the year in the Dutch Open. He led after R2 to win as a 125/1 DYM player.

He had a further high finish in the Scandinavian Masters (T25th). Ended the season well when T12th in the Volvo Masters.

In 1993 he had part of his ribs removed to ease a blood clot under his right shoulder and was out of the game for 18 months.

He is a fine wind player. He'll be 30 in March 1999. Will go to Q School in America to try to earn a US tour card. 11th on O/M.

➤ He is now a proven winner on three continents. He's a confirmed front runner, and a crisp ball striker with a very controlled uncomplicated game. He will surely win again on the Australasian and European tours.

➤ Once you're over your New Year hangover back him for the Victorian Open starting on 7th January. He simply loves the tournament having won it in 1996 and 1997 and finished T6th in 1998.

➤ His two European wins came on courses with a premium on accuracy so don't be surprised if he wins the 1999 Volvo PGA (T16th 1998) on another course, Wentworth, where accuracy is the key.

THOMAS LEVET

Having failed to secure his tour card at Q School in both 1996 and 1997 this year the 30-year-old Paris-born Frenchman played the Challenge tour.

However in April, playing on a sponsors' exemption, he was the 'shock' winner of the Cannes Open. In R3 he shot 65 to take a 4-stroke lead into Sunday. He lost that lead, then showed 'bottle' to birdie the 15th and 17th, and indeed he holed a nine footer on the last to win.

His other high finishes were in the rain-reduced Italian Open (T23rd), the Scandinavian Masters (T25th) and the Lancome Trophy (T18th).

Made his debut for France in the Dunhill Cup winning one of his three matches. 69th on O/M.

➤ I suspect the Cannes win that brought a smile to bookies' faces was a one-off semi-fluke rather than the launching pad for a successful career. It's certainly difficult finding any punter-friendly opportunities emanating from the Frenchman.

JONATHAN LOMAS

The 30-year-old from the town with the wonky spire (Chesterfield) was Rookie of the Year in 1993 when 32nd on the O/M in a year that included a T11th in the British Open and a T3rd in the Benson and Hedges.

After slipping back to 101st on the O/M in 1995 he bounced straight back in 1996 with his first win in the Czech Open. Helped by his switch to the broomhandle putter he ended the year 20th on the O/M.

He struggled again in 1997 before he finished T5th in the Oki Pro-Am to finish 79th in the O/M.

In 1998 he has had only three high finishes in the Portuguese Open (T4th), the Dutch Open (T11th) and the German Open (T13th).

He has three Challenge tour wins, and he won the Novotel Perriers Pairs in 1996 with Steven Bottomley. 85th on O/M.

➤ In many ways he has become the forgotten man over the last two years since his victory, with putting his big problem. Difficult to see him returning to the winners' enclosures in Ryder Cup year unless there is a drastic improvement in his putting.

➤ His best performances in 1996 and 1997 came when he was in fair form having made his recent cuts, whereas in 1998 his Portuguese Open T4th came after he had missed three of his previous five cuts so he's not easy to predict.

➤ His partner Steven Bottomley, like Lomas himself, enjoys the links-type course used for the Novotel Perrier Pairs which they won in 1996 and were T5th in 1998. At a big price (50/1) in a small field (30) they'll be worth an interest in 1999.

PETER LONARD

The 31-year-old Aussie made a big impact in 1997 with high finishes in the Johnnie Walker Classic (T2nd at 66/1), the French Open (T11th), the British Open (T24th) and the European Masters (T4th). As a result he finished 48th on the O/M.

In Australia in that year he beat O'Malley in a play-off to win the Australian Masters and was also 3rd in the Canon Challenge.

In 1998 he had big finishes 'down under' in the Australian Players Championship when 2nd at 20/1 and when 6th in the Greg Norman Holden International.

On the European tour he had high finishes in the Johnnie Walker Classic (T12th), the Heineken Classic (T25th), the Cannes Open (T8th), the Volvo PGA (T5th), the Irish Open (8th), the Canon European Masters (T15th) and the Lancome Trophy (T15th). Led the Volvo Masters by 3 shots at halfway before finishing T12th.

He missed the cut in the USPGA. Uses Queenslander Gary Edwin as his coach. His putting has often let him down this year. 51st on O/M.

➤ He can be noted in match and 3-ball betting for the Canon European Masters (T15th 1998: T4 1997).

➤ His two best European tour performances (the Volvo PGA and the Irish Open) were on courses demanding accuracy so keep him in mind on those tracks in match bets in 1999.

➤ Having made a full recovery from the Ross River Fever that wrecked his life in 1993 and 1994, he has been left with eye problems. His good form in the Volvo PGA followed the prescription of new hard contact lenses.

MICHAEL LONG   D

The 30-year-old Kiwi joined the European tour in 1997 when he made the cut in three quarters of his sixteen tournaments. He ended the season 43rd on the O/M after finishing T2nd in the Johnnie Walker Classic and posting two other top 10s – the Dutch Open (T9th) and the Czech Open (T7th).

In 1998 he had high finishes in the Johnnie Walker Classic (T14th), the Cannes Open (T16th), Turespana Masters (T6th), the Dutch Open (T21st) and the German Masters (T15th).

In the Dunhill Cup representing New Zealand he lost all his three matches. He finished T66th in the British Open. 84th on O/M.

➤ After a disappointing year he will be very keen to do well in 1999.

➤ Must be a leading contender for New Zealand Open (held from 10th December 1998) which he won in 1996.

SANTIAGO LUNA

The Madrid-born 36-year-old Spaniard has had a successful 1998 in which he posted high finishes in the Portuguese Open (he was T6th after R3, then shot a 74 to finish T22nd), the Turespana Masters (T6th), the French Open (T8th), the European Open (T16th), the BMW International (T24th) and the Canon European Masters (T20th).

T35th in the British Open, including an 80 in R3 in blustery conditions.

However his 'big' tournament was the Benson and Hedges (in fine weather) when he was T2nd at 100/1 after scoring 8 under par over the last 36 holes.

He finished 1998 on the O/M.

Since 1991 he has always been in the top 80 and twice in the top 40 on the O/M. His one win came in the weakly-contested Madeira Island Open.

Played well in the Dunhill Cup in the Spanish team that reached the final for the first time. Beat Tiger Woods memorably in the semi-final. Overall he won twice. His very long hitting is well suited to St Andrews.

He joins the European tour when it reaches Europe. 31st on O/M.

➤ With his confidence high after beating Tiger Woods in the Dunhill Cup and with a morale-boosting win in the Hassan Trophy in early November it could well be that we will see a rejuvenated 'Santi' in 1999.

➤ At his very best in still warm and dry conditions he could well land his second win in 1999, possibly in the Turespana Masters.

MALCOLM MACKENZIE

The 37-year-old from Sheffield has struggled in recent years. From 1993 – 1997 his highest O/M finish was in 1996 when he was 78th.

1998 was also a struggle with high finishes only in the South African PGA (T16th), the Turespana Masters (T15th) and the German Open (T7th).

He's now with new coach, Eddie Birchenough. 113th on O/M.

➤ Yet to record a victory, and with just two top 3 finishes this decade he's not a player to follow in outright betting, and no real alternative punting opportunities present themselves.

MIGUEL ANGEL MARTIN

The 36-year-old Spaniard was involved in major controversy in 1997 when he finished 10th in the Ryder Cup table yet was not selected to play on the grounds of unfitness. He was replaced by fellow Spaniard Jose Maria Olazabal amidst much acrimony.

Earlier in that year he had won for the first time when he landed the Heineken Classic at 80/1 in temperatures of 44°C. However a wrist injury stopped him playing from mid-season. He did not return until he played in the Dunhill Cup, losing all three matches. He ended the year 27th on the O/M to end his best-ever, and his saddest-ever season.

In 1998 he had five high finishes before he was once more dogged by the tendon injury in his left wrist.

He was T4th at 33/1 in the Moroccan Open, 21st in the Portuguese Open, T16th in the Cannes Open, T11th in the Spanish Open.

On the eve of the Turespana Masters it was discovered that he had a kidney stone. Told to drink lots of water he went to the loo five times in R1. 'Beware the sick golfer' was proved once more as he went on to finish 2nd at 16/1.

Just 5'6" tall he keeps his head amazingly still when swinging.

➤ At his very best in very warm, still conditions such as those prevailing in his only win in the 1997 Heineken Classic.

➤ If he makes a full recovery his best chances will be in tournaments such as the Spanish Open when he will probably have the weather conditions he requires.

BOB MAY

30-year-old Las Vegas resident Bob retained his card after finishing 109th on the O/M in 1997 which included a T7th in the Benson and Hedges.

In 1998 his 'nappy factor' year, he has played very consistently to record high finishes in the Dubai Desert Classic (T20th), the Moroccan Open (T11th), the Italian Open (T6th), the Benson and Hedges (T15th), the Deutsche Bank Open (T10th) and the English Open (T14th).

He was 74th in the British Open including an 85 in the wind in R3.

Played on the USPGA tour in October when T16th in his home town tournament – the Las Vegas Invitational.

His strength has been his accuracy to the greens, his weakness his putting. A former US Walker Cup player. 72nd on O/M.

➤ Coming from the warmth of the desert he is probably at a comparative disadvantage in windy conditions.

➤ When the weather is warm and his putter is hot he could well make his first European top 4 finish in 1999, and could even post a shock win in one of the lesser tournaments.

➤ He has a solid record in the Benson and Hedges (T15th 1998: T7th 1997) when it has been played in good weather.

➤ Worth noting in the early round 3-ball betting in his 'home' event, the Las Vegas Invitational.

PAUL McGINLEY   F G

The 32-year-old Dubliner joined the tour in 1992 when he was 97th in the O/M. Since then he has progressed, most notably over the last three years.

In 1996 he came from off the pace with 62 in R4 to win his first tournament, the Austrian Open after a two-week break, was T2nd in the Heineken Classic and ended the year 15th on the O/M.

In 1997 he won again when he took the lead at halfway and went on to win the Oki Pro-Am by 4 shots. With three other top 10s in the Cannes Open (T6th), the Dubai Desert Classic (T6th) and the Deutsche Bank Open (T5th) he ended the year 21st on the O/M.

In late 1997 he played superbly to win the World Cup of Golf with Padraig Harrington at 16/1, finishing 4th at 33/1 in the individual rankings.

In 1998 he had high finishes in the Johnnie Walker Classic (T21st), the Heineken Classic (T20th), the Qatar Masters (T21st), the Italian Open (T13th – having led after a 63 in R1), the Turespana Masters (T3rd as a late entrant), the Benson and Hedges (T24th), the Volvo PGA (10th), the Deutsche Bank Open (T22nd), the French Open (T16th), the Scandinavian Masters (T16th), the German Open (T23rd), the European Open (T20th), the German Masters (T6th) and the Volvo Masters (T19th).

In the Dunhill Cup he won just one of his three matches.

A fine player in windy conditions and on links courses. He's a right to left player. 30th on O/M.

➤ Although he has won twice he has yet to win a big event when most of the top players are playing, and there is still a doubt about his R4 nerve when in serious contention despite his 1997 Oki Pro-Am win from the front.

➤ Nevertheless this hugely-talented player has made two very big decisions – to move to a very expensive house in Sunningdale (next door to Darren Clarke) and to change his coach from Bob Torrance to Peter Cowen to improve his short game. He now has both the financial incentive and clear determination to match his undoubted ability as he tries to emulate the achievements of Darren Clarke and Lee Westwood, his Chubby Chandler stablemates. I expect him to post high finishes, including his third win, in 1999.

➤ He will be worth an interest in the Dubai Desert Classic in which he was T6th 1997: T5th 1993 and was going well in 1998 (a 64 in R3) when he injured a rib.

➤ He clearly enjoys the Heineken Classic (T20th 1998: T3rd after 3 rounds 1997: 2nd 1996) so on 27th January have a penny or two each way on McGinley as the tournament starts on the 28th.

➤ He is attached to the K Club in Dublin, home of the European Open. Indeed he has helped in the recent changes to the course that have included narrowing the fairways. He putted badly there in 1998 when T20th, yet played well tee to green. Must be given another chance 'in his own backyard' in 1999.

➤ 2/1 to make the 1999 Ryder Cup team.

JOHN McHENRY

Making decisions always gives people a sense of direction and purpose and creates a positive frame of mind. So it proved for 34-year-old John in 1998 when he and his wife agreed in April that, without a sponsor, he would play for the rest of the year. Until then he had been the house-husband while his wife, Sylvia, went to work.

His reward came in the Irish Open when he was T3rd at 200/1; he was also the 33/1 top Irish player and he won £53,996, so securing his tour card.

The Cork-born guy had three Challenge tour wins in the early nineties and was a Walker Cup player in 1987.

Having secured his card his 1999 aim will be to retain it and to rediscover his best form. 103rd on O/M.

➤ His best chance in 1999 may come in the Dutch Open. It's a track (like the Irish Open) that suits straight hitters, and he'll recall that he shot a 65 in the tournament in 1994.

➤ He has PMAs with France having won there on the Challenge tour in 1991 and recorded a T6th finish in the French Open a year later.

MARK McNULTY   Pb

The 45-year-old from Zimbabwe has been showing signs of being slightly past his best over the last year or so.

He played very well in late 1997 in Sarazen World Open when T3rd at 28/1 on a course where he has a good record.

In 1998 he won the South African Order of Merit for the seventh time after winning the Players' Championship. He also had high finishes in the South African Open (T7th), the South African PGA (T10th) and was 2nd in the Dimension Data Pro-Am.

He was T10th in the English Open.

Missed the cut in the British Open.

Mark suffered with 'tennis elbow' in May and his form has been affected by a continuing wrist injury.

In the Dunhill Cup he won one of his three matches.

With fifteen European tour wins and twenty-nine others worldwide McNulty has been a magnificent player. He is accurate, if short, off the tee. However he has a fine short game and is a brilliant long putter.

➤ After two consecutive years without a European tour victory and with regular niggling injuries I think it is probably fair to conclude that he is past his best. He is therefore given the Pb symbol.

➤ However on the South African tour in the warm weather, when he is at his best, he will continue to post high finishes although he'll rarely be a 'value' betting proposition.

➤ Can be opposed in bad weather conditions in 3-ball betting. He shot 81 on day two of this year's Dunhill Cup for example.

PETER MITCHELL

40-year-old Peter has shown remarkable consistency throughout the nineties. From 1991 – 1997 he always finished in the Top 50 on the O/M.

In 1997 he won the Madeira Open at 40/1 to record his second tour victory and he followed up with another win in 1998 when he landed the Portuguese Open at 66/1 in March.

He also posted high finishes in the Turespana Masters (T23rd), the Benson and Hedges (T18th), the Deutsche Bank Open (T13th), the German Masters (T21st) and the Belgacom Open (T5th).

He missed the cut in the Volvo PGA after a sneeze affected a ligament in his neck!

He missed the cut in the British Open. Had a rib-muscle injury in August and early September.

May be at his best now in warm conditions. 38th on O/M.

➤ His three tour wins have come in tournaments when 'the big boys' are missing and his putter has complemented his accurate approach play. If he is to win again therefore it will probably be in one of the lesser events, perhaps the Turespana Masters.

➤ His strength is his consistent accurate play season after season. He is therefore not a player to oppose in match betting as he makes over 70% of all his cuts (1991-97 inclusive it was 73.48%).

COLIN MONTGOMERIE G M

Last year, after winning the European Order of Merit for the fifth successive year (!), Monty made the momentous decision to play on the European tour rather than move to the States. "My family comes before anything else." In his profile I detailed the advantages that he would get from playing full time in America while saying how refreshing it was to see such a high-profile sportsman having such welcome traditional, if unfashionable, values.

Well 1998 has not brought Monty the major he desires so much, possibly too much. In the US Masters, with the spotlight on Lee Westwood, he played well to finish T8th. He was Number 1 for greens in regulation but T35th for putting. He finished 6 behind O'Meara yet he took 17 more putts! He was the top European (6/1) and top non-American (11/1). This was a fine performance considering he'd suffered a domestic burglary as well as severe American press criticism – labelled 'the Goon from Troon' he was called a 'first-class jerk'. Let's hope that harsh treatment doesn't return for the Ryder Cup.

In the US Open, which was his big chance, he finished T18th. However once more he was heckled by the crowd, and once more he underachieved in the tournament tailor made for his straight hitting.

In the British Open his poor links record continued as he missed the cut.

In the USPGA he had a real chance when 2nd at halfway before a 77 in R3 destroyed his chance. He finished T44th.

After the USPGA he was reunited with his former coach, Bill Ferguson, as he tried to get his swing back into its old groove.

Missed cuts followed in both the European Open and the BMW International as he struggled (a new experience) to find his old rhythm.

Then he won the One 2 One British Masters at 10/1 when not at his very best. It was the second win of the year as he'd landed the Volvo PGA at Wentworth in May when inspired by the nappy factor! (His first son Cameron, had been born earlier that month and Monty had actually cut the umbilical chord.)

His third, and final, win of the year came in late September when he won the German Masters at 10/1.

Earlier in the year on the European tour he'd posted high finishes in the Dubai Desert Classic (T10th), the Benson and Hedges (T5th), the Deutsche Bank Open (T10th), the English Open (T4th), the Irish Open (2nd beaten in a play-off), the Loch Lomond (T7th), the Scandinavian Masters (T16th), the Canon European Masters (T12th) and the Lancome Trophy (T11th).

Ended the season impressively when 3rd in the Volvo Masters to land the O/M for an incredible sixth successive year.

In America he played the 'Florida swing' before the US Masters, missing the cut in the Doral Ryder Open (when jet lagged) and the Players Championship (when upset by poor tee times). 3rd at 20/1 in the Honda Classic and T8th in the Bay Hill Invitational.

In the Dunhill Cup he lost two of his three matches including a defeat by 8/1 chance Z. Lian-Wei.

In the World Match Play he beat Bjorn 4 and 3 in R1 before losing to eventual winner O'Meara 5 and 4 in the QF.

From 1993 he has now won fifteen times on the European tour in the six years to take his total European tally to seventeen.

He has yet to win in the States, although he won the Andersen World Consulting Championship in 1997.

Although winning three times this year he never looked to be playing at his best which is, of course, a compliment as a Monty operating at 85% is better than most others operating at 100%.

His consistent accuracy off tee and fairway had deserted him for a spell in the autumn when he looked mortal as he missed three successive cuts.

A truly world-class player Monty still carries the tag of being one of the world's best players yet to win a major. To succeed in America now I really do think he needs to take a leaf out of Jurgen Klinsman's book. Do you remember when the German football star first arrived at Spurs? He had a reputation as a 'diver' who conned referees into giving free kicks and penalties. At his very first press conference with all the hacks ready to go for him he started by asking them if any one knew where the nearest diving school was. He had, at a stroke, diffused the criticism, won over the press and from then on became a 'cult' figure. He even celebrated his first goal by 'diving' on the grass in a well-thought-out piece of self mockery.

Surely Monty could adopt a similar approach in America, wear a 'Goon from Troon' T-shirt at a press conference and start to lighten up with the press, and so with the galleries. An introduction of Klinsman-like self-mocking humour would surely go down as well in the States for Monty as it did over here for the German.

I spent a large chunk of the opening chapter last year discussing Monty's inability to handle disappointment as he tends to let one bad hole upset him so the next hole is also affected. This inability to focus solely on the present and forget the very recent past is one of Lee Westwood's greatest strengths, yet it's Monty's greatest weakness.

➤ His best chance of a major success is still the US Open because it plays to his great comparative advantage, his accuracy. His full record from 1992 is now 3rd-T33rd-T2nd-T28th-T10th-2nd and this year T18th. Three top 3s and five top 20s in seven starts shows a very solid record. However if he is to win he really must improve his mental skills, and develop a rapport with the press and the gallery.

➤ There are three tournaments in which Monty can be followed with real confidence. They are:
  * The Honda Classic in America (3rd 20/1 1998: 4th 16/1 1997)
  * The Irish Open (2nd 1998: Won 1997: Won 1996).

* The One 2 One British Masters (three wins and two 2nds in five starts!) held at the Forest of Arden near his home.

An each-way bet on the Honda and win bets on the other two would have yielded a nice level-stake profit over the last few years.

➤ Certain to play in the Ryder Cup. Let's remember it was his match against Scott Hoch at Valderrama that secured the European victory.

➤ His tendency to hit the ball high is not suited to links golf when the winds blow, so his British Open record is poor for such a quality player (five missed cuts in seven starts!). In 1999 if the breezes get up at Carnoustie he can be opposed on the spreads.

MARK MOULAND   S

It is now ten years since the 37-year-old Welsh player recorded the second of his two wins, in the Dutch Open (1998).

In the nineties he has only been in the top 50 on the O/M once and that was back in 1990.

In 1997 he had five top 20s to improve to an O/M placing of 62nd. However 1998 has been disappointing.

He had one top 20 in the Cannes Open (T16th), top 30 finishes in the South African Open (T22nd), the Dutch Open (T21st) and the BMW International (T26th), and two top 10s, in the Benson and Hedges (T7th) and the Belgacom Open (T7th). 80th on O/M.

➤ When 'on song' he is a real 'streak' player (with a 61 and two 63s this decade) capable of shooting low scores, as he showed when he shot 64 in R4 of the 1998 Belgacom Open..

➤ Without a top 3 finish in the last eight years the only way you can see him winning again is by making a fast 'streaky' start from a favourable tee time to win a rain-reduced tournament....and it could be the BMW International which was a 36-hole event in 1996 and in which Mark has a solid record (T26th 1998: T12th 1997).

➤ His last win was in the Dutch Open at the Hilversum course in which he's posted a top 20 finish in two of the last four years.

ROLF MUNTZ

29-year-old Dutch player who lives in Belgium. Gained his 1996 tour card via the Q school and ended the year a creditable 63rd after two top 10 finishes and a T3rd in the Spanish Open.

In 1997 he struggled and just secured his card with a T11th in the Lancome Trophy, his only noteworthy finish.

1998 had not seen any progress and he had been troubled with elbow problems until in early October he finished T10th in the Belgacom Open.

Notched his first top 10 since 1996 when T5th at 200/1 in the Qatar Masters. Had a high finish in the Scandinavian Masters (T25th). 99th on O/M.

➤ He'll hope that once past his 30th birthday in March 1999 he can regain the momentum his career had when, as a 21-year-old, he was the British Amateur Champion.

JOSE MARIA OLAZABAL   G

1997 was surely a year that the young (he's now 32) Spaniard will never forget. After missing 1996 because of a right foot injury there was even talk of him becoming wheelchair bound. However he recovered to return to action in the Dubai Desert Classic when T12th before he got his 'comeback' win in the Turespana Masters three weeks later.

After Miguel Martin was declared unfit Olazabal, who was 11th in the Ryder Cup points table, replaced him. He played in all five matches to score 2½ points, although he lost to Janzen in the singles.

He ended the year 9th on the O/M.

In the close season he was T3rd in the Dunlop Phoenix in Japan. In early February he was 2nd in the Greg Norman International in Australia.

On the 1998 European tour he won the Dubai Desert Classic at 16/1 – incredibly it was his seventeenth win on the tour.

He also had punter-friendly finishes in the Heineken Classic (T3rd on his first trip to Australia), the Spanish Open (T2nd at 8/1) and the Italian Open (T2nd at 8/1).

His other high finishes were in the Johnnie Walker Classic (T16th), the Qatar Masters (T17th), the Benson and Hedges (T11th), the Volvo PGA (T16th), the Irish Open (T9th), the BMW International (T18th) and the Volvo Masters (7th).

In the States he was T25th in the Players Championship, T19th in the Freeport McDermott Classic and T24th in the Buick Classic.

In the majors he was T12th in the US Masters, T18th US Open, T15th British Open (69 in R4) and he missed the USPGA cut at a time when he was in poor form off the tee.

Led Spain to its first Dunhill Cup final. He won three of his five matches. 7th on the O/M.

➤ His great strengths are his brilliant short game, his creative shot making and his underrated mental toughness and determination. His major weakness has undoubtedly been his driving which has been a real worry in the second half of the season.

➤ He is best followed on a course in which he can use his brilliant short game to advantage and on which he can be followed when there are wide fairways and tricky 'difficult to read' greens as such courses maximise his strengths and minimise his weakness. Such a course is Augusta, home of the US Masters. His record there on his last nine starts (since 1989) is one win, one 2nd, two other top 10s, only one finish (T42nd in 1992) outside the top 20 and he's made every cut. So in match betting, on the spreads and especially in the top European market he can be followed. So make 'Olly at Augusta' your slogan for the 1999 US Masters.

ANDREW OLDCORN

38-year-old Andrew won his first tournament, the Turespana Masters, in 1993, and his second, the Jersey Open, two years later when he finished 35th on the O/M.

In 1996 five top 10s, including being runner-up in the Irish Open, maintained his progress when he was 34th on the O/M.

In 1997, without a top 10 finish, he slipped back to 86th in the O/M.

However he struggled in 1998, with only a few high finishes – in the Dubai Desert Classic (T10th), the Cannes Open (T16th) and the Dutch Open (T21st after a 66 in R4) until September when he was T4th in the One 2 One British Masters to secure his tour card.

Finished 80th (of 81) in the British Open. 85th on O/M.

➤ Let's remember he was a superb amateur, and it's possibly only self belief that stands between him and a 'shock' win in 1999 – perhaps in the Dutch Open (66 in R4 1998) or the Irish Open (2nd 1996) which both favour straight hitters.

PETER O'MALLEY

The 33-year-old Aussie made his mark in his 'nappy factor' year of 1995 when he won the Benson and Hedges and ended the year 10th on the O/M. It was his second Euro tour win – the first being the 1992 Scottish Open.

1996 was an anti climax when 82nd.

In 1997 he again climbed up the O/M to finish 22nd with a T3rd in the Lancome Trophy, a T5th in the Volvo Masters and a brilliant T7th in the British Open as the highlights.

In 1998 he had high finishes in the Johnnie Walker Classic (T4th at 66/1), the Irish Open (T16th), the British Open (T24th), the One 2 One British Masters (T20th), the Lancome Trophy (T7th), the German Masters (T15th after 65 in R3), the Belgacom Open (T10th) and the Volvo Masters (T4th).

In Australia he won the Canon Challenge by 9 shots as 12/1 favourite – his first win on home soil in eleven years!! He was also T3rd at 8/1 in the Australian Tour Championship. 36th on O/M.

➤ In the 1997 Lancome Trophy he had a very nervy start in R4, and in the 1998 Johnnie Walker Classic he finished double bogey – bogey to throw away a winning chance, so the jury may still be out on his final-round nerve although he has won three European tournaments, one in Australia and the 1995 New Zealand Open.

➤ After finishing T4th this year and T5th last year in the Volvo Masters at Montecastillo he must be noted, especially on the spreads there in 1999.

➤ He can be noted in match bets for the 1999 British Open in which he has posted successive top 25 finishes as he clearly enjoys links golf and he has a fine record in Scotland where he was T7th the last time the tournament was held north of the border in 1997.

➤ Keep O'Malley in mind in 3-ball and match betting for the British Masters – in the last two years he's been T20th (1998) and T12th (1997) and has hit six of his eight rounds at or under par.

➤ He's had successive top 10s in the Lancome Trophy (17th 1998: 3rd 1997) so he'd be worth noting in the outright betting if he's within 4 shots of the lead on the final day.

GARY ORR

The 31-year-old Scot joined the tour in 1993 and since then he has had a series of steady seasons, finishing 30th (1993), 40th (1994), 59th (1995), 41st (1996) and 71st (1997) on the O/M without ever winning.

In 1998 after working on his fitness during the winter he had a fine season, especially early on, again without winning.

He had top 20 finishes in the South African Open (T20th) and the Dubai Desert Classic (T20th).

In late May he was T2nd at 150/1 in the Volvo PGA to record his best-ever finish. Later he was T17th in the Deutsche Bank Open, T6th in the Irish Open and T7th at Loch Lomond after leading after 27 holes.

Made his Dunhill Cup debut for Scotland in October winning two of his three matches.

He missed the cut in the British Open. 28th on O/M.

➤ The doubts about his final-round nerve shown in the 1994 Lyon Open, the 1995 German Open and the 1996 Deutsche Bank Open were confirmed this year in the Volvo PGA as he hit two poor tee shots once he took the lead in R4. It seems clear that, like a racehorse held up for a final-furlong dash, his best chance of winning will be to come 'from off the pace' setting a clubhouse target.

➤ Must be noted in match and 3-ball betting, and as a long-priced outsider in the outright markets, in two tournaments.

 * The Volvo PGA (2nd 1998: 7th 1996: 12th 1995).

 * The Canon European Masters (T25th 1997 including a 61 in R1: T4th 1996: T13th 1994 and T6th 1993).

GREG OWEN

26-year-old Mansfield guy who joined the tour via Q School. By September however he was struggling in 120th place on the O/M after playing twenty events.

However his season was turned round at the Forest Arden course when he finished 7th in the One 2 One British Masters to secure his card for 1999. Considering what was at stake his 70 in R4 was a fine effort. The following week he was T32nd in the Lancome Trophy. Went on to shoot a course-record 62 in R2 of the Belgacom Open before finishing T21st.

89th on O/M.

➤ So 1999 will provide young Greg with a chance to consolidate, albeit in a Ryder Cup year.

➤ His best chances will be in the British Masters, after his fine performance this year, and in the Cannes Open which was his best finish (T47th) before this year.

JESPER PARNEVIK   M G

This is the Swedish guy in the cap with the upturned peak who eats volcanic dust.

33-year-old Jesper joined the US tour in 1996 after winning twice on the European tour – in the 1993 Scottish Open and the 1995 Scandinavian Masters.

In America in 1996 he was 53rd on the Money list after five top 10s including a T3rd at the Greater Milwaukee Open.

He returned to Europe to win the 1996 Lancome Trophy.

In 1997 he had seven top 5 finishes before May in the Bob Hope Chrysler Classic (3rd), the Phoenix Open (2nd), the AT&T (T5th), the Buick Invitational (T2nd), the Honda Classic (5th), the Freeport McDermott Classic (T2nd) and the MCI Heritage Classic (T2nd).

However his big moment came (and went!) in the 1997 British Open. Showing real nerves over the final four holes he finished 2nd for the second time in four years.

His year was to end without a win.

However he played as a wild card in the victorious Ryder Cup team scoring two points.

In 1998 he secured his first US win in the Phoenix Open at 33/1.

He also had high US finishes in the Players Championship (T25th), the Freeport Mcdermott Classic (T12th), the MCI Classic (T18th), the Memorial (T11th), the Buick Classic (T10th), the AT&T (T19th), the Sprint (T13th with 32 pts), the World Series (T11th), and in the National Car Rental at Disney (T4th).

Returning to Europe in late July he won the Scandinavian Masters, for the second time, at 16/1.

In 1998 he was T31st in the US Masters (Number 1 for fairways hit), T14th in the US Open (5th on the putting stats) and was T4th at 50/1 in the British Open. He missed the cut in the USPGA.

A deceptively long hitter. He is a fine iron player. Mainly draws (R-L) the ball.

He now has four wins in Europe and one in America. 14th on the American Money list.

➤ In each of the last two years he has returned to Europe to win a tournament so there's every reason to expect that in 1999 with Europe his primary focus he will do so again.

➤ In each of the last six years he's either won a tournament (1993, 1995, 1996, 1998) or been second in the British Open (1994 and 1997). That's some record!!

➤ 4/1 ON to retain his Ryder Cup place. He will surely have a much, much better chance of securing Ryder Cup points than fellow returnee Nick Faldo.

➤ He retains the M symbol. He's made twelve cuts in his fourteen majors, and he must be worth an interest in the 1999 British Open after his record of three top 4 finishes in the last five years.

JIM PAYNE   D

Leading amateur in the 1991 British Open, rookie of the year in 1992 when he was 33rd on the O/M with three top 3 finishes. He was the winner of the Balearic Open in 1993 when with three other top 10s he was 36th in the O/M. The 28-year-old Grimsby Town fan looked set to do really well after that success.

However serious back problems leading to surgery delayed his progress in 1994 and 1995 before, on the comeback trail, he won the Italian Open in 1996.

Over the last couple of years he has struggled. Without a top 10 in 1997, he's also had a disappointing 1998 with high finishes in the Deutsche Bank Open (T7th), the Irish Open (T16th), the Loch Lomond Invitational (T24th) and the German Masters (T21st).

Married in August. He shot a hole in one in his very next tournament, the European Open. 65th on O/M.

➤ Proved he can cope with rain delays and interruptions when winning the 1996 Italian Open so if he's in contention in a weather-ruined event he can be supported 'in running'.

VAN PHILLIPS

The 26-year-old made an impact in 1997 with his collar and tie, goatie beard and solid all-round game which saw him finish 67th on the O/M when his big finish was T3rd in the French Open.

In 1998 he maintained his progress with a 4th place at 150/1 in the Qatar Masters and a 5th place in the Turespana Masters.

He also had high finishes in the Portuguese Open (T19th), the Volvo PGA (T21st), the English Open (T14th), the Scandinavian Masters (T16th) and the German Open (T13th).

A scratch player at 15, a Walker Cup player at 21, he has progressed well in his twenties.

His excellent early-season form was based on his driving accuracy. Indeed he was Number 1 on the tour at 81.7% when he played the Volvo PGA. This accuracy declined as the season progressed.

His putting has often spoilt his fine approach play. 50th on O/M.

➤ His best form in the last two years has been in the first half of each season.

➤ He has recorded his best finishes when coming from 'off the pace' as in the 1997 Qatar Masters (four birdies in last six holes) and the 1997 French Open (66 in R4 to finish T3rd) whereas he has fallen away when in the lead (1997 Deutsche Bank Open he was the halfway leader than finished T18th).

PHILLIP PRICE G

The 32-year-old from Pontypridd joined the tour in 1991 and has retained his card ever since with his solitary victory coming in the 1994 Portuguese Open which he won on a tough course.

He had a fine 1997 when 39th on the O/M after eight top 20s in a very consistent year.

Played well in the World Cup of Golf for Wales where he was T7th in the individual placings.

In 1998 he made his first seventeen cuts playing with excellent consistency. He posted high finishes in the Johnnie Walker Classic (T16th), the South African PGA (6th where he was top European player), the Dubai Desert Classic (T20th), the Cannes Open (T2nd at 66/1), the Spanish Open (19th), the Italian Open (T13th), the Benson and Hedges (T15th), the Volvo PGA (T11th), the English Open (6th) and the European Open (T2nd after a fast finish to win £108K where, knowing the money at stake, he finished birdie-birdie).

Missed the British Open cut by a shot. 15th on O/M.

➤ He can be followed in blustery, wet conditions.

➤ With his superb consistency he can be supported in match bets.

➤ He may be better when in continuous play week after week rather than after a break.

➤ He must be noted for the English Open (6th 1998: T12th 1997 and T12th 1996) especially in match bets and as nice-priced, each-way outsider.

➤ He's made a fast start in each of the last two years so bear him in mind in match bets in South Africa against other European players.

IAIN PYMAN   D

25-year-old player from Whitby who was the amateur champion in 1993 and was the leading amateur that year in the British Open with a record 281 total.

Having turned pro in 1994 he finished 103rd (1995), 56th (1996) and 66th (1997) on the O/M. During those years his best finishes were a T2nd in the 1996 rain-reduced German Open and a 2nd (after 64 in R4) in the 1997 Oki Pro-Am which secured his card.

In 1998 he has struggled with only one high finish, when he was T7th in the Dutch Open after going 13 under for the final 54 holes. T21st in the German Masters virtually secured his card.

His disappointing 1998 form can be traced to inaccuracy off the tee and an inability to hit sufficient greens in regulation. 118th on O/M so must go to Q. school.

➤ The one event in which he has shown form, and which being weakly contested could give him an opportunity, is the Madeira Open (T8th 1996: T4th 1995).

PAULO QUIRICI

The 31-year-old Swiss player entered 1998 with just four top 10s in 102 tournaments and without a top 100 finish on the Order of Merit.

However in 1998, his 'nappy factor' year he posted high finishes in the Qatar Masters (8th), the Deutsche Bank Open (T17th), the Irish Open (T16th), the Scandinavian Masters (T7th), especially in the One 2 One British Masters (T4th after being the R3 leader) and in the Belgacom Open (T10th).

Suffers from diabetes. 54th on O/M.

➤ Two of his high finishes have been in the European Masters where he was T4th in 1989 and T5th in 1991. Held in his native Switzerland, if he is to cause a shock that could be the tournament in which he does it.

➤ Plays well in bad weather and so must be noted in 3-ball betting in the British Masters at the Forest of Arden where he's finished T4th (1998) and T15th (1997) for a stroke average of 70.87.

MICHELE REALE   D

The 27-year-old Italian's name is pronounced Mikaylee Rayahlee.

In 1997 he was the top player on the Challenge Tour with a truly superb record – Pl 26, eight top 10s, made 21 cuts with a stroke average of 70.65! He won twice, both in play-offs, and was 2nd and T3rd too. He was the first player to win over £50K on the Challenge Tour.

In 1998, as a tour rookie, he found the transition to the full tour was not an easy one. He had high finishes only in the Turespana Masters (T8th) and the Canon European Masters (T20th after a 65 in R4).

High in the driving accuracy stats, it's his short game that has needed improvement. His wife Chiara caddied for him in 1997. This year she's studying Economics! 120th on O/M.

➤ He will take IBC (inspiration by comparison) from Costantino Rocca who also graduated from the Challenge tour, who also came from Northern Italy and who is also sponsored by a brewery company, Peroni.

➤ Showed disappointing nervousness in the Turespana Masters with a 78 in R4 when in contention.

WAYNE RILEY   D

After a 'colourful' early career when the 36-year-old Aussie had a reputation for enjoying himself he made a big impact in his 'nappy factor' year of 1995 when he finished 11th on the O/M after posting five top 10s and winning the Scottish Open, his first success on the European tour.

He followed up in 1996 with another victory in the Portuguese Open and with five more top 10s. He was 16th on the O/M.

However over the last two years his form has dipped. In 1997 he was T4th in the Portuguese Open (as the defending champion) and T2nd in the Moroccan Open, although he made only half of the cuts in his other tournaments to finish 69th on the O/M.

In 1998 it was once more the Moroccan Open (T9th) and the Portuguese Open (T7th after being 2nd at halfway) that saw his highest finishes in a very disappointing year. He will have to go to Q School now.

He has four wins in Australia, the last the Australian Open in 1991 after a 50-foot final-hole putt!

Inaccuracy off both tee and fairway have been his undoing in 1998. Moved from the broomstick putter to the 'ordinary' flat stick by the end of the season. 124th on O/M.

➤ Best recent form has been early in the season, although in 1998 he had problems after breaking a rib at Xmas time in Sam Torrance's house – where else?

➤ It is blindingly obvious, yet his best recent form has been in the Moroccan Open (T9th 1998: T2nd 1997) and the Portuguese Open (T7th 1998: T4th 1997: Won 1996). They are the two tournaments in which he can be followed in match bets and in the outright markets.

JOSE RIVERO   Pb 🍾

Last year the 43-year-old Spanish veteran was awarded the Pb symbol after he had finished 108th (1996) and 95th (1997) on the O/M. Those two years signalled a real decline for the two-time Ryder Cup player who from 1984 – 1995 had always been in the top 50 on the O/M and on six occasions had been in the top 20.

Sadly there has been little sign of him recovering form in 1998. His high finishes came in the Scandinavian Masters (6th), the European Open (T10th) and the Belgacom Open (T17th).

74th on O/M.

➤ He is also awarded the bottle after his collapse in the Turespana Masters where he shot 78 and 76 after he was T3rd at halfway; and in the European

Masters he got into real contention then covered the back nine in 40 with his short putting looking very dodgy.

➤ Best betting opportunities will be in the early round 3-ball betting in the Turespana Masters (T3rd at halfway 1998) and the Portuguese Open (T15th 1997: T7th 1996).

➤ However for the outright markets, no way Jose!

DEAN ROBERTSON

28-year-old Scot who had a solid rookie year in 1995 when 53rd on the O/M after six top 10s including a 2nd place in the Jersey Open.

In 1996 (89th) and 1997 (92nd) the former Scottish amateur champion and Walker Cup player did not really progress.

In 1998 he finished a very creditable T5th at 200/1 in the Volvo PGA. However he did show real signs of nerves in R4 when he took the tournament lead at the 13th and then dropped shots after poor tee shots.

Had a high finish in the Loch Lomond Invitation (T13th after an 'off the pace' 69 in R4) and in the Belgacom Open (T17th). 73rd on O/M.

➤ With just two top 5 finishes in four years he's not a player with a record to encourage betting in the outright markets.

➤ A really good player in windy conditions.

➤ Can be noted in early round 3-ball betting in the Heineken Classic (T8th 1996) and the Benson and Hedges (R1 joint leader 1998).

JON ROBSON **D**

30-year-old player who got into the top 100 on the O/M for the first time in 1996 (66th) after a superb performance when 2nd in the Benson and Hedges in high winds. In 1997 he had two top 10s ending the year 70th on the O/M.

So 1998 has been very disappointing. His high finish was in the English Open (T20th).

He won a car in a long driving contest in Paris in October 1997. His putting has been a major worry in 1998. 161st on O/M.

➤ He offers punters two opportunities:-
* to back him in the Compaq European Grand Prix (66 in R1 in 1998's cancelled event: T6th 1997) on a course that suits his length
* he has a comparative advantage in really windy conditions (remember the 1996 Benson & Hedges) when he can be followed at 'value' prices in 3-ball betting.

COSTANTINO ROCCA **G**

He burst on to the European scene in 1993 when he secured his first tour victories in the French Open and the Lyon Open. He finished the year 6th on the O/M and was a member of the Ryder Cup team that lost to the USA, with some observers doubting his nerve after he failed to secure a point in either of his two games.

He finished 4th on the O/M in both 1995 and 1996.

In 1995 he played in the successful European Ryder Cup side after a season in which he'd not won but had finished six times in the first three.

In 1996 he won the Volvo PGA championship and had two other top 3 finishes.

In 1997 he again made the Ryder Cup team after a solid season in which he finished 12th on the O/M after his fourth win, in the Canon European Masters.

At Valderrama he scored 3 points from 4 including a memorable victory (by 4 and 2) over Tiger Woods in the singles.

In 1998 he made a disappointing start to the year with his long game in disarray. He posted only one high finish before June when he was 15th in the Volvo PGA which he had won two years earlier.

In the second half of the year he had high finishes in the Deutsche Bank Open (T17th), the Dutch Open (T5th at 40/1 (!) after going 15 under par for the last 54 holes), the European Open (T10th) and the BMW International (T18th).

With Ryder Cup points at stake he finished 4th in the Canon European Masters and T20th in the One 2 One British Masters.

In the majors he missed the cut in the US Masters, the US Open and the USPGA. In the British Open he finished T9th after a brilliant 70 in R3 when the stroke average was 77!

24th on O/M.

➤ Ryder Cup years sure do bring the best out of Rocca. In 1993 he won twice, in 1995 he was 2nd in the British Open, in 1997 he was 5th in the US Masters.

So in 1999....expect him to show improved form and let's remember his most consistent performances have been in three tournaments in which he must be noted in match and outright betting.

*The European Open 10th 1998: 5th in 1997 and 1996: 2nd 1995
*The Canon European Masters 4th 1998: Won 1997: 2nd 1995
*The Volvo PGA 15th 1998: Won 1996

➤ 11/10 to make the Ryder Cup side.

MARK ROE   CT

Mark is now very much on the 'comeback' trail. From 1986 to 1994 he had only once been outside the top 50 on the O/M (52nd in 1990), and in 1994 after winning his third tournament, the French Open, he ended the year 9th on the O/M.

However 1995 was an 'annus horribilis' for the 35-year-old from Sheffield who had real personal problems as well as a knee injury. He ended the year 126th on the O/M.

Glimpses of a return to form could be detected in 1996 and late 1997 when he was 3rd in the British Masters.

In 1998 he had high finishes in the Qatar Masters (T21st) and the Cannes Open (T11th).

Married in June. He was T2nd at 125/1 in the German Open and T12th in the One 2 One British Masters in September after leading during R3.

Uses the broomstick putter. 53rd on O/M. Injured a rib in late October.

➤ He will be on the 'comeback trail' in 1999 which will be his first full year on tour since he has completely readjusted his life. He has the ability to win again.

➤ Back him for the 1999 Cannes Open, especially if he has an early R1 tee time so avoiding the gusty winds that spoilt his second round in 1998.

➤ Has real PMAs with France where he's gained two of his three tour wins so remember him for the Lancome Trophy which he won in 1992.

➤ Useful record at the Forest of Arden, home of the British Masters (T12th 1998: 3rd 1997: Top 25 1994: T6th 1993) where he can be noted in 3-ball betting and as a big-priced outsider.

EDUARDO ROMERO   G ☼

The 44-year-old Argentinean, known as 'the Cat', continues to be the most consistent player on the tour. From 1989 – 1994 he made the cut in 84.6% of his tournaments over a six-year stretch.

He briefly played in America without real success and since dedicating himself to Europe once more his consistent accuracy off tee and fairway has ensured that his cut making continues at an amazing high level – 85.7% 1996 and 90% 1997.

He has six European tour victories, the last in 1994.

In 1998 he had top 10s in the Portuguese Open (T4th at 33/1), the Spanish Open (T4th at 33/1), the Loch Lomond Invitational (T2nd) and the One 2 One British Masters (T2nd).

He also posted top 20s in the European Open (T16th) and the Canon European Masters (T20th).

After missing the cut in the Lancome Trophy, after he incurred a penalty shot, he fell down the clubhouse stairs. He then went home to Argentina for treatment.

Missed the cut in the USPGA. After a good start finished T57th in the British Open.

Lost all his three matches representing Argentina in the Dunhill Cup.

At his best in warm, sunny conditions. 21st on O/M.

➤ He is very much a European Tom Watson – a superb tee-to-green straight hitter whose putting from 5 – 8 foot stops him from winning. However even Tom got it right to land the Colonial in 1998 so it's certainly possible that Romero will win again in 1999.

➤ His amazing consistency means you must never oppose him in match bets and always consider him if he's paired against a more erratic 'name' player. He's ideal match-bet material.

➤ He can be supported with confidence on the spreads and in the outright market in the Spanish Open (T4th 1998: T3rd 1997: T4th 1996: T6th 1995).

RAYMOND RUSSELL   D CT

The 26-year-old Scot made a stellar start to his pro career in his first two years when 14th and 16th in the O/M in 1996 and 1997. Indeed he secured a morale-boosting first win on just his fifth appearance when he won the 1996 Cannes Open. In 1997 he had punter-friendly finishes in the Deutsche Bank Open (T5th), the French Open (T3rd), the European Open (T3rd), the British Masters (T4th) and the Oki Pro-Am (4th).

By contrast 1998 has been an 'annus horribilis'. His early-season form and confidence were affected by a virus infection. Without a top 20 finish all season he suddenly found his form, and secured his 1999 tour card, with a brilliant T4th in the British Open after a 66 in R4.

However his swing deserted him after that. His stats for driving accuracy, greens in regulation and putting are all poor, showing that his all-round game really has suffered this year. However he showed some form in September when T11th in the German Masters, and in October when T21st in the Belgacom Open. 63rd on O/M.

➤ Russell's poor year has been completely unpredictable, unwelcome and unexpected. Let's hope it also proves unusual and that the young Scot can regain his form.

➤ Form and confidence usually disappear faster than they return so a watching brief is therefore sensible. However should he return to the form of 1996 and 1997 he can be followed as he had showed plenty of bottle then as he recorded nine (yes nine!) top 5 finishes including his 1996 win.

JUSTIN ROSE   D A

18-year-old amateur Rose became a household name in mid July after a brilliant performance when he finished T4th in the British Open. It was his demeanour, his smile and his enjoyment of the whole experience that really endeared him to everyone. Indeed it became Boy's Own fantasy stuff as he chipped in on the last hole for a 69 in R4.

Everyone on the planet with a microphone then wanted to speak to him amidst a massive media frenzy. He was the next Nick Faldo, the new Tiger Woods as the hype went into overdrive.

It seemed that a sense of proportion was not on the agenda. The fact that he lost in the first round of the English Amateur Championship in early June, and that he missed the cut at Loch Lomond the week before the Open were quickly forgotten.

By turning pro straight after the Open he aimed to secure his tour card for 1999 in the three months of the season then left. At the time it all seemed rather rushed to me, especially as plan A for 1998 had been to stay as an amateur, win the Amateur title, then play the 1999 US Masters.

Rather predictably Rose found the hype, the transition to the full tour and the frenzied nature of the weeks after the Open affected his game.

Cut after cut was missed and when Corals opened their market on players to make the 1999 Ryder Cup they made history – giving a 5/1 quote for Rose, a player who hadn't even made a professional cut!!

Michael Welch, Philip Parkin, Warren Bennett, Lee James and, of course, more recently Gordon Sherry are all examples of brilliant amateurs who turned pro to find hype and heartache rather than success.

➤ Needing a top 10 finish at Chart Hills golf club just to qualify for Q school he shot a 67 in R2 to finish ninth and just made it!

Let's hope he gets his tour card at Q school, and starts to build a successful career in 1999.

➤ In the frenzy after the British Open the following were the 'Magnificent Seven' bets available – JUST-IN case you want to know the odds for those who backed ROSE

* 100/1 To win the 1999 British Open.   Ladbrokes & Hills
* 33/1 To win the 1999 Order of Merit.   Corals
* 25/1 To win a major by the end of 2000.   Corals
* 16/1 To win a European tour event in 1998.   Ladbrokes
* 14/1 To win any of the next five British Opens.   Ladbrokes
* 8/1 To win a major by the end of 2003.   Ladbrokes
* 6/4 To win a European tour event by the end of 2000.   Corals

JARMO SANDELIN   S G

The 31-year-old Finnish-born Swedish citizen now lives in Monaco. He burst onto the European tour in 1995 via the Challenge tour. His impact was immediate, finishing 21st on the O/M after beating Seve to win the Turespana Open. With that win, two 2nds and two other top 10s he was the Rookie of the year.

In 1996 he won the Madeira Island Open. He finished only 55th on the O/M as he played just sixteen events as he also played in the States. However he had progressed as his stroke average had fallen.

In 1997 he ended the year 28th on the O/M after two top 3 finishes in the Lancome Trophy (T2nd) and the Spanish Open (T3rd).

This year he has had top 10 finishes in the Heineken Classic (T8th) the Portuguese Open (T2nd after a 67 in R4), the Lancome Trophy (T2nd), the Belgacom Open (T5th) and the German Masters (T8th after 65 in R4).

His other high finishes have been in the Italian Open (T13th), the French Open (T11th), the Loch Lomond Invitational (T20th), the Scandinavian Masters (T25th) and the European Open (T23rd).

Won the Novotel Perrier Pairs with Olle Karlsson in October at 10/1.

He has huge length, a will to win, proven 'bottle' and real aggression. Well capable of shooting very low scores. He has a fine putting stroke. 23rd on O/M.

➤ In the South African PGA he went from 7 under to 1 over in just one hole as he had more hits than Frank Sinatra taking 12 at the 5th in R2. He had not taken the option of playing a provisional ball. In September in the One 2 One British Masters he was T3rd at halfway before an apparent combination of poor course management and impatience saw him go 14 over par over the last 36 holes.

These examples illustrate the necessity for him to add a degree of cool judgement to his undoubted talent if he is to win again.

➤ "Nobody wants to see my nipples, do they?" he said after the tour banned his see through golf shirts.

➤ Has the length to do really well both in the BMW International (T12th 1997) and the German Masters (T8th 1998).

➤ Clearly he enjoys the Lancome Trophy (T2nd 1998: 2nd 1997) in which his stroke average over the last eight rounds is 68.37 with scores varying from 63 to 74!!

➤ Controversy seems to follow Sandelin around. Last autumn he was involved in a dispute with Phil Mickelson in the Dunhill Cup, and in the 1997 Lancome

Trophy he accused the eventual winner, Mark O'Meara, of moving his ball nearer the hole. In 1998, again in the Lancome Trophy, Lee Westwood said that the Swede's ball had moved when he addressed it on the second green on Saturday. Sandelin maintained that he hadn't grounded the club, and without any other evidence there was no penalty.

If he should make the Ryder Cup team (opening quote 4/1) things might get a little interesting!!

PETER SENIOR

39-year-old Aussie who has been concentrating on the Australian and Japanese circuits. However he returns to the European tour in 1999 for the first time since 1992.

He has won a host of tournaments in Europe, Japan and at home in Australia yet he feels his game is not in the best shape. "My short-iron play is killing me," was the quote from the player who once made better chips than Harry Ramsdens.

In 1998 his best European finish was when he was T4th at 100/1 in the Deutsche Bank Open.

➤ He is a superb wind player and must be noted, especially in 3-ball betting, if in form and there are really blustery conditions.

➤ If he can rediscover his short-iron game he could well post a high finish or two, although it certainly won't be easy in Ryder Cup year.

JEEV MILKHA SINGH

26-year-old Singh was 10th at Q school to earn his 1998 tour card and so became the first Indian golfer to qualify for a place on the European tour.

He had graduated after a steady record of success in the Asia-Pacific region where he had won at least once every year since he turned pro in 1993.

In 1998 he had high finishes in the Heineken Classic (T15th – shot a 72 in R4 in the wind), the Portuguese Open (T12th), the Deutsche Bank Open (T22nd), the English Open (T8th) and the German Open (T20th after a 76 in R4).

Although no relation, Jeev Milkha is very similar to Vijay in that he simply loves to play tournaments.

His putting and bunker play have let him down this year. 104th on O/M.

➤ He may prove to be best when coming from 'off the pace' in warm dry conditions.

➤ A player to note in early 3-ball betting in the English Open (T8th 1998 incl. 69 in R2 and 67 in R3) and the Cannes Open (shot a 67 in R1 in 1998).

ANDREW SHERBORNE

37-year-old tall fella (he's 6' 4" in his slippers) from Bristol. From 1987 to 1996 he'd been in the top 100 on the O/M, then he slipped to 104th in 1997.

He's posted two wins, in the 1991 Madrid Open and the following years Spanish Open.

In 1998 he had a card-saving early success when T2nd at 200/1 in the Qatar Masters.

He later had high finishes in the Cannes Open (T8th) and the Benson and Hedges (T18th).

Accurate off the tee, his putting has been a major problem this year. 78th on O/M.

➤ He's just the sort of big-priced outsider who could provide a shock in the Cannes Open (T8th 1998: T12th 1997).

➤ "I just love Wentworth," so remember Sherborne in the Volvo PGA (T4th in both 1995 and 1996) in 3-ball betting and as a possible long-shot in the outright betting as the course is set up for his accurate driving style.

PATRIK SJOLAND   G

The 27-year-old Swede joined the tour in 1996. He had a very solid first season when 58th on the O/M after two top 10s including a 2nd place in the Italian Open.

However it was 1997 that marked him out as 'a winner about to happen' as he got into the top 20 on the O/M with seven top 10s including four in a superb late-season spell of form in September and October.

1998 saw the promise fulfilled as he posted two more early season top 3 finishes – in the South African Open (3rd at 50/1) and the Qatar Masters (T2nd at 66/1 when he took a par 5 at the last hole when he needed birdie).

His first win came when he won the rain-reduced Italian Open at 66/1 after going 21 under par for 54 holes, making only one bogey.

He then had top 10s in the Benson and Hedges (T7th) and the Volvo PGA (T2nd at 40/1) to give him successive form figures of W-7-2!

Had further high finishes in the English Open (5th at 40/1 after leading after R2), the Loch Lomond Invitational (T20th) and the Dutch Open (T9th).

Went into the final round of the Canon European Masters as the 2/9 favourite with a 4-shot advantage. Showing some nervousness he twice allowed Struver to catch him before he lost to the German in a play-off.

Played for Sweden in the Dunhill Cup in October winning 2½ of his three matches. He had played in the tournament in 1996 when he won three from four. So in seven starts he's lost just once and has a stroke average of 69.86!

35th in the British Open. Missed the cut in the USPGA.

His girlfriend Ulrika caddies for him. She missed this year's Scandinavian Masters after an appendix operation. He attributes their full-time partnership on course for his improved play. Beat Steve Stricker in R1 of the World Matchplay in October before Singh 'slaughtered' him in Q Fs 7 and 6.

Played poorly in the season ending Volvo Masters. 5th on O/M.

➤ Yet to win a 72-hole tournament, he will have learned a lot from the final day of the 1998 Canon European Masters.

➤ He is a superb iron player and a brilliant putter, especially in the 10-15 feet range. Last year his profile said, 'There must be every reason to expect Sjoland to notch up his first win in 1998' and he did. I expect him to win again in 1999 and to take his place in the Ryder Cup side (opening odds 4/7).

➤ He played well at Wentworth in the World Matchplay, and last year no one else in the PGA field could match his 36-hole 12 under par finish. So he can be supported in the 1999 Volvo PGA.

➤ His fine temperament is linked to his car accident (January 1992) after which he lost his spleen and half his liver. "It has given me strength and perspective. I know that if I make a double bogey it doesn't really matter."

DES SMYTH Pb

The one-time Ryder Cup star is now a 45-year-old tour veteran.

In 1998 he had three high finishes – in the Moroccan Open (T14th), the British Open (T15th) and the Scandinavian Masters (T25th).

He has seven tour wins, the last being his only victory this decade when he won the Madrid Open in 1993.

Uses the broomstick putter. 114th on O/M.

➤ 45-year-old Des must be waiting, with his bank manager's blessing, to join the Senior Tour as it really is very difficult to see him winning again. Indeed he hasn't had a top 10 finish for over two years. The Pb symbol is therefore retained.

➤ As always he presents punters with one clear opportunity – to back him in 3-ball betting in really blustery conditions as he's acknowledged to be a fine wind player.

JAMIE SPENCE S

This decade, from 1991, 35-year-old Jamie has been in the top 50 every year (with the exception of 1994 when he was 92nd) and in that time he has just one win when, coming from 'off the pace', he landed the 1992 Canon European Masters after a play-off.

In recent years he's finished 30th (1995), 49th (1996) and 35th (1997) on the O/M.

In 1998 he was T20th in the Loch Lomond Invitational before in September he posted the one high finish he manages each year. It was in the BMW International where he posted a clubhouse target after a 66 in R4 to finish 2nd.

It was his fifth top 5 finish in the last four seasons.

He enjoys a bet and loves horse racing which is really encouraging. However he does support Arsenal which is sad. 43rd on O/M.

➤ A real streak player capable of really low rounds such as his 60 in the Canon European Masters in 1992, and his 61 in the 1997 Cannes Open. Both those were in final rounds so whenever he's on a course that encourages low scoring he can be backed in the final round in 2-ball betting, or even in the outright market as a big-priced outsider if he is about 5 shots 'off the pace'.

➤ He must be noted especially in match betting for the Compaq European Grand Prix (T3rd of R2 finishers in 1998 cancelled event: T6th 1997: T9th 1996) in which he would be worth a bet 'in running' if close up, but 'off the pace', after R3.

SVEN STRUVER G 🐎

The 31-year-old German joined the tour in 1993. Since then he has finished 68th (1993), 41st (1994), 32nd (1995), 70th (1996) and 23rd (1997) on the O/M to establish himself firmly as a leading player and this guy sure knows how to win!

In 1996 his first victory was in the rain-reduced (54 holes) South African PGA after he shot a 63 in R3.

In 1997 he led from the front to gain win Number 2 in the Dutch Open at 100/1.

Then in 1998 he gained his third win when he came from behind to beat Patrik Sjoland in the Canon European Masters at 80/1 after a play-off.

In 1998 he had other high finishes in the South African PGA (T23rd), the Qatar Masters (T13th), the German Open (T23rd), the BMW International (T24th after his putter was stolen – he was 2nd after R2) and the Belgacom Open (T21st after 73 in R4).

He had top 10s in the Cannes Open (T2nd at 50/1), and the rain-reduced Italian Open (T6th).

Won two of his three Dunhill Cup matches for Germany in October.

35th in the British Open. 13th on O/M.

➤ He has now won from the front (Dutch Open 1996), from 'off the pace' (Canon European Masters 1997) and in a rain-reduced event (South African PGA 1995). What's more they were very much on three different courses.

So with three wins in as many years Struver has proved his ability, versatility and bottle. However his patience and temperament are the real extra clubs in his bag.

➤ His two 72-hole wins have come after making six successive cuts (the 1997 Canon European Masters) and after missing six successive cuts (the 1996 Dutch Open) so whether apparently in, or out of, form always consider this guy.

➤ I was most impressed with his last win over Sjoland and feel sure he will have further success.

➤ It is possible that he might become the second German to play in the Ryder Cup for which his opening quote of 4/1 was cut to 5/2 after his European Masters win.

➤ With his fine early-season form in the South African Open (T9th 1997) and especially the South African PGA (T23rd 1998: T12th 1997: Won 1996) remember him in match bets against other more fickle Europeans in those tournaments.

FABRICE TARNAUD

29-year-old Frenchman who has struggled to make an impact since he joined the tour, via the Q. school, in 1995.

He posted two top 10s in each of his first three years, finishing 100th (1995), 84th (1996) and 78th (1997) on the O/M.

In 1998 he had just two high finishes – in the Moroccan Open (T19th after a poor 79 in R1) and the European Open (T23rd).

Usually accurate off the tee, he has been in very poor form with the putter. 92nd on O/M.

➤ His best-ever tour finish, when he was 4th in the 1997 BMW International, came on the back of twelve missed cuts.

➤ After his fine finish in the 1998 Moroccan Open (5 under for the last 54 holes) he should be noted there in 3-ball betting, especially if his putter has 'warmed up'.

STEEN TINNING

The 36-year-old Dane lost his card in 1996 after eleven years on the tour in which he had never posted a top 3 finish, with 1993 his most successful year when he was 63rd on the O/M.

Returned to the tour this year after finishing 8th on the 1997 Challenge tour where he made seven top 10s in 23 starts.

In 1998 he secured his card after three significant finishes in the Italian Open (T6th), the British Open (T35th) and the following week in the Dutch Open (T11th after 4 sub-par rounds). 91st on O/M.

➤ With just one European tour top 4 in over 250 starts he's not one for outright betting.

➤ His best-ever finish came when he was T4th in the 1995 Madeira Open which will surely be the tournament that will provide him with his best opportunity in 1999.

➤ This year he was at his best in July.

KATSUYOSHI TOMORI

The 44-year-old Japanese player had victories in the 1994 Mitsubishi Open and the 1995 Japan Matchplay title and two appearances for Japan in the World Cup to his credit when qualified for the 1997 European tour through the Q School. He was the first Japanese player ever to do so.

In his first year he posted four top 10s, in the Heineken Classic (T8th), the South African PGA (T8th), the Moroccan Open (T10th) and the Deutsche Bank Open (T9th). He ended 1997 80th on the O/M.

In 1998 his progress continued with a fine series of high finishes – in the Spanish Open (T7th – he was T2nd at halfway), the Turespana Masters (T3rd at 80/1), the Madeira Open (T10th after a 76 in R4), the Scandinavian Masters (T11th), the German Open (T7th), the BMW International (T6th after a 64 in R4) and the Volvo Masters (T19th).

Shot a brilliant 70 in R3 of the British Open in which he finished T44th.

An accurate player who lacks length off the tee.

Has been let down by his putting this year. 47th on O/M.

➤ On courses with a premium on accuracy his consistency makes him solid match-bet material if paired with a less reliable player.

➤ His shorter game is suited to the Madeira Open held at altitude. In 1999 he will have a fine chance there to post his first European victory after his T10th this year.

➤ Worth noting in 3-ball betting in the British Open. In his last three Opens he has finished T44th, T24th and T51st.

SAM TORRANCE M.B.E.   G

Smokin' Sam did not win in 1996 or 1997 so he had to watch the Ryder Cup at Valderrama.

However he entered 1998 as a man with a mission. "I've been given a good talent and I want to use it. The difference is I've got to work harder now and take greater care of my fitness to do it. That's why I gave up drink – solely for my health and my golf." He was determined to add to his twenty career wins on the European tour and to try to regain his place in the Ryder Cup side. Remember it was Sam who holed the winning putt in the 1995 Ryder Cup.

He was T4th at 66/1 in the Portuguese Open, T21st in the Spanish Open, and T16th in the Volvo PGA before he won the French Open at 80/1. It was his first win for three years.

Later he had high finishes in the Loch Lomond (T13th), the Scandinavian Masters (T25th), the European Open (T10th), the BMW International (T16th) the Lancome Trophy (T11th after a 64 in R4) and the Volvo Masters (T8th).

Appointed as an assistant to new European Ryder Cup captain Mark James, he is very keen to play in the 1999 Ryder Cup as he will almost certainly be the Captain in 2001.

So once the Ryder Cup points started he continued to post high finishes in the Canon European Masters (T12th) and the One 2 One British Masters (T8th).

From tee to green Sam is usually accurate. However he has often been let down by his putting. 14th on O/M.
➤ Started as a 3/1 chance to play in the Ryder Cup side.
➤ Once the Ryder Cup positions have been finalised he may find it difficult to maintain his motivation in the September tournaments as MLD may set in. He would then be worth opposing in match bets.
➤ Sam has won seven times in Ryder Cup years in the nineties, although he failed to win in 1997, so with his renewed determination expect the moustachioed Scot to notch win 22 in 1999.

JAY TOWNSEND   D

Jay is a 36-year-old from Michigan with a home in Florida. He has played the European tour throughout the nineties with a 2nd place in the 1993 Catalonia Open his best finish.

In 1997 his 3rd-place finish in the English Open secured his card.

In 1998 he has had only four high finishes – in the Heineken Classic (T15th after a fine 67 in the wind in R4), the Qatar Masters (T13th), the Spanish Open (T21st) and the rain-reduced Italian Open (T18th).

He had a shoulder injury in March.

Inaccuracy, especially off the tee, has been a major problem this year. A left-to-right player.

He will have to return to Q School. He's been twice before in 1984 and 1990 and was successful each time
➤ He has PMAs with the Hanbury Manor Course, home of the English Open, as he shot a course record 63 there in 1997 on his way to a 3rd-place finish.

GREG TURNER   G

Greg is a Kiwi who has played with great consistency in recent years. From 1993 to 1997 inclusive he was only once outside the top 30 on the O/M (when 31st in 1996) with his average position 24th, and he made the cut in 78.6% of his tournaments. He also posted wins in the Italian Open (1993), the Balearic Open (1995) and the One 2 One British Masters (1997) to add to his earlier win in the 1986 Scandinavian Open.

Down under in December 1997 he won the New Zealand Open at 16/1.

In 1998 he had high finishes in the Cannes Open (T2nd 33/1), the Italian Open (T13th), the Benson and Hedges (T7th), the Scandinavian Masters (T16th), the Lancome Trophy (T2nd), the German Masters (T21st) and the Belgacom Open (T3rd after going into R4 as joint leader).

Finished T15th in the British Open and was top Aussie at 14/1. Missed the cut in the USPGA.

Played creditably (68 in R1) when T28th in the World Series of Golf. Won all three matches for New Zealand in the Dunhill Cup in October. Can be let down by his putting from under 5 feet. 27th on O/M.

➤ In two of the last three years he has been top Aussie (W 14/1 1998 and W 18/1 1996) in the British Open so do make a note of the 35-year-old Kiwi at Carnoustie in 1999. Let's remember he was top Aussie on that course in the 1996 Scottish Open, has made the cut in each of his last five British Open starts, and won all his three matches at St Andrews in the Dunhill Cup in October 1998.

➤ He has won on the European tour in each of the last three 'odd' years (1993, 1995, and 1997) this decade. There is every prospect that 1999 will continue that sequence.

MILES TUNNICLIFF

30-year-old guy from Leamington Spa who now lives in Southern Spain.

In 1996 he posted six top 10s in an impressive year after he had gained his card via Q School. He was 62nd on the O/M.

Slipped back in 1997 with just one top 10, in the Scandinavian Masters (T8th), to end the year 110th on the O/M.

In 1998 he again struggled although he played in many tournaments. Had a wrist injury from mid September.

His best finishes were in the Spanish Open (T21st), the German Open (T13th) and the German Masters (T21st).

He is simply not hitting enough greens in regulation to give himself real chances of getting into contention.

➤ Now based in Spain, in Marbella he may do best in the Turespana Masters and the Spanish Open (T21st 1998).

JEAN VAN deVELDE

The 32-year-old French guy joined the tour via Q School in 1989, has kept his card ever since and has always been in the top 80 on the O/M. He has just one win in the 1993 Roma Masters, after a play-off.

His best year was 1996 when he was 18th on the O/M after four top 5 finishes in the Heineken Classic (T2nd), the Loch Lomond Invitational (2nd), the Dutch Open (T5th) and the Scandinavian Masters (5th).

In 1997 he slipped to 77th on the O/M.

1998 has seen a significant improvement as he posted high finishes in the Volvo PGA (T16th), the French Open (T16th), the Loch Lomond (T24th), the BMW International (T18th – he had a back spasm and massage on course in R4), the German Masters (T8th) and the Belgacom Open (T17th).

He had top 10s in the Italian Open (T10th), the Scandinavian Masters (T4th), the European Open (T7th) and the Canon European Masters (T7th after a 65 in R4).

Played well in the Dunhill Cup for France in October winning twice in three starts and shooting all rounds at or under par.

Suited by wider fairways and good greens as he is a good putter although he's not the most accurate off the tee. Clearly at his best in sunny, dry weather. 26th on O/M.

➤ He is worth noting in 3-ball and match betting as well as in the outright market in the Heineken Classic (T3rd 1997: T2nd 1996: 6th 1994) where he enjoys the heat and the course.

➤ Has a steady record in the Canon European Masters (T7th 1998) and in 1999, with many 'top guns' focussed on the Ryder Cup, he would be worth a 'nibble' in the outright market, as well as consideration in 3-ball betting.

➤ 6/1 to make the Ryder Cup team.

ANTHONY WALL

The tall 23-year-old attached to Sunningdale played in six events in 1997 without earning a cheque.

He earned his 1998 card via the Q School.

One fair finish when T23rd in the Turespana Masters was the best in a disappointing year until he found form in September in the Lancome Trophy, finishing 6 under for the final 36 holes to finish T7th. The following week he was T28th in the German Masters and then T10th in the Belgacom Open. In that late September spell he'd earned his card for 1999, and in those three tournaments he was 29 under par. 90th on O/M.

➤ I was impressed by his 'bottle' in that last round in the Lancome Trophy. He can now focus on consolidation in a Ryder Cup year.

PHILIP WALTON

The Dublin-born 35-year-old joined the tour in 1983 and has been in the top 100 on the O/M ever since. His best-ever year came in 1995 when he won the Catalonia Open and Murphy's English Open (after a play-off) to finish 13th on the O/M. However his fine year had secured him a surprise place in the Ryder Cup team, and in true Roy of the Rovers style he holed the winning putt!

Since then he had five top 10s in the next two years as he slipped to 92nd (1996) and 64th (1997) on the O/M.

In 1998 he had high finishes when T4th at 200/1 in the Deutsche Bank Open, T11th in the French Open and T11th in the Dutch Open after four sub-par rounds. T35th in the British Open.

Tendonitis with a problem affecting his right thumb was a worry in August when it forced his withdrawal from the German Open.

He now has three tour wins and a wonderful Ryder Cup memory. The question is whether he can build on that. 64th on O/M.

➤ Learned his golf at the Portmarnock and Royal Dublin courses so he's a fine links player and superb when the winds blow. So do note him on the links-style wind-blown Sporting Club course in Berlin, home of the German Open where he could surprise in 1999.

➤ His consistent recent performances in the Dutch Open (T11th 1998: T14th 1997) suggest he must be considered in 3-ball and match betting on the Hilversum course.

STEVE WEBSTER   g y

The 23-year-old from Nuneaton was the top player at the 1995 Q School. However he lost his card in 1996 his rookie year. He regained it at Q School and in 1997, after returning to his original clubs, he hit form to post three top 10s in the Italian Open (T4th), the English Open (T3rd) and the French Open (T7th). He ended the year 63rd on the O/M.

He maintained that progress in 1998 with three top 10 finishes – the Cannes Open (T5th), the Irish Open (T9th) and the German Open (T2nd).

He also had high finishes in the South African Open (T20th), the English Open (T25th), the BMW International (T18th) and the German Masters (4th).

However he hadn't landed the 7/1 bets with Corals on him to win his first tournament in 1998. 37th on O/M.

➤ He's still very young.....and very talented, although he obviously won't find it easy winning in Ryder Cup year.

➤ He has definite PMAs with Germany after his two best 1998 finishes (T2nd in the German Open: 4th in the German Masters) were recorded in that country.

➤ Clearly he's a player well suited to links-type golf as he showed when top Amateur in the 1995 British Open (T24th) and when T2nd in the 1998 German Open on a links-type course. So he'll be worth following for the 1999 German Open in mid June when the 'big boys' will be preparing for the US Open.

➤ Must be noted on the Gut Larchenhof course used for the German Masters which suits his long-hitting style. 4th this year he could post another high finish there in 1999....although 150/1 will not then be on offer.

> He clearly enjoys the Marriott Hanbury Manor course used for the English Open (T25th 1998 and T3rd 1997) so keep him in mind for that tournament in 1999.

ROGER WESSELS

The moustachioed South African joined the European tour in 1995 when he recorded (what is still) his best finish on the tour when T2nd in the South African PGA.

He ended that year 60th on the O/M. However in 1996 with only one top 10 in the Scandinavian Masters (7th) he slipped back to 109th on the O/M.

1997 saw little improvement as he missed the cut in 13 of his 20 tournaments to finish the season 93rd on the O/M.

1998 a 'nappy factor' year after the birth of his first child, a son Mathew, in 1997, saw some improvement.

He had three top 10s in the Qatar Masters (T9th), the Spanish Open (6th), and the English Open (T8th).

He also had high finishes in the South African Open (T22nd), the South African PGA (T23rd), the Dubai Desert Classic (T17th), the Turespana Masters (T23rd), the European Open (T20th) and the Lancome Trophy (T15th).

The 37-year-old won the Canadian Masters in 1994, and the South African PGA in 1991.

Ended the year 57th on the O/M.

➤ Possibly at his best in the early months of the season. He felt he was swinging better than ever in April this year.

➤ He must be noted for the South African PGA played at the Houghton Club to which he is attached. 2nd on his home track in 1995 he would be an outsider with an each-way chance at Houghton in 1999 in mid January.

WAYNE WESTNER

Perhaps it was the blonde rinse that the 37-year-old South African had used early in the year that caused him to lose his form!

Missing cuts with regularity, he was even penalised for slow play en route to missing the cut in the Johnnie Walker Classic.

He had only one high finish when T21st in the Volvo PGA.

For a player who had nine international wins and two on the European tour it has been a very disappointing year. He has still to make the top 30 in any major.

He is a huge hitter although he has been missing two out of every five fairways in 1998. Indeed his long game has been the source of his poor form.

At his best in warm dry weather.

➤ Although he has won the Dubai Desert Classic (1993) he has yet to win on the continent of Europe, and on recent evidence he won't break his duck in 1999.

➤ If he does show in early 1999 that he has recovered his accuracy off the tee then he would be worth noting for the Irish Open where he played very well both in 1997 (T7th) and 1996 (T7th).

LEE WESTWOOD   **G M Y**

Up to 1st November 1997 Lee was clearly a very good player yet he'd only won once in Europe (the 1996 Scandinavian Masters) and twice internationally (the 1996 Taiheiyo Masters and the 1997 Malaysian Open).

However over the following twelve months 'the Worksop Wonder' was to establish himself as a truly world-class superstar winning eight times including his first victory in America and his first in Britain.

It all started in that November (1997) when in 32 days he played five tournaments in three continents, was 70 under par with a stroke average of 68.6, and he won over £537,000! In order he won the Volvo Masters, was 2nd in the Sarazen World Open, in Japan he retained the Taiheiyo Masters title he won in 1996, was T21st in the Dunlop Phoenix also in Japan before he won the Australian Open in Melbourne beating Great Norman at the 4th extra hole of a play-off after catching him at the final hole.

In 1998 on the European tour he had four wins. In early June in successive weeks he won back-to-back the Deutsche Bank Open at 22/1 (shot 61 in R3 with just 23 putts) and the English Open at 10/1 (driving superbly it was his first win in Britain). Later he won the Loch Lomond Invitational at 16/1 and the Belgacom Open at 8/1 after a play-off.

He also had high finishes in the Johnnie Walker Classic (T4th), the Dubai Desert Classic (T6th), the Italian Open (T6th), the Volvo PGA (a never-in-contention T16th), the Irish Open (15th), the Dutch Open (T3rd, after a course record equalling 63 in R1, when 'drained'), the Canon European Masters (T12th) and the German Masters (T6th).

In America he was T13th in the Bay Hill Invitational, T5th at 50/1 in the Players' Championship where he was top European player (7/1) and top non-American player (16/1). He then won the Freeport McDermott Classic at 20/1 in only his seventh US tournament and this despite calling a penalty on himself.

Amidst massive hype he finished 44th in the US Masters at 16/1. Later in the US Open he was T7th and the top European at 9/2. In the USPGA he missed the cut by 5 (!) shots.

In the British Open, the week after he won the Loch Lomond, he was on a $1 million bonus. However he never contended, finishing T55th.

Won one of his three matches in the Dunhill Cup for England. In the World Matchplay after beating Stuart Appleby (8 and 7) and Ernie Els (2 and 1) he lost to Tiger Woods by 5 and 4.

He had a hip injury in August caused he said by overpractising for the USPGA.

Coached by Peter Cowan, Lee is an excellent advert for Chubby Chandler's well-run 'stable' of top pros that also includes (inter alia) Andrew Coltart and Paul McGinley. His caddie is Mike Doran.

6th on the O/M in 1996, 3rd in 1997, he was 3rd again in 1998 after finishing only T12th in the season-ending Volvo Masters after a 75 in R4.

He has a superb all-round game with his driving his greatest asset. Not surprisingly he's in the Top 20 on the stats for driving accuracy, greens in regulation, putting and driving distance (275 yards). However 131st for sand saves (46%) suggests a major area for improvement.

Due to get married on 8th January 1999. He's still only 25!

➤ Lee is now firmly established as a world-class player who must be considered in every tournament he plays. He has already won on all four world tours and is a certainty to win many, many more times so he clearly retains the G and Y symbols.

➤ With his temperament his 'extra club' he must be awarded the M symbol because he clearly has the mentality to match his all-round skill, and so he can be expected to win a major over the next few years.

➤ He will be looking forward to the 1999 British Open at Carnoustie where he was a superb T4th in the 1996 Scottish Open (as a 23-year-old) in bad weather. Without the million-dollar ballyhoo that preceded the 1998 Open he will surely have a major chance of landing his first major.

➤ His record over the last year (from 1st November 1997) of eight wins and only four other top 5 finishes suggest, that like Phil Mickelson, we should back Westwood win only.

➤ In 1998 the hype and pressure before both the US Masters and the British Open appeared to affect him.

➤ A certainty to play in the Ryder Cup team. In 1997 he played in all five matches losing in the singles to Jeff Maggert, but winning two of his four other games when partnering Nick Faldo in Seve's 'dream team'.

➤ In the Italian Open, playing after a break, he claimed he was 'rusty' and it may well be that he's the sort of player at his very best when he's sharp having played a tournament or two. That being the case he'll be a player to oppose when he returns from his planned eight-week break early in 1999.

CLINTON WHITELAW

The 28-year-old South African played the Canadian tour before he joined the European tour in 1997 having secured his card via the Q School.

In his rookie year, 1997, he gained his first win in March in the Moroccan Open as a 100/1 outsider. He had started the final round as joint leader.

Had injury problems later. Ended the year 54th on the O/M.

In 1998 on the European tour he had two high finishes, in the Dubai Desert Classic (T17th) and the Cannes Open (T5th).

As defending champion he finished T33rd in the Moroccan Open.

➤ The exemption for his Moroccan Open victory expires at the end of 1999 so he must improve if he is to stay on the tour in the new millennium.

➤ In a tournament in which outsiders do well his recent record (T5th 1998: 6th 1997) suggests he will do well in the 1999 Cannes Open.

➤ In 1998 he double-bogeyed two of the last three holes when in the lead in the Wild Coast challenge on the South African tour – he finished T6th. As a result he's awarded the bottle!

IAN WOOSNAM M.B.E.   F G

'Woosy' is now taking his Phyllosan and joins Faldo, Torrance, Langer and Rocca as current Ryder Cup players who are now into their forties.

He had won no less than twenty-seven times on the European tour entering 1998 and had been top of the O/M twice (1987 and 1990).

However this year he couldn't add to his sixteen (!) wins this decade.

He's had punter-friendly high finishes in the Heineken Classic (2nd at 22/1), the Dubai Desert Classic (5th) and the Loch Lomond Invitational (T2nd).

He also posted high finishes in the Qatar Masters (T9th), the Benson and Hedges (T18th), the Deutsche Bank Open (T17th), the Irish Open (T9th) and the One 2 One British Masters (T12th after a brilliant 66 in R3). Led the Lancome Trophy at halfway, then with his dodgy back playing up he shot 77 before withdrawing.

In America he was T8th in the Freeport McDermott.

In the majors he was T16th in the US Masters: missed the cut in the US Open: T57th in the British Open: T29th in the USPGA (when he was 2nd top Euro at 14/1).

After beating Darren Clarke in R1 he lost a game he should have won to Tiger Woods at the first extra hole in the QFs of the World Matchplay in October.

His dodgy back has played up, particularly in America during the USPGA, and when he withdrew after 12 holes of the Players Championship.

In the 1997 Ryder Cup he was only used once by Seve in the first two days. He may have felt low when being well beaten (8 and 7) by Fred Couples in the singles.

Right-to-left player. 20th on O/M.

➤ He has generally played well tee to green in 1998. However he has had major problems on the greens, particularly when putting from left to right.

➤ He'll be aiming for his ninth successive Ryder Cup in 1999, for which Corals initially quoted the Welshman at 4-1 ON.

➤ He plays best when fresh after he's rested his dodgy back, so I've no hesitation at all in recommending him for the Heineken Classic at the Vines course which is so well suited to his game. Second in 1998, T6th in 1997, the winner in 1996 he's 31 under par for those twelve rounds!

➤ He can also be followed in Dubai Desert Classic (5th 1998: 2nd 1997: 7th 1996), and noted in match bets for the Benson and Hedges (T18th 1998: 2nd 1997: 12th 1996).

THE USPGA TOUR PLAYERS

Robert Allenby
Stephen Ames
Billy Andrade
Stuart Appleby
Tommy Armour III
Paul Azinger
Doug Barron
Ben Bates
Phil Blackmar
Jay Don Blake
Michael Bradley
Mark Brooks
Olin Browne
Tom Byrum
Mark Calcavecchia
Jim Carter
Brandel Chamblee
Barry Cheesman
Stewart Cink
Brian Claar
Lennie Clements
Russ Cochran
John Cook
Fred Couples
Ben Crenshaw
John Daly
Robert Damron
Glen Day
Clark Dennis
Chris DiMarco
Trevor Dodds
Joe Durant
David Duval
Brad Elder
Steve Elkington
Ernie Els
Bob Estes
Brad Fabel
Brad Faxon
Steve Flesch
Dan Forsman
Harrison Frazar
Bob Friend
David Frost
Fred Funk
Jim Furyk
Jeff Gallagher
Jim Gallagher Jr
Robert Gamez
Brent Geiberger
Kelly Gibson

Bill Glasson
Paul Goydos
Scott Gump
Jay Haas
Donnie Hammond
Dudley Hart
J P Hayes
Nolan Henke
Brian Henninger
Tim Herron
Gabriel Hjertstedt
Scott Hoch
P H Horgan III
Bradley Hughes
Mike Hulbert
John Huston
Peter Jacobsen
Lee Janzen
Steve Jones
Jerry Kelly
Skip Kendall
Tom Kite
Greg Kraft
Matt Kuchar
Hank Kuene
Neil Lancaster
Franklin Langham
Tom Lehman
Justin Leonard
J L Lewis
Frank Lickliter
Bruce Lietzke
Tim Loustalot
Davis Love III
Steve Lowery
Sandy Lyle
Andrew Magee
Jeff Maggert
John Maginnes
Doug Martin
Len Mattiace
Billy Mayfair
Blaine McCallister
Scott McCarron
Spike McRoy
Rocco Mediate
Phil Mickelson
Larry Mize
Frank Nobilo
Greg Norman
David Ogrin

Mark O'Meara
Naomichi (Joe) Ozaki
Craig Parry
Steve Pate
Corey Pavin
Chris Perry
Kenny Perry
Tom Pernice Jr
Lee Porter
Nick Price
Brett Quigley
Mike Reid
John Riegger
Larry Rinker
Lee Rinker
Loren Roberts
Clarence Rose
Scott Simpson
Joey Sindelar
Vijay Singh
Jeff Sluman
Chris Smith
Mike Springer
Craig Stadler
Paul Stankowski
Payne Stewart
Dave Stockton Jr
Steve Stricker
David Sutherland
Kevin Sutherland
Hal Sutton
Phil Tataurangi
Esteban Toledo
Tommy Tolles
David Toms
Kirk Triplett
Ted Tryba
Bob Tway
Omar Uresti
Scott Verplank
Grant Waite
Duffy Waldorf
Tom Watson
D A Weibring
Mike Weir
Kevin Wentworth
Mark Wiebe
Willie Wood
Tiger Woods
Fuzzy Zoeller

AMERICAN TOUR PLAYERS

ROBERT ALLENBY   G Y

27-year-old Robert has four European tour victories, the 1994 Honda Open and the English Open, the French Open and the British Masters in 1996. He ended 1996 after those three wins 3rd on the O/M.

Late in 1996 in Southern Spain he had a dreadful car accident in which he sustained facial injuries and a fractured sternum.

Returning to golf in 1997 he admitted he was only three-quarters fit both mentally and physically. Finished the year 55th on the O/M.

In late 1997 and early 1998 he played consistently on the Australasian tour including a 3rd in the Players Championship, and 2nd in the Schweppes Coolum Classic.

In 1998 on the European tour he was T12th in the Johnnie Walker Classic, T25th in the Heineken Classic, T11th in the Spanish Open (after being joint leader at halfway), T23rd in the Italian Open, T24th in the Benson and Hedges, 7th in the English Open, and T2nd at Loch Lomond (68 in R3 and R4). Finished T8th in the Volvo Masters.

In the Volvo PGA he was 3 under par after R1 but was disqualified on a technicality.

In the British Open he finished T19th, and was 2nd in the top Aussie market.

He then went to play in America on a sponsors exemption to try to secure his 1999 US tour card.

He was T13th in the USPGA, and T4th in the BC Open in September, T17th in the Michelob.

He made the cut in the Sprint (T37th), the Texas Open (T37th), and the Vancouver Open (T28th). He failed to secure his tour card finishing 141st on the M/L.

With four European wins and five 'down under' at just 27 years of age Allenby already has a fine track record.

He's a long driver with a solid all-round game, although his bunker play could be improved. His 'bottle' is shown by the fact that three of his four European wins came after a play-off. He's a fine wind player.

His putting has been variable this year. He is to settle in Florida close to his good friend, Stuart Appleby.

➤ His game is very well suited to links golf and the British Open where he's posted three top 20 finishes in the last four years. He can be supported in match betting, and in the top Australian market where prices may be 'juicy' in 1999 with Greg Norman's return.

➤ If he plays in America in 1999, because "it is so much closer to home" then he can be expected to do well. Perhaps the BC Open (T4th 1998) on the shot-makers' course at En Joie will see his first win.

➤ He will need time to get used to the American courses and American greens. However once adapted watch this guy go....I think we'll be hearing a lot of Allenby in his thirties.

STEPHEN AMES   G

34-year-old Stephen Michael was born in Trinidad and lives in Calgary, Canada.

He joined the European tour in 1993 finishing 49th on the O/M after one 2nd place and four top 10s.

The following year he gained his first win in the Lyon Open.

In 1995 he slipped to 77th on the O/M. He then improved in 1996 with his second win, in the Benson and Hedges International. With four other top 10s he ended that year 13th on the O/M.

In 1997 he was 30th after three top 10s in the Data Dimension Pro-Am (T4th), the Oki Pro-Am (T9th), and most significantly the British Open (T5th).

In late 1997 he finished T3rd at the USPGA Q School to earn his card for 1998. He was the only player there to shoot six rounds at or under 70.

In America in 1998 he got off to a good start when 3rd in the Nissan Open, and T10th in the Bay Hill Invitational. Later he had high finishes in the Shell Houston Open (10th), and the Bell South Classic (T19th).

In the Greater Greensboro Open he was three off the lead before he shot a 78 to finish T30th.

After visa problems in the States he returned to the European tour to post top 25 finishes in the Madeira Open (T19th), the Loch Lomond Invitational (T24th) and the British Open (24th).

He finished T13th in the Canadian Open, and T24th in the Buick Challenge.

He is a highly talented player who was off scratch within six months of taking up the game.

He has secured his 1999 US tour card by finishing 83rd on the M/L.

➤ With his undoubted talent it would not be surprising to see him notch his first US tour win in 1999 (assuming he overcomes his visa problems), possibly in the Shell Houston Open (T10th 1998) in a tournament that has often been won by first-time winners.

➤ He has the sort of solid record in the Volvo PGA (three successive top 20 finishes) that would warrant an each-way interest should he play the tournament in 1999.

BILLY ANDRADE   F G

William Thomas, Billy to his friends, failed by only $5 in 1997 to make the top 30 on the Money list and so qualify for the lucrative Tour championship.

He was 31st after his second-best season which included four top 10s at the Greater Greensboro (T4th), the Players Championship (5th), the AT&T (T7th) and the Memorial (T10th).

In 1998 he had high finishes in the Phoenix Open (T6th), and the Canon Greater Hartford Open (T4th) in a quiet first half of the season. He received a late entry to the USPGA, opened with four birdies in a R1 of 68 before finishing T44th.

He hit form with a vengeance, especially with his putter, in September when T9th in the Greater Milwaukee Open, before in the following two weeks he won the Canadian Open at 66/1 in a play-off against Bob Friend, and was T16th in the BC Open. His win, his first for seven years, was his 3rd on the tour, and of course, it came in his 'nappy factor' year.

In the autumn (sorry, the fall) he was T14th in the Buick Challenge.

He missed the cuts in the US Masters and the US Open.

A fader of the ball, Andrade is a fine putter although short off the tee. 41st on the M/L.

➤ He can be followed with confidence in three tournaments on courses suited to his short hitting, accurate style of play.

*The Canon Greater Hartford Open (14th 1998: T13th 1997: T8th 1995).

*The Greater Milwaukee Open (T9th 1998 with a stroke average over the last 3 years of 67.8!) in which he will have an outstanding chance.

*The BC Open (successive top 20s in the last two years).

STUART APPLEBY Y

Writing this profile brings back the mental pictures of Appleby holding a press conference before the USPGA. His wife, Renay, had been tragically killed in a traffic accident in London on 23rd July and 27-year-old Stuart had decided to return to the tour and to share his thoughts with the press.

"I'm still dealing with trying to feel comfortable out here, to focus on playing golf. That's hard to do. It's not a priority. I'm just taking baby steps right now. I don't know how many I'll need to get back to my best golf.

"I'm trying to be patient. It's pretty hard at times. It's very easy to fall away. You've got to pick yourself back up. I'm trying to get myself on a level, on the course and off it."

In the USPGA he made an appearance rather than a challenge. However his last shot, was a chip in at the 18th in R2.

His season had started so well. He had played successfully in Australia where he was T4th in the Australian Players Championship, T3rd in the Greg Norman Classic, 5th in the Australian Masters, and 2nd in the Australian PGA.

In America he was T10th in the Colonial before he was the 100/1 winner of the Kemper Open (his second American win). Although he had missed the cut in the US Masters he played superbly in the US Open to finish T10th.

He also had high finishes in the Western Open (T9th), the Loch Lomond Invitational in Scotland (T24th) before he missed the cut in the British Open.

After the tragedy he played well in the Sprint to score 23 points, and finish T29th after which he was T21st in the World Series of Golf.

Won two of his four matches for Australia in the Dunhill Cup at St Andrews where he shot 66 on day one. Played the Wentworth course well when losing to Lee Westwood in the World Matchplay in October.

He is an aggressive, competitive player with huge length off the tee. 40th on the M/L.

➤ After the dreadful tragedy of 1998 it would be a real delight to see this talented young player win again in 1999.

➤ He then must be noted whenever there are windy conditions as he is clearly a masterful player. "I grew up in the wind."

➤ If he is to win in 1999 it could be in the Western Open in which his record recently (T9th 1998: 7th 1997) is very good.

TOMMY ARMOUR III

The 39-year-old Texan won the Phoenix Open in 1990 in his best-ever year when he was 35th on the Money list.

Since then he has never finished higher than 140th on the money list although he had success on the Nike tour when he was the first-ever player to win back to back events in 1994.

However 1998 has seen a transformation in his fortunes as he posted a series of high finishes in the Phoenix Open (T2nd), the Buick Invitational (T6th after which he led the US stroke averages), the Hawaiian Open (T21st), the Nissan Open (T6th – led R3 by a shot then shot 73), the MCI Classic (T24th), the Byron Nelson Classic (T25th), the Western Open (T17th), and the Greater Milwaukee Open (T14th – only shot par in R4), the Texas Open (T11th), and the Michelob Championship (T10th).

He's the grandson of British and American Open Champion Tommy Armour. He'll be 40 in October 1999.

Finished the year 52nd on the M/L.

➤ He must have a real chance in the Phoenix Open (T2nd 1998: T15th 1993: Won 1990) in late January.

➤ He's the only player to have posted four successive top 20 finishes in the Texas Open at the LaCantera course. He lives in Dallas, Texas and can be followed in his home state tournament in match bets, on the spreads, and as a 125/1 outsider (his 1998 price) in the outright market.

PAUL AZINGER   CT G

After recovering from cancer in 1994 the 'Zinger' has slowly and steadily found his form.

In 1996 he had six top 20s, and in 1997 he had three top 10s in the AT&T (T7th), the Hawaiian Open (T9th), and the CVS Charity Classic (T9th). He had top 30 finishes in the three US majors.

In 1998 his progress continued with high finishes in the Bob Hope Classic (T24th), the Doral Ryder Open (T15th), the Freeport McDermott Classic (T19th), the Buick Classic (T24th), the CVS Charity Classic (T12th), the St Jude Classic (T7th), the delayed AT&T (T3rd), and the Las Vegas Invitational (T20th).

However it was in the three US majors that he showed his progress – 5th in the US Masters after four rounds at or under par, T14th in the US Open (65 in R4), and T13th in the USPGA.

He missed the cut in the British Open.

He's a superb player in windy conditions. His putting has improved throughout 1998 as he shot up the putting stats by over 100 places in four months from May. 50th on the M/L.

➤ Clearly now well down 'the comeback trail' the big test for him will come when he's in the real heat at the top of the leaderboard again. He won eleven tournaments from 1987 to 1993, and 1999 will I believe see win Number 12.

➤ In the last seven Hawaiian Opens the 'Zinger' had six top 10s including three top 4s. He can be supported in the Sony Open in Hawaii at the Waialae course in January.

➤ The AT&T, in the first week of February, will provide the 'Zinger' with a real winning chance. He won it in 1991, and he was T3rd this year and T7th last.
➤ He will have a real chance in the US Masters. After three high finishes he was 5th in 1998, and with his length off the tees (293 yards) and his 3rd place in the 1998 greens in regulation stats he'll be worth support at Augusta. The point is further developed in Chapter One.

DOUG BARRON

The 29-year-old from Memphis, Tennessee was 116th on the Money list in 1997, his rookie year, with two top 10s – LaCantera Texas Open (T6th) and the Canon Greater Hartford Open (T9th).

In 1998 he had four high finishes – the Players Championship (T18th), the Quad City Classic (T17th), the Greater Milwaukee Open (6th after a 67 in R4), and the BC Open (T7th after four sub-par rounds), and the National Car Rental at Disney (T19th).

109th on the M/L.
➤ His best form in his two years on tour has definitely been in the period from September to the end of the season.
➤ His ability to 'bounce back' with a birdie (or better) after making a bogey (or worse) led to him being ranked 7th in the 'bounce-back' stats in his rookie year. It is a testament to his temperament.
➤ He did not win on the Nike tour, and has yet to post a top 4 or 5 finish on the main tour. Nevertheless he is an improving young player who could well provide a 100/1 plus shock in 1999.

BEN BATES

37-year-old from Florida where he still lives. He earned his 1998 tour card after finishing 12th on the 1997 Nike tour. He won his first Nike tour event, the 1997 Nike Wichita Open in a four-man play-off. It was his 179th Nike tournament.

In 1998 he has done well to post six top 25 finishes – in the Greater Greensboro Open (T23rd), the Shell Houston Open (T22nd), the Canon Greater Hartford Open (T25th), the Quad City Classic (T17th), the Deposit Guaranty Classic (T11th), in the Buick Challenge (T8th) and in the Michelob (T13th).

112th on the M/L.
➤ The Deposit Guaranty Classic, held at the same time as the US Open, is often won by an experienced player. 'Big Ben', after his best-ever finish there (T11th) in 1997, must have an outsider's chance.
➤ His disappointing 74 in R4 of the Greater Milwaukee Open suggests he may need to gain a lot more experience of the 'heat on Sunday' before he can be expected to win.

PHIL BLACKMAR   D

After two wins in the eighties he came back with win Number 3 as a 100/1 outsider in the 1997 Shell Houston Open. He ended that year, his best in the nineties, 32nd on the Money list.

In 1998 he could not maintain that position.

After finishing T25th in the Mercedes Championship he had just two other high finishes – in the Byron Nelson Classic (T15th) and the Buick Open (T8th).

He missed the cut as defending champion in the Shell Houston Open.

He was T33rd in the US Masters. He missed the cut in the USPGA. 136th on the M/L.

➤ Big Phil is one of the few players able to score his height (67). However I doubt if he'll do so consistently enough to post win Number 4, especially as he's 41 and there are now so many 'hot' young players on the tour.

JAY DON BLAKE

40-year-old Jay Don has just one tour win, in 1991. Since that year, which was his best ever, he has finished in the top 70 every year on the Money list, apart from 1993 when he was 86th.

In 1997 he was 65th on the M/L with three top 10s – the Bob Hope Classic (T9th), the Hawaiian Open (T4th) and the St Jude Classic (T5th).

In 1998 he had six high finishes – in the Hawaiian Open (T16th), the Bay Hill Invitational (T17th), the Byron Nelson Classic (T19th), the Kemper Open (T21st) and particularly in the Bell South Classic (2nd at 200/1 to Tiger Woods). He was also T25th in the Michelob Championship.

A left-right fader of the ball. Short off the tee, he's a fine putter. He has had a herniated disc problem. 72nd on the M/L.

➤ In the 1998 Bell South Classic he dispelled doubts about his final-round nerve so the 'bottle' is now removed.

➤ He has now had five 2nd places. However if he is to gain his second win it just might be in the Byron Nelson Classic (T19th 1998: T5th 1995) in May.

MICHAEL BRADLEY

Michael John is a 32-year-old Florida-born and Florida-based player whose steady progress has been halted in 1998 by severe back problems.

After a slow start in 1993 and 1994 when he retained his card but couldn't break into the top 100 on the Money list he finished 85th in 1995, and then made the 'breakthrough' in 1996 when he won the Buick Challenge and had three other top 3 finishes – in the Doral Ryder Open (T2nd), the Michelob Championship (T3rd) and the Sprint International (T3rd). He ended that year 20th on the M/L.

In 1997 he had three top 10s – in the Honda Classic (2nd), the Bay Hill Invitational (T6th) and the St Jude Classic (T5th) to finish 47th on the M/L.

In 1998 he won for the second time when he landed the Doral Ryder Open at 80/1 in his home state. He also had high finishes in the Nissan Open (T24th) and the Greater Greensboro Open (T8th). He finished T29th in the US Masters.

However after severe back problems in May he had surgery for a herniated disc in early June.

Since then on the comeback trail he's finished T12th in the St Jude Classic, and 39th in the World Series. 48th on the M/L.

➤ He is a very good player with a solid swing capable of shooting very low rounds (once shot 59 in a Pro-Am!). If he fully recovers from his back surgery there's every reason to expect this talented player to win again.

➤ Did us a big 80/1 favour when justifying our advice to ".... make a note of him when the tour makes the 'Florida Swing' through his home state, especially in the Doral Ryder Open in which he's had three successive top 20s including a 2nd in 1996."
➤ If his back is in good shape remember him in mid March in his home state for the Bay Hill Invitational in which he was T6th in 1997 after four sub-par rounds.
➤ He simply must be backed for the Fedex St Jude Classic in early June on a course where his recent record (12th 1998: T5th 1997: T6th 1996) is really superb.

MARK BROOKS   CT D

Mark is a 37-year-old Texan, born and bred, who had his mega year in 1996 when he won three times including the USPGA, his first major win. He ended that year 3rd on the M/L.

Since then it's all been downhill.

In 1997, with just one top 10 finish in the Players Championship (T7th), he ended the year 108th on the M/L. The hype, the invitations, all the non-golf ballyhoo had combined with a change of clubs to produce a dramatic loss of form and confidence.

In 1998 he had high finishes in the Freeport McDermott Classic (T19th), the Canon Greater Hartford Open (T12th), the rain-delayed AT&T (T22nd), the Michelob (T17th) and the National Car Rental at Disney (T19th).

He missed the cut in the US Masters. Finished T57th in the US Open, T66th in the British Open and T56th in the USPGA.

A drawer of the ball. He's a superb putter, shown again by the fact that he was T2nd on the putting stats for the 1998 US Open. 129th on the M/L.
➤ He reverted to his old Hogan clubs in July so 1999 will be his first full season with his 'old' clubs. This seven-time tour winner will be on the comeback trail after two very lean years, and he could well post a 'surprise' win at a very big price.
➤ A proud Texan he must be noted in his home-state tournaments particularly in the Colonial, played on his local course at Forth Worth, and also in the Byron Nelson Classic (three top 12 finishes in the last five years).
➤ He plays best in hot and windy conditions.
➤ He must have a real chance in late July in the Canon Greater Harford Open. He won the tournament in 1988, and in 1998, using his 'old' clubs for the first time, he led during R3 and finished 12th.
➤ His British Open record, when he was playing well, was most impressive (T5th 1996: T3rd 1995: T20th 1994) so do remember him in the top US player market (T3rd 33/1 1996: 2nd 66/1 1995) as he'll be an unexposed player at a big price.

OLIN BROWNE

The 39-year-old, who was born in Washington and lives in Florida, entered the 1998 season without a top 3 finish in 129 tournaments.

However in 1997 his accuracy off the tee was the basis for his T5th finish in the US Open. He finished the year 94th on the M/L

In late 1997 he showed signs of improved form when he was 3rd in the Kapalua International in Hawaii.

In early 1998 he had high finishes in the Phoenix Open (T22nd), the Hawaiian Open (T7th), the Doral Ryder Open (T23rd), and the Shell Houston Open (T17th).

Then in July he was the 200/1 winner of the Canon Greater Hartford Open, chipping in for victory on the first extra play-off hole.

Later he was T15th in the CVS Charity Classic.

He was T43rd in the US Open: T62nd in the USPGA, and he missed the cut in the US Masters. T24th in the World series. 47th on the M/L.

➤ His accuracy off the tee is his great strength so he must be noted in 3-ball betting for the US Open where that strength is so important.

➤ In 1999 the season opening Mercedes Championship will be held in Hawaii, and in his last two tournaments there (the 1997 Kapalua 3rd, and the 1998 Hawaiian Open T7th) he's done very well, so he could well justify each-way support as a huge-priced outsider.

TOM BYRUM

Tom had his best year of the decade in 1997 when he made the top 100 on the Money list for the first time. With five top 10 finishes in the Canon Greater Hartford Open (T2nd), the Buick Open (T2nd), the Fedex St Jude Classic (T9th), the LaCantera Texas Open (T10th) and, especially in the USPGA (9th – his best ever in a major) he ended the season 42nd on the M/L.

In 1998 he had high finishes in the Buick Classic (T5th), the Western Open (T22nd), the Greater Vancouver Open (T21st), the Greater Milwaukee Open (T9th after a 67 in R4) and the Las Vegas Invitational (T12th).

He has one tour win in the 1989 Kemper Open.

He'll be 39 in September 1999. He lives in Texas. 116th on the M/L.

➤ His great strength is his driving accuracy. Others players in 1998, such as Olin Browne and Joe Durant have used that strength as the basis for a shock win and Tom Byrum could well do the same in 1999. His middle name is Elliott so I do wish him well!

➤ 38-year-old Tom has a fine record in the Greater Vancouver Open. In 1996 he shot 69 – 64 in the final two rounds; in 1997 he shot 63 – 67 for the first two rounds – if he ever could combine the 1996 finish and 1997 start he'd shoot 19 under which has been a winning total in the last three years. Have a little each way on Tom for the 1999 GVO.

➤ His other main chances would be in the Western Open (T22nd 1998: T13th 1997), and in the Byron Nelson Classic (T2nd 1994 after a six-man play-off) in his home state of Texas.

➤ If backing Tom do make sure you clearly say or write TOM Byrum as he has a younger brother CURT who is also on the USPGA tour.

MARK CALCAVECCHIA   **G**

38-year-old Calcavecchia has certainly made his Mark. He entered 1998 with eight US tour wins as well as four others internationally including one major – the 1989 British Open.

In 1997 he won the Greater Vancouver Open and had high finishes in the Bob Hope Chrysler Classic (2nd), the Phoenix Open (T4th), the Las Vegas International (T4th), the Tour Championship (T4th), the Canon Greater Hartford Open (5th), and notably in the British Open (T10th). He ended the year 14th on the M/L.

In late 1997 he was the 16/1 winner of the Sarazen World Open at the Chateau Elan course.

In 1998 he had top 10s in the Mercedes Championship (T6th), the Bay Hill Invitational (T4th), the Players Championship (4th), the Memorial (T7th) and the Greater Milwaukee Open (T3rd).

He also had top 20s in the Bob Hope Classic (T19th), the Buick Classic (T17th), the Greater Hartford Open (T16th), the NEC World Series (T14th), and the Canadian Open (T13th).

He won his ninth US tournament when he landed the Honda Classic for the second time impressively in March at 40/1.

In the US Majors he was T16th in the US Masters, T44th in the USPGA, missed the US Open cut, and was T35th in the British Open. Poor 29th (of 30) in Tour Championship.

A fader of the ball. He'll be 39 in June 1999. 12th on the M/L.

➤ 'Calc' is a superb player of fairway woods and long irons, with the basis of his game his consistent ability to hit greens in regulation. So when his bunker play and especially his putting are 'in the groove' he posts high finishes – he's had sixteen punter-friendly top 4 finishes since January 1993.

➤ In 1999 back 'Calc' for the Canon Greater Hartford Open (T16th 1998: 5th 1997: 3rd 1996) in midsummer, and for the Canadian Open (T13th 1998: 7th 1996: 2nd 1994, on a course suited to his fade) in September.

➤ I expect him to do very well in January. The Mercedes Championship for 1998 winners should remove 'the rust.....' before later that month he can be backed in the Bob Hope Classic (T19th 1998: 2nd 1997, and in his last five 90-hole tournaments he's had four top 4s and a top 20) and the Phoenix Open (six top 10s and two wins in eleven starts) in successive weeks.

➤ Worth noting, especially for match betting, that he has made the cut in every one of the last seven British Opens and has posted three top 20 finishes in that time, and of course he won it back in 1989.

➤ 'Calc' gets an opening 11/4 quote from Corals to make the US Ryder Cup team. To date he has played in the Ryder Cups in 1987, 1989 and 1991.

➤ He's been in the top 4 in the last three Las Vegas Invitationals. So he'll be 'exposed' and no more than 20/1 but he'll probably go very close again.

JIM CARTER

37-year-old Big Jim from Arizona has never made a real impact during the nineties.

1997 was his best year of the decade when with seven top 25 finishes he was 88th on the money list.

However in 1998 he has had only two top 10s in the Freeport McDermott Classic (T3rd with four sub-par rounds) and the Byron Nelson Classic (T9th).

He also had top 25s in the Nissan Open (T20th), the Canon Greater Hartford Open (T20th), the Quad City Classic (T13th), the Sprint International (T26th with 25 points), the Greater Vancouver Open (T21st), the Texas Open (T11th) and the Buick Challenge (T8th).

Yet to win on the USPGA tour, he has one win on the Nike tour, in 1994. 71st (best in the '90s) on the M/L.

➤ Being very short off the tee it is not easy to see him winning. However he clearly enjoys the Byron Nelson Classic, where his stroke average for the last four years is 68.25, so make a note of Arizona Jim in that tournament in May, particularly in match and 3-ball betting.

➤ Over the last three years he has an impressive stroke average of 68.9 in the Buick Challenge (T8th 1998: 9th 1997: 20th 1996). Each year a 100/1+ outsider 'pops up' in that tournament so in late September it could pay to take a chance and 'Get Carter!'

BRANDEL CHAMBLEE   G

36-year-old Brandel broke into the top 100 on the money list in 1995 (86th) and maintained that improvement in 1996 (94th), and especially in 1997 (70th). During that time he had been second three times – in the 1996 Bell South Classic, the 1997 Quad City Classic and the 1997 Canon Greater Hartford Open.

1998 was to be 'break-through' year when he was the 40/1 winner of the Greater Vancouver Open in late August. He was then in good form having finished 8th in the Buick Open, and 12th, with 44 points, in the Sprint International in his previous two tournaments. In October he was T24th in the Buick Challenge, T10th in the Las Vegas Invitational, and T19th in the National Car Rental at Disney.

Earlier in the season he had posted high finishes in the Hawaiian Open (T11th), the Nissan Open (T20th) and particularly in the Memorial (coming from 'off the pace' to finish T5th).

He missed the cut in the US Open.

Born in Minnesota, he went to Texas University, and lives in Arizona. Good from sand.

37th (best yet!) on the M/L.

➤ A much-improved player who could well go onto further success in 1999.

➤ The fact is that in each of the last three years Chamblee has either won or finished 2nd so he is a very much a player to note, especially when he's in form.

➤ His win came on the back of form figures of 26-8-12 so he's very much a player to note when he's 'hot'. So in 1999, if he has posted solid recent form figures he'd be worth an interest in the Canon Greater Hartford Open (T2nd 1997: 12th 1996) in late July.

BARRY CHEESMAN

39-year-old picked up his second Nike tour win in 1997, seven years after his first win in the 1990 Quail Hollow Open. He ended 1997 6th on the Nike tour order of merit to secure his 1998 card.

In 1998 he equalled his best-ever USPGA tour finish when T10th in the Nissan Open when, coming from 'off the pace', he was 9 under for the final two rounds. Later in the season, in October, he made his biggest-ever cheque when 3rd in the Michelob after shooting 66 in R4.

He also had high finishes in the Honda Classic (T15th), the Kemper Open (T25th), and the St Jude Classic (T12th).

Born in Illinois. He lives in Florida. He'll be 40 in August 1999. 100th on M/L.

➤ He is a very, very long (285 yards), but not always a very accurate, driver (hits less than two thirds of the fairways).

➤ His final 36 holes in the 1998 Nissan Open suggest that he might have an outside chance there in February.

STEWART CINK   G Y

This tall (he's 6'4" in his socks) guy from Alabama who lives in Georgia really made an impact in 1997, his rookie year.

He won the Canon Greater Hartford Open, was 2nd in the Buick Challenge, and had top 10s in the Buick Classic (T6th), and the Bob Hope Chrysler Classic (T9th) to finish 29th on the Money list and so qualify for the Tour championship.

The previous year he'd been the Nike Tour player of the year winning three times, and posting fourteen (!) top 10s in just 21 (a 66.6% strike rate) starts.

In 1998 he had top 10 finishes in the Mercedes Championship (T6th), the Bob Hope Classic (T6th), the Doral Ryder Open (T4th), the Bell South Classic (T5th), and the Canon Greater Hartford Open (T2nd).

He was T23rd in the US Masters: T10th in the US Open.

Came to Britain for the Loch Lomond Invitational (T13th – and was T3rd as Top US player at 5/1) and the British Open (T66th after being 'blown away' in R3 when the wind got to him as he shot 83!).

He also had high finishes in the Buick Invitational (T13th), the Honda Classic (T12th), the Buick Open (T15th), the Sprint (T21st with 26 points), the Texas Open (T11th), the Michelob (T25th) and the Las Vegas (T16th after 64 in R4).

His form dipped from mid August. For example, he missed the cut in the Buick Challenge in his home state in October. Needed a good final round in 'The Disney' to finish in the Top 30 – he shot 76! Nevertheless he's a determined guy with a very solid, athletic swing.

His strength has been his straight hitting, although this started to desert him later in the year. Good from sand. He's had a fine season with his putter. 31st on M/L.

➤ So long as his stats point to a return to the straight hitting which was the basis for his 1996 and 1997 successes he can be followed in four events in the New Year.

➤ He will have a definite chance in the 1999 Canon Greater Hartford Open (T2nd 1998: Won 1997). In the last two years his stroke average is 66.62 (!!) and he's broken par every round.

➤ Held in his home state, expect Stewart to make an Ernest effort to Cink his putts in the Bell South Classic. T5th in 1998 he'll certainly be worth a bob or two for that tournament which starts on April Fools' day.

➤ He can be followed in mid to late June in two tournaments that demand straight hitting.

*The US Open in which his form figures of 16th – 12th – 10th in just three starts must be remembered on the spreads, and in match and 3-ball betting.

*Also worth noting for the Buick Classic in the week after the US Open. He was 6th in 1997, and got the very worst of the tee times and the weather in 1998. It's an event made for his straight hitting.

➤ He was given an opening quote of 7/2 to make the US Ryder Cup team. 2001 seems much more likely than 1999 for his debut.

BRIAN CLAAR

39-year-old Brian was Rookie of the Year in 1986. However he's yet to finish in the top 65 on the Money list, and he entered 1998 without a win, although he was second in the 1991 AT&T.

In 1997 he was T4th in the Deposit Guaranty Golf Classic, T13th in the Hawaiian Open and T18th in the BC Open.

In 1998 he had three top 25 finishes – in the Buick Classic (T24th), the Quad City Classic (T17th), and the Greater Milwaukee Open (T23rd).

Joint leader of the Michelob Championship during R2 till he hit a triple bogey at the final hole.

His best finish was his fourth place in the Greater Vancouver Open.

He'll be 40 in July 1999. 158th on the M/L so Q School beckons.

➤ His best chances will surely be in three tournaments:-
*The weakly-contested Deposit Guaranty Golf Classic (T4th 1997)
*The Greater Milwaukee Open (T23rd 1998: T12th 1996)
*The BC Open (T18th 1997: 5th 1996: 3rd 1994).

LENNIE CLEMENTS   D

Lennie is a 41-year-old San Diegan who is yet to win on the tour. Indeed in his career to date he has had just four top 3 finishes with a 2nd in the 1994 Bob Hope Classic his best finish.

His form has dipped in recent years with only one top 10 recorded in 1997, in the MCI Heritage Classic (T4th).

In 1998 his slump continued with only one significant finish, in the Greater Greensboro Open (T8th).

He was awarded 'the bottle' after his performances in the Buick Invitational, and the Freeport McDermott Classic in 1996.

Short off the tee – he's one of the five shortest hitters on the tour! 182nd on the M/L!

➤ With his lack of length off the tee (254 yards) a massive handicap, so many huge-hitting, hungry young players, his nervy R4 play when in contention and the fact that he's 41 it is very difficult to see him posting his first win.

➤ His most consistent form over the last two years has been in the Greater Greensboro Open (T8th 1998: T13th 1997).

RUSS COCHRAN

Safely past 40 Russ is a highly-experienced pro who had been in the top 100 on the M/L in eleven of his thirteen years on tour as he entered 1998.

1991, when he had his first and only win in the Western Open, was his best year as he finished 10th on the M/L.

In 1998 he had top 25s in the Hawaiian Open (T16th), the Tucson Chrysler Classic (T22nd), the Honda Classic (T22nd), the Bay Hill Invitational (T17th) and the Byron Nelson Classic (T25th).

His two top 10s were in the Buick Invitational (T6th), and the Greater Vancouver Open (T5th).

He was T34th in the USPGA.

Russ is a fine player in windy conditions. His main strength is his consistent iron play helping him regularly to hit two thirds of the greens in regulation. 91st on the M/L.

➤ There is clearly one tournament in which he can be backed both on the spreads, and in the outright market (so long as you take one fifth, or preferably one quarter, the odds the first five places) – it is the Greater Vancouver Open (T5th 1998: T4th 1997: T5th 1996) in which his stroke average for the last three years is just 68.08!

So in the first week of September with the minimum of fuss get on Russ.

JOHN COOK   G

After winning three tournaments in 1992 (to take his career tally to six) he had three barren years from 1993 through 1995.

However Cooky has bounced back with two wins in 1996 to finish 19th on the M/L, and one win and one second in 1997 to finish 28th.

In 1998 he maintained his improvement with his tenth career win when he landed the Byron Nelson Classic at 66/1, showing superb strategic sense in shooting 65 in R4 for a winning total of 15 under par.

He also had top 10s in the Mercedes Championship (T4th), the Doral Ryder Open (T9th), the Colonial (5th) and the World Series of Golf (4th).

He also had high finishes in the Players Championship (T13th), the CVS Charity Classic (T15th), the Buick Open (T23rd), the Greater Milwaukee Open (T18th) and the National Car Rental at Disney (T19th).

43rd in the US Masters: missed the cut in the US Open: 9th in the USPGA. Did not play the British Open.

He is very much a straight-hitting pro who is always high in the greens in regulation stats.

At his best in dry, sunny conditions. 22nd on M/L after finishing T22nd in Tour Championship.

➤ "Let's be clear this guy is a class act!" was the sentence that led his player profile last year. With four wins in the last three years he's proved it, and there's every reason to expect him to go on to further success.

➤ Indeed Corals made him an odds-on shot, 8/11, to make the 1999 US Ryder Cup team. His only appearance in the Ryder Cup to date was in 1993.

➤ He lives at Bermuda Dunes, one of the four courses used for the Bob Hope Classic. He won that tournament in 1997 and 1992 and can be expected to reward support there again in 1999.

➤ It is an interesting fact that multiple-winner Cook from the West Coast has yet to win in Florida on the East. If he is to change that it may be in the National Car Rental at Disney where he's had three successive top 20 finishes.

➤ He'll be worth an interest in May in the Colonial. It's a tournament won by an experienced player, he was 5th in the event this year, and he won his last tournament in Texas.

➤ He simply loves the World Series of Golf. His dad is the tournament manager and, as he was born in Toledo, Ohio, and as he was raised in Akron, he's very much 'the hometown kid'. His recent record there (4th 40/1 1998: T3rd 50/1 1997: 8th 1996) shows that he'd offer first-class each-way value. Let's hope he qualifies for the new 1999 World Series event.

FRED COUPLES   G ≝ ☼

Towards the end of 1997 Fred's father died in Seattle. It was a sad, if expected, end to a troubled year in which Fred had a publicised separation from his fiancee, his back had given him problems, he hadn't posted a tour win and his girlfriend Thais Bren was diagnosed in the autumn as having breast cancer.

So 1998 was very much a 'comeback' year for the ever-popular guy who reached the awkward age of 39 in October.

He returned for the Bob Hope Classic which he won, in a play-off, at 16/1.

He then went on to post high finishes in the Shell Houston Open (3rd), the Byron Nelson Classic (T2nd after taking a triple bogey at the par 3 17th in R4) and the Colonial (T18th), before he won again, this time, landing the Memorial at 25/1.

T2nd at 50/1 in the US Masters, after leading throughout he played the 13th poorly in R4 to lose his momentum.

T53rd in the US Open: T13th USPGA.

In September he married Thais Bren in Paris the weekend before he played in the Lancome Trophy, finishing T9th. He has now won fourteen times on the US tour including the 1992 US Masters, and five times in other tournaments worldwide.

He has a fine all-round game, and at 288 yards has a big advantage in driving distance. His putting from inside four feet has occasionally been wayward.

He'll be 40 in October 1999. Poor T24th in Tour Championship. 9th on M/L.

➤ Fred has now rebuilt his personal life and is clearly a man at ease with himself. IF his back is sound he is surely going to win more golf tournaments.

➤ The season-opening, all-winners Mercedes Championship will be held in Hawaii in 1999 on the course previously used for the Kapalua International in which Fred did so well (2nd 1996: T9th 1995: Won 1994) on his last three appearances. He could well start off with a win there in the New Year.

➤ One way to profit from Fred is to oppose him in R4 2-ball betting when he often loses concentration because he's not in contention (81 in R4 of 1998 British Open, and 76 in R4 of Tour Championship). Because he's a 'name' player the bookies often price up his opponents at juicy prices.

➤ His US Masters record is very good with eight top 10s including his 1992 win and 1998 2nd and he's made the cut in all his starts. His huge length and vast Augusta experience make him a must for match bets, and a player to look for on the spreads.

➤ He simply loves the Bob Hope Classic in which he's a must for match bets and on the spreads. He's had six straight top 10s (W 1998: T9th 1997: T7th

1996: T9th 1993: T6th 1992: 5th 1991) and has had 30 successive straight rounds at or below par.

➤ 5/1 on to make his sixth successive Ryder Cup appearance.

BEN CRENSHAW   Pb

Let's be honest, Gentle Ben's only got a player profile because he's the 1999 Ryder Cup Captain.

46-year-old Ben is now clearly well past his best. A winner of nineteen tournaments including the 1984 and 1995 US Masters, he built a reputation as a world-class putter, golf historian and as a gentleman.

However in 1997, in a year when he had foot surgery, he posted only one top 20 finish.

In 1998 he was consistent in the majors – he missed the cut in all four of them!

➤ He will surely not win again until he joins the roundbellies on the Seniors Tour.

➤ He is clearly a credit to the game, and a credit to himself. However beneath that benign exterior he will be as determined as anyone could be to regain the Ryder Cup for America in 1999.

➤ Expect him to prove a resourceful, shrewd and, yes, a successful captain as the Americans will surely regain the Ryder Cup in 1999.

JOHN DALY

Big John burst onto the scene with his astonishing win in the 1991 USPGA. He went onto win the BC Open (1992), the Bell South Classic (1994) and his second major, the British Open in 1995.

However his golf career had been completely derailed by his off-course behaviour, marital problems and alcoholism during 1996 and 1997.

In 1998 he showed fine early-season form in a series of high finishes in the Phoenix Open (T12th), the Buick Invitational (T16th), the Tucson Chrysler Classic (T18th), the Nissan Open (T4th – his highest finish since the 1995 British Open), the Honda Classic (T4th after 64 in R4) and the Players Championship (T16th).

At the Bay Hill Invitational in March he finished 53rd after a memorable 18 at the par 5 sixth during a R4 of 85.

In the Greater Vancouver Open in R1 he shook uncontrollably on course. His playing partners, Pavin and Frost, helped him. It was a reminder of his on-going battle against alcoholism.

T33rd in the US Masters: T53rd in the US Open (after 69 in R1): missed the cuts in the British Open (including a ten at the 18th in R2), and the USPGA.

Played well for America in the Dunhill Cup winning all of his four matches. His game is ideally suited to St Andrews where, of course, he won the British Open.

A good long putter he has an underrated touch around the greens. Massively long off the tee. 77th on the M/L.

➤ After his encouraging first half to the 1998 season the Pb symbol is removed.

➤ Well worth opposing in final round 2-ball betting if he's out of contention as he showboats, plays to the gallery, and gives common sense a swerve. He's then often at a 'value' price, providing members of the 'wide-awake club' with a real betting opportunity, eg in the 1998 Las Vegas he shot 77 in R4 losing his 2-ball to Weibring (69) at 5/4!

➤ He played his best golf this year early in the season and I expect that to be his pattern from now on.

➤ He may be at his best therefore in February when in successive weeks he plays the Nissan Open (T4th 1998) and the Tucson Open (T18th 1998).

➤ In all seriousness I do hope he could spend some time with Arsenal's Tony Adams who would surely be able to comfort, support and, above all, offer real hope.

ROBERT DAMRON   g y

Born in Kentucky 26-year-old Robert now lives in Florida.

Made an impressive start to his tour career in 1997 when he was 53rd on the M/L after he'd posted four punter-friendly top 5 finishes in the Buick Classic (T3rd), the Fedex St Jude Classic (T3rd), the Greater Greensboro Classic (T4th) and the Doral Ryder Open (T5th).

In 1998 he had high finishes in the Buick Invitational (T16th), the Tucson Chrysler Classic (T14th), the Freeport McDermott Classic (T12th), the Memorial (T11th), the Western Open (T20th), the St Jude Classic (T7th) and in October in the Las Vegas (T12th after being R2 jt leader).

Missed the cut in the USPGA.

➤ He's a fine player, good from sand with a sound swing who I expect to go on to win golf tournaments.

His two years on tour have followed the same pattern as he has shown fine form in the first half of the season before his form has dipped over the later months.

➤ He must be expected to do very well in the Bay Hill Invitational. He lives next to the course, knows every blade of grass, and was T11th (after four sub-par rounds) in 1997 and was R1 leader after a 64 in 1998 before finishing T29th. Back him in the early 3-balls, and as an outsider with a real chance on the spreads and in the outright. 81st on the M/L.

➤ There are two other tournaments in which his two year form is very impressive.

*The Memorial (T11th 1998 and T21st 1997) in which all his rounds (stroke average 70.28) have been under par. He'll have a real chance at very big odds there in 1999.

* The Fedex St Jude Classic (T7th 1998 and 3rd 1997) in which his form makes him an each-way must bet.

GLEN DAY   S g

Glen entered 1998 as just another journeyman pro, who was yet to notch his first win. In his four years on the US tour he'd been 45th (1994), 91st (1995), 73rd (1996) and 98th (1997).

In 1998 he played his best-ever golf, posting a whole series of high finishes in the Phoenix Open (T6th), the Players Championship (T2nd after being in the leading group throughout), the Freeport McDermott Classic (T3rd after a 64 in R1), the MCI Classic (2nd after a 67 in R4), the Memorial (T11th), the Fedex St Jude Classic (3rd), the Canadian Open (T4th) and the National Car Rental at Disney (11th after 73 in R4).

He also had top 25 finishes in the Bob Hope Classic (T24th), the Byron Nelson Classic (T25th) and the AT&T (T22nd).

T23rd in the US Open. T29th in the USPGA. He missed the cut in the British Open. T18th Tour Championship.

He was a European tour player before moving to the States.

Sarcastically, Glen Day became known as 'All Day' to his peers as he played so slowly. His improvement this year is probably because he has quickened up his play. It will also be a reflection of contentment as a happy family man with two young daughters. Even his best friend is his caddie!

His putting has improved a lot this year.

Fader of the ball.

He retains the S symbol as a streak player capable of very low scores. 15th on M/L.

➤ With no fewer than five top 4 finishes he has had a remarkably consistent season although he's still to record his first win.

➤ He'll be a big price against the big names in the Memorial in early June. He was 9 under for his last three rounds in 1998, and T10th in 1997 so do remember in the Memorial to back GLENN on Thurs-DAY, June 3rd.

CLARK DENNIS

Clark is a 30-year-old Texan who came into 1998 very much as an 'unknown'. OK he was T3rd in the 1990 Hawaiian Open, had a solid (65th on the M/L) season in 1994 and was a Nike tour winner in 1993, yet there was little reason to expect him to have such a consistent year.

He posted a whole string of high finishes in the Greater Greensboro Open (T16th), the Byron Nelson Classic (T9th after 63 in R3), the Colonial (T14th), the Kemper Open (T3rd to equal his best ever finish), the Western Open (T9th), the delayed AI&I (I25th after a 63 in R4 at Poppy Hills) and the Texas Open (T11th).

He missed the cut in the USPGA.

Came over for the Loch Lomond Invitational finishing a creditable T11th (2nd top US player at 10/1).

Had an 18 foot on the last green for a 59 in the 1997 Nike St Louis Golf Classic – he missed it to shoot 60!

His form has taken off since he passed his 30th birthday. Being 29 can be a dodgy age for golfers as well as for the rest of us. 75th on the M/L.

➤ This guy's strength is his straight hitting. Let's remember he was T6th in 1994 US Open so he sure knows where the fairways are. Such players (remember straight hitters Olin Browne and Joe Durant's wins this year) can win a tournament when they are on a suitable course and the putts start to roll in. So in 1999 Dennis could well notch his first victory.

➤ He must be noted as a Texan for his home state tournaments particularly in the Byron Nelson Classic (T9th 1998 including a 63 in R3), and also in the Colonial held on his own home course at Forth Worth (T14th 1998).

CHRIS DIMARCO

30-year-old New York born and Florida based player who secured his 1998 card by finishing 3rd on the 1997 Nike tour money list in a season in which he won the Nike Ozarks Open and posted seven other Nike top 10s.

In 1998 he regularly appeared high on the leaderboards, especially in the second half of the season, only to fall away with relatively poor final rounds.

In the Kemper Open (79 in R4), in the Buick Open (74 in R4), in the Canadian Open (73 in R4 despite a final-hole eagle – finished T9th) and the BC Open (72 in R4 – finished T9th) he was in contention before he let his chance slip on the Sunday. So he must be given the 'bottle'.

In the US Open, too, a 77 in R4 saw him finish T32nd.

Finished T25th in the Canon Greater Hartford Open.

He has a very unusual putting stroke. Not a convincing player in the wind as he showed in the Kemper Open. 111th on the M/L.

➤ Clearly his achilles heel is his R4 nervy play. However others before him (Duval for example) appeared 'bottlers' yet eventually they learned how to win and he may well do so, too.

➤ Nevertheless on the evidence of 1998 the betting opportunity he provides is for us to oppose him in R4 2-ball betting.

➤ His best chance will probably lie in the weakly-contested Deposit Guaranty Classic in which he posted his best-ever finish T3rd in 1994.

➤ It may well be that his first tournament success comes either when he's made a fast start in a rain-reduced tournament, or when he comes from 'off the pace' in R4 to set a winning clubhouse target.

TREVOR DODDS

39-year-old Namibian-born guy who lives in Minnesota. In 1997 he was 5th on the Nike Tour money list winning the 1997 Nike Miami Valley Open as well as posting eight other top 10 finishes.

In 1998 he made the big breakthrough when he was the 125/1 winner of the Greater Greensboro Open in a play-off after shooting 69 in R4.

He also had top 10s in the Hawaiian Open (3rd), the Freeport McDermott Classic (T8th), and the Bell South Classic (T10th), as well as top 25s in the Buick Invitational (T22nd), and the AT&T (T13th).

Missed the cut in the US Open: T57th in the British Open: T62nd in the USPGA: T36th in the World Series of Golf.

He'll be 40 in September 1999. 33rd on M/L.

➤ Finished top of the Canadian Order of Merit in 1995 and 1996 after notching six wins in those years. So remember him for the Canadian Open, especially in the early-round 3-ball betting in which he was a tasty 3/1 R1 winner in 1998.

➤ Now that he's got the confidence from his first US win he must be noted in the early-season South African tournaments in a country he knows so well.

JOE DURANT   S

34-year-old Joseph Scott finished 100th on the M/L in 1997 after finishing an impressive 3rd the previous year on the Nike tour M/L after eight top 10s including a victory in the Nike Mississippi Gulf Coast Classic.

However he ended 1997 the Number 1 ranked player on the tour for Total Driving so his breakthrough in 1998 could have been anticipated. It came when he was the 125/1 winner of the Western Open. Although he started R4 four shots behind Vijay Singh he played with courage and skill to post his first tour win.

He also had high finishes in the Shell Houston Open (T12th), the Kemper Open (T21st), the Canon Greater Hartford Open (T16th), the Fedex St Jude Classic (T12th) and the World Series of Golf (T7th after a fine performance at 4 under par).

After a 68 in R1 he finished T32nd in the US Open before his breakthrough victory. He missed the cut in the British Open having qualified due to his superb form from April to June.

Finished T38th in the USPGA.

Born in Florida where he lives. 43rd on the M/L.

➤ If he could develop and improve his short game to match the consistency of his driving he would be a player in regular contention.

➤ With driving accuracy the key to the River Highlands course, home of the Canon Greater Hartford Open, Joe must have a first-class chance there in 1999. His performances in the last two years (T16th 1998: T17th 1997) suggest that he'll be worth a wager next year, especially if he gets an early tee time.

➤ He led the Honda Classic during R4 in 1997 before he slipped back to finish T5th. A more confident player now he'll have a real chance in that tournament in early March.

DAVID DUVAL   G M Y F

Make a note of the date.....Sunday, 12th October 1997....certainly it's one David Duval will never forget because after appearing to be a final-round bottler he won his first tournament, the Michelob Championship at the first extra hole of a play-off.

Since then he simply can't stop winning. One week later he landed the Walt Disney, again at the first extra play-off hole, and then two weeks later he won the $720,000 first prize in the season-ending Tour Championship. He became the ONLY player in USPGA tour history to win his first three tournaments in consecutive starts.

In 1998 he's had four more victories – in the Tucson Chrysler Classic in late February at 20/1, in the Shell Houston Open in early May at 11/1, in the World Series of Golf at 20/1 in late August and in the Michelob Championship, as defending champion in October, at 9/1.

He also posted high finishes in the Mercedes Championship (T6th – after 73 in R4), the Bob Hope Classic (T4th), the Bell South Classic (T14th), the

Colonial (T14th), the Memorial (3rd) and the Canon Greater Hartford Open (T7th).

Came to Europe in September to finish T2nd in the Lancome Trophy after a double bogey at the last.

In the US Masters he played superbly. Leading into R4 he was outputted by O'Meara to finish T2nd at 33/1. After an indifferent start he was T7th in the US Open. Finished T11th in the British Open. Missed the cut in the USPGA. Never in contention T8th in Tour Championship.

2nd on the M/L in 1997, he was the clear Number 1 in 1998.

An immensely strong, fit player with a fine all-round game. A fader of the ball he hits it 'miles' off the tee. His consistency is shown by the fact that going into the Tour Championship he had made top 10s in half of his 22 starts!

High in all the leading stats, his lowly position in sand saves (T114th) suggests that, like Westwood, this is one area for significant improvement.

➤ Last year I suggested, "he's very much a player to keep on your side. He is a certain winner of many tournaments over the next few years." He's certainly justified those comments – and they still apply.

➤ He is now without question the best player on the planet without a major victory. However his strong all-round game and proven winning record suggest he'll put that right over the next year or two so he is given the M symbol without hesitation.

➤ He clearly goes well fresh as he showed when, after a week's skiing, he won the Tucson Chrysler Classic.

➤ If he misses a cut don't be concerned – his Tucson win came after a missed cut and his World Series victory after two missed cuts!

➤ He will be looking forward to the New World Golf Championship events, especially the NEC Invitational on the Firestone course where he won this year. In a small field he'll be worth a win bet.

➤ There are three other tournaments in which he can be supported.

*The Bell South Classic (T14th when tired 1998: T2nd 1997) on a course suited to his driving.

*The Memorial (three top 3s in the last four years). His R4 scoring average there in the last four years is a magnificent 68.25!

*The Players Championship (T18th 1998: T4th 1996) on his local course at Sawgrass.

➤ He rewarded this book's tip last year for him to win the 1998 Money list at a tasty 16/1. He could well win it again in 1999 and looks a solid bet to finish in the first four for the third successive year.

BRAD ELDER

The 1997 Jack Nicklaus College Player of the Year turned professional in mid May. In his first pro tournament, the Colonial, he missed the cut. In his second, the Memorial he was T48th, while in his third he followed a 63 in R2 with a 78 in R3 to finish down the field in the Kemper Open.

Yet to post a top 20 finish on the tour.

Sadly Elder has been diagnosed as having a rare bone disorder, Kienbock's Disease, which causes a painful loss of circulation. It seems that the illness is under control now.

➤ Very highly rated. He's even been called the next Davis Love III!
➤ His 63 in R2 of the Kemper Open will be worth remembering in late May next year in that event's 3-ball betting.

STEVE ELKINGTON   CT G

The 36-year-old 'Elk' this decade, up to this year, had won eight times, and he'd finished in the top 25 on the M/L in six of the eight years.

In late 1997, with Jeff Maggert, he won the Diners' Club tournament in December at 6/1.

In 1998 after a poor T19th in the Mercedes he played in Australia for the first time since 1995. He finished T3rd at 16/1 in the Greg Norman Holden Classic.

However back on the American tour he was plagued by a series of health problems. His sinus difficulties continued and he had a severe viral infection in May, and a neck injury in June which forced his withdrawal after R1 of the British Open.

30th in the US Masters.

He found his form from mid August. He was a superb 3rd at 100/1 (!) in the USPGA, finishing as the top Rest of the World and Aussie player. He finished T6th in the AT&T.

Then, in early October, he was the impressive winner of the Buick Challenge at 33/1. He then played well for Australia in the Dunhill Cup to win three of his four matches at St Andrews. 42nd on the M/L (playing only 16 events).

➤ The simple fact is that 'Elk' has now won six times in the last five years despite all manner of health problems. When fit and healthy he's a superb, competitive player with a classic swing who has improved his putting. He really must be expected to do very very well in 1999.
➤ Must be supported (if fit) on the spreads and in the outright betting for the Players Championship in late March. He's won it twice already (1991 and 1997) at Sawgrass on one of his favourite courses.
➤ "I always feel comfortable playing this tournament," and Steve Elkington's USPGA record gives the reason – 3rd 1998: T3rd 1996: Won 1995: T7th 1994: T14th 1993 and T18th 1992. In the last seven years he's only once finished outside the top 20 (when T45th in 1997) and his average position has been 13th. Such astonishing consistency can be backed either on the spreads or in the top Australasian market where he was an 11/2 winner in 1998. If he's fit in mid-August the 35-year-old, with arguably the best swing on tour, must be backed.
➤ If he's in good health he would love to win the Shell Houston Open held near his home in Houston. 3rd there in 1997 he'd have a really big chance there in 1999.

ERNIE ELS   D G F Y 🏇

Ernie started 1998 having won five times on the American tour including the US Open in 1994 and 1997. He also had secured no less than twenty other victories worldwide.

Although 1998 turned out to be a big disappointment to the tall South African he did start the year brightly. He was the convincing winner of the South African Open at 9/2, was 2nd in the South African PGA and topped the South African O/M.

In the Johnnie Walker Classic his 73 in R4 let Tiger Woods in to force a play-off and then Tiger's momentum took him to victory. Ernie was 2nd at 10/1.

He was T3rd in the Dubai Desert Classic before joining the American tour. He won the Bay Hill Invitational at 20/1 in Florida in March.

He was T11th in the Players Championship, T10th in the MCI Classic and T16th in the US Masters.

However from May he was never really at his best. He had tennis elbow then, and later from June he had recurring back problems.

Although he was T7th in the Memorial he was only T49th in the US Open, T29th in the British Open and T21st in the USPGA.

He missed the final day cut in the Sprint International and was a poor 19th in the World Series.

In the Dunhill Cup in October he won three of his five matches as he helped South Africa retain the trophy at St Andrews. He went on to play in the World Matchplay at Wentworth where he was beaten by Lee Westwood in the quarter-finals. Finished T8th in the season ending Volvo Masters.

The problems he faced were perhaps best illustrated in the Irish Open when during a 78 in R4 he lost his temper, threw a club and nearly decapitated his caddie. For such a mild guy to act like that highlighted his frustrations.

To add to his woes his South African home has been burgled.

However Ernie announced his engagement in April, and will marry his fiancee Liezl in December.

Ernie is a long-hitting, accurate driver with an easy, languid style. His length regularly gives him eagle chances on the par 5s. One of his great strengths is that he makes few mistakes so that he is at his best, as in the US Open, when par is a good score. His putting let him down as his general form worsened over the latest months of the season.

36th on the M/L after 15 tournaments.

➤ 1999 could be a very good one for Ernie. He'll be a married man on the 'comeback trail', and if his back is OK he can surely be expected to regain his best form.

➤ Last year I pointed to his tendency in R4 to 'throw away' tournaments he had previously dominated. He did it in the 1997 Buick Open, and he did it again this year in the Johnnie Walker Classic. So when Ernie is apparently cruising from start to finish to an easy win and is odds on entering R4 he can be opposed then both in 2-ball betting and by an each-way player with a strong final-round record.

➤ The Buick Classic and Big Ernie go together like Bill Clinton and stained dresses. Big Ernie's record there (W1997: Won 1996 by 8 shots: T4th 1995: 2nd 1994) is sensational, although this year to the bookies' delight he withdrew after nine holes of R1 with his problem back. Expect normal service to be resumed in 1999 when Ernie will be a must bet.

➤ I expect that in his thirties he'll do really well, especially when and if he's inspired by 'the nappy factor'.

➤ He will be worth a bet (if he's in form) in the Sprint International. From 1995 – 1997 he scored 83 points, more than anyone else and in 1999 he could run away with this. So in August get your betting boots on and Sprint to the bookies to back Ernie in the Sprint.....or els you'll lose out on a big opportunity.

BOB ESTES

32-year-old Bob was 32nd on the M/L in 1993 before he made the breakthrough in 1994 when he won the Texas Open, finishing that year 14th on the M/L.

However he had a dreadful 1996 (149th M/L) before the first green shoots of recovery were seen in his 1997 stats – Number 1 in sand saves, Number 1 for scrambling, No. 2 for total putts and 5th in R4 scoring averages.

That consistency continued in 1998 when he posted four punter-friendly top 5 finishes in the Bay Hill Invitational (T2nd at 100/1), the Greater Greensboro Open (3rd at 28/1 after bogeying both the final holes when in the lead), the Fedex St Jude Classic (4th) and the Greater Vancouver Open (T5th at 25/1).

He also had top 10s in the Nissan Open (T6th), the Honda Classic (T7th) and the Freeport McDermott Classic (T8th), and top 20s in the Bob Hope Classic (T19th), the MCI Classic (T14th), the Bell South Classic (T19th), the Byron Nelson Classic (T12th) and the Texas Open (T11th).

T24th in the British Open: T34th in the USPGA. 28th (of 30) in Tour Championship. 28th on M/L.

➤ His final round resolve has been questioned this year, especially after the Greater Greensboro Open. However his 1994 win was from the front and I think it will pay to give him the benefit of the doubt so let's file Estes in the 'winner-about-to-happen' category.

➤ He must have a leading chance in the St Jude Classic. His four-year stroke average is 68.71 so in mid June have a little on 'Big Bob' for the St Jude.

➤ He's also a 'must' bet on the spreads and in the outrights for the Greater Vancouver Open (T5th 1998: 3rd 1997) where he averages 67.5 for his last eight rounds.

➤ In the Scottish Open at Carnoustie in 1996 he was the top American when he finished T11th in dreadful weather. He was also T3rd at 66/1 in the top US betting when the Open was last played in Scotland. So he'll be worth a small each-way interest at a huge price in the top American betting at Carnoustie for the 1999 British Open as his 'form' will be unexposed.

➤ 10/1 to be a 'surprise' player in the 1999 US Ryder Cup side.

BRAD FABEL

Bradley Scott is a 43-year-old guy who lives in Tennessee and after 14 years on tour he's yet to win although he has been 2nd twice – in the 1997 Buick Open and the 1990 Canon Greater Hartford Open, and he's won twice on the Nike tour.

In 1998 he had two punter-friendly top 5 finishes in the Kemper Open (T3rd) and the Quad City Classic (T5th). He also had high finishes in the Bob Hope Classic (T10th), the Byron Nelson Classic (T25th) and the Texas Open (T25th).

Although T28th he was one of only six players in the Memorial to shoot four sub-par rounds.

Missed the cut in the US Open: T71st in the USPGA.

His lack of length off the tee is a handicap. 105th on the M/L.

➤ He has now posted four top 5 finishes in the last two years.

➤ Has a useful record on the LaCantera course, home of the Texas Open (25th – 14th – 11th in the last three years including a 64 in R2 in 1998). Could cause a surprise by getting a top 5 place there in 1999 when coming from 'off the pace'.

BRAD FAXON   g

Brad is now 37. He has five American tour wins, and one in Australia.

In 1996 he was 8th on the M/L after posting nine top 10s including four 2nd place finishes; in 1997 he was 10th after six more top 10s including his last win in the Freeport McDermott Classic.

However he ended 1997 with off-course personal problems as he faced divorce proceedings.

In 1998 he has never really 'fired on all cylinders'.

He's had high finishes in the MCI Classic (T14th), the Greater Greensboro Open (T23rd), the Buick Classic (T12th), the Sprint (T6th with 36 points), and the Canadian Open (T22nd).

Came to Europe in late September to play the Lancome Trophy (T34th) and the German Masters (T28th).

T26th in the US Masters: T49th in the US Open: T11th British Open and T13th in the USPGA.

Off the tee he is neither long (263 yards) nor always accurate. However his putting is legendary and he is rated by many as the world's best with 'the flat stick'. 74th on the M/L.

➤ There's every reason to expect that Brad will be a more settled and more focussed player in 1999, a Ryder Cup year. He's quoted at 3/1 by Corals to make the US team again having played for them in 1995 and 1997.

➤ Well worth an interest in late April in the Greater Greensboro Open on a course where he's done well (23rd 1998: 2nd 1997: 7th 1995: 15th 1994), and in mid May he can be supported in the Colonial (2nd 1997: T5th 1995: T5th 1994) where he's been in the top 5 in three of the last five years.

➤ Can be safely opposed on the spreads and in the outright for the US Open where his driving regularly lets him down. His record is really poor. In 13 starts his best finishes have been T33rd (1994 and 1989).

➤ He has made the cut in each of the last five British Opens (11-20-32-15-7 are his form figures) so remember him for match bets as he rates the British Open as 'the Olympics of Golf'.

STEVE FLESCH   G

By winning the 1997 Nike tour championship 31-year-old Steve moved up to 4th place on the Nike tour M/L to earn his US tour card.

In 1998 he made a big impact, especially in the first half of the season.

He was top of the Greens In Regulation stats, and my selection as a 200/1 outsider, going into the Freeport McDermott Classic. He finished 2nd. T13th in the USPGA.

He also posted high finishes in the Honda Classic (T15th), the Greater Greensboro Open (T23rd), the Shell Houston Open (T12th), the Byron Nelson Classic (T25th), the Colonial (T10th), the Kemper Open (T11th), the Western Open (T22nd after a 75 in R4), the Canon Greater Hartford Open (T25th), the CVS Charity Classic (T12th), the Sprint International (T6th) and the Buick Challenge (T6th).

His other big finish came when he was T3rd as an 80/1 DYM player in the Bell South Classic.

A left hander, Steve was T9th in the 1996 Sarazen World Open after qualifying for it by a victory in the Malaysian Open.

Born in Ohio. He lives in Kentucky. 35th on the M/L.

➤ He has had a really promising 'rookie' year. Second seasons can be difficult, however he's no baby at 31, and he's been around, playing in Asia a lot. He's a neat, solid player with a fine all-round game and great length. His ability both to read and pace his putts can be improved. Nevertheless he's just the sort of player to post a first win in 1999.

➤ Must be expected to go well in the Entergy Classic on the English Turn course where he was 2nd this year.

➤ His debut in the Sprint International (T6th) was very promising, and he must be worth an interest in that event in August 1999.

➤ It's worth noting that his best performances have come on the back of solid cut-making finishes.

➤ Although not too accurate off the tee his superb iron play has put him very high in the Greens In Regulation stats. The long Sugarloaf course with four par 5s suits him so he can be followed in match bets, on the spreads and in the outright market for the Bell South Classic (T3rd 1998).

➤ Last year it was Steve who? this year it's just 6/1 that Steve appears in the Flesch in the Ryder Cup.

DAN FORSMAN

40-year-old Daniel Bruce, Dan to you and I, lives in Utah. He has four wins to his name on the US tour, the last in 1992 when in his best season he was 10th on the M/L. His decline in recent years is shown by his end-of-year Money list positions – 112th 1994: 93rd 1995: 123rd 1996: before a revival with two top 3s in 1997 when he was 56th.

In the close season late in 1997 with C Matthews he was T2nd at 50/1 in the JC Penney Classic.

In 1998 he had a series of very solid finishes, in the Shell Houston Open (T6th), the Byron Nelson Classic (T25th), the Colonial (T10th), the Memorial (T23rd), the Kemper Open (T25th), the Western Open (T9th), the Quad City Classic (T17th), and the Texas Open (T25th).

Safely past 40 Dan is very much a family man. 99th on the M/L.

➤ He is awarded the bottle after entering the final round of this year's Shell Houston Open in the lead only to shoot 74 and finish T6th. He also shot 77 in R4 of the Kemper Open to fall down the leaderboard to finish T25th. Lost the lead over the final holes in the 1997 Walt Disney Classic, and famously (when at his very best) he made a quintuple bogey 8 (!) at the 12th in the 1993 US Masters when in contention.

➤ A very accurate iron player his putting has often let him down.

➤ Must be noted in the close season JC Penney Classic for man/woman teams. T7th in 1996, he was T2nd at 50/1 (!) in 1997 with C Matthews.

➤ He's a proven player on the Oakwood course (W 1985: 2nd 1988) so 'Dan the man' can be expected to play well in the 1999 inaugural John Deere Classic on one of his favourite tracks.

➤ His accuracy makes him a player to have on your side in match bets.

➤ His best chances of victory Number 5 will be if he can set a clubhouse target coming from 'off the pace' in the Shell Houston Open or the Kemper Open in which he's got very solid form.

HARRISON FRAZAR

"What a great way to make a living.....I consider everything about this job wonderful"....not surprising considering the form shown this year by the 27-year-old six footer from Dallas, Texas.

In 1997 he won the Nike South Carolina Classic to finish 13th on that tour's M/L to earn his tour card.

In 1998 he was T16th in the Greater Greensboro Open before he posted two very high finishes in successive weeks in May. He was T2nd at 150/1 in the Byron Nelson Classic beating Fred Couples in his R4 2-ball. With his card safely secured he was 4th at 100/1 the following week in the Colonial.

Had further high finishes in the Western Open (T9th) and the AT&T (T25th).

One of the longest hitters on tour (289 yards). His sand save stats point to an area where there is clear scope for improvement.

Uses Justin Leonard's coach, Randy Smith. 63rd on the M/L.

➤ Showed nerves in the Memorial to finish T38th after being T3rd at halfway. His iron play was also nervy in R4 of the Colonial although his score was solid because of a series of par-saving putts. So he's still to learn about handling the final-day pressure on a Sunday.

➤ Strong and fit he played 36 holes on the final day of the 1997 Nike South Carolina classic to win.....so if he's involved in a 'survival of the fittest' two round Sunday in 1999 he'd sure have PMAs.

➤ Worth noting in May in his home state when the tour hits Texas. He knows the courses and their Bermuda greens so well.

➤ One of only three players to shoot four rounds at or under par in the Greater Greensboro Open this year when T16th. He will be worth a small investment at very big odds in that tournament in 1999.

➤ 16/1 (is that all?) to make the US Ryder Cup team.....surely they're skinny odds!

BOB FRIEND

35-year-old Bob quit trying to make it as a competitive player in 1996 and taught golf for a season instead. He needed a really low final round at Q School to earn his 1998 tour card. He shot a 63, got his card and turned 1998 into a success story.

He won the Panama Open in January to kick start his year and posted two early season top 10s – in the Honda Classic (T7th) and the Byron Nelson Classic (T6th after a 63 in R1 at Las Colinas).

However in late August/early September he really hit form when he followed his T11th in the Greater Vancouver Open with a 2nd at 150/1 in the Canadian Open, losing in a play-off to Billy Andrade. They were his best-ever USPGA tour finishes.

His 1998 success has been built on his accuracy off the tee. 57th on the M/L.

➤ His best-ever year followed the birth of his first daughter and second child last November. The 'nappy factor' has certainly worked for Bob Friend.

➤ He wasn't even a household name in his own household in 1997, and now he has retained his card, pocketed a few dollars and boosted his confidence. The question is whether Bob who? can become Bob (the punter's) Friend in 1999.

➤ If he shows up well in the early-season driving accuracy stats. we'll know he's maintained the platform on which his 1998 success was based.

DAVID FROST

South African born, Dallas-based 'Frosty' will be 40 in September 1999. He's got a superb winning record with ten US tour wins, and eight others world-wide. He had his best year in 1993 when he was 5th on the M/L. He entered 1998 after three finishing 50th (1995), 54th (1996) and 50th (1997) on the M/L.

In 1998 he was 2nd at 33/1 in the South African Open on the European tour in February.

In America he had a disappointing year with just one top 20 finish when he finished T14th as defending champion in the Colonial.

T26th in the US Masters (4th on putting stats): T44th British Open, T56th USPGA.

Won three of his five matches in the Dunhill Cup at St Andrews to help South Africa retain the trophy. 148th on the M/L.

➤ It could be that a once-fine player is in decline and merits the Pb symbol. I think that would be a premature judgement as Frosty could well catch fire and win again. Let's remember he won the 1997 Colonial after two winless years.

➤ From 1995 to 1997 he has a stroke average in the Memorial of less than 69.5. So if you forget his 1998 missed cut you would give him a real chance there in the first week of June.

➤ In each of the last three years he's been placed in the Rest of the World betting in the US Masters. So come Augusta follow Frost for a cool each-way bet in that speciality market.

➤ In each of the last two years he's been placed at 25/1 and 33/1 in an early-season European tour event in South Africa.

FRED FUNK   G

Born in Minnesota 42-year-old Fred now lives in Florida. In recent years he has been a very consistent player. 26th on the M/L in 1995 after two wins, 21st in 1996 after another victory, and 38th in 1997.

In 1998 before June he had high finishes in the Nissan Open (T15th), the Doral Ryder Open (T23rd), the MCI Classic (T24th) and the Greater Greensboro Open (T6th).

Then in the first week of June he had laser surgery on his eyes before he was T3rd in the Kemper Open after a very poor 77 in R4.

Hit form in successive weeks in July when T4th at 50/1 in the Canon Greater Hartford Open, T5th in the Quad City Classic, before he won the Deposit Guaranty Classic at 12/1.

Went on to post high finishes in the CVS Charity Classic (T25th), the Buick Open (T15th), the Greater Milwaukee Open (T7th), the BC Open (T16th), and the Texas Open (T20th). Finished 2nd at 28/1 in the Buick Challenge in October and T7th in the National Car Rental at Disney. Trying to win from the front in the Buick, he lost at the first play-off hole to Steve Elkington.

Missed cut in US Masters. T23rd USPGA. Disappointing T24th (of 30) in Tour Championship.

Fred is the classic American tour pro who hits it very straight yet often struggles on the greens.

He is always very high on the driving accuracy stats, and always very low on the stats for putting and driving distance (267 yards). Stock shot is a draw. 23rd on M/L.

➤ Clearly at his best in the second half of the season with four of his five victories coming in or after July.

➤ In 1999 he must be supported for the Canon Greater Hartford Open in late July on a course that suits his game. His T4th 50/1 finish this year was despite a triple bogey at the par 3 eighth in R4.

➤ However if there is one event in which we should back Fred in 1999 it's the BC Open in September. In the last four years his stroke average is 69.46 and, of course, he won there in 1996.

➤ He can be followed with confidence in the Michelob Championship which, with its three par 5s, suits the shorter accurate hitters like our Fred. From 1995 through 1997 he finished T8th, T3rd and 4th for a stroke average of 68.5. So let's forget his 1998 par display as he was suffering from MLD after the previous week's play-off defeat.

➤ Only 6/1 to make the US Ryder Cup team.

JIM FURYK   G M 🌧 Y

James Michael, or Jim to his friends is the 28-year-old guy with the oddest swing on the planet!

However he's made a big impact in his years on the tour. 78th on the M/L in 1994; he was 33rd in 1995 after winning the Las Vegas Invitational; he won the Hawaiian Open in 1996 to finish 26th, and in 1997 although not winning he showed astonishing consistency to post 13 top 10s, including three 2nds and a 3rd, to end the year 4th on the M/L.

He also made his debut in 1997 in the Ryder Cup beating Faldo in the singles.

In 1998 he had high finishes in the Hawaiian Open (T21st), The Tucson Chrysler Classic (T9th), the Doral Ryder Open (T9th), the Honda Classic

(T12th), the Bay Hill Invitational (T8th), the Greater Greensboro Open (T11th), and the Byron Nelson Classic (T15th).

Then in successive weeks in late May he was 2nd at 25/1 in the Colonial, and 4th at 22/1 in the Memorial.

Two weeks later he lost in a play-off, to J P Hayes, in the Buick Classic after driving into the rough off the tee!

Tied 7th in the Western Open before astonishingly his form slumped in late July as he missed successive cuts in the CVS Charity Classic and the USPGA.

Playing the Canadian Open for the first time he was T22nd before he was made the favourite (why?) for the BC Open in which he finished T25th.

Secured his third tour victory when he won the Las Vegas Invitational at 33/1 in October.

4th in the US Masters: T14th in the US Open: T4th in the British Open: Missed cut in the USPGA.

Accuracy off tee and fairway and a brilliant cross-handed putting touch have been his trademarks. Has had a poor season from bunkers in 1998. A fine player in windy conditions.

It may be that like other players, such as Lee Westwood, the Birkdale breezes during the British Open weakened his swing and his inability to hole key R4 putts dented his confidence. However, he can emerge in 1999 back to the 'old' cut making 'Mr Consistency' that we know so well. 3rd in Tour Championship to finish 3rd on M/L.

➤ He can be followed with confidence on the spreads, in match bets and in the outright markets for the Colonial (2nd 1998: 8th 1997) and the Memorial (4th 1998: 2nd 1997).

➤ His record in the majors is superb. In 14 starts he's made 13 cuts, and posted six top 6 finishes! He's been 4th in the last two British Opens, and T14th, T5th, T5th in the last three US Opens. The big question is can he really make things happen when it really matters? Has he got that 'touch of magic' to turn a 4th into a win? The answer probably is Yes, let's hope it's in 1999 – so he retains the M symbol.

➤ Must be followed on the spreads in the US Open in a tournament tailor made for his accuracy. T14th – T5th – T5th finishes make him a cracking bet so long as he's in fair form come next June.

➤ When in his usual form he must never be opposed in match bets.

➤ Living in Florida his next victory could well be in his adopted state perhaps in the Doral Ryder Open in which he shot 62 in R2 this year on his way to a T9th finish.

➤ In the last three years he has an impressive stroke average of 67.8 in the Byron Nelson Classic so in May have a little on Slim Jim when he travels to Texas.

➤ May be worth opposing as defending champion in the Las Vegas. In 1996 as defending champion he was T22nd.

➤ 7/1 ON to make the US Ryder Cup team.....and he would be a likely candidate for a wild-card place if he didn't automatically qualify.

JEFF GALLAGHER

34-year-old Jeff gets his first player profile because in 1998 he's twice beaten his previous highest US tour finish.

He was T10th in the 1996 Freeport McDermott Classic, and the Colonial in the same year. However this year having got his tour card via Q. School he's been T6th in the Nissan Open (69 in R4), and T8th in the Buick Open.

He also had high finishes in the Freeport McDermott Classic (T12th) and the AT&T (T13th).

T4th in the Bell South Classic entering the final day he shot an 80 to earn the 'bottle'.

Brother of Jim Gallagher Jr. Has one Nike tour win, in 1991. 113th on the M/L.

➤ He obviously enjoys the Freeport McDermott Classic (T12th 1998: T10th 1996). However, especially after his Bell South Classic finish this year, it's not easy to visualise him winning.

➤ With two J Gallaghers in the same tournament the scope for confusion is massive. It once more illustrates the point that bookmaker-punter friction is increasingly in the area of sportsbetting not horseracing.

JIM GALLAGHER JR   D Pb

37-year-old Jim is a proven winner of five US tournaments who has lost form over the past three years.

In 1995 he was 8th on the M/L after winning twice. However since then the former Ryder Cup player has really struggled with all aspects of his game.

76th on M/L in 1996, he was 145th in 1997.

In 1998 he showed fair form in the Shell Houston Open (T17th) and the Bell South Classic (T24th) before he played really well in the Colonial to finish T6th.

However he has not been able to build on that performance. 161st on the M/L.

➤ Sadly he must be given the PB symbol.

➤ If there is to be a 'comeback' success it will probably be in the St Jude Classic (Won 1995: T10th 1994: 4th 1992).

ROBERT GAMEZ   D 🎂

Gamez is a 30-year-old from Las Vegas. A talented player who won twice in 1990 as a 21-year-old.

However from 1995 – 1997 he's been 89th, 89th, and 86th on the M/L. During those three years he missed the cut 54% of the time!.

In 1998 in windless and warm weather he was T16th in the Hawaiian Open after a disappointing 72 in R4.

However he was involved in a road accident at the Kemper Open in June and did not return until the Quad City Classic five weeks later.

His putting has been poor in 1998 and he's one of the very poorest bunker players on the tour. 195th (!!) on the M/L.

➤ Safely past 30 let's hope he can recover his form in 1999. However his short game must improve significantly if he's to make any impact at all.

➤ Born and raised in desert conditions he plays best in warm, humid conditions.

➤ He has solid form in the St Jude classic (T12th 1997, after a 64 in R4: 2nd 1992) and will have 'homefield' advantage in the Las Vegas Invitational (2nd 1994). They will provide him with his best opportunities in 1999.

BRENT GEIBERGER g

30-year-old son of Al Geiberger who won eleven times on the US tour.

Born and raised in California where he now lives. Gained his 1997 tour card through Q School finishing his rookie year 62nd on the M/L with a 2nd in the Texas Open his best finish in a solid first season.

In 1998 he made an impact early on when T2nd in the Phoenix Open, T6th in the Buick Invitational, T21st in the Hawaiian Open and T7th in the Honda Classic.

Started R4 of the Buick Open T6th. Playing with Tiger Woods he shot 74!

He was T11th in the Greater Vancouver Open, T22nd in the Las Vegas and a superb 3rd in the National Car Rental at Disney to finish the season well..

Missed the cut in the US Open: T71st in the USPGA.

Longish hitter (273 yards), his sand save stats are poor. 49th on the M/L.

➤ He hit the water off the 17th in the Phoenix Open when joint leader and he has shot nervy final rounds in the 1997 Shell Houston Open and the 1998 Buick Open. It's probable that his best chance of securing his first victory will be when coming from 'off the pace' to post a winning clubhouse target – perhaps in the Greater Vancouver Open (T11th 1998: T12th 1997).

➤ An improving player who has now posted three top 3 finishes in his two seasons on tour.

KELLY GIBSON D

34-year-old Kelly had his best year in 1996 when 69th on the M/L after he had his career best finish when T3rd in the Las Vegas Invitational.

In 1998 he has failed to progress. Solid finishes in the Buick Invitational (T22nd), the CVS Charity Classic (T15th), and the Greater Vancouver Open (T15th) were his best efforts.

A long hitter (283 yards) he is not always accurate so is suited by wide fairways, long courses and four par 5s. He must now go to Q School after finishing 139th on the M/L.

➤ He was in contention in the Canadian Open before he shot a 76 in R4 (he'd shot a 78 in R4 in that tournament in 1994, too), and he led the Phoenix Open at halfway only to fall away to finish T27th.

➤ So his best chances of winning will undoubtedly be on par 72 (four par 5s) courses with wide fairways suited to his long hitting when he can come from 'off the pace' without too much pressure. His best chances therefore may be in the Las Vegas Invitational (T3rd 1996: T15th 1995) and the Walt Disney Classic (T17th 1997).

BILL GLASSON CT G

38-year-old Bill qualified for the season opening Mercedes Championship by winning his seventh tournament, the 1997 Las Vegas Invitational. However it was no surprise that he could not play because of injury.

He's had twelve operations that have continually wrecked his career. Nevertheless in 1998 he posted high finishes in the Bell South Classic (T5th after a 66 in R4), the CVS Charity Classic (T7th), the World Series of Golf (T11th), the Texas Open (T11th), and the Buick Challenge (3rd).

Missed the cut in the US Masters: T13th in the USPGA. A long driver who drives the ball a huge distance through the air so he has a big length advantage when a course plays short after rain. 84th on the M/L.

➤ If there's one player I expect to have a really good year in 1999 and to record a victory it would be Bill Glasson. A proven winner with plenty of bottle he can be expected to post a series of big finishes.....if he stays healthy, fit and well.

➤ "My goal is to be the first person to become eligible for the Ryder Cup and politely decline," as he reckons he's not a match player.

➤ Glasson was 2nd in 1997 at the English Turn course so he could well be the first winner of the Entergy Classic there in early May.

➤ He is genuinely 'must-bet' material for the Bell South Classic. In the two years it's been held at Sugarloaf he's finished T19th and T5th. If his 1998 R4 was added to his first three rounds in 1997 he'd shoot 14 under......and win.

PAUL GOYDOS

34-year-old Paul is a Californian who broke through in 1996 when he won the Bay Hill Invitational to end the year 44th on the M/L. In 1997 he had five top 10s to finish the year 61st.

In 1998 he had high finishes in the Bob Hope Classic (T24th), the Quad City Classic (T13th), the Deposit Guaranty Classic (T2nd at 66/1), the St Jude Classic (6th), and the Buick Open (T15th).

Finished T34th in the USPGA.

Won once, in 1992, on the Nike tour.

Often he seems to play better than he scores. 82nd on the M/L.

➤ The early-season tournaments in his home state of California, especially the Bob Hope Chrysler Classic (T24th 1998: T7th 1996 after being the R2 leader), will give Paul his best chance of his second win.

➤ Worth noting in the St Jude Classic (T6th 1998) in mid June.

➤ 12/1 to make the US Ryder Cup team.....not a bet to make me thinks!

SCOTT GUMP

Florida resident Scott is a 33-year-old still seeking his first win. Joining the tour in 1991 he had never finished in the Top 80 on the M/L as he started 1998.

He had high finishes in the Bell South Classic (T19th), the Western Open (T22nd), the CVS Charity Classic (T19th), the AT&T (T23rd after a 67 in R4), and the Texas Open (T8th). Shot a 62 in R2 of the Canon Greater Hartford Open before he finished a disappointing T36th.

His big finish came when he finished 2nd at 66/1 in the Quad City Classic.

T23rd in the USPGA after being T2nd at halfway.

He has two wins on the Nike tour.

He is very accurate, although very short (264 yards) off the tee. Needs to improve his short game to match his driving accuracy. 73rd on the M/L (his best yet).

➤ Other players have notched their first win on the basis of accuracy off the tee, and Gump could do so too.

➤ He'll be a very big price for the Doral Ryder Open in his home state in early March and he would be worth consideration then if his early season stats are sound.

JAY HAAS

Jay is now a 45-year-old US tour veteran. He's been in the top 90 on the M/L every year since he joined it in 1977. He's played in the Ryder Cup twice (1983 and 1995) and the Presidents Cup in 1994.

He's won nine times, and been second on eleven occasions, although he's not won since 1993.

In 1998 he had high finishes in the Nissan Open (T10th), the MCI Classic (T24th after being halfway leader), the Memorial (T23rd), the St Jude Classic (T7th), the AT&T (T6th) and the Texas Open (T2nd at 50/1).

T12th in the US Masters (T1st for fairways hit): missed the cut in the British Open and the US Open: T38th USPGA.

Not surprisingly he's not long off the tee at 265 yards. However he has a sound, well-proven swing. 56th on the M/L.

➤ If he is to notch his tenth tour win it will be in one of the two tournaments in which his record is so good.

*The St Jude Classic (T7th 1998: Won 1992) where the Zoysia grass suits his sweeping style.

*The Texas Open – 2nd 1998: 2nd 1996: 8th 1995, and his last win was in this tournament, albeit on a different course.

➤ As an accurate player who regularly makes the cut he must never be lightly opposed in match bets.

➤ Worth noting that he may have nine victories yet he has never won in Florida.

DONNIE HAMMOND   Pb

41-year-old Donnie has an unusual swing with very low hands at address. He has struggled in recent years finishing 136th (1995), 165th (1996), and 106th (1997) on the M/L. Indeed his two victories came in the eighties, the last in 1989.

In 1998 he had three top 25s, in the Greater Greensboro Open (T23rd), the Shell Houston Open (T22nd), and the Canon Greater Hartford Open (T25th). 167th (!) on the M/L.

➤ Short off the tee it's not easy seeing Hammond, at 41, winning for the first time this decade in Ryder Cup year. He's therefore awarded the Pb symbol!

➤ His game is clearly suited to the Canon Greater Hartford Open. He was in the lead there in R3 this year until, at the 17th, he had more hits than the Beatles, to shoot a ten and lose all chance!

DUDLEY HART   S G

Born in New York, 40-year-old Hart now lives in Florida. Recovered from wrist surgery to record his first tour win in 1996 when he won the rain-shortened Canadian Open. He finished that year 47th on the M/L.

In 1997 he had two high finishes – in the Sprint International (4th), and the St Jude Classic (2nd) to end the year 60th on the M/L.

In 1998 he played well again with high finishes in the Phoenix Open (T8th), the Doral Ryder Open (T15th), the Players' Championship (T25th), the Greater Greensboro Open (T11th), the Shell Houston Open (T4th after 67 in R4), the Kemper Open (13th), the Western Open (T3rd after 63 in R4) and the Buick Open (T12th – T3rd at halfway).

High in the stats for sand saves and driving accuracy his putting is his weakness.

81st of 81, in the British Open after 85 in the wind in R3. 53rd on the M/L.

➤ He proved with his brilliant 80/1 win in Subaru World Open in November that he is very much a player to note in 1999.

➤ A streak player (62 in R3 1998 Subaru World Open: 63 in R4 The Western Open) who can be expected to win if his putting stats look good early in the season.

➤ Improving, safely past 40, with confidence high and with two wins and four top 4s in the last 2½ years, he's a player you must keep on the right side in 1999.

➤ "It sets up well for my game," says Dudley about the Glen Abbey course, home of the Canadian Open, which he won in 1996. So take Hart and back Dudley there in 1999.

➤ Must be noted in match bets, spreads and the outright in the Greater Greensboro Open (T11th 1998 and a good record there in the early years of this decade) where his chance may be underrated by the bookies.

➤ 14/1 to make his US Ryder Cup debut in 1999.

J P HAYES

33-year-old JP was born in Wisconsin and lives in Texas. Secured his 1998 tour card at the 1997 Q School, and what a year it's been for him. In June in the rain-reduced 54-hole Buick Classic he sprang a real 250/1 shock when he got into a play-off, and proceeded to beat Jim Furyk.

He was T3rd in the rain-reduced AT&T.

Finished T18th in the Greater Milwaukee Open, and T20th in the Buick Challenge.

Won once on the Nike tour in 1996 in Florida.

Missed the cut in the British Open and the USPGA. 51st on the M/L.

➤ With both his big 1998 finishes coming in 54-hole events he has still to win a 'normal' 72-hole event. Nevertheless he played well to beat Furyk, and his 67 in R3 of the AT&T was impressive.

➤ Born in Wisconsin he is very much the hometown kid in the Greater Milwaukee Open (T18th 1998) in which he can be expected to play well again in 1999.

NOLAN HENKE   S

Nolan Jay had three wins, three 2nds, and three 3rds as he entered 1998. The 34-year-old Florida-based guy was disappointing in 1997 ending the year 111th on the M/L after just one top 10 when T8th in the Shell Houston Open.

In 1998 he had top 20s in the Phoenix Open (T14th) and the Quad City Classic (T17th).

However he found good form from late July recording top 4 finishes in the CVS Charity Classic (T4th), the Greater Milwaukee Open (T3rd incl a 62 in R2) and the BC Open (3rd at 50/1 after disappointing 72 in R4). Finished T7th in the National Car Rental at Disney.

Right to left player. 65th on the M/L.

➤ His putting can be very good and this has helped him to record at least one top 3 finish every year (apart from 1997) this decade.

➤ His final rounds when in contention over the last three years have not been too good. So if he's to post win No. 4 it will probably be when he comes from 'off the pace' with a hot putter to set a clubhouse target, perhaps in the Greater Milwaukee Open (T3rd 1998: 3rd 1996: 17th 1995).

➤ Must have a chance in the Phoenix Open in late January – he won it in 1991 and played well there this year when T14th.

➤ His streaky style makes it usually unwise to oppose him in early round 3-ball betting.

BRIAN HENNINGER   S

Californian born Brian Hatfield....now there's a middle name to conjure with......is a 33-year-old who now lives in Oregon. He joined the tour in 1993 and had to return to Q School in 1996 to keep his card.

His best season was in 1994 when after winning the rain-shortened Deposit Guaranty Classic he was 63rd on the Money list.

In 1998 he had two top 10s, in the Colonial (T8th), and the BC Open (T9th), and top twenties in the Honda Classic (T15th), the Deposit Guaranty Classic (18th), and the CVS Charity Classic (T19th).

He has three wins on the Nike tour, both in 1992.

His stats tell his story – top 20 for putting, bottom 20 for driving accuracy. At 275 yards he's in the top 50 for driving distance. 114th on the M/L.

➤ Let's remember in the 1995 US Masters he led the field into the Sunday before finishing T10th. He has a highly-talented short game so is well able to shoot very low on occasions.

➤ Sadly for him the Pleasant Valley course on which he's a good record (home of the CVS Charity Classic) is no longer a tournament course.

➤ If the stats ever show that he has found accuracy off the tee (unlikely but possible) then he can be followed at huge prices as his short game could then win him a tournament.

➤ Played during the week of the British Open the weakly-contested Deposit Guaranty Classic (18th 1998: 10th 1997: T16th 1996: W 1994) will be the tournament that Hatfield Henninger will have ringed in his 1999 diary as his very best opportunity.

TIM HERRON

Tim is a 28-year-old who now lives in Scottsdale, Arizona. He burst onto the tour in 1996 when he won the Honda Classic in only his seventh event, and then in 1997 he won again when landing the LaCantera Texas Open. So in his first two years he'd won twice and finished 39th and 33rd on the M/L.

In 1998 he had top 10s in the Tucson Chrysler Classic (T4th at DYM 100/1), the Doral Ryder Open (T9th), the Byron Nelson Classic (T9th) and the Memorial (T7th), and top 25s in the Greater Greensboro Open (T16th), the St Jude Classic (T12th), the AT&T (T19th after a poor 74 in the final round), the World Series (T24th) and the Buick Challenge (T14th).

T53rd US Open: 75th and last in the USPGA.

His massive length off the tee (281 yards) is a great advantage especially on the par 5s so he has plenty of eagle chances. However his driving accuracy stats are always poor, and he doesn't make the top 90 for sand saves. 54th on the M/L.

➤ OK 'Lumpy' is inconsistent, yet he does know how to win and his record shows he does best when in form, and on a course he likes.

➤ A very good wet-weather player as he proved when winning his first event, the Honda Classic.

➤ "I'm real comfortable on this golf course," he said describing the LaCantera course used for the Texas Open. 6th in 1996, winner in 1997, he missed the cut this year as defending champion. 'Normal service' can be resumed in 1999 on one of his favourite courses.

➤ His length is a big help in the Memorial. T8th in 1997, T7th in 1998 his stroke average for these two years is 69.57, so in a tournament in which there'll be all the 'name' players Lumpy may be 100/1 again in 1999 in which case he'd represent excellent value.

➤ Living in Arizona expect him to make an impact in late February in the Tuscon Open. T4th this year, with wide fairways and four par 5s it suits Herron really well. Worth support on the spread, and in match and outright betting.

GABRIEL HJERTSTEDT   D F

This 28-year-old Swede became the answer to a super pub quiz question.....name the first Swedish golfer to win on the USPGA tour.....when landing the 1997 BC Open at 200/1. It was his only top 25 finish of the season so, although a winner, he finished 89th (!) on the M/L.

In 1998 he played well to finish T6th in the season opening all winners Mercedes Championship.

However since then he's had only two significant finishes, in the Byron Nelson Classic (T25th) and the Greater Milwaukee Open (T9th).

Missed the cut (79 – 78!) in the US Masters and the USPGA. 157th on M/L.

➤ Not long off the tee (272 yards). Not in the top 100 for driving accuracy, in the bottom 30 on the putting stats, and in the bottom 10 for greens in regulation – facts that speak for themselves.

➤ It is now clear, as I suggested last year, that his win in the 1997 Ryder Cup week in a low-quality field was a (big) flash in a (small) pan!

➤ If he wins in 1999 it will be very very surprising so don't expect to see Gabriel Steig Johan Eric receiving a trophy again late on a Sunday night on Sky telly.

SCOTT HOCH ☼ G �

43-year-old Hoch came in to 1998 as a player with a proven winning record. He had six international victories as well as eight on the American tour including one in each year from 1994.

Indeed from 1994 when 11th on the M/L he has always finished in the top 20, and in 1996 (9th) and 1997 (6th) in the top 10.

In 1998 his astonishing consistency continued with top 10s in the Tucson Chrysler Classic (T9th), the Nissan Open (T6th), the Doral Ryder Open (T7th), the Players Championship (T5th), the Kemper Open (2nd), the Western Open (T7th), the Canon Greater Hartford Open (T7th after being R3 joint leader), and the CVS Charity Classic (2nd).

He had top 20s in the Freeport McDermott Classic (T12th), the Shell Houston Open (T12th), the Colonial (T18th), the St Jude Classic (11th), and the World Series (T9th).

T16th US Masters: Missed cut in US and British Open: T29th USPGA. T21st Tour Championship.

Although a proven winner 'Hoch the Choke' has developed a reputation as a 'bottler' because he's now had thirteen 2nd places in the States. The most famous came in the 1989 US Masters when he missed a tiddler to gift the tournament to Faldo.

He'll never be nominated for a Nobel Peace prize as he's had a 'diplomacy bypass' operation.

Over the years his consistency (24 top 4 finishes in the last five years) has made him a punter's friend.

Short off the tee at 269 yards. His game is based on his accuracy off the tee and the fairway. However his bunker play has let him down this year. In much better form in the first half of the season. 17th on M/L.

➤ 5/1 on to retain his Ryder Cup place. Let's remember he made his debut in 1997 when he was the top US points scorer.
➤ He has yet to win in Florida where he now lives.
➤ Can be expected to post a series of high finishes again in 1999. His best chances may lie in the three tournaments in which his accuracy is rewarded.
*The Players Championship T5th 1998: 2nd 1997: top 20 1996
*The Kemper Open: three top 3 finishes in the last six years
*The Greater Milwaukee Open: his four-year stroke average is 67.87, and he won it in 1995, and 1997.
➤ He's a player who should never be opposed in match betting.
➤ He hates the British Open. In only three starts (missed cut 1990: T68th 1995: and missed cut 1998) he's shown that cold, windy, seaside golf is not for him. So if he's contractually obliged to play the British Open he can be opposed with real confidence. Scotland will not become Scott-land at Carnoustie in 1999.

P H HORGAN III 🍾

38-year-old PH (it's Patrick Henry actually) struggled in 1997 to end the year 105th on the M/L. He therefore retained his tour card obtained through his high Nike tour money list finish (7th) in 1996.

In 1998 he had top 25s in the Doral Ryder Open (T15th – after taking a 7 at the last in R4 of 74 when partnered with Tiger Woods), the Freeport McDermott Classic (T12th), and the CVS Charity Classic (T25th after 74 in R4).

Had a top 10 in the Deposit Guaranty Classic when T5th.

T44th in the USPGA.

He has three Nike tour wins.

Short off the tee at 269 yards, his strength has been his driving accuracy. His iron play, and his short game especially from sand can be improved. 126th on the M/L, he missed retaining his card by $4,205!

➤ Last year he was awarded the bottle after a 75 in R4 of the Texas Open when in contention. This year after 74s in R4 of both the Doral Ryder Open and the CVS Charity Classic he keeps it!

➤ If he's to make a breakthrough win it will surely be when coming from 'off the pace' with the two most likely tournaments.

*The Greater Milwaukee Open (T6th 1997). He lives near the River Highlands course which is his 'home' track.

*The Deposit Guaranty Classic (T5th 1998). He was easily the best in this year's tournament over the last three rounds (19 under) and has a definite chance in this 'third division' event.

BRADLEY HUGHES   g

Brad is a 31-year-old Aussie who gained his 1998 tour card via Q School having lost it in 1997 when he had only one big tournament, when he posted his best-ever US finish, in the BC Open (T8th).

1998 started well when after finishing T8th in the Greg Norman Classic he was the 40/1 winner of the Australian Masters. In R1 he broke the course record with a 63 playing superbly in windy conditions. It was his 5th Aussie success.

In America he found form in late July when T2nd in the CVS Charity Classic, and in September when T4th in the Canadian Open, and in October when T4th in the Michelob.

T25th in the Texas Open.

Coach is Roham Dummett. He is very high on the all-round driving stats. 80th on the M/L.

➤ He shows up with the very best players very high in greens in regulation. However his putting is very variable. It was brilliant over the last two rounds in the Canadian Open when he went cross handed. If he can improve on and around the greens (his sand saves stats are shocking) he could well win one of the tournaments when the 'name' players are missing.

➤ Clearly enjoys the LaCantera course, home of the Texas Open, where he was the halfway leader in 1997, and T25th in 1998, and the Kingsmill course, home of the Michelob tournament, where he was T4th in 1998 11 shots better than his visit twelve months earlier.

➤ His accuracy, and ability to play in the wind are well suited to the Shell Houston Open (T9th 1996). If his early-season putting stats show improvement he'd be worth an interest there in the outright, 3-ball and match betting markets.

MIKE HULBERT

New York born 40-year-old Mike now plays out of Bay Hill, Florida.

He's had three career wins, the last in 1991, when he was 24th on the M/L, his highest finish this decade.

In 1998 he had high finishes in the Phoenix Open (T14th after a 63 in R1), the Greater Greensboro Open (T16th), the Shell Houston Open (T17th after 73 in R4, when T5th after R3) and the St Jude Classic (T20th).

His big finish however was in the Canadian Open in September when he came from 'off the pace' to finish 3rd.

At 270 yards he's increased his length by 10 yards off the tee.

His short game, from sand and on the greens is always his weakest area. He even putted one handed (now that is desperate stuff!) three years ago. 88th on the M/L.

➤ Now safely past 40 he's posted a top 3 finish in each of the last five years so he's liable to 'pop up' at big odds sometime in 1999 – perhaps early on (January) in the Phoenix Open (T14th 1998: T7th 1997 with a 63 in R1 this year), or later on (in June) in the Fedex St Jude Classic (T20th 1998: T9th 1997).

➤ Has played well in the Buick Invitational in recent 'odd' years – T2nd 1997; 2nd 1995 so perhaps 1999 will see him "in the frame" at big odds again.

JOHN HUSTON   g S

You probably thought Johnny Ray was a singer you remember from years ago, well he's also a 37-year-old Illinois-born golfer who now lives in Florida.

John had a really poor year in 1997 when because of a shoulder problem he finished 141st on the M/L with just one top 10 finish, in the Colonial (9th). He used a one-off exemption as a top 50 career money winner to retain his 1998 tour card.

And didn't he just make a real comeback!

He was T10th in the Bob Hope, and T8th in the Phoenix Open before he ran away with the Hawaiian Open, winning by 7 shots at 50/1 on the back of a missed cut. He set all sorts of records as he shot 31 birdies and finished 28 under par.

His second win came in the National Car Rental at Disney, also at 50/1 after a 66 in R4.

He had other high finishes in the Tucson Chrysler Classic (T22nd), the Doral Ryder Open (T2nd), the MCI Classic (T10th), the Shell Houston Open (T12th), the Bell South Classic (T5th), the Colonial (T18th), World Series (T24th), the Michelob (T6th) and the Tour Championship (T11th).

T23rd in the US Masters (2nd in putting); T32nd US Open: T11th British Open: T13th USPGA – so he made all four cuts in the majors.

Played the Dutch Open to finish a never-in-contention T11th.

This year his improvement is partly due to the fact that since January he has slept on a magnet-laced mattress to alleviate tendonitis and bursitis.

Huston is a classic example of a fine player who, after a really bad season, becomes fully fit and on the comeback trail posts a victory and a series of high finishes.

He has always had an excellent short game and a brilliant touch. This year he's added accuracy to the greens.

Long off the tee at 270 yards. 10th on M/L.

➤ 4/1 to make his Ryder Cup debut in 1999.

➤ He now has five wins, four of them in Florida. He could well win again in 1999, especially if his early-season stats show that his newly-found accuracy has been maintained.

➤ Can be expected to play really well in the US Masters where his record is very good – in nine starts he's made every cut, and posted five successive top 25 finishes. Remember to follow him at Augusta in 1999 in the early-round 3-ball betting, in suitable match bets and if you want a massively-priced outsider to come from 'off the pace'.

➤ Can be followed with confidence in the Doral Ryder Open. Held in his 'home' state of Florida, he won it in 1993 and was T2nd in 1998.

PETER JACOBSEN

44-year-old Jake is well known for founding "Jake Trout and the Flounders", a group that also features Larry Rinker and Payne Stewart, for winning six US golf tournaments, and for letting his caddie 'Fluff' move on to Tiger Woods's bag.

His form slumped after his father's death in 1992. However in 1995 refocussed he won the AT&T and the Buick Invitational back to back, and at the end of a superb 'comeback' season he finished 7th on the M/L.

Injury ruined 1996, and in 1997 he had two top 10s to finish 82nd on the M/L.

In 1998 he had high finishes in the Hawaiian Open (T11th), the Byron Nelson Classic (T19th) and the Sprint (T13th – 32 points).

However it was in September in the BC Open that he had his big finish when 2nd at 80/1.

Relaxed, and fun loving, he now has business interests which take up a lot of time.

He's always been a fine ball striker. Tends to draw the ball. At 276 yards he's also long, but this year he has been inaccurate off the tee. However his achilles heel has always been his putting. 92nd on the M/L.

➤ His exemptions for his 1995 successes have now expired so he knows he must retain his tour card on his own merits in 1999 so he can be expected to show improved form.

➤ The West Coast celebrity events suit his extrovert personality and the wide fairways suit his game. So he can be noted as an outsider 'with a squeak' in the Bob Hope Classic in January. After all he's already won it once – in 1990.

LEE JANZEN   G🏇

Florida-based Lee is a 34-year-old guy who started 1998 very much on 'the comeback trail'. He'd not won since 1995 when he won three tournaments finishing the year 3rd on the M/L.

In 1998 he had high finishes in the Phoenix Open (T14th), the Buick Invitational (T22nd), the Players Championship (T13th after shooting 79 (!) in R4), the MCI Classic (T18th), the Shell Houston Open (T4th after leading with 7 holes to play), and the Kemper Open (T21st).

His big moment came in the US Open when the R4 jitters that stopped him winning the Shell Houston and the Players Championship stayed at home. He played superbly in that final round (68) to catch and beat Payne Stewart to win his second US Open.

Went on to the Western Open to finish T3rd.

T33rd US Masters: T24th British Open: Missed cut in the USPGA. T24th (of 30) in Tour Championship.

He now has eight tour victories including two US Opens.

His great strength is his accuracy. He is a superb short-iron player. He was top in greens in regulation in the US Open. He has putted well again this year. Right-to-left player with a good temperament. 20th on M/L.

➤ His accuracy and sound putting will put him into contention again in 1999 when he could well win again, possibly in the Kemper Open (T21st after an 8 in R3; T14th 1997: Won 1995: T4th 1994: T7th 1993).

➤ 4/1 on to make the Ryder Cup for the third time.

STEVE JONES

Safely past 40 now Steve has seven US tour wins, the most important being the 1996 US Open. In that year he was very much on the 'comeback trail' after the accident in 1991 that put him on the sidelines until 1995.

He ended 1996 22nd on the M/L, and in 1997 he proceeded to consolidate and then improve his position to 20th after winning the Phoenix Open and the Canadian Open.

In 1998 he won again when landing the Quad City Classic at 20/1 from a weak field in early July.

He also had top 25s in the Hawaiian Open (T11th), the Players Championship (T25th), the Byron Nelson Classic (T25th), the Buick Classic (T24th), the Sprint (20th), the World Series (T21st), the Canadian Open (T13th) and the Texas Open (T11th).

His other top 10 was in the Bob Hope when T4th.

T26th in the US Masters (2nd in G.I.R): missed US Open cut: did not play in USPGA.

An accurate player, he's a very streaky putter. When he's hot he's hot, and when he's not he's not! 38th on the M/L.

➤ With four wins, including a major, in the last three years he's a proven winner and proven front runner.

➤ Finds it difficult to defend his titles. He's yet to post a top 10 in recent years as a defending champion. In the 1997 US Open (T60th), the 1998 Phoenix Open (T34th) and the 1998 Canadian Open (T13th), he's failed to sparkle.

➤ Last year, I nominated him for the Bob Hope Classic and he finished T4th at 28/1. He will have a first-class chance there again in 1999 after his T4th – T9th finishes in the last two years.

➤ Based in Arizona, Jones is a fine player in desert conditions and now that he won't have the burden of being the defending champion he could well

win the Phoenix Open again....after all he strolled home in 1997 by eleven shots!
➤ Yet to win in Florida.
➤ 7/2 to fulfil his ambition to make his Ryder Cup debut in 1999.

JERRY KELLY

32-year-old Jerry lives where he was born in Madison, Wisconsin. Joined the tour in 1996 finishing 59th on the M/L after four top 10s including a 2nd in the Greater Milwaukee Open after a play-off. He followed that in 1997 with three top 10s to be 103rd.

In 1998 he had high finishes in the Tucson Chrysler Classic (T18th), the Nissan Open (T20th), Honda Classic (T22nd), the Greater Greensboro Open (T11th after 76 in R4), the Shell Houston Open (T6th – after 68 in R4), the Bell South Classic (T14th), the Kemper Open (T25th), and the Deposit Guaranty Classic (T7th).

T4th at halfway in the Players Championship he shot 77 in R3 and ended T31st.

➤ His round-by-round stats point to his weakness. In 1997 he was T150th for final-round scoring yet 4th for R3 scoring. When the heat goes up so do his final-round scores!

In the 1996 Greater Greensboro Open (77), the 1997 Shell Houston Open (74), and the 1998 Greater Greensboro Open (76) he's shot disappointing final rounds when in contention so he's awarded the bottle. 87th on the M/L.

➤ Became a first-time dad, of a son, in mid August so expect him to be inspired to improved performances in 1999 by 'the nappy factor'.
➤ With his record it's crystal clear that if he's to win it will be when he shoots a low final round from 'off the pace'. His best chances of doing that must be in the two tournaments in which he's done so well in the past two years.
  *The Greater Greensboro Open (T11th 1998: T19th 1997).
  *The Shell Houston Open (T6th 1998, T6th 1997).
➤ His home town tournament is the Greater Milwaukee Open (T8th 1997: 2nd 1996) on a course suited to his game. Worth noting there 'in running' if fairly close up yet 'off the pace'.

SKIP KENDALL G

Skip is a native of Milwaukee who now lives in Florida. He made a poor start to his career when 129th on the 1993 M/L, was 164th on the M/L in 1995 to lose his card again. Then in 1997 he had two top 10s, in the Buick Invitational (T9th) and the Sprint International (3rd) to end the year 74th on the M/L.

In 1998 he played very consistently to post high finishes in the Bob Hope Classic (T8th with all five rounds under 70), the Phoenix Open (T14th), the Hawaiian Open (T16th), the Nissan Open (T13th after 73 in R4), the Greater Greensboro Open (T11th after 78 in R4), the Shell Houston Open (11th), the Colonial (T18th), the Western Open (T17th), the Greater Milwaukee Open (T23rd after 65 in R4), the BC Open (T9th) and the Buick Challenge (5th after 63 in R4).

His big chance came when he got into a play off, with Scott Simpson, for the Buick Invitational only to lose it and finish 2nd. At that stage of the season he was 2nd on the tour's stroke-average stats.

His T10th USPGA was an indication of his quality.

At 270 yards 34-year-old Skip is not a long hitter. His improved results are to a large extent based on his improved putting. 32nd on the M/L.

➤ Skip is a fast-improving player who will be boosted by the 'nappy factor' in 1999 having become a first-time dad in June. Last year I suggested he could provide a 'surprise win' in 1998, and losing in that play-off, he nearly did.

➤ Living in Florida I expect him to make an impact in 1999 when the tour takes 'the Florida Swing'. He will be at tasty prices in the outrights for the Bay Hill Invitational (19976 R2 leader), and the Doral Ryder Open.

➤ He would surely have a big chance in the weaker field for the BC Open in September. He shot four sub-par rounds when finishing T9th in 1998.

➤ Born in Milwaukee he's the 'hometown boy' in the Greater Milwaukee Open (T23rd 1998 after 65 in R4: 12th 1997).

TOM KITE   Pb

49-year-old Tom is surely counting down the days until 9th December 1999 when he's 50 and eligible to make a pot of gold with the roundbellies on the Seniors tour.

With nineteen American tour wins, and three others worldwide Tom as a superb record.

However in 1998, with MLD setting in after he led his side to Ryder Cup defeat at Valderrama, he couldn't post a top 20 finish although he did have top 25s in the Buick Invitational (T22nd), the Players Championship (T25th after being 3rd at halfway), and the Byron Nelson Classic (T25th).

38th US Masters: 43rd US Open: T35th British Open: missed cut in USPGA. Right-to-left player. Plumb last for sand saves this year.

➤ He is now clearly past his best and surely he won't get his 20th win in 1999.

➤ However when betting next Millennium on the Seniors tour Tom will regularly enter into our calculations.

➤ A crazy 12/1 to make the next US Ryder Cup team, perhaps in the mistaken belief that he'll be given a wild card.

GREG KRAFT

34-year-old Gregory Thomas had a poor 1997 when 139th on the M/L. So he started 1998 without a win and with two 2nd places (1993 Walt Disney Classic: 1994 Western Open) as his best finishes.

In 1998 he had high finishes in the Bay Hill Invitational (T13th), the Bell South Classic (T24th) and the Buick Classic (T12th).

He made two very big cheques, in the Hawaiian Open (T4th) and the Western Open (T5th after a poor 75 in R4).

In the USPGA finished T23rd after shooting 65 in R3. A fine putter with a good short game, he must improve his accuracy off both tee and fairway. 94th on the M/L.

➤ During the USPGA he said "I haven't been as sound before as I am now. I haven't been as focussed and dedicated."

➤ One of those players who must be watched on the early season stats. If he's improved his greens in regulation, and driving accuracy stats then as a good putter he'd be first-class value at massive prices.

➤ His best chances will surely be in the Western Open (T5th 1998: 2nd 1994) and the weakly-contested Deposit Guaranty Classic (T3rd 1996).

MATT KUCHAR   A

20-year-old Matt lives in Florida and has been written up as the next golden boy of American golf.

He won the US Amateur title in 1997.

Made a big impact on the wider public through his big smile en route to finishing a very impressive T14th in the 1998 US Open.

In the US Masters he was T21st.

Played in the Bay Hill Invitational (missed cut) and the Bell South Classic (T36th). Came to Britain to miss the cut in both the Loch Lomond and the British Open. Finished down the field in the Buick Challenge.

Apparently, and surely wisely, he has no immediate plans to turn pro as he continues his studies.

It may also be that his swing may not stand up to the rigours of the pressure of the pro game.

Uses his extrovert father, Peter, as his caddy. His dad has already talked about managing his son's eventual pro career.

➤ If he's to make a successful pro career he will surely need to break away from his dad's influence by seeking both a professional caddy and professional management.

➤ 10/1 (from 7/1) to make the US Ryder cup team.....which must surely be a bet to avoid!

➤ With Justin Rose, Matt Kuchar, Hank Kuene, and Sergio Garcia all promising amateurs I have absolutely no doubt that it will be the Spaniard who has the glittering career!

HANK KUENE   A

US Amateur golf champions are always worth noting, and in 1998 22-year-old Hank Kuene won the title in August beating Tom McKnight 2 and 1.

He later made his debut in a USPGA tournament in the Texas Open after receiving a sponsor's exemption.

"I was more nervous swinging on the driving range than I was at any point in the US Amateur," and it showed as he missed the cut after shooting 77 and 72.

He comes from a golfing family. His elder brother Trip was beaten in the 1994 US Amateur final by a certain Tiger Woods, and his sister Kelli is on the LPGA tour.

However it's not just been one big breeze as he'd been addicted to alcohol as a teenager and went to a rehab centre. Well over that now, hopefully he can focus on his golf.

Justin Leonard is a family friend. He also shares the same coach, Hank Haney, as Mark O'Meara whom he's known for many years.

Massive driver – hitting it 300 yards off the tee. Needs to improve his wedge play to create more birdie chances.

➤ He'll be playing in the 1999 US Masters.

NEAL LANCASTER

36-year-old Neal is a 6 footer from North Carolina who has only once finished in the top 100 on the M/L, and that was in 1994 when he won the 36-hole rain-reduced Byron Nelson Classic in a six-man play-off.

Since then he has struggled with only one top 10 in 1995, two in 1996, and none in 1997.

In 1998 he had top 25s in the Doral Ryder Open (T23rd), the MCI Classic (T24th), the Memorial (T16th) and the Canon Greater Hartford Open (T20th).

4th in the Greater Greensboro Open and T8th in the Buick Challenge (disappointing 71 in R4).

Missed the USPGA cut.

Can be a brilliant putter. Poor in 1998 from sand. He is well down the stats for driving accuracy.

Led the 1996 LA Open after R3 only to 'bottle' it in R4 with a 77 to finish T6th. 86th on the M/L.

➤ He lives near his birthplace in North Carolina so his 'home' tournament is very much the Greater Greensboro in which he was a very solid 4th at 150/1 this year. He can be followed there in 1999 in the 3-ball betting and as a 100/1 plus outsider who could win if coming from 'off the pace'.

FRANKLIN LANGHAM

30-year-old Franklin lives in Georgia where he was born.

Secured his 1998 tour card by finishing 6th at Q School.

In 1998 he was T19th in the Freeport McDermott Classic, T12th in the Shell Houston Open, T12th in the St Jude Classic, and T25th in the BC Open.

In the Deposit Guaranty Classic he lost a 4-shot lead on the back nine to finish T2nd.

Has one Nike tour win, in 1993, in a play-off.

Has putted well in 1998 but played poorly from bunkers. 117th on the M/L.

➤ Understandably nervy when he got his winning chance this year.

➤ He has so far proved to be the sort of player to do well on courses on which he has already proved himself. So in 1999 he can be expected to play well in the Shell Houston Open having recorded his best-ever finish there when T12th this year.

TOM LEHMAN   CT G F 🐎

Thomas Edward is the guy who suddenly hit the big time in his thirties. From 1994 through 1996 he won four tournaments, the Memorial (1994), the Colonial (1995), and then in 1996 the British Open and the Tour Championship. He finished 4th (1994), 15th (1995) and 1st (1996) on the M/L.

In 1997 he finished 19th on the M/L although he won the Loch Lomond Invitational at 20/1 on the European tour.

In 1998 he was T14th in the Phoenix Open, T6th in the Tucson Chrysler Classic, T22nd in the Bay Invitational, T2nd in the Players' Championship, T14th in the MCI Classic, T11th in the Memorial, and 3rd in the Buick Classic the week before he finished T5th in the US Open. T9th in the AT&T after 71 in R3, T15th in the National Car Rental at Disney, and 15th in the Tour Championship.

As defending champion he was T9th in the Loch Lomond Invitational. Then he injured his shoulder at Southport's fairground so went on to miss the cut in the British Open.

T29th in the USPGA. He had earlier missed the cut in the US Masters after an 80 in R1.

He has now won four times in the States and twice internationally.

Losing one and a half stones in weight by July led to him pulling shots. 25th on M/L.

He's a straight-hitting player with immense length whose stock shot is a draw (R- L). His short game has improved although his putting was placed in 'intensive care' over the later stages of the season. He'll be 40 in March 1999.

➤ Lehman, after going two years without a win on the US tour, will be a very determined guy on the 'comeback trail' in 1999. I expect him to win at least one tournament.

➤ Last year I suggested he was worth an each-way interest in the Players Championship (6th 1997: T8th 1996: and three earlier top 15s) on a course suited to his accuracy. Tom obliged when 2nd at 33/1....let's go for him again each way in 1999 for the Players.

➤ Lehman could well be the first winner of the Sony Open in Hawaii in January as his record on the Waialee course (6th 1997: T4th 1996: T2nd 1995) is very good

➤ His recent record in the US Open is quite astonishing, T5th 1998: 3rd 1997: T2nd 1996: 3rd 1995. So he can clearly be followed in match bets and on the spreads. However his inability to vary his standard 'draw' shot and his occasional poor putting touch may stop him winning again in 1999.

➤ Must have PMAs with the Memorial where he secured his first tour win in 1994 with a 20 under par total which is still a record. T11th this year he could well win it again in 1999.

JUSTIN LEONARD   G Y

Justin Charles Garret is the 26-year-old Texan who showed real promise in 1995 when 22nd on the M/L after posting seven top 10s and two 2nd places, in the Texas Open and the Western Open (T2nd).

In 1996 he landed his first win in the Buick Open, and came second in the Phoenix Open on the way to finishing 11th on the M/L.

In 1997 he progressed to 5th on the M/L winning the British Open, and the Kemper Open and finishing 2nd in the USPGA, and T3rd in the Western Open.

In late 1997 he was a late replacement for Fred Couples as he partnered Davis Love III to represent the USA in the World Cup of Golf to finish 3rd at 2/1 (!!).

In 1998 he was 2nd in the Tucson Chrysler Classic, before he won the Players Championship impressively at 50/1 in late March.

He was T8th in the Colonial, T16th in the Memorial, only T25th when favourite for the Kemper Open, T9th in the Western Open, and T2nd in the Texas Open after a bogey-bogey finish!

T8th in the US Masters: T40th in US Open: missed USPGA cut. As defending champion was T57th in the British Open after an 82 in R3 in the bad weather. T5th in Tour Championship.

His form dipped later in the season before he was T6th in the Las Vegas.

Mainly hits the ball right-left. Justin is a meticulous player with a simple, solid swing, and a very reliable putting routine and putting stroke. A tough competitive player. 8th on M/L.

➤ He has now won on the American tour in each of the last three years, as well as the 1997 British Open. There is every reason to expect him to win again in 1998.

➤ He does not play particularly well in the early-season Californian tournaments where he can safely be opposed in suitable match bets.

➤ He can be followed with confidence in all forms of betting in the Western Classic in early July. His record really is simply the best (T9th 1998: 3rd 1997: 8th 1996: 2nd 1995).

➤ He's only played in the Colonial four times (T8th 1998: 13th 1997: 10th 1996: 5th 1995) and as a proud Texan in his home state he can be expected to do well there again in 1999. Back him on the spreads, in match betting and, if a fair price, in the outright market.

➤ 7/1 on to retain his Ryder Cup place.

J L LEWIS

38-year-old Texan resident J L was 7th on the 1997 Nike tour money list to earn his tour card. In 1998, with his wife Dawn caddying for him, he was T6th in the rain-reduced Buick Invitational, T23rd in the Buick Open and T20th in the Texas Open.

Played superbly in October in the Buick Challenge to shoot four rounds in the sixties, including 68 in R4, to finish 4th. T13th the following week in the Michelob championship after 72 in R4. He finished T15th in the National Car Rental at Disney.

Reaches the awkward age of 39 in July 1999. 104th on the M/L.

➤ After nervy final rounds in the Canadian Open (82) and the Greater Milwaukee Open (76) he played superbly on Sunday in the Buick Challenge (68). If he can maintain that final round 'bottle' he could well post another high finish in 1999.

➤ He obviously wants a new car as his best career performances have all come in the Buick-sponsored tournaments – the Buick Challenge (4th 1998), the Buick Invitational (T6th 1998) and the Buick Open (T23rd 1998: T17th 1995). So let's remember that J L always moves up a gear when Buick are the sponsors!

FRANK LICKLITER G

29-year-old Frank Ray lives in the state of Ohio where he was born.

In 1997 he was 107th on the M/L after top 10s in the Canadian Open (T4th), the Greater Milwaukee Open (T8th), and the Quad City Classic (T5th).

In 1998 he had high finishes in the Phoenix Open (T8th), the Hawaiian Open (T7th after 72 in R4), the Nissan Open (T20th), the MCI Classic (T6th), the Western Open (T17th), the Quad City Classic (T13th after starting R4 T3rd, he shot 72), the CVS Charity Classic (T15th after 70 in R4), the Texas Open (T20th after 71 in R4), and the Buick Challenge (T20th), and the Michelob Championship (T6th after 72 in R4).

T18th in the US Open: T4th in USPGA including 68 in R4 when he beat O'Meara in his 2-ball.

Suffered, on his own admission, some MLD after his USPGA effort.

Poor old Frank has a degree in Sociology – that's the subject that studies people who don't need studying by people who do!

His very consistent year has been based on solid driving accuracy and improved putting. Sand save stats are poor. 45th on the M/L.

➤ His performances in the US Open (T18th) and the USPGA (T4th) were superb, exemplifying his much-improved form. His obvious weakness has been his poor R4 scoring when in contention However he'll have taken heart from his final round in the USPGA.

➤ He is just the sort of fast-improving, accurate player to win in 1999.

➤ He'll be 30 in late July 1999, and that can often kick start a major improvement (ask Jean Van de Velde). Could well cause a surprise especially in the second half of 1999, perhaps in the Canadian Open (T4th 1997) or in the John Deere Classic (T13th 1998: T5th 1997). He can be supported in both those events.

BRUCE LIETZKE

47-year-old Texas resident has thirteen tour victories with his last win in the 1994 Las Vegas Invitational.

In 1998 he was 2nd at Bob Hope Classic, T13th in the Players' Championship, and T17th in the Shell Houston Open.

A left to right player.

Plays very rarely these days yet still very competitive on the course. 79th on the M/L from just 10 starts.

➤ Played in 1998 on a special exemption as a top 25 career money winner.

➤ Always worth serious consideration in close-season events – as he is not a 'name' he's often 'value' (eg 25/1 winner, with Scott McCarron, of the 1997 Shark Shoot-out).

➤ Worth noting in the early 3-ball betting in the Bob Hope Classic (2nd in 1998 and 1997 (!)). It's an event that suits his laid back style.

TIM LOUSTALOT

Tim who? (Loss, tu, lot is the pronunciation) is a 33-year-old Californian who now lives in Scottsdale, Arizona.

Earned his 1998 tour card via Q School and went on to make his best-ever USPGA finish in July when T2nd in the Deposit Guaranty Classic.

He was also T13th in the Canadian Open after an 'off the pace' 68 in R4.

He's won twice on the Nike tour, in 1992 and 1996. 152nd on the M/L so Q School awaits.

➤ Accuracy from tee to green is his strength, and putting is a definite weakness. If he can show up well early in 1999 in the putting stats his accuracy could well land a 'shock' win and certainly gain a top 5 finish.

➤ Living in the desert he'll feel at home early in the season in the Phoenix Open and the Tucson Open.

DAVIS LOVE III   G S

34-year-old Davis is a superb player who started 1998 with twelve American tour victories, including his first major the 1997 USPGA. Apart from 1995 when he was 33rd, he has never been lower than 12th on the M/L.

In 1997 he was 3rd on the M/L after winning twice. In late 1997 he won the Kapalua at 8/1 in Hawaii, and playing with Justin Leonard took USA to 3rd place in the World Cup of Golf.

In 1998 he had high finishes in the Buick Invitational (T3rd), the Doral Ryder Open (T7th) and the Bay Hill Invitational (T17th after being jt leader at halfway), before he won the MCI Classic (at 20/1 after shooting 74 in R4) for the fourth time.

He was T5th in the Memorial, T17th in the Buick Classic, T22nd in the AT&T, T21st in the Sprint, 3rd at 14/1 in the World Series and 5th in the Las Vegas.

T33rd in the US Masters (after 78 in R4): missed cut in the US Open: 8th in the British Open: T7th as defending champion in the USPGA. T8th in Tour Championship.

Went to Japan in late April to be the runaway winner of The Crowns by 8 shots winning over 21 million Yen! His back problems have recurred this season, particularly after he returned from that Japanese trip in May.

In October he was 2nd at 14/1 in the National Car Rental at Disney after having a 4-shot lead going into R4 when he shot 71.

His form in the majors 'took off' after his son was born. The point was fully developed in his player profile in last year's volume. 11th on M/L.

➤ At his best he makes golf look very easy. He is a very, very long driver although not always accurate. His achilles heel is his putting and bunker play. Nevertheless he's won on the US tour every year (apart from 1994) this decade and he'll doubtless win again in 1999.

➤ 8/1 on to make the American Ryder Cup team for the fourth successive year.

➤ His R4 scoring early in the season in the Players Championship (80), the Bay Hill Invitational (76), the Freeport McDermott (75) and the US Masters (78) came in consecutive weeks and showed a disturbing trend that continued in the Memorial (73) in late May, and 'the Disney' (71) in October.

➤ His early-season target is the US Masters so he tends to be at his peak in April when he can be expected to play well in the 1999 Greater Greensboro Classic which he won in 1992.

➤ His huge hitting off the tee is ideal for the US Masters. However his Augusta problem is his putting.

	Final Pos	Rank for putting
1997	T7th	T36th
1996	T7th	T44th
1995	2nd	T17th

So if you back him at Augusta you're expecting his putting there to improve a lot.

➤ In 1997 he went straight from playing in the Ryder Cup to win the Buick Challenge. I think he could well do the same in 1999 although he may be suffering MLD as I'm sure America will win the Ryder Cup. Nevertheless keep him in mind for the Buick Challenge in late September.

➤ Must be expected to post a high finish in the Las Vegas Invitational – in the last six years he's won it once (1993), and had two top 5 finishes.

STEVE LOWERY **S**

Stephen Brent is a 38-year-old Alabama-born, Florida resident who has generally been high in the money list in recent years – 44th (1997). 80th (1996), 37th (1995) and 12th in 1994 after his only win to date in the Sprint International.

In 1998 he had top 25 finishes in the Bob Hope Classic (T24th), the Bay Hill Invitational (T22nd), the Memorial (T23rd) and the CVS Charity Classic (T19th).

He had top 10s in the Tucson Chrysler Classic (T4th), the Freeport McDermott Classic (T3rd including 66 when first out in R2), the Buick Classic (9th) and the Texas Open (T4th after 64 in R4).

T44th in USPGA.

Can be aggressive and, on his own admission, complacent.

Steve will reach the dodgy age of 39 in October 1999.

Long off the tee at 276 yards, he sets up a lot of eagle chances on the par 5s. His putting has been inconsistent and below average this year, and his sand save stats are also poor. He still requires his iron play to compensate for his inaccuracy off the tee. 70th on the M/L.

➤ He'll be worth an interest in July in two tournaments – the Motorola Western Classic (3rd 1997: 6th 1995) and the Deposit Guaranty Classic (T4th 1997).

➤ Last year I nominated him for the Freeport McDermott Classic for which he was T3rd at 80/1. This year the tournament is renamed the Entergy Classic, and with three successive top 7 finishes he'll be worth another each-way bet.

➤ A real streak player well able to shoot low rounds, especially final rounds, when off the pace (60 in R4 1997 Buick Challenge: 64 in R4 1998 Texas Open).

SANDY LYLE **Pb**

Alexander Walter Barr Lyle, Sandy to the golf world, is now safely past 40, and has spent 1998 trying to retain his tour card now that his 10-year exemption for winning the 1988 US Masters has ended.

He has four other US wins, the last in 1988: and twenty others worldwide, the last in 1992.

In 1998 he had high finishes in the Tucson Chrysler Classic (T14th), the Kemper Open (T25th), the Canadian Open (T7th) and the BC Open (T25th) as he made a bid to retain his card.

Finished T20th in the German Open.

Missed the cut in the US Masters: fine T19th in the British Open.

At 146th on the M/L Sandy's off to the Q. School. May return to play in Europe.

➤ His brilliant 75 in R3 of the 1998 British Open in rain and wind was a reminder that he's one of the best players around when he puts on his waterproofs – so let's remember that in 3-ball betting next time the weather's poor for Sandy.

➤ Clearly his game is suited to the Kemper Open. He was 5 under par with two to play this year and with one more birdie would have finished T3rd.....before he hit a quintuple bogey 8 at the 17th in R4. He also shot a 69 in R1 there in 1997. So in the early 3-ball betting remember Sandy for the Kemper in late May.

➤ His two highest US finishes in recent years have been in the heat of the desert – in the Phoenix Open (10th 1996), and the Tucson Chrysler Classic (T14th 1998). So if Sandy, is to post a really big finish in 1999 it will probably be in one of those desert tournaments, or in the Kemper.

ANDREW MAGEE   g F S

36-year-old Magee lives in Arizona. He's retained his card every year since joining the tour in 1985. His best year by some distance was 1991 when he won twice to finish 5th on the M/L.

He has four wins in all, the last in 1994.

In 1997 he finished 30th on the M/L after seven top 10s including second places in the BC Open (T2nd), and the Greater Vancouver Open.

In 1998 he had top 5 finishes in the Bob Hope Classic (3rd at 50/1 after being joint leader going into R5), the Memorial (2nd), the Buick Open (3rd after 64 in R4) and the Texas Open (T4th at 28/1).

He also had high finishes in the Tucson Chrysler Classic (T6th), the Honda Classic (T22nd), the Bay Hill Invitational (T10th), the Sprint (T15th – 31 points), the Canadian Open (T13th) and the Las Vegas (T22nd).

T31st US Masters: missed cuts in US Open and British Open: T21st USPGA.

Fader of the ball. A long hitter at 275 yards. For the second successive year by finishing 30th on the M/L he got the last place in the Tour Championship where he was T21st.

30th on M/L.

➤ With seven punter-friendly top 5 finishes in the last two seasons Magee is clearly a player to note, and one who could well land win Number. 5 in 1999.

➤ With two of his four wins in 'desert' tournaments and living in Arizona he simply must be supported in the Tucson Chrysler Classic (T6th 1998: T10th 1997).

➤ His points tally in the Sprint Invitational is going up each year 22 – 27 – 31 and he'll be worth a bet in late August in the sort of tournament you could see him winning at 80/1, just as Steve Lowery did in 1994.

➤ The Canadian Open (three successive top 20s) suits his 'fade'. With the 'big names' missing he could well win this event in 1999.

➤ 5/1 (from 6/1) to make his Ryder Cup debut in 1999.

JEFF MAGGERT

34-year-old Jeff joined the tour after topping the 1990 Nike tour M/L in a season when he won twice, was 2nd three times and made the cut in 91% of his tournaments. In 1991, his rookie year, he was 68th on the M/L.

Since then he has always been in the top 40 with his best year 1994 when he finished 9th.

From 1994 – 1997 he averaged eleven top 10s a year yet could not win. Indeed he has only one victory, in the 1993 Walt Disney Classic.

In 1998 he was T4th in the Honda Classic, T2nd in the Bay Hill Invitational, 2nd in the Shell Houston Open, T5th in the Buick Classic and T5th in the Greater Vancouver Open.

He was also T16th in the Greater Greensboro Open: T18th in the Colonial: T8th Texas Open: T8th in the Buick Challenge.

T23rd US Masters: T7th in US Open: missed British Open cut: T44th USPGA. 16th in Tour Championship.

Played in the 1994 Presidents Cup, and 1995 and 1997 Ryder Cups.

Although short off the tee at 265 yards his great strength is his driving accuracy. In 1998 he's much lower for greens in regulation than for driving accuracy, suggesting that his iron play has sometimes let him down. Sand saves much improved this year (T168th 1997).

27th on M/L.

➤ If you want a moment of his time never say 'Just a second' – he's now got some frightening near-miss statistics. He's been 2nd twelve times, has led into R4 eight times yet has won once!

➤ "....there's still a kind of a big empty hole there that I'm trying to fill." He sure ain't filled it as in the last five seasons he's not won yet he's had ten 2nds and four 3rds! Whatever else he is, on the stats he's clearly not a winner. So he retains the 'bottle'.

➤ He's now taken a lead into R4 of the Shell Houston Open four times; indeed he's been 2nd three times in the past five years (1998, 1996 and 1994). It's the tournament on his own Woodlands course. Last year I suggested "he'll go close there again," and he did. Can be supported in match bets and on the spreads as he'll be thereabouts again in 1999.

➤ His game is ideal for the Buick Classic with his form figures now 5th – 2nd – 2nd – 8th. He can be supported with confidence in that tournament in the last week of June.

➤ Can be profitably opposed in 3-ball betting if he's the halfway leader. He shot 76 in R3 in the 1998 Honda Classic when leader at halfway.

➤ If he is to win again it will probably be when leading in a weather-reduced tournament, or by coming from 'off the pace'.

➤ Worth noting in the relaxed close-season tournaments. He won the Diners Club tournament, at 6/1, with Steve Elkington in December 1997.

➤ 5/2 to retain his Ryder Cup place. Let's remember he beat Lee Westwood in the singles at Valderrama.

➤ His recent US Open record (T7th: 4th: T97th (!): T4th: T9th) shows four top 10s in five years so he can be followed on the spreads, in match betting, in early round 3-ball betting and as a big-priced outsider.

JOHN MAGINNES

30-year-old John lives in North Carolina although born in Georgia. He hit a purple patch of form from mid June on the Nike tour during which he had form figures of T4th – T14th – T3rd – T28th – Won – T3rd and T14th in successive weeks. It proved again what a positive effect becoming 30 can have on a player.

On the main tour he was T5th in the Deposit Guaranty Classic, T15th in the Greater Vancouver Open, T25th in the Texas Open, T18th in the Greater Milwaukee Open (74 in R4), T16th in the Greater Greensboro Open and T25th in the Michelob from only eight starts. 153rd on the M/L. He'll earn his 1998 tour card via his Nike tour successes. Twice a winner on the Nike tour.

Short off the tee. Best-ever finish when T2nd, after losing in a play off, in the rain-reduced 1996 Buick Challenge.

➤ Living in North Carolina it is no coincidence that in 1998 he played well in his home state in the Greater Greensboro Open (T16th) and on the Nike tour Greensboro Open (T3rd after 65 in R4). So in 1999 in late April keep him in mind in the early 3-ball betting for the Greater Greensboro Open.

➤ In both the Greater Milwaukee Open (74 in R4), and the Texas Open (R1 + 2 10 under: R3 + 4 level) he showed nerves when in contention.

➤ His short, accurate game is best suited to the Greater Milwaukee Open (T18th 1998: T12th 1996).

➤ The Deposit Guaranty Classic is always weakly contested, and he'll have a real chance there in 1999 after his T5th finish this year.

DOUG MARTIN   D

32-year-old Doug had his best season in 1997 when 64th on the Money list after top 10s in the Honda Classic (T5th), the MCI Heritage Classic (T9th) and the Buick Challenge (T6th).

In 1998 he had top 25 finishes in the Buick Invitational (T16th), the Tucson Chrysler Classic (T22nd), the Bay Hill Invitational (T17th), the Colonial (T18th) and the Buick Open (T23rd) before he made his first top 10 of the season in the National Car Rental at Disney (T7th after 72 in R4).

Missed the cut in the US Open

Former US Walker Cup player. Born in Ohio, he lives in Kentucky. 102nd on the M/L from 33 (!) starts.

➤ Very short off the tee at 257 yards, he's at a massive disadvantage on the par 5s. However his driving accuracy is his strength so he's at his best on shorter courses with less than four par 5s.

➤ He has yet to win, and with only one top 3 finish since 1995 he's not a player to follow in the outright markets. Given his lack of length it's difficult seeing him winning.

LEN MATTIACE

31-year-old Len now lives in Florida. In 1997 he had four top 20s on the way to finishing 77th on the M/L.

In 1998 he had three top 10s, in the Doral Ryder Open (T9th), the Players Championship (T5th after a quintuple bogey (!) on the penultimate hole in R4), and the Canon Greater Hartford Open (T9th including his second hole in one on the tour).

He also had high finishes in the Freeport McDermott Classic (T19th), and the MCI Classic (T18th).

Was the joint leader at halfway in the Memorial before he shot 73-76 to finish T31st.

Missed the USPGA cut.

Mootees (that is how you say his surname) is a fine putter and very good bunker player. However inaccuracy off the tee is his big problem. Very short driver at 263 yards.

Number 1 Junior in America in 1985 and a member of the 1987 Walker Cup team. 68th on the M/L.

➤ With his inaccuracy off the tee and his good short game he is well suited to the wide fairways of the Walt Disney Classic in his home state (T3rd 1997).

➤ Must earn the bottle for his 8 at the par three 17th in R4 of this year's Players Championship, and for his final-36-hole collapse in the Memorial.

➤ Could 'pop up' in the frame at big odds on the wide fairways of the Bob Hope Classic (T17th 1997) next year.

BILLY MAYFAIR   G

32-year-old Billy was born in Phoenix and now lives in Scottsdale Arizona.

He came into 1998 with three wins, two of which were in his best-ever year of 1995 when he was 2nd on the M/L.

In 1998 he won twice. He won the Nissan Open at 100/1 on 1st March, and the Buick Open at 125/1 in August.

When he's 'hot' he keeps his form well. After his first 1998 win he was 2nd at 66/1 the following week in the Doral Ryder Open. In August in the week after his second win of the year he played very well to finish T7th in the USPGA, (T4th at 50/1 in top US player betting).

He was T22nd in the Tucson Chrysler Classic, 20th in the World Series, T21st in the Sprint, T6th in the Michelob and T13th in Tour Championship.

Missed US Masters cut: T52nd British Open. Not long at 270 yards. However he's usually fairly accurate off the tee. Number 1 for sand saves in 1995, he was poor in bunkers in 1997 but excellent again this year. Has a very quirky putting stroke which somehow works. 16th on M/L.

➤ Make no mistake....this guy may be inconsistent but when in contention he sure knows how to win. He has posted four wins and six 2nds in the last four seasons and they have all been at big prices.

➤ Can suddenly find his form after missing cuts.

➤ Mayfair must be followed when he does hit form as he's well capable of playing top-quality golf in successive tournaments.

➤ Living in the desert he could provide a surprise in the 1999 Tucson Chrysler Classic or the Phoenix Open.

BLAINE McCALLISTER   D

40-year-old Blaine is based in Florida. He has five tour wins including two this decade, the 1991 Texas Open and the 1993 BC Open. His best year was 1989 when 15th on the M/L. He has struggled over the last three years.

In 1998 he had just two top 20 finishes, in the Bob Hope Classic (T19th), and the Kemper Open (T11th). However 66 in R4 of the National Car Rental at Disney saw him finish 125th on the M/L to keep his card.

➤ He's had just one top 4 finish in the last four years so he's not one for the outright markets.

➤ High in greens in regulation, his stats for putting and sand saves are poor. However if the 1999 stats show an improvement in his short game he could well spring a surprise and post a high finish at huge odds, possibly in the Deposit Guaranty Classic (T4th 1997).

SCOTT McCARRON   D

This 33-year-old Californian based player joined the tour in 1995 and secured his tour card after finishing 3rd in the Las Vegas Invitational.

In his second season, 1996, he won the Freeport McDermott Classic, finishing the year 49th on the M/L, and in 1997 he won again when landing the Bell South Classic which in a season of seven top 10s saw him finish 25th on the M/L.

In 1998 he has had high finishes in the Mercedes Championship (12th), the Phoenix Open (T8th), the Byron Nelson Classic (T6th), the Colonial (T18th), the Quad City Classic (T5th) and the Buick Open (T15th).

At 25/1 won the Shark Shoot-Out in the close season in late 1997 with Bruce Lietzke.

T16th US Masters: T40th US Open: missed cut USPGA.

A huge hitter at 290 yards. He has plenty of eagle chances on the par 5s. However his driving accuracy and greens in regulation stats show that he has often been wayward. 69th on the M/L.

➤ Must be noted and backed for the Phoenix Open (T8th 1998: T7th 1997) on a course suited to his game.

➤ In three starts he's been T10th 1996: T30th 1997: T16th 1998 in the US Masters. It's a course which suits long-hitting players with its four par 5s and wide fairways. So remember Scott for match bets at Augusta.

➤ Will have PMAs with the Entergy Classic having secured his first tour win on the English Turn course in 1996.

➤ You would expect his game to be well suited to the Bob Hope Classic (T20th 1997) in his home state, so if you have a spare BOB, or two, put them on Scott and let's HOPE McCarron will oblige.

SPIKE McROY

30-year-old guy from Alabama makes his debut in this book. Winner on the Nike tour.

5th at 1997 Q School to earn his tour card.

He was 6th in the rain-reduced Buick Invitational to post his highest-ever finish. Had high finishes in the Bell South Classic (T19th) and the AT&T (T13th after 67 in R3).

When in contention in the Canadian Open shot 75 in R4 to fall off the leaderboard.

Reasonably accurate off the tee, although at 260 yards he is very short. Has had putting problems this year, although he was 2nd in the 1997 World Putting Championship. 145th on M/L.

➤ Very difficult to make a case for him in any tournament. However his first top 20 on the tour came in the 1997 Deposit Guaranty Classic (T19th) so he can be expected to play well there next year.

ROCCO MEDIATE   CT

Rocco Anthony is now 36 and based in Florida. He has two tour wins, the last the 1993 Greater Greensboro Open.

Since his major back surgery in 1994 he's struggled to recapture his best form.

In 1997 he was 101st on the M/L with just two top 10s, in the Buick Open (T8th) and the Greater Greensboro Open (T9th).

In 1998 he had top 25 finishes in the Tucson Chrysler Classic (T22nd after 73 in R4), the Doral Ryder Open (T23rd after 76 in R4), the Colonial (T18th after 74 in R4), the St Jude Classic (T20th) and the Las Vegas (T20th).

Best finishes came in the Sprint Invitational (5th with 37 points) and the National Car Rental at Disney (T4th).

Missed the cut in the USPGA.

Reverted to the shorter putter for the Players Championship where he shot 67 in R1, eventually finished T57th.

He led the tour for consecutive cuts made (17) after Singh missed the US Masters cut.

Short at 270 yards. He's found the greens well this year but his putter is still 'cold'. 78th on M/L.

➤ After his T4th in 'the Disney' he said he may finally be over his 1994 back surgery. "I'm enjoying golf now more than ever before." So in 1999 a fully fit Rocco will be a player to watch on the comeback trail.

➤ Worth following as a 100/1 outsider, and in the early 3-ball betting for the Players Championship at Sawgrass (five top 15s including two top 6 places and a 67 in R1 in 1998). Fully fit in 1999 he could represent exceptional 'value'.

PHIL MICKELSON   G ♨ Y M F

Phil is still in his twenties, he was 28 in June, yet he's now won thirteen tournaments on the American tour. Indeed his first tour success was as a 20-year-old amateur in the desert tournament, the Northern Telecom in 1991.

He joined the tour in 1992. Playing only ten events he finished 90th on the M/L. Since then he's been 22nd (1993), 15th (1994) and 28th (1995). In 1996 he won four times, in the Nortel Open, the Phoenix Open, the Byron Nelson Classic and the NEC World Series, to finish 2nd on the M/L. In 1997 he won twice, in the Bay Hill Invitational (his first win east of the Mississippi) and the Sprint to end the year 11th on the M/L. In 1998 he won the season-opening Mercedes Championship at 14/1. He had high finishes in the Players Championship (T8th), the MCI Classic (T3rd at 20/1), the Greater Greensboro Open (T6th), and the Byron Nelson Classic (T6th).

Then in six days in August he won over $626,000. A final round 67 in the rain-delayed AT&T tournament took him to victory on the Monday, and then he was T2nd at 18/1 as the defending champion in the Sprint International. His

AT&T win also brought him a west-coast bonus. Went on to finish 2nd in the World Series of Golf at 12/1.

Finished T12th in the US Masters: T10th in the US Open (Number 1 on the putting stats): T34th in USPGA: 79th (of 81) in the British Open. 17th in the Tour Championship.

Mickelson's greatest strength is his short game. He has a superb ability to invent shots with his 'vertical take-off' parachute lob from close to the green a trademark.

However his long game is underestimated. He has huge length, is a really pure ball striker although he can be wayward off the tee. Very competitive. He has a superb putting stroke.

He'll be 29 on 16th June 1999. 6th on M/L.

➤ Let's be quite clear....this guy's win to tournament ratio is simply first class, and the best on the tour. Since 1992 in 140 tournaments (up to the 1998 Tour Championship) he has now won thirteen i.e. 9.28% which translated into betting terms is about 19-2 against.

In non-majors the ratio is 13 wins from 120 (10.83% or odds of a little less than 17-2).

Put simply on the stats of his career to date Mickelson is 'value' in any non-major if he's available at 9/1+!!

➤ He has now won in every year from 1993 onwards, and in the last three years he's won eight tournaments in 64 starts (up to the 1998 Tour Championship).

➤ Usually a player with Mickelson's win record has more 2nd and 3rd places than wins. Yet Phil is different – if you combine his 2nd and 3rd places together (10) he has less than his number of wins (13). The motto is clear – when backing Mickelson back him to win!

➤ He can be followed in tournaments that clearly suit his game.

*The Sprint International. He loves desert tournaments and has kept good records here to help him with club selection. Winner in 1997, 2nd in 1998 – he averages 36.6 points over the last three years.

*The Byron Nelson Classic (T6th 1998: T12th 1997: Won 1996).

*The World Series of Golf (2nd 1998: 2nd 1997: Won 1996: 4th 1995) becomes one of the 'new' tournaments on the World Tour in 1999, and Phil will probably be its first winner.

*This year as defending champion he played poorly in the Phoenix Open. Expect him to resume normal service there in late January as he loves desert tournaments.

➤ He is clearly now, with Montgomerie, the world's best player yet to win a major. His big chance will come in the US Masters. His game is ideally suited to Augusta and undoubtedly he will win there one day....it could be that like Davis Love III he needs the pressure lifting from him 'by the nappy factor'. Perhaps Daddy Phil in his thirties will land both the USPGA and the US Masters.

➤ Tends to hit the ball too high to be really effective in links golf. May come to Britain earlier in future to improve his preparation for the British Open.

➤ He is so competitive that when really out of contention in the final round of a tournament he loses concentration, and can then be safely opposed, for example he had final rounds of 75 in the Phoenix Open and 78 in the British

Open. Therefore when he is way down the field he'll be worth opposing in 2-ball betting.
➤ He is a certainty (no offers) to make the US Ryder Cup team for the third successive time.

LARRY MIZE

Larry has now blown out his 40th birthday candles. He has four American tour victories, and another four worldwide. His great triumph came when he famously chipped in to beat Greg Norman to land the US Masters in 1987.

He slipped down the money list in recent years from 13th in 1993 (after two wins) he's been 42nd, 67th, 67th and 99th in 1997.

In 1998 he had high finishes in the Hawaiian Open (T11th), the Honda Classic (T15th after 66 in R4), the MCI Classic (T10th), the Kemper Open (T14th) and the Buick Challenge (T14th).

His big chance came in the Canon Greater Hartford Open. He finished T2nd losing to Olin Browne (who chipped in) on the first play-off hole.

T52nd in the British Open: missed cut in US Masters.

A very good putter his great strength is his superb driving accuracy. He may not hit it far (265 yards), but he sure does hit it straight. 62nd on the M/L.
➤ Showed in this year's Canon Greater Hartford Open that he could still post win Number. 5.
➤ He can be expected to play well in the Kemper Open after posting three top 15 finishes in the last four years so remember him there, especially in match bets.
➤ Although he missed the cut this year his Augusta record in the US Masters is very good with eight top 30 finishes in his last ten starts. So he can be noted there again in suitable match bets.

FRANK NOBILO   🎂CT G M D

38-year-old Frank is a New Zealand born Florida resident who has ten international wins and one, the 1997 Greater Greensboro Classic, on the US tour.

23rd on the 1997 M/L was his best year in the States.

In 1997 he had high finishes in the Mercedes Championship (T10th), the Phoenix Open (T14th), the Greater Greensboro Open (5th) and the Memorial (T16th).

Missed the cut in the US Masters, the British Open and the USPGA. T40th in the US Open.

Was T3rd in the Australian Masters.

Won two of his three matches for New Zealand in October in the Dunhill Cup.

Fired his caddie during the season. Badly injured by a stray golf ball on a range in August. He needed 30 facial stiches.

Nobilo has a fine swing and is a very good mid-to-long iron player with a solid record, especially on tough courses. Remarried in July with Ernie Els as a witness. He'll be 39 in May 1999. 108th on the M/L.

➤ After a very disappointing year Nobilo will be a player to note in 1999. After all in each of the previous five years he'd won at least once in USA, Europe or in the Far East so he'll be on the 'comeback trail' next season.

➤ He must have solid prospects in the Memorial (T16th 1998: 7th 1997) where he's been 16 under par for his last six rounds.

➤ As a quality player in his thirties who has still to win a major he fits perfectly the identikit of a future winner of the USPGA. He could be a tasty price, too in 1999.

GREG NORMAN   CT 🐎 F g

43-year-old Greg started the 1998 season with eighteen US tour wins, and 55 (!) others worldwide. Yet he'd only won one major, the British Open (1993 and 1986) twice.

In 1997 'The Great White Shark' was 7th on the M/L after winning twice, the St Jude Classic and the NEC World Series of Golf. He was also 2nd in the Canadian Open, T2nd in the Memorial, T3rd in the Kemper Open and T5th in the Bell South Classic.

In 1998 as always he played poorly in the season-opening Mercedes Championship to finish T27th.

He won his own, Greg Norman Holden Classic in Australia after shooting 67 in R4.

Came 6th in the Dubai Desert Classic on the European tour. In America he missed the cut in the Doral Ryder Open and the US Masters before he withdrew from the Players' Championship with a shoulder injury. It required an operation in Colorado and kept him out for the rest of the season.

A superb player, true sportsman and brilliant ambassador for the game of golf.

➤ Has a golf-led business empire with offices in New York, Florida and Sydney generating income of over $1 million per day.

He'll be 44 in February 1999 and the big question must be whether his emphasis on business has really taken away his appetite for competitive golf at the highest level.

➤ If he's clearly at or near his best come early June then he'd have a first-class chance in the Memorial in which his record is superb – 2nd 1997: Won 1995: 2nd 1994: T4th 1993: Won 1990!

DAVID OGRIN

41-year-old Texan resident Ogrin finished 34th (1996), and 36th (1997) on the M/L, his highest finishes since he joined the tour in 1983.

His only win to date was in the 1996 Texas Open.

In 1997 he had high finishes in the Tucson Chrysler Classic (T22nd), the Deposit Guaranty Classic (T21st), the St Jude Classic (T20th), the Buick Open (T15th) and the Greater Milwaukee Open (T14th). Joint leader after R2 of the Las Vegas before finishing T36th!

So he's had a disappointing year without a single top 10 finish.

Missed US Open cut.

Short off the tee at 267 yards. Over the last two years he's been very low in the greens in regulation stats. His bunker play and putting have been solid in 1998. A fader of the ball.

130th on the M/L.

➤ His exemption for his 1996 win has now expired so he knows he must improve to retain his card in 1999.

➤ If his accuracy off the tee can get back to its usual high standard he could well go close in 1999, and possibly even notch his second win.

➤ Must have a leading chance in the Deposit Guaranty Classic (T21st 1998: 13th 1997: T5th 1996) in July when the 'big boys' are in the US Open.

➤ As a Texan he can be noted in the Shell Houston Open (T8th 1997) in match bets.

MARK O'MEARA   G 🐎

What a year it's been for the 41-year-old from Florida where he's Tiger Woods's neighbour and best friend. Coming into 1998 Mark had won fourteen US tournaments and six internationally. However he'd been a major underachiever in the majors with just three top 10s this decade. 1998 was to change all that.

At Augusta he won the US Masters at 66/1 after a birdie – birdie finish, and in a play-off against Brian Watts he landed the British Open at 40/1 on one of his favourite courses, at Royal Birkdale.

His superb patience, steely determination and brilliant course management had combined with his accurate iron play and brilliant putting to give him two majors within four months....and it couldn't have happened to a nicer guy...."this won't change him," said his wife....and it hasn't.

He had other high finishes when T2nd in the Mercedes Championship, T6th in the Bob Hope Classic, T22nd in the Honda Classic, T24th in the MCI Classic, T15th in the Byron Nelson Classic, T3rd in the Kemper Open and T7th in the World Series of Golf.

In Europe he was 3rd in the Deutsche Bank Open, T2nd in the Lancome Trophy as defending champion, and, representing America, he won three of his four matches in the Alfred Dunhill Cup.

He played superbly to win the World Match Play in October, beating Tiger Woods by 1 hole in the final to crown a great year.

In Australia he was 6th in the Australian Masters.

He was T32nd in the US Open; T4th in the USPGA. T13th in the Tour Championship.

A brilliant mid-iron player and rock-solid putter. Accurate off the tee (generally) and an excellent strategist who plays the percentages. 7th on M/L.

➤ Last year I suggested his big chance in a major would come in the year 2000 in the US Open on his favourite Pebble Beach course, (where he's had five (!) wins), for which I suggested 50/1 was a good price. Well he won't be more than half those odds next year now!

➤ If it's not wrecked by El Nino the AT&T at the start of February will give O'Meara a chance to make his Mark early in the year. "I play it like a chess game." So make your move to the bookies early on 4th February to have a little on 'The Prince of Pebble'.

➤ He has a fine record in the Bob Hope Classic in California (where he's had seven wins). He's had four top 6 finishes in the last eight years including three top 4s.

➤ His accuracy is tailor made for the Kemper Open where he's had three top 4 finishes in the last four years, and where he can be expected to do well again in 1999.

➤ 'No offers' to play for America in his fifth Ryder Cup in 1999.

NAOMICHI (JOE) OZAKI

42-year-old Japanese player is the younger brother of Masashi (you can call him, Jumbo) Ozaki.

Finished 1997 115th on the M/L after posting his first top 4 finish when T2nd in the Buick Open.

In 1998 he had four high finishes in the Players Championship (T18th after being joint leader at halfway), the Freeport McDermott Classic (T12th: R1 + 2 8 under then R3 + 4 3 over), the Kemper Open (T25th), the Buick Classic (T12th) and the Western Open (T9th after 73 in R4).

T35th in the British Open.

Very short driver at 267 yards. 121st on the M/L.

➤ He has only one top 4 finish so he can be safely ignored in the outright betting.

➤ Japanese Joe can be safely opposed in final-round 2-ball betting when he's in contention, and in R3 3-ball betting when he's in the top 4 at the halfway stage of any tournament. His record merits the award of the bottle.

➤ Can be followed in R1 & R2 3-ball betting in Florida tournaments such as the Doral Ryder Open (1996 halfway leader), and the Players Championship (1997 halfway leader).

CRAIG PARRY

Nicknamed 'Popeye' because of his muscular appearance Parry is just 5' 6" in his socks. He's a 32-year-old Aussie with an American base in Orlando, Florida.

He's won fourteen tournaments worldwide although he's still to notch his first American win.

From 1992 to 1997 he's been placed between 43rd and 65th on the M/L with seven top 3 finishes including four 2nd places, in the 1994 Honda Classic, the 1995 Colonial, the 1996 Byron Nelson and the 1996 Buick Classic.

In 1997 he posted three punter-friendly top 5 finishes, in the Honda Classic (T5th), the St Jude Classic (T3rd), and the Texas Open (5th).

In the close season he was T2nd at 33/1 in the Dunlop Phoenix in Japan after a six-week break. Won the Schweppes Coolum Classic at 10/1 in December.

In America in 1998 he was T6th in the Bay Hill Invitational (3rd at 25/1 in the top non-US betting), T14th in the Bell South Classic, T10th in the Colonial (with four sub-par rounds), T8th in the Kemper Open (76 in R3 when T2nd after R2) and T9th in the World Series (22/1 winner in top non-US betting).

Missed the cut in the British Open: T71st USPGA.

Won three of his four matches for Australia in the Dunhill Cup at St Andrews.

T2nd at 11/1 (75 in R4) in the first event on the 1998-99 Australasian tour, the Ford Championship.

Poor showing this year in greens in regulation. High in sand save stats, his putting has improved in 1998. Only 269 yards off the tee. Moves the ball left to right. 98th on the M/L from 16 starts.

➤ His best chance of recording his first American win will surely be when he comes from 'off the pace' as he has shown major R4 jitters, notably in the 1990 British Open and the 1992 US Masters.

➤ His record recently in the Kemper Open (T8th 1998: T7th 1994: T7th 1993) suggests that he can be followed in early-round 3-ball betting, and 'in running' if a little 'off the pace' after R3.

➤ Worth noting in the Colonial (T10th 1998: 2nd 1995) especially in 3-ball and suitable match bets.

➤ He will be worthy of support in February in the Australian Masters at the Huntingdale course (won 1996: Won 1994) which he knows so well.

➤ Clearly goes well fresh as he showed when playing really well in the 1997-98 close season.

➤ If he represents Australia once more in the Dunhill Cup remember his St Andrews record is Pl 11 W 9, so he can be followed in 2-ball betting. His stocky, low centre of gravity style is ideal for the windy conditions there.

STEVE PATE

Steve is a 37-year-old nicknamed 'The Volcano' in his early days because of his volatile nature.

His best year was 1991 when he won the Honda Classic on the way to finishing 6th in the M/L.

Played poorly in 1995, and in 1996 he played only three times after a major road accident in January (right hand and wrist broken) and a fall in August (left wrist injured).

In 1997 he was 95th on the M/L with top 10s in the Western Open (T7th), the Canon Greater Hartford Open (T9th), the Buick Challenge (T9th) and the Colonial (T10th).

In 1998 he played well to finish T2nd in the Phoenix Open, T6th in the Buick Invitational, T9th in the Tucson Chrysler Classic, T15th in the Honda Classic before he won his sixth tournament when he was the 125/1 winner of the CVS Charity Classic in after 67 in R4. It was his first win since 1992. Later was T14th in the World Series, T25th in the BC Open, T17th in the Michelob and T12th in the Las Vegas.

T32nd US Open (T2nd on putting stats). Missed USPGA cut.

Not long off the tee at 272 yards. A low ball hitter, he's good in windy conditions. 34th on the M/L.

➤ Californian born and bred he must be noted for the Buick Invitational at Torrey Pines. He was the leader going into the final round this year, and of course he won it in 1992.

➤ He has a useful record in Hawaii in the Kapalua International including rounds of 63 (1998) and 64 (1995). So with the season-opening Mercedes Championship held there in 1999 he'd be a player to note in match bets and as an outsider at a massive price.

COREY PAVIN
g CT

Corey is now at that dodgy age of 39. His glittering career includes fourteen US tour wins, ten internationally, and appearances in the Presidents Cup twice and the Ryder Cup three times. His memorable victory was in the 1995 US Open.

From 1991, when he was at the top of the money list, he was always in the top 20 until 1997 when he slumped to 169th.

In 1998 there have been some signs of a real recovery. He was T25th in the Byron Nelson Classic, 10th in the Texas Open and T10th in the Michelob Championship.

He missed the cut in all four majors for the first time.

At his best 'Crazy' is a magical shot maker with a superb capacity to invent and execute shots. He compensated for his lack of length off the tee with a magnificent short game. His steely competitive edge made him a formidable Ryder Cup player. 155th on the M/L.

➤ His best chance probably lies in May in the Colonial on a course which requires accuracy and shot making rather than length, and where he's won twice (1985 and 1996) and been second twice (1992 and 1990). If he's clearly on his way back by then Pavin would be a shrewd wager in match betting or as a big-priced outsider.

➤ In September and October in the Texas Open (10th) and the Michelob (T10th) there were real signs of a comeback. In 1999 Corey could well become the comeback kid posting a win at big odds.

➤ Must be noted for the Texas Open (19th 1998: 11th 1996) in which he's shot ten consecutive rounds at or under par.

➤ 14/1 (from 16/1) to play in the 1999 US Ryder Cup team....and how the Americans missed him at Valderrama.

CHRIS PERRY
g

Chris, born in North Carolina, lives in Ohio. Topped the Nike M/L as that tour's player of the year in 1994. However he has struggled on the main tour. In 1996 he was 112th on the M/L, before in 1997 he had his best-ever year when 48th after finishing T2nd in the BC Open and T5th in the Byron Nelson Classic.

In 1998 however he played consistently well with high finishes in the Bob Hope Classic (T16th), the Memorial (T16th), the Kemper Open (T25th after 65 in R1), the Buick Classic (T10th), the Western Open (T22nd), the CVS Charity Classic (T25th), the Buick Open (T23rd) and the Sprint (19th).

However September was to be his month because after finishing T3rd at 80/1 (62 in R2) in the Greater Milwaukee Open, he won the BC Open at 25/1 (after 67 in R4) in his 378th tournament!

Later was T8th in the Buick Challenge.

270 yards off the tee, he is a consistent player. He's had a poor year from sand. 39th on the M/L.

➤ A most consistent player who must be kept on the right side in match bets.

➤ Has usually looked likely to post a high finish rather than a win. However now he's won he could well go on to further success in 1999.

➤ He has a useful record in the Kemper Open including 2nd place in 1987, and after a 65 in R1 this year he said "I feel like I can play this golf course". He'll be worth an interest there in late May.

➤ Living in Ohio the Memorial (T16th 1998) is his local tournament, so remember him there in match and 3-ball betting.

➤ His 1998 win came in a tournament where he'd been placed (T2nd) the previous year. On that basis the 1999 tournament in which to follow him must be the Greater Milwaukee Open (after his T3rd there this year).

➤ Sure to go close in the John Deere Classic in July held on the Oakwood course where his record (T3rd 1996 and two top 20s) is solid.

➤ Introduced by Corals at 8/1 to make the 1999 Ryder Cup. He'd have to win at least two big tournaments to have any chance so it would be best to back him at big outright odds rather than that skimpy 8/1.

KENNY PERRY

38-year-old Kenny has been in the top 100 of the M/L every year since he joined the tour in 1987 with his best year in 1996 when 13th on the M/L.

He's had three tour wins, the last the 1995 Bob Hope Chrysler Classic.

However in 1997 he struggled, coming 90th on the M/L with T4th in the Phoenix Open his best finish. In 1998 he showed improved form in the Hawaiian Open (T16th), the MCI Classic (T10th), the Colonial (T6th), the Kemper Open (T14th), the Canon Greater Hartford Open (T9th) and the Quad City Classic (3rd at 20/1).

T10th in the USPGA.

Played in the 1996 Presidents' Cup team. Number 1 on tour in 1996 for R4 scoring average.

Fairly long at 278 yards. He does not show up well for sand saves, or driving accuracy. 58th on the M/L.

➤ "I'm a hot-weather player. Being from Kentucky, it's kind of my climate," so clearly Kentucky Kenny is at his best when the temperature is high.

➤ Can be noted in match bets for the Memorial. He won it in 1991 and has had top 20s in 1995 and 1996.

➤ His USPGA record is solid having made all eight cuts, finished 2nd after a play-off in his home state in 1996, and T10th in 1998. Worth noting for that final major in match betting.

➤ The one tournament I'd nominate him for in 1999 would be the Canon Greater Hartford Open (T9th 1998) on a course that suits him.

➤ If you ever back him for cash or credit always give his christian name and initial very clearly!

TOM PERNICE JR.

39-year-old Tom lives in Minnesota where he was born.

Gained his 1998 tour card via Q School.

He has had high finishes in the Nissan Open (T24th), the Quad City Classic (T13th after an 'off the pace' 63 in R4), the Sprint (17th), the Greater Vancouver Open (T11th) and the Greater Milwaukee Open (T18th after 66 in R4).

Secured his tour card when he shot a 67 in R4 in the rain delayed AT&T to finish 2nd at 250/1. Finished 15th in the Las Vegas, and T19th in the National Car Rental at Disney.

He'll be 40 in September 1999. A long hitter at 280 yards. Yet to win on either the Nike or the USPGA tour. 55th on the M/L.

Came in to play the Hassan Trophy in November at the last minute. Finished a very creditable 2nd after losing to in-form Santiago Luna in a play-off.

➤ There can be no doubt at all that his game is suited to the Greater Milwaukee Open where he posted his best-ever tour finish in 1997 when 4th, and where he had a top 20 this year. His two-year stroke average is exactly 68 with seven of his eight rounds in the sixties. He could well provide a big shock there in 1999, especially if coming from 'off the pace'.

LEE PORTER

32-year-old guy from North Carolina. Has played the Canadian tour, the South American tour, the Asian tour and the Nike tour. Earned his 1998 tour card via 3rd place at Q School.

In 1998 he had high finishes in the Kemper Open (T25th), the St Jude Classic (12th after 66 in R4), the Greater Vancouver Open (3rd after 66 in R4) and the Las Vegas (T16th).

Showed up well early on (67 in R2) in the US Open before slipping to T32nd.

Very short off the tee at 258 yards, his forte is his driving accuracy. 95th on the M/L.

➤ In 1998 he has shown an ability (St Jude Classic and Greater Vancouver Open) to shoot low on Sundays when not in contention.

➤ Having posted his best ever finish in the Greater Vancouver Open this year he'll have PMAs when he returns there next year.

➤ Would love to qualify for the 1999 US Open in his home state. If he does he'll be worth remembering as a 'value' outsider in the R1 + R2 3-ball betting.

NICK PRICE   G 🐎

Nicolas Raymond Liege has a career record as solid as his names. 44-year-old Nick started 1998 with fifteen US tour wins and twenty others worldwide. He has twice won the USPGA major, in 1992 and 1994, and the British Open in 1994.

He hit absolutely stunning form in 1993 and 1994 when he won a total of nine times on the US tour to finish top of the money list in each year.

In 1997 he won the MCI Classic to finish 17th on the M/L.

In December 1997 he won the Sun City Million at 9/1 proving he had fully recovered from the rib injury he'd had since the World Matchplay in October.

In 1998 he started well when T4th in the Mercedes. On the South African tour at 11/4, playing as defending champion, he was the easy winner of the Dimension Data Pro-Am.

On the European tour he was T3rd as defending champion in the South African PGA.

In America he was T8th in the Players Championship, T6th in the MCI Classic, T22nd in the Western Open and T21st in the World Series, playing below his best.

In Europe he was T22nd in the Deutsche Bank Open and T3rd in the Dutch Open.

He won the St Jude Classic at 16/1 in early August. Missed the US Masters cut: 4th in US Open at 66/1 finishing top in the Rest of the World market: T29th in British Open after an 82 in the R3 winds: T4th in the USPGA at 20/1.

Representing Zimbabwe in the Dunhill Cup in October at St Andrews he won all his three matches.

Plumb last of 30 in season-ending Tour Championship. 26th on M/L.

High on the stats for total driving. With Nick it all boils down to his confidence with the putter. When he's putting well he can be followed with confidence.

Started to wear a cap – "very itchy at first".

➤ Last year's advice to oppose him in match bets in the US Masters came off this year when he missed the cut. The advice stands, as although ironically he holds the course record there he's never really comfortable at Augusta.

➤ Nick has already proved, both in America (the 1993 and 1994 Western Opens) and in South Africa (1997 and 1998 Dimension Data Pro-Am) that he can successfully defend a championship. So in June he'll be worth a bet to win the Fedex St Jude Classic again. He's a great record there as he won it in 1993 and 1998, and has also finished 2nd, 3rd, 5th and 6th. "I like the course. The greens have always been a little on the slow side and I think that helps me to be a little more aggressive with my putter."

➤ He has a fine record at Cog Hill, home of the Western Open, where he notched back-to-back wins in 1993 and 1994. In 1999, if he's not drained after being in contention in the previous week's US Open, he'll be worth support.

BRETT QUIGLEY

29-year-old Brett lives on Rhode Island. Earned his 1997 tour card via the Nike tour where he was 5th on the M/L, after winning the Nike Philadelphia Classic.

In 1997 just retained his card when 128th on the M/L with T12th in the Greater Vancouver Open his best finish.

In 1998 he had his best-ever finish when T4th in the Hawaiian Open. Also posted high finishes in the Nissan Open (T24th after 75 in R4), the Memorial (T23rd), the Quad City Classic (T17th after an 'off the pace' 65 in R4) and the BC Open (T9th).

Nephew of former PGA tour player and Senior tour winner Dana Quigley.

He'll be 30 in August 1999. 127th on the M/L.

➤ Has had a poor season putting. However his strength is his accuracy to the greens as he's a fine iron player. Also long at 279 yards. He's just the sort of improving player to make his mark in his thirties.

➤ He made the frame once this year (T4th Hawaiian Open) and could well post another big finish or two in 1999 perhaps in the Nissan Open (5 under after 54 holes this year) in February.

MIKE REID

Michael Daniel is known as 'Radar' because of his accuracy. The 44-year-old from Utah has two tour victories but none this decade.

He's struggled over recent years. In 1997 he had his best year since 1990 by finishing 73rd on the M/L after he was T2nd in the Hawaiian Open.

In 1998 he was T4th in the Hawaiian Open, T18th in the Tucson Chrysler Classic, and after a 62 (!) in R4 finished T4th at 200/1 in the Texas Open.

T49th in the US Open (T2nd for putting).

Usually accurate off the tee. However at 256 yards he's at a huge disadvantage on the par 5s. 123rd on the M/L.

➤ Shown signs of pressure when in contention in R4 in the 1997 Las Vegas Invitational and the 1997 Buick Classic, whereas he came from 'off the pace' (62 in R4) in the 1998 Texas Open to finish T4th.

➤ So if he's to land his first win this decade it will surely be when he's in the lead after a fast start from an early tee time in a rain-reduced event, or when coming from 'off the pace'.

➤ His straight hitting is suited to the Buick Classic (T6th after R3 in 1997) where he can be noted in match bets. His Hawaiian Open record (T4th 1998: T2nd 1997) suggests he'll be an outsider with a real chance in the Sony Open in Hawaii in January.

JOHN RIEGGER

Big John lives where in the state where he was born, Illinois. 35 years old he was 10th at Q School to earn his 1998 tour card.

In 1998 he had a series of top 30 finishes in the Canon Greater Hartford Open (T20th), the Buick Open (T23rd), the Sprint (T29th), the Greater Vancouver Open (T28th), the Fedex St Jude Classic (T26th) and the Texas Open (T20th).

270 yards off the tee. His surname is pronounced ree-ger. 162nd on the M/L.

➤ The question is whether, if he retains his tour card via Q. School, he can turn top 30s into top 10s, and top 10s into a first win. His consistency in the second half of the season is encouraging.

➤ He has PMAs with the Fedex St Jude Classic where he posted his career, best finish in 1993 when T12th, and where he was T26th this year.

LARRY RINKER

41-year-old Larry lives in Florida. His best year was 1985 when 30th on the M/L. This decade he's only once broken into the top 100 on the M/L, in 1992 when he was 95th.

In 1998 he had only four high finishes, in the Phoenix Open (T14th), the CVS Charity Classic (T12th), the St Jude Classic (T20th) and the Sprint (T21st), until he showed real courage to finish T12th in the National Car Rental at Disney (68 in R4) to finish 120th on the M/L and keep his card. His form improved after he became an active member of the newly-formed Tour Players' Association. Perhaps it boosted his confidence.

Very short driver at 258 yards – 40 yards behind Daly. Apart from sand saves he shows up poorly in all the stats.

➤ Very difficult to find a punting possibility although early round 3-ball betting in the Bob Hope Classic is a real possibility after his 63 in R1 in 1997 en route to a T9th finish.

➤ His brother Lee is in the next player profile. Two L Rinkers......a bookies' nightmare!

LEE RINKER

Lee is the 38-year-old younger brother of Larry. He now lives in Ohio.

His best year was in 1997 when 59th on the M/L after finishing 2nd in the Byron Nelson Classic, and T2nd in the BC Open.

In 1998 he had top 25 finishes in the Doral Ryder Open (T15th), the Players Championship (T25th), the Freeport McDermott (T8th), the Buick Classic (T17th) and the BC Open (T25th).

29th in the USPGA. Like his brother he's yet to win. 110th on the M/L.

Usually an accurate, if short, driver his bunker play and putting let him down.

➤ He has a stroke average over the last two years of 69.87 in the BC Open (T25th 1998: T2nd 1997 after 66 in R4) so that may offer him one of his best opportunities in 1999.

LOREN ROBERTS   CT g

43-year-old Roberts is one of the 'name' players on the USPGA tour. From 1994 to 1997 he was in the top 30 of the M/L posting five wins and making the top 10 in 28% of his tournaments. His brilliant, world-class putting earning him the nickname of 'Boss of the Moss'.

In 1998 he's had top 25 finishes in the Bob Hope Classic (T19th), the Nissan Open (T15th), the Kemper Open (T21st), the Western Open (T22nd), the CVS Charity Classic (T7th as defending champion), the World Series (T5th), the Texas Open (T4th at 20/1) and the Michelob (T13th).

Missed the US Masters as he injured himself, breaking a couple of ribs sneezing! T29th in the British Open and T65th in the USPGA. So it's been a disappointing year in which he's had recurrent back problems.

Played in the 1994 Presidents Cup and 1995 Ryder Cup team.

He makes up for his lack of length off the tee with first-rate course management, brilliant wedge play and first-rate putting. 60th on the M/L.

➤ 1998 has therefore been his first winless year since 1993 so he'll be doubly determined to find the winners enclosure in Ryder Cup year for which he's given a 3/1 (from 4/1) quote by Corals to make the US team. However his niggling back problems may prevent him from lining up at Brookline.

➤ In 1999 Roberts can be followed in three tournaments if he's free from any back problems:-

* "I feel comfortable here. The course fits my game. I like the surroundings and I can visualise well." Roberts thoughts on the Greater Milwaukee Open are backed up by his record (62 in R1 in 1998: T2nd 1997: W 1995: 2nd 1994).

* "I can visualise the shots off the tee." So it's not surprising to find that in the Bay Hill Invitational (T6th 1997: Won 1995: Won 1994) his record is first class.

*No quotes here for the Texas Open just a solid record on the LaCantera course where he can plot his way round. 4th 1998: 14th 1997: 3rd 1995 he has a course stroke average of 69.42.

CLARENCE ROSE

41-year-old Rose left professional golf from 1992 to 1995 playing just 18 times because his son Clark had cancer. With his son's recovery he rejoined the tour in 1996, and yes, you've guessed it, he won. His shock victory came in the Sprint International when the Rose really bloomed. He ended that year 41st on the M/L.

In 1997 he retained his card when 97th on the M/L with high finishes in the Tucson Classic (T5th), the Greater Milwaukee Open (T5th) and the Buick Classic (T6th).

In 1998 the guy from North Carolina had just four top 25s, in the Shell Houston Open (T22nd), the Bell South Classic (T12th), the Buick Open (T23rd) and the BC Open (T16th). Missed the cut in the US Open.

However without a top 10 its been a poor year, and his exemption for winning in 1996 has now expired.

Accurate off the tee and fairway his short game usually lets him down. 142nd on the M/L.

➤ Was the 80/1 shock winner in late 1997 of the JC Penney Classic, with Amy Fruhwith. So he must be noted in the relaxed end of season events.

➤ Born and raised in North Carolina where he still lives, he would love to do well in his home state tournament, the Greater Greensboro Open in which he was 2nd back in 1987.

SCOTT SIMPSON

In 1997 43-year-old Scott fell out of the top 125 on the M/L for the first time since joining the tour in 1978. So he used his top 50 career money exemption to retain his tour card.

In 1998 he won the Buick Invitational, in a play-off, at 150/1 in February.

His only other high finish came when he was T25th in the Kemper Open.

Missed the cut in the US Masters: T58th in the US Open: missed cut in the USPGA.

He now has seven US tour wins and four others worldwide. He won the 1987 US Open.

At his best he's a straight hitter who knows how to win. 64th on M/L from 19 starts.

➤ Last year's profile pointed to the Buick Invitational, held in his home town of San Diego as the tournament for him, and how right that turned out to be. However he'll find it very difficult in 1999 as defending champion.

➤ A relaxed family man. He used to commute from Hawaii so he'll be looking forward to the 1999 Mercedes Championship when it will be played in Hawaii.

JOEY SINDELAR

40-year-old Joey joined the tour in 1984, and had been in the top 100 on the M/L in every year since (apart from 1994) until he had a disappointing 1997 when 114th.

In 1998 he had top 10s in the Tucson Chrysler Classic (T9th), the MCI Classic (T6th), the Canon Greater Hartford Open (T9th) and the Buick Open (T6th after 64 in R4).

He also had top 25s in the Doral Ryder Open (T23rd after 75 in R4), the Buick Classic (T17th), the Canadian Open (T13th), the Michelob (T17th), the Las Vegas (T22nd), and the National Car Rental at Disney (T19th).

T43rd in US Open: T38th in USPGA. 61st on the M/L.

➤ Coming from the 'Big Apple' the core of his problem has been his bunker play, and especially his putting in the 5 – 8 feet range which often prevents him turning his generally accurate approach play into wins.

➤ Showed improved form this year after his 40th birthday with a top 10 finish in May, June, July, and August.

➤ His record in recent years in the Canadian Open is really impressive (T13th 1998: T7th 1996: T14th 1995) on the Glen Abbey course. If his putter gets hot next September he could win it!

VIJAY SINGH   G F 🐎

This is now my fifth golf betting annual and there has only been one player who has been in my players to follow in each of the previous four volumes....yes it has been Vijay....and in my first book the advice was, 'Do keep Singh on your side as a punter. He is, put simply, a world-class player who must be expected to win more tournaments at good prices.'

Well he's proved it, especially over the last two years.

In 1997 he won the Memorial and the Buick in America, to finish 16th on the M/L, and he also won the World Match Play Championship at Wentworth and the South African Open. In 1998 he was T13th in the Mercedes, T22nd in the Phoenix Open, and as defending champion was T9th in the South African Open.

On the Florida swing he was T4th at 33/1 in the Doral Ryder Open, 2nd at 25/1 in the Honda Classic, and T22nd in the Bay Hill Invitational.

He was T24th in the MCI Classic, a poor T68th as defending champion in the Memorial and T24th in the Buick Classic.

He was 2nd at 50/1 in the Western Open putting cross handed after going into R4 with a 2-shot lead before shooting a 72! In the Canon Greater Hartford Open he was T12th after a 62 in R4 with the back nine in 28!

As defending champion he was T8th in the Buick Open.

Then in a golden fortnight in mid August he won the USPGA, his first major, at 50/1 and then the following week won the Sprint at 33/1 with 47 points.

He had other high finishes in the World Series (T14th) the Canadian Open (T22nd) and the National Car Rental at Disney (T12th).

In Europe he was T2nd in the German Masters.

Missed the cut in the US Masters: T25th in US Open: T19th in the British Open (joint first at 11/1 in Rest of the World market).

Easily beaten by Mark O'Meara (11 and 10) in the World Match play semi-final where he was the defending champion.

Led the Tour Championship from the start only to be caught by Hal Sutton at the 72nd hole. He then lost at that hole in the play-off. His fine performance took him to 2nd on the M/L.

Played in the Presidents Cup in 1994, 1996 and will play again in December 1998.

His huge length off the tee gives him a great advantage, especially on a damp course with little 'run' on the ball. He is very consistent with a solid all-round game. His weakness has always been his putting. However now he's gone back to the conventional putter putting cross handed he's improved. Nevertheless his form on the greens can be variable.

He'll be 36 in February 1999. Moves ball L-R (fade).

➤ With four wins in America and two others worldwide in the last couple of years Vijay has justified my faith in him. There is every reason to expect him to go on to win more tournaments.

➤ Last year his profile clearly pinpointed his 50/1 USPGA triumph which I know from the response helped many readers. This year I suggest we back him in March on 'the Florida swing'. He recorded back-to-back wins last year. He must have a chance of doing another double in early March in the Doral Ryder Open (sixteen consecutive par or sub-par rounds and T4th 1998), and then in the Honda Classic (2nd 1998). In his adopted 'home state' he can be followed in match bets, on the spreads and in the outright markets in those tournaments.

➤ He can also be supported in the Buick Classic (two wins and two top 25s in his last five starts) in the week after the US Open.

➤ Yet to make the top 15 in the US Masters he's not a player in love with Augusta where he missed the cut this year after 53 (!) consecutive cuts. In his last ten rounds there he's shot 74 or more six times, (including an 80 and an 82), and has a stroke average of 74! Worth opposing on the spreads.

➤ His knowledge of Augusta makes him a player to note in the early-round 3-ball betting. This year he shot 68 in R2 and was 3rd on the putting stats.

JEFF SLUMAN   g

41-year-old Slu started 1997 with an unusual, indeed a unique record. He had never won a 'normal' tournament yet he had won a major, the 1988 USPGA. He'd been in the top 20 on the M/L twice (1992 and 1988).

In 1997 he won the Tucson Chrysler Classic at 100/1 to record his first 'ordinary' win after eight 2nd places. He ended the year 34th on the M/L.

He improved again in 1998 with three really big tournaments. He was 3rd at 66/1 in the Colonial, 2nd after a play-off in the St Jude Classic, and he won the Greater Milwaukee Open at 33/1 in September.

He also had top 20s in the Hawaiian Open (T16th), the Byron Nelson Classic (T12th), the Buick Open (T15th) and the Michelob (T10th).

Missed the cut in the US Masters: T10th in the US Open after 68 in R4: T27th in the USPGA. T11th in the Tour Championship

Became a first-time dad in April so the 'nappy factor' has already worked.

Slu is the classic case of the US pro who is not long off the tee, but is consistent, straight-hitting and must always be considered on courses suited to his game. 21st on the M/L.

➤ He has now won or been 2nd in each of the last five years.

➤ He will be worth support on the spreads, in match and in outright betting, in the Colonial where his shot making and short-but-accurate style is so well suited. 2nd in 1996 and 3rd this year, he has a stroke average over the last four years of 68.5!

➤ Slu must be given a sound outsider's chance in the 1999 USPGA which will be held in his own home state. With confidence boosted by his recent successes, and in a tournament he likes, (in thirteen starts he's made twelve cuts and, of course, he won in 1988!) he will be worth supporting.

➤ Must be worth an interest in his other home-state tournament – the Western Open held at Cog Hill, Chicago in which he's got a solid record (3rd 1997: 13th 1996: 6th 1994 and he shot the course record of 62 in 1992).

➤ His game is really well suited to the Kingsmill course, home of the Michelob, where he'll be worthy of support in October (T10th 1998: T11th 1997, T8th 1995).

➤ 5/1 (from 6s) to make his Ryder Cup debut as a 42-year-old!

CHRIS SMITH

29-year-old Chris was given 'battlefield promotion' in 1997 from the Nike tour to the full USPGA tour having won three Nike tour events.

He played in six tournaments, made every cut and finished 4th at 100/1 in the CVS Charity Classic. As a result I put him up last year in Chapter One as the young American player to follow.

Well 1998 has been a great disappointment with only two high finishes, in the Deposit Guaranty Classic (T7th), and the AT&T (T9th).

His inconsistency was shown in the Canadian Open where he followed 66 in R1 with a 77!

In 1998 he has had two major problems – inaccuracy off the tee and a desperate year with the putter.

He'll be 30 in April 1999, and past that dodgy age of 29. Lives in Indiana. Very long at 282 yards. 144th on the M/L.

➤ The best plan will be to take a watching brief, monitor his early-season stats and if they show real improvement off the tee and on the greens he'd be a player to note because after five Nike tour victories he knows how to win.

➤ His form could well return after his 30th birthday in April 1999.

➤ He can be expected to do well again in the Deposit Guaranty Classic (T7th 1998).

MIKE SPRINGER

Mike had his golden season in 1994, his nappy factor year, when he won twice to finish the year 13th on the M/L. Since then he's never been in the top 100 on the M/L, and has posted only one top 3 finish in the 1997 Kemper Open.

In 1998 he had top 25s in the Canon Greater Hartford Open (T14th after 65 in R4), the Quad City Classic (T17th), the CVS Charity Classic (T23rd: leader at halfway he shot 72 in R3), the Greater Vancouver Open (T15th), the BC Open (T20th after 73 in R4), the Texas Open (T11th) and the Las Vegas (T22nd).

So another disappointing year for the 33-year-old from California.

Off the tee his inaccuracy this year has taken on Ballesteros-type proportions. 124th on the M/L.

➤ Mike will never be a Springer in the market but if he is to create a 'shock' it could be in the Deposit Guaranty Classic (T4th 1997) held in July – the month in which he showed his best form this year.

CRAIG STADLER   D F

'The Walrus' can hardly be accused of being a fashion trend setter. Pants that fit are not for the unmistakable figure of the 45-year-old who has won twelve times on the US tour, twice in Europe, and twice elsewhere. His big victory came in the 1982 US Masters.

The beard, the baggy pants and the best golfing non verbals around make Stadler compulsive viewing.

Since he joined the tour in 1977 he's always been in the top 70 on the M/L, and five times he's been in the top 10 including 1992 when he was the tour's no. 1.

In 1998 he's slipped down the M/L after just two top 10s, in the Honda Classic (T7th) and the Bay Hill Invitational (T10th), although he did post top 20s in the Buick Invitational, the Memorial (T11th), and the Buick Classic (T12th).

T41st in US Masters: T38th USPGA. Fades the ball. Born in California, he lives in Colorado. 85th on the M/L.

➤ Usually at his best on the West coast in the earlier part of the season.

➤ His best chance of another victory probably lies in the Buick Invitational (T13th 1998: T2nd 1997: Won 1994) in February in which Californian-born players like 'the Walrus' do so well.

PAUL STANKOWSKI

29-year-old Paul hit the headlines in 1996 when he won the Bell South Classic on the way to finishing 52nd on the M/L.

In 1997 he improved further to post five top 10s including a 13rd in the Tucson Chrysler Classic, as well as his second win in the Hawaiian Open. He ended that year 21st on the M/L.

So 1998 had been disappointing with only one top 10, in the Bob Hope Classic (T10th), and just four other top 20s, in the Mercedes Championship (T13th), the Phoenix Open (T12th), the Deposit Guaranty Classic (T18th) and the Greater Vancouver Open (T11th), before he hit form in mid October in the Las Vegas (T6th).

T39th in the US Masters. He missed the cut in the US Open and USPGA.

A fine player in windy conditions.

Long hitter at 275 yards. His putting has been a real problem this year. Born in California, he lives in Texas. 96th on the M/L.

➤ His exemption for winning expires at the end of 1999 so he's every incentive to regain the form he showed in 1996 and 1997.

➤ He's shown sound form in the desert in the last couple of years so he's worth noting for the Phoenix Open (3rd after R3 this year), the Tucson Chrysler Classic (T3rd 1997), and the Las Vegas Invitational (T6th 1998).

PAYNE STEWART **G**

Instantly recognisable in his plus fours Payne is a 41-year-old one-man fashion show who lives in Florida.

He's had nine tour wins and seven other victories across the world. From 1982 he'd been in the top 45 on the M/L every year until 1994 when he slumped to 123rd. However he bounced back in 1995 with his last win in the Shell Houston Open, to end the year 12th on the M/L

He had elbow surgery in December 1996 after finishing 33rd on the M/L, and in 1997 he was 40th with a 2nd in the Honda Classic and a T3rd in the Bay Hill Invitational his big finishes.

In 1998 he had top 25 finishes in the Buick Invitational (T22nd), the Tucson Chrysler Classic (T18th), the Byron Nelson Classic (T19th), the Colonial (T18th), the AT&T (T19th after 67 in the final round) and the Buick Challenge (T14th).

He had a top 10 in the Players Championship (T8th after 65 in R4), and top 4 finishes in the Nissan Open (T4th at 50/1), the MCI Classic (T3rd at 66/1 after 72 in R4), the Greater Vancouver Open (2nd after being R3 leader) and the Michelob (T4th).

Led the US Open from the start until in R4 he was caught and passed by Janzen. He finished 2nd at 80/1.

T44th British Open: missed cut USPGA T24th Tour Championship.

Represented USA in the Ryder Cup four times; in the World Cup twice; and the Dunhill Cup once. Tends to draw the ball. Good wind player.

Inaccuracy in his approach play has been a problem occasionally this year. 19th on M/L.

➤ He has now had thirteen top 4 finishes in the last four years to confirm what a consistent player he is. However his R4 scoring average, particularly when in contention, is not good.

➤ His record in the Greater Vancouver Open (2nd 1998: T6th 1997) would have been two successive victories if he had played well in the final round each year. Must have a first-rate chance of winning this event in 1999.

➤ You can give the bookies some Payne by backing Stewart to win the MCI Classic in April. He's won it twice (1989 & 1990), was T3rd this year and when the wind blows shows real guts in the gusts.

➤ Yet to win on the West Coast.

➤ 7/2 to make the 1999 Ryder Cup team for the fifth time.

DAVE STOCKTON JR

30-year-old son of a famous father who was a US Ryder Cup Captain and winner on the USPGA tour and currently on the Seniors tour. Junior is not finding it easy to emulate Dad's feats.

In 1997 he was 146th on the M/L after a best finish of T8th in the BC Open.

In 1998 he was T7th in CVS Charity Classic (after 71 in R4) and T15th in the Greater Vancouver Open in another disappointing year.

274 yards off the tee.

Played poorly from bunkers this year.

Lives in California where he was born. 132nd on the M/L.

➤ A fine putter, if Junior retains his tour card via Q. School he could show much improved form in 1999.

➤ He can be followed in the Canon Greater Hartford Open (T3rd 1994: T2nd 1995) which has given him his two best finishes so far in his career.

➤ Has useful form (T5th 1996) in the Las Vegas Invitational where the wide fairways suit him. Would have a chance at a huge price there in October.

STEVE STRICKER   G M 🐎

Steve is the 31-year-old guy who burst on to the scene in 1996 when he was 4th on the M/L after winning both the Kemper Open and the Western Open.

However in 1997 it all went pear shaped (what have pears done to offend us?) as he slumped to 130th on the M/L with just one top 10 when T7th in the Quad City Classic, after changing his clubs.

Last year's profile suggested 'this guy will comeback with a bang in 1998', and that's what he did as he posted a series of top 10 finishes, in the Hawaiian Open (T7th), the Bay Hill Invitational (T6th), the Byron Nelson Classic (5th), the Kemper Open (T8th), the Western Open (T5th), the Greater Milwaukee Open (2nd after a 63 in R2) and the Buick Open (T6th after 72 in R4).

He also had high finishes in the Phoenix Open (T22nd after 64 in R1) and the Tucson Chrysler Classic (T22nd).

T52nd in the British Open: he was T5th in the US Open and 2nd in the USPGA. T5th in the Tour Championship.

Beaten by Sjoland in a close game (by 1 hole) in R1 of the World Match Play in October.

Became a first-time dad to daughter Bobbie Jean (lovely name) in August. 'Nappy-factor' inspiration can be expected in 1999. Wife Nikki used to act as his caddie. His coach, Dennis Tiziani, is his father in law and golf coach at the University of Wisconsin.

Showed a cool temperament in his 1996 wins although he has 'wobbled' this year in R4, notably in the Buick Open. He has putted well this year and his bunker play is now much improved. Long off the tee he can still improve the ratio of fairways hit.

Now lives in Florida. 13th on M/L.

➤ With two top 5s in the 1998 US majors, and seven other top 10s, this guy has clearly 'come back with a bang'. He can be expected to win in 1999.

➤ Indeed I believe he is a good bet to land the 1999 USPGA. He fits the identikit in every respect – he's a quality player, a proven winner who's yet to win a major and he's in his thirties.....and in 1999 it will be held in the state where he went to University so he'll feel comfortable there.

➤ He could well have a golden patch in July 1999 which starts with the Motorola Western Classic and moves on to the Greater Milwaukee Open. He could win either, he may win both.

➤ His Western Classic record (T5th 1998: Won 1996) is first class as he feels at home there because he studied at Illinois University.

➤ Next to a major he wants to win the Greater Milwaukee Open held in the state (Wisconsin) where he was born. Over the last three years (2nd 1998: 12th 1997: 3rd 1996) he has a stroke average of 67.08!

➤ Worth a small each-way bet at long odds for the 1999 Money list. After all he was 4th in 1996, and he's a better 'nappy-factor-inspired', and hungrier player now than he was then so he's sure worth the risk. What's more he'll play in the February World Championship event although he'll miss the season-opening Mercedes tournament for 1998's winners.

➤ Went to 8/15 from 4/6 to make his Ryder Cup debut in 1999.

DAVID SUTHERLAND

David is the younger brother of Kevin whose profile follows.

In 1997 he had two top 10s in the Greater Milwaukee Open (T2nd), and the Greater Vancouver Open (T6th) on his way to finishing 84th on the M/L. It was his best-ever year.

In 1998 he had top 25 finishes in the Phoenix Open (T22nd), the Honda Classic (T22nd), the Players Championship (T16th), the Shell Houston Open (T22nd), the Sprint (18th) and the Greater Milwaukee Open (T23rd after 66 in R4).

70th in the USPGA.

Poor stats for both Driving Accuracy and putting show the key weaknesses which have prevented him posting a top 15 finish this season. 122nd on the M/L.

Lives in California.

➤ He will be looking forward to the Greater Milwaukee Open after finishing 23rd this year after his T2nd there in 1997. His two-year stroke average there is a very impressive 68.

KEVIN SUTHERLAND

34-year-old Kevin is the elder brother of David. Like his brother he had his best year in 1997 when 52nd on the M/L after four top 10s including his career best finish, in the Shell Houston Open (2nd).

In 1998 he was T3rd in the rain-reduced Buick Invitational, T15th in the Nissan Open, T7th in the Honda Classic, T22nd in the Bay Hill Invitational, T7th in the Buick Classic, T25th in the Canon Greater Hartford Open, T20th in the St Jude Classic, T15th in the Greater Vancouver Open and T14th in the Greater Milwaukee Open.

Inaccuracy off the tee has been his major problem this year. Lives in California. 66th on the M/L.

➤ Must be noted in the Canon Greater Hartford Open (T25th 1998: T13th 1997: T9th 1996) and the Honda Classic (T7th 1998).

➤ Like his brother he likes the Greater Milwaukee Open where over the last three years his stroke average is 68.5.

HAL SUTTON

Hal is now 40 years old. He was the 'golden boy', the next Jack Nicklaus after winning seven tournaments from 1982 to 1986 including the USPGA.

However this decade he lost his way in 1992 and 1993 before he showed real improvement in 1994 when 29th on the M/L, and in 1995 when he won the BC Open to end that year 32nd.

Slipped back again in 1996 to 109th.

In 1997 he was T3rd in the Buick Challenge, T4th in the Shell Houston Open and T4th in the MCI Heritage Classic, ending the year 54th on the M/L.

In 1998 he had top 25 finishes in the Nissan Open (T13th), the Players Championship (T18th), the Bell South Classic (T24th), the Western Open (T22nd), the Deposit Guaranty Classic (T14th), the Buick Open (T12th) and the Greater Vancouver Open (T15th).

He had top 10s in the Greater Greensboro Open (T8th after being R2 joint leader), the Shell Houston Open (T6th after 68 in R4), the Kemper Open (T8th), the Quad City Classic (T9th after 65 in R4) and the Buick Challenge (T8th).

He had top 4s in the Byron Nelson Classic (T2nd) and the Canadian Open (T4th) before he won, for the ninth time, in the Texas Open with a fine, front-running performance.

Won the Tour Championship at 40/1 after beating Vijay Singh in a play-off. He had played superbly, especially from sand, in the final round. So he finished 5th on the M/L.

He has had a superb season, showing up well in all the major stats.

He has always been a superb ball striker whose putting has prevented him winning more often.

➤ Becoming the father of twins in February will mean that he will rarely, if ever, play more than two weeks in a row compared to his normal pattern of four in a row. As a result he may find it difficult to repeat the consistency he showed this year. It might be a rare case of the '(double) nappy factor' not working!

➤ He has a fine course record in the Canadian Open (T4th 1998: 11th 1997: 4th 1995). If his putter is hot he will surely go very close in 1999.

➤ He can be followed with confidence in the Byron Nelson Classic where his stroke average over the last three years is a most impressive 67.2.

➤ 3/1 (from 7s) to play in the 1999 Ryder Cup for the first time in twelve years.

PHIL TATAURANGI

Phillip Mikaera is a 27-year-old Kiwi who finished 96th on the M/L in 1997 after posting two top 10 finishes, in the Canadian Open (3rd), and the Canon Greater Hartford Open (T9th).

In 1998 he had four top 25 finishes, in the Freeport McDermott Classic (T12th after 75 in R4), the Shell Houston Open (T22nd after an 'off-the-pace' 68 in R4), the Byron Nelson Classic (T19th) and the BC Open (T20th). He posted his best-ever finish in October when a superb 2nd, to Duval, in the Michelob to retain his card.

Missed the cut in the US Open.

Played brilliantly for New Zealand in the 1992 Eisenhower Trophy, the World Amateur team championship.

Won the Australian PGA Championship in November 1996. Won once on the Nike tour. Inaccuracy off the tee has been a big problem this year. 89th on the M/L.

➤ His best chances may come in the tournaments later in the season such as the Canadian Open (3rd 1997) and the BC Open (T20th 1998) in September when the 'big names' are not playing.

ESTEBAN TOLEDO

This 36-year-old guy was born in Mexico and now lives in California.

Earned his 1998 card via the Q School and has made an impact most notably when T3rd in the Bell South Classic and T7th in the CVS Charity Classic (after a 64 in R4). He also had top 25 finishes in the Freeport McDermott (T19th), the Kemper Open (T25th), the Deposit Guaranty Classic (T21st) and the Greater Vancouver Open (T15th).

Es-tu-bann-toe-lay-doe may be an ex-professional boxer but he doesn't punch his weight off the tee with his driving distance only 260 yards. However his great strength is his accuracy off both tee and fairway. 93rd on the M/L.

➤ If he can maintain the accuracy shown this year his 1999 progress will depend on his putting.

➤ Best chance of a top 5 finish will probably be in the Deposit Guaranty Classic (T21st 1998: T16th 1994).

TOMMY TOLLES   D

Tommy is a 32-year-old guy born in Florida who now lives in North Carolina.

He was 116th on the M/L as a rookie in 1995. Made a big impact in 1996 when he had five top 5 finishes with a T3rd in the USPGA the highlight. He ended the year 16th on the M/L.

In 1997 he was 27th on the M/L after finishing 3rd in the US Masters, and T5th in the US Open.

However 1998 has been very disappointing with just one really-high finish when T3rd in the Kemper Open after a 74 in R4. Finished T9th in the Tucson Chrysler Classic after a double bogey at the last hole when a par would have given him a T4th finish. He also posted top 25 finishes in the Doral Ryder Open (T23rd after 74 in R4) and the Honda Classic (T22nd after 73 in R4) as well as a top 20 when T15th in the National Car Rental at Disney.

Missed the cut in the US Masters and the USPGA.

He has generally been so inaccurate off the tee that he has struggled all season. 115th on the M/L.

➤ Once more this year his R4 scoring when high on the leaderboard has been disappointing. If he is to win it will surely be after coming from 'off the pace' with a low score in R4, or when after making a fast start he finds he's won a rain-reduced tournament.

➤ "I still try to win a tournament with one shot instead of playing 72 holes." This comment suggests that patience and course management are not his greatest strengths.

➤ His best chances will surely come on courses with wide fairways. So the Bob Hope Classic clearly suits him. He was T3rd in 1995, T5th in 1997 (after 46 (!) birdies) and he was 19 under par in 1998 before he managed an 80 in R5 this year.

➤ If he proves he's back to form his record (T7th 1997: 3rd 1996) on the English Turn course should be remembered in May when the Entergy Classic begins.

DAVID TOMS   g S

31-year-old Toms lives in Louisiana where he was born. He got into the top 100 on the M/L for the first time in 1997 when he was 49th after notching his first win in the Quad Cities Classic.

In late 1997 he was 2nd in the Kapalua International in Hawaii.

In 1998 he had top 25 finishes in the Mercedes (T22nd), the Bob Hope Classic (T19th), the Bay Hill Invitational (T17th), the Greater Greensboro Open (T23rd), the Canon Greater Hartford Open (T20th), the AT&T (T13th), the Sprint (11th with 34 pts) and the Greater Milwaukee Open (T23rd).

He had top 4 finishes in the Tucson Chrysler Classic (T2nd), and the Quad City Classic (4th as defending champion).

Played the back nine in 29 in a R4 of 64 in the US Masters to finish T6th. Missed the USPGA cut.

Won twice on the Nike tour. Not long at 271 yards. 44th on the M/L.

➤ He's now had a win and three other top 5 finishes (four if you include the 1997 Kapalua) in the last two years.

➤ Must be given a real chance in the Greater Milwaukee Open where over the last three years his stroke average is 68.75.

➤ Worthy of support at 50/1 plus in the Tucson Chrysler Classic in late February. He had a good record on the Tucson National course when it was one of two courses used for the Northern Telecom Open (3rd 1992: T9th 1996), and this year he was T2nd.

KIRK TRIPLETT

Kirk is the 36-year-old guy who has won more money than any other non-winner on the USPGA tour. He's had six 2nd places and has developed a reputation as a player who loses his nerve when in contention.

However his consistent play has seen him finish 38th (1994), 29th (1995), 65th (1996) and 39th (1997) on the M/L in recent years.

In 1998 he had top 20s in the Bob Hope Classic (T10th), the Nissan Open (T15th), the Byron Nelson Classic (T15th), the Colonial (T18th after 71 in R4), the Memorial (T16th after 73 in R4), the Deposit Guaranty Classic (T7th), the AT&T (T13th), the Sprint (T15th) and the Las Vegas (T8th).

Fades the ball. A very accurate player. However this year he's struggled with his putter. 59th on the M/L.

➤ He is best followed in the early-round 3-ball betting when his skill rather than his nerve is on display as his R4 scoring when in contention has never been good.

➤ If there's one player who would be the likely winner of a rain-reduced event it would be Triplett. After all he was the 40/1 'winner' of the 1996 voided AT&T.

➤ There can be no doubt at all that his game is very well suited to the Annandale course, home of the Deposit Guaranty Classic, where his form figures for the last four years are 7th – 13th – 2nd – 4th. His four-year stroke average of 68.44 is better than any other player so he should win......however the big doubt will be his ability to handle the pressure in R4.

➤ With two top 10s in the last four years he clearly enjoys the Las Vegas Invitational. He's had some low early-round scores so do note him in R1 and R2 3-ball betting.

TED TRYBA

Ted is a 6'4" 31-year-old good-looking guy who lives in Florida.

His best year came in 1995 when he won the Anheuser Busch Golf Classic on the Kingsmill course, ending the year 39th on the M/L.

In 1996 he was 131st, and in 1997 80th on the Money list.

In 1998 he had high finishes in th Doral Ryder Open (T15th), the Byron Nelson Classic (T19th), the Memorial (T7th after 73 in R4), the Greater Vancouver Open (T4th), the Texas Open (T11th), and the National Car Rental at Disney (T15th).

Fairly long off the tee at 276 yards although his driving accuracy stats over the past two years point to his key weakness. He's never been a particularly good putter. 67th on the M/L.

➤ He was very nervy in R4 of the Greensboro Open (77) and disappointed in R4 of the Memorial (73) when in contention. He will have to improve his final round resolve if he's to win again. Sadly Ted's got the bottle for not having 'the bottle'.

➤ However he's posted at least one top 4 finish in each of the last four years and he'll probably do so again in 1999. If so it will be in the later stages of the season from mid September onwards, especially in the BC Open (stroke average 70.26 over last four years: T4th 1998), the Texas Open (made last three cuts: 11th 1998), the Michelob at his favourite Kingsmill course (W 1995: 3rd 1996), and the Walt Disney Classic (T3rd 1997: T2nd 1995).

BOB TWAY

Bob is the very tall (he's 6'4" in his slippers) guy from Oklahoma who had his golden year in 1986 when after four wins he was 2nd on the M/L.

Lost form earlier this decade, from 1992 through 1994, before he won again in 1995, the MCI Classic, to finish 20th on the M/L. In 1996 he was 35th and in 1997 he was 43rd.

In 1998 he had high finishes in the Bob Hope Classic (T10th), the Buick Invitational (T16th), the Tucson Chrysler Classic (T6th), the Doral Ryder Open (T9th), the Players Championship (T18th after 69 in R4), the MCI Classic (T18th), the Bell South Classic (T5th), the Byron Nelson Classic (T19th), the Memorial (T16th), the Buick Classic (T7th), the Buick Open (T15th), the Sprint (T6th), the Canadian Open (T25th), the Buick Challenge (T20th) and the Las Vegas (4th at 50/1 after being the R3 leader).

Missed the cut in the US Masters and the British Open. 3rd at 66/1 in the US Open: T13th in USPGA. T8th in the Tour Championship.

With seven career wins this guy has a sound record. He is the classic straight-off-the-tee pro who has a clear comparative advantage when there is a premium on accuracy. Sadly he often posts top 10s instead of top 4s or victories because of his average putting.

"I hit the ball low coming from Oklahoma so that helps me in the wind," so Bob can be followed when its blowing! 24th on M/L.

➤ After another very consistent year he can be expected to play steady, accurate golf again in 1999, especially after May when he's blown out the 40 candles on his birthday cake.

➤ Passing 40 has had a liberating and inspiring effect on a number of players and I expect Tway's form to blossom as a result. I expect him to win in 1999.

➤ He says he really enjoys the desert tournaments, so he can be noted for the Tucson Chrysler Classic (T6th 1998: T17th 1997), the Sprint International (T6th 1998) and the Las Vegas (4th 1998 and winner 1990).

➤ His accuracy is tailor made for the US Open where he's real value in match bets and on the spreads. 3rd this year and T5th in 1997 are two excellent back-to-back finishes. This year he was also 3rd top US player, and 3rd on Surrey's handicap.

➤ He grew up locally in Marietta so he loves the Bell South Classic having won it in 1986 and been 2nd in 1989. In its two years on the new Sugarloaf he has posted a T19th 1997, and a fine T5th this year after going 14 under for the last 54 holes. He'll be worth support on the spreads there in 1999.

➤ He has rock-solid form in the Byron Nelson Classic (T19th 1998: T5th 1997, 9th 1995) and must be followed in that event in 1999 as it will be one of his first as a 40-year-old!

➤ 6/1 to make his US Ryder Cup debut in 1999.

OMAR URESTI S

You-rest-ee is a 30-year-old Texan guy who was given his Christian name in honour of actor Omar Sharif. He has yet to make an impact on the tour as, so far, retaining his card has been his main preoccupation.

In 1998 he had top 25 finishes in the Bob Hope Classic (T24th), the Players Championship (T18th), the Buick Classic (T17th), the CVS Charity Classic (T19th) and the St Jude Classic (T20th).

His best finish came when he was T5th in the Greater Vancouver Open.

Missed the cut in the US Open. His iron play has often let him down. Only 267 yards off the tee.

Keeps the streaker symbol for having made nine consecutive birdies in the Nike tour in 1994.

Born in Austin, Texas where he now lives. He has one win on the Nike tour. 107th on the M/L.

➤ He led the 1997 Bay Hill Invitational after three rounds before finishing T3rd. It was his best-ever finish and could well inspire him to play well there again in March.

SCOTT VERPLANK   G CT M

34-year-old Scott was born in Dallas Texas, and now lives in Oklahoma.

Has suffered with elbow injuries and ill health. He is a diabetic. He won the 1985 Western Open as an amateur and the 1988 Buick Open as a pro.

Missed most of the 1991, 1992 and all of the 1993 seasons because of his elbow problems. In 1994 he was 97th, and in 1995 55th on the Money list. His form slumped in 1996 (171st) and in 1997, playing on a medical exemption, he was 159th.

However in late 1997 he was the Number 1 player at the Q school which he won by 6 shots.

In 1998 he was T14th in the Phoenix Open (76 in R4 after being joint leader after R3), T10th in the Nissan Open, T11th in the Players Championship, T9th in the Western Open, T9th in the Quad City Classic (64 in R4), T12th in the St Jude Classic, T9th in the Canadian Open, T25th in the Michelob and 3rd at 80/1 in the Las Vegas.

He had three top 5 finishes – in the Greater Greensboro Open, he was the leader after R3 and after birdieing the last he forced a play off which he lost to Trevor Dodds. In the Bell South Classic he was T5th after a 65 in R4, and in the Buick Open he was 2nd after 64 in R4.

T49th US Open: T54th USPGA. T5th Tour Championship (impressive performance).

So 1998 has seen Verplank firmly establish himself on the comeback trail.

Shows up reasonably well on all the main stats and is an impressive 5th on the all-round ranking. 18th on M/L..

➤ Make no mistake.....this guy can play. He was a top amateur, the US Amateur Champion in 1984 and he's won twice. Having gone close this year and shown his bottle by birdying the last hole to force the Greater Greensboro Open play-off he's a player to note. I expect him to post a win at big odds in 1999.

➤ He has a useful record at the Glen Abbey course (2nd 1988 and T9th 1998) so remember him for the Canadian Open in September.

➤ His comeback victory, could well be in the John Deere Classic on the Oakwood course where he's posted three consecutive top 10 finishes. He simply cries out for support there in late July.

➤ Could make an early-season impact in the Phoenix Open where he led this year after R3 before 'contention rust' set in. Definitely worth support on the spreads and as a big-priced outsider.

➤ Given a 14/1 initial quote to make the Ryder Cup team.

➤ Could even do a 'Steve Jones' and win the US Open at 150/1 as a 'comeback kid' in 1999

GRANT WAITE   D

Last year I held out high hopes that this 34-year-old Kiwi might post a shock win this year because I had been impressed by his play when he lost in a play-off to Duval in the Michelob. He ended that year 68th, his best ever, on the Money list.

However in 1998 he has been rather disappointing. He posted six top 20s, in the Honda Classic (T15th), the Bay Hill Invitational (T13th), the Shell Houston Open (T17th), the Bell South Classic (T12th), the Deposit Guaranty Classic (T11th), and the Canon Greater Hartford Open (T16th after 75 in R4 which he started as joint leader).

Missed the cut in the US Open and the USPGA.

Won once in America in 1993 after which he lost his way trying to remodel his swing.

This year, like last, his poor stats for both sand saves and putting tell their own story. 118th on the M/L.

➤ If he is to win again he really has to find a magic touch with his putter. Watch his early-season putting stats and if they're good then he'd really be an outsider to note.

➤ Driving is his strong suit, and the Bell South Classic is held on a drivers' course so he must be seriously considered there in April 1999 after his T12th this year.

➤ When in the lead last year at halfway in the BC Open and this year after R3 in the Canon Greater Hartford Open he played nervously. He's probably better coming from 'off the pace'.

DUFFY WALDORF

36-year-old James Joseph, Duffy to the golf world, was born in Los Angeles and now lives in California. He has one tour win, the 1995 LaCantera Texas Open. He's been 35th (1995), 30th (1996) and 51st (1997) on the M/L in recent years.

In 1997 he had four top 4 finishes, in the Michelob Championship (T2nd), the Buick Invitational (2nd), the LaCantera Texas Open (4th) and the Las Vegas Invitational (T4th).

However in 1998 he's had only one top 4 when T4th in the Canon Greater Hartford Open.

His other high finishes were in the Hawaiian Open (T11th), the Freeport McDermott Classic (7th after 74 in R4), the Western Open (T20th), the Greater Milwaukee Open (T23rd) and the BC Open (T25th).

T38th in the USPGA.

His inconsistency was shown in the National Car Rental at Disney. He led with a 63 in R1 then shot 78 in R2!

Very long hitter. He shows up well in greens in regulation. However his putting and especially his bunker play have been very poor this year (again!). 103rd on the M/L.

➤ Every year for the last five years he's posted at least one top 4 finish and he'll probably do so again in 1999 given the accuracy of his approach play.

➤ His best chances will probably be in

*The Greater Milwaukee Open (T23rd 1998: T9th 1996: T6th 1995) where in the last four years he's had 15 of his 16 rounds under par, and has a stroke average of 68.56.

*The LaCantera Texas Open (4th 1997: Won 1995) in which he has done very well in 'odd' years.

TOM WATSON

Tom is counting the days to the 4th September 1999 when he'll count the candles on his 50th birthday cake and ring his bank manager to widen their vaults as he joins the roundbellies on the Seniors tour.

In 1998 he posted two high finishes early on, when T2nd in the Phoenix Open and 2nd in the Hawaiian Open. He then won the Colonial at 66/1 playing superbly in R4 alongside Furyk, to shoot 66 to record his 34th win!!

Led into the final round of the AT&T only to shoot 72 and finish T9th.

Missed the cut in all four majors. Played fewest events (14) of any player qualifying for the Tour Championship, where he finished T18th. 29th on M/L.

➤ Accuracy from tee to green has always been his trademark and when his putting from under 4 feet has been steady he's won.

➤ The MCI Heritage Classic is a tournament he likes. He's won it twice and could do well there again in 1999.

➤ He'll be worth many a flutter in the Seniors tour events where his accuracy will be so vital. Just look at how well straight-hitting Hale Irwin has done.

➤ He's never won in Florida on the Bermuda grass.

➤ 7/1 to make the Ryder Cup team. He played four times in the eighties and was the US captain 1993. Tom in the 1999 team as a 50-year-old? I'd want 50/1 rather than 7/1.

D A WEIBRING

Donald Albert, known as plain DA, is a 45-year-old who lives in Texas.

He has five tour wins, the last in the 1996 Canon Greater Hartford Open.

In 1998 he posted one high finish, in the Quad City Classic (T5th).

One of the shortest drivers on tour. However he is accurate off the tee. Runs his own golf business. Suffered from Bell's palsy (a form of facial paralysis) over the last two years. 149th on the M/L.

➤ His exemption for winning in 1996 expires at the end of 1998 so expect DA to show improved form in 1999.

➤ Must be followed in the John Deere Classic (5th 1998: W 1995: W 1991: W 1979) in which his record when it was known as the Quad City Classic was, as you can see, first class.

➤ DA has proved that he can win for a second time on a favourite course when landing the Quad City Classic for the second time in 1995. So in 1999 you can visualise him winning the Canon Greater Hartford Open for a second time on 1st August.

➤ Could spring a 100/1 shock in the Las Vegas Invitational. He was 2nd in 1991, and was an impressive 8 under for his three rounds at Summerlin this year when T16th.

MIKE WEIR

Canadian born, Mike is a 28-year-old guy who now lives in Utah.

On the Canadian tour he was rookie of the year in 1993. Earned his tour card via the 1997 Q School.

In 1998 he had four high finishes, in the Freeport McDermott Classic (T19th after 68 in R4), the Sprint International (T21st), the Greater Vancouver Open (T5th) and the BC Open (T7th after 71 in R4).

272 yards off the tee. He's had big problems this year on the green and with his driving accuracy. Left-handed player. He'll be 29 in May 1999. 131st on the M/L.

➤ Clearly at his best from mid August he can be followed in the Greater Vancouver Open in the first week of September. Played in the land of his birth he's posted his best-ever tour finishes there (T5th 1998: T5th 1997).

KEVIN WENTWORTH

Kevin is a 30-year-old Californian who gained his 1998 tour card via Q. School.

In 1998 he posted six top 20 finishes after August, in the St Jude Classic (T12th), the Greater Vancouver Open (T15th), the Greater Milwaukee Open (T9th), the Buick Challenge (T14th), the Michelob Championship (T13th) and the Las Vegas (T10th).

Won the 1997 Philippines Open. Left-handed player.

272 yards off the tee. His greens in regulation, driving accuracy, and sand save stats were all in 'intensive care' until his form improved after August. 119th on the M/L.

➤ Having played, and indeed won, in the Far East, with his post-August form to boost his confidence, and now safely past thirty, he'll be keen to establish himself as a tour regular.

➤ On this year's evidence he's clearly a player to note later in the season.

MARK WIEBE

Mark is a 41-year-old big guy (6'3") from Colorado who has two wins, in 1985 and 1986.

In 1996 he was T2nd in the Nissan Open, and in 1997 he was 2nd in the Kemper Open after going into R4 with a 3-shot lead.

In 1998 he had five high finishes in the Bob Hope (T10th), the Freeport McDermott (T3rd), the Memorial (T23rd), the Western Open (T22nd) and the CVS Charity Classic (T7th).

Has poor stats this year for greens in regulation and driving accuracy. Short off the tee at 268 yards. 106th on the M/L.

➤ He's suffered this year with involuntary shaking of his hands. It's not the 'yips' as it happens off the course as well as on it. It could be an allergic reaction, a chemical imbalance, or even a possible start of Parkinson's disease.

➤ With his illness and the memory of his nervy final round in the 1997 Kemper Open it's difficult to see this short-hitting guy in his forties winning for the first time for thirteen years.

➤ He'll be looking forward to the new tournament, the Reno Open held in his own home state of Colorado in August.

WILLIE WOOD

Just fourteen years ago Willie was a guy with a really big future. He'd been a US Junior Champion, a member of the 1983 US Walker Cup team, and from 1984-86 he'd been 61st, 49th and 52nd on the Money list. Then tragedy as his wife had cancer and died in 1989. His career nosedived.

Remarried in late 1995, he became a dad in April 1996. Relaxed, refocussed and re-partnered with 'nappy factor' inspiration he won the 1996 Deposit

Guaranty Classic in July on only his second tour event of the year. The previous week he'd played really well on the Nike tour in Buffalo. He ended the year 87th on the M/L.

In 1997 with only one top 10, in the MCI Heritage Classic he was 121st on the M/L.

In 1998 he had two top 4 finishes – in the CVS Charity Classic (T4th) and the Sprint (T2nd). He also had top 20s in the Kemper Open (T14th) and the Canon Greater Hartford Open (T16th).

He was T21st in the US Masters.

His putting, as in the 1998 Sprint and the 1996 Deposit Guaranty Classic, can be brilliant and he shows up very highly in the sand save stats.

However he's only average for accuracy off the tee and fairway. 76th on the M/L.

➤ His solid short game and his need for wider fairways is suited to Augusta (T21st 1998: T12th 1997) although his lack of length will prevent him from getting into real contention. However he can be noted there in the US Masters in rounds 3 and 4 where he's shot 70-70-71-68 in the last two years to be 9 under for those 72 holes.

So have a little on Willie over the last couple of days at Augusta at 'value' prices in the 2- and 3-ball betting.

➤ An interesting 'trick' question to ask your friends. Can you name two professional golfers with the name of WEST WOOD? Your mate will get Lee Westwood straight away, but it's surely 1000/1 against him (or her) getting Willie West Wood!! Yes that's right Willie's middle name is West....Wood you believe it?

TIGER WOODS   G Y F

The Tiger burst on to the golf scene at the end of the 1996 season when he played in just eight tournaments. He was in the top 25 in the last seven, and he won the Las Vegas Invitational at 50/1, and the Walt Disney Classic at 16/1. He was also placed in the BC Open (T3rd at 40/1) and the Texas Open (3rd at 22/1). He finished 24th on the M/L. That late-season burst however was only the prelude to 1997, the Year of the Tiger.

He won four times to top the Money list with victories in the Mercedes Championship, the Byron Nelson Classic, the Western Open and famously in a record-breaking US Masters which he won easily by 12 (!!) shots.

In 1998 on the European tour he scored a memorable victory in the Johnnie Walker Classic. A 40/1 chance starting R4 8 shots behind Els he shot 65, forced a play-off, and won.

On the American tour he started the season with high finishes in the Mercedes Championship (T2nd after 64 in R4), the Buick Invitational (T3rd), the Nissan Open (2nd beaten by Mayfair in a play-off) and the Doral Ryder Open (T9th).

His form dipped when he was T13th in the Bay Hill Invitational with his 77 in R4 his worst as a pro. He was then a poor T35th in the Players Championship.

In May he gained his only US success of the year when he was the 15/2 winner of the Bell South Classic. After finishing T51st in the Memorial he withdrew from the Kemper Open with a back problem – his first withdrawal because of injury since turning pro.

He was T9th as defending champion in the Western Open, T4th in the Buick Open, T4th in the Sprint (he was 18th on normal scoring), T5th in the World Series of Golf and T7th in the National Car Rental at Disney.

In the 1998 Majors he was the only player to have four top 20 finishes. T8th in the US Masters, T18th in the US Open (never in contention), 3rd in the British Open after a birdie-birdie finish, and T10th in the USPGA (after having a 2-shot lead at halfway).

So overall Tiger had thirteen top 10s in twenty US starts and finished the year having made 17 consecutive cuts.

In the Dunhill Cup he played superbly at St Andrews to win three of his four matches. However the 'tiddler' he missed at the last to lose to Santiago Luna could come back to haunt him on that course in future.

In the World Match play at Wentworth, although full of cold, he beat Ian Woosnam (at the 37th), and Lee Westwood (5 and 4) before losing a superb final to Mark O'Meara by just one hole.

Poor display when 20th (of 30) in season-ending Tour Championship.

Tiger's four truly great strengths are his massively long drives, his superb long-iron play, his competitive nature and his ability to extricate himself from trouble.

His massive length means that if he uses his driver on say 10 holes he is actually playing a course some 400 yards shorter than the majority of his opponents!

However he has three key weaknesses. The most notable is probably his putting, as his lowly position (128th) on the stats illustrates. In the British Open for example, he lost his chance by being too aggressive on the medium-long putts. His sand save stats are also unimpressive for a player of his quality. Although his bunker play has improved his putting has often created the poor stats in this category.

He has also found it difficult to control the distance with his short irons which has often negated his earlier excellent play from the tee.

However 1998 has seen a more mature, a more consistent and a more thoughtful Tiger. He is clearly maturing as a golfer showing a much more strategic approach than in the past.

4th on the Money list.

➤ Obviously he's a player who will go on to win many tournaments, although the back problem in 1998 was a potentially worrying development. However, as I pointed out last year, his biggest problem will be to find any deep personal happiness given that he lives in a goldfish bowl.

➤ Tiger's sole American success in 1998 came in the Bell South Classic where, after a three-week break, on a 7,200+ yard, par 72 (four par 5s) course with his dad in good health he was the 15/2 winner.

Studying the pattern of his successes shows clearly that three conditions are necessary for Tiger to be backed with confidence.

*He must be playing after a break. All his five wins in his two full seasons, and six of his seven wins in total have all preceded by a break of at least one week. Tiger is at his best fresh so he certainly merits the F symbol.

*He enjoys the greatest comparative advantage on long par 72 courses with wide fairways and four par 5s as such tracks play to his greatest strength – his driving.

*Tiger showed in 1997 that he underperformed when his dad was ill. If his dad should become ill in 1999 Tiger could be opposed with confidence.

➤ There are two courses tailor-made for Tiger.

*The Augusta course, home of US Masters, with its wide fairways and reachable par 5s really does suit him. The sensational runaway winner in 1996 and T8th in 1997. I expect him to win the tournament in 1999.....if his Dad is well.

*The St Andrews course. How Tiger must be looking forward to the British Open in 2000. He showed in the Dunhill Cup that his massive hitting on the wide expanses of 'The Old Lady' puts the ball well past the fairway bunkers to set up really-low scores. It may not be the most original selection I've ever made but he'll surely be a worthy favourite to land the first British Open of the new century.

➤ He must be noted if he plays in the 1999 Sprint International. Its special points scoring system suits his aggressive style. This year playing there for the first time he was not at his best yet finished 4th, although on normal scoring he'd have been 18th!

FUZZY ZOELLER   D Pb

Frank Urban Zoeller, Fuzzy to you and I, has won ten US tournaments including the 1979 US Masters.

However in 1997 without a top 10 finish he was 148th on the M/L, and kept his tour card by using a one-time exemption for being among the top 50 on the career money list.

At 47 Fuzzy needed a good 1998. In the close season a vision test revealed dominant eye problems which led to new glasses which were paid for when he picked up $69,000 when T8th in the Bob Hope Classic.

However he's only had four other big finishes, in the Greater Greensboro Open (T23rd), the Canon Greater Hartford Open (T25th), the AT&T (T6th after 65 in R4) and the Canadian Open (T13th).

Missed cut in US Open.

He's retained his tour card. His game at its best is based on accuracy off the tee and the fairways. 101st on the M/L.

➤ After his 'glory' year in 1994 when he posted five 2nd places to end the year 5th on the M/L he's had just one top 3 finish in four seasons. Clearly Fuzzy is past his best.

➤ It's virtually impossible to see him winning for the first time since 1986. However he can be expected to shoot occasional low rounds, especially in the 'celebrity' events so remember him in R1 and R2 in the AT&T which he won in 1986 and in which he shot 65 this year, and in the Bob Hope (T8th 1998: 2nd 1994).

➤ Like Tom Watson he can look forward to earning a fistful of dollars on the Seniors tour.

1998 EUROPEAN TOUR STATISTICS

The GUARDIAN PERFORMANCE DATA (reproduced by kind permission) for the 1998 EUROPEAN TOUR SEASON including the Belgacom Open, but excluding the Volvo Masters is as follows. The first 40 players in each list are shown.

STROKE AVERAGE

		Dr Acc (%)
1	Darren Clarke	69.56
2	Colin Montgomerie	69.74
3	Lee Westwood	69.84
4	Ernie Els	69.91
5	Jose Maria Olazabal	70.30
6	Patrik Sjoland	70.48
7	Thomas Bjorn	70.53
8	Miguel Angel Jimenez	70.59
9	Bernhard Langer	70.62
10	Greg Norman	70.63
11	Nick Faldo	70.69
12	Sam Torrance	70.85
13	Robert Karlsson	70.86
14	Ian Woosnam	70.89
T15	Paul McGinley	70.90
T15	Retief Goosen	70.90
17	David Gilford	70.91
18	Andrew Coltart	70.95
19	Eduardo Romero	70.97
20	Peter Baker	71.01
21	Alex Cejka	71.01
22	Peter O'Malley	71.02
T23	Peter Mitchell	71.03
T23	Pierre Fulke	71.03
25	Jean Van de Velde	71.04
26	Costantino Rocca	71.06
27	Per-Ulrik Johansson	71.11
28	Gordon Brand Jnr	71.12
29	Padraig Harrington	71.14
30	Phillip Price	71.16
31	Ian Garbutt	71.19
T32	Paul Broadhurst	71.21
T32	Robert Allenby	71.21
34	Mats Lanner	71.24
35	Stephen Leaney	71.28
36	Mark James	71.30

37	Joakim Haeggman	71.31
T38	Mathias Gronberg	71.35
T38	Russell Claydon	71.35
40	Jarmo Sandelin	71.39

DRIVING ACCURACY

		Dr Acc (%)
1	Pierre Fulke	76.1
T2	David Gilford	74.2
T2	Michele Reale	74.2
T2	Adam Hunter	74.2
T5	Miguel Angel Jimenez	74.0
T5	Stephen Bennett	74.0
T7	Colin Montgomerie	72.9
T7	Van Phillips	72.9
9	Paul Eales	72.4
T10	Pedro Linhart	71.9
T10	Andrew Oldcorn	71.9
12	Lee Westwood	71.7
13	Ross McFarlane	71.3
14	Francisco Cea	71.2
T15	Mark McNulty	71.1
T15	Ian Garbutt	71.1
17	Peter Baker	70.8
18	Paul McGinley	70.5
19	Peter O'Malley	70.4
20	Jose Coceres	70.1
21	Phillip Price	70.1
T22	Des Smyth	70.0
T22	Fabrice Tarnaud	70.0
24	Steve Alker	69.9
25	Peter Mitchell	69.8
26	Chris Van der Velde	69.7
27	Andrew Sherborne	69.6
28	Soren Kjeldsen	69.5
T29	Eduardo Romero	69.4
T29	Alex Cejka	69.4
31	Gary Orr	69.2
T32	Per-Ulrik Johansson	69.0
T32	Fredrik Henge	69.0
T32	Tony Johnstone	69.0
T32	Raphael Jacquelin	69.0
36	Darren Clarke	68.9
37	Paul Affleck	68.7
38	Patrik Sjoland	68.6
39	Bob May	68.4
40	Peter Senior	68.2

DRIVING DISTANCE

		Dr Dist (Yards)
1	Emanuele Canonica	295.8
2	Angel Cabrera	288.8
3	Steve Webster	283.1
4	Ernie Els	282.5
5	Carl Suneson	282.2
6	Paolo Quirici	280.3
7	Darren Clarke	279.3
T8	David Thomson	278.5
T8	Colin Montgomerie	278.5
10	Clinton Whitelaw	278.4
11	Santiago Luna	278.3
12	Scott Henderson	278.0
13	Joakim Rask	277.9
14	Anthony Wall	277.4
15	Francis Howley	277.2
16	Ignacio Garrido	276.8
17	Klas Eriksson	276.2
18	Thomas Bjorn	275.9
19	Jon Robson	275.5
20	David Carter	275.1
21	Lee Westwood	274.9
T22	Per-Ulrik Johansson	274.8
T22	Olivier Edmond	274.8
T22	Kalle Brink	274.8
25	Alex Cejka	274.7
26	Anssi Kankkonen	274.6
27	Retief Goosen	274.5
28	Robert Karlsson	274.3
29	Peter Senior	274.2
30	Derrick Cooper	274.1
T31	Jose Maria Olazabal	273.6
T31	Ivo Giner	273.6
T33	Stephen Allan	273.3
T33	Robert Allenby	273.3
35	Fabrice Tarnaud	273.1
36	Mats Lanner	273.0
37	Raphael Jacquelin	272.6
38	Greg Chalmers	272.5
39	Michael Jonzon	272.3
40	Greg Owen	272.1

GREENS IN REGULATION

		GIR (%)
1	Alex Cejka	78.5
2	Colin Montgomerie	76.2

T3	Peter Baker	75.7
T3	Darren Clarke	75.7
5	Miguel Angel Jimenez	75.3
T6	Peter O'Malley	74.9
T6	Ernie Els	74.9
8	Ian Garbutt	74.8
9	Bob May	74.5
10	Andrew Coltart	74.3
11	Jose Maria Olazabal	73.6
T12	Lee Westwood	73.5
T12	Ian Woosnam	73.5
14	Peter Mitchell	73.4
T15	Mark McNulty	73.1
T15	Patrik Sjoland	73.1
17	Bernhard Langer	72.8
18	Eduardo Romero	72.7
19	Eamonn Darcy	72.4
20	David Gilford	72.1
21	Robert Allenby	71.8
T22	Craig Hainline	71.7
T22	Pierre Fulke	71.7
T22	Francisco Cea	71.7
25	Retief Goosen	71.5
T26	Santiago Luna	71.4
T26	Costantino Rocca	71.4
28	Raphael Jacquelin	71.1
29	Angel Cabrera	70.9
T30	Per-Ulrik Johansson	70.7
T30	Michele Reale	70.7
32	Ross Drummond	70.6
33	Sven Struver	70.1
T34	David Carter	69.9
T34	Phillip Price	69.9
36	Stephen Leaney	69.8
T37	Ignacio Garrido	69.6
T37	Jean Van de Velde	69.6
T39	Adam Hunter	69.4
T39	Malcolm Mackenzie	69.4

SAND SAVES

		Sand Saves (%)
1	Tony Johnstone	81.6
2	Phillip Walton	77.5
3	Joakim Haeggman	77.3
4	Per-Ulrik Johansson	75.6
5	Olle Karlsson	74.2
6	John Bickerton	72.9
7	Stephen Bennett	72.0

T8	Bernhard Langer	71.4
T8	Ignacio Garrido	71.4
10	Stephen Allan	70.5
11	Ernie Els	69.2
12	Angel Cabrera	69.0
13	Retief Goosen	67.3
T14	Mark McNulty	66.7
T14	Greg Turner	66.7
16	Sam Torrance	66.3
17	Adam Hunter	66.1
18	Mark Roe	66.0
19	Martin Gates	65.8
20	Ian Woosnam	64.9
21	Per Haugsrud	64.5
22	Thomas Bjorn	63.8
T23	Wayne Westner	63.2
T23	Jose Maria Olazabal	63.2
25	Diego Borrego	62.5
26	Miguel Angel Jimenez	62.0
27	Paul McGinley	61.5
T28	Jamie Spence	61.0
T28	Daniel Chopra	61.0
T30	Paul Affleck	60.6
T30	Jose Coceres	60.6
32	Jeff Remesy	59.7
33	Pedro Linhart	59.6
34	Raymond Russell	59.2
35	Andrew Sandywell	58.9
T36	Darren Clarke	58.6
T36	Bob May	58.6
38	Jonathan Lomas	58.3
39	Steve Alker	57.8
40	Paul Eales	57.6

PUTTS PER GREEN IN REGULATION

		Putts/GIR
1	Seve Ballesteros	1.731
T2	Russell Claydon	1.736
T2	Robert Karlsson	1.736
T2	Darren Clarke	1.736
5	Paul Broadhurst	1.740
6	Padraig Harrington	1.746
T7	Gordon Brand Jnr	1.749
T7	Jay Townsend	1.749
9	Greg Chalmers	1.750
10	Patrik Sjoland	1.752
11	Bernhard Langer	1.753
12	Andrew Beal	1.757

13	Daniel Chopra	1.758
14	Mark James	1.760
15	Paul Lawrie	1.762
16	John Bickerton	1.765
T17	Ernie Els	1.766
T17	Jose Maria Olazabal	1.766
T17	Paul McGinley	1.766
20	Joakim Haeggman	1.769
T21	Jean Van de Velde	1.770
T21	Lee Westwood	1.770
T21	Olle Karlsson	1.770
24	David Howell	1.771
25	Mats Hallberg	1.774
26	Phillip Price	1.775
27	Per-Ulrik Johansson	1.779
28	Jarmo Sandelin	1.780
T29	Miguel Angel Jimenez	1.781
T29	Jamie Spence	1.781
T29	Paolo Quirici	1.781
T32	Tom Gillis	1.783
T32	Retief Goosen	1.783
T34	Mark Davis	1.784
T34	Ian Woosnam	1.784
T36	Steve Webster	1.785
T36	Dean Robertson	1.785
T36	Mathias Gronberg	1.785
T39	Greg Turner	1.786
T39	Steen Tinning	1.786

PUTTS PER ROUND

		Putts/Round
1	Seve Ballesteros	27.9
2	Jay Townsend	28.4
3	Russell Claydon	28.5
T4	Padraig Harrington	28.6
T4	Andrew Beal	28.6
T6	Paul Lawrie	28.8
T6	Paul Broadhurst	28.8
T6	Daniel Chopra	28.8
T9	Robert Karlsson	28.9
T9	Greg Turner	28.9
T9	Gordon Brand Jnr	28.9
12	Greg Chalmers	29.0
T13	John Bickerton	29.1
T13	Joakim Haeggman	29.1
T15	Jarmo Sandelin	29.9
T15	Mathias Gronberg	29.2
T15	Mark Davis	29.9

T18	Mark James	29.3
T18	Thomas Bjorn	29.3
20	Andrew Sherborne	29.4
T21	Olle Karlsson	29.4
T21	Paul McGinley	29.4
T21	Sam Torrance	29.4
T21	David Howell	29.4
T21	Mats Hallberg	29.4
T21	Lee Westwood	29.4
T27	Jose Rivero	29.5
T27	Mark Mouland	29.5
T27	Gary Evans	29.5
T27	Fredrik Jacobson	29.5
T27	Steen Tinning	29.5
T27	Roger Wessels	29.5
T27	Dean Robertson	29.5
T27	Thomas Gogele	29.5
T35	Martin Gates	29.6
T35	Paolo Quirici	29.6
T35	Thomas Levet	29.6
T35	Stephen Scahill	29.6
T35	Katsuyoshi Tomori	29.6
T35	Jean Van de Velde	29.6

EUROPEAN CHALLENGE TOUR RANKINGS

The top 15 earn their 1999 European tour (category 10) cards

				£
1	Warren Bennett	(Eng)	(19)	81052.66
2	Per Nyman	(Swe)	(22)	37196.46
3	Massimo Scarpa	(It)	(17)	35523.54
4	Roger Winchester	(Eng)	(22)	33796.07
5	Ricardo Gonzalez	(Arg)	(16)	33159.05
6	John Bickerton	(Eng)	(14)	30205.86
7	John Mellor	(Eng)	(21)	30015.06
8	Fredrik Lindgren	(Swe)	(21)	28864.58
9	John Senden	(Aus)	(10)	28769.86
10	Soren Hansen	(Den)	(21)	27984.22
11	Max Anglert	(Swe)	(20)	27522.95
12	Jorge Berendt	(Arg)	(17)	27194.62
13	Christopher Hanell	(Swe)	(23)	26884.19
14	Stephen Gallacher	(Scot)	(22)	26673.37
15	Darren Lee	(Eng)	(16)	26133.85

1998 EUROPEAN ORDER OF MERIT

1 Colin Montgomerie	41 Craig Hainline	81 Michael Campbell
2 Darren Clarke	42 Pierre Fulke	82 Nick Faldo
3 Lee Westwood	43 Jamie Spence	83 Andrew Beal
4 Miguel Angel Jimenez	44 Robert Allenby	84 Michael Long
5 Patrik Sjoland	45 Angel Cabrera	85 Andrew Oldcorn
6 Thomas Bjorn	46 Thomas Gogele	86 Jonathan Lomas
7 Jose Maria Olazabal	47 Katsuyoshi Tomori	87 Marc Farry
8 Ernie Els	48 David Gilford	88 Raphael Jacquelin
9 Andrew Coltart	49 Massimo Florioli	89 Greg Owen
10 Mathias Gronberg	50 Van Phillips	90 Anthony Wall
11 Stephen Leaney	51 Peter Lonard	91 Steen Tinning
12 Peter Baker	52 Ian Garbutt	92 Fabrice Tarnaud
13 Sven Struver	53 Mark Roe	93 Olivier Edmond
14 Sam Torrance	54 Paolo Quirici	94 Gary Evans
15 Phillip Price	55 Per-Ulrik Johansson	95 Paul Eales
16 Stephen Allan	56 Olle Karlsson	96 Daniel Chopra
17 Robert Karlsson	57 Roger Wessels	97 Per Haugsrud
18 Bernhard Langer	58 Mark James	98 Mark Davis
19 David Carter	59 Mats Lanner	99 Rolf Muntz
20 Ian Woosnam	60 Tony Johnstone	100 Roger Chapman
21 Eduardo Romero	61 Mats Hallberg	101 Rodger Davis
22 Russell Claydon	62 Paul Lawrie	102 Eamonn Darcy
23 Jarmo Sandelin	63 Raymond Russell	103 John McHenry
24 Costantino Rocca	64 Philip Walton	104 Jeev Milkha Singh
25 Greg Chalmers	65 Jim Payne	105 Stephen Field
26 Jean Van de Velde	66 Jose Coceres	106 Paul Affleck
27 Greg Turner	67 Joakim Haeggman	107 Domingo Hospital
28 Gary Orr	68 Scott Henderson	108 Seve Ballesteros
29 Padraig Harrington	69 Thomas Levet	109 Francisco Cea
30 Paul McGinley	70 Dennis Edlund	110 Barry Lane
31 Santiago Luna	71 Michael Jonzon	111 Silvio Grappasonni
32 David Howell	72 Bob May	112 Miles Tunnicliff
33 Retief Goosen	73 Dean Robertson	113 Malcolm Mackenzie
34 Alex Cejka	74 Jose Rivero	114 Des Smyth
35 Paul Broadhurst	75 Fredrik Jacobson	115 Soren Kjeldsen
36 Peter O'Malley	76 Peter Senior	116 Tom Gillis
37 Steve Webster	77 Derrick Cooper	117 Mathew Goggin
38 Peter Mitchell	78 Andrew Sherborne	118 Iain Pyman
39 Gordon Brand Jnr	79 Brian Davis	119 Klas Eriksson
40 Ignacio Garrido	80 Mark Mouland	120 Michele Reale

1998 USPGA TOUR STATISTICS

The official USPGA stats for the 1998 season, up to but excluding the season ending Tour Championship, are as follows. The first 40 players in each list are shown.

SCORING AVERAGE

Scoring Leaders is a weighted scoring average which takes the stroke average of the field into account. The statistic is computed by taking a player's total strokes for the year, adding an adjustment figure, and dividing by the total rounds played for the year. The adjustment figure is computed by determining the stroke average of the field for each round played. This average is subtracted from par to create an adjustment figure for each round. A player accumulates these adjustment figures for each round he participates in.

		Average
1	Tiger Woods	69.10
2	David Duval	69.14
3	Nick Price	69.40
4	Davis Love III	69.43
5	Jim Furyk	69.58
6	Mark O'Meara	69.64
7	John Huston	69.67
8	Ernie Els	69.71
9	Fred Couples	69.77
10	Payne Stewart	69.84
11	Scott Hoch	69.88
12	Steve Stricker	69.95
T13	Jesper Parnevik	69.96
T13	Bob Tway	69.96
15	Vijay Singh	69.97
16	Mark Calcavecchia	70.01
17	Glen Day	70.06
T18	Lee Janzen	70.12
T18	Scott Verplank	70.12
20	Hal Sutton	70.16
21	Tom Lehman	70.17
22	Justin Leonard	70.18
23	Stewart Cink	70.21
24	Bob Estes	70.23
T25	Steve Jones	70.25
T25	Jeff Maggert	70.25
T25	Loren Roberts	70.25
28	Phil Mickelson	70.28
29	Fred Funk	70.30
30	Craig Parry	70.37
31	Skip Kendall	70.40
32	Steve Flesch	70.42
33	John Cook	70.43

34	Paul Azinger	70.44
35	Kenny Perry	70.45
36	Jeff Sluman	70.48
37	Billy Mayfair	70.50
38	Chris Perry	70.58
39	Steve Pate	70.62
40	Tommy Armour III	70.67

DRIVING ACCURACY

Driving Accuracy is the percent of time a player is able to hit the fairway with his tee shot.

		%
1	Bruce Fleisher	81.4
2	Larry Mize	80.4
3	Jeff Maggert	79.5
4	Fred Funk	78.7
5	Tim Loustalot	78.5
T6	Joe Durant	78.4
T6	Hal Sutton	78.4
T8	Scott Gump	78.0
T8	Lee Porter	78.0
10	Tom Byrum	77.7
11	Clark Dennis	77.4
T12	David Edwards	76.6
T12	Nick Price	76.6
T12	D A Weibring	76.6
15	Kirk Triplett	76.4
16	Esteban Toledo	76.3
17	Bob Friend	76.1
T18	Jim Furyk	76.0
T18	Frank Lickliter	76.0
20	Scott Hoch	75.9
T21	Fulton Allem	75.7
T21	Mark Carnevale	75.7
T23	Paul Goydos	75.1
T23	Loren Roberts	75.1
T25	Olin Browne	74.8
T25	Blaine McCallister	74.8
27	Justin Leonard	74.7
T28	Billy Mayfair	74.6
T28	John Morse	74.6
T30	P H Horgan III	74.5
T30	Tom Lehman	74.5
32	Fuzzy Zoeller	74.2
33	Mike Reid	74.0
34	Joe Daley	73.9
T35	Jay Haas	73.8
T35	Dudley Hart	73.8

T37	Pete Jordan	73.6
T37	Skip Kendall	73.6
39	Ben Bates	73.5
T40	Jimmy Johnston	73.4
T40	Duffy Waldorf	73.4

DRIVING DISTANCE

Driving Distance is the average number of yards per measured drive. Driving distance is measured on two holes per round. Care is taken to select two holes which face in opposite direction to counteract the effects of wind. Drives are measured to the point they come to rest regardless of whether they are in the fairway or not.

		Average
1	John Daly	299.4
2	Tiger Woods	296.1
3	Harrison Frazar	289.8
4	Fred Couples	289.6
5	Scott McCarron	289.1
6	David Duval	285.9
7	Barry Cheesman	284.1
8	Phil Mickelson	284.0
9	Vance Veazey	283.9
10	Kelly Gibson	283.0
11	Steve Jones	281.7
12	Steve Flesch	281.6
13	Tommy Armour III	281.5
14	Chris Smith	281.3
15	J L Lewis	281.2
16	Tim Herron	281.1
17	Kenny Perry	280.4
18	Davis Love III	280.3
19	Gary Hallberg	280.1
T20	Jim Gallagher Jr	279.7
T20	Bradley Hughes	279.7
22	Jay Delsing	279.6
T23	John Adams	279.4
T23	John Huston	279.4
25	Stuart Appleby	279.3
T26	Robert Damron	279.0
T26	Vijay Singh	279.0
T28	Richard Coughlan	278.2
T28	Duffy Waldorf	278.2
30	Tom Pernice Jr	278.0
31	Mark Calcavecchia	277.9
32	R W Eaks	277.7
T33	Craig Barlow	277.4
T33	Steve Lowery	277.4
T33	Brett Quigley	277.4

36	Paul Azinger	277.3
T37	Ted Tryba	276.5
T37	Grant Waite	276.5
39	Peter Jacobsen	276.3
40	Keith Fergus	276.0

TOTAL DRIVING

Total Driving is computer by totalling a players rank in both driving distance and driving accuracy.

		Total
1	David Duval	58
2	Duffy Waldorf	68
T3	Bradley Hughes	70
T3	John Huston	70
T3	Hal Sutton	70
6	Nick Price	73
7	Dudley Hart	89
8	Blaine McCallister	95
9	Dan Forsman	101
10	Brandel Chamblee	108
11	Davis Love III	109
12	Tiger Woods	111
13	Mark Calcavecchia	112
14	Richard Coughlan	113
T15	Joe Durant	115
T15	Kelly Gibson	115
T15	Steve Jones	115
18	Ben Bates	117
19	Brent Geiberger	118
20	Robert Damron	120
21	Billy Mayfair	121
22	Phil Mickelson	122
23	Tom Lehman	124
24	Tommy Armour III	129
25	Jim Furyk	131
T26	Mark Carnevale	132
T26	Lee Janzen	132
T28	Fred Funk	133
T28	John Riegger	133
T28	Craig Stadler	133
T28	Grant Waite	133
32	P H Horgan III	135
33	Kenny Perry	137
34	Russ Cochran	139
T35	Glen Day	140
T35	Harrison Frazar	140

T37	Scott Hoch	144
T37	Kirk Triplett	144
T39	Bob Gilder	145
T39	Skip Kendall	145

GREENS IN REGULATION

Greens In Regulation is the percent of time a player was able to hit the green in regulation (greens hit in regulation/holes played). Note: A green is considered hit in regulation if any part of the ball is touching the putting surface and the number of strokes taken is 2 or less than par.

		%
1	Tom Lehman	71.2
2	Hal Sutton	70.9
3	Dan Forsman	70.7
4	Steve Flesch	70.5
5	David Duval	70.4
6	Steve Jones	70.1
7	Mark Calcavecchia	69.9
8	Kirk Triplett	69.5
9	Bradley Hughes	69.4
10	Duffy Waldorf	69.2
11	Blaine McCallister	69.0
12	Larry Mize	68.9
T13	John Huston	68.8
T13	Rocco Mediate	68.8
T15	John Cook	68.7
T15	Paul Stankowski	68.7
17	Joey Sindelar	68.6
18	Lee Janzen	68.5
T19	Brett Quigley	68.3
T19	Bob Tway	68.3
T21	Jay Don Blake	68.2
T21	Gary Hallberg	68.2
T21	Andrew Magee	68.2
T21	Vijay Singh	68.2
T25	Paul Azinger	68.1
T25	Scott Hoch	68.1
27	Davis Love III	67.9
28	Esteban Toledo	67.8
T29	Fred Couples	67.7
T29	Grant Waite	67.7
31	Scott Verplank	67.6
T32	Russ Cochran	67.4
T32	Clark Dennis	67.4
T32	Joe Durant	67.4
T32	Jim Furyk	67.4
T32	Jeff Sluman	67.4
T32	Tiger Woods	67.4

T38	Mark Carnevale	67.3
T38	Skip Kendall	67.3
T40	Craig Barlow	67.2
T40	Dave Barr	67.2
T40	Brandel Chamblee	67.2
T40	Keith Fergus	67.2
T40	Scott Gump	67.2
T40	Nolan Henke	67.2
T40	Steve Lowery	67.2

PUTTING AVERAGE

Putting Leaders measures putting performance on greens hit in regulation. For each green hit in regulation the total number of putts are divided by the number of greens hit in regulation. By using greens hit in regulation we are able to eliminate the effects of chipping close and one putting in the computation.

1	Rick Fehr
2	Stewart Cink
3	David Duval
T4	John Huston
T4	Davis Love III
6	Steve Stricker
7	Dave Stockton Jr
8	Bob Estes
9	Jim Furyk
10	R W Eaks
11	Mark O'Meara
T12	Glen Day
T12	Chris Perry
T12	Loren Roberts
T15	Billy Andrade
T15	Lee Janzen
T17	John Daly
T17	Brad Faxon
19	Greg Kraft
T20	Scott Hoch
T20	Scott Verplank
T22	J P Hayes
T22	Skip Kendall
24	Andrew Magee
T25	Tommy Tolles
T25	Bob Tway
T27	Brian Henninger
T27	Craig Stadler
T27	Payne Stewart
39	Len Mattiace
31	Fred Couples
32	Jeff Maggert
T33	Paul Azinger

T33	Franklin Langham	
T35	Robert Damron	
T35	Trevor Dodds	
T35	David Ogrin	
T38	Steve Pate	
T38	Mike Springer	
T40	Bobby Gage	
T40	Justin Leonard	

SAND SAVE PERCENTAGE

Sand Saves is the percent of time a player was able to get "up and down" once from a greenside sand bunker. Note: This up and down is computed regardless of score on the hole.

		%
1	Keith Fergus	71.0
2	Len Mattiace	69.8
3	Kirk Triplett	66.7
4	Justin Leonard	65.2
5	Fuzzy Zoeller	64.9
6	Billy Mayfair	63.3
7	Esteban Toledo	63.2
8	Craig Parry	63.0
9	Stewart Cink	62.9
10	Steve Stricker	62.6
11	Dudley Hart	60.9
12	Robert Damron	59.9
13	Curtis Strange	59.8
T14	John Morse	59.4
T14	David Ogrin	59.4
16	Payne Stewart	59.3
17	Willie Wood	59.2
T18	Brandel Chamblee	58.9
T18	Lee Porter	58.9
20	Tommy Armour III	58.7
21	Sonny Skinner	58.6
22	Clarence Rose	58.2
T23	John Daly	57.5
T23	Greg Kraft	57.5
T25	J P Hayes	57.4
T25	Mark Wiebe	57.4
27	Jeff Sluman	57.2
T28	Stuart Appleby	57.1
T28	Brad Fabel	57.1
T28	Doug Martin	57.1
31	Mike Brisky	57.0
32	Bruce Fleisher	56.9
33	Craig Barlow	56.7
34	Mike Weir	56.6

T35	Fred Couples	56.4
T35	Tom Lehman	56.4
T37	Skip Kendall	56.3
T37	Jeff Maggert	56.3
T37	Scott Verplank	56.3
40	Jay Don Blake	56.0

ALL-ROUND RANKING

The All-Round statistic is computed by totalling a player's rank in each of the following statistics; Scoring Leaders, Putting Leaders, Eagle Leaders, Birdie Leaders, Sand Saves, Greens in Regulation, Driving Leaders, and Driving Accuracy.

		Total
1	John Huston	146
2	David Duval	207
3	Davis Love III	239
4	Fred Couples	294
5	Scott Verplank	297
6	Tiger Woods	330
T7	Glen Day	333
T7	Hal Sutton	333
T7	Bob Tway	333
10	Skip Kendall	344
11	Jim Furyk	346
12	Lee Janzen	347
13	Mark Calcavecchia	360
14	Steve Jones	361
15	Brandel Chamblee	365
16	Steve Stricker	368
17	Steve Flesch	389
18	Billy Mayfair	391
19	Paul Azinger	406
20	Dan Forsman	411
21	Stewart Cink	413
22	Robert Damron	420
23	Kirk Triplett	423
24	Scott Hoch	440
25	Tommy Armour III	463
26	Bob Estes	468
T27	Jeff Maggert	469
T27	Nick Price	469
29	Joe Durant	473
30	Justin Leonard	480
31	Andrew Magee	481
32	Ben Bates	490
33	Chris Perry	497
T34	Larry Mize	504
T34	Payne Stewart	504

36	Kenny Perry	512
37	Vijay Singh	514
38	Tom Pernice Jr	525
39	Paul Stankowski	531
T40	Stephen Ames	534
T40	Phil Mickelson	534

THE 1998 AMERICAN MONEY LIST

1 David Duval
2 Vijay Singh
3 Jim Furyk
4 Tiger Woods
5 Hal Sutton
6 Phil Mickelson
7 Mark O'Meara
8 Justin Leonard
9 Fred Couples
10 John Huston
11 Davis Love III
12 Mark Calcavecchia
13 Steve Stricker
14 Jesper Parnevik
15 Glen Day
16 Billy Mayfair
17 Scott Hoch
18 Scott Verplank
19 Payne Stewart
20 Lee Janzen
21 Jeff Sluman
22 John Cook
23 Fred Funk
24 Bob Tway
25 Tom Lehman
26 Nick Price
27 Jeff Maggert
28 Bob Estes
29 Tom Watson
30 Andrew Magee
31 Stewart Cink
32 Skip Kendall
33 Trevor Dodds
34 Steve Pate
35 Steve Flesch
36 Ernie Els
37 Brandel Chamblee
38 Steve Jones
39 Chris Perry
40 Stuart Appleby
41 Billy Andrade
42 Steve Elkington

43 Joe Durant
44 David Toms
45 Frank Lickliter
46 Lee Westwood
47 Olin Browne
48 Michael Bradley
49 Brent Geiberger
50 Paul Azinger
51 J P Hayes
52 Tommy Armour III
53 Dudley Hart
54 Tim Herron
55 Tom Pernice Jr
56 Jay Haas
57 Bob Friend
58 Kenny Perry
59 Kirk Triplett
60 Loren Roberts
61 Joey Sindelar
62 Larry Mize
63 Harrison Frazar
64 Scott Simpson
65 Nolan Henke
66 Kevin Sutherland
67 Ted Tryba
68 Len Mattiace
69 Scott McCarron
70 Steve Lowery
71 Jim Carter
72 Jay Don Blake
73 Scott Gump
74 Brad Faxon
75 Clark Dennis
76 Willie Wood
77 John Daly
78 Rocco Mediate
79 Bruce Lietzke
80 Bradley Hughes
81 Robert Damron
82 Paul Goydos
83 Stephen Ames
84 Bill Glasson

85 Craig Stadler
86 Neal Lancaster
87 Jerry Kelly
88 Mike Hulbert
89 Phil Tataurangi
90 Brian Watts
91 Russ Cochran
92 Peter Jacobsen
93 Esteban Toledo
94 Greg Kraft
95 Lee Porter
96 Paul Stankowski
97 Colin Montgomerie
98 Craig Parry
99 Dan Forsman
100 Barry Cheesman
101 Fuzzy Zoeller
102 Doug Martin
103 Duffy Waldorf
104 J L Lewis
105 Brad Fabel
106 Mark Wiebe
107 Omar Uresti
108 Frank Nobilo
109 Doug Barron
110 Lee Rinker
111 Chris DiMarco
112 Ben Bates
113 Jeff Gallagher
114 Brian Henninger
115 Tommy Tolles
116 Tom Byrum
117 Franklin Langham
118 Grant Waite
119 Kevin Wentworth
120 Larry Rinker
121 Joe Ozaki
122 David Sutherland
123 Mike Reid
124 Mike Springer
125 Blaine McCallister

THE RYDER CUP PLACINGS
(as of 28th October 1998)

EUROPEAN TEAM RANKING

1	Colin Montgomerie (Scot)	318020.00
2	Miguel Angel Jimenez (Sp)	165610.00
3	Sven Struver (Ger)	146775.00
4	Robert Karlsson (Swe)	128830.00
5	Lee Westwood (Eng)	124426.57
6	Jarmo Sandelin (Swe)	98824.12
7	Patrik Sjoland (Swe)	97710.00
8	Pierre Fulke (Swe)	74130.00
9	Darren Clarke (N Ire)	69090.00
10	Per-Ulrik Johansson (Swe)	65665.00
11	Gordon Brand Jr (Scot)	64223.81
12	Costantino Rocca (It)	56731.11
13	Fredrik Jacobson (Swe)	55211.00
14	Alex Cejka (Ger)	54646.67
15	Steve Webster (Eng)	50000.00
16	Jean Van de Velde (Fr)	46973.33
17	Sam Torrance (Scot)	46362.50
18	Paolo Quirici (Swi)	42537.14
19	Ignacio Garrido (Sp)	42071.11
20	Peter Mitchell (Eng)	40400.00

UNITED STATES TEAM RANKING

1	Mark O'Meara	652.500
2	David Duval	602.500
3	Jim Furyk	458.000
4	Tiger Woods	456.875
5	Steve Stricker	387.500
6	Davis Love III	367.500
7	Fred Couples	357.500
8	Phil Mickelson	331.250
9	Lee Janzen	295.000
10	Payne Stewart	292.500
11	Billy Mayfair	262.500
12	Fred Funk	255.000
13	Mark Calcavecchia	252.500
14	Bob Tway	233.333
15	Jeff Maggert	225.000
16	Justin Leonard	219.375
17	Glen Day	212.500
18	John Cook	205.000
19	Scott Hoch	193.000
20	Hal Sutton	191.250

X21052 (T)